Fabricating Pleasure

George Melchior Kraus, Bridge and Castle. Courtesy of the Stiftung Weimarer Klassik Herzogin Amalia Bibliothek. Photo by Sigrid Geske.

Fabricating Pleasure

Fashion, Entertainment, and Cultural Consumption in Germany, 1780–1830

KARIN WURST

WAYNE STATE UNIVERSITY PRESS
DETROIT

K R I T I K

German Literary Theory and Cultural Studies
Liliane Weissberg, Editor

A complete listing of the books in this series
can be found online at http://wsupress.wayne.edu

© 2005 by Wayne State University Press,

Detroit, Michigan 48201. All rights reserved.

No part of this book may be reproduced without formal permission.

Manufactured in the United States of America.

09 08 07 06 05   5 4 3 2 1

Library of Congress Cataloging-in-Publication Data

Wurst, Karin A.

Fabricating pleasure : fashion, entertainment, and cultural consumption in Ger-

many (1780–1830) / Karin Wurst.

p. cm. — (Kritik)

Includes bibliographical references and index.

ISBN 0-8143-3131-9 (hardcover : alk. paper)

1. Middle class—Germany—History. 2. Amusements—Germany—History. 3. Popular

culture—Germany—History. 4. Germany—Social conditions. I. Title. II. Kritik

(Detroit, Mich.)

HT690.G3W87 2005

305.5'5'0943—dc22

2004017868

∞The paper used in this publication meets the minimum requirements of the Ameri-

can National Standard for Information Sciences—Permanence of Paper for

Printed Library Materials, ANSI Z39.48-1984.

For Benjamin

Contents

CONTENTS

Acknowledgments

I WOULD LIKE TO acknowledge the generous assistance of a number of institutions and colleagues. The early research phase for this study was facilitated by an All University Research Grant from Michigan State University. I am grateful for the anonymous evaluators of the grant proposal and my department chair at the time, Georg Peters, for enabling me to accept the grant and take a research leave.

I am especially grateful to the libraries and collections that assisted with material and with providing illustrations, in particular, Angelika Barthel at the Stiftung Weimarer Klassik; the staff at the Landesbibliothek Baden-Württemberg, Stuttgart; Peter Berg at Special Collections, Michigan State University; Elke Schwichtenberg at the Bildarchiv Preußischer Kulturbesitz, Berlin; Gerald Köhler at the Theaterwissenschaftliche Sammlung Universität Köln; and Dagmar Gengnagel at the Thüringer Universitäts- und Landesbibliothek in Jena.

Thanks go also to the anonymous reviewers who evaluated the manuscript for Wayne State University Press, above all to the Kritik series editor, Liliane Weissberg, whose enthusiasm for the project was very important to me, and to the wonderful staff of Wayne State University Press, in particular to the copyeditor, Jonathan Lawrence.

An earlier version of parts of chapter 7 appeared under the title "Spellbinding: The Body as Art/Arts as Body in *Attitüden*" in the *Lessing Yearbook* 32 (2001): 151–81; an earlier version of parts of chapter 6 appeared under the title "The Self-Fashioning of the Bourgeoisie:

Bertuch's *Journal des Luxus und der Moden*" in the *Germanic Review* 72.3 (1997): 170–82. I appreciate the permission to reprint.

Many colleagues—too many to mention by name—have offered comments and engaged with bits and pieces of the book at various conferences over the last years, I gratefully acknowledge their input. Several wonderful students here at Michigan State University have engaged with the material over the years in formal classroom settings and in informal after-hours discussions in the hallway or at get-togethers. I very much appreciated their energy and probing questions—with special thanks to Ken Munn and Angelika Krämer.

For his unwavering practical support in the daily activities of maintaining family life, I am deeply grateful to my partner in life, Doyle Brunsen. The book is dedicated to our son, Benjamin, whose ways of exploring his environment have given me the gift of seeing the world with fresh eyes and to appreciate the simple pleasures.

Introduction

ENTERTAINMENT, DEFINED AS OCCASIONS for creating pleasure, added an important dimension to the lifestyle and self-definition of the middle class. Pleasure provides the affective motor for the forms of cultural entertainment and material consumption that occupied the leisure of the (upper) middle class. Yet many critics from the eighteenth century to the present associate pleasure and entertainment with trivial and inconsequential amusements and thus dismiss both concepts. Although the effects of a work of art on human beings were theorized extensively from the Enlightenment to the classical period, pleasure and entertainment were usually devalued in favor of the moral or idealist impact of a work of art. Roland Barthes summarized this trend in *The Pleasure of the Text,* where he argued that historically pleasure has been called either "idle or vain, a class notion or an illusion," and that almost every philosophy repressed hedonism: "Pleasure is continually disappointed, reduced, emptied, in favor of strong, noble values: Truth, Death, Progress, Struggle, Joy etc."[1] These condemnations turned attention away from a serious analysis of the function of pleasure and entertainment in the formation of middle-class identity. It is this area that my study examines. It seeks a fuller account of late-eighteenth-century culture, one that does not exclude the material aspects of cultural life but argues for an analysis that addresses the interplay of material and nonmaterial aspects of culture.

My analysis of pleasure and entertainment is concerned with their cultural and social meanings. It raises the following questions: Which changes in values and habits produced a departure from ascetic values dominating middle-class values earlier in the century toward an acceptance and even celebration of pleasure and entertainment in middle-class culture?[2] How do these concepts take on social and cultural meaning? What role do the emergent print culture and the increased interest in material (fashion, interior design) and visual culture (travel, landscape gardens, theater as spectacle, living pictures, diorama, panorama) as exemplary—yet by no means comprehensive—sites play in the formation of both concepts, or vice versa? Finally, I hope to restructure the manner in which concepts of entertainment, pleasure, and consumption are explored by challenging the unwritten rule that these topics are undeserving of study due to their mix of self-indulgence, insatiability, and irrationality. Instead, I see the areas of everyday life that are governed by the forms of entertainment and the positive affective experience (pleasure) they constitute as a compelling, albeit largely unacknowledged, part of what Nancy Fraser calls the "powerful informal pressures" derived from the operation of taste as "protocols of style and decorum" that are characteristic of the bourgeois public sphere.[3]

Studies on pleasure have surfaced only recently. Catherine Cusset examines the ethics of pleasure in the French libertine movement, and Roy Porter and Marie Mulvey Roberts's collection of essays offers glimpses on various aspects of pleasure in eighteenth-century England. Mulvey Roberts rehearses the dominant reasons why writing about pleasure is one of the great taboos in criticism. Pleasure is marginalized because of a class bias; by its association with "immediate gratification, the pleasurable has been devalued partly because it has been seen as being more accessible to the populace than to the elite."[4]

In the German critical tradition, the disinterest in pleasure and entertainment stems from the dominance of an elite concept of literature, philosophy, and the arts (and their institutionalization) created at the end of the eighteenth century. This classicist aesthetic denigrates the entertainment function of literature and art in favor of their autonomous character that avoids social and economic entanglements. Modern criticism in the idealist tradition of Immanuel Kant followed suit and belittled entertainment by defining high art as a subversive force that opposes the false harmonies created by bourgeois tastes and morals.[5] Theodor Adorno's influential theoretical framework—although based on early-twentieth-century conditions—nevertheless colored the debates on "trivial" or popular tradition of non-autonomous forms of culture in earlier historical periods. The entertainment value of an artifact signaled its triviality. The most frequently critiqued aspects of popular or mass culture were its status as a product to be sold and purchased, its ability to seduce audiences away from high culture with "easy" pleasures and false harmonies, and its alleged tendency to create passive audiences that become susceptible to manipulation and techniques of totalitarianism.[6] Yet this theoretical framework is unsuitable to grasp the historical specificity of the late-eighteenth-century cultural public sphere. I see the cultural public sphere as a nuanced and interrelated continuum. It ranged from the critical literary discourse, which Habermas theorized, to the contemplative and disinterested pleasures of autonomous art (i.e., pleasure that brackets out desire as theorized by Kant and the idealist tradition, which Stanley Corngold recently reexamined in *Complex Pleasures*),[7] to the forms of cultural entertainment and consumerism associated with the increasingly important informal and self-regulatory modes of lifestyle and taste.

Rather than accepting the canonized disregard of classicism (1786–1805) and romanticism (1798–1830) for the dilettantish or "popular" as evidence of a split between high and low culture, I read this disdain as a sign of anxiety about the transformation of culture into a dynamic field of forces. Eighteenth-century cultural critics, literary critics, and artists tried to come to terms with these uneasy tensions and with this jostling of forces by creating aesthetic hierarchies. Martha Woodmansee even suspects that the modern concept of "art" was "invented to stem the commercialization of literature."[8] Critics dismissed art forms that privilege the senses, rely on direct and unmediated accessibility, and provide entertainment by stimulating the imagination and fostering self-illusory fantasies. The role of entertainment and pleasure in the formation of cultural taste and (high) cultural literacy remained precarious and embattled.

A devaluation of sensory experience in knowledge formation in favor of abstract cognition contributed to the disinterest in the affective disposition we call pleasure as it manifests itself in entertainment. The ensuing lack of prestige was aggravated (or, in part, created) by a disinterest in precise definitions and thus of theoretical accounts of the concepts of pleasure (*Vergnügen*) and entertainment (*Unterhaltung*) oscillating between specific instances and activities and a certain disposition toward events. For definitions and discussions that do not theorize these terms as Other or as a negative foil to the disinterested pleasure theorized by Kant, we have to look beyond the theoreticians of high culture to popular discourse—in particular, to the periodical press of the time. For example, the influential, long-running *Journal des Luxus und der Moden* (1786–1827), which accompanies the time frame under investigation, speaks of the time devoted to leisure, in which individuals seek forms of entertainment (*Zeit[ver]kürzungen*) that provide pleasure (*Vergnügen*), which in turn is characterized by a vigorous stimulation of the senses and the mind.[9] Entertainment is the specific activity that creates the positive affective disposition (pleasure), which is based in an increased level of stimulation. The pursuit of this excitation is the affective motor for cultural consumption.

The popular philosophy of the *Journal des Luxus und der Moden* places high value on innovation—and the stimulation it provides—as the dynamic that drives most forms of entertainment and is responsible for the increase and diversity of cultural practices and artifacts defining the middle-class lifestyle. Although devalued in high theory, the sensual perception of the environment and the self remained an important factor in cultural life during the time frame under investigation.

In many ways, this position revisits earlier traditions that were by then out of favor, in particular Joseph Addison's *The Pleasures of the Imagination* (which appeared in *The Spectator* in 1712 in eleven installments),[10] which established the fine arts as desirable sources of recreation—the mind seeks diversions in cultural practices, as the mind likes to be occupied—and connoisseurship. In the German context, the latter concept deteriorated to the considerably less flattering term "dilettantism" by the end of the century. The dilettante response to cultural products must have been pervasive, because Johann Wolfgang von Goethe and Friedrich Schiller felt it necessary to offer a theoretical exploration, which was intended for publication in the *Propyläen*. The outline "Über den Dilettantismus" ("On Dilettantism" 1799)[11] discusses the usefulness and harm on contemporary culture of dilettante, nonprofessional engagement with poetry, the visual arts, music, dance, architecture, and theater. Goethe and Schiller acknowledge that in certain cases the dilettante occupation with the arts sharpens the powers of perception and can lead to a greater development of a sense of aesthetics.[12] Yet the dominant trend attributed to the dilettante is that he or she uses the arts as a form of entertainment, as a pleasurable pastime, and as a playful activity, which Goethe and Schiller reject as a misuse of the arts. Despite this influential critique, it is precisely this function that seems to become the cultural reality.[13] At the same time, Goethe and Schiller also sense that dilettantism has a social legitimizing function for the emerging middle class.[14] Both interwoven aspects—entertainment and social distinction—become important features of cultural life around 1800 and beg analysis.

In its practice more than in its theoretical adumbration, the *Journal des Luxus und der Moden* revisits positions from earlier in the century, namely Charles Batteux's often ignored third category in the history of aesthetics, situated between the mechanical arts, which are designed to satisfy human needs, and the fine arts, whose end is pleasure. The arts of the first kind employ nature as they find it, solely for use and service. The fine arts do not use nature at all but instead only imitate it, each according to its own principles.[15] The third category combines utility and pleasure. Originally reserved for architecture and rhetoric, this category proves useful for the new interest in fashion and interior design. It bestows a certain polish upon useful items for the comfort of middle-class life in order to make them suitable for use, social distinction, and, above all, to the emotive dimension of pleasure.

Several interrelated factors played a role in creating the importance that came to be attached to sensations, emotions, and desires. By the 1780s—influenced by the literary movements *Empfindsamkeit* (1740–80; sensibility) and *Sturm und Drang* (1767–85; Storm and Stress) that championed emotions and sensations—the individual had learned to react not only to actual physical stimuli but, more importantly, to imaginary stimuli and mental images, and to manipulate them to heighten their pleasurable effect. These shifts in attitudes with their emphasis on imaginary pleasures, in turn, encouraged modern conceptions of romantic love[16] and its celebration in romance novels. Both fostered an emotional dimension of consciousness and the modern characteristic of savoring imaginary pleasures.[17] People celebrated the stimulating joys of longing and suffered disillusionment when the desired object (or person) was obtained, only to start the cycle of desire anew.

The desire for new stimulation, for novelty, is the dynamo at the core of all forms of entertainment and is responsible for the increase and diversity of cultural practices. This spiral of desire and disillusionment, which requires frequent stimulation of the senses, produces what I will call cultural consumerism. Bearing a certain structural resemblance to the celebration of passion as a fleeting emotion that craves perpetual renewal and savors new stimulation, cultural consumerism manifests itself in distinct yet related strands. On the one hand, an interest emerged in material culture, an appetite to adorn the body and its surroundings with fashionable goods; on the other hand, we see a hunger for new cultural practices and innovations in traditional genres. Although these strands are usually discussed in separate studies or even in different disciplines, I argue that they are deeply intertwined. As we will see in chapter 6, the varied print culture—especially the periodical—is instrumental in creating an interest in material culture and in making these objects part of the system of culture. The dynamics of the objects of material culture, their emphasis on change and innovation, in turn, influences, for example, print culture, which reacts by offering a greater variety of specialized publications and by adding features such as illustrations that were prompted by the objects of material culture described in its pages.

Similarly, the visual stimulation, the interest in looking, the sensual indulgence of the gaze, altered the theater experience and created new genres, such as the living pictures, panorama, and diorama. The focus shifted from the spoken word to the specular event. In addition, vision, which during the Enlightenment was tied to rationality, organization, and concept formation, took on new dimensions.[18] By the end of the century, vision became linked to the sensual impact of looking at stimulating objects on the one hand—the concepts of *Schaulust* and *Augenschmaus*—and the imaginary pleasures of visualizing, in daydreaming and fantasizing, on the other. The first trend manifests itself in an interest in elaborate stage sets for the theater and in new visual art forms such as the panorama and the diorama. The latter form of visualizing, closely linked to the former, can be detected in the new periodical literature on fashion and design in the increasing interest in illustrations allowing the viewer to imagine him- or herself in the depicted situations, in exotic lands and times, or in an imaginary altering of one's lifestyle and body image. These visualizations were fostered by the illustrations in the fashion magazine or by the depiction of luxury items, offering (imaginary) visions of enhancing the bourgeois lifestyle. They were also created by new reading practices, allowing for daydreaming, a playful identification with the characters and situations in a text, trying on different roles and living out fantasies, and in embodying cultural artifacts in *Attitüden* and living pictures. Those forms of entertainment that provide not only direct stimulation of the senses such as the pleasure derived from looking but also occasions for culturally acquired modern fabrication of imaginary pleasures became especially desirable and are therefore placed at the center of this study. The theater experience, an occupation with fashion, and the periodical print culture—the most important forms of entertainment—allow for this kind of pleasure, one that is heightened by the imaginary aspect coupled with the sensual impact of looking.

I suggest that the pleasure driving cultural entertainment as an enrichment of everyday life played a larger role in the formation of (upper-)middle-class identity and its differentiation than previously thought. Cultural entertainment played an important role in the process of self-culturation and the formation of taste. Whether the middle class enjoyed novels, followed the latest fashion depictions and descriptions in journals, or designed new interior spaces, they interpreted not only the objects under contemplation but also their own identities. In this context of increasing class differentiation we find an "extremely anxious production of endless discriminations between people who are constantly assessing each other's standing."[19] By reading about the practices of others—be it in the actions of fictional characters or descriptions of cultural practices in magazines—consumers not only shaped their own individualities but also learned how to read other consumers, linking the pleasures of the imagination with "social calculation."[20]

Furthermore, just as the readers of romance novels experience the state between desire and satisfaction as pleasurable, consumers began to experience the gap between the desire to possess and the actual purchase as pleasurable. As people integrated the connotations associated with the desired object into their own self-image (the stylish house, the elaborate garden, and the fashionable dress) and fantasized about the possibilities of their lives, they created a form of consumerism that combined material and cultural aspects.

At the same time, the identity formation of the individual is not a given but becomes an (ad)venture and a task negotiating between the inner self and its embodiment, between the mind and body one has and the mind and body one might acquire.[21] While the history of the mind in the formation of the bourgeoisie has largely been written, the link to the body, its embodiment, has just begun to enter into focus. Cultural studies invited a reevaluation of the role of the body in identity formation at the end of the eighteenth century. The body's adornment (fashion), environment (interior design and garden culture), and movement (travel) allow it to come into focus.

Complex shifts in the composition of the upper middle class as well as the trend toward urbanization and proto-industrial production of luxury products (e.g., porcelain and silks) created a larger and more affluent middle class.[22] The new mentality of deriving pleasure from a state of desiring enticed the middle class to spend more money not only on fashionable goods but also on other forms of cultural entertainment as a regular part of their lifestyle. In the urban centers, cultural activities such as frequenting the theater, to some extent the opera, and other performances became regular pastimes for increasingly larger layers of the middle class. More people had the means to travel for entertainment. The resorts and spas were no longer the exclusive privilege of the nobility. Descriptions of these forms of entertainment in the periodicals of the time and in autobiographical texts suggest that they played an important part in the creation of the middle-class lifestyle and thus in the identity formation of the middle class.

At the same time, with taste as their organizing principle, these forms of cultural entertainment and consumption also became central in assigning status and cultural capital in the more differentiated modern society emerging at the end of the eighteenth century. After all, the upper middle class did not define itself solely through education, high culture, and economic strength—as historians foreground (Jürgen Kocka)—but also through the forms of everyday culture (*Alltagskultur*), the pleasurable cultural enrichment of everyday life in these forms of entertainment. The concept of *Bürgerlichkeit* becomes less a simple legal category than a complex perception of social status that is based on a number of criteria ranging from financial and professional aspects to taste and *Bildung* working together to produce a distinct lifestyle,[23] one that manifests itself in the forms of self-representation as aesthetic practice.

Methodologically, this study is informed by Pierre Bourdieu's comprehensive theory of culture, which analyzes the interplay of the various social and cultural spheres of influence (fields), including the ordinary, everyday consumption and the aesthetic realm, which provides the tools for the analysis of the bourgeois lifestyle.[24] Bourdieu's definition of lifestyle as the extensive manifestation of class, economic, cultural and symbolic capital, fields of influence, and habits informs this study. Taste as a symbolic ordering principle governing the forms of entertainment and cultural consumption negotiates cultural and social position within a more permeable social system emerging during the time under investigation. *Bildung* and taste negotiate matters of inclusion and exclusion and aid in the formation of various communities within the middle class. Yet I see these concepts as layers in the self-fashioning of the bourgeoisie that are not simply analogous but play distinct, flexible roles. Although *Bildung*, especially the humanistic education associated with Humboldt's education reforms, seeks to enhance the social, economic, and political position of the bourgeoisie on the national level, on which *Bildung* becomes a currency that is valid throughout the German states and thus forms the basis of the middle-class lifestyle and taste, the latter concepts allow for more individualistic manifestations that permit unique formations of communities within the middle class. Merchants, the early industrialists, the various groupings among the civil servants (teachers, university professors, the various professionals in the bureaucracy), intellectuals, journalists, physicians, and others form distinct communities, as we will see in our discussion of the forms of entertainment as an important part of their lifestyles and their distinct symbolic forms. Social practices such as fashionable dress, forms of sociability, the distinctive use of food and drink, and the personal environment of the styles of interior design, architecture, and garden architecture represent these symbolic forms, which are closely connected to the forms of entertainment that fashion distinct regional and group-specific middle-class lifestyles. A cultural studies approach, which illuminates artifacts and contexts, allows us to "read" texts, visual images, objects of material culture, and cultural practices so that we can determine their symbolic function. This promises new insights into the birth of the modern individual—not as conceptualized outside and independent of the cultural marketplace but within it and deeply interwoven with it—in this important period in German culture.

The time between 1780 and 1830 was selected because we notice a new emphasis on entertainment and an expansion and diversification of cultural activities. At the same time, this period represents a "complex period of transition and transformation in German history"[25] and a time of significant and rapid changes in cultural history. The few decades after the French Revolution have been called a veritable time of social experimentation for the middle class.[26] These changes are part of a complex transformation and modernization process in which the corporate estate society became more differentiated and functionalized.

The decades under consideration thus denote a time of crisis and transition, a decisive step into modernity, a time of profound change paving the way for social, technological, economical, and political modernization.[27]

Modernity is characterized by the awareness of historicity, a belief in growth and change, an enjoyment of novelty, the growing desire to know, the thrill of discovery, and the awareness that the "natural" can be manipulated and improved, whether it be in animal breeding or in horticulture. The veritable "garden-mania"[28] that had gripped the middle class contained not only an aesthetic element and provided a source of entertainment and a site for informal sociability but also allowed the interested dilettante to experiment in botany. The fashionable trials to create as many variants and colorings of flowers represent practical applications of the science of the day. As in other areas, the specialized periodical press plays an important role in the popularization of horticulture, in attempts at cultivation and classification.[29] These advances in applied sciences made larger segments of the middle class "receptive of scientific activity, of technological change, of modern compared with traditional methods."[30] Often, the lessons in particularly spectacular scientific experiments (the wonders of nature displayed through telescopes, microscopes, and electrical apparatuses) became the object of entertaining public lectures. I will not discuss this aspect in this study, since Barbara Stafford has already offered substantial insights into these phenomena.[31] Other examples that I do not cover here include visits to the emerging public museums, collections, and zoos, the observation of air balloons, and so forth, as Gerhard Tanzer has described these activities in detail.[32]

Politically, the era under investigation was defined by significant reform movements: the absolutist reforms before 1789 and the bureaucratic reforms after 1800.[33] Ambitious reform programs, usually fueled by the need for revenue, were initiated by princes and driven and implemented by intellectuals (absolutist reforms under enlightened absolutism). In an intermingling of interests, the state—in need of civil servants as administrators to implement reforms—opened positions to middle-class professionals and intellectuals, who, steeped in Enlightenment philosophy, were attracted to these positions in the hope of promoting Enlightenment principles and transforming absolutism into enlightened absolutism.[34] The complex interplay among cultural, philosophical, and economic change fostered political change. The nobility depended on economic strengthening of the state to maintain its power. It thus allowed or even encouraged changes, which in turn altered the face of absolutism.[35] The more massive financial reforms after 1806—creating state budgets, centralizing the financial administration, and drawing distinctions between public and dynastic finances—required the expertise of bureaucrats.[36] Both waves of reform created opportunities for middle-class intellectuals to enter the service of the state, thus fostering the strengthening of the middle class and the creation and implementation of reforms. These reformist tendencies were intended not only to better the economic situation of the ruler and state but also to avoid social unrest and revolutionary leanings. Reforms were often suggested to the ruler by his middle-class advisers. Creating a sense of movement and progressive change, these reforms were credited for the fact that intellectuals regarded the conditions in Germany as less severe than in France, for example, and generally considered the German states as responding to reformist political pressure. This process cannot be explained by traditional concepts of an innovation's threat to a stable position but must be seen as a field of sometimes opposing, sometimes symbiotic or supporting forces in cultural, social, and political practices. The discussions regarding the cultural self-definition of the middle class have to be seen in this political context with its field of power relationships.

The period examined in this study was further defined by the Revolutionary Wars (1792–95), the Napoleonic Wars (1796–1815), and the conservative restructuring of Europe with the Carlsbad Decrees (1819). At the beginning of our time frame, the numerous German states were still organized in the Holy Roman Empire of the German Nation. By 1806 this entity no longer existed; the French Revolution, along with the wars and political destabilization it created, disbanded the precarious balances of power within Europe. By 1820 the first experimentation with constitutions and representative assemblies occupied the German states. The middle-class intellectuals participated in these discussions shaping the fate of the middle-class identity within the emergent debate on formations of community and nation. We see the desire for participatory forms of government limiting the absolute powers of the rulers. The cultural realm became a testing ground for self-regulatory practices. One example would be the non-enforcement of sumptuary laws which allowed the self-regulatory system of fashion to emerge, creating a new ordering principle.

In terms of social changes, the overarching pattern is the change from an estate society, in which position and rank was based on birth and lineage, to one based on achievement, that is, on function. Society's social differentiation can be seen in the construction of the self-reflexive individual, in the changing concepts of interpersonal relationships (friendship, love, marriage, and family), in changes in the legal and economic systems and in consumerism, in changes in theology, sciences, philosophy, and pedagogy, and in the concept of culture. A most important shift in the structure of the family enabled—and was enabled by—the separation of work and household. This development was accompanied by the intimization of the family, in which the relationship between the couple is based on a love match and in which the socialization and emotionalization of the children became an important task for mothers. This, in turn, was enabled and produced by the Enlightenment belief that education and pedagogy should foster the individual's full potential. The belief in human development and perfectibility depended on the changes in theology and science, enabling the historicization of human development into a unique personality or subjectivity.

In sociopolitical terms, we observe the increasing separation of the public and private spheres, where politics and morality as well as law and morality become differentiated. The transformation of cultural practice could not have occurred without the changes in the other systems, and vice versa. These changes must be regarded as uneven and unsystematic, occurring with their own individual dynamic.

Changes in the role of literature are of special importance because literature reflects and comments on the individual within the complexity of his or her social context. Furthermore, the diverse reading practices that emerged during this time fostered reading as a form of entertainment indulging in the powers of the imagination. The new periodical literature also very concretely introduced readers to new foreign products and practices, thereby creating interest in those practices and products before they were part of everyday life.

In the field of economics, new forms of finance capitalism, based on Protestant ethics, helped the middle class to acquire the wealth that enabled and fostered cultural consumption. These consumer goods in turn enabled acts of self-definition and collective definition.[37] With the specialization of work and the split into defined times for work and leisure, entertainment became ensconced in leisure and associated with relaxation and thus contrasted with the (mental) exertion of work. Changes in technology began to introduce machines producing energy and labor, significantly changing the middle-class lifestyle and helping to produce more wealth. As the middle class became more affluent, more money could be spent on cultural artifacts and activities, which came to define the middle-class lifestyle. Pre-industrialism made more so-called luxury items available, which could then be utilized for the beautification of the domestic sphere as a culturally valid practice. Yet the economic argument does not suffice as a mode of explanation for these changes. Greater affluence does not necessarily mean that more money is spent on cultural activities, on entertainment, and on consumer goods; instead, changes in attitudes and values regarding cultural practices and material culture bring about these changes in behavior. Thus economic and financial behaviors were enabled by changes in the (cultural) self-definition of the (upper) middle class. Extensive reading practices created—among other things—material desires, leading to increased willingness to consume. The increased consumer demand in turn accelerated the production of consumer products. Technical inventions such as more comfortable and efficient means of transportation (e.g., improved coaches) allowed for greater mobility, thus increasing people's spatial environment, while artificial lighting, which extended the time for leisure activities, expanded people's temporal environment and altered leisure practices significantly.

Cultural life and entertainment experienced during leisure served to distinguish the middle class from the nobility, but by the last decades of the eighteenth century they also served as a means to create new distinctions, to produce new forms of social stratification within the middle class itself. At stake at this historical juncture was no longer the oppositional identity formation created to wrest the cultural and economic supremacy from the nobility. Instead, we note the differentiation within the middle class, which is negotiated in terms of what has been labeled "cultural capital" (Bourdieu) or (cultural) taste. This contentious process of establishing cultural competence as a means for the self-differentiation of the middle class represents the larger framework for the investigation of entertainment and pleasure within the context of the functionalization (modernization) of society.

I therefore regard the changes in the cultural marketplace as a (necessary) differentiation of the cultural arena and as bound up with the diversification of its consumers and their altered mentalities and values. This is not simply a deterioration of tastes and a simplification of forms to appeal to a broader (possibly less educated) audience but rather a complex restructuring of cultural valorizations. Nonprofessional, dilettante (in the parlance of the day) cultural practices created a third dimension, a cultural public sphere bridging the gap between the domestic sphere and the public realm. In this mediating sphere, with its forms of sociability, the limitations of the emerging modern society with its differentiated functions could be addressed, covered up, or, to a degree and for brief periods, overcome. Cultural practices such as entertainment during leisure forged new communities beyond the family and close personal friends. The most significant of these are the communities of readers created by and creating the various forms of the periodical press. In historically broad terms, Benedict Anderson has discussed the role of what he labels "print capitalism" in the emergence of a new form of "imagined community." With the rise of the vernacular, which in turn was codified by the printed text, it became possible to reach a much larger readership. Readers could conceive of themselves as members of a group by participating in the same reading experience without actually having to come in contact with each other.[38] While Anderson's concern is with the role of the formation of imagined communities as a stepping-stone to the construction of the nation, my concern here is with the dissemination of modern mentalities. The latter are caught between the specialization of a functionally differentiated society and the increasing degree of standardization and nonspecialization within cultural practices. Ernest Gellner sees standardization in education, literacy, and broad access to forms of communication as the prerequisites for modern societies. Print culture is of primary importance in the formation of the shared habits of modern men and women such as "literacy," a modern concept of time, "work habits," "social skills," and cultural literacy.[39] As decisions about cultural entertainment and leisure are arguments about power and control, they are also implicitly political.[40] Although differentiated into distinct groupings with particular interests, a number of publications of general interest, such as Johann Justin Bertuch's (1747–1822)[41] *Journal des Luxus und der Moden*,[42] offered the general parameters of modern cultural literacy and of taste. Such publications negotiate between the formation of commonalities in communities and the prized individuality of the modern subject. Cultural discourses, especially those that are highly effective, attractive, and thus popular—in other words, those that produce pleasure and are thus highly desirable—play a major role in this self-fashioning of the middle class.

Toward the end of the eighteenth century, the cultural realm in a symbiotic relationship with the economic realm constituted the primary site for the self-constitution of the middle class. At this point, culture becomes the major field of contention, where conflicting interests and competing needs begin to differentiate an earlier, more monolithic understanding of culture. I do not see this process as a unidirectional form of coercion or manipulation in the name of taste or as an internalization of normative standards that simply take the place of the hegemonic powers of absolutist sumptuary laws, as Appadurai argues. With respect to the English context, Appadurai considers the prescription of taste as "no less effective in limiting social mobility, marking social rank and discrimination, and placing consumers in a game whose ever-shifting rules are determined by 'taste-makers' and their affiliated experts."[43] Rather, the formation of taste driving (cultural) consumption, and with it the forms of entertainment, is less unidirectional and more self-reflexive. It is vigorously discussed and highly contested. As I will show in chapter 6, it is not immediately clear who the so-called "taste-makers" are and what the agenda is as it shifts and changes depending on the context. However, taste and the cultural practices that it drives do mark rank and social position and assist in group formation. Yet at times it encourages social mobility, while at other times it discourages it. The study of entertainment—in this larger context—participates in studying the symbolic orders in which intersubjective meanings and cultural and social practices are formed and challenged. Examining the multiple layers of discourses, meanings, practices, and codes that fabricate the discourses of pleasure and entertainment, this book participates in the discussion of the discursive reorganization of cultural and social value systems in this central period in German cultural history.[44]

After I explore in chapter 1 the methodological framework of cultural studies for the analysis of pleasure and entertainment, chapter 2 illuminates the sociohistorical context, the emergence of the modern middle class, its differentiation, and its conception of culture. Chapter 3 reconstructs the role of *Empfindsamkeit* (sensibility) and the role of the new love paradigm and the changes in mentalities they fostered. In their construction of desire and longing, both were essential for the reconceptualization of pleasure and entertainment discussed in chapter

4. Chapter 5 discusses various forms of cultural consumerism. In chapter 6, taking Bertuch's *Journal des Luxus und der Moden* as my example, I examine the relationship between print culture and the discursive creation of material culture. With a focus on clothing fashions as a most obvious form of consumerism, I show how instrumental this form of print culture was in the creation of the middle-class lifestyle and how, in turn, the desire for new information and stimulation began to drive and alter print culture itself. This chapter further explores the various functions of fashionable clothing as an expressive medium that integrated the body as a cultural production into identity formation. Chapter 7 explores entertainment (including music and art and the fashionable cultural practice of living pictures) in its social context of middle-class sociability. Chapter 8 discusses several forms of fashionable entertainments (travel, visits to landscape gardens, and the enjoyment of the private gardens) and the stimulation they created. The final chapter explores those pleasurable diversions that foreground the pleasures of looking, thus altering practices in conventional genres such as theater and painting.

1

The Role of Cultural Studies
in Historicizing Entertainment

The discourses of objects and practices of cultural consumption as means of entertainment (*Unterhaltung, Zeitverkürzung*) that provide the emotive disposition of pleasure (*Vergnügen*) comprise the topic of this book. By "discourse" I mean the linguistic side of a larger formation of specialized knowledge that enables, organizes, and accompanies social differentiation and functionalization. My term "cultural consumption" captures the interplay of the symbolic and socioeconomic aspects of the middle-class lifestyle and at the same time suggests the dynamic aspect of entertainment. It encompasses objects of both high and everyday culture ranging from books and the theater to fashion and fashionable pastimes, which become increasingly consumed as entertainment during leisure. Because fashion craves novelty, it encompasses the tendency to constantly require new stimulation and innovation, leading to a voracious appetite for the consumption of new products and practices. The emergence of an entertainment culture (the theater and print explosion) and the availability of luxury objects (the book as status object, fashion in dress and the domestic environment, the imports of coffee, tea, china, muslins, and chintzes) influenced the norms that people had formerly used "to explain the material world and to make its artifacts meaningful."[1]

The attempt to reconnect the objects of material culture with nonmaterial cultural practices and to ground both in their socioeconomic context, of course, goes against the grain of aesthetic theory in the wake of Kant. His decisive revolutionary break with previous aesthetic theory formulated in his *Critique of Judgement* (1790),[2] postulating an autonomous concept of art, separated the modern conception of the arts from other artifacts. The non-instrumental character of art, which contains its inner completion within itself, separates it from other forms of cultural production. The emergence of this decisive model is usually theorized in its innovation for philosophy as a discipline. On occasion, other implications have been pointed out: Kant's model has been explained as an opposition to the growing commercialization of culture, especially literature, toward the end of the century. Woodmansee reads aesthetic autonomy as a defensive strategy designed to protect high culture from the encroachment of commercialization, which was perceived as pushing the elite concept of art to the periphery of cultural practices. Although these economic aspects are certainly of central importance, my own approach focuses on changes in mentalities and lifestyles within the context of the economic exploration. Other critics have argued that the conception of autonomous art responds to a political crisis in Enlightenment public culture, that is, the fear of a politicized Enlightenment.[3]

THE OTHER OF HIGH CULTURE

By using the term "cultural consumerism," this study also seeks to distance itself from the problematic implications of the conventional terminology naming cultural practices that do not belong to high culture. Yet the conventional usage—"trivial," "mass," or "popular" culture— is misleading with regard to the late eighteenth century and does not capture the historical specificity of what has been made out to be the Other of high culture. "Mass" culture suggests larger numbers of members, participation by the lower class, a sense of a significant potential for actual physical assembly, and a highly efficient culture industry that mass-produces artifacts and imposes them on the masses. These factors were not given in our time frame. The mark of "triviality" suggests a negative value judgment about the quality (or lack thereof) of the given artifact or practice but says little about the historically specific function of the artifacts thus labeled. "Popular" culture suggests not only an opposition to "high culture, learned culture or liberal culture"[4] but also a groundswell of interest in a given cultural artifact or practice arising from many layers of society—mostly, however, from the lower classes. This implication of popularity is not suitable for the concept of culture described in this study, which is clearly an upper-middle-class phenomenon that takes great pains to distinguish its practices from those of the lower classes. Both terms, with their association of mobs and masses, fail to capture the specificity of our time frame, which is, instead, characterized by forms of small-group activity and more intimate forms of sociability negotiating new forms of community in a crumbling estate society with its shifting configuration of family and work.

Furthermore, all three terms imply binary opposition as their form of classification, which assumes that this phenomenon can be reduced to two opposing values. Although this way of thinking, theorizing, and creating paradigms has long been the dominant approach to deal with high culture's Other, it is not suitable to my investigation, which considers entertainment as provided by cultural practices ranging over a continuum. In any case, the discussion of pleasure and entertainment is clearly affected by this binary construction of alterity. High culture became built up and legitimized as the dominant model, as we will see when tracing the historical development of the binary model of culture in the eighteenth century and its critical reception.

For late-eighteenth-century Germany, the formation of this cultural divide was discussed primarily with respect to literature. Only by implication does this debate yield insights into other cultural practices, such as the aestheticization of the domestic sphere, fashion, and travel as sites of entertainment. Elements of everyday culture or lifestyle were not part of serious discussions and did not receive much critical attention. The overview will show how this binary model relegated entertainment that produced pleasure to the realm of the irrational and body-centered sensuality. I argue that this dichotomy is reductionist and fails to explore what I see as the less orderly and less clear distinctions between cultural practices and their functions over a continuum of culture.

The shift in reading practices, for example, added new journalistic tasks to literature's unique manner of knowledge formation. Presenting information on consumer goods or on other cultures helped to create a whole range of other cultural practices, such as fashion and leisure travel. What was perceived as a split into high and low literature—and

3

what I label a differentiation of the cultural scene—emerged at that historical moment when the educational level lost its relative uniformity. Leading to increasing specialization, this differentiation can be read as a failure of the Enlightenment project to retain a progressive concept of a monolithic culture, striving for an ever greater realization of one's own human and educational potential. The result was a specialized professional reader (critics, authors, and journalists to some extent, etc.) on the one hand and a general predominantly recreational readership with diverse educational preparations on the other. Both groups—which are themselves differentiated and not monolithic—require distinct things from literature. The recreational reader expects practical advice, direction, and discussion of certain current issues and problems as well as entertainment. The forms of playful imag(in)ing are a dominant aspect of the entertainment function of recreational reading. The professional reader might read as a professional reader in one area but for entertainment or advice on other occasions and in other areas.

Nevertheless, the theory of a split into two separate cultural spheres became the dominant critical model throughout the nineteenth century, with various emphases, and survived until the anthropological turn in literary studies, the recent dominance of cultural studies. While the discussion ostensibly centered on the rise of "trivial" or "mass" literature, what was really negotiated was the role of pleasure and entertainment in culture. Derived from an examination of reading for entertainment, three main lines of argument—as we will see below—were usually associated with the creation of pleasure: pleasurable cultural consumption provides a certain freedom from the rigor and discipline associated with (high) culture, it grants momentary liberty from the pressures of "reality" and thus operates as a social safety valve (Greiner), and, at the same time, it can serve as a stepping-stone or means to a more fully developed cultural taste (Beaujean).[5] These arguments also imply that the products are characterized by aesthetic simplicity, accommodating the unsophisticated tastes of the less educated.

All arguments dismiss these forms as inferior to true cultural competence. The latter is based on the Kantian aesthetics of pure disinterested, sublimated, distinguished, or "complex" pleasure (Corngold). Modern cultural critics followed suit and constructed mass culture as the Other in order to advocate certain positions, to foster social and intellectual control, or to displace traits that a society considers undesirable. As Dana Polan points out: "Indeed, in the way that some cultural anthropologists have shown how much the constitution of a society depends on that society's ability to construct some sort of Other on which to focus its disapprobation so that its own mainstream social relations may seem normal, mass culture has become one of culture studies' most recurrent Others—as a repository and a stereotypic cause of all social ills of life under capitalism."[6] By linking pleasure and entertainment with mass culture, they become relegated to the storehouse of alterity and thus devalued. Moreover, there is a simplistic tendency "to denigrate that other primarily because it allegedly provides pleasure to the consumer."[7] As we will see, not only did the negatively perceived link between culture and consumption dominate the discussion from its very beginning, but its role as Other also obscured its additional functions such as the part it plays in social differentiation, or as an important affective motor for advances in culture and civilization. These latter functions, not the role as Other to high culture, are at the center of this study. I am therefore not interested in value judgments or in discussing the relative merits of artifacts.[8]

BEYOND A BINARY MODEL

We have to keep in mind that for this stage in cultural differentiation it is problematic to speak in reductive dichotomies such as the opposition between "simple" and "complex" or "ideological" and "subversive." Instead, all cultural forms are potentially contradictory, blending progressive and regressive elements and serving specific uses that vary in any given context. Polan cautions that the reliance on the "stable existence of a whole series of reductive dichotomies" and the "assumption that a number of different dichotomies are parallel, equivalent, or even interchangeable—as is the case in the process by which an opposition of 'simple' and 'complex' is mapped onto opposition of 'mass culture' and 'high culture'"—can actually block the analysis of cultural politics because it overlooks the specificity of the various functions.[9] Tania Modleski also points to the theoretical problem with this tendency of the theorists of making mass culture into the Other of whatever, at any given moment, they "happen to be championing."[10] Attributing phenomena to the realm of mass culture has become a facile way to avoid dealing with the artifact in a systematic manner, a way to dismiss what does not fit the dominant paradigm under investigation. Used as a negative foil—which seemingly warrants no closer scrutiny—it foregrounds the object under investigation at the moment, while the negative foil remains relatively unexamined. My book argues against this tendency in the analysis of culture in the eighteenth century.

As far as I can tell, there are no grand narratives of the pleasures of cultural consumerism as a counterpart to Max Weber's influential *The Protestant Ethic and the Spirit of Capitalism*[11] that illuminate this early phase of middle-class cultural differentiation before we can speak of consumer culture. Despite the fact that pleasure and entertainment represent a central cluster of concepts connecting the economic and cultural discourses in their impact in the construction of bourgeois identity, they remain under-researched. Making explanatory connections among culture, leisure, entertainment, and pleasure has not been central to German eighteenth-century studies.

For this particular historical situation, it does not suffice to follow the traditional schools of cultural criticism—which assume this kind of firm binary classification—such as that of the Frankfurt school with its emphasis on the role of high culture and its pessimistic view of the manipulated masses, or that of the Birmingham school with its optimistic view of mass culture and its belief in the audience's potential resistance to mass culture's manipulation.[12] Although both have been formulated with twentieth-century conditions in mind, they nevertheless influenced the discussion on mass culture in general—even when dealing with earlier moments in history (Huyssen, Bürger)—and thus deserve a short review of their relevant points.[13]

According to Adorno and Horkheimer, only high art could keep alive the utopian promise once held by religion. It could fulfill this function only because it defined itself in opposition to the material reality, by its insistence on autonomy and on freedom of purpose (*Zweckfreiheit*). High art, defined as a negative category, is the subversive force that opposes the spurious harmony linked to bourgeois taste and morals. Mass culture, on the other hand, became linked with cheap and easy pleasure that reconciles consumers with their material surroundings. This critical paradigm links entertainment with capitalism and its ills such as urbanization and alienated city life where a plethora of easy "false" pleasures fill people's desperate emptiness. The standardization of working life that produced a bored, numbed, and passive worker was replicated by a standardized culture industry that offered only pseudo-individualized stimulation to the bored consumer. Adorno views the culture industry as a deeply ideological apparatus; thus the work of art should distance itself from the material conditions of everyday life.[14]

Herbert Marcuse's theory on affirmative culture reads it as a dialectical phenomenon that stabilizes a problematic social reality by offering compensation for the alienation of modern life by holding up a mirror of a better, more humane world. Accordingly, the split into two cultural realms—the dichotomy between products of high and low culture—thus expresses the truth, that is, the negativity of social reality. Low culture is the shadow of high culture, its bad conscience.[15] For the modernist, entertainment cannot be part of (high) culture because the pleasure it provides is associated with bourgeois manners, morals, and habits.[16] High art had dedicated itself to an attack on pleasure in part because pleasure was the province of mass art. Thus modernism was repelled by an art that is "consumer-oriented and comfortable, let alone luxurious."[17] The autonomy of modernist aesthetics suppresses not only the trivialities of life but resists the lure of mass culture and abstains from pleasure as well as from the pleasure of pleasing an audience.[18] High art's refusal to entertain coupled with its disdain for the material context was an important impetus for the differentiation of the cultural realm.

While Marxist criticism and its most influential and sophisticated manifestation, critical theory and *Ideologiekritik,* legitimized the integration of economic and political contexts in the study of cultural artifacts, it focused on the sphere of work and production, paying less attention to its flip side, leisure and entertainment. As outlined above, the Frankfurt school's concept of high art as refuge from alienated work theorized a concept of art in which the kind of pleasure associated with entertainment had no place. The latter terms became associated with mass art and consumerism, which displayed similar marks of alienation as capitalist work. Since many important literary critics who produced the seminal studies on the critique of absolutism and the nobility in eighteenth-century Germany were influenced by the Frankfurt school, *Ideologiekritik,* and Marxist criticism, their emphasis was on the exploration of the Protestant work ethic (Weber) and on (high) cultural production. These were seen as the center of the self-image of the emergent bourgeoisie. This approach was, of course, justified, as the theoreticians in the early eighteenth century indeed emphasized self-discipline and repression of desires. They created an elaborate system of ethics and morality that was based on self-control. Leisure, entertainment, and pleasure were at best marginal concepts and at worst vilified as part of the nobility's lifestyle.[19]

Apart from not being taken seriously, the objects of cultural consumerism have been deeply implicated as ideological and coercive by the Marxist tradition. Yet the multi-causal nature of change and the participatory nature of the consumer do not warrant the reliance on this underlying model of oppressors and oppressed.

I am also not pursuing the possible utopian element of so-called mass culture in the tradition of Marcuse or especially Hans Magnus Enzensberger. They argued against the Frankfurt school's claim that the culture industry imposes false needs on its audience, instead claiming that mass culture's success depended on its ability to address people's real needs.[20] I do not wish to argue that the forms of cultural consumption discussed in this book serve any overtly emancipatory utopian purpose but instead that they have very specific historically determined social functions.

My cultural studies approach reconnects the cultural objects and events with their context and focuses on the multiple layers of discourses (i.e., economic, historical, aesthetic, anthropological) that have an impact on entertainment, exploring how these spheres influence and alter each other in a fluid, continually evolving exchange. By treating the genesis of the middle-class concept of cultural entertainment as unstable and historically constructed, this study problematizes the simplistic dichotomies dominating the debates. A closer look will reveal that it is more accurate to talk about a complex network of force fields serving a variety of interests and needs. Among other things, the pursuit of pleasure resulted in voluntary participation (and not coercion) and shaped middle-class cultural consumerism with its demands for goods, services, and practices, facilitating and creating the bourgeois lifestyle. This, in turn, led other members of the same class to invest in the means of production for these desirable goods and cultural practices. The resulting increase in variety allowed for a larger selection of cultural practices and artifacts for the consumer. Each new activity and product implied the potential for another, producing an escalating, self-generating system that insisted on its own transitoriness. The transitory nature of these cultural practices and objects was contained in its valorization of novelty, in, for example, the term "fashion" (*Mode*), which contained the seeds of its own obsolescence. This self-regulatory system was much more unsystematic and contingent (contingent is what can take place in many different ways or not at all) than any binary model can suggest.

8

This study hopes to explain how the mechanisms by which entertainment and the pleasure it creates came to be important forces in the fabrication of new cultural practices linked to the nascent consumer culture. Furthermore, it explores the impact of cultural consumerism on the self-fashioning of the middle-class lifestyle as an important part of identity construction. Consumer culture has received recent attention by historians, anthropologists, sociologists, and economists. The consumption of goods and of cultural practices displays similar features. Their entertainment function is one important common denominator; the other is their ability to convey meaning and render visible aspects of one's identity. It is therefore useful to take a closer look at studies on consumerism.

The more recent studies pick up on the classic studies on the modernization of societies—the study of the legal, economic, industrial, and other revolutions (Durkheim, Weber, Marx, Simmel, and Sombart)—but with a new emphasis on the area of consumer demand, some arguing the case of a consumer revolution that preceded the industrial revolution.[21] These studies explore the "new categories of goods, new times, places and patterns of purchase, new marketing techniques; new ideas about possessions and materialism; changed reference groups, lifestyles, class mobility, diffusion of patterns, product symbolism, and patterns of decision making."[22] None of them focus specifically on the German context, and they situate the birth of consumer society at different historical points. They are nevertheless important and pertinent for our context because the German states were influenced by French and especially English consumer behavior and goods—albeit to different degrees and at different times. The fact that the consumer revolutions were situated in different historical periods is instructive because it points to the different functions and manifestations of a seemingly similar phenomenon.

Grant McCracken situates a consumer revolution at the Elizabethan court in late-sixteenth-century England when courtiers were induced to spend. Elizabeth I used expenditure as a means to govern— a convention she might have learned from observing Italian Renaissance courts. It is there that the court had become a kind of theatrical spectacle and that luxury had become a means of government. "The supercharged symbolism of the monarch's court, hospitality, and clothing became the opportunity for political instruction and persuasion."[23] Objects could be made to convey the monarch's validity of government, goals for the kingdom, or qualities of power and majesty. The consumer boom among courtiers was one consequence and served as a means of social positioning and competition for the political favors of the monarch. This is, of course, the model of conspicuous consumption that Norbert Elias developed. He saw the absolute ruler, most notably Louis XIV and the Court of Versailles, as the model that was imitated to a greater or lesser degree by the rulers in the German states and which was to arouse the opposition of the middle class (*Die höfische Gesellschaft*). At the same time, in his study on the civilizing process (*Der Prozeß der Zivilisation*) he considers this process an evolution of both behavioral and material aspects of culture. More sophisticated behaviors—for example, those relating to the consumption of food—required more elaborate and differentiated utensils and more refined dishes. With the suppression of aggressive and instinctual behavior, self-consciousness about the perception of one's person and actions by others increased along with refinement and ritualized conduct, which, in turn, required and was enabled by a larger variety of goods and cultural practices.[24]

I am using the convergence of these two models by Norbert Elias to analyze the decades under consideration here. His "saving-for-future-profit model" as the dominant economic pattern for the middle class (which he contrasts with the status-consumption model of the aristocracy in *Die höfische Gesellschaft*) needs to be fused with his insights into the civilizing process with its proliferation of goods, cultural objects, and practices (*Der Prozeß der Zivilisation*). This leads to a more appropriate and complex model of consumption by the various layers of the middle class at the end of the eighteenth century. Their pattern of consumption takes on aspects of status consumption—cultural objects and practices become markers of refinement and thus symbols of social positioning—within an overarching saving-for-future-profit model. Fiscal discipline constituted an important first step in the building of middle-class wealth and power and assured greater returns in the long run. Although the middle class began to advocate spending for cultural consumption, it clearly advocated living within one's means. During the time under investigation, the middle class reformulated the concept of "luxury" by deemphasizing the individual implications (and thus the moral liability the term had held for an oppositional identity formation) and by instead stressing the social usefulness of spending for the larger community and thus for the civilizing process. At the same time, the refinement of taste associated with the civilizing process influenced the reinterpretation of luxury.

For the German context, my own reading situates the emergence of middle-class consumption as an important factor in identity formation around 1780. It was assisted and in part prompted by the emergence of the periodical press with its invitation to consume. The format of a periodical in itself trained the readership to expect a similar reading experience at regular intervals (monthly in the case of the *Journal des Luxus und der Moden*), and its illustration and subject matter set the stage for consumption. In the first half of the century, the middle class was hostile toward the extravagance and luxury of the nobility (the Protestant ethic and its condemnation of luxury), linking it to a lack of moral values, to debauchery, and to lasciviousness. By the 1780s, with periodicals such as the *Journal des Luxus und der Moden,* the attitudes toward luxury underwent a careful and deliberate reinterpretation. Bolstered by economic theory and the emphasis on the cultural (or civilizing) value of consumption, the reinterpretation of "luxury" associated consumption with culture, as we will see below.

Neil McKendrick et al. and Colin Campbell situate the birth of consumer society in the eighteenth century (both with emphasis on England) because it was at that point that the middle class was able to enjoy a larger variety of goods. McKendrick focuses on the production, marketing, and advertising side of consumption in the course of the eighteenth century. Campbell sees the origins of consumption in a particular mentality (that of the individual in Romanticism) with its insistence on the uniqueness of the self, which was realized through various experiences and creativity.[25]

McCracken's observation of an intensification of consumer activity during the eighteenth century also holds true for the German situation, albeit to a lesser degree: "Consumption was beginning to take place more often, in more places, under new influences, by new groups, in pursuits of new goods, for new social and cultural purposes."[26] I argue that intensified cultural consumption took on a number of different but related functions, such as social differentiation and (cultural) entertainment within the middle-class lifestyle in the process of middle-class identity formation and negotiation.

This study takes part in the exploration of the signifying power of culture, in examining its mediating properties, the way in which men and women create their material surroundings or distance themselves

11

from them and attempt to gain control over material phenomena through symbolic representation. By reading culture through the lens of entertainment, the study offers a fresh look at the meanings and values that defined the middle class. By examining how its members negotiated the conditions of their existence, I focus on the relational communicative processes between subjects in the interstices of texts and contexts. This study shows how cultural practices—such as literature, periodicals, and (theatrical) performances and objects of material culture (fashion and other luxury goods)—as forms of entertainment driven by the desire to experience pleasure constituted an important part of the emergent consumer culture and middle-class self-definition.

Cultural studies of the eighteenth century will, of course, have to take the findings of historiography and social history as the context for the cultural practices into consideration. This study also makes use of the materials and social and cultural practices unearthed by *Kulturwissenschaft;* my main focus, however, will be on the discursive creation of the cluster of concepts "entertainment," "leisure," and "pleasure" within these new cultural practices. The study differs from works in anthropology and *Kulturwissenschaft* in its perspective. I do not provide an empirical account of what people actually did for entertainment; the examples will only serve as illustrations of a more abstract and theoretical account of the discourse of entertainment.

Taking entertainment as the focal point, the study moves between describing specific instances of its manifestation in cultural artifacts and providing a theoretical framework. The book is thus concerned both with a series of exemplary cultural artifacts and with the development of discourses that render these culturally significant. Therefore this study builds the diversities and contentions informing cultural construction and representation and its sociopolitical contingencies into its critical reflection. When discussing specific examples from literary and cultural primary texts, I attempt to focus on less-well-known (non-canonical) texts wherever possible to further expand our understanding of the late eighteenth century.

In particular, I am interested in how the various manifestations of entertainment enhance and are enhanced by cultural and economic activity and what function this interrelationship plays in the emergence and establishment of the social stratification of the middle class. In other words, by taking entertainment as my reference point, I would like to offer another reading of the distinct pattern of the birth of modern (consumer) culture in Germany, where it was more closely associated with education and culture (*Bildung*) than in other countries. In addition, the traditional critical disinterest in the close ties of culture and consumption and the foregrounding of the cultural aspect distinguish the German development to a degree from that of its European neighbors.

This study examines the various forms of cultural production in connection with other cultural practices in their sociohistorical context. In doing so, a considerably less homogeneous picture of the eighteenth century emerges. For example, in the diverse print culture of the time period under investigation, a complex and often contradictory discourse on fashionable consumption as the motor for economic and cultural advancement of a nation emerges. Multiplicity as an inescapable condition of culture[27] has, until recently with the methodological proliferation of cultural studies, not been valued—and has even been suppressed—in the study of eighteenth-century German culture. A relatively homogeneous view of eighteenth-century Germany based on a narrow literary canon (Gottsched, Lessing, Goethe, Schiller), a limited methodological arsenal (the Protestant work ethic), and an emphasis on rationality in philosophy remained in place. When the student movement in West Germany called for the democratization of culture, criticizing the canon of high culture, more authors and texts were added to the canon (e.g., J. M. R. Lenz, Büchner, Jacobin literature, etc.). Determined by the sociohistorical or Marxist reading of literature, especially authors whose works lent themselves to a political and socially critical reading (*Ideologiekritik* or *Sozialkritik*) were rediscovered and integrated into the canon. Yet the studies of texts outside the realm of high culture—periodicals, almanacs, and above all *Trivialliteratur*—explored predominantly their function as escapism. Despite the change of focus, the system of valorization in itself remained largely uncontested. Denouncing the elitism of Weimar classicism while illuminating the positions of social or ideological critiques of the Storm and Stress writers or the Jacobins did not fundamentally challenge the underlying valorization of high culture as aesthetically normative.

It was not until the women's movement unearthed a wealth of texts written by women that the canon debate began in earnest. The relationship between cultural valorization and gender began to destabilize accepted norms and values. By pointing out the influence of institutionalization and professionalization on the formation of cultural values, feminist criticism initiated a serious analysis of the relationship between canonized artifacts and marginalized, neglected, and dismissed forms of cultural practice. By problematizing gender-specific educational and social practices and by examining strategies of inclusion and exclusion, cultural values lost their aura of quasi-"natural" normativity and appeared, instead, as culturally constructed.

My cultural studies approach takes these contestations into a broader context—of which gender is only one of many facets—by simultaneously illuminating several discourses that affect cultural production and reception. It denaturalizes the disciplining operations of cultural valorizations and examines how they function in society and become socially meaningful. One important part of the function of culture is entertainment.

In broader terms, this multidimensional grasp of cultural studies in historicizing entertainment adds a new layer of differentiation to the debate surrounding the emergence of the public sphere and the rise of civil society in late-eighteenth-century Germany. The most important—albeit frequently critiqued—account of the emergence of the public sphere, Jürgen Habermas's *Strukturwandel der Öffentlichkeit* (1962) (*The Structural Transformation of the Public Sphere* [1989]), serves also as the foundational text for this study, but with important additions and modifications. Habermas described how the literary public sphere—the world of literature and the periodical press as well as certain forms of sociability, the salon and the coffeehouse—served as a site where private people could engage in critical debate. This literary public sphere was seen as a springboard for a politicized public sphere. The modern state becomes a bureaucratic apparatus, which Habermas sees as an institutional structure separate from the person of the ruler and his court.[28] He sees a central function of the modern state in the regulation of economic activity on the side of private people as the economic activity becomes separated from the household economy.[29] I agree with Habermas's assessment that the rise of capitalism limits the influence of church and court in the commodification of culture. Taken out of its traditional context, art becomes autonomous and requires a critical debate of its merits, creating the literary public sphere. Rational communication is the medium with which private individuals make sense of the meanings of the cultural product stripped of its representative qualities as embodiments of institutional power (that of the church or the court).

Yet I would contend—as have Habermas's critics—that the exclusive focus on the literary sphere creates an undue focus on a perceived homogeneity of the self-representation of the public with a predominant focus on a critical oppositional identity formation. *Structural Transformation* has thus been criticized not only for basing itself on predominantly textual material but also for misreading the process of subject formation in literary texts—which it uses to make the point of the rational-critical examination of texts. Most recently, Jonathan Hess, with recourse to Jochen Schulte-Sasse and Dorothea von Mücke,[30] summarizes the newer trends in eighteenth-century scholarship that offer a correction to Habermas's position:

> Recent literary criticism tends to stress the way eighteenth-century literature participates in the new forms of subjectivity. Habermas, however, blindly follows the conventions of eighteenth-century fiction: he reads *Pamela* and *Werther* as authentic documents of a genuine subjectivity, not as fictional narratives that purport to be true and in doing so help foster certain modes of subjectivity. In and of themselves, such works lack reflective clarity about this subjectivity, Habermas insists, and therefore they naturally engender a rational-critical discourse in which individuals gain clarity and enlighten themselves about the "genuine experiences of their new privateness."[31]

Habermas's early study overlooks not only the self-reflexive complexity of eighteenth-century texts but also, for example, the moralizing tendency of theater, which strives to instill norms in the individual, thus actively participating in the process of subject construction.

Furthermore, Habermas's belief in the rational-critical subject, which he later modified under the influence of poststructuralism and the postmodernism debates in his *Der philosophische Diskurs der Moderne*,[32] precluded his addressing other areas of culture not devoted to critique. These are the areas of material culture, the self-presentation of the body and its physical environment, and the entertainment function of culture. By including these aspects, we arrive at a more complex dynamics of class formation.

In Habermas's account, middle-class values are based solely on those of high culture, which depends on the exclusion of other forms of cultural practice and their practitioners. Due to this exclusive focus on rational-critical debate and high culture, he overlooks those groups that could not participate in this idealized sphere, for example, women and less-educated men.

Habermas initially overestimated (in the first edition of his *Strukturwandel der Öffentlichkeit*) the coherence of the literary public sphere, which he saw as forming a homogeneous group structured by the democratic medium of critical reasoning (*Räsonnement*), but later he modified his position (1990 edition) and spoke of competing public spheres. Habermas's correction has been critiqued as not going far enough by, among others, Erich Schön, whose arguments, based on his work on the reading craze, are of importance for my context. While Habermas assumes that the public sphere transforms itself from a critical public sphere into one of cultural consumption in the nineteenth century, Schön argues for a stronger emphasis on the aspect of cultural consumption and a deemphasis of the critical aspects already in the eighteenth century.[33] My own study extends Schön's description beyond the aspect of reading to other forms of cultural consumption. Thus I see this study as part of a revision of the arguments that focus predominantly on reading as *the* form of entertainment in the eighteenth century. Engelsing, for example, argues that because patriarchal forms of sociability had lost their appeal by the end of the century, the middle class was looking for alternate forms of public social exchange. They were centered around the book—and reading as the dominant form of sociable entertainment—as long as other forms of entertainment (e.g., sports, music, politics, and hobbies) did not compete.[34]

My study will show that the interest in reading—and the consequent proliferation of the market with its many distinct forms of reading materials—was, from the onset, intricately linked to other forms of entertainment that developed parallel to reading. With regard to reading practices, Roberto Simanowski also rethought the sequential nature of Engelsing's argument as a parallel development of the critical and the consuming audience instead and situated both in the eighteenth century.[35] His argument must be expanded to include the other forms of entertainment described in this study as the motor for the expanding sphere of cultural consumerism, which is instrumental in creating the middle-class lifestyle. This lifestyle represents an important counterpart of and supplement to the critical rational subject of high culture.

After all, both the pleasure that the forms of entertainment bring and the socialization in the aestheticized domestic sphere are important parts of subject formation. For some members of the middle class, the creation of a certain lifestyle represented the dominant focus (i.e., for women); other members (the cultural elite, consisting predominantly of men) could focus on it to a greater or lesser degree at will. Habermas's monolithic concept of culture ignores these more multifaceted cultural practices. Instead, I would argue that we are dealing with multiple public spheres that created and were created by a range of diverse cultural practices of which reading and literary discourse is only one, albeit a central one.

By examining a lifestyle issue such as entertainment, we are able to look beyond high culture and its representatives at these diverse practices and their practitioners. Recent work on sociability has pointed to its importance well beyond the formal salons and reading societies that Habermas theorized. In contrast to Habermas, we will see that the various forms of sociability included not only both genders but also other aspects of culture and entertainment in the formation and differentiation of middle-class identity.[36] In the formation of middle-class identity, commerce and consumption interconnected in certain reading practices and in the forms of comprehensive socialization in the family. The latter was not limited to emotional values, familial love, and friendship, as Habermas argued, but includes the forms of entertainment, consumption, everyday culture, and the formation of taste as a prerequisite of and a supplement to high culture.

Pierre Bourdieu's work is useful to my study because it addresses several of these issues and offers a methodological framework for the analysis of lifestyles. Bourdieu points to the relationships among social institutions, systems of thought, and the symbolic power of culture and its artifacts. For example, he confirms that, among other functions, art and cultural consumption fulfill a social function in their legitimization of social differences. Bourdieu's analyses of culture stress the importance of cultural artifacts and forms for the enforcement and reproduction of social hierarchies. Cultural consumption displays and consequently legitimates social differences. The formation of taste is instrumental as an organizing principle that helps to situate people on the continuum of their class. Bourdieu thus offers a critique of notions of the universality of the aesthetic sense on the one hand and of assumptions of autonomy that see (high) culture as devoid of external determinants on the other; he points, instead, to the intermingling of symbolic and economic power.[37]

Poised between a neohumanist concept of the individual as determining his or her destiny and the poststructuralist view that sees the individual as a mere intersection of various discourses, Bourdieu's concept of *habitus* (habit) contains a degree of agency while also taking account of discourses or structures outside the self, determining it to some degree. Habit thus reintroduces a form of subjectivity and agency into cultural analysis that structuralism and deconstruction had dismissed as idealistic. Habit denotes the dynamic interplay of structure and action, society and the individual. It represents a "theoretical intention . . . to get out from under the philosophy of consciousness without doing away with the agent, in its truth of a practical operator of object constructions."[38] Habit is a system of durable dispositions, that is, of principles that generate and organize practices and representations. Habit can also be described as a "feel for the rules of the game," a *sense pratique* that allows people to act and react in an almost unconsciously determined way that is second nature to them in specific situations. The long-term socialization in the various practices of culture is important for the formation of habit. It is everyday culture (*Alltagskultur*) that instills this practical sense.

Bourdieu's concept of "field" grounds the subject in an objective social context, offering another way to bridge the chasm between idealistic, humanistic approaches focusing on the subject and materialistic, structural, and deconstructive positions focusing on the material conditions or the discourse as determining features. While the exclusive focus on the subject ignores the social ground that molds consciousness, the sole emphasis on discourse fails to account for the contributions and representations individuals make to shape the social conditions. Therefore, symbolic features of social existence are entwined with the material conditions, yet without one being reducible to the other. Fields (the economic field, the educational field, the cultural field, etc.) are defined as structured spaces with their own laws of functioning. A field's structure is determined by the relationships among the positions that agents occupy in the field. Field is thus a dynamic concept. Within each given field, individuals compete for specific resources. In our case, in the cultural field, we are dealing primarily with symbolic power, which, though not reducible to economic capital, is linked to it. Symbolic capital is the degree of accumulated prestige (through academic capital—degrees, position, etc.—or linguistic capital) in a mix of knowledge and recognition ("connaissance" and "reconnaissance").[39] While economic capital is that which is immediately and directly convertible into money, cultural capital—the more important concept for Bourdieu—is accumulated in forms of cultural knowledge, competencies, and dispositions in the form of internalized codes that equip the agent with appreciation for and competence in deciphering cultural relationships and artifacts. Bourdieu defines cultural capital as an assembly of acknowledged and valued cultural resources and powers—expressed, for example, in educational qualifications—that can be "invested" in order to ensure social power. Particular cultural constructs and practices have historically been privileged by, among other things, their position in institutions or in educational settings and by the critical practices that surround these institutions. The possession of and access to valorized practices become the expression and the guarantee of social dominance.[40] Access to culture exists only for those who understand it. Comprehension relies on a learned decoding operation that is based on the values established in the given field and thus requires much more than the direct and immediate apprehension of the work. It is the result of a sustained process of inculcation, a long exposure to the works, and their reinforcement by the educational system. This process can result in the aesthetics of Kantian "pure" taste, which is based on a refusal of "impure" taste (a taste that is reduced to the pleasure of the senses) as well as on a refusal of the facile.

Bourdieu argues that this refusal is not universally accessible but is the dividing line between the cultured and the uncultured. Kant's definition suggests an educational opportunity, a process by which pure pleasure could eventually be achieved. Bourdieu challenges the notion of progressive refinement toward the appreciation of artistic autonomy; he sees the denial of the natural enjoyment as a function of social differentiation of legitimating social differences. Many rules of true appreciation are unconsciously internalized through repeated exposure and are thus closely linked to the cultural practices of one's family within its class.[41]

By necessity, this form of socialization within the middle-class lifestyle invites the inclusion of everyday practices that go beyond traditional high culture and includes the contribution of both genders. The increasing attention to the children in the middle-class household—

with its early childhood home schooling, specific children's literature, and the emergent exposure to exhibitions and museums, as well as to leisure travel, clothes, pets, toys, and music—provides a significant basis for the acculturation of its members. This process of socialization and acculturation takes place under the primary initial guidance of the mother. I would argue that these practices, which go beyond the scope of this study and deserve their own investigation, lay the groundwork for the continuum of culture, though they do not guarantee access to high culture.

It will become obvious in chapter 6 that the delineation of what constitutes taste permeates not only the discussions of high culture but all areas of cultural life. The negotiation of this competence is an important aspect of this study on entertainment and pleasure. This acquisition of taste within the domestic sphere and the family is therefore of utmost importance to the emergence of a continuum of cultural practices and of cultural consumerism, whereas traditionally more emphasis was placed on the formation of taste within the formal institutions of education. After all, the emerging universities and secondary schools at the end of the eighteenth century attempted an academization of this knowledge in the concept of *Bildung,* in a utopian desire to overcome the arbitrariness of one's social position by birth.

In his historical and sociological contextualization, Bourdieu situates the accelerated movement toward artistic autonomy and the values associated with it at the dawn of the industrial revolution and the reaction of the movement of Romanticism to it:

> The development of a veritable culture industry and, in particular, the relationship between the daily press and literature, encouraging the mass production of works produced by quasi-industrial methods—such as the serialized story (or in other fields, melodrama and vaudeville)—coincides with the extension of the audience. This can be attributed to the expansion of primary education, which turned new classes (including women) into consumers of culture. The development of the system of cultural production is accompanied by a process of differentiation generated by the diversity of the publics at which the different categories of producers aim their products. Symbolic goods are a two-faced reality, a commodity and a symbolic object.[42]

As I do in this study, Bourdieu links the expansion of education with the creation of new audiences with different needs. As I do, he links the differentiated audience with new (less monolithic) modes of reception and production. My analysis differs in that I do not link this diversification of the audience and its modes of cultural consumption directly to the industrial revolution; instead, I consider these factors as precipitated by the change of mentalities fostered by the values and dispositions we came to label sensibility (*Empfindsamkeit*) and Storm and Stress (*Sturm und Drang*) in German cultural history in the period preceding the industrial revolution.

Beyond exploring the interrelationships among high culture, cultural consumerism, and material culture, we need to address the expressive properties of material culture. In our analysis of the techniques of cultural and intellectual history, we need to pay attention to figurative language, to allusions, to imagery, and to the ways in which material culture achieves the outward expression of ideas—in other words, to how culture is made material (or vice versa), to how processes that constitute culture might be discovered in the concrete objects of material culture. We will therefore examine a cluster of cultural categories and cultural principles centered around the concept of entertainment in a historically specified framework.[43]

2

The Differentiation of the Middle Class

The strengthening of the middle class and the transformation of the cultural sphere was brought about by a number of intrinsically linked social and perceptual factors.[1] The accepted opinion is that the bourgeoisie defined itself as differing from the nobility. In contrast, I argue that we have to distinguish two waves in this fluid construction of middle-class identity. The first wave is indeed characterized by an oppositional self-fashioning of middle-class identity as morally superior to that of the nobility. However, this is not the whole story. By the 1780s the oppositional formation began to lose its urgency. I would argue that the oppositional external differentiation is followed by a second wave of intraclass differentiation in which the members of the different communities within the middle class define themselves in contrast to each other. They do so primarily though their lifestyles. A brief discussion of both moments in the identity construction of the middle class—even though the first is well researched—serves as the necessary context for the discussion of the forms of entertainment and the sensations of pleasure they create.

In this process of differentiation, a more completely nuanced understanding of culture plays the dominant role. While the changes in the cultural marketplace—or the early culture wars leading to the displacement of the monolithic Enlightenment culture—have been

23

explored in detail, the fact that this cultural divide also created moments of internal differentiation for the middle class has not explicitly entered the critical discourse and thus deserves elaboration. This new concept of culture was closely associated with the economic strengthening of the middle class. A most striking example of this nexus can be observed in the modernity associated with the center of a cosmopolitan consumer culture of Hamburg associated with the merchants and commerce. It contained traces of the Enlightenment project's monolithic concept of culture as well as the new elite concept of high culture with its implied Other—non-elite culture (and its close link to cultural consumerism and entertainment).

In addition, the specificity of this new blended or "hybrid" concept of culture in Germany[2] was, in part, determined by the unique personal constellations—associations between members of the nobility and the bourgeoisie—that created centers of culture such as the unique culture associated with the city of Weimar. In addition to being a bastion of high culture, Weimar displayed forms of sociability in the salon of Johanna Schopenhauer, for example, which featured important forms of entertainment that transcended class barriers. Weimar was also home to a significant entrepreneurial spirit in the figure of Friedrich Justin Bertuch. Advisor to the court, businessman, entrepreneur, well connected, and an influential publisher, Bertuch played an important role in the creation, promotion, and establishment of many layers of cultural consumerism that transcended the barriers between the nobility and the (upper) middle class. Both Weimar and Hamburg are exemplary as central yet distinctly different sites for the differentiation of the bourgeoisie because they displayed a wide range of representative practices that I associate with the forms of entertainment and cultural consumption.

These kinds of constellations alert us to the fact that at this point in the historical development of the middle class it is no longer useful to speak of oppositional formations and to treat intermediaries such as Bertuch—or Goethe for that matter—as either naive or self-serving reformers or collaborators betraying the interest of their class (Wilson). Instead, it might be more useful to look at this (second) stage in the development of the middle class in eighteenth-century Germany as a moment of differentiation, when alliances are no longer drawn along class lines but are based on common economic and cultural interests. The names—Bertuch on the one hand, Goethe and Schiller on the other—are indicative of at least two distinct yet interwoven variants of this differentiation of the bourgeoisie. Associated with Goethe and Schiller is, of course, the neohumanist model of classicism with its idealist self-fashioning and careful discursive attention to high art. They drew the lines of demarcation to other groups with the help of the prescriptive concept of *Bildung*. The latter was elaborated most clearly in Schiller's complex dialectics of the concept of *Spiel*—the interplay between sensuous experience and (rational) control—and the notion of *Lebenskunst*. In his concept of *Lebenskunst* with its prerequisite of *Bildung*, Schiller considered art—and especially its central concept of beauty, the interpenetration of matter and form—as indispensable to being human.[3] In contrast, Bertuch, as we will see, stands for a more diverse and comprehensive, yet less integrated, understanding of "lifestyle" that can include elements of *Bildung* and *Lebenskunst* but also of the forms of cultural consumption driven by the pursuit of pleasure. His endeavor is characterized by its fluid, self-regulatory taste formation. Bertuch is a driving force for the fabrication of "pleasure" propelling cultural consumption, which he facilitated with his many economic and cultural enterprises. His ventures formed alliances according to common interests and economic, social, and cultural aspects. His concept of culture found extensive expression in the *Journal des Luxus und der Moden* and other periodicals, which helped to accomplish and give expression to the process of differentiation of the bourgeoisie around 1800. This process of differentiation of middle-class identity, a reshaping of the textures of everyday life, is the context of this study. I am not suggesting that one form of identity construction was simply replaced by another but rather that shifts and modifications altered its formation in which some elements were retained, some modified, and some replaced by others. The first phase of oppositional identity formation brought about important shifts in mentalities and cultural, social, and material interests that necessitated new ways of living together. As we will see, while the intimate nuclear family remained the most important core of bourgeois intimacy, it developed forms of sociability and entertainment that reached beyond its parameters and formed larger alliances and communities.

THE OPPOSITIONAL IDENTITY FORMATION OF THE MIDDLE CLASS, 1700–1780

The implicit political critique of the absolute state took place primarily in the cultural arena; literacy, education, and literature therefore played a major role in the self-constitution of the bourgeois class. Because of the delayed cultural investment in the development of the German language as the vehicle for educated dialogue, literary production was initially tied to other professions, such as university teaching, the pulpit, and other occupations devoted to education and scholarship. The movement to employ German as the learned language to replace Latin expanded general interest in education and literacy and ultimately led to a popularization of knowledge. The development of the vernacular also provided the necessary structural changes, which enabled "nonprofessionals"—men and women who were previously excluded by a lack of formal education and training—to participate in cultural practices.[4] The concept of the independent professional writer divorced from obligations of other professions and patrons emerged.[5] At the same time, our modern notion of a readership and literature was formed.[6]

These were important aspects in the cultural (and implicitly political) self-fashioning of the bourgeoisie. The cultural sphere had to be won over by the emerging bourgeoisie that aspired to social leadership: therefore the struggle over the definition of culture constitutes a struggle for intellectual, moral, and philosophical leadership. In the early stages of the Enlightenment the bourgeoisie attempted to wrest the cultural leadership away from the court culture of the nobility. This oppositional self-definition of the middle class emphasized humanistic values and a strong work ethic as a secularized version of Protestant ideals (Weber).

Work, frugality, and economic discipline represented not only a means of self-improvement but a critique of the status consumption practiced by the nobility.[7] Historically and theoretically informed literary criticism on the eighteenth century has in essence taken this position since the 1970s.[8] The most important sociohistorical literary criticism had therefore focused on a model in which the middle class wrests the moral and cultural hegemony from the nobility in an attempt to render the society based on estates superfluous.[9]

Up to and including the seventeenth century, cultural hegemony was firmly in the hands of the nobility and the courts. As Antonio Gramsci defined it in his *Prison Notebooks,* hegemony describes two connected phenomena: on the one hand, the state's preservation of authority through arranged concurrence rather than coercion, and on the other, the leadership of one class or group in relation to other social classes or political groups.[10] The different manifestations of hegemony operate within "civil society," the realm of "the private," and the domain of "culture" rather than within the institutions of the state. According to Gramsci, social control can be sustained only by both hegemonic and coercive activity. The political structures of the absolute state were paralleled and confirmed by the display of status and rank in the cultural sphere and by the corresponding status consumption. The nobility was bound to the court not only through political, economic, and social ties but by the expectation of their contribution in the cultural realm, in the display of splendor. If any social group aspires to social dominance, it must first assert its intellectual and moral leadership.[11] The dominant culture can be understood as the site of hegemonic representations. "It is also, therefore, a sphere that must be won over by any social group aspiring to social leadership: struggles over the definition of culture can thus be seen as struggles for intellectual, moral and philosophical hegemony."[12] Cultural production in eighteenth-century Germany was dominated by this shift of cultural hegemony as the German middle class carved out a distinct discursive space in opposition to that of the aristocracy and the courts. By emphasizing rational judgment and enlightened critique, the bourgeoisie was able to establish its moral and intellectual superiority. This cultural strategy represents a form of empowerment because it usurps cultural dominance. By claiming the universality of middle-class values, it devalues the nobility's symbolic display of political and cultural power. One important example is the oppositional character of the discourse of sensibility with its core unit, the middle-class family. It was based on mutual respect, friendship, and love—in short, on ideal humanitarian values—and thus represented a model for a progressive public sphere. The other important (related) feature of the middle class's oppositional self-definition is the economic aspect. Jürgen Kocka—although painting with broader strokes and addressing a longer historical period—notes that the *Bildungsbürgertum* had a certain respect

> for individual achievement on which they based their claims
> for rewards, recognition and influence. They shared basically
> positive attitudes towards regular work, a propensity toward
> rational lifestyles. . . . Emphasis on education (rather than on
> religion) characterized middle-class views of themselves and
> the world. Simultaneously, education (Bildung) served as the

basis on which they communicated with one another, and which distinguished them from others who did not share this kind of classical education. There was much respect for scholarly pursuits (Wissenschaft) and a particular aesthetic appreciation of music, literature and the arts.[13]

At the core of these changes of mentalities are the related concepts of temporalization, discipline, and self-discipline. While the theoretical model of the oppositional formation of the middle class provides the larger context for this study, it has to be modified. For the time frame in question, this process of distancing and oppositional moral and aesthetic identity formation in the move to wrest cultural, moral, and economic supremacy from the nobility was facing new challenges and tasks.

DIFFERENTIATION AND MODIFICATION OF MIDDLE-CLASS IDENTITY, 1780–1830

The time span in the cultural history of the German nation-states under investigation here is characterized by the internal adjustment of the dominant ideology which no longer functions as an organic and convincing relational whole. The internal stress, turmoil, and change are reflected in discourses negotiating and reshaping consent. During periods of increased renegotiations, many social components and discourses attempt to become hegemonic and prescriptive. The aesthetic treatises and the increased discussion of the value and nature of cultural practices became crucially important and a highly visible sign of change. They represent an attempt to account for the significant increase in belletristic texts, as we will see below. The increase in the availability of cultural practices and objects required new forms of orientation. As taste became an important organizing principle, it allowed the various layers of the middle class to create their own lifestyles with their unique forms of entertainment. These cultural practices could be used for the purpose of social differentiation and distinction within the context of late-eighteenth-century Germany.

Traditional historians, examining political, economic, and religious trends in the German states, focus on the backwardness of the political and economic system in comparison with the more centralized nations, in particular France and England. Alexander Gerschenkron's hypotheses explaining the pattern of industrialization were highly influential in establishing this interpretative grid. According to his paradigm, the German states are considered a backward country. As Robert Lee summarizes: "The more backward the country, the more active was the role of institutional factors, such as the banks or the state, and the greater the pressure on consumption levels in order to facilitate capital formation."[14]

Recent historical research differentiated this view, albeit with a different focus. While traditional schools had viewed the Holy Roman Empire as an inadequate structure because it had failed to become a nation-state—and this view had influenced sociohistorical and Marxist studies of literature (the *deutsche Misere* model)—recent historical studies revised many of these earlier positions. Historians have since argued that this decentralized political system worked effectively and even assured a certain power balance and stability in Europe.[15] They also point to the intense modernization taking place during our time frame.

Another often-mentioned liability as cause for Germany's backwardness were the borders limiting economic and political centralization. Yet these borders were permeable for the transfer of knowledge and education. Less monolithic than the more centralized countries, many cultural and educational centers with different educational, religious, and philosophical agendas were conducive to a diverse cultural life. This situation created and enabled a variety of opinions and schools. In addition, the larger number of cultural centers created a greater need for civil servants, educators, artists, and intellectuals across the many territories. For the middle class, this peculiarity also provided greater access to cultural activities throughout the land. These factors contribute to the strengthening of cultural life in Germany and set the stage for the legendary cultural self-definition of the German middle class as the architects of the *Kulturnation*.[16] Of course, we have to keep in mind that these transformations are limited to a small segment of the population, a fact that is borne out by the tensions between the stories that the different disciplines tell with regard to this time in history. While historians (especially traditional historians) lament the backwardness of Germany in the eighteenth century, cultural historians and literary scholars celebrate the decisive step into modernity in the cultural realm.

The apparent tensions between history and cultural history are productive because they force us to examine the complex relationship between historical events and cultural developments. In addition, these thick descriptions (to use Clifford Geertz's phrase) also remind us of the limited scope of what in cultural history appears as an all-encompassing role of culture. This cultural activity was limited to a fairly small part of the general population when even in the most advanced states, such as Saxony, the most industrialized and urbanized state in the Confederation, 72 percent of the population lived and worked on the land.[17] As a recent introduction into the history of this period summarizes:

> German society and economy in the 1810s appeared to have changed very little from the days of Martin Luther. The overwhelming majority of Germans lived in farmhouses or country villages near the fields where they worked. Transportation throughout the Confederation remained difficult, even for farmers and villagers who rarely ventured far off. There was little sense of time as an entity: it was still marked by the changing seasons, by the rising and setting of the sun, and occasionally by the ringing of church bells.[18]

The tensions and seeming contradictions that these two images of Germany produce are seldom thematized in studies dealing with cultural history. In my study they are also little more than a footnote cautioning us to keep in mind that all generalizations have to be thought of as qualified by regional differences—even if (for the sake of readability) this is not always explicitly stated in my study. The investigation of entertainment and cultural consumption refers predominantly to the less than 30 percent of the population who lived in the urban centers, the members of the third estate, the (upper) middle class, and members of the lower nobility.

The lower nobility, who increasingly had to compete with members of middle-class intellectuals and professionals for positions, were to some degree participants in the realm of culture that I am examining. At this point in history, the German upper middle class consisted of predominantly higher civil servants, theologians and ministers, professors, and writers but also members from the lower nobility, wealthy merchants, and businesspeople.[19] Yet the tensions between Germany's large agrarian population and the urban middle class at the vanguard of culture might not be unimportant to the differentiation of culture. As social mobility becomes a factor due to the influx of people into the urban labor pool, the realm of culture becomes a major field of cultural and social positioning.

The increasing economic vitality of the emerging middle class has become a (frequently unexamined) commonplace as a mode of explanation for the increasing cultural dominance of the middle class in Germany during the course of the eighteenth century leading to the eventual dissolution of corporate society and the estates. Frequently the economic strengthening is uncritically associated with the production side of economic development and ignores the side of consumption, which is of greater importance for my context. The centers for economic and cultural change were the cities and towns.[20] "It was here that social and economic development found its clearest expression."[21] Economic advancement flourished in the cities around the many large and small courts in the numerous principalities of the German states and in the Republican city of Hamburg. Initially, the agents of change in this pre-industrial urbanization could be found among the administrative elite who served the courts and among the bourgeois elite active in business, the professions, and commerce. Representing the connective tissue between court and city, these elites provided intellectual, cultural, and economic leadership.

My definition of the constitutive factors determining the middle class is informed by the cultural definition of the Kocka school. Yet I would not want to equate cultural self-definition with Kocka's notion of self-definition through *Bildung,* which is exclusively tied to high culture. As a glance at the actual cultural practices shows, the exclusive concentration on high culture is misleading and does not tell the whole story about the formation of the middle class. The impact of leisure activities and entertainment on economic development, for example, is not accounted for in this focus on *Bildung* and high (neoclassical) culture. Kocka's view of *Bildung* ignores consumption as an important ingredient in the formation of the modern middle class, while Kaschuba extends *Bürgerlichkeit* (the cultural identity of the German middle class) as a historically variable cultural practice and social status to a variety of factors ranging from property and profession to taste and *Bildung*[22] and, at least, alludes to the role of entertainment practices and consumer goods in the role of bourgeois identity formation. After all, goods on which the "consumer lavishes time, attention, and income are charged with cultural meaning." Consumers use the meaning of consumer goods to express cultural principles, cultivate ideals, create and sustain lifestyles, construct notions of the self, and create (and survive) social change.[23] These strategies assisted the German middle class in its internal differentiation and in group formations. Unlike the concept of *Bildung,* which is one of the unifying features of the middle class that separates its members from those of other estates, lifestyles allowed internal groupings and communities within the middle class to differentiate themselves from each other. While *Bildung* united the members of the same class—intellectuals, civil servants, the various layers of the merchant community, and so forth—the various lifestyles in which certain forms of sociable (cultural) entertainment played important roles distinguished the various groups.

THE SITE OF ENTERTAINMENT IN MIDDLE-CLASS LIFE

Contrary to what one might expect, the Enlightenment focus on rationality and effectiveness did not translate into a general condemnation of leisure and entertainment. The stance was not one of hostility but rather of a rational organization of leisure and entertainment. In the context of modernization and the transformation into a functionally organized society, a new sense of time emerged. As Koselleck has pointed out, one of the most important innovations brought about by the middle class was establishing the rational, disciplined, and effective use of time as a commodity.[24] Work, organized in a place away from home, therefore required new habits such as punctuality and diligence.

The need to coordinate and synchronize meetings and activities created the need for schedules and time management. Both an increased volume of work and a more anonymous business atmosphere accompanied the increasing functionalization and specialization. This necessitated a disciplined and regulated work ethic and also a more clearly defined sense of time (*Arbeitszeit,* business hours) when work or business was conducted and clients, customers, and business associates could expect to be seen.

For the most part, under enlightened absolutism the offices of civil servants were already moved out of the immediate vicinity of the court proper. Work was usually tended to between nine and twelve and from three to six. The time between these blocks was devoted to dining, rest, and many times a recreational walk. Around the middle of the century, the division between work and entertainment was fluid and largely unregulated; although the workday seemed to comprise most daylight hours, it was interrupted by times of entertainment, visits, eating and drinking, walks, and even games. The work pattern of merchants, a group that is significant for our investigation, is a case in point. After breakfast they conducted business at the exchange, which was often followed by a visit to a coffee- or clubhouse for conversation, games, and reading, then lunch, coffee, and a walk.[25]

This tendency had important ramifications for leisure and entertainment. Yet increasingly the overall trend was toward a strict separation between work and leisure entertainment in which work was privileged. The prime hours of concentration were reserved for the strenuous activities of work or one's professional obligations in the morning and afternoon, while entertainment became relegated to the evenings. The focus on the rational use of time implied a clear hierarchization: the best (most productive) hours of the day should be devoted to work; entertainment and relaxation should conclude the day, since one does not like to return to work after a pleasurable activity.[26] The evening and night became the sites dedicated to the pleasure that the forms of entertainment create. It was considered a sign of refinement to carve out more time in the evening for leisure.[27] At the same time, this shift suggested a deemphasis on the more physical activities (physical games, horseback riding, etc.) in favor of more sedentary mental activities (theater, reading, conversation, etc.). This increase in evening and nighttime activities was greatly facilitated by the advances in artificial light by the turn of the century. During the course of the time period under investigation, the separation of work and leisure entertainment became more established, although it varied depending on the profession, social group, and gender. The effect was that especially for middle-class men, the more distinct separation of work and leisure pushed entertainment increasingly into the evening and nighttime hours. This suggests a higher level of self-regulation and self-discipline. With this more distinct compartmentalization came the association of the importance of work and the relative lack of importance associated with leisure. The pleasures that entertainment provided were assigned to the less important part of the day. The tensions between the prestige and value attached to productive work and duty on the one hand and the desire for more leisure entertainment on the other produced a new middle-class lifestyle, one that retained the rigors of the business day while also adopting many leisure practices not unlike those of the nobility. The middle class extended the day well into the night and fused previously incompatible lifestyles.

This change in mentality and practice was aided by new cultural phenomena such as the abandonment of alcoholic beverages during the workday and the consumption of the now fashionable coffee and tea first thing in the morning, during the day, and as the beverage of choice for informal get-togethers in the evening.[28] The stimulation derived from coffee consumption facilitated and supported the self-discipline of the Protestant ethic of the middle class. Together with technical inventions such as the Argand lamp, it extended the day and created more time for leisure after the day's work was done. Technical inventions such as gas lighting for outdoor and indoor use were celebrated by the *Journal des Luxus und der Moden*—along with many other technical inventions that made everyday life more convenient and comfortable—as important steps in the cultural development of the middle class, the state, and the nation.

The flexibility of setting one's own working hours and interspersing them with leisure activities became associated with only the most privileged professions. This underscores that the sense of time is not only historically variable but that the segmentation of time and seasons reserved for certain activities also varies by class, social group, profession, age group, and gender. While the spheres associated with work, professionalism, science, and even art were identified with discipline and rational behavior, the domestic sphere and its forms of sociability (under which I subsume the family, love relationships, friendship, and cultural entertainment) were ruled by sentiments, by the value system of sensibility.

For women, this separation between work and leisure became more complicated as the image and role of women constructed within the discourse of sensibility relegated women's activities primarily to the domestic sphere. Here, a melange of emotive and cultural tasks bridged work and leisure. The creation of the emotional value system of the family, the aestheticization of the private sphere as well as the middle-class forms of sociability—connecting both spheres—represented women's work as well as women's entertainment. Assuming a fusion of work, creativity, and entertainment represents a departure from the major feminist criticism that characterized middle-class women's situation in later-eighteenth-century Germany as enforced domesticity. Feminist critics such as Bovenschen, Becker-Cantarino, Cocalis, Frevert, Hausen, Heuser, and Meise emphasized the important role that women began to play in the intimization of the family and in the socialization of the children, and they discussed the strategies of coercion that seduced women into this role.[29] While I do not wish to minimize this role—which was certainly enforced on them by the patriarchal system—my focus in this study looks beyond the fact that female domesticity was enforced and instead on the power that the creation of an enhanced domestic environment afforded to women. As the domestic realm became increasingly important as a "heaven on earth"[30] and a compensatory site sheltering its members from the negative effects of the external area of paid work, so did women's power and influence grow. Women provided—in addition to the efficient functioning of the household and the intimization of the family—a pleasurable realm for the entertainment of the family as recreation, relaxation, and stimulation. In orchestrating the forms of entertainment, women played an important role in cultural consumption by shaping the everyday cultural environment of the middle class.

In their roles as wife and mother, women had to combine organizational work with emotional work. They not only provided a comfortable, aesthetic, and stimulating recreational domestic sphere but also had to create and sustain an intimate refuge, a melange of *Zärtlichkeit* (sensibility), friendship, and eroticism. Women enabled men to enjoy the pleasures of sensibility as an escape from the world of work by providing possibilities for fulfillment in familial love and in cultural life. This blend of tasks and functions within the domestic sphere constituted a large portion of women's identity, while men's identity was more distinctly split into separate functions that dissociated the emotional sphere of the family and the rational sphere of work outside of the house. Elisa von der Recke's play *Familien-Scenen oder Entwickelungen auf dem Maskenballe* (Family Scenes, or Developments at the Masked Ball) illuminates this complex task of the family within a more functionalized society in exemplary directness:

> Don't let us forget that men live for the state. He is the provider and protector of his family, and he encounters a thousand unpleasant details in his profession and he is faced with innumerable slights in his interaction with people. Agitated, exhausted, and annoyed, he hurries home to the companion of his life. Therefore it is little wonder that he

gets upset at the first thing that grates on his raw nerves. Shouldn't tender love, with pleasant patience, remove everything that could annoy him? Yes, dear Julie, we have to try to create a heaven on earth for the companion of our life that makes him forget that humans so frequently turn God's beautiful world into hell.[31]

Although the emotional work of women in the family has been discussed extensively, their distinct form of cultural work remains underexplored. As mothers, they did not only socialize intimacy and familial love and provide gender-specific education for their children. This "heaven on earth" also provided cultural nourishment in the form of elementary education and entertainment. Creating a pleasant domestic environment represented a major impetus for the diversification of culture and cultural consumption. Within the household, women's roles became redefined. The general assumption is that women lost significant economic powers with the removal of the sphere of production outside of the household and to the consumption side of the economy. However, by the end of the eighteenth century, domestic consumption became a major dynamo for the overall economic development; thus the role of women as the main organizers of the household was redefined—not necessarily diminished—within the household economy. The traditional emphasis on the production side of economic development and the value attached to paid work contributed to the neglect of the importance of domestic cultural practices and consumption as a significant motor for the cultural development of the middle class. As had happened decades earlier in the much-admired "modern" Britain, "home demand was of central importance to eighteenth century commercial capitalism" and "would be 'the ultimate economic key to the Industrial Revolution.'"[32] "The home became the primary site for consumption on a broad social scale and women gained significant authority over the relations of new objects to human activities therein, creating what we think of as domesticity."[33] Bourgeois women created a unique form of domestic culture, one that fused the areas of consumption with those of culture. As the primary architects of what I will call cultural consumerism, their role becomes crucial in a redefinition of the formation of middle-class identity.

It is therefore too simplistic to speak of a dualism between "nature" (family) and "culture" (the public sphere of larger society), as the systems-theoretical approach, for example, suggests.[34] Far from being "natural," this unique realm of cultural formations carefully created a pleasurable ambience enriching the domestic sphere (with a variety of reading materials, fashionable objects of interior design, luxury items, musical instruments, etc.) and sensitized its members to cultural values, thus laying the foundation of taste. Here the habits—in Bourdieu's usage—as a system of dispositions, as principles that generate and organize practices and representations, are fashioned and adapted without presupposing a conscious, specific goal. Acquired in the informal cultural sphere of the home is the "feel for the rules of the game," Bourdieu's *sense pratique,* a sense of acculturation as the foundation of all formal education and cultural learning. The importance of childhood for the acculturation of social practices, the practice of public speaking (e.g., in memorizing and reciting poems, in music lessons and musical performances), and the use of toys that not only taught scientific principles but also instilled a sense of scientific inquiry cannot be underestimated. This factor in the overall development of culture is usually ignored in favor of the forms of "professional" culture. In the realm of professional culture, closely linked with the institutions of higher learning, art forms are created by professionals, not dilettantes. While access to culture is based on comprehension (an acquired decoding operation based on the values established in the given field), it is nevertheless the result of a sustained process of inculcation, a long exposure to the cultural artifacts and practices. These practices can be enforced and formalized by the educational system. While formal education can be acquired in schools and at the university, and thus represents a significant moment of social mobility, true competence can only be socialized in the family over a long period of time. These mentalities and cultural habits receive their all-important start and their differentiation in the domestic culture of the family. These cultural practices pave the way for new forms of sociability and entertainment as expressions of new forms of living together:

> Sociability flourished and informally or formally reorganized bourgeois lives and their environments with patterns of social interaction: birthdays, parties for children, walks in the recently created promenades, excursions to the country,

musical soirees, balls, visits to cafés and to museum societies. Many of these occasions and forms of sociability were new to the bourgeois lifestyle.

Besonders die aufblühende neue Geselligkeit formt mit ihren vielfältigen informellen wie organisierten Beziehungs-mustern nun die bürgerlichen Lebensläufe und Lebenswel-ten um. Die Geburtstage und die Kinderfeste, die Spaziergänge auf gerade eingerichteten Promenaden und Ausflüge ins städtische Umland, die Hausmusikabende und die Bälle, die Caféhausbesuche und die Abende in den Museumsgesellschaften—viele dieser Anlässe und Formen waren in der bürgerlichen Geselligkeitskultur vorher unbekannt.[35]

This form of domesticity provides an important link to the larger public sphere, especially in the form of public leisure culture with its various forms of entertainment. As both men and women participated either together or separately in these entertainment practices, the family was linked to the larger community. Nevertheless, women were the main architects of the middle-class lifestyle with its range of cultural practices.

Of course, these largely self-regulatory cultural practices require a certain level of economic power (*Lebenshaltungsniveau*) and thus limit social mobility to a certain extent:

It means at any rate not only to live relatively free from want but also to maintain a certain level of bourgeois sociability and social duties. Those who, while not lacking in education, do not have the financial means to participate more or less regularly in the forms of bourgeois sociability, the afternoon teas, the excursions, the balls, the dinner invitations, the club memberships, will eventually exclude themselves.

Es bedeutet jedenfalls, nicht nur relativ frei von Mangel leben, sondern darüberhinaus noch einen bestimmten Aufwand bügerlicher Geselligkeitsformen und -pflichten tra-gen zu können. Wem es zwar nicht an Bildung, jedoch an Existenzmitteln fehlt, um sich jener "bürgerlichen Gesellschaft" der Teenachmittage, der Ausflüge, der Bälle, der Essenseinladungen, der Vereinsmitgliedschaften mehr oder weniger regelmäßig anzuschließen, der schließt sich auf Dauer selbst aus.[36]

Not only the financial resources but also significant freedom in the distribution of one's work-leisure pattern and a significant amount of leisure were necessary prerequisites to an elaborate entertainment culture.

The role of entertainment in bourgeois identity bears distinct traces of Enlightenment thought. The Enlightenment discourse not only established a clear separation between work and leisure but also sought to provide a balance between the two.[37] An ordered and regulated balance between work and entertainment was believed to foster the well-being of the population. Entertainment limited to leisure had an important function in the pursuit of happiness, harmony, and balance. The organization of a balanced rhythm between work and pleasurable entertainment not only optimized work attitudes but also led to a higher degree of contentment and happiness.[38]

The emergence of leisure and entertainment has also been associated with the Enlightenment's call for self-actualization. The Enlightenment discourse did not envision leisure as idleness but rather considered it the most important time for the construction of the self in the private sphere. Leisure did not consist merely of rest and relaxation from the demands of work; under ideal circumstances, it was devoted to edification and entertainment.[39] During the Enlightenment, entertainment was rational and useful; it not only provided a counter-sphere to work but also served as the most important site for self-improvement, self-education, and the cultural self-definition as a class. Reading (ranging from moral weeklies and similar publications to fiction), visits to the theater, conversation, and so forth constituted the building blocks of the Enlightenment's project for general nonprofessional pleasurable self-edification. Taking place during the time devoted to leisure, entertainment was thus considered useful and pleasurable in the self-fashioning of the middle class. It is therefore misleading to assume that the self-discipline associated with professional work is nonexistent in leisure. Instead, a disciplined and productive use of leisure is at the heart of the discussion on entertainment. The eighteenth-century usage of entertainment makes clear that absolute freedom, passivity, and repose were not considered desirable characteristics of entertainment. On the contrary, the intensification and higher degree of efficiency of work is paralleled by a tendency to intensify the experience of pleasurable entertainment as part of the bourgeois identity formation. Self-edification not only focuses on *Bildung* but also places a premium on fostering sensibility and the powers of the imagination. Enhanced sensibilities become a prerequisite for the intensification of the sensation of pleasure.

3

Changes in Mentalities

THE DISCOURSE OF SENSIBILITY

To explain the new entertainment function of culture, we have to look at the discursive shifts and the mentalities that enabled them.[1] Discourses as functional units ensure the success of social communication by offering general patterns of orientation in order to facilitate and simplify communication. The discourse of sensibility (*Empfindsamkeit*) becomes an important structure of orientation in a changing society that increasingly problematizes the relationship between the individual and society. As the Enlightenment vision of a demystified rational society that orients itself around worldly happiness displayed its limitations in social communication, the new discourse of *Empfindsamkeit* addressed these shortcomings.[2] Sensibility's focus on the emotional and relational creation of ethics—instead of a rational, rule-based morality—promised not only to appeal to a larger segment of society but was also more self-regulatory. After all, once the ability to experience strong emotional bonds is established, this disposition was thought to produce the proper moral response in an infinite number of contexts. The sensual quality of emotion—rather than strictly rational deductions—allows people to determine the quality of the object. Barker-Benfield offers a deft summary of the culture of English sensibility:

41

The word denoted the receptivity of the senses and referred to the psycho-perceptual scheme explained and systematized by Newton and Locke. It connotated the operation of the nervous system, the material basis for consciousness. During the eighteenth century, this psycho-perceptual scheme became a paradigm, meaning not only consciousness in general but a particular kind of consciousness, one that could be further sensitized in order to be more acutely responsive to signals from the outside environment and from inside the body. While sensibility rested on essentially materialists, proponents of the cultivation of sensibility came to invest it with spiritual and moral values.[3]

Moral sense theory draws an analogy between sensual pleasurable emotions and the moral quality of the object.[4] *Empfindsamkeit,* according to the dictionary definition of the time, is a morally qualified sentiment, "a tender quality of the mind, the heart and the senses, through which man receives an immediate and strong sense of his duties and experiences an effective drive to do good" ("eine 'zärtliche Beschaffenheit des Verstandes, des Herzens und der Sinnen, durch welche ein Mensch geschwinde und starke Einsichten von seinen Pflichten bekömmet, und einen wirksamen Trieb fühlet, Gutes zu thun'").[5] The innate moral sense allows more direct and efficient understanding of one's responsibilities. Furthermore, it is available to everyone, thus increasing benevolence in social relationships.

Both meanings of the term—the moral and ethical tenderness toward others characterized in particular feelings of friendship and love (*moralische Zärtlichkeit*), on the one hand, and the development of a heightened sensibility, the ability to experience sensual stimuli in a heightened physical sensibility of nerves and senses (*physische Empfindsamkeit*),[6] on the other—are important for our study. The first is central to the development of the sentimental love paradigm, the intimization of the family, and new forms of sociability. The second created the increasing interest in imaginary and sensory pleasures: the reading craze, the indulgence in imaginary pleasures, the interest in specular entertainment, and in the sensual impact of nature coupled with the desire to spend time in nature (landscape gardens). Especially the pleasures of life in the garden in an ideal manner exemplify the symbiotic nature of these activities. The garden mania represents an ideal embodiment of the sentimental lifestyle. The informal life in the garden allowed for the intimate exchange between friends and lovers, between married couples, and between parents and children.[7] Closer to nature and away from formal social responsibilities, the middle class could focus on their individuality, their feelings, emotions, and sensations.[8] At the same time, it allowed the heightened sensibility to indulge in the sights, sounds, smells, and sensations of nature. The slower pace at the garden allowed its inhabitants the repose to indulge the wandering gaze as light, weather, and the colors and shapes of flowers provided an ever-changing canvas. In addition, the less structured days—requiring less formal dress, formal entertaining, and therefore less preparatory work—allowed more time for the indulgence in reading, fantasizing, and daydreaming.

Sensibility is not only a pattern of social orientation and recognition that disciplines the relationship to others; it also regulates the concept of the self and, most importantly for our context, expands the individual's knowledge about him- or herself through self-observation. It fosters paying attention to the most minute sensations, feelings, and reactions produced within the self in the relationship to the surroundings.[9] The intense experience of the self—derived from detailed self-observation of one's present and past (memory)—increased the refinement and complexity of emotional responses. This construction of the prized individualism depends on the intensification of the discourse and communication about the self, as evidenced in many autobiographies, autobiographical texts, and biographies of the period and also in the *Bildungsroman* as a historical and philosophical construct.[10] The intense focus on self-perception is associated especially with youth.[11] Youth is the "socially sanctioned period of time for the development of subjectivity."[12] At the various life stages, the sites for self-fashioning change. This study focuses predominantly on adulthood, when the members of the middle class have settled into their various professions and when entertainment and work are separated.

THE ROLE OF LITERATURE

The role of literature and the epistolary culture was paramount in creating a shift from oral personal communication to communication through the written word within the discourse of sensibility. Literature served as the dominant arena where these shifts in values were explored, established, and critiqued. Within a more differentiated society where individual functions (e.g., economy and science) become more special-ized and professionalized, literature becomes the only discourse in which the complexity of many discourses in their impact on the individual could be discussed.[13]

These tasks were accomplished in two distinct forms of reading: work-related, goal-oriented reading and reading as entertainment by the *Lese-Dilettant*,[14] separating the cognitive understanding of the text (*Sinnbildung*) from the sensual reading experience (*literarisches Erleben*).[15] In this study, reading refers predominantly to the latter, which emphasizes "enjoyment, pleasure, delight, and participatory reading or . . . being affected by the text" ("Genuß, Vergnügen, Lust, Beteiligung am Text . . . oder Betroffenheit").[16]

In the linguistic creation of sensibility, literature did draw upon the tradition of rhetoric in the creation of ethos and emotion. How-ever, unlike the grand passions and pathos of the baroque, rhetoric is now enlisted to move its audience in a pleasant, gentle way by selecting persons and objects from one's everyday environment, such as family relationships, friendship, love, and empathy (Lessing's concept of *Rührung*). Stylistic innovations (e.g., the heavy use of apotheosis and ellipsis, which suggest the topos of the unspeakability of the emotion, of psychological vocabulary and the frequent reference to tears, the transformation of past events into the present, and the general sense of emphasis) created modes of speaking about one's sentiments[17] and enhanced one's ability to produce a more differentiated and complex repertoire of sentiments. These innovations also fostered a tendency to identify with the fictional characters and thus allowed a different mode of conceptualizing pleasure. Identification and empathy tie the fictional experience to the imaginary life of the self, altering and enriching the self's mental script, that is, the way individuals think about themselves.

In popular philosophy and especially in literary texts, the family becomes a site and a symbol for the values of sensibility because it appears as the most "natural" social unit embodying empathy. The for-mation of this discourse responds to inadequacies in the existent value system and experiments with new constellations leading to its reformu-lation. The discourse of family has to be seen as anticipating concrete historical change and thus enabling new social forms to emerge.[18] The family offers new forms of self-definition and orientation in a changing social context and compensates for the increasing demands of a func-tionally organized society. As production moves outside the household, work becomes more professionalized and efficient. Changing economic patterns dissolved the "household" into more specialized (and more effective) areas in which its members had to redefine their roles. This reconfiguration was part of the change from an agrarian, physiocratic system based on production, by which one meant agrarian and demographic fertility, to a mercantilist and precapitalist economic system based on trade and commerce. This change provides the first impetus for an economic upturn in the middle class. It also required a different model of living together in the family. The family becomes the main source for emotional relations and, in turn, serves as the model for social relationships in general. With the increased functional concentration on intimate emotional relationships between the couple and between the parents—especially mothers—and their children celebrated in the literary discourse of the day, expectations rose. The individual's happiness depended on his or her familial context. This was especially true for women, who were largely restricted to the familial realm. This exclusivity would become an important liability that threatened to destabilize the institution. As an important topic, familial relationships began to occupy literature, which not only fostered these relationships but also dealt with their contradictions.

The realm of family and friends compensated for the demands made on the individual by the functionally organized society. Its members learn to react in different ways to the various demands on their life; they compartmentalize it. Sensibility, reserved for the familial intimate realm, competed with the rational self-discipline associated with the achievement-oriented economic and professional lives of its members in the public sphere. The differentiation of various functions into separate compartments of social life produced the dissociation of work and family life. At the same time, this dissociation came to be linked to gender and regarded as natural. The construct of the *Geschlechtscharaktere* (the idea that the sexes are different by nature and thus naturally responsible for different social tasks) firmly grounded this division of labor, areas of functionality, and even mentality. Yet the cultural consumption discussed in the following chapters constitutes another dimension of women's lives that expands their role beyond the intimization of the family.

Limiting sensibility to a small, intimate circle removes from larger society (economy and politics) the responsibility of providing fulfillment of individual hopes and dreams. This, in turn, made other realms of society more efficient and rational. Economic, legal, and political realms are absolved from providing satisfaction and happiness and thus can focus on utmost efficiency.[19] The private realm of the family—and especially love, the relationship between the couple—becomes the responsible agent for the emotional well-being of its members. The new intimate relationship within the private sphere becomes the focus of emotional energies.[20]

THE ROLE OF THE LOVE PARADIGM
IN THE CONSTRUCTION OF DESIRE AND LONGING

The primary site for the intensification of emotionality and creation of desire is the private sphere of the intimate family and especially the marriage as love match. The desire fueling erotic love is the most obvious example of the creation of a general sense of desire and longing. The celebration of the family as the ideal nucleus for the value system of sensibility placed particular emphasis on a new concept of love. Sentimental love, as a form of communication and a structure for identity formation, began to replace the older family alliance model. The discourse of love as a semantic system with its own logic is the most important strand within the discourse of sensibility. Cultural formations of sexuality and love are systems that determine the thinking, feeling, and action of individuals.[21] They played an important role in the strategic battle against the value system of the nobility and thus in the oppositional identity formation of middle-class values.[22]

Based on one of the central categories of sensibility—namely, *Zärtlichkeit* as a tempered relational attitude to others—love was based on this moderate, controlled emotion devoid of the darker forces of sexuality and passions that, due to their excessive nature, were considered dangerous and disruptive for social well-being.[23] What the discursive formation of love and sensibility have in common is that they both foster the intense and exclusive intimate communication with a few chosen others and the intense observation of one's own emotional reactions.

As soon as the discourse of sensibility had established itself as the dominant means to achieve happiness in communication with lovers and friends, its high intensity and exclusivity, which limited it to a small circle, was perceived as restrictive. Its exclusivity precluded wider social integration and pitted the domestic against the other areas of life. Its intensity allowed the prized individuality to find expression only with one person with whom the utmost intimacy dissolved all boundaries.[24] Yet because the chances of finding this one intimate soul mate became increasingly slim, the danger of remaining monologic remained great. The subject desiring the most intimate communication faced the risk of remaining without response and could thus be thrown back onto his or her own subjectivity, leading to isolation, estrangement from society, and a lack of social integration.

This had an impact not only on friendship but, most importantly, on the concept of love. The anxiety surrounding this failure of social integration by not achieving the desired love match is one of the dominant themes in eighteenth-century canonical and noncanonical literary texts. One of the central contradictions of this new form of marriage match was that reciprocity, the necessary condition of love matches, cannot be forced or achieved by will alone.[25] At the same time, the individual had to work on the construction of his or her uniqueness in order to attract a like-minded mate. The acculturation of the mind and the senses as well as the body (fashion) and its surrounding (the domestic sphere) became important tasks on the path toward individualization. For women, the issue of beauty as part of identity construction becomes even more relevant than before. Beauty advice and even topics of personal hygiene thus find their way into the new forms of journalistic publications (e.g., the *Journal des Luxus und der Moden*) intended for the (upper) middle class, where sensibility and individuality first established these new forms of communication and social integration. The desire to create the most attractive, highly individualized personality plays a central role in the flourish of cultural activities ranging from the reading frenzy to the increasing interest in the aestheticization of the domestic sphere. It also becomes a form of entertainment because it allows the indulgence in imaginary pleasures.

Because happiness and pleasure became relegated to the familial realm, especially to the couple, finding a suitable partner became most urgent. For men, the failure to find an ideal mate meant missing out on a vital part of the value system of sensibility enriching their private lives. However, it did not touch the very core of self-definition, work and/or creativity. For women, this model of integration becomes even more problematic because it determines not only their chances for self-definition and happiness but also their legal, social, and economic position. For them there existed only the illusion of freedom in the love paradigm of sensibility. Freedom was limited to the moment of choosing a mate, and this moment of selection thus became all-important.[26] Literature took the lead role in the discussion, examination, and problematization (or celebration) of this moment. Feminist criticism has pointed to the dilemma associated with this constellation. Sigrid Damm discussed the very visible and unusually accessible example of Cornelia Goethe to illustrate the ambivalence of the love paradigm for women. Educated and socialized within the value system of sentimentality, Cornelia Goethe addresses in her autobiographical texts all its contradictions. Not only do love and marriage play the central role in her imagination, but she is also aware that the moment of selection is very important. Moreover, she recognizes that romantic love has to be accompanied by financial security. Fully aware of the role that physical attraction plays in attracting a suitable mate (and considering herself not beautiful), she sees her chances in finding a suitable attractive mate diminished.[27] In addition, women were limited in their self-determination by the social circle of the family; therefore, the connections fostered by the family and friends remained de facto an important factor, further limiting freedom in the choice of a mate.

Once married (Cornelia marries her brother's friend Georg Schlosser, a civil servant and intellectual), she soon comes to experience other contradictions associated with marriage as love match. She finds the division of labor between the emotive work of women in the family and the demands of organizing and supervising a household difficult. The more mundane and "unglamorous" business aspect of leading a household was often overlooked, leading to massive crises of self-definition for men and women but especially for the latter. As with many other women of Cornelia's generation and social standing, the prudent management of a household was ignored in her education. Instead, the value system of sentimentality dominated her socialization, fostering the valorization of individualism in the cult of sensibility.

The role of romance novels is unique in this context; they not only helped to create this dilemma but also masked it by having their romantic plot end at the altar. At the same time, they allowed for an endless cycle of identification with the lovers, reliving the joys of anticipation and celebrating longing with each new novel. The fantasy life that resulted from this practice was perceived as pleasurable and became an important form of entertainment, as the reading-craze phenomenon suggests. The preoccupation with one's emotional reactions became an important source of pleasure and enjoyment. While the love relationship is highly individualized and removes the lovers from their social responsibilities,[28] marriage, on the other hand, is a socially integrated unit with its own set of gender-specific responsibilities.[29]

The most dominant and, for our argument, most interesting aspect of the new love paradigm is the creation of desire. Sexual attraction within the love match, based on immediate gratification, was considered common. It did not provide enough space for the creation of individualism and was therefore separated from the creation of erotic desire. Erotic desire as an imaginary pleasure substituted mental or emotional stimuli for physical stimuli. Since this way of fostering and maintaining desire is hardly possible in marriage—making this new concept of marriage as "love match" so problematic—the fantasy is nevertheless nourished in literature, especially in romance novels. They set the stage for cultural consumption as a form of indulgence in imaginary pleasures, in which the celebration of longing becomes perceived as immensely pleasurable.[30]

Goethe's *Werther* could be considered the formative example for the creation of longing in the discourse of sensibility. Prohibitions and separations (self-imposed) are the conditions that produce and maintain desire. The prohibition creates what it forbids, the desired object.[31] It is not (sexual) fulfillment but withholding and anticipatory fantasies that create desire.[32] Because real barriers are falling, artificial, self-created obstacles stand between the lovers to maintain erotic desire.[33]

Other contemporary manifestations of maintaining desire can be seen in the distinct pattern of erotic refusal that J. M. R. Lenz displayed in his life patterns and in some of his literary texts. He falls in love with unavailable women (especially those around Goethe, to whom he had a strong artistic and social/emotive attraction): Friederike Brion, the married Cornelia Goethe, and Frau von Stein. He constructs plots in which the protagonist falls in love with a woman whom he knows only by hearsay and who, in addition, is unavailable because she belongs to another class and is engaged to be married (*Der Waldbruder* [*The Hermit*]). These patterns can be seen as attempts at maintaining erotic desire, drive, and the pleasures of the imaginary.

As fleeting emotions, desire and passion crave perpetual renewal. "Newness" becomes highly prized. Of course, middle-class morality did not allow for the possibility of a perpetual string of consecutive liaisons. As the system of erotic love enters a self-critical phase, we find in literature and in social practice many examples of the re-separation of desire and the physical and emotive comforts of love in marriage. This is accomplished, for example, by directing the desire at a third person, as can be observed in fiction (Goethe's *Stella*, Karoline Schlegel's *Düval und Charmille*, a dramatic text based on actual events)[34] and in biographical patterns (Goethe's own relationship to the married Frau von Stein, and Gottfried August Bürger's erotic attachment to his first wife's sister).

Elise Bürger's farcical short dramatic text "Die antike Statue aus Florenz"[35] provides an especially ingenious and, in its sarcasm, unmasking portrayal of the contradictions of marriage based on a love match and its relationship to cultural practice. Here, a wife complains to her sister about the recent lack of desire or love from her husband, who after his initial attraction has seemingly lost interest. The wife suspects that he is directing his erotic desire at another woman. The sister knows better. The husband, in the privacy of his study and concealed from his wife, admires the beauty of antique statuary. Instead of having an affair, he found the perfect solution to create erotic desire and longing that can never be fulfilled and thus remains in the realm of the pleasurable imaginary. Each new visual reproduction in books or each plaster replica provides the desirable element of novelty. Each depiction provides a new and fresh stimulus for desiring fantasies.

The wife plays a trick on the husband to redirect his erotic desire back at her by secretly taking the place of a life-sized replica of a female antique statue that was destroyed in transit. As he admires the beauty of his "new acquisition," it comes to life in a playful re-creation of the Pygmalion myth. The husband is "cured" of his fantasies, and the wife vows to keep his interest by constantly re-creating herself. The spectator must assume that she intends to do this by role playing and by transforming her body through fashion. The text displays thus two— for our context—important tasks of cultural practices. The consumption of cultural products (here the statuary) can produce erotic desire in the realm of the imaginary. It helps to create a rich fantasy life replacing (or accompanying) a less-than-perfect "reality." Beyond this function and that of pleasurable distractions, cultural practices can also create an impression of the reinvention of the self, as in the concept of fashion. These variances defamiliarize the individual ever so slightly and therefore hold too much closeness and boredom at bay, postponing the crisis of the love match ad infinitum. Elaborate cultural constructs of the love discourse in romance novels and other imaginary pleasures were created in an attempt to sustain desire.

An unusually frank testimony to this problematic complex of the modern marriage with its contradictory multiple functions and tasks in the context of cultural practices can be found in the description of the stormy marriage between Elise Hahn and Gottfried August Bürger. Their long-distance romance was initiated by literature: Hahn fell in love with Bürger's poetry, most likely expecting the man to be like the poet. The seduction of the text invites identification, playfully allowing the reader to take on the imaginary roles provided in the text. In this case, the fantasies prodded her to engage in a literary dialogue with the author. She sent him an admiring poem, and he asked to meet her after she had sent him a picture of herself, underscoring the role of beauty in the level of attractiveness in women. The couple decided to live the fantasy and get married.

Once they married, the initial erotic attraction could not be sustained and the relationship suffered. After all, within the love paradigm the exclusivity of the attachment and the demand of everlasting erotic desire were contradictory demands. Yet both are at the core of the modern concept of marriage that emerged at this time. In marriage there can be friendship, tenderness, and sexual fulfillment but no sensual desire—the latter because, as Gallas adds with Jacques Lacan, you cannot desire what you already possess.[36] The disappointment with the impossibility of sustaining desire within a long-term relationship soon leads to serious disagreements. Bürger accuses his wife of being sexually insatiable and of having affairs.

In addition, he considers her preparation and ability as the organizational head of the household unsatisfactory. She accuses him of a lack of romance in their marriage and of treating her as a housekeeper rather than a lover. Disappointed that he pays attention only to his work, she tries to find a realm outside the emotive and organizational work of the family for her own self-definition. The creation of a cultural realm apart from the intimate familial relationship created a buffer to the choking exclusivity of the emotive tasks in the family. She maintains a separate circle of friends, and her correspondence and an active social life expand her world. For Elise Bürger these forms of cultural entertainment become an important part of her self-definition, compensating for the shortcomings of the contradictory concept of romantic love in marriage, in which familiarity works against maintaining desire. Her cultural practices defamiliarize the humdrum of daily existence by creating an extrafamilial realm for her self-definition (her forms of entertainment consist of visits, reading circles, picnics, dances etc.). Her husband's anger (he considers these activities trivial, immoral, and self-indulgent) stems from the fact that this redirection of erotic desire creates pleasure only for her rather than being channeled into creating a pleasant and pleasure-filled domestic sphere for her family. After all, a culturally enriching domestic sphere took pressure off the exclusive focus on the couple and the maintenance of erotic desire in marriage.

While this might be an extreme example, the underlying pattern is not atypical and reveals the crisis of the love match: the unsustainability of desire in a companionate marriage. Cultural entertainment thus becomes a necessary diversion as a refuge from the exclusivity of the relationship between the couple as leisure time increased and became highly valued. As the intensity of the new companionate marriage—with its focus on the emotional bonds of the couple and the dominance of family life—became restrictive, leisure activities, the cultural aspects of domesticity, and its extension into public leisure culture became more important. At the same time, the desire that drives erotic love creates a general sense of desire and longing that allows people to experience the resulting tension, enhanced by the increased sensibilities, as pleasurable.

4

The Concepts of Pleasure and Entertainment

As pleasure and entertainment were theorized *ex negativo* by philosophy, aesthetics, and literary and cultural historiography, there are no comprehensive theories of pleasure. Nevertheless, it is important to point out that the issues of entertainment and pleasure were closely tied not only to the "arts" and the history of aesthetics but also to the rise of the middle class. After all, it was with the emergence of the middle class (initially in England) that the question of the appropriate pleasurable use of leisure arose. During the time under investigation, entertainment becomes an occasion for self-actualization.

Martha Woodmansee reads the foundational text of modern aesthetics, Addison's *The Pleasures of the Imagination* (1721), as a pedagogical project, as a contribution to the literature of leisure-time conduct. It "takes readers on a guided tour of one after another of the fine arts in order to recommend, as preferable to less 'innocent' sources of recreation, the amateur activities that would come to be known as 'connoisseurship.'" She goes on to explain that it was in the first instance a "solution to the 'problem' of leisure—in a word, as a 'refined' spectator sport—that the arts came together under a single concept" in the early eighteenth century.[1] As her focus is on the modern conception of

53

art, Woodmansee does not pursue the aspect of entertainment any further.

The arts became a central form of entertainment for the emerging bourgeoisie to fill the newly acquired leisure. A glance at the history of aesthetics contextualizes our debate. This overview will be conducted in two steps: first, in this chapter, in a general survey that does not distinguish between the "arts"; and second, in the next chapter, in a more specialized look at literature.

The entertainment function of art was enabled by the change from a rational, rule-based normative aesthetic to an aesthetic that focused on the effects of the work of art on the human psyche and emotions. This change introduced a less monolithic concept of art that allowed wider access to cultural objects. In the dominant German aesthetics of the middle of the century, Sulzer's *Allgemeine Theorie der schönen Künste,* we read: "the true business of the arts is to awaken sentiments" ("das eigentliche Geschäfft der schönen Künste ist, Empfindungen zu erweken").[2] Once the role of the arts in producing pleasant sentiments and sensations was justified, the door was opened for the new cultural practices providing entertainment.

The pleasures that the entertainment practices produce have their roots in two dominant strands of aesthetics: in the effects of the beautiful and in the stronger impact of the sublime. Associated with the beautiful, "that quality in bodies by which they cause love, or some passion similar to it," are the social pleasures of "good company, lively conversation, and the endearment of friendship."[3] Regarding the sublime, "whatever is fitted in any sort to excite the ideas of pain, and danger, that is to say, whatever is in any sort terrible, or is conversant about terrible objects, or operates in a manner analogous to terror, is a source of the *sublime* . . . it is productive of the strongest emotion which the mind is capable of feeling."[4] Burke associated the qualities of power, vastness, infinity, difficulty, and magnificence with the sublime.[5] The notion of the sublime can be read as a reaction to a greatly expanded sense and knowledge of space. The arts could no longer offer an imitation of potentially infinite nature and thus turned to depicting the sentiments, the human reactions to this new understanding of the world. Instead of imitating nature, the arts now depict the emotional reaction to nature.[6]

Moses Mendelssohn's aesthetics foregrounds the powerful effects of the arts in moving an audience. By the end of the century, he referred to what can no longer be grasped rationally and sensually but can only be created by our imagination as art. In this complex mixed sensation, the perceived discomfort, the horror, is mastered and thus transformed into a pleasurable experience (in the sublime, *das Erhabene*), as mastery was experienced as pleasurable.[7] The sublime merely alludes to terror. Aestheticizing terror in this manner represents its mastery.[8] This particular dimension of pleasure formation—or, more accurately, pleasure enhancement or intensification—will become important in the analyses of some of the forms of entertainment: in the enjoyment of the gothic on the stage, in novels, in travel descriptions, in landscape garden design, and to a certain extent in the monumental forms of the panorama and diorama. Yet the sensation of pleasure created by these cultural practices cannot be adequately grasped with the concept of the sublime alone. Instead, these forms break down the delineation of aesthetic categories and reassemble them anew. Using Schiller's concepts of the sublime, the pleasant, and the beautiful (the good, as the fourth category is not useful in our context), we have to construct a mix between these categories to describe these phenomena (*das Angenehme, das Erhabene,* and *das Schöne*).[9] While Schiller did not consider the pleasant (*das Angenehme*) as worthy of being considered in the context of art because it appeals primarily to the senses,[10] in the entertainment culture under investigation it plays an important role.

Moritz, describing the short history of aesthetics as one in which the principle of pleasure has replaced the principle of imitation, is instrumental in creating the conceptual split into pure and disinterested pleasure ("uneigennütziges Vergnügen") and a negatively perceived pleasure. Art does not have a purpose outside itself; it exists only for the sake of its own perfection. The recipients lose themselves in the contemplation of the beautiful object; this forgetting of ourselves is the "highest degree of pure and disinterested ('uneigennützig') pleasure which beauty grants."[11] All other forms of giving pleasure to an audience were valorized negatively; and this "seems to mean, indulging [the] appetite for spectacle."[12]

The influential *Journal des Luxus und der Moden* counteracts this bifurcation of culture in its focus on topics from high culture and everyday culture and everything in between. In its discussions of the variety of cultural practices, the periodical offers a comprehensive source for the concept of entertainment and the pleasure—as moments of profound well-being—it creates.

In its descriptions of entertainment and pleasure, the *Journal* seems to revisit older positions, for example, the tradition associated with Addison, who provided an early blueprint for the mental and affective faculties associated with aesthetic pleasure. He had argued for the arts as leisure-time entertainment. For him, they provided an alternative to both the rigors of work and the kind of mental effort required for serious pursuits, on the one hand, and the baser pleasures offered by the directly sensual delights (presumably wine and women), on the other. Describing the pleasures of the imagination, Addison argued that they did not "require such a Bent of Thought as is necessary to our more serious Employments, nor at the same time, suffer the Mind to sink into that Negligence and Remissness, which are apt to accompany our more sensual Delights, but like gentle Exercise to the Faculties, awaken them from Sloth and Idleness, without putting them upon any Labor or Difficulty."[13] The forms of entertainment do not require disciplined and focused labor of the brain but instead offer gentle stimulation. He associated pleasure with the care of the self, since the forms of entertainment that produce the disposition we call pleasure have a positive influence on the body and the mind. They are able to disperse grief, melancholia, and, in particular, the modern affliction of boredom.

Furthermore, these forms of entertainment are primarily visual and provide the pleasure of looking "either literally or imaginatively."[14] Addison considered sight the most perfect and delightful of all our senses because it fills the mind with the largest variety of ideas, converses with its objects at the greatest distance, continues the longest in action without weakening, and resists satiation.[15] This was part of a significant emancipation of the senses in the Enlightenment, which paved the way for modern empiricism, the primary reliance on the powers of observation, experimentation, and experience. The senses, and particularly sight, became the primary tools for experiencing the world. This reorientation from allegory to observation also signals a measured and limited legitimation of sensuality. Self-observation further enhanced the validity of sensuality in the formation of the modern self.

Reviving traces of this older notion, the *Journal* also places the gentle, pleasurable activity of the mind—the imagination and the senses—at the core of its concept of pleasure in the modern context of cultural consumption. Advocating pleasure as an important part of the care of the self, the *Journal* points to a cluster of terms associated with entertainment. In a list of opposing terms (leisure/work, pleasure/boredom, as well as spirit/senses), the *Journal* outlines the social and psychological parameters of modern entertainment.

By selecting the city of Hamburg as the site for a discussion of entertainment, the publication links entertainment with an icon of modernity. Hamburg was a modern urban area with a strong middle class, which fashioned its identity independently from a court. This modern port city with access to the trade of the world is frequently mentioned in discussions of pleasure. Hamburg's unique political situation as a republic with a liberal immigration policy allowed for trans-European connections fostering capital infusions and commerce and enabled it to serve as an intermediary for trade in luxury goods from the colonies owned by Spain, England, Holland, and Portugal. Hamburg became the quintessential modern city where the consumer found a vast variety of goods enabling cultural consumption.[16] Consequently, a wealthy middle class emerged which created a sophisticated lifestyle in its city dwellings and country houses that rivaled courtly culture. The *Journal* describes entertainment and pleasure in Hamburg as follows:

> Hamburg's inhabitants do not engage in the typical leisure activities merely out of boredom or to escape empty hours of passive repose (unlike the inhabitants of some Italian or Upper Saxon Cities) but in order to recuperate after the strain of business—be it that of mental or physical work. They are looking for pleasure but at the same time seek in this pleasure something more, something which occupies their spirits and senses most vividly.

> Der Hamburger geht nicht (wie etwa der Bewohner mancher italiänischen oder obersächsischen Stadt) bloß aus Langeweile oder um dem Müßiggange zu entgehen, sondern um sich nach Anstrengung in Geschäften, Kopf- oder Handarbeiten zu erholen, von diesen zu den gangbaren Zeitkürzungen über. Er sucht zwar Vergnügen, aber in diesem Vergnügen zugleich etwas mehr, etwas das seinen Geist oder seine Sinne lebhaft beschäftigt. (2:253)

The passage argues against the contemporary commonplace, the notion that entertainment fills the mental vacuum and, above all, that it is a merely passive undertaking.[17] *Zeitkürzungen* (leisure) implies a stretch of time that can be filled with activities unrelated to work. Entertainment is linked to leisure and seen as separate from paid work, from the responsibilities of the office or shop. Entertainment is contrasted with the strain of business activity and with intellectual and physical work. As a pastime, entertainment compensates for the toil of work. At the same time, it is conceived as an activity, not merely passive repose (*Müßiggang*).

Boredom (*Langeweile*) and idleness (*Müßiggang*) signal an inappropriate and wasteful use of leisure. According to Grimms' *Wörterbuch*, *Langeweile* had obtained its modern meaning as *otium taediosum*, which foregrounds the unpleasantness of having too much time on one's hands without meaningful occupation.[18] *Müßiggang* (*otium, vacuitas, vacatio*) also emphasizes the absence of "Geschäften und Abhaltungen"[19] with a more negative connotation than the related positive term *Muße* ("musze = gelegenheit, freie zeit etwas zu thun").[20] *Muße* offers freedom from utilitarian purposes and the opportunity for self-improvement and entertainment. This free time serves as a means for regeneration and recuperation from the stress and strain of physical or mental work. It therefore needs to be filled with a pleasurable activity, *Vergnügen*, which implies that "the spirit or the senses are actively engaged" ("etwas das seinen Geist oder seine Sinne lebhaft beschäftigt"; *Journal* 2:253). Intellectual or sensual stimulation was believed to be at the core of the sensation of pleasure that the forms of entertainment provide.

The associations of *Vergnügen* are not in opposition to the ideology of progress and change. Just as the overall sense of modernity valued progress and development, the forms of entertainment are not characterized as passive repose. After all, ambition and progress were values that are closely associated with middle-class identity, as the Protestant work ethic valued the useful recreational activity more highly than idleness. Meaningful forms of entertainment presuppose (mental or sensual) vivid, even vigorous activity. On the other hand, the activity should not resemble strenuous (mental) work and should not display the severity of study, the drudgery of contemplation, or the fatigue of profound speculation. This early Enlightenment argument resembles those made during this period with regard to the reading practices of women, whose delicate nerves, easily moved by sensations, were considered unsuited for sustained intellectual work.[21] By the end of the century, reading as a leisure activity was seen as a counterpart to rigorous, disciplined work for both men and women.

Associated with *befriedigen* or *erfreuen*,[22] *vergnügen* had achieved the meaning of "to satisfy and gratify" (*zufriedenstellen, befriedigen*)[23] in the eighteenth century; it suggested "comfort" (*Behagen*), "delight in" (*Wohlgefallen*),[24] "pleasurable stimulation" (*angenehme Gemütserregung*), and "cheerfulness" (*Gemütsheiterkeit*),[25] and it replaces the French loan words *Amüsement* and *Pläsir*.[26] *Vergnügen* is the translation of the Latin *voluptas* ("pleasure"). "In the sense of pleasant stimulation, pleasure is sometimes used synonymously with the individual event creating the pleasurable sensation and thus with entertainment."[27] As the positive counterpart to the negative reaction to the sensation of boredom, *Vergnügen* is the reaction to the sensation created by a vigorous stimulation of the senses or the spirit; it is the capacity to react to stimuli in a certain (positive) manner.

Keeping in mind the imprecise distinction in the *Journal* (as a reflection of the popular parlance in the eighteenth century) between these terms, and especially between *Vergnügen* as sensation and event, I distinguish between entertainment and pleasure by considering the former as the varied, deliberately selected or created occasions, practices, and events that produce the psychological disposition of pleasure. Pleasure is not a state of being in itself but a certain quality of experience that the individual seeks to repeat as frequently as possible. "Not properly in itself a type of sensation, pleasure is a term used to identify our favorable reaction to certain patterns of sensation. Desire is the term used to refer to a motivational disposition to experience such patterns, and this is typically triggered by the presence in the environment of a recognized source of pleasure."[28]

A concept related to pleasure is that of *Genuss* as highly pleasurable enjoyment. As a sub-aspect of pleasure, *Genuss* also underwent a significant—and analogous—transformation during the age of sensibility. Wolfgang Binder's discussion of enjoyment observes that early in the century, *Genuss* was connected to objects that everybody could enjoy, such as spring, youth, beauty, and love. In the second part of the century an important reflexive form appears that extends the range of feelings to the all-important enjoyment of the self, *Selbstgenuss*.[29] This parallels the mutation of the concept of *Genuss*: the self experiences pleasure not only when stimulated by physical objects and actual sensory inputs but also in the feelings they produce. The pleasure associated with this activity is different from earlier forms of experiencing pleasure, which was, in general, tied to real activities and their stimuli. "The former is the ancient pattern, and human beings in all cultures seem to agree on a basic list of activities which are 'pleasures' in this sense, such as eating, drinking, sexual intercourse, socializing, singing, dancing, and playing games."[30] The modern pattern, on the other hand, regards objects as mere stimuli producing the pleasurable sensation, which, in turn, becomes a greater source of pleasure than the original stimulus because it could be artificially manipulated and thus heightened.[31] This capacity to take pleasure in sensations themselves, not only in the objects or actions that precede them, sets the stage for the modern ability to react to and savor imaginary stimuli. The new form of pleasure as a "potentially ever-present possibility" required that the "individual's attention is directed at the skilful manipulation of sensation."[32] The Enlightenment's privileging of sight yielding "primary pleasures of sight" proved essential as it supplies the imagination with images, pictures, and ideas that can then be manipulated, conserved, altered, and enhanced in the secondary pleasures of the imagination.[33]

One of the foundational myths of human individuation in Greek antiquity—the story of Eros and Psyche—already suggests the human capacity to enhance the simple primary sense of pleasure of food, drink, music, and sexual intercourse with the desiring gaze, with a visual transgression of the given. The desire to see and to know as a symbol of curiosity and desire, coveting more than one has, can enhance the simple pleasures. The beautiful Psyche (her name means either "soul" or "mind") was condemned to death by the jealous Aphrodite, but Aphrodite's son, Eros, rescues Psyche and takes her to his castle, where she lives in luxury and where disembodied voices bring her delicious food, drink, and music. Eros visits her at night. The only condition is that she not see him. Discontent with the simple pleasures, she desires to see him. One night her curiosity leads her to light a candle, and her desiring gaze wanders over Eros as he sleeps. When the hot wax drips on him, he awakens in a fury and banishes her. Aphrodite intervenes again and sets Psyche to work at four seemingly impossible tasks. After she accomplishes these tasks—not by outwitting or manipulating others, like Odysseus, but by cooperating with and accepting the help of others—she is rescued by Eros, who asks Zeus to make her immortal. They are married among the gods, and she gives birth to Pleasure

(Voluptas). Pleasure thus is the product of heightened secondary desire that does not rely on the immediate luxuries and delights (simple primary pleasures) but insists on the insatiable desire to see, the indulgence in the wandering gaze, to create a secondary, heightened form of pleasure.

Curiosity as the essence of inquiry suggests the dissatisfaction with the status quo, the simple if luxurious pleasures provided by the disembodied voices and the invisible body of Eros. Inherently unstable, it signifies the trend to pursue something more than is in your possession. In the Psyche myth, as in our eighteenth-century context, the transgression of curiosity manifests itself as a kind of ocular appetite (*Schaulust*) and is potentially limitless. Unlike its more famous counterpart of the myth of individuation, the story of Odysseus, who triumphs over the seductive pleasures with self-discipline and violence against himself and others, the myth of Psyche acknowledges the value of pleasure in the dynamic creation of the self.[34]

In this sense, the ability to extract pleasure is a cultural achievement and thus an acquired—not merely a natural—reaction. Cultural entertainment as the occasions for pleasure is therefore dependent on the shift from sensations to emotions, not unlike the shift from visual images that lead to mental images. Because emotions connect physical sensations and mental images, they are necessary for the deliberate control of stimuli. This self-regulatory control is not only a means for self-control but also enables individuals to conjure up the pleasure in the absence of actual stimuli. It is precisely this ability to retain and transform visual pictures into mental images that allows for the limitless potential of the pleasures of the imagination.

This growth in self-consciousness creates greater autonomy in the deliberate creation of one's own emotional state. No longer solely based on the manipulation of objects from one's surroundings, this new emotional state controls the meaning of the stimulus. "Individuals employ their imaginative and creative powers to construct mental images which they consume for the intrinsic pleasure they provide, a practice best described as day-dreaming or fantasizing."[35] Likewise, descriptions could create a more vivid impression than the sight of the object itself. Textual descriptions in novels or nonfictional materials had a profound impact on creating the pleasures of the imagination, the capability to envision things, persons, and situations, to create mental scenarios and to experience them in a pleasurable manner. Recreational readers could indulge in the kind of fantasies that suited their taste. This in essence created a new state of mind through the amplification of the imagination.[36]

Images are elaborated on and modified in order to increase pleasure; at the same time, they contain the element of possibility, thus introducing longing. According to Campbell, the unique feature is that "wanting rather than having is the main focus of pleasure-seeking." The "process of day-dreaming intervenes between the formulation of a desire and its consummation; hence the desiring and dreaming modes become interfused, with a dream element entering into desire itself." Campbell continues this line of argument by noting that "the state between wanting and obtaining, or between desire and satisfaction is thus no longer one of frustration or negative emotion but is experienced as pleasurable." Because imag(in)ing capabilities are infinite and unlimited, the consummation or actuality lags behind the fantasy, moving the attention away from the object or event in question.[37] Imag(in)ing—that is, the emotive and cognitive process of signification—becomes the source of pleasure. The change from the physical presence (e.g., of a lover) to a presence as sign only (in the sense of a self-created presence of the lover in one's imagination) creates this kind of pleasure. In the more limited context of reading for pleasure, Simanowski comes to a similar conclusion when he interprets this embodiment of the sign, the producing of a world in one's imagination, as the true pleasure that reading conjures up.[38] Beyond the primary visual pleasure of looking, the secondary heightened pleasure flows from ideas of visible objects, which can be manipulated by the mind.[39] The realm of the imagination allows for the free combination of elements of various forms of plot continuation, as well as substitutions that turn the reader into the author of his or her own fantasy. This provides the secondary sensation of pleasure that can counteract the tedium of the mundane.

Pleasure is further defined by its negative counterpart, painful boredom. The tedium of routines, of repetition, of sameness, the lack of change, and the fear of stagnation produce boredom. To relieve this monotony, modern individuals want to experience new impressions and to be stimulated by a never-ending string of sensations. The mind seeks diversions and prefers to be occupied. Dwelling for too long on one object or impression produces the negative sensations of satiety and monotony, from which one seeks remedy in fresh and new perceptions.

The craving for novelty manifests itself in the emerging interest in fashionable consumption—be it in fashions for the body and its environment or in the voracious appetite for new reading materials and spectacles. The mind likes the uncommon and the surprising that gratify curiosity momentarily, that refresh and mentally relieve cognitive, intellectual, and sensual satiety. It seeks diversions and wants to be occupied. In the words of the *Journal*, the modern individual wants to be "amused, vividly occupied, and surprised" ("amüsiert, lebhaft beschäftigt, überrascht seyn" [2:253]). The stimulation through contrasts and novelty helps to pass time quickly, which is perceived as pleasant. Time that seems to stand still has a negative impact on the psyche. Stagnation and boredom, the perceived slow passing of time, had already been associated with a depressed state of mind during the Enlightenment and rococo. Heinrich Brockes's poetry advocated the modulations of the soul in the form of dietetic and cultural stimulations.[40] The view that a pleasurable state of being is linked to the proper functioning of the body, the unimpeded flow of its vital fluids—which proper stimulations of any kind, be it laughter, music, or coffee and tobacco supported—was advocated by the medical knowledge of the time.

If we use this account to explain the description in the *Journal*, we can understand why mere repose without exposure to various stimuli would not be experienced as pleasurable and thus cannot be entertaining. More important, because work tends to be repetitive—especially as it becomes increasingly specialized and takes place in a relatively unchanging environment—the varying occasions for pleasurable stimulation and changing environments have to be sought in the forms of entertainment during leisure. The enjoyment associated with leisure that interrupts the discipline of work increases people's performance and was thought to maintain physical and mental health. Tasks can be carried out more efficiently, which enhances professional reputations and even contributes to financial gains. Furthermore, the equilibrium creates a pleasant disposition, which in turn increases popularity and thus enhances sociability. Both further enhance the overall well-being of the individual.[41]

Yet work and the forms of entertainment begin to display distinctively different cognitive and emotive responses to the objects of exploration. The increasingly specialized work requires focused and sustained attention and a utilitarian orientation to a specific goal. In his literary exploration of entertainment in *Die Wahlverwandtschaften*,[42] Goethe has the character of the Captain associate work with seriousness and discipline ("Ernst und Strenge") which depends on the logical sequencing ("reinste Folge"). Rule-based, hierarchically organized, and following logic, the achievement orientation of work requires disciplined mental exertion. The extended span devoted to this kind of discipline was experienced as displeasure ("Unlust"). The contrasting forms of entertainment, on the other hand, allow the mind and senses to wander on a whim and roam by association. They celebrate instability instead of order, freedom instead of necessity. They allow for spontaneity and immediacy. The Captain equates the opposite of disciplined work with life ("Leben") itself, which he characterizes as given to delightful contingency and chance ("Willkür") and an absence of strict logic and consequence ("Inkonsequenz"). This distinction echoes that of Goethe and Schiller's abandoned dilettantism project—yet with an important difference. What the theoretical polemical sketch denounces as dilettantism (and contrasts with true mastery and artistry), the fictional account labels as "life" in all its contingencies.

Rudolf Vaget describes the complexity and ambivalence of the dilettantism project that goes far beyond the 1799 sketch and which he sees as a profound personal issue for Goethe that has ramifications beyond an aesthetic critique of the time but goes to the core of an analysis of the psychology of artistry.[43] Its socio-psychological aspects are important for the discussion of cultural practice as forms of entertainment. Goethe's early discussions of the dilettante undergo significant changes and waver between sympathy for the socio-psychological condition and aesthetic condemnation. He lays the theoretical groundwork and creates categories for later explorations in his review (1772) of Sulzer's *Allgemeine Theorie der schönen Künste*. Here, Goethe distinguishes between the true practicing (Promethean) artist and the theoretical critic, who is not creative, and on a lower level between the dilettante and the "wahren Liebhaber."[44] The dilettante is also not productive and has only a superficial understanding of the subject, while Goethe sees the *Liebhaber* "as a receptive but uncreative art lover"[45] in a more positive light. At the same time, Goethe begins to see the *Liebhaber* as one who derives pleasure also from the practice of the art in question ("Mitwirkend genießt," "Dichtung und Wahrheit")[46] and who with careful training and diligence might come close to the mastery of the artist. Until his frustrating encounter with the visual arts in Italy,

Goethe seemed to see himself in this category of apprentice or student. This experience of limitation prompted him to realize that it was an illusion to think that he could achieve mastery in several fields, and he consequently relegated his own production in the visual arts into the category of dilettante or *Liebhaber*. Vaget aptly calls this realization "a painful ironic renunciation, which tries to find serenity even in the deep disappointment" ("schmerzlich-ironische Entsagung, die noch der tiefen Enttäuschung eine heitere Seite . . . abgewinnt").[47]

With a clear realization of the modern division of labor requiring specialization in one area, Goethe begins to foreground the entertainment value of those cultural practices that are not one's primary field:

> I hope and wish to at least reach the same level of achievement as a music dilettante, who is able to create sounds from his sheet of music that please him and others, that is how I'd like to create a harmony on paper that pleases and delights me and others with me.

> Ich wünsche und hoffe es nur wenigstens so weit zu bringen, wie ein Musickliebhaber, der wenn er sich vor sein Notenblatt setzt, doch Töne hervorbringt, die ihm und anderen Vergnügen machen, so möchte ich fähig werden eine Harmonie auf's Blatt zu bringen und andere mit mir zu unterhalten und zu erfreuen.[48]

Upon his return to Weimar and his disappointment about cultural life in Weimar and Germany, his thinking on dilettante practices takes on a more critical tone with a pedagogical and polemical agenda that found its clearest expression in the dilettantism sketch. Nevertheless, he introduced forms of sociability in Weimar, for example, his *Freitagsgesellschaft*, where an interested group (the Duke, Voigt, Knebel, Wieland, Meyer, and Herder) assembled in his house for an exchange on topics in the arts and sciences. While Vaget tends to read this assembly as a step in the direction of his later pedagogical *Kulturprogramm* of which the dilettantism sketch is an important part,[49] I see this form of sociability as an extension of his realization of the limited access the modern individual has to the increasingly specialized fields within the arts, letters, and sciences and an attempt to contain this limitation by seeking information and access to as many areas as possible—despite the realiza-

65

tion that true, comprehensive mastery is not possible. The pleasurable stimulation by new insights, the pleasure of learning as an enrichment of the self, seems to dominate. With the introduction to the *Propyläen* a more polemical and rigorous distinction between the artist and dilettante cultural practices emerges. While the first is characterized by strict discipline, work, and strict adherence to the aesthetic laws in a gradual and systematic training toward mastery, the latter is prone to shortcuts and lacks the necessary discipline and training.[50] Likewise, the *Propyläen* sought to educate the audience so that they could become experts ("Kenner").[51] Certain forms of dilettante practice can serve as steps toward true appreciation, as is discussed in detail in the sketch. Unless this pedagogical task is realized, dilettante practice is seen as more harmful than useful.[52] Yet the second sketch underscores Goethe's ambivalent position, which eventually led to the abandonment of the dilettantism project. Vaget attributes the abandonment of the project to Goethe's reluctance to stringently condemn dilettante practices due to his biographical affinity with dilettante practices (the visual arts and the sciences).[53] Focusing on the social condition of the dilettante practice instead, this study attributes the abandonment of the project and Goethe's ambivalence and his reluctant acceptance of dilettante practices to his intuitive grasp of the perils of modern differentiated and specialized society, which only allows mastery in one field. Abandoning this modern playful engagement with cultural practices—as consumption or non-expert participation—would signify a decisive impoverishment of the bourgeois lifestyle.

If the artist is depicted as a "worker" (in addition to inborn talent, the Promethean impulse of the view of the artist in the young Goethe is gradually replaced by an emphasis on work and discipline), his training and activity display structures similar to those of other professionals. Both demand intellectual focus, discipline, and rigor, while nonprofessional cultural practices as forms of entertainment are free of these aspects and can indulge the senses at will and seek new stimulation with the ultimate goal of achieving the sensation of pleasure. The utilitarian, rule-based, and reality-based nature of productive work or artistry needs the repose of nondirectional, undisciplined cultural practice. The goal orientation and the basic belief in linear progress associated with the professional and economic sphere of work can be interrupted by the forms of entertainment that are subject to fashionable change.

The powers of the imagination and of fantasy liberate the mind from the orderly, restricting, and limiting structures of the patterns required for professional work. Curiosity (the drive to see and know) and impulse, which resist control, guide the (visual and mental) gaze. Haunted by monotony and discipline, the modern mind becomes addicted to the novelty and freedom of the primarily visual pleasures that the modern forms of entertainment provide. This explains not only the new fascination with change and innovation (as evidenced in the middle class's emphasis on fashion and fashionable physical surroundings) but also the preoccupation with the potentially unlimited free play of the imagination, the indulgence in the pictures created by the mind. While the early Enlightenment and rococo culture insisted that the creation of pleasure avoid any semblance of excess, of passion, a lack of balance, the new forms of entertainment contained the potential for unlimited excess.

This active interest in cultural innovation, in a rapid sequence of new impulses, originates from the ability of sensations to act as stimuli that create an "excited" state in humans. Campbell writes: "It is thus not the substantive nature of sensations but their stimulative potential which is most directly pertinent to pleasure-giving." Excitement resists immediate assimilation. Since a stimulus can only be recognized in a given context "as something apprehended by a sense organ against an existing background of sensations," a stimulus is by its very nature only momentary and requires a steady stream of new or changing stimuli.[54] It is therefore the change and variety of sensations and the imagination's ability to manipulate them—rather than any inherent quality—that yield pleasure. Repetitive activities or invariable surroundings would not be considered pleasurable. Providing an element of surprise, a new object diverts the mind momentarily and refreshes by averting the satiety of the ordinary. Thus the sight of the uncommon is perceived as pleasurable.

The instability, the potential for unlimited excess, and the randomness of the forms of entertainment that produce pleasure distinguish the concept of *Unterhaltung* from its more famous and more carefully theorized idealist sister concept of *Spiel* (play). The subcategory of *Spiel* in the sense of game is a voluntary action or pastime that takes place within a certain time and place according to conventional and voluntarily adopted rules.[55] The fact that a game provides stimulation and a certain tension makes it one form of entertainment among many others. As a speculative philosophical concept, Schiller uses *Spiel* as a symbol for the aesthetic condition of human beings,[56] as the realm of freedom from external conditions and a sense of internal or moral duty that creates *Glückseligkeit* (bliss) (*Journal* 2:312). As are the forms of entertainment, his concept of play is a reaction to the differentiation and specialization of modern life with its separation of sensual and intellectual powers.[57] The contributors to the *Journal des Luxus und der Moden* do not explicitly critique specialization but accept it as necessary for human cultural development and seek to compensate for the discipline of specialized work by offering a discussion of a wide variety of forms of entertainment and comforts—even luxuries—that enhance the middle-class lifestyle by adding pockets of pleasure to the mundane. Schiller sees in the increasing specialization, in the separation between the arts and the sciences, in the increasing specialization in the sciences, and in the areas of work a one-dimensional impoverishing development of the individual that he at the same time, however, considers necessary for the progress of society as a whole: "I'll gladly admit that individuals cannot flourish in this division of their being; however, the species could not have made progress without it."[58] Specialization leads to the fragmentation of work and play and thus results in a loss of harmony and balance, impoverishing the individual. Both Schiller and the popular positions that the *Journal* represents recognize this price of modernity already in this early phase of modern social, economic, and scientific differentiation. Schiller questions whether humankind is destined to forsake individual harmony (and happiness) for the sake of progress. He sees it as the task of the modern individual to seek a higher form of harmony to replace the one that culture destroyed: "It must consequently be wrong that the development of the individual ability sacrifices the totality, even if the laws of nature point in this direction. Thus we have the task to re-create this totality in our nature, which artifice had destroyed anew in a higher art."[59] Both positions consider culture and the civilizing process not only the reason for this alienated state of affairs but also as the only means for a cure.

Yet they differ considerably in the specifics, as can be seen in the distinction between Schiller's concept of *Spiel* and the concept of *Unterhaltung* in the popular philosophy of the *Journal*. Schiller sees this higher form of culture, which has to prevent the one-dimensionality of modern man, as a dialectical synthesis between intellectual desire (*Formtrieb*) and sensual nature or the material condition (*Stofftrieb*) which creates the tension and impetus to seek and reach for harmony.

He labels the drive toward synthesis the *Spieltrieb*. While the first compels us to act according to either physical or moral constraints, the drive to play combines both in a precarious momentary balance. It fuses the demands of the intellect with those of the senses: "he should sense because he is intellectually aware, and he is aware because he senses." The sensual drive seeks change "so that time has content," while the intellectual drive seeks continuity "so that there not be a change."[60] "The drive to play thus, in which both work together, will encourage one's disposition in a moral and physical manner; it will transpose humans into a state of physical and moral freedom because it sublates all coincidences and all demands."[61] Schiller considers this dialectically harmonizing play to be at the core of art as the force that allows humans to experience their true double nature (*Doppelnatur*). He explains the synthesis of the sensual and intellectual drive or the trend toward the material (*Stofftrieb*) and the formal (*Formtrieb*) with the example of the ideal beauty of a Juno Ludovisi: "Irresistibly moved and attracted to the first, and kept at bay by the latter, we find ourselves in a heightened state of calm and movement, and a wondrous sentiment arises for which reason knows no concept and language has no name" ("Durch jenes unwiderstehlich ergriffen und angezogen, durch dieses in der Ferne gehalten, befinden wir uns zugleich in dem Zustand der höchsten Ruhe und der höchsten Bewegung, und es entsteht jene wunderbare Rührung, für welche der Verstand keinen Begriff und die Sprache keinen Namen hat").[62] To retain the disinterested nature of play—which has to remain an *Idee*—it has to abstract from every desire to possess or desire in reality. It is only in this tension that the harmony of the "art of living" (*Lebenskunst*) can be achieved.[63]

In contrast, the forms of entertainment creating pleasure do not attempt to fuse these opposing forces but rather alternate them. Schiller's synthesis as *Lebenskunst* clearly takes place in the realm of ideas alone, along the Kantian principles of disinterestedness, while the forms of entertainment and the sense of pleasure they produce clearly have an impact on "reality." The powers of the imagination are not exclusively at free, disinterested play but seek to alter the environment of the individual. They create a lifestyle that offers the utmost variety, alternating between moments of concentration and relaxation, work and play, duty and freedom, restraint and indulgence.

The *Journal* does not pin its hopes on the utopian dialectics of harmony that the individual has to achieve through *Bildung* in an elite concept of high art. Although the editor or contributors do not make this explicit, the overall design suggests a considerably less ambitious solution. Accepting the basic split in the modern individual that can no longer be truly overcome or transcended in a dialectical synthesis, the *Journal* seems to suggest that rather than bemoaning the compartmentalization of modern life, the individual should develop the sensual and intellectual facets of his or her personality and enhance and vary them as much as possible. The tedium of work can be relieved momentarily by forms of entertainment that offer a qualitatively different experience. If the sphere of work demands intellectual focus, discipline, and rigor, the forms of entertainment can engage the senses, especially the free-roaming indulgence of the gaze in the forms of specular entertainment. The utilitarian, rule-based, and reality-based nature of productive work could be interrupted with the imaginary pleasures that reading, for example, could launch.

Furthermore, if the utilitarian sphere of work and its social relationships display a rigid hierarchy, the forms of sociable entertainment allow the individual to create different, more flexible social relationships. Sociability allowed people to assemble based on common interest and personal affinities, creating alternate forms of community. In the forms of sociable entertainment, people shared the cultural pleasures of conversation, music, engagement in the visual arts, and the consumption of culinary delights with people freely and voluntarily chosen. If the scientific or professional specialization required the one-dimensional development of certain faculties, the forms of entertainment allow a nonprofessional (dilettante) development of other faculties, be it in art, literature, music, or the popular sciences of horticulture and landscape design. The goal orientation and the basic belief in linear progress associated with the professional and economic sphere of work can be interrupted by the forms of entertainment that are subject to fashionable change, as fashion brings a moment of contingency and random change when compared to the linear thought of progress. The former allows the individual to drift on the wave of innovation without necessarily having to control it. The demand of aesthetic control over artifacts, as prescribed by *Bildung* and its concept of high art, mirrors the discipline of the workplace. This mode of cognition and experience can be interrupted by forms of entertainment that are creative in producing an aesthetic environment that brings together a whole range of areas of freedom from sheer utility and discipline.

Less absolute, less ambitious, and less exclusively dependent on *Bildung* than the notion of Schillerian "play" and the artistic mastery celebrated in the dilettantism project, entertainments consist of a range of cultural practices that alter the lifestyles of individuals and affect the development of society by altering, for example, the relationship to consumption and thus expanding the range and variety of cultural practices enhancing everyday life. These cultural activities—by necessity of a nonprofessional nature—are part of maintaining mental health, of caring for the self, in an increasingly specialized world as the playful powers of the imagination and of fantasy liberate the mind for a moment from the orderly, restricting, and limiting structures of the patterns required for work. People crave new experiences to enhance their lives.

CULTURAL CONSUMPTION AND THE CREATION OF PLEASURE

The spiral of desire and disillusionment is central for the explanation of the dynamics of cultural consumerism and entertainment. Just as the consummation of passionate love never measures up to the anticipatory fantasy, the perfected pleasures produced by the forms of entertainment, once consumed, quickly lead to disillusionment. The desire for new stimuli or new objects to start the cycle of longing anew results in the perpetual striving to "close the gap between imagined and experienced pleasures." The cycle of "desire-acquisition-use-disillusionment" interweaves the pattern of romantic love and cultural consumption.[64] As we discussed in the previous chapter, these patterns mutually reinforce each other. Erotic love assumes the unique individual in constant need of improvement, and cultural consumption allows him or her to re-create the mind, the body, and its environment in the imagination. These images could then be pursued and potentially realized, driving cultural consumption. Similarly, the hunger for new art forms or innovative use of genre conventions and a varied and stimulating physical environment is the dynamo at the core of entertainment.

The fashionable household and its variety of cultural practices linked culture and consumption. This cultural consumption is composed of cultural activities (e.g., reading, the theater, the arts, and spectacles) and the objects of material culture (e.g., fashion, fashionable interior design, the use of luxury products, etc.). The allure of (luxury) objects influenced the mental images of the self, improving it, making

71

it more attractive, more cultured, and more sophisticated. The individual incorporates the object or practice into the image of him- or herself, into his or her imaginary life. This strategy addresses the gap between the "real" and the "ideal," between the present and a more desirable future. This process has its roots in the teleological Enlightenment project of continuous self-improvement. Cultural consumption can be used as a means to bridge the gap between one's present lifestyle and an imagined and anticipated ideal condition.

I would argue that pleasure as the motor for entertainment and the cultural enrichment of everyday life played a larger role in the formation of the upper middle class than previously thought. The act of coveting an object or cultural practice, of longing, produces the anticipatory pleasure. This is especially important for "high involvement" goods such as houses, carriages, and clothing, which "individuals buy . . . in order to take possession of a small concrete part of the style of life to which they aspire."[65] While this fantasizing about imaginary possibilities is pleasurable in itself, it also serves as a preparation for social positioning within one's class or peer group. Cultural objects and practices serve well in this capacity because they make "abstract and disembodied meaning extant, plausible, possessable, and, above all, concrete."[66] In this new middle-class lifestyle, not only education and cultural practices but also "consumer goods carry cultural meaning."[67] Consumers "use the meaning of consumer goods to express cultural categories and principles, cultivate ideals, create and sustain life-styles, construct notions of the self, and create (and survive) social change."[68] This behavior is at the root of the consumption of luxury items, which began to drive and stimulate the emergent modern economy.

At the same time, these objects and artifacts both stabilize and destabilize people's existence because they signify what their owners are, on the one hand, and what they hope or long to be, on the other. More importantly, this destabilization introduces a potential for change into the identity formation of the middle class. As a self-regulatory system, fashionable consumption introduced a momentum, a valorization of change, into the lifestyle of the middle class. Consumer goods, charged with meaning, are signal objects in the process of self-transformation to which the modern (European) world became committed in the course of the eighteenth century.

The instability is, for example, underscored by what economists have labeled the "Diderot effect."[69] A new object begins to demand new companion objects that are in keeping with the message of the object, and this dynamic gradually moves the standard of consumption upward. The *Journal* created the idea that all objects surrounding the body must create one harmonious whole, forming *in toto* an important part of one's lifestyle and, with it, middle-class identity. "Clothes determine the furniture in a room, the table setting, company, carriages, servants and the like. Everything must harmonize, otherwise it will not look pleasant."[70] Yet it is debatable whether the increasingly higher levels of consumption themselves are the sole locus of pleasure; I would argue that it is also to a large degree the anticipatory imaginary energy, described above as desire and longing, that is experienced as pleasurable. The pleasurable event seems to be experiencing the desire—of which certain material things are the objects—not the actual act of taking possession of the object. The resulting diffuse desires or longings, the yearning for something "better,"[71] or at least something new, becomes a central feature of the modern mentalities and extends into all areas of cultural practice. This form of desire is instrumental in the increasing appetite for innovative and diverse cultural offerings as the mind seeks ever-new stimuli.

Of course, the pleasure stemming from the imaginary use of cultural consumption also has an important economic dimension. With the consumption of nonessential goods ("luxury items" in the parlance of the day), an important economic stimulus was created that helped to strengthen the middle class. While the *Journal* acknowledged and fostered the immense interest in fashionable goods from England, it also advocated the creation of new industries in the German states: "As is well known, it is the plan and design of this journal to make Germany more aware of its own enterprises."[72] By 1800, new industrial and commercial centers had formed especially along the Rhine (Frankfurt, Cologne), administrative cities (*Residenzstädte*) grew significantly, and agricultural production and variety increased and even showed signs of increased prosperity. This created new opportunities to consume a greater variety of essential and nonessential goods. For the first time, a larger part of the middle class than before was able to acquire objects— luxury items—that had previously been reserved for the members of the nobility and thus restricted by sumptuary laws.

The bourgeoisie no longer bought only what need dictated but instead what was fashionable at the time. Items that were traditionally inherited or bought only once in a lifetime might now be bought several times in a lifetime. The availability of goods increased, as the pages of the *Journal* demonstrate. England, where consumption played an already established role at this time, served as a model for the modernization of the German states. As in England, the increasing availability of goods in permanent stores changed the nature of consumption drastically: "What were once available only on high days and holidays through the agency of the markets, fairs and itinerant peddlers were increasingly made available every day but Sunday through the additional agency of an ever-advancing network of shops and shopkeepers."[73] Albeit with an eye on the British context, historians have pointed out that the consumer revolution preceded the industrial revolution which would "answer to and vastly stimulate needs and appetites (for white bread, tea, china cups, cotton prints, and muslins)."[74] With a delay in time and to a lesser degree, the same holds true for the German situation.

Magazines and other forms of periodical literature provided information on the latest—often English—trends ranging from fashion to landscape architecture and horticulture, which created interest and enabled a larger segment of the middle class to participate in such novelties. The *Journal* was accompanied by an *Intelligenzblatt,* which went beyond providing information about new products and offered actual purchasing information and advertisements. Thus the press cannot be underestimated as a transregional sales agent. Publications such as the *Journal* constitute a central nexus between the marketplace and the cultural practices of consumers. In many instances, these publications were instrumental in creating consumers by presenting objects as desirable and by facilitating their acquisition; the *Journal* not only served as advertiser but in certain cases also as merchant by providing contact addresses, accepting orders, and so forth. The *Journal* firmly fused culture and consumption and was therefore essential in the creation of cultural consumption by allowing the material aspects of culture to come into view.

With the changes in attitudes and behaviors as well as in production techniques and advertising, the stage was set for the industrial revolution of the following century as the analogue of the "consumer revolution." Examples of the gradual development of a luxury industry over the course of the eighteenth century are the proto-industrial production in Silesia, Saxony, and the Rhineland. Furthermore, substantial population growth after the middle of the century and increased accessibility to markets aided a general expansion of industrial production. "The eighteenth century also witnessed the development of larger units of centralized production (*Manufakturen*) whether in Bavaria, the electorate of Mainz or Schleswig-Holstein, often as a result of direct state initiatives reflecting a concern to reduce unemployment and to promote the sale of luxury goods."[75] The availability of luxury goods, in turn, enhanced and created more interest in the cultural activities associated with the beautification of the middle-class domestic sphere and its cultural activities.

Fine porcelain had been a highly desirable luxury item for the nobility since 1710 with the foundation of Meissen by August King of Poland and Elector of Saxony. It quickly became an indispensable accompaniment of splendor and magnificence for the nobility at court. Württemberg, Mainz, The Palatinate, Bavaria, and Brandenburg were some of the smaller territories with a porcelain factory.[76] The increasing interest in the domestic sphere and its cultural activities, such as the consumption of tea and coffee as a social event, also produced an interest in fashionable tableware among the members of the middle class. Dietary changes and the vessels in which these new foods and beverages were consumed enhanced each other.

Especially the consumption of tea and coffee was accompanied by a host of implements to prepare the beverage, special storage cabinets, a variety of cups and saucers, pots and containers for cream and sugar, and table linens. A layering of pleasures surrounded the objects. The aesthetic objects themselves provided pleasure with their intricate patterns, contrasting vivid colors, and color combinations that delight the eye and invite the gaze to wander following the visual power of the serpentine line, leading the eye on a pleasurable chase. The eye takes pleasure in the intricacies of patterns, in the contrast and combination of colors. Beyond this interest in the material objects associated with the consumption of tea and coffee, their consumption occasioned rituals and sparked new forms of sociability. These innovations increased the interest in new forms of hospitality and sociability and thus created a demand for specialized publications such as cookbooks, which were practically non-existent in the modern sense before 1700. Garden books fostered (and were, in turn, created by) not only the aesthetic aspects of gardening but were also motivated by an interest in new vegetables and fruits for the fashionable modern table. Resulting in a more complex cuisine, this innovation required new and additional methods and utensils for its preparation and, above all, its presentation. The aesthetic presentation of food and beverages increased the interest in decorative serving dishes in the style of the time, which subjugated them to the laws of fashion and change.

The *Journal* was instrumental in providing information and illustrations of the latest in imported—and later to an increasing degree domestic—pottery.[77] Yet china and pottery were not the only luxury items that began to embellish the (upper) middle-class household. The increased domestic production of linens, silks, and other materials was a necessary prerequisite for a number of fashionable items from clothing to draperies, curtains, and furniture coverings. Hamburg boasted a significant production of luxury textiles, printed cottons (finished by hand with the colors that could not be used for printing by female workers [*Schildermädchen*]), silks, and some finished products such as stockings and silk flowers. Another important area of luxury production was the manufacturing of sugar in which the raw material was refined into the finished product, the sugar cones, by the confectioners (*Zuckerbäcker*).[78] This, in turn, added a wide variety of sugar-based luxury foods to the available selection.

Many towns and cities had developed a considerable manufacturing and trading record, especially in linen and silk trades. The availability of these new sources for fabric enabled and fueled the increased interest in fashion. These products allowed fashion to be domestically produced, thereby relieving the dependence on imported goods and not only providing a greater variety but also increasing its affordability. In turn, the manufacturers were dependent on a vibrant fashion culture for creating new and, most importantly, perpetual/perennial demands for luxury goods to adorn the body and its domestic backdrop.

The notion of fashionable change speeding up the cycle of consumption beyond necessity is especially important for the stimulation of the luxury industry. The interrelationship of increased production and availability of goods, information on luxury goods in certain segments of the press, and an awareness of design changes (fashion) created an awareness of the elasticity of demand and a sense of the dynamic effect of consumption.[79] The *Journal* and related publications were, again, instrumental in creating and feeding these ever-changing desires and thus assisted in the creation of pleasure. Of course, fashionable design changes and the public's favorable reaction to them presuppose the economic means to do so. In addition, the legal right to participate in fashionable consumption has to be granted in form of the non-enforcement of sumptuary laws.

As the urban middle class's economic influence, and with it their degree of consumption, increased, wider levels of the middle class were affected as merchants, artisans, craftspeople, and storekeepers responded to their demands with increased service and goods. Trade and commerce became more differentiated, providing for the desirable merchandise beyond necessity as craftspeople began to specialize in the production of luxury goods. Milliners, hatters, ribbonmakers, perfumers, and hosiers replaced the general talents of simple tailors and seamstresses. The middle class assumed the dominant role in social, intellectual, and economic life. City life had its economic base in commerce and trade rather than in agriculture. At this point, the emergence of these new cultural practices and forms of cultural consumerism had destabilized the more monolithic concept of culture that dominated the eighteenth century until the 1780s. This change is based on the assumption that social and cultural experience and consciousness are mutually constitutive, that the material aspects of experience both mold and are molded by the discourse in which they are perceived. It remains to be explained how an essentially ascetic economic behavior—as described by the dominant theory of Weber's *The Protestant Ethic and the Spirit of Capitalism*—based on rational spending and the accumulation of wealth could pave the way for the industrial revolution.

The key has to be seen in the patterns of consumption preceding the industrial revolution. The conventional wisdom of the accumulation of wealth in the middle class does also not explain how this group was induced to spend this new wealth, how it was seduced into extended consumption. Increases in spending cannot be explained by the growth of the middle class alone. In short, a change in attitudes regarding spending and consumption must have occurred. These changes took place in the cultural arena, more specifically in the force field of the rise of romance novels, erotic love, and modern identity construction, all of which valued a rich imaginary life. Campbell explains part of this nexus:

> The essential activity of consumption is thus not the actual selection, purchase or use of products, but the imaginative pleasure-seeking to which the product lends itself, "real" consumption being largely a resultant of this "mentalistic"

hedonism. Viewed in this way, the emphasis on novelty as well as that upon insatiability both become comprehensible.

The modern consumer will desire a novel rather than a familiar product because this enables him to believe that its acquisition and use can supply experiences which he has not so far encountered in reality. It is therefore possible to project onto this product some of that idealized pleasure which he has already experienced in daydreams, and which he cannot associate with those familiar products currently being consumed.[80]

The consumer's imagination incorporates the cultural product or practice into his or her fantasy life, thus transforming his or her identity. These changes in turn produce new desires, starting the cycle of cultural consumption anew. The individualistic middle-class identity formation—seeking exclusive erotic attachment to an equally individualistic other—emphasizes the construction and presentation of the best possible identity in order to attract a like-minded mate. At the same time, the daydreaming about romantic possibilities was fueled by and fueled the popular novel. Both reinforced each other in this form of mental hedonism, which also had an important consumption side to it. In the construction of middle-class identity, cultural consumption in its material and nonmaterial manifestations played an important role. The middle-class lifestyle depended to a large degree on a vibrant cultural life and an emotionally nourishing and entertaining domestic sphere.

This mentalistic hedonism, or what I have labeled imaginary pleasures, is also a by-product of the process of civilization as Elias explored it. As people began to exercise control over their emotions and desires, they also replaced direct action on their desires with imaginary or symbolic actions on the one hand and with the scopophilic desire of watching others or by experiencing symbolic objects through the gaze on the other. This trend accounts for the interest in theatrical spectacles and in reading for pleasure.

As we have observed, cultural consumption could distract from the intensification of the emotive connection between the family members and especially between the couple. After all, these relationships could be perceived as stifling due to their conceptual contradictions (the fusion of fleeting passion and long-term commitment based on an emotive relationship).[81] An individualized and broadly defined range of cultural activities provided another realm for the identity formation of men and especially of women in order to take the pressure off the emotive sphere of the family and limit the predominance of its emotionalization. More importantly, the beautification of the domestic sphere provided an important area of creativity for women beyond the mere organizational work of running a household.

In this sense, the self achieves a "newness" that, in turn, might defamiliarize the all too familiar and thus assist in maintaining desire. Especially women—as the primary keepers of the domestic sphere—were induced to practice this form of cultural self-renewal. Extending one's selection of luxury products for the house, entertaining in more refined ways, turning meals into cultural events by regulating the body language and stylizing the presentation of food, and turning the natural seasons into social seasons by underscoring the occasion by proper and distinct attire—all these practices allowed for and required more knowledge, taste, and creativity to orchestrate. Women were responsible for organizing and providing cultural entertainment in the domestic sphere and beyond—outings, visits to the theater, opera, and other performances, as well as visits to art collections and travel.

In addition to the imaginative pleasure-seeking to which these objects and activities lend themselves, the actual selection of the products or activities in the creation of cultural entertainment is yet another source of pleasure because it allows for creativity and the playful construction of a whole system of taste. It provided an area for aesthetic discernment based on knowledge of basic patterns as well as the deviations. Taste depended on the degree of exposure to the whole gamut of cultural activities and practices. The pleasure they created was heightened by the association of other ideas or practices with those evoked by the activity or object that produced the reaction in question. The more the mind is "enriched by a variety of kindred and corresponding imagery," the more a cultural practice can be enjoyed.[82]

On a nonprofessional level, the members of the middle class could create a unique individualistic lifestyle, which, like fashion (on which it is based), requires understanding and knowledge of the model in order to create the unique deviation that bespoke one's individualism. This comprehensive understanding of culture becomes an important part of the self-fashioning of the middle class. Cultural classification and stratification—"distinction" in Bourdieu's terminology—was most explicitly negotiated in periodicals, and most notably in the pages of (fashion) magazines that described and depicted the latest products for the adornment of the body and its environment.

Bringing momentum into middle-class life, cultural activities such as fashions for the self and the home allow for innovation for each season (or social occasion), thus periodically reinventing the self and its surroundings. Yet contemporaries also expressed concern over this sense of unrest that these new attitudes had created and advocated a simpler, more contemplative life:[83]

> The spirit of restlessness, of change, and of fluttering from one object to another remained far removed from those spirits who quietly enjoyed what they rightfully acquired and did not constantly seek novelty. They used their time for useful activity and carved out time to contemplate their destination and the salvation of their soul.

> Geist der Unruhe, des Flatterns und Wechselns blieb fern von diesen Gemüthern, die in rechtlich erworbenem Besitze gern ruhten, bei'm stillen Genusse des Vorhandenen nicht immer nach Neuem strebten, Zeit für nützliche Beschäftigung, und Stunden der Sammlung gewannen, um über ihre Bestimmung und das Heil ihrer Seele nachzudenken. (3:111)

The excessive momentum and restlessness that this dynamic created in its pursuit of novelty and ever greater pleasures were perceived as undesirable by some who preferred time to be filled with more important and useful occupations. Critics saw entertainment as a frivolous distraction that created a number of social ills, including "immorality, theft, malcontent and frivolity of the servants, excess, waste, debt, and destruction in the economy of the household and of the happiness of their members" ("Sittenverderbniß, Diebstahl, Ungenügsamkeit und Uebermuth der dienenden Classe, Verschwendung, Schulden, Zerrüttung im Hauswesen und Zernichtung der häuslichen Glückseligkeit" [3:106]).[84] In order to negotiate between the advocates and critics of the entertainment of cultural consumption, the *Journal* engaged in a debate on the issue of "luxury." After all, a necessary prerequisite for the creation of this new middle-class lifestyle was the reinterpretation of luxury, one that no longer vilified or moralized against self-indulgence but praised the entertaining consumption of luxury items as a significant motor stimulating not only the economy but cultural progress.

THE DEBATES ON "LUXURY"

The *Journal* does not argue for suppressing consumption and repressing the pleasure it provides but instead for their reasonable increase and management. It carefully contextualizes the concept of "luxury" as a key moral and economic issue:

> If we are allowed to use an image, luxury is like a staircase in a building and thus essential for the use of the house. A smart person climbs and descends it slowly; a child or a fool runs down carelessly and breaks his neck. Thus the concept of luxury is as relative as that of good and evil.

> Luxus, wenn uns erlaubt ist ein Bild zu brauchen, ist wie die Treppe in einem Gebäude; unentbehrlich zum Gebrauch des Hauses. Ein Kluger steigt langsam auf und ab; ein Kind oder Wahnsinniger stürzt sie unvorsichtig herab, und bricht den Hals. Ebendaher ist der Begriff vom Luxus so relativ als der vom Guten und Bösen. (1:25–26)

The house of culture requires the proper use of luxury items to function. Yet the uses that the various groups make of it can be more or less appropriate and are thus open for evaluation. The editor thus felt compelled to discuss criteria for its proper use. Insisting on a discussion of the context underscores the notion that both cultural practices such as fashion as well as intellectual, moral, or economic positions are not only in constant flux but also that they are relativized by their context in a complex interplay of discourses. The call for contextualization also fosters an important reinterpretation of luxury, which detached it from its earlier use as a key concept in the oppositional identity formation of the middle class. At the stage in the development of the middle class under investigation here, luxury items were used to provide pleasure while also negotiating status within the middle class. The resulting cultural and economic competition, in turn, enhanced the status of the middle class as a whole and helped to create its cultural and social domination.

Following early Enlightenment polemics, luxury had been associated with the nobility and their ability to display status and rank.

Considering it as wasteful, excessive consumption, Enlightenment critics had constructed their own position in opposition to this form of luxury. Using moral and economic arguments, they associated luxury with aristocratic splendor as a demonstration of the ruler's political, economic, and cultural power. The economic frugality that Weber theorized in *The Protestant Ethic and the Spirit of Capitalism* as defining the middle class of the earlier decades of the eighteenth century valorized luxury negatively. Instead of the status consumption of the court, the middle class adopted a saving-for-future-profit model.[85] At the same time, the moral argumentation had associated luxury with lasciviousness and indulgence, which had made it a key concept to be used against the lifestyle of the nobility during the phase of oppositional identity formation. The concept of luxury required a significant reinterpretation to make it useful for the self-definition of the middle class. The *Journal* was instrumental in this reevaluation. With the integration of "luxury" into the self-fashioning of middle-class identity, a new stage in the identity formation of the middle class emerges.

In mercantilist theory, the chief responsibility for inducing economic activity through consumption lay with the rich, who were encouraged to spend freely. An initial insistence on middle-class frugality and on saving in order to accumulate economic power was gradually replaced by a new sense of economic comfort that encouraged increasing layers of the middle class to participate in an expanded level of consumption. This redefinition detached the concept of luxury from its traditional association with sin and amoral conduct. In the reinterpretation of luxury by the middle class, it becomes linked with culturally and economically productive sophisticated domestic consumption. It no longer means sheer opulence and quantity but rather elegance and variety, displaying not only the cultural taste of its owner but the capital of pleasure. This was only possible through a significant reconceptualization of luxury from its early Enlightenment condemnation as a sign for the decadence of the court and the estate system. Discussions in the *Journal* and other venues on the proper use and function of luxury are instrumental for the acceptance of the concept of luxury into middle-class mentality by the end of the century. This reinterpretation is achieved—in good Enlightenment fashion—by classification, by distinguishing degrees of luxury, by listing its advantages and disadvantages, and by outlining the dangers. The *Journal* saw itself as stimulating the economic climate in order to improve the cultural climate. These subtle transformations can be observed in the debates on "luxury" in the *Journal*.

The debate on "luxury" attests to two competing economic theories and systems: the physiocratic ideas, based on the strength of agriculture, and the precapitalist expansionism, based on commerce. The first criticizes fashionable consumption of luxury items as extremely wasteful, while the second celebrates consumption as the most powerful engine driving the economy and also stimulating culture, science, and education:

> Luxury, says the devotee of the physiocratic system, is the plague of all nations! It wastes a pure yield, turning it into fruitless expenses; hindering reproduction; enervating the physical strength of the nation; loosening all feeling for morality and honor; ruining the well-being of families; leaving the state with hordes of beggars!
>
> Luxury, says the financier and technologue, is the richest source for the state, the mightiest lever of industry, and the strongest force behind the circulation of money. It erases all traces of barbaric mores; creates the arts, sciences, trade, and commerce; increases the population and the energies of the state while bringing pleasure and happiness to life!

> Luxus, sagt der Anhänger des physiokratischen Systems, ist die Pest der Staaten! Er verschwendet den reinen Ertrag zu unfruchtbaren Ausgaben; hindert die Reproduction; entnervt die physikalischen Kräfte der Nation; lößt alles Gefühl für Moralität und Ehre auf; zerrüttet den Wohlstand der Familien, und liefert dem Staate Schaaren Bettler!—
>
> Luxus, sagt der Finanzier und der Technolog, ist die reichste Quelle für den Staat; der allmächtige Hebel der Industrie, und das kräftigste Triebwerk der Circulation. Er verwischt alle Spuren der Barbarey in den Sitten; schafft Künste, Wissenschaften, Handel und Gewerbe; vermehrt die Population und die Kräfte des Staats, und bewürkt Genuß und Glück des Lebens! (1:23)

The periodical takes the side of progress (a free-market position) and considers the consumption of luxury items based on the perennial principle of novelty as an important impetus not only for economic and social advancement but also for the cultural advancement and enrichment of the (middle) class, the state, and the nation. Consumption produces opportunities for the arts and sciences and fosters commerce, trade, and the crafts, thereby improving the level of culture and civilization. As a progressive force, the consumption of luxury items not only benefits the individual but also has a positive effect on the larger communities, be it the state or the nation.

For my investigation, the last line of the quote is central: luxurious consumption provides pleasure, well-being, and happiness; it is entertaining ("bewürkt Genuß und Glück"). Entertainment becomes linked to economic and material well-being and to cultural sophistication. Increased consumption is seen as the prerequisite for cultural entertainment. Therefore, a closer look at the discourse of economic development as it is established in the *Journal* is instructive. We do not find an unqualified celebration of consumption. The contributor to the *Journal* makes a point to distinguish among three gradations of luxury—*Wolleben* (living well), *Hochleben* (living exceedingly well), and *Ueppigkeit* (excessive consumption)—of which only the first two are portrayed in an entirely positive light:

> Living well is available to all people on earth as soon as they can earn more than they need to cover their basic necessities. And the burning desire to reach this stage and to indulge is the mightiest dynamo of industry, the arts, inventions and taste, in short, it drives most human endeavors.

> Wolleben will und kann jeder Mensch auf der ganzen weiten Erde, so bald er sich etwas mehr, als seine ersten nothwendigen Bedürfnisse des Lebens erwerben kann; und eben der heiße Wunsch dahin zu kommen, und sich gütlich zu thun, ist die mächtigste Triebfeder der Industrie, der Künste, der Erfindungen und des Geschmacks, kurz des größten Theils der menschlichen Thätigkeit. (1:24)

The desire of every human being to live well, that is, to live above the subsistence level, creates an enormous impetus not only for the economy but also for civilization—the arts, inventions, and taste—for most areas of human endeavor. Financial stability is also the prerequisite for the expansion of entertainment. More importantly, living well or enjoying oneself ("sich gütlich zu thun") takes place during leisure and seems to consist of the entertainment that fills this time span.

The second, higher level of consumption, *Hochleben,* is reserved for the more affluent:

> To live exceedingly well is reserved for the elite and the rich and is in part derived from a sense of competition with others and in part from a hunger for pleasant sensations that are so easily within reach.

> Hochleben will und kann der Vornehmere und Reiche; theils aus Hang sich vor Andern auszuzeichnen, theils aus Durst nach angenehmen Empfindungen, die er sich so leicht verschaffen kann. (1:24)

The desire to live well and to indulge in comforts that go beyond the basic necessities of life seems to be an innate trait of all peoples of this earth, but the stage of indulgence and consumption, reserved for the rich and powerful, serves an additional purpose. It creates a register of distinctions that set people apart. Their indulgence in pleasures they can easily afford is positive for the state because it creates employment and wealth for other segments of the population. In short, it aids in the circulation of money. In fact, it was seen as the duty of the wealthy to spend freely.

The *Journal* is directed at the upwardly mobile and upper middle class, at those who can afford luxury items without suffering hardship. Only excesses (*Ueppigkeit*)—that is, when monies that are needed for the necessities are spent on luxury items or the expense supersedes the income—are detrimental to the general welfare. In other words, reasonable consumption is advocated, while excessive luxury beyond the appropriate individual comfort zone is discouraged. The *Journal* does sound a note of caution about the danger of extravagance to those groups that cannot afford it, namely the merchants, craftspeople, and servants.[86]

The argument is that people in these groups might live above their means. The luxury items are in principle available for sale to them but might exceed their limited income, making consumption imprudent. This in turn could lead to their financial ruin. While merchants might have significant income one day, excessive spending and the natural fluctuation of their profession make them vulnerable to financial disasters on a large scale. Rich merchants were known for their interest in luxury items—elegant coaches, a large number of servants, lavishly furnished houses, and lavish gardens—as status symbols of their professional success: "As soon as a merchant has accumulated 100,000 guilders, he has to have a coach and a garden. His consumption increases with his income, and the smallest financial setback might throw him back into the mud" ("Sobald es ein Kaufmann auf 100 000 Gulden gebracht hat, muß er seine Equipage und seinen Garten haben. Sein Aufwand steigt mit seinem Vermögen, und dann ist der kleinste Schlag imstande ihn wieder in den Koth zurückzuwerfen").[87] Especially the leisure gardens, with their significant cost for maintenance and their low use value, were a quintessential luxury item.

Rather than advocating restraint and frugality, the *Journal* teaches the proper management and use of luxury and pleasure. Acknowledging the physiocratic position regarding the negative effects of excessive consumption, the magazine concedes that the indulgence in luxury articles by those who cannot afford them can lead to a variety of social ills ranging from debt to prostitution. If middle-class women have a tendency to live above their means, men will be reluctant to marry them. Because men cannot afford to marry, they instead seduce lower-class girls or frequent prostitutes. This in turn causes many women of the bourgeoisie to remain unmarried and those of the lower classes to prostitute themselves for luxury items (1:183–85). This cautionary scenario advocates moderation and social responsibility in the use of luxury and (cultural) consumption. While celebrating the circulation of luxury items as a means for upward mobility, the *Journal* nevertheless does its part in policing access to luxury items by discouraging the lower layers of the middle class to participate in this process of acculturation.

The pleasure that entertainment creates is the motivating force behind the luxury of spending for nonessential cultural practices. Social and economic hierarchies carefully structure access to cultural entertainment and the pleasure it provides. The *Journal*'s discussion of its proper use replaces external regulations—such as sumptuary laws—with (self-)discipline. Yet it is important to point out that during this period under investigation, when the differentiation of the middle class takes place, self-discipline is no longer characterized as restraint, frugality, thrift, and the accumulation of wealth but rather as the proper and prudent use and management of resources in order to achieve the greatest return in cultural capital and the enhancement of the middle-class lifestyle.

Taste makes use of the faculties of the mind and the senses which discern between the proper and improper use of cultural (and economic) capital. Taste as the faculty that can discern beauty, which provides pleasure from imperfection, which produces dislike,[88] can be acquired and cultivated. Everyone has the potential for improving the natural capability of taste. Similarly, this form of self-discipline is a self-regulatory mechanism that negotiates the proper distribution of restraint and spending, of work and entertainment, and of necessary tedium and desirable pleasure.

In addition, overindulgence in luxury items hints at the seductive and addictive nature of consumption. Consumption as entertainment is so seductive because the pleasure it creates can be endlessly repeated (within the limits of the purse, of course—which is why it is discouraged for the less affluent). The availability of a plenitude of goods, the emergence of fashionability (which, of course, suggests that the item will soon be unfashionable and obsolete) not only in clothing but in items of interior design and (garden) architecture, creates a steady stream of wants to satisfy the desire produced by the given cultural object or activity.

The surge of commercial activity that was enabled by the saving-for-future-profit model and allowed a standard of living above subsistence level was then augmented by an increase in consumption that contributed not only to a surge of commercial activity but also—closely linked—to the establishment of a leisure culture and cultural entertainment. The *Journal* teaches not only about matters of taste but also of the necessary self-discipline that the individual needs in order to balance frugality and consumption, need and want.

The growing interest in leisure-time entertainment and the increase in commercial activity during the period under investigation required not only more leisure but also a higher level of affluence. Social signs of affluence are "increased consumption of food, . . . increased expenditures on houses, increased pre-occupation with fashion, a boom in books, music, entertainment and holidays."[89] More leisure and even a slight rise in affluence stimulate desire for self-improvement and social mobility. This is achieved through a higher level of consumption of goods and a higher degree of participation in cultural activities. Evidence for this trend can be seen in the significant importance of reading (the emergence of specialized periodical reading materials, the institution of reading societies and circulating libraries).

This complex reinterpretation of luxury is taken up by highly successful members of the middle class. They are able to renegotiate the original contradiction between their own rational use of money (saving for future profit) and their lifestyle (consumption) in various ways that distinguish them from other subgroups within the higher middle class. The merchant elite in Hamburg—most notably Georg Heinrich Sieverking, Johann Michael Hudtwalker, and Johann Arnold Günther—discussed the topic at one of the meetings of the Patriotische Gesellschaft:

> Luxury consists of the means for the selective satisfaction of needs, comforts, pleasures, and splendor. . . . Everybody has the right and the duty to create comfort and pleasure for himself, in some cases he may also impress with external splendor, and it is meritorious when he thus encourages and nourishes the arts and the crafts. . . . A certain degree of luxury is inseparable from the Enlightenment.

> Luxus ist Aufwand für ausgesuchte Befriedigung der Bedürfniße, der Bequemlichkeit, des Vergnügens, des Glanzes. . . . Jeder hat das Recht und die Pflicht sich Bequemlichkeit und Vergnügen zu verschaffen, in manchen Fällen darf er auch durch äußern Glanz imponieren, und es ist verdienstlich, wenn er dadurch Gewerben und Künsten Nahrung und Aufmunterung schafft. . . . Ein gewisser Grad des Luxus ist durchaus von der Aufklärung unzertrennlich.[90]

I would argue that the evidence from the *Journal* suggests that the asceticism of the early Enlightenment, with its exclusive focus on inner values, which usually went in tandem with a rejection of physical comforts and above all with splendor, is replaced with a justification of these material comforts. The reasonable, measured indulgence in objects of material comfort and pleasure are seen not only as a right but also as a duty because they foster commerce, manufacturing, and the decorative arts, leading to more refinement and to a higher level of culture. In addition, a certain amount of luxury in the satisfaction of needs, the provision of comforts, and the indulgence in pleasurable forms of entertainment and even in splendor in the care of the self is the right and the duty of the individual, as an enriching lifestyle plays an important part in the proper care of the self. The roots of this imperative to achieve mental and physical well-being, even happiness, by pursuing measured pleasures can be found in rococo culture with its psychology of delight ("Psychologie der Lust").[91] Mauser looked beyond the reading of the rococo as the playfully lascivious celebration of nature and saw the serious core of rococo culture in the realization that human beings distinguish themselves from other creatures by their ability to enjoy pleasure and experience happiness and that they thus should actualize this potential: "Joy and pleasure are the measure and expression of happiness, whereby both concepts do not denote exuberance but a condition of measured enjoyment" ("Freude und Vergnügen mit Maß sind Ausdruck dieser Glückseligkeit, wobei beide Begriffe nicht Ausgelassenheit meinen, sondern einen Zustand des maßvollen Genusses").[92] The rococo culture considered the biodynamic harmony of mind and body as the prerequisite for health and happiness. What distinguishes this earlier stage of the care of the self from the one explored in our time frame is that the rococo credited the beauty of nature with providing the sensual stimulation of the simple pleasures (those of vision, hearing, taste, and smell)[93] as the source of happiness, while by the turn of the century the pleasures were more culturally enhanced. As we discussed in this chapter, the sensual delights are manipulated and heightened by the powers of the imagination and extended by an increasing range of entertainments that could provide pleasure. The creation of pleasure no longer depended on nature alone but looked to cultural forms of entertainment and luxury items to create the sensation of pleasure.

Yet the underlying concern is a similar one. The Enlightenment belief in progress and self-determination resulting in the ideal of the autonomous subject placed the responsibility for the pursuit of happiness in the hands of the individual. Happiness consists of a delicate balancing act, a biodynamic balance of body and soul in accord with "nature." The individual has to take active steps in his or her care so that he or she does not fall victim to the symptomatic disease of the eighteenth century, melancholia. After all, the responsibility for the failure to achieve fulfillment and happiness fell squarely on the autonomous subject.[94] Since the medical knowledge considered melancholia an affliction of the body and the mind, caused by a compromised flow of the vital fluids (*Säftetheorie*), it was treated with physical and mental forms of stimulation to increase the impeded flow of vital fluids. This beneficial stimulation of the body consisted of changes in temperature, increased activity, and changes in diet, while the mind was stimulated with forms of entertainment—for example, with music, travel, and other diversions.[95] This laid the groundwork for the use of pleasure and luxury to enhance the middle-class lifestyle—body and mind. Stimulation that produces the sensation of pleasure thus becomes not only acceptable but indeed a necessary part in the care of the self.[96]

5

Cultural Consumerism

THE ROLE OF READING

The importance of reading cannot be underestimated in the diversification and specialization of cultural activity. It not only created the ability to delight in imaginary pleasures but also fostered the new taste for novelty so noticeable in the voracious appetite for reading. As discussed in chapter 3, *Empfindsamkeit* and *Sturm und Drang* had placed new emphasis on fostering emotions, and these emotions, as states of high arousal, began to be experienced in their potential to produce intense pleasures. This contributed considerably to the socialization of pleasurable emotions. It became clear that not only physical stimuli but also mental images could produce the sensation we call pleasure. The role of reading for pleasure (ludic or playful reading), of non-work-related reading, is of paramount importance for the ability to experience imaginary pleasures. Emotions could be manipulated and enhanced through sentimental fiction. The culturally constructed ability to manipulate feelings (i.e., to determine their nature and intensity) was a necessary step in creating the ability of modern men and women to produce "mental images which they consume for the intrinsic pleasure they provide."[1]

Reading for entertainment is the most popular (and most frequently analyzed) form of cultural consumption. For men, this kind of reading, while not providing important truths, yields entertainment and pleasure, or at least stimulates and satisfies curiosity and thus offers an alternative to work-related reading and thinking. Just as the body requires repose and rest, so does the mind. As the professionalization and specialization of working life increased, the energy and general knowledge required to appreciate complex cultural forms decreased and the demand for qualitatively different forms of relaxing entertainment increased proportionately.

For women, whose socially ascribed work in the home allowed for more leisure, and who—due to the naturally "more vivid imagination" ascribed to them—supposedly do not relish serious tasks, reading was an especially important way to fill the empty hours. Reading for pleasure is thus a matter of mental hygiene, a way of caring for one's self. Contemporaries argued that for women in particular—but also for other persons who have much free time on their hands—entertaining diversions are desirable because they provide refuge from the saddest boredom ("traurigsten Geschäftslosigkeit").[2] Ludic reading sparked by curiosity and boredom was the result of the modern functionalization of society, through which a large segment of the population no longer had the time, energy, and, most importantly, the educational prerequisites to enjoy all areas of high culture. Characterized by passivity, the ludic reader is no longer actively engaged (*Tätigkeit*) but is said to be merely occupied (*Beschäftigung*).

The easy consumption of trivial literature is often explained by reference to its formal elements, which are said to emphasize non-integrated scenes that serve as individual but cumulative sites for the imagination. Because such literature contains numerous, fairly self-contained parts, the recipient is not forced to maintain an overview of the whole at all times, and hence less concentration and attention are required. Some authors deliberately stressed individual scenes or images, sentimental groups, or interesting situations in preference to a stringent whole.[3] Reading became firmly established as a leisure activity and thus became separated from the productive hours devoted to work and livelihood. At the same time, reading became linked with pleasure.

Audiences searched for more than practical advice or edification in the reading material they selected. They derived entertainment from certain reading practices that could be applied to the whole range of available reading materials. These practices include selecting certain favorite passages as occasions for strong identification or—more importantly for our context—as springboards for daydreams. This selection fostered the ability to create mental scenarios that "improve on reality" by imaging circumstances that propel the reader out of his or her ordinary situation into a uniquely pleasurable context. These scenarios are usually linked to extraordinary situations surrounding romantic love, amazing adventures, or fame and fortune.

This particular reading practice exists between fantasy and directed thought. As readers become absorbed in the text, reflexive awareness and self-consciousness are momentarily relegated to the background and words are replaced by images. The reader experiences the hallucinatory pleasure of being propelled from one emotive scene to the next.

Through this form of reading, the individual acquired the art of arranging and rearranging images from his or her actual surroundings or from memory, thus creating an "improved" mental image. This "control" over one's (imaginary) environment is experienced as pleasurable. The educated middle class's extensive reading practices and common practice of dabbling in the visual arts fostered the ability to manipulate mental and then physical painted images to produce new effects and to create pleasing emotions. After all, drawing and painting lessons were an intrinsic part of the middle-class lifestyle.

Bertuch's *Journal des Luxus und der Moden* characterizes the effect of this reading practice as a kind of dreamlike suspension between the real and the possible. People delight in being kept in a dreamlike state ("wunderbaren Traume erhalten zu werden") and in continuously oscillating between the conditions of their lives and the imaginary possibilities ("stets zwischen dem Reiche des Wirklichen und des Möglichen träumend hin und her zu schweben" [1:369]). Reading fostered this type of fantasizing and the production of elaborate imaginary scenarios. Because these scenarios contained the element of possibility, they were distinguished from pure fantasy.

Contemporaries expressed concern over this reading practice, considering it a sign of underdeveloped taste and of a lack of cultural sophistication. Those who indulge in this practice are frequently compared to children who replaced fairy tales with fiction.[4] Reading is compared to pleasurable children's play: the magic of a storyline or plot, the recurrence of a familiar experience, the security derived from the fulfillment of conventional structures, the predictability of a controlled imaginary landscape.

Yet even the critics had to acknowledge the fascination of novelty and the extraordinary. Ludic reading is characterized by the tension between familiarity and novelty, and this kind of reading provided occasions for comfortable, safe stimulation that allowed readers to select an optimal level of arousal.[5] Reading-produced fantasy, unlike dreams, can never become overwhelming and is completely under the control of the reader. The familiarity precludes too high a degree of difficulty or aesthetic innovation and makes ludic reading effortless. Effortless pleasure stems from the appropriate degree of stimulation for the given context, situation, and reader. As Victor Nell writes, "The pleasurableness of an aesthetic stimulus does not lie on the same dimension as its interest value or complexity. Berlyne has demonstrated that pleasure reaches its peak at moderate levels of complexity, whereas very uniform stimuli, and those that are highly complex, tend to be aversive."[6] Since the appropriate level of stimulation is highly contingent on the context, the reader can select reading materials that provide the desired level of conflict and degree of stimulation.[7] The educated eighteenth-century reader could select the level of complexity by choosing from the continuum of reading materials available to him or her—often in a single publication (e.g., in almanacs or pocket books).

Interesting and often neglected factors in the discussions of reading practices are the physical changes in reading practices from reading aloud in groups to silent and solitary reading.[8] The physical-sensual loss of the performance aspect of reading helped to focus on the production of meaning and on the imaginary experience of reading. At the same time, more comfortable furniture, designed particularly for reading, soon appeared in advertisements in the pages of magazines like Bertuch's *Journal* (fig. 1). Reading chairs served multiple functions in the bourgeois household. They provided physical comfort for extended leisurely reading, stilling the body and privileging the optical sensations and the imagination. At the same time, they became status symbols in the middle-class lifestyle, displaying pride in the cultural activity of reading (fig. 2).

The sense of effortlessness associated with ludic reading stems from the "absence of any response demands."[9] The privacy of a solitary reading experience required no public reaction to the text. In addition, by offering freedom from (intellectual) censure, the experience provides a realm of imaginary role-play and psychological experimentation.

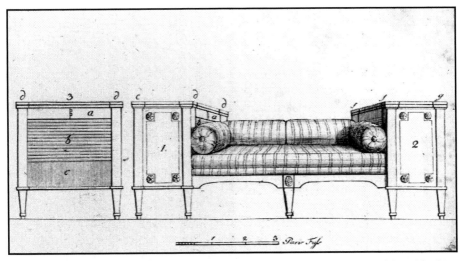

1. An English reading bed in *Journal des Luxus und der Moden* 3 (1788). Courtesy of the Bildarchiv Preußischer Kulturbesitz Berlin. Photo by Dietmar Katz.

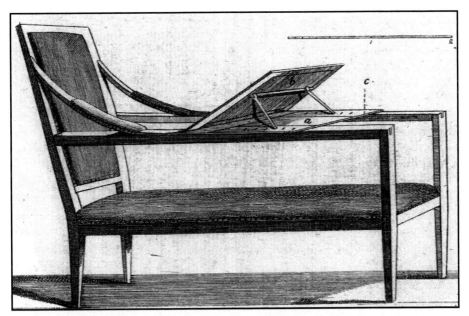

2. Reading chair in *Journal des Luxus und der Moden* 14 (1799). Courtesy of the Bildarchiv Preußischer Kulturbesitz Berlin. Photo by Dietmar Katz.

This fantasizing associated with reading could serve as a rehearsal process for the reader's own issues requiring resolve.

The powers of the imaginary were fostered by certain genres in particular—for example, in the popular historical novels, ballads, and the chivalric and gothic. These genres tend to provide pleasurable stimulation in a fictionalized presentation of history. The historical sources are retold in literary language, and the historical sequence of events is interrupted with anecdotes. The material was presented in such a way that readers could reexperience the events and use their imagination to participate in them. A heavy reliance on pictorial representations assisted in stimulating the imagination. The most famous and widely imitated ballads were those of Gottfried August Bürger (1747–94), in particular his chilling "Leonore" (first published in 1774 in the *Göttinger Musenalmanach*).[10] The pleasures that ballads provide lay in their sensory effects. Their proto-cinematic quality created illusions of immediacy. Topics, images, and linguistic features were carefully selected to produce the strongest effects possible. A tight, easily accessible plot and an effective pace, a sequence of impressive imagery, and the inclusion of dialogues and lyrical elements such as onomatopoeia, parallelisms, and assonances heighten the seeming immediacy and stir the emotions and imagination. The frequent use of ballads in almanacs bespeaks their popularity.[11]

The reading craze was propelled by this desire to repeat the sensation of pleasure that this experience provided. Readers selected reading materials that displayed the same basic structures with only slight variations. The underlying desire for repeated stimulation is contained in formulations such as "addictive reading," "reading craze," and "reading mania" and in the association with the voracious ingestion of food, with gluttony ("Bücher verschlingen"). Critics compared fashionable books that lend themselves to this kind of reading to highly appealing food that seduces the senses—especially when presented in attractive vessels—but fails to nourish and thus leaves the consumer hungry for new fare.[12] The very nature of this form of reading drives its repetition in an attempt to repeat the pleasure it produces.

The pleasure of reading is often combined with other forms of entertainment, creating doubled pleasures, for example, with the sensual enjoyment of tobacco, wine, coffee, and tea; with going for a stroll; and with reading in nature. This layering of pleasures was represented not only in literature but also in visual representations. The educated middle class had themselves depicted as readers in portraiture in all stages of life, from childhood to old age.[13] This indicates that reading was an important part of the self-image and thus the identity formation of the middle class. In many illustrations we can observe this integration of the book into everyday activities as part of the daily chores or occupations, especially of girls and women. Almanacs, illustrated books, and journals often incorporated depictions of reading scenes in important points of the publication, such as the frontispiece or the cover illustration.[14] A fashionably dressed woman is depicted reading as she takes a stroll (fig. 3).[15] Nies sees the positive integration of the book into middle-class activities as a sign that the education by the book has to be supplemented by the social world around it, thus limiting the value of the book as educator of the middle class. My emphasis, in contrast, is on the entertainment function of the book as it is incorporated into other pleasurable activities, thus creating a pleasurable mélange of nature and culture, heightening the sensuality and the pleasure of the event.[16] Schön has argued that peripatetic reading is an attempt to bridge the discrepancy between physical immobility during normal seated reading and the vividness and movement depicted in the text.[17] This might explain the reception of certain especially arousing texts, such as *Werther,* but the more likely explanation, especially for illustrations of reading women (and men) on the promenade, is that two or more highly pleasurable forms of entertainment are layered to heighten the pleasurable effect of the entertaining activities. At the same time, the combination of reading and other pleasures demonstrates people's fashionable taste in cultural practices. The fashionable presentation of the body, the activity of walking with the visual stimulation it provides, the entertainment of intermittent conversation, and the cultural prestige value of the book as icon are layered to heighten the pleasurable qualities. These images sell the whole package of culturally refined entertainment to the readership of the *Journal* and offer models for imitation or identification, thereby contributing to the formation of the middle-class lifestyle. Even professional readers seem to have enjoyed this layering of pleasant activities and combined (or alternated) going for walks in nature or the garden with reading.[18]

Reading was not only a solitary form of entertainment that created a private, individualistic pleasure but also an important part of social interaction. It was part of the social interaction in gatherings for afternoon coffee or tea (*Kaffee- und Theekränzchen*) and at parties and

T. 20

3. Lady reading in *Journal des Luxus und der Moden* 20 (1805). Courtesy of the Thüringische Universitäts- und Landesbibliothek Jena.

dinners in private homes. Here, reading aloud, largely abandoned by the end of the century in favor of silent reading, was still part of a series of possible forms of entertainment—games, card games, charades, amateur performances of dramatic scenes or even plays,[19] performances of attitudes and tableaux, music, savoring visual art, discussing and sharing the latest almanacs and pocket books, eating and drinking, and enjoying fashionable tableware in front of the backdrop of the aestheticized domestic sphere and its inhabitants. Andrea Van Dülmen also describes instances where reading aloud was a regular activity during the informal forms of sociability taking place in the beloved gardens of the middle class.[20] In this social context, reading was only one of many forms of cultural entertainment. The entertainment value provided by these cultural practices facilitated social communication by creating a comfortable ambience that allowed varying degrees of social engagement and a variety of stimuli.

The Diversification of Print Culture

The importance of the varied print culture beyond the book had long been underestimated because it was associated with entertainment in the domestic sphere and thus thought to be of lower cultural value than the literary work published in book form. This is surprising because Habermas, in his 1962 study, had clearly described a varied print culture in his discussion of the formation of the literary public sphere. Although the more recent translation and second edition of *Structural Transformation of the Public Sphere* spawned considerable theoretical debate,[21] various forms of (nonliterary) print culture and the role of material culture have not received adequate treatment that would examine their impact in the formation of the literary public sphere and in fostering a cultural community.[22]

The structural transformation of the public sphere was accomplished by two symbiotic developments: the intense net of communication evolving within the bourgeois private sphere, on the one hand (Habermas), and the self-destruction of the *Gelehrtenrepublik,* the *res publica litteraria,* the communication system of the university-trained community of scholars (*literatus:* fluent in Latin, university trained, and published), on the other.[23] By the late eighteenth century (somewhat later than in Habermas's analysis), the immense expansion of the literary marketplace restructured the mix of literature in favor of belletristic literature. Belles lettres constituted 21.45 percent of the book market by 1800 and 29 percent by 1810, which broke the dominance and the close ties of the community of scholars with the book market. The discourse of the community of scholars retreated into the university while opening the ever-expanding field of public debate to nonspecialists or dilettantes.[24] As the scholars withdrew to the university by the end of the century, a parallel institution, the periodical press, took over the communication of knowledge to a lay audience. In addition, scholars began to write in the vernacular and also contributed to the general discussions, thus increasing the volume of literary communication significantly. This further deemphasized the monopoly of knowledge traditionally reserved for the scholarly community and stressed the contributions of laypersons.[25]

The increase in the periodical literature was enabled by this development and at the same time allowed a larger group of authors to publish their works because, overall, it published established authors next to novices, even, on occasion, encouraging its readers to submit their own pieces. All genres saw a significant increase in literary production between 1770 and 1800.[26] An increased interest in education and literacy (by the end of the century almost all German states introduced mandatory schooling for all) as well as changes in the literary marketplace and in the intellectual climate facilitated the emergence of a larger group of writers than was previously possible.[27] The increase in readership and in the variety of reading materials (journals, almanacs, weeklies, monthlies, newspapers, etc.) enabled the professionalization of literary production. A truly staggering number of publications on all aspects of middle-class culture—some for special groups, such as women and children and youths, others directed at all adult readers—provided a significant range of reading materials for the entertainment of the middle class. Their focus ranged from travel and geography, history, art, music, literature, fashion, science and technology, pedagogy, politics and current events, theater, and theology to the ultra-current newspaper.[28]

From 1766 to 1800 the number of writers who could live on their writing increased from 2,000–3,000 to 10,650.[29] By fostering the democratization of education, literacy, and discourses of cultural competence, the Enlightenment participated in the demise of its own originally monolithic concepts. The expanding literary production was accompanied by changes not only in its aesthetics but also in its reception. These transformations were theoretically reflected in the emerging debate on "trivial" literature—or in the parlance of the day, the phenomena of dilettantism (production, author) and entertainment (reception, reader). An indicator of the valorization of culture within the bourgeois concept is the discussion of *Lesesucht,* of addictive reading for pleasure. This change in the literary marketplace was caused by the deprofessionalization of authorship and the creation of dilettante authors, the unspecific concept of literary genius, the appreciation of a quasi-"natural" work without artifice, and the absence of firmly established poetic rules.[30] At the same time, many publications paid for their contributions and provided some income for the authors, thus creating a new form of semi-professionalization. Editors also drew honoraria, which could be quite significant. For the publishing houses this was also a lucrative undertaking. To ensure their market share, they were interested not only in attracting a variety of interesting new authors and works but also in engaging the famous authors as contributors and, if possible, as editors. Mutually desirable and financially lucrative, this arrangement contributed to the success of the periodical print culture. Goethe, for example, used the periodical literature not only to his own financial advantage but also to reach a larger audience. Of course, as a successful author he could select how and when he wanted to use this medium.

Professional readers—for example, professors, critics, and some authors—were critical of or disinterested in this part of the literary marketplace, despite the fact that many important works were first published in these venues before they appeared in book form. The publications could contain avant-garde pieces by the most famous contemporary authors next to pieces by more popular writers—men and, often, women, even of the audience themselves. Almanacs, in particular, contained a selection of poetry and other literary forms in verse, excerpts from unpublished drama, epos, elegies, and so forth published anonymously with the explicit invitation to the readership to send in appropriate material.[31] Although York-Gothart Mix cautions not to overestimate the actual printed contributions by dilettantes,[32] the fact that laypersons were encouraged to participate as authors and recipients challenged the monopoly of the *Gelehrtenrepublik* and the professional writers and contributed to the establishment of a broader cultural public sphere.

The periodical literature also played an important role in the commercialization and commodification of literature. It became an integral part of cultural consumerism; it produced short-lived objects that were replaced at regular intervals and as such was fully integrated in the economic system. Innovation and novelty in presentation and content made it a product of fashion, carrying in it the seeds of obsolescence and demanding a replacement product. The pleasure of reading became commercially available. Initially, almanacs and pocket books were quite affordable and thus made this pleasure more widely available than the book.

The time from the 1770s to the turn of the century displays a previously unheard-of rapid succession of poetic trends and literary fashions, resulting in an eventual coexistence of various movements from the avant-garde elite writers of classicism and romanticism to the late representatives of Enlightenment, rococo, and *Empfindsamkeit*. The plurality of the literary styles was complemented and in a sense enabled by the variety of the periodical print culture. Although a few almanacs were used to advance a certain poetic program, the variety of the materials, topics, and literary styles was not only a hallmark of the periodical literature but contributed significantly to its entertainment quality, providing pleasurable stimulation while also fulfilling a desire for public literary communication.

Historical Development of the Binary Model

By the last decades of the eighteenth century, the anxiety over the increased literary production provoked sustained poetological discussions in which the literary avant-garde attempted to bifurcate culture by attaching cultural value exclusively to the products of high culture. By implication, this debate is also a discussion of the proper role of cultural production and consumption. Overall, the poetological gesture directed at this new phenomenon was one of warding off, of containment, of limiting the ever-increasing flood of literary texts and objects of cultural consumption. It was based on a resistance to, an abstention from, and a suppression of the "seductive lure of mass culture."[33] The elite writer (or poet) withdrew from the demands of the broad audience and distanced himself from the middle-class audience to avoid being functionalized as a means for social and economic progress. The agenda and purpose of the debate on mass culture is not one of serious analysis or exploration but of containment and denouncement. The educated elite attempted to hold onto their position of power by rhetorically denouncing the entertainment and pleasure associated with other non-autonomous cultural artifacts. In aesthetic theory, this cultural politics surfaces in Schiller's review of Bürger's ballad as a prelude to his *Aesthetic Letters,* which was read as a reaction against populism and an overt privileging of the sensual elements in literature.[34] Nevertheless, my examination of the *Journal des Luxus und der Moden* suggests that cultural consumption was firmly entrenched in the lifestyle of the bourgeoisie, just as the almanac culture attests to the enormous diversification of reading as a fait accompli. Cultural consumption as it was presented in the various forms of print culture consisted of a wide range of practices on a continuum, which classicist aesthetics attempted to classify and thus artificially split into binary oppositions for rhetorical purposes in such publications as the sketch on dilettantism. Daniel Purdy argues even more pointedly that classicist aesthetics can be regarded as a backlash against commodity culture.[35] Both Woodmansee and Purdy see the classicist aesthetic as based in opposition to the forms of cultural consumption. The entertainment value and the kind of pleasure the artifact in question was to produce were at the core of the negotiations of value. Yet because of the underlying defensive posture, the "noncomplex" pleasures produced by the forms of cultural consumerism must be culled from the negative examples designed as a foil to foreground the complex pleasures of high art.

As a means of explaining the failure of the Enlightenment's monolithic concept of culture and the privileging of a new understanding of high literature over what was perceived as an onslaught of inferior works, three main aspects of the discussions are of relevance for our topic. First, there is the attempt to distinguish two forms of pleasure with the ultimate goal of establishing an understanding of the complex pleasures afforded by high literature. Second, a cultural hierarchy is established with the argument that the other forms of pleasure are said to derive from a failure to "master" the text. Third, this argument is couched in gendered terminology and discussed as a power relationship in which certain groups display a lesser degree of cultural literacy or mastery.

The goal was to suppress the destabilizing allure of mass culture and to encourage artists and writers to resist pleasing a larger audience—a move that, however, put the author in direct conflict with the modern literary market, in which literature had become a commodity. As literary production increased, the traditional outlets for publicity—advertisement and reviews in the appropriate journals—became quickly overburdened. Increasingly, marketing was left to the publishers, who were, of course, interested in increasing the popularity of the piece in

103

question. In lieu of the detailed reviewing practices in journals to guide and to aid taste formation with regard to individual texts, the debate moved to a general debate on aesthetics. It is within this debate that the jostling for the maintaining of cultural hegemony took place; here the battle for intellectual, moral, and philosophical dominance of the intellectual elite was fought.

At the same time, this convoluted discourse on the proper forms of pleasure that culture was to provide reveals the ambivalence of the Enlightenment project. By "Enlightenment project" I mean the secularization of all aspects of life by a firm belief in progress in all areas of human endeavor. This required a large-scale pedagogical endeavor to educate the middle class to become mature and self-reliant and to eventually acquire the necessary self-discipline to strive for constant improvement. From its inception, the project contained certain contradictions that came to the fore by the end of the century and drove the bifurcation of culture. For our context, the most important ones are the unresolved conflict over who—that is, which social groups—should be brought into full participation in the Enlightenment project through education and self-education seemingly intended for everybody. Complex constructions of public and private use of *Räsonnement* (critical reasoning) attempted to reconcile individuals with their political context but failed to resolve the contradiction that certain groups—for example, women and the lower class—were limited from a full participation in the Enlightenment project. It also could not anticipate the issues associated with an increased specialization that further jeopardized the monolithic concept of education and *Bildung*. Habermas's initial overestimation of the coherence of the literary public sphere structured by the democratic medium of *Räsonnement* (modified in the foreword to the 1990 edition, which speaks of competing public spheres) was symptomatic of the ambivalence in the Enlightenment discourse itself. By ignoring the economic and social aspects, that discourse failed to understand the dynamics and the interwoven nature of economics and culture in the kind of "progress" it had helped to create. Progress resulted in a more functionalized and differentiated society with different needs and desires. Yet these desires could not be contained by the prescriptive education projects associated with certain aspects of classicism and romanticism as heirs of the Enlightenment project; instead, they spilled over into cultural consumption and thus became an important impetus for the forms of cultural entertainment.

The Differentiation of Pleasure

The diversity of readers' educational preparation and the difference in reception situations (leisure vs. professional reading, reading in educational settings, etc.) required a differentiation within the poetological discourse.[36] By the end of the century we notice a distinctly negative valorization of sentiment and feeling as an aesthetic response to works of literature when compared with, for example, Lessing's earlier concept of aesthetic sensibilities in his *Hamburgische Dramaturgie* (1769)—in particular his understanding of sympathy (*Mitleid*), in which he argues that feeling, while being stimulated by the aesthetic object, is most important in its relationship to the self and the reflection on this feeling by the self. According to Rolf Grimminger, Lessing's aesthetic pleasure consists of a unified relation of sympathy and identification with the work of art.[37] This reflection is not merely rational but also mediated by feelings.[38]

The aesthetics of affect opened the floodgates for the immense increase of literature and helped to make literature a commodity. At the same time, it was unable to supply effective categories to classify this new outpouring. The 1750s theorem that all human beings react in the same manner to artifacts if their sensibilities (*Seelenvermögen*) are natural did not stand the test of time, as Sulzer's *Allgemeine Theorie der schönen Künste,* which was conceptualized in 1751 and completed significantly later, in 1771–74, shows.[39] Sulzer refined his earlier concepts and conceded that perceptive faculties can vary in maturation. Introducing a dichotomy between "interesting" (*interessante;* the usage of this term differs from conventional usage in that it is used to describe the opposite, i.e., fashionable writing emphasizing novelty) and "softish" (*weichliche*) literature, he argued that aesthetic pleasure must lead to activity within the soul, not to inactive daydreams, "not to comfortable, limp or idle and passive reveries or musings . . . but to activity and effectiveness of the soul" ("angenehmen schlaffen und passiven Träumerei . . . sondern zu Thätigkeit und Würksamkeit der Seele").[40] As we will see, the ability to savor imaginary pleasures (daydream) was underestimated in its ability to produce desires and wishes that lead to significant changes in mentalities.

In reaction to the flood of fashionable literature, Sulzer formulates two distinct forms of pleasure: first, the "interesting" art, which stimulates inner activity (*Thätigkeit*) and effectiveness (*Würksamkeit*)

105

and activates the readers, allowing them to react independently and freely to the text; and second, the voluptuous, sensual, and passive pleasure produced by fashionable literature. The latter form of pleasure is enjoyable because it entertains and lulls us into a quiet state of mind.[41] In his *Vertraute Briefe,* Johann Gottfried Hoche condemns trivial literature's seduction to revel in the pleasure of sentiment as daydreaming which has little to do with an appropriate response to art.[42] This distinction, which concedes that there are two distinct forms of pleasure, is an important development for our context; it is taken up again by Karl Phillipp Moritz with more of a quantitative than qualitative slant.[43] Readers of fashionable literature foreground pleasure—the pleasure of experiencing their own emotions evoked by literature—whereas for readers of high literature, pleasure is a subordinated by-product of their experiences.[44] In the latter, the distancing contemplation of the work will lead to a comprehension of its form and thus to a higher form of pleasure. In the second edition of his *Versuche über den Geschmack und die Ursachen seiner Verschiedenheit* (1776; Berlin, 1790), Marcus Herz distinguishes between experiencing pleasure and deriving pleasure from pleasure.[45] Addiction to pleasure and to sensual desires are the earmarks of this negatively defined pleasurable reaction to the artifact.

Goethe extends this distinction between the pleasure as a dark, indefinite sensation that is affected only by the artifact (but is not determined by it) and the pleasure derived from the contemplation of value of the object.[46] In the first instance, people consider the artifact merely an occasion for entertainment, as a springboard for their own thoughts and feelings, which essentially have little to do with the object in question because the sensation itself is experienced as pleasurable. Schiller pushes this negatively theorized form of pleasure further in the direction of an almost bodily sensation: for him the focus on emotion and the senses has little to do with the beauty of art but belongs to the realm of the pleasurable (*das Angenehme*), which merely pleases the senses through dissolution (*Auflösung*) or relaxation (*Erschlaffung*), in the voluptuous purging of the body through, for instance, tears, in which the spirit (or a rational response) is neglected.[47]

Kant then complicates the relationship between pleasure and judgment by introducing a paradox, suggesting in the *Kritik der Urteilskraft* (*Judgement of Taste*) (1790) that pleasure is posterior to judging the object.[48] Yet at the same time, Kant affirmed that the sentiment of delight is the first reaction to the object, which is unhampered by moral or cognitive interests ("ohne alles Interesse").[49] Aesthetic delight is immediate. The contradiction can be explained by assuming that Kant is talking about two distinct forms of pleasure, the initial delight on the one hand and the complex pleasure based on the refraction of the attunement of the faculties, "one that follows the judgement and finally validates it," on the other.[50] It is this first understanding of pleasure, which is hardly ever theorized, that becomes the more important concept for this study. To dissolve the Kantian contradiction, Corngold ingeniously describes aesthetic feeling as a circular movement: "For on the circle as a figure of thought, propositional moments, like points on the circumference, lose the elementary distinction of sequence. . . . Any point on a circle, and therefore . . . either point of pleasure, can be read as the starting-off point." He continues: "What is the relation of reflection on the cognitive faculties to the mood of pleasure it finds there? The act of reflection, and its particular intentionality, cannot be without power on the mood of the faculties. Is not the 'mere reflection' itself the creation of the mood it finds?"[51] The uncomplicated pleasure, the mood or sensation that forms of cultural consumption provide, is immediate and—while it allows for this hermeneutic movement of oscillating between the mood created by the object and its contemplation—is liberated from any compulsory cognitive judgment that has to validate it.

Although the discussions of pleasure produced by the text vary, the complicated relationship between thought and feeling, between reason and imagination—in short, the tension between the faculties—makes up their core. This tension between concept formation and imagining, between conceptuality and imagination, creates complex pleasure. "Thus pleasure can serve as the spur to interpretation."[52] "Its [high art's] pleasure is in an objective sense intentional: it aims at understanding all the time it suspends the possibility of final satisfaction. It is in this field of expectation, as a function of the intensity of longing, that something like a disclosure, a knowledge of one's own, could come to light."[53] What the more general concept of pleasure explored in this study has in common with this complex pleasure produced by high art is that just as "literary pleasure is dependent on intelligibility dawning,"[54] on a momentum that spurs further occupation with the text and that can never be quite satisfied, cultural consumerism produces desires that can never quite deliver what they promise and thus keep desire flowing.

Friedrich Schlegel isolated a new aspect of the pleasurable effect that is important for my delineation of entertainment and pleasure, the valorization of novelty. Although he regards this emphasis on novelty as a negative earmark of trivial literature, his emphasis not only on strong stimuli but, above all, on the need for a constant stream of new impressions is an important aspect of the pleasures derived from cultural consumerism. In a negative assessment of trivial literature, Schlegel states:

> As long as there are effects and as long as they are strong and new, then the audience does not care how (in manner or material) they are achieved, nor are they interested in how the various effects create a unified whole.

> Wenn nur gewirkt wird, wenn die Wirkung nur stark und neu ist, so ist die Art, wie und der Stoff, worin es geschieht, dem Publikum so gleichgültig, als die Uebereinstimmung der einzelnen Wirkungen zu einem vollendeten Ganzen.[55]

He assumes that the pleasurable effect is derived from strong and repeated stimulation that does not reflect much on how it is achieved. The trivial reader gives him- or herself up to the seduction of the text. As a remedy, as an antidote to textual seduction, the theoreticians prescribe a distancing contemplation of the architecture of the text, which results in its mastery and in the independence of the recipient from the enslavement by the emotions.

The Renunciation of Noncomplex Pleasure

Johann Christoph Friedrich Bährens's *Ueber den Werth der Empfindsamkeit besonders in Rücksicht auf die Romane* (On the value of sentimentality especially with respect to novels; Halle, 1786) and Johann Gottfried Hoche's *Vertraute Briefe über die jetzige abentheuerliche Lesesucht und über den Einfluss derselben auf die Verminderung des häuslichen und öffentlichen Glücks* (Intimate letters on the current adventurous addiction to reading and its influence on the diminishing domestic and public happiness; Hanover, 1794) postulate two distinct modes in both production and reception, "mental passivity" versus "mental activity" ("geistige Trägheit" versus "geistige Beweglichkeit"). The human condition is characterized by a desire to remain in familiar patterns. Charting new territory requires effort and the suppression of our innate tendencies.[56] This trend of taking pleasure in the familiar and playful, which does not require any serious intellectual work, leads to lethargy. For our discussion of pleasure and entertainment it will be important to reexamine this argument. After all, the interest in novelty, the stimulation by looking, is a form of breaking out of familiar patterns to stimulate the senses, creating a more diverse and elaborate cultural environment.

Bährens further argues that, in the reception of high literature, effort is required to perceive the unity of the formal construct whereby reason perceives the overall design and imagination visualizes the details: in order to appreciate and do justice to beauty in a work of art, we have to actively strive to grasp its totality. "The comprehension of this unity demands reason; the perception of manifoldness [demands] imagination" ("Die Erkenntniß dieser Einheit erfordert—*Vernunft;* die Vorstellung der Mannigfaltigkeit—*Einbildungskraft*)."[57] Imagination becomes linked to sensuality and passivity and has to be mediated by the active powers of reason for a true appreciation of aesthetic pleasure. In this argument, the trivial reader (and spectator), one who passively and sensually absorbs the literary text or the spectacle, is merely a slave who does not master the text through active reason. Of course, this discomfort with the seductive powers of literature—which is, of course, a vital part of its entertainment value—is not new but goes back to Plato, who saw the entertaining stories with their powers to absorb the listeners as a threat to the rational and moral basis of culture.[58]

In "Über den Dilettantismus" (1799), Goethe and Schiller expressed a similar idea when they denounced the dilettantes as lacking the power to create an architecture that subjects the material to the form:

> What the dilettante lacks is a feeling for architecture in the highest sense, this power which creates, forms, constitutes; of which he has only a vague notion but succumbs to the material, instead of conquering it. Instead of mastering the text, the dilettante yields to the material.

> Was dem Dilettanten eigentlich abgeht, ist Architektonik im höchsten Sinne, diejenige ausübende Kraft, welche erschafft,

bildet, konstituiert; er hat davon nur eine Art von Ahnung, gibt sich aber durchaus dem Stoff dahin, anstatt ihn zu beherrschen.[59]

The terminology suggests a female positionality. While dilettante literature and its recipient are primarily interested in the content, that is, the subject matter, high literature strives to distance the recipient from the subject matter or material and does not merely yield to it—so the discussion goes.

Similarly, Schiller contrasts the false pleasure of the passive reader, who is merely interested in the subject matter and its sensual allure, with the genuine aesthetic response of the trained reader's free and distancing play.[60] To counteract this focus on one's own sensation, to limit the subjective arbitrariness, and to turn the attention to the artifact, Goethe and Schiller in the sketch on dilettantism suggest that the recipient is to focus on the thorough and knowledgeable examination of the literary "constructedness" and a sustained attempt to understand the work, departing from the sensual looking to making spiritual connections between the elements of the work.[61]

Contemplative reception that prompts the recipient to distance him- or herself from his or her particular interests is the true earmark of high art. Schlegel also considers certain art forms—that is, "more common art" ("gemeinere Kunst")—as degenerations of high art, since they appeal only to lower sensual attractions. Although the trivial text offers a variety of surface features, its spirit remains the same: confused paltriness ("verworrene Dürftigkeit"). This kind of literature plays with adventurous or childish images in order to stimulate indolent desires ("schlaffe Begierden zu stacheln"), to tickle dull senses ("stumpfe Sinne zu kitzeln"), and to cajole raw lust ("rohen Lüsten zu schmeicheln"), leading to intoxication and raw sensuality.[62] These art forms appeal to an audience that has no interest in formal considerations but is primarily focused on the content and its sensual appeal. Because the sensual reaction is not mediated and distanced by the intellect, it becomes insatiable, and this leads to addictive consumption.

The arguments against excessive reading ranged from medical (it was damaging health because of the unnatural sitting position), to economic (it wasted valuable time that should be spend on work or on education), to moralistic (the excessive stimulation of the imagination was often connected to sexual self-gratification) condemnation.[63] This argumentation connects bodily pleasures with those of the imagination, hinting at sexual arousal and at the indulgence in (sexual) fantasies provoked by the love scenes depicted in romance novels. Juxtaposing reading with an unleashing of the powers of the imaginary suggested that the sentimental romance novel set women, in particular, up for seduction. Reading women were considered both attractive and willing objects of men's erotic attraction, as contemporary writers point out.

Marianne Ehrmann's play *Leichtsinn und gutes Herz: Oder die Folgen der Erziehung* (Triviality and a good heart: Or the effects of education)[64] portrays the heroine, Lotte, as indulging in novels when she is first seen by Count Treuberg, who is attracted immediately to the middle-class girl reading by the banks of a river. As female readers were considered to possess a more developed sensibility than their nonreading sisters, they were expected to indulge in the pleasures of the imagination, which, in turn, made them more susceptible to seduction, especially by raking males. As Barker-Benfield writes, "Other eighteenth-century writers also suggested that rakes represented the attractions of 'the world,' of prodigality, playfulness, and sexual pleasures to women, who expressed the same attraction directly too. In other words, rakes were symbols of women's own potential sensual liberation."[65] After successfully seducing Lotte, Treuberg loses all desire for her and leaves her alone in her anguish and depression. As we see in this example, the debate on the pleasures of reading were closely linked to fostering the pleasures of the imagination, with their implicit link to sensuality.

Cultural Hierarchies: Gendered Terminology as an Expression of Power Relationships

Another line of argument was initiated by Sulzer, who warned that excessive emotion or sentimentality was to be avoided because it would make readers soft, weak, and unmanly. Creating an oppositional system to account for the new modes of creation and reception, criticism redefined high literature by creating an Other—that is, the concept of trivial or mass literature. The terminology inscribing this other literature ("weichlich," "schwach," "unmännlich" ["soft," "weak," "unmanly"])[66] is encoded as female, starting the long tradition of inscribing the trivial tradition as woman.[67] This dichotomy established a notion of alterity that lends more credence and power to the male-encoded norm of high culture while devaluating other cultural productions.

Sensing the failure to establish his concept of autonomous art in

111

light of the increasing diversification of the audience, Goethe emphasized the absence of a masculine spirit in the contemporary arts in his *Gespräche mit Eckermann* (Conversations with Eckermann):

> Yet all these paintings are lacking something, i.e., the masculine [principle]. Remember this word and underline it. The paintings are lacking a certain penetrating vigor, which was present everywhere in earlier centuries and which is missing now and not only in works of the visual arts but also in all other arts. A feebler generation is alive today of which one cannot determine whether it is such by nature or by weaker education and nurturing.

> Allein doch fehlet diesen Bildern allen etwas, und zwar: das Männliche. Merken Sie sich dieses Wort und unterstreichen Sie es. Es fehlt den Bildern eine gewisse zudringliche Kraft, die in früheren Jahrhunderten sich überall aussprach und in dem jetzigen fehlt, und zwar nicht nur in Werken der Malerei, sondern auch in allen übrigen Künsten. Es lebt ein schwächeres Geschlecht, von dem sich nicht sagen läßt, ob es so ist durch die Zeugung oder durch eine schwächere Erziehung und Nahrung.[68]

Goethe connected this "unmasculine" weakness with a certain socially produced cultural "Überfeinerung" ("over-refinement")[69] that effected the impotent and sentimental theater.

The professionalized elite poet was always male and connotated as such. The poetological discourse producing this split into mass/low or trivial literature and high/elite literature displayed from its onset a distinctly gender-specific terminology. The social inequality and hierarchy created by the cultural construction of sex into gender was transferred into the institutional discourse of poetology as a semiotic apparatus, a system of representation, as we will see in the following discussion. The fact that the dichotomies—"aktiv/produktiv/wirkend" and "passiv/rezeptiv/leidend"—parallel the terminology describing the sexes was confirmed by Christa Bürger: "Schiller's definition of dilettantism defines itself through the oppositions active/productive/effecting to passive/receptive/enduring which almost literally correspond with Humboldt's concept of the oppositional nature of the sexes."[70]

This discursive strategy assigned a hierarchical relationship to various forms of literary production. The association with a female positionality not only devalued non-elite or trivial literature but established a close association between women's writing and trivial literature. And with this argumentation, the dominant poetological discourse excluded women's literary production from the realm of high art. Following Humboldt's anthropology, women's literary production is by its very nature of dilettante origin.[71] Moreover, Goethe's definition of the true professional artist versus the dilettante focused on proper formal education and training. The list of qualifications include "pursuit of art according to scientific principles, acceptance of an objective art, methodical sequence and gradation, calling and profession."[72] Goethe's account demonstrated how the gendered poetological discourse and the social and educational discourses strengthen each other. The effect of this mutual reinforcement of the representational and social gendering of high literature as male might be at the heart of one of Schiller's comments regarding his thought of building a theater for the performance of tragedies only and, moreover, to performing a play exclusively for men on a weekly basis.[73] Goethe did not reject the idea for ideological reasons but for practical, financial ones. The statement acknowledged the contemporary situation where pure and autonomous high art could not sustain itself because of the diversity of the audience's taste. When inferior literary tastes—that is, "those spoiled by the diverse, confused offerings on the German stage"[74]—are mentioned, oftentimes reference is made to women. This historically established separation between art and dilettantism placed women into the latter group.

The cultural discourse encoded artistic creativity, the powers of the "second maker," as male. At the same time, the second maker, the artist, turns nature, subject matter, and the material—all encoded as female—into a work of art. As Christine Battersby writes, "Creativity was displaced *male* procreativity; male sexuality made sublime."[75] Artistic creation is also portrayed as a form of erotic desire between the (male) poet and his (female) text.[76] The trivial author is seen as the lesser creator with less control and power over his material and text, becoming more like the material that the writer is unable to master, like nature, like woman. This kind of writing is weak, soft, and effeminate, and the relationship thus acquires undertones of the homoerotic—or, in the value system of the time, of perversion. But it was not only the relationship between author and his creation that was altered, for the erotic pleasure between reader/spectator—also encoded as male—and the text was thus altered analogously. The reader/spectator is a slave to the text rather than its master. These implications served to devalue this nonmastering production of trivial writing as a pleasure-seeking perversion of "true creation." By association, these value judgments also colored the opinion of other forms of entertainment.

As Erich Schön pointed out, toward the end of the century the readership may have consisted predominantly of women. Women's educational preparation, which stopped short of formal literary competence,[77] as well as their social position within the house and the representation of their "natural" gender identity (*Geschlechtscharaktere*) influenced the formation of their literary tastes. If women composed a large part of the audience and readership, their expectations must have had a significant impact on the literary taste of the time. Hans Friedrich Foltin—following Ludwig Tieck and Wilhelm Hauff—argued that women were the primary audience of *schöne Literatur* around 1800. He stressed that certain structures—for example, the disjunctive plot and the emphasis on descriptive individual scenes—favor a trivial reading, which was performed primarily by women.[78] The "feminization" of culture in the German states is equated with the emergence of mass culture.

Women as the aesthetically lesser trained spectators resisted a more disciplined and mastering (i.e., male-encoded) aesthetically aware mode of reception in the theater and in their reading practices. We can assume that the art of perception in the theater must likewise be trained. The culturally valorized, educated-male-encoded mode of spectatorship and reading was characterized not by a sense of pleasure-seeking but by forcing one against one's will to perceive the various genres in a specific manner. Thus reading in this sense was an application of rational, educational, and achievement principles (*Leistungsprinzip*).[79] In a December 1765 letter to his sister, the young Goethe recommended the following: "Take one piece after another, in sequence, read it attentively, even if you don't enjoy it; read it nevertheless. You have to force yourself when reading [*Gewalt anthun*] . . . and not just seek pleasure when reading. When you are finished reading, close the book and contemplate it."[80] It is apparent that throughout Goethe's life, his influential voice regarded women in general as dilettantes rather than true artists.[81]

Typical for the idealist response to non-elite culture was the insistence that these art forms appeal to an audience that has no interest in formal considerations but is primarily focused on the content and its sensual appeal. Because the sensual reaction is not reconciled with and restrained by the intellect, it becomes voracious, thus contributing to addictive consumption.[82]

Both the idealist and the late-Enlightenment critics considered non-elite culture a deterioration in cultural values and tastes, albeit for different reasons. Critics associated with the late Enlightenment focus predominantly on the fact that these products undermine the virtues of a civilization ("die gute Sitte wurde unterwühlt").[83] The social concern seems to stem from the fear that the consumers of "mass" culture would lose self-control and thereby become less disciplined and effective as productive members of society, endangering the cultural hegemony of the middle class and its values. The cultural arena is obviously seen as a practice field for social values and behaviors. In other words, the role of pleasure and entertainment is defined *ex negativo,* as lack and as a cultural and social ill. While at times using similar arguments, the concept of entertainment was criticized by the idealist response through an insistence on the autonomy of the work of art, which was to erase or negate the mundane reality and re-create it instead as a product of the imagination or as the abstract foil of reality. The latter critique became the more dominant and institutionalized critique (grammar school, university, professional criticism in reviews, etc.).

However, large segments of the audience around 1800 (not just women) remained dilettante readers.[84] Reading societies (*Lesegesellschaften* and the more exclusive and expensive *Lesekabinette*) did not focus on high literature or avant-garde literature but on informational and entertaining reading materials.[85] It seems plausible, therefore, that women as a distinctly visible group were singled out to account for the changes within the general reception practices.

Although this line of argument focuses on the fact that women displayed trivial aesthetic practices more distinctly, women's influence on literary tastes as spectators, readers, and writers remains unexamined. The simplistic linking of trivial viewing and reading habits with women—rather than with educational preparation and, more importantly, with social changes (the greater functionalization and differentiation of society)—obscured the increasingly differentiated cultural identity of the middle class. The mode of reception that was attributed to women represented that of an increasingly larger portion of the general audience caused by the shrinking numbers of semiprofessional readers and spectators and the expanding ranks of leisure-time consumers of books, plays, and other cultural artifacts. By using the gender-related terminology to mark the dichotomies between high and trivial literature, the poetological aesthetic discourse misread the changes in the social and economic discourses and created a prescriptive insistence on high art forms. The strategy did not explain the social changes but simply warned writers of becoming too effeminate. The quasi-moralistic association of women and triviality not only ignored the function of non-elite forms of culture but also obfuscated the social causes for the decline in reader- and spectatorship: the overall general decline of the educational preparation and the social position necessary to adequately respond to the demands of autonomous art.

It seems plausible that the poetological discourse devalorizing trivial literature as feminine or effeminate was also reacting to the real and perceived cultural influence of women on the tastes of the time in an attempt to ward off the feminization of culture. As women became the main architects of leisure entertainment, cultural consumption, and sociability—in short, of the middle-class lifestyle—they gained considerable informal power within the household. Schiller, disappointed about the reception of his *Anthologie auf das Jahr 1782,* deplored the taste of his audience, remarking that the tone of his anthology was obviously "too unique, deep and masculine" to please the "honeyed prattlers male and female."[86] The juxtaposition of their poor taste and his serious and masculine one served to deplore a decline—a trivialization and feminization—of culture. In this light, women's cultural participation, usually marked as absent, excluded, and marginalized, has to be taken into account. More likely than not it did matter what women wrote and produced and how they consumed literature; otherwise it would have not produced such a level of anxiety and debate. On the other hand, this focus on the poor taste of women and their role as contaminators of high culture in a quasi-moralistic argument fails to account for the social changes responsible for making women such an important part of the readership. As we will see below, women, as the primary architects of the domestic sphere, with its emotionalization of family life, its cultural ambience, and its entertainment quality, looked to cultural practices (especially literature) for inspiration, advice, and the discussion of issues and values that occupied the private sphere.

The Critical Debate on the Split
between High and Low Culture

While the debate focused ostensibly on the emergence of trivial literature, at the core of these negotiations was the role and function of entertainment and pleasure provided by cultural activities. Whether acknowledged or not, pleasure and entertainment became the main point of contention in this debate.

The first critical historical accounts of the phenomenon of so-called trivial literature can be found by the end of the nineteenth century (Appell, Müller-Fraunreuth). These accounts pick up on certain arguments that had emerged in debates of the previous century, such as the lack of formal discipline, its escapist tendencies, and the not (yet) adequately developed taste. For the discussion of methodology it suffices to show how pleasure and entertainment become firmly linked to high culture's Other, how this process is used to dismiss tendencies that are deemed undesirable at any given time. This dismissal, however, fails to acknowledge the different kinds of alterity (and fails to distinguish among them), thus overlooking important functions of entertainment.

One of the first critics in the nineteenth century, Johann Wilhelm Appell, considered *Unterhaltungsliteratur,* or *schöne Literatur,* to be a cancer in the cultural and political life in Germany, affecting not only the lower classes but also the more cultured groups, and especially women of all age groups, who waste their time on the "soft cushion of platitude" ("weichen Polster der Platitude") and spoil their taste for more rigorous fare.[87] Likened to a dangerously spreading disease of the social body, the entertainment that trivial literature brings is seen as harmful to productivity and (self-)discipline, making people mentally lazy and thus interfering with the socializing function of culture. The rhetoric bespeaks the perceived threat of the encroaching mass culture. The strong terminology used (e.g., "gemeinschädlich" [dangerous] and "geistestödtend" [lethal to spirit and soul]) and its fervor indicate that the cultural arena was considered a preeminent site for the socialization of desirable values. Any interest in pleasure is vilified as the coarse lust for entertainment ("groben Unterhaltungsgelüst"); authors and artists who accommodate this desire are characterized as blind and despicable minds ("elende Köpfe"), their readership and consumers as an uneducated heap ("ungebildeten Haufens").[88] With recourse to Johann Heinrich Merck, Appell considers it detestable that there are writers who consider it their profession to provide entertainment.

117

Labeling the large readership expecting entertainment an indiscriminate "heap" suggests that he does not offer a differentiation of the new type of readership. The entertainment provided is referred to as facile and nonrigorous, derived from banality, clichés, and triteness.

Obviously, cultural control is equated with social control. It is implied that similar strategies are at work in dealing with cultural artifacts and in social behaviors: delayed gratification, control, mastery, the ability to distance oneself, and discipline. While the link between aesthetic control and social control under German idealism was more tentative and focused more on the side of aesthetics, the social argument became more and more important in discussions of the late nineteenth century.

In these early studies, no serious attempt was made to discuss trivial literature's possible functions beyond the mere mention of the compensatory, of escapism for the masses.[89] By the end of the nineteenth century, Carl Müller-Fraunreuth characterized trivial reading as "moral gluttony," as an addiction that reduces public and private happiness.[90] He assigned it a distinctly conservative outlook, one that limited revolutionary energies and maintained the status quo by simply venting political and other frustrations. For Müller-Fraunreuth, trivial literature channeled energies away from revolutionary tendencies. The indulgence in pleasurable but objectionable and questionable ("bedenklichen, ja verwerflichen Kost") cultural fare is considered moral gluttony ("moralische Freßsucht") that reduces public and private happiness, fosters criminal behavior, limits revolutionary energies, and simply vents political and other frustrations.[91] The implication is that art should foster social control, which, in turn, would increase public and private happiness, advance good citizenship, and free revolutionary energies.

As another explanation for the disastrous "fatal" attraction to mass culture, Müller-Fraunreuth suggests that the desire for more imaginative fare that appealed to the senses by focusing on the unusual, unexpected, and even inexplicable was a backlash against the worn-out rationalism of the Enlightenment. The dissatisfaction with the dominance of reason allowed a host of charlatans to surface dealing in the occult, dabbling in mesmerism, faith healing, and alchemy ("Schwärmer und Schwindler," "Geisterbeschwörer," "Wunderthäter," "Goldmacher").[92] Gustav Sichelschmidt argues similarly. The interest in the German national past, specifically that of the rather unspecified middle ages, served to provide positive and strong heroes with whom disillusioned citizens could identify. He attributes this yearning for the past to a crisis in political self-confidence.[93] The implication is that this is merely an escapist strategy which in itself merely compensates for political weakness. The hypothesis is that mass culture is fueled by the venting of thwarted revolutionary energies and represents compensatory imaginary action that provides an outlet for everyday frustrations. The argument is of limited value because it assumes that the segment of the population which constituted the consumers of mass cultural artifacts was interested politically in and indeed frustrated with their political and social reality. The fact that the argument about the compensatory nature of mass culture is put forward by its opponents suggests that it could well be a projection and interpretation of perceived frustrations—that is, the frustrations of the elite or their assessment of their imagined frustration is projected onto the consumers of mass culture. Therefore it is a questionable assumption that the consumers of mass culture themselves experienced their cultural practices as compensatory and necessarily born out of frustrations of a political or social nature. The hypothesis of the compensatory function of mass culture is a reductive argument that severely limits the exploration and analysis of this phenomenon. However, his diagnosis of the tedium of cultural over-refinement (*Zivilisationsmüdigkeit*) which led to a cult of the lower instincts and the primitive seems to be more an ahistorical projection by the critic.[94]

At the same time, both Sichelschmidt and Kurt-Ingo Flessau emphasize the documentary value of trivial literature.[95] Sichelschmidt considers trivial literature to be a good documentary indicator of the values of a given period because of its consumability for everyone, especially for women, whose realm of interest—the family—was utilized.[96] Martin Greiner considers the escapist tendencies important as a means of alleviating tensions, of letting off steam. He views trivial literature as a coping mechanism to deal with the realities of everyday life.[97] In this line of argument, entertainment becomes a safety valve, allowing people to momentarily withdraw from the frustrations of modern life.

Marion Beaujean, on the other hand, regards trivial literature as a necessary by-product of the development toward autonomous art, which increasingly larger parts of the audience could not fully appreciate. What she perceives as a lack in the proper development of literary taste I consider a result of the higher degree of differentiation of social and cultural life. Furthermore, the forms of pleasure derived from cultural activities such as reading—differentiated, of course, by gender—change throughout the life span. The boy alters his reading practices as he enters formal educational structures, and again after he enters a profession. Different yet also differentiated paths of cultural entertainment can be determined for girls and women. In addition, the more distinct separation of work and leisure creates new reading practices and at the same time allows readers to select the mode of reading suitable for the given situation. The concentrated reading for work was relegated to the important daytime hours, while reading for entertainment occurred during the evening and nighttime. Literature's easy consumability is often explained by its formal elements, which are said to emphasize the attention paid to individual nonintegrated scenes and which serve as individual but cumulative sites for the imagination. Literature on both ends of the cultural spectrum uses some of the same elements, yet they are used to a lesser degree in high literature and are usually tempered with moments of disillusionment, such as irony, tragic outcomes, the demise of the good characters, and the fortune of evildoers. Furthermore, high literature is often self-reflexive and points directly or indirectly to its fictionality, while mass literature stresses its realism, what Foltin calls its "truthfulness." Foltin cautions against isolating individual stylistic or structural means as belonging to either high literature or mass literature and thereby making them the criteria of quality or lack thereof; he instead suggests seeing how they function in each context.[98]

Even if we note a departure from the predominantly evaluative categories, overall, critics of the twentieth century recycle many of the arguments. Their responses fall into two basic categories: first, those based on critical theory (*Ideologiekritik*), which consider the trivial reader and consumer as manipulated victims of the culture industry (Adorno); and second, psychological approaches to the function of *Trivialliteratur*, which explore the nexus between certain forms of socialization, reception, and cultural expectations.[99] Winfried Fluck considers popular culture a means to negotiate problems of socialization in a pleasurable manner,[100] and Jochen Schulte-Sasse's most advanced position within this discourse on the dichotomization of culture reconstructs the positive aspects of identification. This (positive) side of the coin of the suspension of the reality principle momentarily suspends the protective shield of our identity, which is focused on competition and the discipline of our emotions ("konkurrenzorientierte" and "affektdisziplinierte Panzerung unserer Identität").[101] Schulte-Sasse reads the products of entertainment culture as a form of psychological hygiene, as a form of mental health. Similarly, my own reading refers to the forms of cultural entertainment with Foucault's terminology as an important form of the care of the self, which offers alternative forms of experiencing and reacting to the environment. The forms of entertainment not only offer activities that are not influenced by competition and ambition, that do not focus on the disciplining forces exerted on the self—and, I would add, are not goal oriented, focused, and useful. They also do not make an attempt at dialectically transcending the modern split between rational and sensual forces in modern individuality that Schiller's concept of *Spiel* theorized. Instead, the pleasure that the forms of entertainment create offers a momentary respite punctuating everyday life. It offers alternative modes of experience and communication to the discipline and monotony of work and the intensely emotionalized family life.

Inadequacies of the Binary Model

The ensuing binary model opposing high art and mass culture is by itself not a suitable model to theorize the differentiation of the cultural sphere in eighteenth-century Germany. A closer look at the growth of the culturally literate middle class revealed a wide range of cultural competencies and interests. Because cultural histories tend to favor innovation and to construct well-defined groups, we hear those voices more distinctly that formulate explicit cultural programs, literary and aesthetic theories, and traditionally published and reviewed primary works. The canonized voices of Gottsched, Lessing, Klopstock, Herder, and others created a discourse of middle-class self-definition in contrast to an Other—the court and courtly culture. By the end of the century these voices had proliferated and the message was no longer as clear but became contested. The effectiveness of courtly culture as Other from which the middle class distinguished itself had lost its function as a unifying power. Due to the successful push for literacy and education, more people became readers and writers. A number of new forms of publication—for example, almanacs, pocket books, magazines, and the more journalistic forms of writing—tried to capture these more diverse educational preparations and cultural tastes contributing to the diversification of cultural competence. It does not suffice to say that mass culture represents a transgression from the norm (of high culture). Simple binary oppositions between norm and transgression cannot distinguish between different alterities, that is, between specific differences. After all, Germany at the turn of the century is not a monolithic political entity, and shifts in cultural representations and interests differ within the different states, between urban cultural centers and the agrarian areas, and between the various cultural centers themselves.[102] This differentiation over the range of culture becomes most apparent in the periodical press.

The Periodical Press

Almanacs, pocket books, calendars, and journals became easier to sell than the book with its lack of visual appeal. They are part of a new multilayered, varied, and, above all, entertaining reading culture, and they contributed significantly to the diversification of cultural practices.[103] Different types of almanacs address themselves to subgroups of the middle class. To become and remain successful in an increasingly competitive market, periodicals had to consistently attract a significant number of readers. As Kirsten Belgum explains: "The success of a periodical publication depends on its ability to win over a substantial and consistent share of the reading market. This in turn means the publication has to provide its readers with attractive material on a regular and dependable basis. In other words, the popularity of the press is a measure of its ability to present readers with identities that are readily understandable and acceptable."[104]

Periodicals either attracted a broad audience of fairly educated men and women (e.g., the *Journal des Luxus und der Moden*) or specialized in attracting a particular audience and tailored the publication to their specific needs (e.g., the *Leipziger Taschenbuch für Frauenzimmer: Zum Nutzen und Vergnügen auf das Jahr 1804* or the *Taschenkalender auf das Jahr 1798 für Natur- und Gartenfreuden: Mit Abbildungen von Hohenheim und andern Kupfern*). Others attracted those middle-class readers who were not necessarily consumers of the latest literary works but rather enjoyed the preselected variety of a literary almanac or of a *poetische Blumenlese* (collection of poetic flowers).[105] The popularity of a publication depended on its ability to assume a useful and entertaining function in the context of the middle-class lifestyle. Periodicals presented points of view with which the audience could identify. The *Journal des Luxus und der Moden* was able to achieve its level of success by serving a whole range of functions. Its editor, Justin Bertuch, and his son, Carl, who took over in 1807, were able to shift emphasis in reaction to the changing tastes of its readership. Title changes—in 1813 the name was changed to *Journal für Luxus, Mode und Gegenstände der Kunst*, and in the following year it became the *Journal für Literatur, Kunst, Luxus und Mode*—took the distinct shift in general reader interest into account. The publication also reacted to other changes in the political and cultural climate of the day, directing, for example, significant attention to the topic of Napoleon in the years between 1806 and 1815. In its last decades, at the dawn of the industrial age, it paid increasing attention to technical inventions (gas lighting for homes and workplaces, steam engines, and new transportation technologies). In addition, the *Journal's* visual appeal, the quality of its illustrations, and its overall presentation also contributed to its success.[106] The *Journal* had procured the services of the painter Georg Melchior Kraus, who did most of the illustrations until his death in 1806. The illustrations attracted the attention of the audience; Bertuch, the savvy businessman and publisher, was also an intellectual and sensitive cultural critic who understood the needs and desires of the readership and, in turn, created new demands. He paid particular attention to the *Journal's* advertisements, which not only utilized the written word but added high-quality illustrations that served as samples of the publication he happened to be advertising.[107] For Bertuch—and he was typical for the major publishing houses of the day—the function of periodical literature was its ability to popularize knowledge in all areas of interest to the middle-class lifestyle so it could be used to make everyday life more comfortable, interesting, and pleasant.[108]

Illustrations specific to the publication played an important role in the popularization Bertuch and others envisioned. The *Journal* contained predominantly fashion plates but also had etchings of furniture and decorative objects as well as of modern inventions. The gardening magazines contained biological illustrations, the political publications contained caricatures (*London und Paris*), and the geographical works sported maps and charts. Many times, Bertuch's etchings were colored by hand, which represented a significant increase in prestige as well as price.[109]

With the increase in the number of readers, it became possible to offer more specialized publications. As specialized periodicals appeared, they reinforced and shaped other areas of the entertainment culture of the time. A case in point are the many periodicals on gardening or the fashion journal. Cultural practices such as gardening and fashion could not have gained their stature and importance without the periodicals. Other popular topics were scientific pocket books and publications focusing on travel.[110] It might be instructive to take a brief look at some of the titles in circulation:[111] *Almanach für Damen* (1801);[112] *Karikaturen Almanach mit 9 illuminierten Blättern nach Hogarth und Lichtenberg* (1801);[113] E. A. W. Zimmermann's *Almanach der Reisen, oder unterhaltende Darstellung der Entdeckungen des 18then Jahrhunderts in Rücksicht auf Länder- Menschen- und Produktenkunde für jede Klasse von Lesern;*[114] and Solbrig's *Almanach der Travestieen und Parodieen* (1816).[115]

Pocket books also boast a variety of different interest foci, ranging from information on urban fashions (*Hamburger Taschenbuch der Moden und des Luxus* [1802]);[116] collections of literary works by a single author or collection of authors (*Taschenbuch von Wieland und Goethe* [1804]);[117] illustrated accounts of Carnival and its fashions (*Taschenbuch, für Freunde u. Freundinnen des Carnevals mit Illuminierten Kupfern* [1804]);[118] titles such as *Das goldne ABC für Herren und Damen ausser der Ehe. Ein Taschenbuch* (1809);[119] *Legenden* (1813);[120] Solbrig's *Taschenbuch der Deklamation* (1814);[121] to the *Taschenbuch für Mineralwassertrinker* (1820).[122]

The palm-sized *Leipziger Taschenbuch für Frauenzimmer: Zum Nutzen und Vergnügen auf das Jahr 1804* (1804)[123] offers a whole range of topics for incorporation into the daily life of middle-class women. Addressing women who are interested in cultural as well as household matters, it offers information on literature, geography, gemology, biography, poetry and songs (some with music scores), short prose narratives, essays on materials and merchandise, diet and health, scenes from novels in installments, several illustrations, and a fold-out pattern for needlecraft.

Calendars, the most old-fashioned genre among the periodical literature, usually intended for a general or less educated audience,[124] could also display specialization, as in the *Taschenkalender auf das Jahr 1798 für Natur- und Gartenfreuden. Mit Abbildungen von Hohenheim und andern Kupfern* (1798).[125] In addition to the thematic contributions to gardening or other topics, calendars offered an extensive calendarium—typical for this genre—indicating holidays, the phases of the moon, the constellations, length of days, information on the planets, dates for the medical practice of bleeding and purging, predictions and rules regarding the weather, and practical suggestions and advice. Organized in columns, they also offered space for notes ("Schreib-kalender"), which could not only serve as a to-do list but also as a brief diary documenting the events of the year.

The new periodical press focused on many different topics designed for different audiences and extended the thematic range of print culture significantly. They included illustrations—depending on the topic—geographical maps, sketches, statistical charts, and architec-tural and technical drawings of various kinds. The careful aesthetic pre-sentation, the well-designed cover, illustrations, and other decorative elements, as well as the thematic plurality of the illustrations were the elements that the public appreciated. Illustrations created much of a publication's entertainment value. The subtitle often mentioned the number of illustrations contained in a particular publication, suggest-ing their high value. Illustrations for optical explanation and entertain-ment grace the pages of publications for all audiences, from children to the most sophisticated readers.[126]

The reader could select from the range of materials within each publication depending on the particular situation (i.e., whether one wanted to read for entertainment or edification, or how much time one could spend at any given reading). This differentiation of reading prac-tice was accompanied by a differentiation and specialization of tastes, which supported the creation of more specialized publications address-ing particular interests.

Men, educated single women, and girls seemed to prefer the genre of literary almanac (*Musenalmanach*), in which most of the famous authors of the time published. Almanacs did not offer second-rate literature or simplistic poetic material. In their mixture of estab-lished and new writers, their variety of topics, and their appealing mode of presentation, they filled diverse needs. Some literary almanacs addressed themselves to the sophisticated educated audience and also offered progressive, innovative poetic treatises and materials. Many important canonized works were first published in almanacs, pocket books, and journals (e.g., Schiller's *Musenalmanach*, 1796–1800). Others were intended for more general or popular edification and entertainment; these publications often included musical scores and etchings (many by the most famous composers and artists of the time) in a careful aesthetic presentation. They cannot be equated with trivial literature, since they play an important role in the differentiation of literary tastes.[127] Married women preferred pocket books for women (*Frauenzimmertaschenbuch*), which contained fashion plates, economic topics, and prescriptions for health and beauty along with short pieces of literature. Calendars also included a mixture of informative, educational pieces next to shorter literary pieces (often serialized). Among the three periodical genres, the calendar was aimed at the least-educated middle-class readers. Some calendars were aimed at children and young people for educational purposes.

Almanacs, pocket books, and calendars constituted the transitory genre between books and newspapers. These new genres helped in making reading "portable" by leading it away from the limited mode of consumption in the private library or office. This represents a new attitude toward books, making the knowledge and experiences contained in them truly portable and accessible in all situations.[128] As adviser and entertainer, this new type of book became integrated into many other cultural practices, such as forms of sociability, travel, and outdoor recreation, and could be easily integrated into everyday activities,[129] especially for women who spent more time in the home.

Most importantly, the periodical print media helped to produce and mirror the complex entertainment needs of the middle class, which displayed a wider variety of pleasurable responses to cultural objects and practices. Of course, this range of pleasurable responses was in itself to a large degree created and socialized through the print culture. The reader learned to select the kind of pleasure he or she desired at any given moment of leisure. This ranged from the specular pleasure derived from the illustrations and the aesthetic appearance of the volume itself, the stimulation of fantasies and daydreams of adventure and love stories, the indulgence in strong emotions (the shudder of the supernatural, the stimulation of the sublime), to the more cerebral pleasures the avant-garde pieces offered. Most importantly, variety and novelty were perceived as pleasurable because they alleviated boredom. The lively mix of literary genres, topics, and modes of presentation, as the earmark of periodical literature, contributed to this sense of novelty.

The entertainment quality achieved by the mix of pleasures created by the aesthetic presentation on the one hand and the reading material on the other was not lost on "serious" authors like Goethe. He published his epos *Hermann und Dorothea*—which he considered quite suitable for a larger audience due to its integration of the historical event of the century, the French Revolution—in the literary pocket book *Taschenbuch für 1798* in editions ranging from the most luxurious to the more modest and affordable. The most luxurious edition had a cover of silk in which a medallion, flowers, and grapevines were woven. It contained numerous illustrations by famous artists, among them Chodowiecki, J. W. Meil, and Eduard Henne.[130] Beyond functioning as books, these kinds of publications served as status symbols indicating the sophistication of taste (linked to one's economic status). A letter by Goethe's mother to her son upon the receipt of two of these volumes suggests the function of the almanac as prestige object: "Hufnagel considers all who don't yet own the pocket book or don't carry it in their pocket a Hottentot. Elisa Bethmann had to buy one of the most expensive copies in his presence."[131]

At the same time, these publications, especially the almanacs directed at women and the pocket books for women, also participated significantly in cultural consumerism. Not only were they based on the perennial principle of novelty, of receiving new information in a fashionable new form, but they were themselves also a product of material culture and thus signified the up-to-date cultural capital of its owner and reader. Periodical print culture served not only as a conveyor of cultural information and a source of entertainment but also as a material object. It had an important signifying function as, for example, gifts or as decorative items for display in the home. These objects conveyed the degree of culturation of the giver and the recipient. The elegant pocket books made for fashionable and useful Christmas, New Year's, and birthday gifts, and as such they played a role in the symbolic social exchange between acquaintances or family members. As gifts, these material objects could be carefully nuanced and tailored to the recipient, the occasion, the degree of luxury required by the event, or the relationship between giver and recipient.

These almanacs boasted extravagant and fashionable decorations. They were printed on expensive tinted paper, contained colored prints and integrated placemarkers, and sported colored and gold-tone edges as well as fashionably designed covers made from a variety of materials. They served not only as a means to indulge in imaginary pleasures, to be entertained by the spectacle of illustrations and a stimulating variety of topics and presentations of different cultural practices (musical scores, embroidery patterns, etc.), but also as a means to convey social

127

and cultural status. They did so by treating the fashionably designed and decorated almanac as a signifier for cultural capital and as an object of cultural consumerism. The decorative aspect was emphasized to such a degree that critics soon ridiculed these publications as fashionable accessories in the interior design of the home rather than reading materials, thus underscoring their—negatively connoted—entertainment value.

For about sixty years, these forms of the periodical print culture not only created the pleasure of reading for a large segment of the middle class, both male and female, but also provided clear evidence of the important role that reading played as a form of cultural entertainment.[132] Their popularity faded after the Biedermeier period as they had to compete with newer forms of periodical literature: the journals (*Zeitschriften*), the illustrated family magazines such as the famous *Gartenlaube*,[133] and, most importantly, the newspaper.[134] The excessive appetite for up-to-date news found its way into the caricatures of the day as a signal of superficiality and a penchant for sensationalism, especially in women.[135]

Overall, the features that made periodical literature highly entertaining were the same ones that were the most criticized, belittled, and ridiculed. The critique of the fashionable periodical literature was commonplace and almost a matter of bon ton with intellectuals and professional readers. Even Daniel Nikolaus Chodowiecki, one of the foremost illustrators of periodical literature, felt the need to caricature its use as superficial entertainment in his well-known illustration "Almanac Mania!! Calender—Narr. Manie d'almanacs," in which men and women gather to intently examine a tiny almanac or pocket book.[136] Nevertheless, we should not underestimate the importance of the periodical press in the creation of the literary public sphere and—most importantly for my study—the formation of the cultural public sphere. It shaped and provided knowledge in every area of cultural consumerism addressed in this study. In particular, the modern phenomenon of fashion could not have emerged without the discourse on fashion in the periodical press, as we will see in the next chapter.

6

The Fashion Journal [Bertuch's *Journal des Luxus und der Moden*] and the Construction of the Material Culture of Fashion

Fashion visualizes the interrelationships among luxury items, economics, and the journal print culture in an exemplary manner and is therefore representative of many forms of cultural consumerism and entertainment defining the middle class. The complex nexus of journal culture, the economic development of the urban areas, and the phenomenon of fashion and luxury items is but one important strand in the multi-causal exploration of the new forms of entertainment.

The increasing economic vitality of the emerging middle class has become a commonplace explanation for the increasing power of the middle class in Germany during the course of the eighteenth century. Yet this economic vitality would not have been possible without the emergence of different types of print media. The decades around the turn of the century (1780–1830) demonstrate a vigorous growth of the commercialization of cultural information for the middle class. New, specialized publications with unique foci demarcated and, at the same time, increased the diverse interests of the middle-class reading public. The expansion of a print culture for a general audience and the increasing range of specialization in the print culture, especially the periodical, is inextricably linked to this interest in the fashionable expansive (and expensive) cultural refinement and beautification of the private sphere. These activities, in turn, fueled economic development by creating new demands for more—and more diverse—offerings. With greater cultural diversification, the social fabric of the middle-class gained greater complexity.

The creation of this culture of adornment, predominantly flourishing in the cities, which the periodical press distributed throughout the provinces, represents both an economic and a cultural factor in the self-fashioning of the middle class, and it required knowledge, taste, time, and, of course, financial resources. As travel outside the city was still rather cumbersome, the creation of the culture of fashion required an urban environment, one that facilitated acquisition of goods and services and ensured a more convenient social life as a major site for fashionable display. The increasingly widespread interest in luxury items for personal adornment was dependent on the new urban economy and was at the same time an important factor in its creation. The aestheticization of the private sphere—and its bodies—created an important site for leisure entertainment, offering a kind of self-fulfillment that the realm of work could not provide. An important part of work for women, it was also a significant cultural activity, an entertaining and pleasurable occupation that could provide personal gratification.

The most prominent and all-encompassing example for this nexus is Friedrich Johann Justin Bertuch's (1747–1822)[1] *Journal des Luxus und der Moden* (1786–1827).[2] This publication is central as a source for my study because its readership comprises that subgroup of the middle class under investigation here: the well-to-do upper middle class with an active interest in cultural practices. The *Journal* had a large circulation in the German states and within Europe (as high as twenty-five hundred according to some estimates) and was relatively expensive,[3] but it was not quite as exclusive as one of Bertuch's other journals, *London und Paris* (1798–1805). The publication was instrumental in creating a far-reaching concept of fashion that not only encompassed fashionable clothing but referred to a wide spectrum of cultural practices. It did so in the context of descriptions of historical changes in lifestyles. In addition, the *Journal* not only discussed important forms of entertainment but constituted itself a form of entertainment.

The *Journal* was the first important publication of the genre of "fashion magazine" turned best-seller in the German states that flourished in the center of cultural refinement and high culture of Weimar.[4] While an earlier attempt (1758) at a fashion magazine—the *Mode- und Galanteriezeitung*—in Erfurt had failed, by now the readership had a firmly established appetite for the objects of print culture. Bertuch's reputation and business skills gave the magazine an air of sophistication and ensured quality.[5]

Addressing a male and female educated readership and considering itself a (self-critical and self-reflexive) chronicle of cultural development, the *Journal* contained information not only on the latest cultural development in theater, literature, and the visual arts (as well as information on other countries and their cultural lives) but also—and most importantly—on the latest styles in fashion, furniture, interior design, carriages, and travel. A central document of the culture of the time, the *Journal* represents a complex middle-class position exemplifying a range of cultural practices across the continuum of culture associated with entertainment. It offered commentary on high cultural practices (notices about theater performances, new literature, art, exhibitions, etc.) and discussions of the economic and scientific aspects undergirding modern cultural practices (information on the latest coaches, iron rail transportation, modernization of sanitary conditions, and convenience in the home). It exemplified a complementary vision of culture distinct from late-Enlightenment and idealist positions yet mindful of both. The *Journal* was, for example, instrumental in fostering an increase in consumer products by describing and thus advocating a desire for the embellishment of all areas of material culture. With the attached *Intelligenzblatt* (advertising supplement),[6] Bertuch's *Journal* provided stimulation and direction for the consumption of cultural artifacts and activities that came to define the middle-class lifestyle in Weimar and beyond.

The creation of this culture of adornment required not only financial resources and time but also knowledge and taste. The *Journal* was instrumental in developing the latter two. The reason for the journal's immense success lies in the fact that it was able to combine educational and high-cultural aspects with entertaining and economic aspects. Bertuch's philosophy of culture, articulated in the first issue's introductory statement, is noteworthy because it relies for justification on a combination of the public good and the individual good. The consumer desires created by publications such as the *Journal* resulted in demands for luxury goods, which, in turn, stimulated the domestic economy into producing these goods, thus providing employment and more money for larger segments of the population. At the same time, this enhanced the individual's life by providing goods that not only increased consumers' productivity and comfort but also provided pleasure and entertainment, enhancing the quality of life.

The entertaining world of luxuries and fashions created and was in turn shaped by magazines and other publications. One could not have flourished without the other. The title of this chapter underscores the importance of the new specialized print media in the construction of material culture and for creating a community of educated consumers. This print media also participated significantly in creating a cultural community or a cultural public sphere where the use of objects of material culture became a topic of communicative exchange and nuanced self-definition. This argument broadens Habermas's concept of the literary public sphere to include the whole range of cultural practices as a site for the negotiation of cultural values within the middle class.

FASHION AS LUXURY ITEM

In economic terms, fashion may be the most readily visible luxury item of the time. More affordable than fashionable furniture and changes in interior and exterior design, it displays the quintessential dictate of novelty, changing with each season and clearly exceeding the necessary. As a luxury item, fashion is caught in the controversy between the proponents of the older, physiocratic ideas and the modern precapitalist expansionism based on commerce (discussed in the previous chapter). Critics arguing against fashion's wastefulness and excesses often take their arguments from these older agrarian principles, while proponents celebrated it as the most powerful engine driving commerce and stimulating the economy as a whole. A vibrant economy, so the argument goes, activates culture, science, and education. As discussed above, the *Journal* takes the side of progress and considers fashions based on the perennial principle of novelty an important impetus not only for economic and social progress but also for the cultural advancement and enrichment of a nation or state. When the economy is pushing with full steam ahead, serving as the dynamo for emerging industries, it will also benefit commerce and, with it, cultural spending, which in turn enables the arts and letters to flourish. In the discussion of luxury, the *Journal* articulates the legitimation of reasoned and prudent—not excessive— consumption.

To avoid the appearance of being uncritical and advocating unbridled consumerism, the *Journal* offers a classification and definition of several gradations of luxury and by implication comments on spending on fashionable clothing (1:24). Reasonable consumption is advocated, while excessive luxury beyond the appropriate individual comfort zone is discouraged. In many respects the *Journal* aligns itself with Adam Smith's *Wealth of Nations* (1776), which not only considered the aristocratic consumption and luxurious ostentation beneficial for the larger public (because it circulated the riches into the middle class) but also advocated basic luxuries in the form of durable commodities such as houses and furniture (including what we would hardly consider luxury items today, such as soap, linen, wool, salt, commercially grown food, candles, etc.).

The *Journal* also imag(in)es social mobility through fashion. It suggests the possibility of willfully creating a social persona that does not correspond to one's "natural" station in the social hierarchy. Cultural activity and cultural consumerism can create social mobility. While the role of education in the creation of social mobility with respect to intellectuals has been extensively studied and theorized in literary criticism and history, the role of decorative culture in the creation of social mobility has received little attention. Yet social mobility based on educational and professional achievements was more often than not accompanied by changes in lifestyle and thus in cultural practices.

Excursus: Fashion as Oppositional System

Earlier in the century, dress and fashion were areas where the body in the political realm of absolutism was contested. Dismantling the bodily presentations, the function of clothes as unambiguous indicators of status and rank at court, dislodged the body from its stable position within the complex system of power under absolutism. This questioned the assumption that class distinctions correspond to naturally given differences between the classes. Moral sense philosophy's emphasis on "natural" sentiments had made a similar argument by postulating that all human beings have essentially the same potential for morality. Differences are not innate but arise from an uneven development of moral character. The moral and ethical value system conceptualizes this equality that demystifies and dismantles the superiority of the nobility. The discourse of fashion, for example, allowed the bourgeoisie to distinguish itself from the politically codified system of dress that precisely situated the body within the spectacle of absolute power.[7] This move is often interpreted as the destruction of the artificiality of the aristocratic notion of personhood in order for the natural human (stripped of all privilege) to emerge. It assumes that if the outer layers of artifice are torn away, the natural essence will emerge. Without the rigid conventions that governed social relations under the absolutist system, the individual personality emerges.

It has become commonplace to argue that the conceptual abandonment of the structures of cultural life at the courts (and along with it its fashions) provided greater freedom, the abolishment of impermeable boundaries, rules, and regulations. In bourgeois tragedy, the virgin daughter becomes the object of desire for the aristocratic seducer, who is seduced by her as the beautiful embodiment of the bourgeois value system. Lessing's Emila Galotti and her simple (wedding) dress, "natural" hairstyle, and unconventional use of jewelry are a symbolic representation of the middle-class virtues she embodies. The famous "Werther fashion" is another example of (male) oppositional dress with which the middle class communicates its alliances or its lack thereof. The construction of the new middle-class subjectivity within the philosophical, aesthetic, and cultural discourses was embodied and made visible in these markers. The body is, in turn, read as the transmitter of information about its inner reality. Its involvement with representation is at the core of the discussions on fashion. The attention to ascertaining social rank by the consideration of clothes that could be read as unambiguous signals of class identity was replaced by a system of knowledge that attempted to understand the uniqueness of the individual clothed body in order to catch a glimpse at what was presumed to lie beneath. Under the premise that the exterior corresponded with the interior reality, knowledge of the body's interior below the surface became possible. As Daniel Purdy writes:

> This epistemological requirement was reinforced by medical arguments that insisted that clothes adapt themselves to the unique characteristics of the body they covered. Within this new model, garments were not considered signs of rank, instead they served to mediate between public discourses and an isolated subjectivity hidden within the body. The new techniques for scrutinizing the clothed body presumed that the object of their investigation existed below or beyond the limits of observation and that clothes were a means of knowing this inner character.[8]

This is not to say that bourgeois fashion was in effect able to radically dismantle the noble dress code or change the public dress code of absolutism, or that bourgeois fashion was not influenced by courtly fashions. Yet dress and fashion were areas—the other important area being literature—where the spectacle of the body in the political realm of absolutism could be contested. Purdy considers the *Journal* an important player in the dissociation of bourgeois dress from that of the court: "Bertuch juxtaposed the codified layers of feudal dress with restrained, utilitarian style that focused on the body as a natural organism and the person as an intellectual and economic producer."[9]

While both the epistemological and utilitarian arguments are important aspects of the use of dress in middle-class identity construction, my study focuses on a third argument. The development and cultural refinement of bourgeois taste—seemingly providing greater freedom and mobility than the value system associated with the court—nevertheless created an intricate system of cultural distinctions. Taste becomes the new yardstick with which the representation of social and personal identity is gauged. It replaces direct social control and assigns social status. Thus this seemingly essential equality of human nature and a "natural" morality and sense of aesthetics is not really a sign of democratization but rather of a sophisticated and complex system of self-regulation. Consequently, my emphasis is on fashionable dress as a system of distinction with which groups or communities are defined.

SOCIAL DIFFERENTIATION THROUGH FASHION

Fashion plays a visible part in this system of subtle cultural distinctions structuring the growing and rather amorphous middle class. This structuration process plays itself out, for example, in the tension between cultural capital (taste) and economic capital (wealth). The fashion system illuminates the social mobility inherent in the new understanding of culture, which was theoretically accessible to everyone. Yet the *Journal* did not ignore the potentially problematic ramifications of social mobility. Cultural capital could, after all, be used for inclusionary as well as exclusionary purposes. It could consolidate a group identity by keeping undesirable elements out.

The *Journal* made this culture of adornment available to a large audience and thus created interest and knowledge. Due to the relative accessibility of the print medium (magazines were more affordable than the older forms of disseminating fashion information, i.e., the fashion doll), those tiers of the middle class that were previously excluded from the elite culture of adornment could now participate in the discourse of fashion.[10] Some of the illustrations in the *Journal* could also serve as patterns for imitation (fig. 4). Members of the middle class could try on and thus create potential identities for themselves. Earlier critiques of the seductive qualities of finery beyond one's social standing had a decisive moral overtone. For example, in Jakob Michael Reinhold Lenz's *Die Soldaten* the acceptance of fashionable accessories is seen as the first step on the path to social climbing, which is equated with the moral downfall of the middle-class woman. Contemporaries were concerned about the possibility of social masking—for example, that servants had access to their mistresses' discarded clothes and that new modes of distribution in secondhand shops made clothes available to people who would normally be unable to afford them. Not only could these people dream or fantasize themselves into a new social role, but the fear was that this trend could actually enable one rank to slide into another.

The *Journal,* while acknowledging the moralist position, does not use moralistic argumentation but instead assumes a sliding scale of cultural tastes and offers insight on how to improve taste and cultural capital, which can place members of the middle class at more or less prestigious positions. In contrast to Veblen,[11] I argue that for the *Journal* fashionable consumption is not limited to social climbing but offers a complex range of historically changing negotiations of social position within the middle class. Fashion constitutes a self-regulatory system that constantly renegotiates the differentiation of taste in the context of other discourses. These (the systems of distribution, economic resources, lifestyle, social conventions), in turn, might enhance or limit it.[12]

THE VALORIZATION OF NOVELTY

The *Journal*'s monthly charting of fashionable change intensified communication by providing information at a rapid pace (1:29). Allowing the magazine to react more quickly to the trends and changes in fashion, its mode of publication participated in and perpetuated the ever-increasing rate of turnover of styles and became instrumental in creating the phenomenon of fashion. Change can only be accomplished if there is a rapid source of information dissemination, and the fashion

4. A young German woman in a morning dress in *Journal des Luxus und der Moden* 9 (1794). Courtesy of the Bildarchiv Preußischer Kulturbesitz Berlin. Photo by Dietmar Katz.

journal fills that bill. The short wait for the next issue of the monthly contributed to the acceleration of the fashion process. The reader could be informed about and prepared for seasonal dress much more quickly than was previously possible.[13]

The focus on rapidly changing cultural practices and objects altered the nature of the print medium itself. The focus on novelty and change determined the editors' choice of genre (monthly) with its variety of short contributions on many different topics and aspects of culture. Inscribing its own obsolescence, the individual issue is but a transitional object; the publication is consumed like the cultural objects it describes. While offering variety, the publication nevertheless retains a fixed order of general topics (1:30). Foregrounding novelty, the periodical publication visualized change. Its subject matter, fashion, embodied novelty and change as well as commodification—all of which are markers of modernity.

As the publication gathered and collected the new trends, it in essence created the new fashion trend by giving it contours and assigning it the status of a model for any given style. In addition to valorizing change, the *Journal* therefore helped to establish fashionable culture—culture based on the perennial principle of novelty—as a range of signifying practices creating and organizing social life.

This obsession with novelty and the desire for new impressions and sensations is at the root of self-adornment and cultural activity. The innovation in fashionable dress allows persons to appear in a new light, and thus one does not tire of their beauty. In his short novel *Die Wahlverwandtschaften* (*Elective Affinities*), Goethe offers a perceptive image of this leisure culture and its pleasures. Among other topics, he addresses the uses of fashion:

> Her new, fashionable clothes greatly improved her [Ottilie]: for since people's charm is conveyed through external appearances, so one seems to see them afresh, and ever more charmingly, when their characteristics are conveyed in new surroundings.

> Die neuen modischen Gewänder erhöhten ihre Gestalt: denn indem das Angenehme einer Person sich auch über ihre Hülle verbreitet, so glaubt man sie immer wieder von neuem

und anmutiger zu sehen, wenn sie ihre Eigenschaften einer neuen Umgebung mitteilt.[14]

This same preoccupation with change, newness, and freshness is also at the core of cultural entertainment. Innovation that provides stimulation is perceived as a source of pleasure in bourgeois society. The preoccupation with the discourse of fashion as a prime embodiment of rapid and continual change is therefore an important source of pleasure.

In explaining the rapid and continual changing of styles, one of the many contributors to the *Journal* theorizes change as a deviation from the narrow line of beauty as a harmonious balance, which is destabilized by the exaggeration of certain trends. These tip the balance seeking a new harmony from a number of innovative new options (4:25). If fashion's innermost core is change, it becomes a marker or symbol for the concept of change, as discussed above. The term *Moden* ("fashions") in the journal's title refers to more than clothing, encompassing all aspects of a cultured lifestyle that are subject to perennial deliberate change and value novelty. Fashion's focus on change also discussed its categories, principles, and processes on a general level and with broader implications.

The system emerging from this theory of change represents an open, self-regulating one in which the tension between innovation (new ideas) and the standard or model (eternal truths) resolves itself by adjusting or abandoning the model when enough exaggerations, excesses, and new impulses destabilize the balance, starting the process of creating momentary models anew. The structure of the *Journal* parallels this destabilizing effect by depicting and describing a number of options considered as the model and at the same time advocating individual modifications in other contributions, thus creating the conceptual dispositions or avenues for the valorization of change. These structures set the stage and allow for the emergence of self-regulatory systems, no longer regulated by (sumptuary) laws but by a balance between consensus formation and dissent.

Bertuch even invites his readers to collect interesting information for him, giving the impression of an open forum for information on fashion (1:32). Throughout its long life, the *Journal* also included the views of its detractors in order to maintain the air of seriousness. The *Journal* exemplifies this form of change by making the point that—relying largely on independent contributors—it voices a range of positions, resisting reconciliation or the formation of an unambiguous editorial stance but visualizing instead the instability of positions. A telling example for this strategy is the debate on the controversial topic of the corset. The editor invites female contributors and a female judge to weigh the arguments for and against the practice. Whether this debate was orchestrated by the editors or arose spontaneously—I suspect the latter—it features input by the readers and is structured as a debate.[15] The issue of body shaping was a controversial one. Since the editor of the *Journal* obviously did not want to play devil's advocate for the continued use of the corset, he invited a "qualified" woman to write the piece in its defense: "We turned over the defense of the corset to an intelligent lady, who is the fortunate mother of two beautifully proportioned children and who through her experience and intelligence was a suitable judge as requested by our anonymous correspondent, and asked for her opinion" (1:109).[16] The correspondent defends the corset with the argument that men who have no firsthand experience should not conduct the debate, since they not only overestimate the inconvenience and dangers to women's health but are disingenuous in that they admire a slender build while condemning the means to achieve it (1:112). This discussion alluded to the relationship between fashion, in this case underwear, and desirable feminine shapes. Hinting at the eroticization of women through body shaping, the contributor explains that the excesses of tight lacing are caused by the celebration of women's waiflike shape ("schlanken Erlenwuchs") in cultural representations (1:113) in the context of the modern erotic love paradigm. The female judge decides against the use of the corset.

The system's resulting instability and transitory nature are an intricate component of its design, as is the unpredictability of change. Ingenious creativity, playfulness, and chance, not reasoned planning, spark innovation.[17] The lack of prestige and the serious consideration of material culture opened the door for this kind of argumentation. Cognizant of the tension between the master narrative of progress in the Enlightenment tradition and the indeterminacy of novelty, and thus departing from the grand narrative of change as deliberate linear progress, it allowed people to think in different ways about change. Because the new options have to be selected from a large number of possibilities, and because this selection cannot be determined causally and cannot be anticipated, it is contingent or arbitrary with unpredictable outcomes. It is as likely that the new fashion colors are selected from jewel tones as it is that they are chosen from pastels. As the technical and economic advances made available a larger, more complex environment to choose from—for example, a larger, more affordable selection of cloths and materials—the choices become less predictable. At the same time, other systems or discourses regulating cultural and social life limit the range of options from which new impulses arise. Each one operates as a continual unstable contingent process; each system consolidates trends to create a model or an established position, only to be destabilized by the unpredictability of innovation. These discourses in turn influence and limit each other. The fluid, complex system of self-regulation will constantly renegotiate the differentiation of taste in the context of other discourses. They might in turn enhance or limit it (the system of distribution, economic resources, lifestyle, social conventions, etc.), thus experimenting with a way of theorizing change that explains culture as a complex interplay of a set of systems, each governed by its own unpredictability.

The discussions on Paris fashion as the ultimate status symbol illuminate this kind of interplay of discourses or interfacing of systems. At first glance it seems that access to Paris fashions is primarily limited by financial restrictions. However, cheaper copies soon become available, and the originals and copies are resold in secondhand shops and even in outdoor public markets, thus becoming available to larger circles. The *Journal* discusses an example from the city of Cassel (1:82), where outdoor markets sell the latest slightly used fashions from Paris. A new mode of distribution coupled with the attitude that clothing is disposable lifted some of the financial barriers to its access.

However, this potential for a degree of equality in the consumption of cultural products—based on their "affordability"—became immediately modified. The system of taste begins to limit the system of economics. Even though fashion requires a degree of similarity and common features in order for it to be recognizable as a particular style, it nevertheless allows, even requires, a certain amount of individual interpretation based on one's taste. The consumer with discriminating taste (i.e., cultural capital) will soon become aware of this trickle-down effect of fashion and will abandon this particular style once it has become common (1:85).[18] As soon as the latest style has become stale due to excessive access to it—that is, once its novelty has worn off— new influences modify it. Of course, economic capital can be used to discourage or preclude this trickle-down effect. The journal mentions cases—for example, artificial fantasy flowers (1:96) or the finest imported painted muslin and lace (1:98)—in which the price precluded the integration into less affluent circles, virtually guaranteeing exclusivity. Georg Simmel's influential theory of fashion as a means for social distinction and imitation focuses on this phenomenon as the main impetus for fashionable change:

> As soon as the lower layers of the middle class begin to acquire the new fashion and transgress the markers set by the upper layers, and thus crumble uniformity of the symbolic cohesion, the upper layers turn away from this fashion and onto a new one, by which they distinguish themselves from the broad masses, and the game starts all over.

> Sobald die unteren [Stände K.A.W.] sich die Mode anzueignen beginnen und damit die von den oberen gesetzten Grenzmarkierungen überschreiten, die Einheitlichkeit in dem so symbolisierten Zusammengehören jener durchbrechen, wenden sich die oberen Stände von dieser Mode ab und einer neuen zu, durch die sie sich wieder von den breiten Massen differenzieren, und an der das Spiel von neuem beginnt.[19]

The *Journal* sees this process as more complex than mere social climbing. The fluid, complex system of self-regulation will constantly renegotiate the differentiation of taste in the context of other discourses that might in turn enhance or limit it (the systems of distribution, economic resources, lifestyle, social conventions).

This discursive construct of novelty—based on an open-ended concept of non-intentional and not necessarily meaningful change and contingent selections (selections that could always lead to different results and which cannot logically be predetermined and have an air of randomness)—relativizes both the Enlightenment belief in linear progress carrying the individual to ever-higher levels of culture as well as the idealist design of a deliberately integrated self as contained in its notion of *Bildung*. If the latter is based on the categories of discrimination that are based on rational values, the randomness of fashionable change contested this dominance by offering a competing conceptual register.

Although intellectuals and representatives of high culture regarded this kind of instability as threatening and unsettling, and fashion's self-reflexive drive toward self-perpetuation and autonomy as without reference and meaning, the middle-class position of the editor, advocating a broader definition of culture, regards it as playfully stimulating and therefore as pleasurable. It not only satisfied the desire for stimulation by novelty but created the sense of endless possibilities. The examination of fashion is thus also a study of the cultural implications of the modernity emerging toward the end of the eighteenth century. Ann Hollander therefore sees fashion as displaying the same logic as other modern arts.[20] The random, open-ended selection process, which chooses from a variety of cultural options and, in turn, is subject to change, which is modeled by fashion, is a main, if not the main, element of entertainment, linking it closely with the emergence of modernity. By incorporating change, that is, by altering the aspects of the personality—in this case, the shaping of the concept of the body or social differentiation through fashion—the self becomes destabilized. The *Journal*'s emphasis on change functions to underscore an understanding of the self as changing and therefore as historically constructed.

Fashion, as a very visible and obvious sign of change, becomes an easy target for profound and far-reaching cultural anxieties. These concerns arise from the difficulty of maintaining the vision (or, more appropriately, the fiction) of a self-determined subjectivity based on one's own free will (Kant). The gesture therefore is one of warding off of what is perceived as the disintegration of the stable self as it was constructed and celebrated in high culture.

By focusing on fashion in clothing and other cultural practices as examples with its follies, unpredictabilities, and deliberate and contingent features, the *Journal* relativizes both the Enlightenment belief in linear progress and the idealist design of a deliberately integrated self.

The valorization of novelty, this particular form of nonlinear historical dynamics, thus serves as an irritant and as a means for self-reflexivity in the self-fashioning of middle-class (autonomous) subjectivity. It also represents an opportunity for the emergence of an alternate realm for the playful pleasures and forms of entertainment that mass culture began to provide.

Beyond experimenting with a way of theorizing change that explains culture as a complex interplay of a set of systems, each of which is governed by its own non-logic, Bertuch's argument functions on a more pragmatic level as well. A highly cultured man himself, Bertuch is aware of the unconventionality of this experiment and therefore familiar with the discomforting destabilization that contemporaries associated with the notion of fashion. Of course, associating fashion with a lack of discipline, excess, playfulness, sensuality, and falseness devalues it as inconsequential. Many contemporaries, especially men of letters, considered fashion journals and their subject matter a highly problematic genre.[21] By situating fashion within a number of discourses—in particular, economic, social, and aesthetic—the editor wants to ensure that the publication transcends the odium of a frivolous, superficial, and inconsequential monthly. The *Journal* gives the impression of explaining and, to a degree, managing and overseeing the randomness of progress in modernity. In order to combat the commonplace criticism associated with fashion, Bertuch provides a detailed theoretical description of fashion and its usefulness and includes essays by authorities like Benjamin Franklin that examine the role of fashion for the body politic. By demonstrating that thoughtful people discuss the topic of fashion, the editor suggests that fashion—and, by implication, other cultural practices that provide convenience, comfort, and entertainment—is a subject to be taken seriously.

By the end of the eighteenth century, fashion magazines were no longer the only opportunity to indulge the pleasure of looking at the latest fashions and novelties—at least in the urban areas. Shopping increasingly lost the stigma of drudgery as more luxury goods became available and were displayed more aesthetically. Bertuch's *London und Paris* (1799) describes the seduction of a well-stocked store that magically draws people in to browse and shop.[22] As ready-made goods became displayed in shop windows and glass cabinets in eye-pleasing presentations and were offered with fixed pricing, the traditional marketing tradition with its unpleasant mingling in crowded and often dirty outdoor stalls was replaced. The aesthetics of consumption encouraged people to absorb the stylized representations of goods, allowing for a whole range of persuasive and informational stimuli to affect the spectator's/consumer's imagination. This created a previously nonexistent distance between looking and purchasing. The rhetorical object of the marketplace had changed. It now evoked the desire to browse rather than a directed need to purchase certain predetermined items. An increased selection required the customer to make choices, which entailed surveying all the available options. The dissociation between the browsing and the actual purchase became even more pronounced later in the nineteenth century with the introduction of the department store and its catalogs as major cultural primers that showed the middle class how to dress themselves, furnish their homes, and spend their leisure.[23]

Like the new form of materialist and empiricist science and its theories of cognition that characterize modernity, shopping (and with it the new retail trade) is visually oriented—it is a form of visual and imaginative appropriation. Images in the imagination have their base in objects perceived initially by sight. As Erin Mackie writes: "Things become cognitive and affective objects through the gaze. It is in this sense that we consume and acquire the objects we look at, incorporating them into our mental and emotional landscapes. And because looking operates as a mode of acquisition, the discourse of the gaze overlaps with the discourse of consumption."[24] The enchantment of the consumer/spectator by a well-stocked display of fashionable goods in store windows gradually became an ideal form of entertainment. Window shopping created a sense of profound pleasure because it displayed all the earmarks of entertainment by combining leisured activity, the enjoyment of novelty, and the intricate combination of visual and imaginary pleasures. To accommodate and facilitate this kind of shopping, retail facilities underwent significant transformations. The aesthetic display of objects not only required significant overhead for the procurement of display cases and windows setting the stage for an aesthetic display of goods, but it also altered the space of the store and its relationship to the community by opening it up to the street. The new store design drew the gaze through windows and invited the customer in by making the transition between street and shop as easy to overcome as possible. This trend not only invited consumption but also rendered shopping recreational. The entertainment aspect of shopping became apparent early in England, where shopkeepers and cultural critics began to complain that a large portion of the clientele shopped to cure their "spleen and vapors," disturbing the stores' aesthetic arrangement and display without resulting in a purchase and thus profit for the shopkeeper.[25] As we discussed above, the entertainment value derived from novelty and from visual stimulation that stirs the imagination and thus holds boredom and depression (ennui and melancholy) at bay was considered an important part of the care of the self. Addressing all these aspects of entertainment, shopping seems like an ideal form of recreation to forestall boredom and provide a powerful potion promoting mental health—if only for a short while.

Although this change took place in Germany on a lesser scale than in much-admired London, the difference was only one of degree. London occupied the leadership position in the creation of a market for mass consumption. Already by 1770, German visitors had been amazed by the vast assortment of goods on display, as noted by Georg Lichtenberg, who marveled at the variety of goods and their availability at all hours of the day and in every location.[26] Sophie La Roche's description of her stay in London in 1786 is another example of this kind of specular attraction. She notes not only the abundance of goods but also the mode of seductive display in a brilliantly lit environment:

> Behind the great glass windows absolutely everything one can think of is neatly, attractively displayed in such abundance of choice as almost to make one greedy. Now large slipper and shoe shops for anything from adults down to dolls, can be seen; now fashion-articles or silver or brass shops, books, guns, glasses, the confectioner's goodies, the pewter's wares, fan's etc. . . . There is a cunning device for showing women's materials. Whether they are silks, chinzes, or muslins, they hang down in folds behind the fine, high windows so that the effect of this or that material, as it would be in the ordinary folds of a woman's dress, can be studied.[27]

This kind of suggestive display of material for women's clothing appeals to the imagination. Looking at the object is only part of the pleasure, as the customer is invited to see how it would lend itself to incorporation in her own clothing. It invites an imaginary anticipation of the image the consumer hopes to create for herself. In their minds, the consumers integrate the desirable objects into their lifestyles. Visual acquisition and imaginative consumption are significant forms of entertainment and produce considerable pleasure.

La Roche also confirmed the pleasure created by the sheer wealth of variety in one of the premier shopping streets in eighteenth-century Europe, Oxford Street:

> First one passes a watch-making, then a silk or fan store, now a silversmith's, a china or glass shop. The spirit booths are particularly tempting . . . here crystal flasks of every shape

and form are exhibited: each one has a light behind which makes all the different coloured spirits sparkle. Just as alluring are the confectioners and fruiterers, where, behind the handsome glass window pyramids of pink apples, figs, grapes, oranges and all manner of fruits are on show. We inquire the price of a pineapple and did not think it too dear at 6s. Most of all we admired a stall with Argand lamps situated in a corner house and forming a really dazzling spectacle. Every variety of lamp, crystal, lacquer and metal ones, silver and brass in every possible shape.[28]

Bertuch's *London und Paris* discusses the lure of window displays in London's Strand in great detail, not only noting the wealth of objects and the mode of display but also commenting on the fact that there is always something new to be discovered.[29] This novelty factor draws people into the store over and over again.[30] It was only a matter of time until the same phenomenon surfaced in the large cities in Germany, particularly Berlin and Hamburg.[31] The fashionable spas already displayed temporary booths of (decorative) luxury items for the seasonal shoppers.

This practice of display and selection also changed work patterns within the middle-class household. If the lady of the house had the necessities and food items picked up by the servants, decorative items or items for which there was a significant selection were no longer procured by the servants.

In the meantime, the colored fashion plates illustrating the pages of the *Journal* fulfilled the function of elaborate display, allowing people in the provinces to participate in the emerging consumer culture. As forms of advertisement, both the shop window and the illustration created an interest in luxury goods by fostering desire and longing. Consumers imagined how they would incorporate the items in their own lifestyle. Then they imagined and planned the transformation of the self to match this imagined vision. The creation of these images and fantasies was a form of pleasurable entertainment.

THE SELF AS CULTURAL PRODUCTION

Bertuch's famous contemporaries in Weimar, notably Goethe, Schiller, Herder, and Wieland, remained indifferent or hostile to this and other (fashion) journals. Herder's condemnation combined economic and moral arguments.[32] Time that could be utilized for the cultivation or construction of the intellectual, emotive, and spiritual aspects of the self is instead wasted on an inconsequential and superficial facet of the self that could only uneasily coexist with the value attached to personal integrity and authenticity. By displaying rapidly and continually changing styles, these publications created false desires and distractions that threatened the stability of the private sphere, especially the family. Women were singled out as especially prone to the fickleness of changing tastes and the undisciplined indulgence in consumer pleasures. Due to their "naturally" undisciplined, weaker constitution and their responsibility for the workings of the domestic sphere, they (so the complaint implied) were seduced into excessive, continual spending. This strained the family resources and led women to neglect their families by spending time on fashion, on updating their wardrobes, and the fashionable decoration of the home. The implication is, of course, that more "important" functions of the middle-class household and the family were neglected, such as the proper education of the children. This condemnation suggests that Herder—and he is fairly representative in this—not only regards this focus on change as dangerous but also foregrounds the utilitarian aspects of the domestic sphere. This (dominant) line of argument disregards the family and its forms of sociability as an important cultural site where objects of material culture serve as means for creative and pleasurable practices.

This argumentation dissociates the cultural practices surrounding the beautification of the home and its cultural ambience from high cultural practices and corresponds to a prominent trend in the intellectual culture of the time, namely, to dissociate culture from its material and economic aspects. This trend was paralleled by the non-utilitarian concept of education (*Bildung*) and (high) culture celebrated under idealism. The heavy use of manufactured art objects (around 1800 these were mostly copies of the highly fashionable Roman and Greek art) for the beautification of the domestic sphere was seen as a degradation of the original autonomous artwork. Used as decorative objects, the artifacts no longer provided edification but instead offered only momentary pleasure. The distinction was influenced by Kant's valorization of "pure" aesthetic judgment, according to which the relative purity of observations can be achieved only through the proper training of the mind through sustained education.[33]

The culture of adornment and its economic implications were dismissed in the celebration of *Bildung* and thus were not valorized in the self-definition of the intellectuals. Yet judging by the advertisements for copies of statuary, it becomes clear that the cultural elite purchased the plaster casts of neoclassical statuary, as one could find them at the studio of the court sculptor in Weimar, Gottlieb Martin Klauer (1742–1801). He advertised in the most sophisticated periodicals of his time: the *Merkur* (1782) and the *Intelligenzblatt* of the *Journal des Luxus und der Moden* (July 1787).[34] Obviously, there is an implicit strand in the cultural imagination that links "true" or professional education with material asceticism, which ignores its material base and the very important socialization within the family and the domestic sphere. If we do not want to dismiss as hypocrisy this schism between the rhetorical condemnation of these decorative objects as non-art and the actual practices of cultural consumption, we have to assume that high art and the decorative arts fulfilled different functions in the middle-class lifestyle. There seems to have been a time and place for both. The middle-class lifestyle consisted of many layers of culture, such as social communication or conversation, reading (and even writing) as a social event, the reception or production of musical performances, the appreciation of the visual arts as participant or spectator, the opportunity to travel, and the increasing playfulness of childhood and its toys, among others. Within the context of an aestheticized domestic private sphere we find myriad forms of cultural consumption. As forms of cultural socialization they represented a crucial—albeit often unacknowledged—part of identity construction. After all, the material capital of the domestic environment created the favorable conditions for the acquisition of cultural capital.

An important aspect of this ambience for the formation of one's cultural capital in the domestic sphere is the cultural attention lavished on children. This took the form of specialized reading materials, children's books, and age-specific and often instructional toys and educational games, signaling that more time and money were spent on children, their clothing, furnishings, and activities, and the special appointment of play areas in the garden. Bertuch's sketch of a garden in his *Allgemeines Teutsches Garten Magazin* that paid particular attention to the needs of the children allows a glimpse at the care lavished upon children's development in all areas. In this elaborate garden there was ample lawn for games, places for bowling and swinging, quiet corners where children could read, a space to dance and make music, spaces in the garden house where the collections of the father could serve as teaching tools, a teaching plantation where the father could teach botanical and horticultural principles, few flowers, and no water features, which could endanger the children.[35] Special clothing for children and infants became commercially available.[36] The fact that parents, which meant predominantly mothers, spent their leisure time with the children was somewhat of a novelty. It was an effect of the enlightened attitude of benevolence in child rearing propagated by pedagogues. The socialization and education of children became an important factor in leisure-time entertainment. At the same time, this often unacknowledged cultural life in the home laid the important groundwork (Bourdieu's *habitus*) for the acculturation of its members. The nexus of conveying knowledge, entertainment, and the formation of taste was ideally represented in Bertuch's *Bilderbuch für Kinder* (1790–1830), a most ambitious, carefully and lavishly illustrated encyclopedia for children. Regarding intellectual and sensual forms of knowing as complementary, he combines the pleasure of looking with providing information and uses both to stimulate the imagination. In this kind of visual education he conveys the importance of attractive and correct illustrations that accustom the child to true depictions, beautiful shapes, and correct proportions, impressions, and concepts, thus instilling good taste. Offering information and the pleasure of the gaze (*Schaulust*), the illustrated encyclopedia for children socialized visual education. By offering this in small doses on a periodical basis, it heightens and prolongs the pleasure of its young readers.[37]

Everyday cultural practices (in their material and nonmaterial manifestations) served as the necessary preconditions for the socialization and acculturation that make high culture possible. The dismissive reaction to this cultural realm by intellectuals helped to usher in a social differentiation within the middle class and was directed primarily at the proto-industrial and merchant tier within the middle class in a quest for cultural dominance. This differentiation strategy is the other important context in which the frequent critiques of fashion as materialistic, disruptive, frivolous, and distracting have to be seen. This line of argumentation would later inform most theories of fashion until the most recent present, when cultural studies allowed for a less dismissive approach to forms of material culture.[38]

By its very presence and apparent success, the *Journal* advocated the desirability and importance of culture as a whole range of practices, not only elite high art. Yet Bertuch's vision of the interplay of the various cultural systems stood in contrast to the position that was to become the dominant one, one that was suspicious of the onslaught of increasing and eventually competing cultural activities. In the 1780s, the attack on fashion's triviality—its distracting of people from more "valuable" forms of cultural (i.e., high cultural) entertainment, which required the concentrated, sustained attention of its participants—marked this process as a deterioration of culture rather than its enrichment. Competing forms of cultural pursuits—such as the preoccupation with fashion and the periodical print culture, which ostensibly requiring less time, effort, intellectual preparation, and mental work—were perceived as a threat to the concept of middle-class culture. The seduction of entertainment was regarded as a menace to what was imag(in)ed to be a monolithic, disciplined, and achievement-oriented concept of high culture.

READING THE FASHIONABLE BODY

The presumption that the culturally constructed exterior of the clothed body mirrored the character of the individual necessitated a discussion of the body's surface markings as clues to the reality hidden within the body. This proved essential in a system of knowledge that sought to construct and read the unique characteristics of individual bourgeois subjectivity. As personal identity and idealized subjectivity became the earmarks of the bourgeois self, the *Journal* constitutes an important arena for the examination of the relationship between physical appearance and character. A contribution to the *Journal* elaborates:

> The physiognomy of male dress allows more reliable glimpses at character, costumes, ways of thinking and acting than the forms of the forehead, nose, mouth, chin, etc., which often suffered accidents and thus represent an unreliable exterior. Many times it is the hat (if not part of a uniform) and the form and manner in which the man wears and carries it that is the true mirror of the brain it covers.

> Es giebt für das Auge des Kenners eine Physiognomik des männlichen Anzugs, die vielleicht sicherere Schlüsse auf Charakter, Sitte, Denk- und Handlungsart erlaubt, als die Formen der Stirn, Nase, Mund, Kinn u.s.w. die häufig durch

Zufall gelitten haben, und also ein falsches Schild von dem Bewohner am Hause aushängen. Oft ist der Huth (wenn eine Uniform ihm nicht den Schnitt giebt) die Form, die Art wie der Mann ihn setzt, trägt und hält, ein ziemlich treuer Spiegel des Gehirns, das er deckt. (1:137)

The *Journal* argues that the physiognomy of dress (i.e., the cultural presentation) is more reliable than that of the physical features of the body and face (i.e., nature) because the latter can be altered by accidents and mishaps while the first requires deliberate choice and therefore exhibits clearer signals of the wearer's character. The clothed body is seen as the better indicator of individual subjectivity because it requires an act of self-creation, an inventive combination and blending of biological and cultural attributes. Clothing functions as a means for self-expression and will be read by others who judge its wearer. The deliberate change of the kind of clothes a person wears is associated with changes in his or her self-image.[39]

By teaching the art of the culturally studied and calculated presentation of the clothed body, the *Journal* by implication also argues for social mobility. Neither lineage and heritage nor upbringing and socialization necessarily determine the individual. The free will to obtain cultural knowledge, which can be satisfied by publications such as the *Journal,* enables a deliberate and purposeful identity construction beyond mere appearances. This constructivist position acknowledges the role clothes and fashion play in the formation of the self. The *Journal* argues that if the vestimentary forms begin to show seriousness and modesty, this will, in turn, have an impact on the inner values (3:53). The interrelation and mutual influence of behavior, character, and appearance is then used for a fairly crude moralistic argument. Bolstered by medical arguments, the contribution in the *Journal* surmises that by discouraging revealing clothes, especially those baring the neck, arms, and cleavage, the health of women would be greatly improved by creating "stronger mothers, who, unassailed by vapors, give life to happy and healthy children" ("stärkere Mütter, von keinen Nervenkrämpfen geplagt, [die] frischen und lebensfrohen Kindern das Daseyn geben") (3:114). Vigor and health are associated with strong moral character, which, in turn, can be produced by the appropriate modest clothes. In this argument, the vestimentary envelope participates in the creation of the social body for both the private and the public sphere.[40]

At the same time, clothing exerted an influence over the wearer's conduct.[41] After all, during the eighteenth century the body emerges at the center of perceptual philosophies, thus becoming increasingly objectified in both aesthetic and scientific analyses. Examining the clothed body was considered an effective technique to understand the psyche, the inner qualities of another human being. The discussions in the *Journal* presumed that a hidden personal truth could be gleaned from bodily appearances. Not only could facial features tell about a person's psychological makeup, but the clothed body could reveal a person's social character. As personal identity and idealized subjectivity became the earmarks of the bourgeois self, fashion becomes an important arena for the self-definition of the middle class.

While also delineating the distinction between public and private fashions, the *Journal's* emphasis, however, is clearly on the apparel of the private sphere ("das Negligé"), not on the official dress ("voller Anzug") (1:134). It is therefore primarily focused on the construction of the private cultural and social body. We need to keep in mind, however, that the official dress for specific occasions, usually in context with functions at court, was the much more limited and overall less important segment of clothing. Private dress, which accompanied the normal day-to-day business activities and social occasions, was by far the more important one and received more attention in the pages of the fashion magazines.

In the forum of the fashion magazine, the ethics and morality of the time are far less cerebral, conceptual, and abstract than in other discourses; instead, they become embodied as the fashion magazine takes the body into consideration in the creation of its own sense of morality. In this regard, it is an embodied ethics. In addition, the presentation and discussion of the fashionable body create and establish taste and teach how to read this subtle system of cultural values. Only the expert knowledge of this system of exterior signs creates an interpretative framework for what was assumed to be hidden underneath, the subjectivity of the individual. Since individual subjectivity cannot be seen, appearances have to be taken as conjectures about the inner qualities, thus creating the need for a detailed and extensive system of signs.

FASHION AS SYSTEM OF KNOWLEDGE

The *Journal's* overreaching gesture promotes the aestheticization of everyday life, including the body. It assumes that all people, regardless of race, nationality, or class, strive for self-adornment, and furthermore that members of the human race want to distinguish themselves from each other.[42] The universal human desire for beautification of the body and its surroundings, for the cultural construction of the self, springs from the thirst for novelty and variety. The degree of variety, ornamentation, and attractiveness of the fashion is an indicator of the degree of cultural sophistication and enlightenment of a people or a nation. Fashion is thus a form of acculturation—a means by which individuals and groups learn to be visually at home with themselves in their culture. It relates to particular codes of behavior and rules of ceremony and place. It denotes and embodies conventions of conduct that contribute to the etiquette and manners of social encounters. The way people clothe their body is an active process for constructing and presenting a bodily self. With the help of publications such as the fashion journal, the tangible objects of material culture became culturally meaningful in their manifestation of conceptual systems of difference. They taught how to define categories of person (by the differential distribution of clothing, color, shape, fabric, and level of ornamentation or by rank, sex, marital status, occupation, etc.) as well as categories of time, place, and activity that are represented in clothing. Fashionable clothing uses material objects as a cultural practice which is part of the culture that structures social communication. Although I would agree with McCracken that clothing can be seen as a means by which "cultural categories and principles are encoded and made manifest,"[43] his conclusion that this code is closed—that it does not allow for infinite combinations but provides a set of fixed messages—has to be qualified. The *Journal* foregrounds change as the core of fashion, and this change is ongoing. After all, the discourse of fashion negotiates a delicate balance between established categories and destabilizing innovations and personalization. The *Journal* thus discusses fashion as an important strand in the fabric of culture, as a prominent site for the creation of the social body. It links the representation of the biological body to the social body and shows how its transformations were linked to the emergence of modern social organizations. As such, the discussion of fashion brings the biological body into the general and popular discourse. Fashion and the body are intricately linked, and one could not fully exist without the other. Clothes are a means of constructing the social body to which others react.

The *Journal* sets out to offer overviews on the ebb and flow of changing fashions as models or samples it has constructed from trends it has observed. Hoping to assist in making sense of the world of luxuries and fashionable change, it wants to teach the proper judgment and use of clothing (1:28).

The *Journal* assists the reader not only in gauging and reading the fashionable environment but also in producing it. It taught its readership how to integrate and orient itself within this complex system, not only making readers aware of the general trends—the general framework and rules—but also offering an understanding of how this framework could be modified and personalized in the creation of one's individuality. The nuanced reading and reconstruction of fashionable clothing to express one's understanding of the norms and rules while at the same time being able to personalize and modify it according to one's sense of style is the mark of cultural sophistication (1:98). The small degree of creativity in the construction of the self reveals good taste and cultural knowledge. Readers learned the art and skill of negotiating between the ideal image presented and the realities of their own lifestyle in a complex mutual process of approximation. It is not that readers were manipulated into blind imitation; instead, the *Journal* fueled desires for a certain lifestyle, which, in turn, created new wants and needs.

In order for a style to emerge as fashionable, enough people have to buy into its general premises. However, to allow for the prized individual subjectivity, subtle differences within given (fashionable) frameworks have to be encouraged as means of distinction. The tension between individuality and conformity drives cultural consumption. This tension provides the framework for the elaborate but subtle system of cultural distinctions, which constitutes a form of momentary regulation, normativity, and control. This reveals one of the frequently noted paradoxes of fashion: it renders conformity and offers individualization at the same time.[44] Dress was "both used as an indicator of social conformity, and paradoxically, also individualized to the wearer's taste and personality,"[45] creating the need for a detailed and extensive system for the interpretation of these signs.

FASHION AND THE COMPARTMENTALIZATION OF THE BOURGEOIS LIFESTYLE

Not only did fashion's rapid change help to create, visualize, and underscore the modern sense of time (Koselleck), but the variety of styles helped to create and express the increasingly compartmentalized life of the bourgeoisie. Fashion underscored seasonal changes in dress; several illustrations in the *Journal* depict specifically winter or summer clothes. The period of time during the summer that many families spent in the country in their gardens was marked by the deliberate informality of dress. Men are said to take off their frocks, hats, and wigs and to put away their walking sticks as soon as they enter the private sphere of their beloved garden. We even read of men who enjoy the early mornings and evenings in their gardens dressed in their dressing gowns (*Schlafrock*) and slippers.[46] Women's informal dress (*Negligé*) was simpler in cut and ornamentation and was made of washable materials, allowing for more movement and comfort. Dress for the time in the country was marked more by comfort and informality than by a focus on the differentiation within the middle class.

The more formal winter season, with its array of sociable entertainment, required a more differentiated wardrobe that accented the uniqueness of the various occasions for which it was worn. Leisure itself was divided into many social occasions, which were underscored by the appropriate dress such as "morning gowns, tea gowns, dinner gowns, walking dress, traveling dress, dress for the country," which "matched and expressed the compartmentalized, obsessionally subdivided life of the bourgeoisie."[47] Clothes specific for the occasion help to make the occasion what it is; they provide definition, clearly distinguishing one occasion from another. Clothes and other attributes of the "proper" lifestyle turn a natural part of the day into a cultural and social construct, an occasion. At the same time, dress assigned the occasions various degrees of importance through its level of formality or informality. Putting together the appropriate fashionable ensemble for the occasion was not only an important pastime in itself but also structured and underscored the social activities of the day.

The relationship between clothing and sociability becomes apparent in those contributions in the *Journal* that describe everyday life, contemporary customs, and lifestyles. In a letter from a newlywed daughter to her mother (and its reply), the negotiation of status through fashionable clothes in their relationship to social occasions become apparent. The daughter explains:

> The involvement in social life is very high these days, and it is *bon ton* to visit one another in one's *Negligé* [informal

morning dress] for breakfast in the garden. Then the men go to work and the women remain together until lunch, after which they return home and then dress for the afternoon visits. That's how things proceed day after day. I have to admit that I find this lifestyle oppressive because it does not allow me to enjoy my domestic space and focus on important things. Alas, can I withdraw from this lifestyle? May I retreat and possibly risk that the whole town makes fun of me? Or that I destroy relationships with families and other relationships that my husband is engaged in and thus harm his position and mine in his eyes? You know he is pleasant and good and allows me to do as I wish, but you also know that it is important to him that we are reputed to have a fashionable house and lifestyle.

Der Hang zum gesellschaftlichen Leben ist sehr groß, und es ist jezt *bon ton,* des Morgens, im *Negligé,* im Garten zum Frühstücke zueinander zu gehen. Die Männer gehn dann an ihre Arbeit, und die Weiber bleiben zusammen bis zum Mittags-Essen, wo dann alles nach Hauße geht, und sich erst nach Tische wieder zur Nachmittags-*Parthie* anzieht. So gehts einen und alle Tage. Ich muß bekennen, daß mich diese Lebensart drückt, weil sie mir nicht erlaubt in meinem Hauße zu leben, und mich zu sammeln. Allein kann und darf ich mich ihr entziehen? Darf ich mich absondern, und es wagen, daß vielleicht die ganze Stadt über mich spottet? Oder, daß ich Familien und andere Verhältnisse, in denen mein Mann hier steht, dadurch zerreiße und ihm, oder mir selbst bey ihm schade? Sie wissen er ist gefällig und gut; ihm ist alles recht was ich thue; aber Sie wissen auch daß er etwas darauf setzt, daß unser Hauß den Nahmen habe, es sey von gutem Ton. (1:153–54)

The daughter feels overwhelmed in what she senses is a careful negotiation of the interplay of social interactions with its material accoutrements (fashion, the unique form of sociability, eating as a social event, the proper ambience) and status. Taste, cultural refinement, and knowledge are the skills that come to define women's role in the aestheticization of the domestic sphere. The daughter realizes that the carefully crafted and "designed" informality of the breakfasts is not simply a form of leisure entertainment but an important aspect of networking and community building within this layer of the middle class, as are the more formal social occasions in the afternoon. These after-lunch activities are visually set apart from those in the morning by more elaborate dress. Clothing underscores and defines the social activities of the afternoon. The daughter's letter solicits advice about the creation of an appropriate lifestyle and the negotiation between personal interests and social obligations. With this kind of exchange, the *Journal* itself takes on an advisory function in the creation of the appropriate middle-class lifestyle.

The Fashionable Domestic Environment

As Norbert Elias has pointed out, objects of consumption—not the least of which changed the domestic environment significantly—played an important role in the civilizing process and, to extend his argument, in the identity formation of the bourgeoisie. Interiors changed: furniture and furnishings became subject to fashionable change; wallpapers, fabrics, mirrors, and clocks reflected the tastes and financial status of their owners. The fashionable house and the carriage (which increased one's range of mobility and just now became available for the middle class) served as the backdrop for the most conspicuous change, the fashionable wardrobe. These material objects also function as signs that require careful interpretation. The aesthetic environment, the middle-class home (and its extension, the garden), became not only an important context for the fashionable body but helped to define it. The rich tapestry of middle-class culture was woven of many strands—the decorative arts, design, art, literature, and music. As Elizabeth Wilson pointed out: "It was the beginning of the idea of the Self as Work of Art, the 'personality' as something that extended to dress, scent and surrounding, all of which made an essential contribution to the formation of 'self'—at least for women."[48]

As the house became more of a focus for an increasingly important leisure lifestyle for both men and women, it becomes imbued with new qualities. Contemporaries point out the desirability of neatness and cleanliness of the domestic space as the prerequisite for the elements of refinement. The traditionally larger communal spaces gave way to distinct rooms with specific functions, offering more privacy and room for

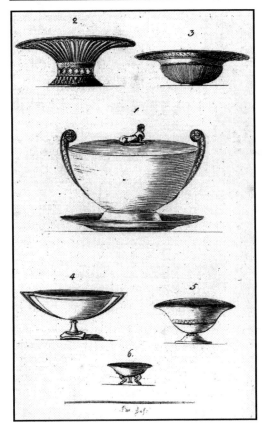

5. Elegant bowls in *Journal des Luxus und der Moden* 16 (1801). Courtesy of the Bildarchiv Preußischer Kulturbesitz Berlin. Photo by Dietmar Katz.

individual and solitary occupations. The use of fashionable wallpaper and paint, of wainscoting, of rugs and carpet, of fashionable draperies and curtains, and of more elaborate new furniture made from more expensive woods than simple oak—all selected on the basis of one's individual taste—became the backdrop for other items of consumer culture. The new furniture displayed the objects of consumer culture that marked the bourgeois lifestyle: books, chinaware, tableware, musical instruments, and visual artifacts (smaller-scale paintings, porcelain statuary and figurines, children's toys, and mirrors) (see figs. 5–7).

At the same time, consumer artifacts become selected as representations of aspects of the purchaser's personality. La Roche, for example, writes: "I bought a seal really expressive of my present mood and past

6. Two fruit bowls in *Journal des Luxus und der Moden* 4 (1789). Courtesy of the Bildarchiv Preußischer Kulturbesitz Berlin. Photo by Dietmar Katz.

fortune; namely a female figure leaning on a ruined pillar, looking back along the road she had come."[49] Once integrated into the interior design of the study as part of her writing desk, this object can be "read"—it invites interpretation not only of the thing itself but also in its relationship to its purchaser. Its functional nature is supplemented by its representational value. Decorative items for the household were being purchased by the individual who owns them—unlike in previous time, where household items were usually family heirlooms and did not express the taste or individuality of their current owner but rather signified tradition and one's heritage.

The fact that this particular item was purchased on a trip as a souvenir added another dimension to the signifying quality of cultural artifacts as narratives about their owner's lifestyle and tastes. As markers of events and places, they embodied memories and could trigger a replay of the situation and place in which they were acquired in the imagination of their purchaser, thus representing a significant source of imaginary pleasure.

Travel for pleasure also increased the variety of fashions and goods brought back as souvenirs. Silks, woolen and linen goods, jewelry, perfume for the adornment of the body, fine furniture, silverware, curios, natural objects, coins, books, and engravings for decorating one's environment imparted novelty into domestic life.[50]

The prominence of books and libraries, reading tables, and decorative desks in the interior design of the bourgeois household suggested not only that reading was an important activity but that it had become a cultural status symbol with which people could symbolize their distinctive inner qualities. As we discussed above, reading materials helped people learn how to enrich their emotional life and learn how to feel.[51]

7. Wallpaper and wall decoration in *Journal des Luxus und der Moden* 2 (1787). Courtesy of the Bildarchiv Preußischer Kulturbesitz Berlin. Photo by Dietmar Katz.

They also served as consumer goods that conveyed their owner's status. These objects show that people had become "at home" with their reading material, that they had integrated it into their daily practice, and that it had become a great source of pleasure of which they wanted to avail themselves as often, as long, and as conveniently as possible (figs. 8–11).

New reading chairs, for example, allowed their users to read longer and with less strain on the body than traditional chairs. Writing tables that conform to the body's need and range of movement extended the user's stamina. Physical comforts made activities more conducive to be experienced as pleasurable, and therefore a higher degree of comfort contributed to the activity's use as entertainment. Overall, the interior design was significantly embellished with decorative furniture such as the fashionable tables or shelves that included plants, flowers, and often birdcages (figs. 12–13).

The steady stream of fashionable changes created a momentum for consumption. As layers of the middle class became larger and more diverse, their tastes also displayed a wider range and their appetite for novelty in cultural artifacts increased. After all, the bourgeoisie defined itself primarily as a cultural elite instead of as an economic force. Yet culture and economics were closely linked, as we observed in the emergence of a literary marketplace, the significant increase of literary production, and the diversification of cultural production and consumption. The middle-class lifestyle was based not only on the all-important principle of education and the popularization of knowledge through the emergent print culture but also on consumer goods' expression of cultural categories and principles.[52] As a by-product of increasing social differentiation and social mobility, the use of culturally significant goods and practices could serve to express and read social identity in an increasingly anonymous society, setting the stage for the modern society that was to become a "cohesive society of perfect strangers."[53] Cultural objects and practices carried messages, requiring individuals to acquire the code to decipher these messages, in essence shaping individuals as consumers. In this line of argument, consumption became an important aspect of the construction of subjectivity at the end of the eighteenth century.

As we discussed above, the new patterns of consumption were both a cause and an effect of idealist conceptions of the individual, insisting on the singularity and sovereignty of the individual and its

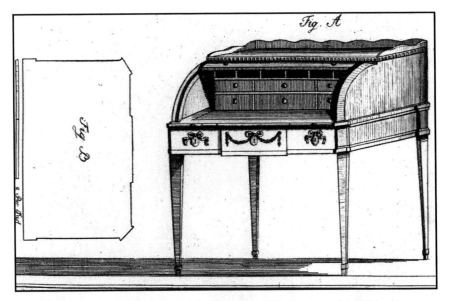

8. Ladies' desk in *Journal des Luxus und der Moden* 8 (1793). Courtesy of the Bildarchiv Preußischer Kulturbesitz Berlin. Photo by Dietmar Katz.

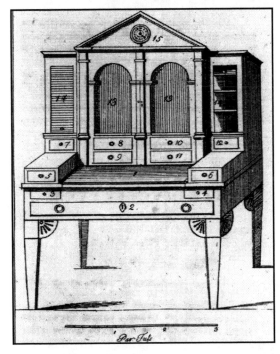

9. Ladies' writing cabinet in *Journal des Luxus und der Moden* 17 (1802). Courtesy of the Bildarchiv Preußischer Kulturbesitz Berlin. Photo by Dietmar Katz.

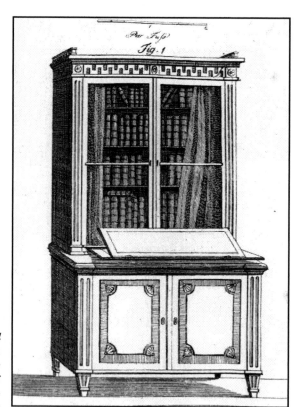

10. Book cabinet in *Journal des Luxus und der Moden* 11 (1796). Courtesy of the Bildarchiv Preußischer Kulturbesitz Berlin. Photo by Dietmar Katz.

11. Writing utensils in *Journal des Luxus und der Moden* 14 (1799).Courtesy of the Thüringische Universitäts- und Landesbibliothek Jena.

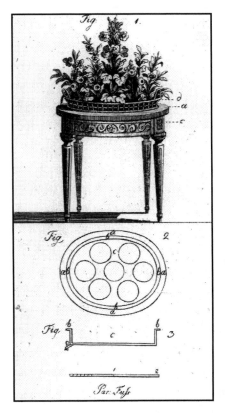

12. A portable garden or flower table in *Journal des Luxus und der Moden* 7 (1792). Courtesy of the Bildarchiv Preußischer Kulturbesitz Berlin. Photo by Dietmar Katz.

13. Flower table with birdcage in *Journal des Luxus und der Moden* 24 (1809). Courtesy of the Thüringische Universitäts- und Landesbibliothek Jena.

realization through experience and creativity. McCracken's assessment of changes in English society is also valid in principle for late-eighteenth-century German society: "In short, the eighteenth century saw a transformation of consumption and the world in which it took place. Consumption was beginning to take place more often, in more places, under new influences, by new groups, in pursuit of new goods, for new social and cultural purposes. The 'world of goods' was steadily making itself co-extensive with the new world of social life."[54] Families carefully assembled the cultural objects and practices that would serve to constitute and signify their identity as a social unit. When compared to the previous pattern of identity formation—that is, one based on inherited household items and clothing and heirlooms—the new pattern represents a decisive step into modernity. Individuals are no longer firmly protected, defined, and limited by lineage and the traditions of the family in its social position; the new system is more open, offers choices, is subject to change, has a higher degree of instability, and relies on personal initiative and taste. With the previous pattern, families inherited not only objects but the meanings signified by them, while the modern pattern required the family to construct its own meaning. Along with this freedom of choice—these visions of infinite possibilities—arrived a loss of traditions and the stability and security attached to them.

Descriptions of the forms of sociability in the famous Reimarus household in Hamburg allow glimpses at the new forms of interior architecture and design that created the new spaces for these forms of sociable entertainment. This kind of informal entertainment, which had become representative for the educated middle class, had certain material prerequisites. The architecture of the house had to provide the proper space for an informal exchange between the living rooms in which one entertained and the study, which by now was placed next to the living room to allow for family interaction during leisure hours—even if certain work-related tasks are conducted in the adjoining yet separate study.[55] This form of predominantly intellectual work was a source of prestige and was not relegated to a back room. At the same time, intellectual work often required that a certain amount of work spilled over into leisure, and in certain fields the border between leisure and work was less distinct than in others. This was true in particular for intellectuals, writers, and artists but also for physicians, teachers, and merchants, to name only a few.

As early as 1788, the *Journal* praised the architectural design changes in the layout of the middle-class home that added a study connected to the living room, where the middle-class professional could take care of his paperwork, correspondence, and reading while still being connected to the activities of the other family members:

> The middle-class man cannot make do with only one living room. With the increase of written negotiations and an extended correspondence, and the currently expected level of literacy, he needs a study or library in which he can complete these tasks without interruptions. If possible, these should connect to the living room, so that he can easily speak with his wife.

> Der bürgerliche Mann vom Mittelstande kann sich nicht mehr mit Einer Wohnstube begnügen. Bei den vermehrten schriftlichen Verhandlungen, dem außerordentlich erweiterten Briefwechsel, und der jetzt allgemein erforderlichen Belesenheit braucht er ein Studier- oder Expeditions-Zimmer, in welchem er dieses alles ungestört verrichten kann, und zwar soll dies auch wo möglich mit dem Wohnzimmer Verbindung haben, damit er zu jeder Zeit mit seinem Weibe sprechen kann.[56]

The spatial environment is intricately linked to the activities of the household with its increasing emphasis on entertainment during leisure. The creation of an environment appropriate for domestic work, leisure, entertainment, and sociability demanded a considerable amount of knowledge regarding the products of the material culture for the home. The increasingly specialized periodicals and their illustrations offered important models and became important tools for the formation of taste regarding the objects of material culture.

THE *JOURNAL*'S ROLE IN THE BEAUTIFICATION OF THE DOMESTIC SPHERE

The *Journal* significantly assisted in the task of beautification. Reporting, for example, on the latest chairs, desks, and occasional furniture, the editor gives a systematic verbal account accompanied by pictorial representations. Illustrations offer visual information on the objects regarding both their usefulness and their aesthetic qualities. Often objects are dissected into their relevant parts. The nuanced reading and reconstruction of the fashionable environment, expressing one's understanding of the norms and rules while at the same time being able to personalize and modify it according to one's sense of style, is the mark of cultural sophistication; crude, direct imitation is not (1:98). The small degree of creativity in the construction of the environment is what reveals taste and cultural sophistication.

The necessity of cultural refinement that included dress and the domestic environment as a prerequisite for social mobility did not escape contemporaries. The late-Enlightenment popular philosopher Christian Garve pointed to the interrelationship between (cultural) knowledge and material in the gradual creation of middle-class identity. Unless he is born into a fashionable and opulent household, the member of the middle class equips himself and his household in stages, according to how much his increased wealth will allow him to purchase at any given time. In most instances this will lead to a mixture between old and new, yet with the goal of eventually replacing the old with the new as soon as circumstances allow.[57] Publications such as the *Journal* created the knowledge and this trajectory in the pursuit of cultural refinement.

Beyond the aesthetic appeal of the domestic environment as a reflection of its inhabitants' taste, the *Journal* underscored the importance of the physical comfort it provides for the body. English furnishings served as the much-imitated models. Discussions and pictorial representation of furniture and technical innovations were designed to provide a comfortable environment. Aesthetic and well-functioning heat sources, which many times corresponded in coloring and design with the other furniture in the room, offered increased comfort in the winter months.[58] These modern heating and light sources extended the time available for leisure-time activities. The Argand lamp, for example, significantly prolonged the time span available for reading and socializing and thus significantly restructured leisure. But even for these useful articles, the *Journal* insists on the importance of aesthetic properties and in their aesthetic usage to show people in the best possible light.[59]

Bertuch recommends the items for the beautification of the domestic sphere not only to his middle-class readership but also to the nobility. He suggests furniture designs for adoption at the court. In his discussion of new, fashionable light fixtures, for example, he expresses plans to show more examples by German artisans and recommends that the courts buy these domestic products in order to stimulate the economy. He argues for the consumption of domestic luxury items to break the predominance of exported luxury items.[60] As with other items of cultural consumption, the distinctions between the classes begin to be less important than issues of taste and levels of consumption.

THE CARE OF THE BODY AS ENTERTAINMENT

The care of the body was not only seen as a social responsibility and as a means to enhance the body's ability to experience pleasure; it also produced a series of practices that could be experienced as pleasurable in themselves. In popular philosophy and the medical discourse of the time, the perfectibility of the mind had its counterpart in the perfectibility of the body.[61] This link began to free the care of the body from the earlier association with vanity. By connecting the pursuit of the care of the body—and, by association, of beauty and attractiveness—with health and "naturalness," the door was opened to a host of cultural practices and the material objects associated with them.

In the beautification of the face, the medical discourse and its popularization in the periodical press—for example, in the *Journal*—emphasized those products that were not perceived as harmful and which underscored the health of the skin and cleanliness. Rubbing the skin clean, combing and brushing the hair, and other hygienic measures such as cleansing the teeth were part of the beauty routine. They were part of the *cosmetica medicamenta* (remedies to heal the skin from blemishes) that began to replace the decorative cosmetics.[62] If the latter were used, they should seem natural and offer a similacrum of natural beauty. The reevaluation of cosmetics in the medical discourse and popular philosophy (which can only be alluded to here) opened the door for its increased use by the middle class. Not unlike fashion, it is both part of the civilizing process of refinement and social distinction within the middle class. In addition, the nexus of cosmetics, beauty, health, happiness, and self-fulfillment was part of the immensely popular field of dietetics and macrobiotics (a bibliography on the subject lists two thousand titles in 1801).[63] It signals the importance that began to be attached to the care of the body to prevent illness, foster the physical and mental well-being of the self, and achieve beauty. This well-being is an important prerequisite to the enhanced ability to perceive the stimulation of the forms of entertainment as creating the sensation of pleasure.

Functional furniture and implements—such as the shaving table for men, new heaters for bathwater, and the creation of bathrooms in general—facilitated the care of the self, making it easier to integrate hygiene into the daily routine and rendering it less tedious. Affording the care of the body a distinct place and time in daily life signaled a higher degree of valorization of the body and resulted in more sensitivity to its real and perceived needs. The numerous articles on medical issues bespeak the new interest in the body. Maintaining a healthy body is seen not only as the prerequisite for daily activities but also as an appropriate canvas for adornment. Health and beauty are conceptually linked: health is seen as the only and most unfailing means to achieve beauty. The editor therefore includes contributions on cleanliness as a means for the construction of a healthy body as the basis not only for beauty but, more importantly, for a healthy mind. In addition to dispensing beauty advice based on the scientific and (more often than not) conventional or anecdotal wisdom of the time, the *Journal* provides information on the latest technical inventions. The (relatively) modern bathroom, which consists of a heatable room near the kitchen, took advantage of the water supply for the hot-water heater and the wastewater disposal (2:169). Yet the advice on the necessity of bathing obviously did not find enough followers when it was first published (1790). The *Journal* took the topic up again a few years later—this time with the recommendation of the editor himself and supported by the preeminent medical authority of the day in Weimar, Christoph Wilhelm Hufeland, who attributed the frequent occurrence of gout and afflictions of the nerves in German society to the failure to take advantage of the health benefits of an immersion in water (2:139). He hoped to convince the readership of its virtues by offering a brief history of the bath.

We have to keep in mind that the sanitary conditions in the often old houses in the cities were poor; often the chamber pots were placed in the bedroom or the kitchen, the space for bathing facilities was limited, and transporting and heating water was a major undertaking.[64] These material conditions—rather than a lack of interest—might have discouraged people to follow the advice. By giving practical technical suggestions for how to overcome the unpleasant conditions for the care of the body, the *Journal* rendered the activities in question more pleasurable and thus more desirable. Innovations in heating systems, plumbing, and fixtures created a more convenient and luxurious site for the care of the body, yet as is often the case in the *Journal* and many other publications by Bertuch, there seems to be a need to use pleasure not as an end in itself but as a means to a higher end. In this case, the implied argument is that by making it more pleasant for people to take baths, they will indulge, and this, in turn, would have significant health benefits. Thus it was not the pleasures in their own right but the medicinal function of the care of the body that was foregrounded.

Especially in the gardens of their summer residences, many families included bathing facilities, which they placed inconspicuously at the end of the garden behind shrubs and hedges. These ranged from small enclosures for a primitive tub, to a simple tub outside in an arbor, to the most elaborate and luxurious pavilions with marble tubs and sitting rooms. Even the most famous garden theorist, the philosopher Christian Cayus Lorenz Hirschfeld, discusses bathing facilities and their placement and design, thus attesting to the desirability of these modern conveniences. They should be secluded and hidden from curious glances in a low spot, or behind bushes and in the shade of low-hanging branches. The pleasurable sensation of the water can be enhanced by the olfactory pleasures of fragrant shrubbery and flowers.[65] Unlike the *Journal,* which sees the need to foreground its health benefits, Hirschfeld—not surprisingly for a designer—emphasizes the aesthetic qualities but also, maybe less expected, the sensual elements of bathing facilities. A scented environment enhances the pleasure of the bath by its sensual impact. Andrea van Dülmen discusses more elaborate luxurious facilities, such as those in the garden of the Brentanos in Rödelsheim. A contemporary reports:

> "Under shrubbery a narrow entrance to a bathing temple opened up. Light white fabric covers the walls of the forehall dimly lit by a cupola and the bathing alcove with its mirrors and sofas and the partially sunken white marble basin." Maxe von Arnim . . . completes this description: "There was a small Greek temple, in which a marble basin invited the bathers. In the bath you were not bored because behind a large mirrored pane was a *volière* in which many colored birds flew to and fro. When we wanted to take a bath, the uncle had rose petals scattered throughout the whole room."

> "Da öffnete sich unter einem Gebüsch der schmale Eingang

zu einem Badetempel. Zarte weiße Gewänder bedecken die Wände der durch eine Kuppel dämmernd erhellten Vorhalle und der Badenische mit ihren Spiegeln und Sofas und der halbversenkten Wanne aus weißem Marmor." Maxe von Arnim . . . vervollständigt diese Schilderung: "Da war der kleine griechische Tempel, in dem ein Marmorbassin zum Bade einlud. Im Bad wurde einem die Zeit nicht lang, denn hinter einer großen Spiegelscheibe sah man eine Volière, in der viele bunte Vögel hin und her flogen. Wenn wir baden wollten, ließ der Onkel den ganzen Raum mit Rosenblättern bestreuen."[66]

Comfort and aesthetics combine to indulge all of the bather's senses. The pleasant visual appearance of the environment is complemented by the olfactory delight of the rose petals and the shrubbery around it; the cool of the marble and the warmth of the water stimulate the skin's sense of touch, and the sounds of the birds and the other aural stimulations of nature in the garden round out the multisensory experience. Even in this form of entertainment with its layering of multiple sensations, care is taken to avoid the boredom of absolute stillness. The "bird-theater"—the fashionable *volière*—invites the gaze to wander, following the movements of the birds.

If the garden was located on a natural river, bathing facilities were created to take advantage of these desirable features. The occupants partitioned off stretches of river with large sheets for privacy and created inconspicuous access for bathing and swimming.

In addition to bathing at home and in private gardens, the *Journal* also advocated public bathing facilities in clean rivers and streams and encouraged investors to provide such safe and healthy facilities in every city (e.g., the so-called bathing boats [*Badeschiffe*]) (2:174).[67]

The care of the body as a form of entertainment was also advocated in the traditional form of summer entertainment, the visit to the spas, which began to attract larger numbers and more diverse groups of visitors. Since the medicinal advantages of the spas were beyond dispute at the time, the *Journal* focused its attention on making the experience as comfortable as possible so that people, especially women, could take full advantage of all the forms of entertainment offered there. It advocated the so-called *Bad-Uniform,* innovative new clothing designed to make the spa experience more healthful. By simplifying the fashion to an uncomplicated uniform, women would be able to partake more readily of the opportunities for exercising their bodies and improving their health. Simple uniforms required less time for dressing and hence left more time for walking and other healthful outdoor activities (1:104–7). Women's traditional formal dress limited them to playing cards, knitting, and similar sedentary activities, thus restricting the healthful effects of the spa treatment, which depended largely on exercise in addition to drinking from the mineral springs. More informal, less binding dress made walking, dancing, and other physical forms of entertainment more comfortable and thus encouraged them.[68]

The "call for riding outfits for women" ("Aufforderung und Vorschlag zu einer neuen Reitkleidung für Damen" [2:57–65]) suggests that more functional and attractive riding clothes for women would encourage more women to take part in this form of entertainment. The text argues that women have obtained a more equal status in recent times, as evidenced by the fact that there are female poets, hunters, warriors, and equestrians who equal their male counterparts in skill and ability. Proper dress reconciles femininity—the softness of her character—with expert riding skills, allowing women the healthful and pleasant occupation of riding without jeopardizing feminine modesty (2:64). Seemingly unimportant forms of cultural practice (suitable riding fashion) created cracks in the ostensibly firm contours of gendered identity (*Geschlechtscharaktere*) by increasing women's physical and symbolic range of mobility. Dress played an important enabling role in this process.

The care of the body as a prerequisite for health is also addressed in the description of modern inventions such as the *Gymnastikon* (2:132–37), an exercise machine working upper and lower body at the same time. It was said to produce as much exercise as a walk of two to ten miles within one hour, all in the comfort and privacy of one's own room. It could be modified for feeble or disabled persons and could be equipped with tables for reading and writing. This efficient, healthful leisure-time activity could replace the few forms of physical entertainment remaining in modern society: strolling along the promenades, dancing, badminton ("Federball"), and pool ("Billiardspiele"). Other physical forms of entertainment, such as various indoor ball games, rocking horses ("Schaukelpferde"), ringtoss ("Ringelrennen"), and the various modifications of bowling ("verschiedenen Modificationen des Kugel- und Kegelschiebens") (2:133), had fallen out of favor by this time.

Beyond the physical benefits of these forms of pleasurable occupation, the most fashionable outdoor activities also had important mental benefits, as they provided an important source of stimulation, as we will discuss in more detail in chapter 8. The facile stimulation of the senses and the imagination that the skillfully cultured nature could provide was considered immensely beneficial for the visitors' mental health. The domestic garden, the landscape garden, travel, and spas reinserted the body into nature—albeit a culturally transformed nature designed to heighten the stimulation of a natural setting.

FASHION AND GENDER

In the *Journal,* fashion was not limited to the female body but depicted and described both male and female fashions. The comprehensive approach to fashion lent an air of seriousness and importance while at the same time ensuring a wider audience for the publication. In addition, the inclusion of the male fashionable body—if to a lesser degree—suggests that fashion could play a signifying role not only in the narrow confines of the domestic sphere, as the nucleus of the private sphere, but also in the public sphere.

Fashion critics have predominantly followed J. C. Flügel's argument from his *The Psychology of Clothes* (1930)[69] that this change in masculine dress toward the dark suit and away from the flashy fashionable clothing of the courtier signals a "great masculine renunciation" focusing all attention on women as the purveyors of fashion and all that was associated with it. With regard to the gendering of fashion in the *Spectator,* Mackie suggests that "men are admonished to keep their distance from this feminized arena of signification; their bodies, it is implied, are emasculated by the marks of the mode. Sexual difference removes bourgeois women more completely from the arena of production, relegating them more and more to the spheres of leisured consumption. At the same time it puts certain kinds of consumption and leisure activities outside the bounds of the properly masculine."[70] For the gendering of fashion as forwarded in the *Journal,* this is no longer a valid (or at least not an exclusive) explanation. This discussion must be read in the context of the earlier oppositional identity formation, where the perceived simplicity associated with masculine dress seems to suggest the exclusive focus on inner values such as stability and reliability. This understated dress code was more than a means of distinguishing the bourgeois from the courtier. At the same time, it became linked with and a sign of an almost obsessive gendering of character and identity, culminating in the notion of *Geschlechtscharaktere*.

This change represented not a renunciation of social difference but a sign of a shift in attention at the end of the eighteenth century to more subtle distinctions with which males distinguished themselves from other males within their own class. Custom tailoring, the subtle nuances of fabric and cut, the details in lining and undergarments, and the quality of construction and assembly offered occasions for subtle distinction. They did not erase the sartorial marks but merely replaced them with different ones. The subtlety of male fashions suggested a seriousness and stability of character and a focus on inner values— seemingly avoiding the negative aspects associated with expressive fashion, such as excessive consumption, faddishness, and fickleness—while capitalizing on fashion's positive associations. The latter included a sense of going with the time, of modernity, and "newness," and of utilizing fashion's visualization of taste as a marker of social distinction in men's private and public dress.

It is true that during the eighteenth century men's and women's clothes began to differ markedly. Dress and fashion played an important role in the construction of gender. As Elizabeth Wilson writes, "Fashion is obsessed with gender, [it] defines and redefines the gender boundary."[71] Fashion became more and more associated with women and less with men, although the *Journal* discusses men's fashion as well, especially in its earlier issues. Yet throughout its life the *Journal* made a point of addressing both male and female readers. As we discussed above, the bourgeois woman's appearance increasingly became an artistic production. Individualized romantic love and the marriage market based on personal attraction are causes for this need for uniqueness within similarity. Fashion is an important means of creating this desirable distinctiveness.

Other studies have pointed to the competition to get noticed as one of the reasons why especially women indulge in fashion. Since women have a passive role in courtship, the only way to influence the very important outcome is to stand out from the crowd; thus Vischer sees fashion as an indicator for "the mania to trump others in attracting men."[72] The *Journal* cautiously acknowledges the role of fashionable clothing in making women more attractive to men: "If indeed it is true that women keep the purpose of fashion's role in pleasing men in mind to some degree then it follows that they should know what pleases them" ("Uebringens, wenn es wahr ist, daß die Frauen bei ihrem Putz auch, wenigstens nebenbei, den Zweck haben, den Männern zu gefallen, so folgt daraus, daß diese doch wissen müssen, was dazu gehöre, um ihnen zu gefallen" [3:13]). The *Journal* thus offers to educate women in what men like.

Clothing not only defines and redefines gender boundaries but is one of the most important cultural implements for articulating and territorializing human corporeality—for mapping erotogenic zones and for affixing a sexual identity.[73] While middle-class oppositional dressing condemning the lasciviousness of courtly fashions focused on restraint, self-control, and "affect transformation" (Elias), it also created ways to manage attention to the body.[74] More importantly for our topic, as part of the civilizing process, fashion creates a dialogue between the natural and the artificial and is thus an important means to foster erotic attraction because it conceals and reveals at the same time:

> For women, dress beautifies, it covers flaws, emphasizes forms that nature did not emphasize enough. Women are given more choices, they are able to charm by veiling and unveiling, they can alter their appearances with a different cut, colors, or contrast of coloring. Like a world traveler, she can choose from all national costumes. . . . She can conceal her body with the mask of dress heightening and accenting her charms.

> Bei ihr [Frau] verschönert das Kleid, es bedeckt die Mängel, es hebt Formen mehr hervor, welche die Natur nicht zulänglich geschaffen. Ihr sind größere Spielräume der Wahl gegeben, sie übt die Zaubereien der Entblößung und Verhüllung, sie wechselt mit dem Schnitt, alle Farben und Farbengegensäze stehen ihr zu Gebote. Wie ein großer Reisender hüllt sie sich in alle Nationaltrachten. . . . Sie weiß ihren wahren Leib durch eine vollständige Maske zu verbergen, ihre Reize zu verherrlichen, sie im höchsten Preise anzubringen. (4:27)

In addition, the eroticization of the body and the quest for novelty in fashion help to retain desire and longing within the confines of a stable, long-term relationship. The *Journal* hints at the role of clothing in the self-transformation primarily of women in order to retain newness. If this transformation, this play of revealing and hiding the body, is achieved with rare and exotic materials, the effect is even more rarefied and unique ("je ferner das Material herkommt, je teurer, desto beliebter" [4:31]).

In erotic attraction, the fantasy of the body became more important than direct (visual or physical) access to the body. Concealment hints at the hidden body and allows for the sensations produced by the memory or the anticipation of the (nude) body to be experienced as pleasurable. This involvement of the pleasures of the imagination participates in the cultural transformation of sexuality into erotic desire.

Indulging the gaze while avoiding the touch created the necessary distance for the powers of the imagination to thrive. The manipulation of clothing to create the fantasy is as pleasurable a form of entertainment as enjoying the gaze in which the observer objectifies the subject of the gaze "in the pursuit of scopophilic and voyeuristic pleasures."[75] The ideology of the time suggests that erotic desire is gender-specific. Men take an either more active (scopophilic) or more passive (voyeuristic) pleasure in looking at the female body as an object of imaginary pleasures. Women, on the other hand, derive the pleasures of fantasy from manipulating their image through decorative arts in order to entice the male gaze in which they then see themselves mirrored and validated.[76]

7

Sociability and Entertainment

EPISTOLARY CULTURE AS A FORM
OF SOCIABLE ENTERTAINMENT

Reading in the tradition of the urban conversation that the *Spectator* and the *Tatler* had introduced to the German states—and the participation in an epistolary culture were probably the most important forms of sociable entertainment during the time frame under investigation. Letters not only reported about events but built and rearranged alliances. The exchange of letters with acquaintances and friends contributed to the bourgeois change of mentalities. As a communicative exchange between private citizens within the private sphere yet transcending the domestic realm of the family, it extended people's immediate social nexus. Epistolary exchanges became important means not only of self-analysis and self-expression but also of friendship and sociability (*Geselligkeit*). The cult of sensibility (*Empfindsamkeit*)—so important for the development of the desiring self at the core of cultural consumption—would not have been possible without the extensive and intensive scrutiny of one's personality in these (written) exchanges. The new form of epistolary writing, emphasizing the primacy of inner cogency over external rules and rejecting the learned mechanical organization of letter writing, empowered women and nonprofessional men to take part in this cultural activity, contributing significantly to the creation of a broader cultural public sphere for the bourgeoisie. Gellert's treatise *Briefe, nebst einer praktischen Abhandlung von dem guten Geschmack in Briefen* (Letters and a practical guide to good taste in letters) (1751) considered women especially suited for this new epistolary form and regarded his exchange with Christiane Karoline Lucius (1739–1833) as exemplary.[1] With their pedagogical, social, and cultural functions, there are multiple spheres of influence among private letters, (auto)biographical writing, essayistic writing, and epistolary novels. In addition to the famous male correspondences—Goethe's being the most prominent, of course—women like Sophie La Roche and Elisa von der Recke also maintained expansive correspondences in which travel descriptions, letters, and autobiographical reflections played an important role.

Beyond the well-known letters on literary taste formation such as the letter exchanges between Lessing and Mendelssohn on tragedy ("Lessing-Mendelssohn Briefwechsel zum Trauerspiel"), epistolary culture also plays a vital part in the enhancement of a more broadly defined cultural taste, especially for women. In addition to the traditional moral conduct books such as Campe's *Väterlicher Rath an meine Tochter* (Advice of a father to his daughter), books like Sophie La Roche's *Briefe an Lina* (Letters to Lina) (1785)[2] combine advice on moral education and conduct[3] with advice on the proper use of material culture in the creation of the bourgeois lifestyle (*Lebensart*) and its forms of sociability.[4] These letters focus on the development of taste regarding dress, interior design, cooking, the presentation of food, and the use of decorative items as conversation pieces and means to please the eye of the inhabitants and visitors of the domestic sphere. It becomes clear that the proper display of taste is considered a marker of one's social standing, cultural capital, and prestige.[5]

Experimental in nature, letter writing played an important role in the development of thinking and especially feeling and was thus instrumental in the change of mentalities that came to be associated with the age of sensibility. Epistolary exchanges fostered self-awareness and established emotionally intimate relationships by exploring the crevices of the soul and giving voice to feelings, longings, and wishes. Letter writing played an important role both in the discursive formation of new gendered social identities and in the social formations of friendship and erotic love. Letters became a codification of intimacy. For many women, the epistolary exchange with distant friends represented significant social connections.[6] Beyond fostering sustained intellectual and emotive exchange, epistolary culture discovered not just the other but also the self. Both actual letter exchanges and epistolary novels were intended for public consumption. These texts took on the role of entertainment for readers as they observed the lives constructed in the pages of these intimate texts.

Epistolary novels (La Roche's *Die Geschicte des Fräulein von Sternheim* [The story of Lady Sternheim, 1771], Goethe's *Die Leiden des jungen Werthers* [The sufferings of young Werther, 1774], La Roche's *Rosaliens Briefe an ihre Freundin Marianne von St*** [Rosalie's letters to her friend Marianne von St**, 1780–81]), autobiographical writings (Goethe's *Dichtung und Wahrheit* [Truth and fiction, 1811–33]), diaries, and autobiographically inspired fiction, constituting the individual genres of epistolary culture, developed interpretative and literary skills and the powers of the imagination. As novels suggested the immediacy of the correspondence, actual correspondences strove for literary qualities. Writers like Bettina von Arnim (1785–1859) foregrounded the literariness of their correspondence by altering original letters and creating new ones.

The most famous examples of epistolary forms of sociability as a form of entertainment—as a kind of long-distance salon—are the letters by Karoline Günderrode (1780–1806), Caroline Schlegel-Schelling (1763–1809), Sophie Mereau (1770–1806), and Rachel von Varnhagen (1771–1833). An interesting example is von Varnhagen's *Bildnisse*,[7] edited by her husband after her death, which represents an epistolary construct of a "literary" salon transcending the present and instead spanning Rachel's lifetime. A selection of letters from those correspondents who were interesting to her throughout the various stages of her life were arranged in epistolary vignettes (*Bildnisse*), with a biographical sketch added by her husband. He not only created a particular biographical persona of his wife, which emerged from the letters of famous contemporaries to her, but also shed light on the lives of her correspondents, contributing to a description of cultural history (*Zeitgeschichte*).

These forms of entertaining self-analysis were not only instrumental in effecting significant changes in mentalities associated with the discourse of sensibility but also constituted an important facet of middle-class sociability as entertainment that extended beyond family and friends to the (local) community.

THE STRUCTURATION OF MIDDLE-CLASS SOCIABILITY

In addition to solitary forms of entertainment, the new semiprivate culture of sociability was an important site for many forms of cultural entertainment for the (upper) middle class. Many forms of cultural entertainment and consumption were only possible within the social dynamic of the group. Beyond being a (historically variable) system of interpersonal relationships, constituting an integral part of the middle-class lifestyle between the intimate family and society at large, sociability was an important aspect of the pleasurable enrichment of everyday culture. Gatherings included not only friends and family members but also guests, which, depending on the household, could include business associates, academic colleagues, and visiting travelers (usually famous contemporaries, writers, intellectuals, artists, etc.). The larger and more varied the groups participating in sociability were, the higher the degree of novelty and pleasurable stimulation. Shifting and changing groupings were considered desirable as new members and constellations brought a new impetus and dynamic into the forms of sociability.

Although the forms of sociability around 1800 included association with friends, this has to be distinguished from the concept of friendship as it is more broadly conceived. Sociability lacks the stability, durability, intensity, and intimacy of friendship. Both have a similar broadly conceived goal, the care of the self, but they take different paths and fulfill unique needs. The discourse of friendship—with its roots in the conduct literature (*Klugheitslehre*) of the seventeenth century[8]—flourished earlier in the century as a dominant social-ethical category ensuring mutual trust and support. It stabilized the social fabric by offering a sense of reliability counterbalancing the decrease in the integrative hierarchical powers of absolutist society. Friendship had an important literary component as literature played the decisive role in creating models and patterns for the underlying change of mentality associated with the formation of the bourgeoisie.

In the formation of bourgeois identity in the early part of the century, sociability was already theorized as an important prerequisite for (mental) well-being of the individual.[9] In an obvious contrast to forms of social engagement at the court, the Enlightenment periodical *Der Gesellige* (1748–50)[10] suggested that sociability was based on a cluster of social virtues: equality instead of social gradation, voluntary action instead of following orders, trust instead of fear, empathy instead of affect.[11] Grimm defines sociability (*Geselligkeit*) as the inclination and ability to enjoy the company of others and to enjoy socializing with them, as following the rules and duties of sociability, and as the activity of socializing itself.[12] Sociability not only expressed a desire to be in the company of others but also entailed a duty to foster one's social skills, which were seen as essential for the functioning of societies with a higher level of differentiation. Both sociability and friendship foster social skills governing the proper conduct in word and action that were desirable for the middle class: "He who wants to be sociable has to be polite, agreeable, quick and talkative and observe all rules of proper conduct" ("Wer gesellig seyn will, der muß freundlich, höflich, gefällig, munter, gesprächig seyn, und alle Pflichten der guten Aufführung beobachten").[13] Proper conduct in the company of others entailed maintaining a friendly demeanor, avoiding excessive fashionability and frivolity in clothing and expression, refraining from any coarse behavior, and observing the given social distinctions and regulating the forms of social give-and-take: "The sociable person represents the proper balance between the too personal and the too distant" ("So steht der Gesellige für den rechten Mittelweg zwischen dem Zu-Persönlichen und dem Zu-Distanzierten").[14] An extensive list of (practical) rules concerning the intersocial conduct governing everyday life in various settings is at the heart of Adolf von Knigge's extensive late-Enlightenment treatise on desirable middle-class deportment in *Ueber den Umgang mit Menschen* (1788). With the gesture of the popular philosopher, he hopes to give practical advice for harmonious conduct and the regulation of a wide range of social relationships and individual behaviors, since "it is unwise to dismiss the innocent social conventions if one wishes to live and exert influence in society" ("es ist nicht weise gehandelt, die unschuldigen Gebräuche der Gesellschaft zu verachten, wenn man in der Gesellschaft leben und würken will").[15] Proper social conduct and interpersonal skills lay the groundwork for a meaningful, successful, harmonious, and pleasurable middle-class lifestyle.

The discourse of friendship had intensified within the movement of sensibility (c. 1770) and added a significant emotional (and individualistic) dimension to the earlier ethical emphasis on mutual social support and reliability. Already in *Der Gesellige* we see the close link between sociability and friendship. The sensual, emotive dimension to

friendship provided the core that organizes sociability.[16] Sociability signifies an important part of the civilizing process.[17] It functions as a
social, psychological, emotional, and ethical utopia.

Habermas sees literary-critical communication as the important
part of the literary public sphere where the middle class formed its positions on the way to the political public sphere. Lepenies (and also
Arendt)[18] considers sociability a form of social experimentation in class
transcendence, or a utopia—yet without true political persuasiveness.

The critical and the utopian dimensions of sociability began to
lose their effectiveness in the last decades of the eighteenth century.
Mauser attributes this decline to the emergence of national sentiment
as a force of social organization.[19] Enlightenment and sentimental
sociability were based on the idea that personal value and affinity
allowed the individual to join the group at will and also leave it again.
The concept of a nation assumes that the association of the *Volk* is historically determined and that a national community supersedes individualistic tendencies. I would argue that by the end of the century, both
of these dimensions of sociability become supplemented by the forms
of entertainment with their pursuit of the sensation of pleasure and psychological well-being.

Sociability represents a notable confluence of bourgeois forms of
entertainment within fluid, loosely assembled groups. It contributes to
the enhancement and aestheticization of everyday life and represents a
significant part of the middle-class lifestyle. Konrad Feilchenfeldt's
argument that sociability took on the dimension of performativity, of
the staging of one's aesthetic *habitus*,[20] is certainly an important part of
this understanding of the concept. While his sociopolitical focus—
developed with the Jewish salon in mind—is on sociability as the playful creation of an alternate (intercultural) social reality, my focus is on
both the differentiation and display of middle-class identity, that is, on
the performativity of *habitus* as well as the pleasurable enrichment of
the everyday lifestyle. For many forms of entertainment the social
aspect was a prerequisite; they could only be enjoyed in the company
of others.

The aestheticization of life is reminiscent of Schlegel's romantic
ideal of the poeticization of life and Schleiermacher's understanding of
sociability as a forum that extricates the individual from mundane,
everyday culture and thus contributes to true *Bildung*.[21] For Schleiermacher both the sphere of work and, more originally, the domestic realm

are sites of alienation that hinder *Bildung*. The entertainment value of sociability, its "amusement," stems from the loose, free-flowing structure of the event with its variety of activities, the heterogeneity of talents, and the diversity of the participants' viewpoints and backgrounds. Schleiermacher admits that in his form of sociability—spanning a wide variety of cultural practices—the core is by necessity dilettante culture.[22] Yet while Schleiermacher clearly distances his concept of sociability from the utilitarian sense that it embraced in Enlightenment thought, he also distances himself from the ascetic classicist notion of *Bildung*. He does so with a bad conscience, it seems. Because Schleiermacher sees sociability as self-reflexive, it can serve as a site for *Bildung*.[23] *Bildung* rescues his concept of sociability from the odium that classical and romantic thought associated with its inherent dilettantism.

Yet the concept of sociability developed in this study differs from that of both Schlegel and Schleiermacher as it extends to all areas of culture (not only to high culture), especially everyday culture and even technology. It encompasses a whole realm of cultural influences. These range from the journal culture enhancing cultural practices and the middle-class lifestyle, to the aesthetics of the new garden culture, to fashion in dress and design, to the culture of food, and to technical innovations. Thus by definition, sociability was a phenomenon of the (dilettante) culture of consumption ranging over a continuum of activities and was not limited to high culture. Sociable entertainment culture helped to create a "middle ground" of taste that could accommodate the various levels of interest, educational preparations, and specializations and participate in the formation of the particular community. Sociability's goal is to provide a setting for the various forms of entertainment that offer variation to the bourgeois lifestyle and thus provide enough stimulation to keep boredom at bay. Unlike Schleiermacher, I do not see sociability as an alternative realm to the tedium of everyday life, as a kind of modern version of an earlier culture of festivals (*Festkultur*). Instead, the forms of entertainment, as an important part of sociability, enrich and enhance the everyday experience by sprinkling it with bits and pieces of sociable entertainment, thus altering and transforming the overall middle-class lifestyle itself. The intervals between festivals and workdays become shorter and the delineation between the two less pronounced. Sociability thus reshapes the strict distinction between work and entertainment—between the tedium of the "everyday" and "special occasions"—and thus enhances the middle-class lifestyle.

This form of sociability is not based solely on literature and critical discourse, as Habermas suggests, but includes the whole range of cultural practices and many forms of cultural consumption, which represented different yet also very important aspects of the formation of a cultural public sphere. The material design of the domestic sphere expressed and helped to shape the status of its inhabitants and their lifestyle as the cultural objects and practices mirrored important aspects of middle-class identity formation and group differentiation.

These forms of entertainment within the sociability of the domestic sphere constitute a site between the private sphere and the public sphere yet without direct or explicit political "directedness." As an extension of the domestic forms of sociability, they also extended the informal gathering and more or less casual meeting of friends and acquaintances into cultural realms outside the home, such as the theater and other performances, the museum, promenades in popular areas, and balls.

These forms of (extended) sociability were attended by personal friends, business associates, and visitors and combined the sensual pleasures of food and drink with the less physical pleasures of conversation, reading, enjoying the aesthetics of the gardens, looking at artwork, listening to and making music, and frequenting the theater. They ranged from informal breakfasts with colleagues and their wives to its most formalized manifestation, the salon. The gatherings at private homes for forms of cultural entertainment (e.g., conversation, readings, enjoyment of the latest literary and visual artifacts, food and drink) differed not so much in the forms of entertainment as in the level of sophistication, the degrees of consumption, the social and intellectual status of the guests, and the level of disposable wealth.

Goethe's novel *Die Wahlverwandtschaften* offers unique glimpses into the phenomenon of dilettante culture (*Liebhaberei*) as an expression of modern mentalities (garden mania, tableaux, and other forms of entertainment). I see this novel in close relationship with the dilettantism sketch. In the novel, Goethe embodies the mentality that drives the dilettante and which he contrasts with true cultural competency, or "art."[24] The contributions in the *Journal des Luxus und der Moden* not only allow glances at these forms of social entertainment but, more importantly, provide guidance in how to organize these events, how to dress for them, and what kind of ambience to create. For example, a description of a breakfast for which colleagues and their wives gather before the men head off to work explains to the reader the proper decorum, dress, hospitality, and conduct. It also makes clear that these kinds of gatherings provided a layer of communication situated between the professional level and the personal level. Sociability provided a transitory sphere between the family and the larger social network.

While this form of small, quasi-intimate gathering between friendship and professional exchange was appropriate for certain occasions and group identities within the middle class, others required more elaborate and formal evening gatherings. Some forms of sociability were limited to men, such as the daytime visits to the coffeehouses as a break from the office by the wealthy Hamburg merchants, or to women, such as the daytime visits to the homes of other women. Beyond enhancing the sphere of the mundane by interrupting it with pleasurable social activities, as forms of symbolic socialization these practices and the material surroundings associated with them helped to shape mentalities, habits, tastes and preferences. They thus formulate the social values of a group or social figuration (Elias) while allowing for individuality and differentiation. "Figuration" resembles Bourdieu's concepts of "field" and "habit," according to which social beings are situated in a net of intellectual, affective, social, economic, and geographical interdependencies. Figuration according to Elias is the observable net of interrelationships of interdependent human beings that manifests itself in symbolic representations and specific formations. It is not a static concept but a process of differentiation and functionalization of society that takes place within a net of interdependent discourses. In this transformation of the corporate society into a modern society, the symbolic forms of representation within sociability played an important role. The individual strands of these figurations are not intentional linear processes of transformation but rather contingent processes of dynamization, of the interplay of social interaction with which the individual participates in the social construction of "reality."

Sociability denotes a flexible, loose, momentary assembly of participants during moments of leisure for the common goal of entertainment. It therefore required an elaborate organization of instances of entertainment. They were governed by affective factors (pleasure), by a similarity of lifestyles, and by an "intent to gather."[25] These instances of sociability allowed for the functionalization of society by interspersing compensatory moments with the rigorous and more inflexible realm of professional and working life. By providing connections and negotiations among various spheres and creating larger and ever-shifting fluid communities, sociable entertainment offered important spaces where taste and thus social positioning could be negotiated. This net of social connections was important for the formation of the self-definition of the middle class and the differentiation within this class.

The forms of sociability often reached beyond the particular region and connected people throughout the German states and Europe. Especially within certain groups, such as the intellectuals or the merchants, the members visited other highly visible members of their layer of the middle class on their travels. Making use of introductory letters or taking advantage of the *jour fixe* to introduce themselves or renew earlier contacts, they created a sense of community within this specific group.

Like the periodical press, conduct literature allows glimpses at how eighteenth-century contemporaries viewed the nexus between lifestyle (cultural practices, education, the aestheticization of the domestic environment, the fashionable, well-dressed body), sociability, and the projection of one's identity to others. More overtly than in her novels, La Roche in her epistolary conduct collection of letters *Briefe an Lina,* written to an adolescent girl in preparation for her role as woman of the house, illuminates this nexus. In her virtual "room-by-room" tour through Lina's middle-class household, La Roche gives a systematic overview of the bourgeois lifestyle. The description of the parlor, where visitors are entertained, is especially relevant as the site for first impressions. The maternal friend emphasizes the importance of the pleasant, yet not opulent, decor as a suitable backdrop for the hosts, who in this context will appear upbeat and competent. This first impression is important because reading the appearance of the interior design (and the dress of the inhabitants) gives the visitors good insights into their social position and their taste; these indicators allow the guests to situate their hosts within the layers of the middle class. In addition, a pleasant material environment will encourage conversation because it has a positive effect on the psychic disposition and mood of its occupants.[26] Certain material objects, such as the coffee and tea machine, proved a magnet for sociability, serving as a point of assembly and a conversation opener. As the physical environment plays an important role in influencing the mood of its occupants, care must be taken to create the greatest possible level of comfort and stimulation. By providing pleasure, the beautified domestic sphere—enhanced with tasteful objects of material culture—plays an important role in the mental and physical well-being of its inhabitants and their guests.

This self-fashioning of the individual through forms of sociability occurs in an active exchange with others and with the environment, thus alleviating the by-products and effects of modernization: isolation, the experience of loneliness, and the sense of lack of control over the social and physical environment.[27] This compensatory function of sociability took place not only in love and friendship but also in the forms of companionship, in entertainment, in conversations, and even in such insignificant forms of exchange as culturally elevated gossip, such as, for example, the fashionable phenomenon of theater mania (*Theatromanie*).

As a media/celebrity event, the theater took its place in "conversations of gentlemen," among other topics such as horses, dogs, and women of ill repute.[28] The popularity of the theater as a social event, divorced from any critical assessment of it as an art form or of the intricacies of specific performances, manifested itself in the practice of using names of actors as the solutions to crossword puzzles in newspapers. The divorce of the famous actor Unzelmann was the talk of the town; a large number of anecdotal or descriptive articles on matters related to the theater indicate widespread interest. The entertainment value of this particular manifestation of *Theatromanie* as a topic of conversation and gossip has little to do with the artistic or specular entertainment of the institution but rather takes on an independent social function. People derive enjoyment from anecdotal stories about public figures, in particular those whose profession makes them risqué to begin with, such as actors. Titillating stories about Iffland's alleged homosexuality or about the affairs, divorces, and remarriages of other actors were obviously more effective than gossip about completely unknown persons. At times the gossip was consumed by people who had only the most distant acquaintance with the subject matter. As a means of social group formation and differentiation, it allowed individuals to demonstrate that they were conversant in current affairs, aware of the fashionable trends or popular public persons. It served as a topic of noncontroversial conversation. One could easily establish rapport with others who most likely felt the same sense of amazement over the follies of the famous, thus aiding in the formation of a sense of belonging to a group by creating a common object of amusement or contempt. Just like appropriate clothes, activities, and houses, such inconsequential aspects of cultural life played a part in group formations within the middle class.

While this socializing function aided in the formation of a sense of belonging to a group, it also allowed for differentiation. After all, people were able to determine which kind of gossip they participated in and to what degree. Stories and newspaper reports about details on the progress of the new theater building also seem to have been popular. Instead of signaling a special affinity for the theater as institution, these stories constitute yet another topic for conversation that had the air of a higher level of sophistication than the more personal topics, especially those involving sexuality. Within the forms of cultural consumption of *Theatromanie,* levels of relative sophistication could distinguish the participants.

Other aspects of *Theatromanie* manifested themselves in art objects offered for general consumption. It was, for example, in vogue to produce and sell etchings of specific favorite scenes from theater and opera, such as the coronation procession from Schiller's *Die Jungfrau von Orleans.* They popularized certain aspects of these performances while at the same time integrating them into the decor of the middle-class household. Nonprofessional journals discussing the performance often focused on the most spectacular scenes and thus popularized them considerably. The *Journal* (3:136–38) praises the performance of Schiller's *Die Jungfrau von Orleans* in Berlin as superb and discusses the famous coronation scene in detail.[29] The same scenes can still be found in a contemporary calendar print (see fig. 24).

Once in a while a play became so fashionable—for example, F. H. Himmel's *Singspiel, Fanchon,* that it found its way into popular material culture. "A la Fanchon" was attached to anything from candy, cakes, and pipes to clothes and shoes and signifies an early phenomenon of idolization and possibly clever marketing.

As in *Theatromanie,* in conversations about literature and/or the reading and production of texts about art and music and their practical components, cultural value systems came under informal investigation. Yet unlike formal or professional criticism, these forms of exchange and orientation were unsystematic, subjective, spontaneous, and interrupted by associations, personal anecdotes, or gossip. The goal was not education, the search for truth, or the "correct" reading of a phenomenon but rather to be entertained by the pleasures of playful discovery. By avoiding the search for "eternal truths," this activity presupposes identities that are open to and value constant change, not necessarily a development to higher levels of *Bildung*. It represents a practice of bridging the degree of specializations in a functionalized society, of spanning the growing divide between the increasingly professionalized world of culture and cultural criticism and general consumers. We should keep in mind that a certain—relatively uniform—level of a humanistic education was limited to specific life stages, for example, that of university-educated young males before they immersed themselves in the various careers. In later life stages, the specialized professional life is no longer conducive to a thorough expertise in all areas of culture. Instead, the creation of a dilettante culture with its form of cultural entertainment allowed participation in the whole range of cultural activities to varying degrees.

Offering glimpses at possible harmonious integration of the self and its environment, this kind of nonprofessional, dilettante aesthetic experience produced a form of pleasure that integrated the sensual, psychological, and intellectual. This kind of aesthetic pleasure has been compared to a form of utopia that compels people to strive for an integrated development of the intellectual, sensual, and imaginative capabilities of the individual toward "completeness."[30]

These kinds of gatherings were organized as a mixture of whole-group activities and decentralized events. Loose groupings of people assembled for different activities, which they could leave for a different group at any time, within the same room or setting.[31]

SOCIABLE ENTERTAINMENT AND THE FORMATION OF COMMUNITIES

Friedrich Nicolai's form of sociable entertainment is representative for the wealthy middle-class intellectual and businessman. His gatherings were by invitation and took place in his new house furnished with all the modern luxuries of the time, the latest in fashionable furniture and design.[32] Due to Nicolai's far-reaching reputation as an intellectual and writer, artists and intellectuals traveling through Berlin visited him. They brought their cards to his bookstore in the first floor of his house, and a shop assistant prepared a list of visitors from which Nicolai selected the guest list for his Sunday invitations. In a time before public clubs or casinos, this could easily have been the literary and social center of middle-class life in Berlin, in which the solidity of hospitality was coupled with an appropriate degree of middle-class luxury.[33]

Another type of sociability could be found in the household of Johann Albert Reimarus (1729–1814). The medical doctor and professor of natural sciences at the Akademisches Gymnasium in Hamburg became known as a host of heavily attended teas at which family members joined friends, acquaintances, travelers, and business associates. On several evenings of the week the family stayed at home and opened their doors to guests and acquaintances who stayed as long as they wished. In these gatherings no one was noticeably in charge of leading the conversation. People participated or listened, and very few expectations or demands were placed on the guests to participate. This provided a stress-free environment where everyone felt at ease. The layout of the space was conducive to various forms of entertainment. Journals, illustrated books, and pictures invited the curious and provided more topics of conversation. In these gatherings it was not considered impolite to withdraw for a time to read or leaf through magazines:

> Here truly *bon ton* and informal sociability reigned; the visitor is put at pleasurable ease by what is and is not done for him or her. The family is frequently at home in the evenings, and everybody who is part of the regulars is allowed in. . . . People come and go, they stay for a short time or for longer periods. Nobody is anxiously keeping the conversation going and therefore it easily flows. . . . No subject is excluded and nobody feels pressure because he or she knows that he or she does not exert any and so time passes pleasantly seemingly without effort. Available are always several periodicals, newspapers, or a rare publication or a valuable book with etchings, which is pleasurable to look at because of its rarity and novelty. The guests are not embarrassed to peruse these artifacts and the others do not consider this as impolite. Often this activity provides new material for conversation. . . . In this household one can spend a whole pleasantly diverse evening without taking refuge in (card) games.

> Hier herrschte wahrhaft guter Ton und ungezwungener Umgang, und der Besuchende fühlt sich angenehm durch das, was man für ihn thut und—nicht thut. Die Familie ist mehrentheils Abends zuhause, und jedermann, der einmal

eingeführt worden ist, wird eingelassen. . . . man kommt, man geht, man bleibt längere oder kürzere Zeit. Niemand ist ängstlich die Unterhaltung aufrecht zu erhalten, und eben darum geht sie immer ihren Gang. . . . Kein Gegenstand der Unterredung ist ausgeschlossen; jedermann fühlt sich ohne Zwang, weil er weiß, daß er niemanden welchen auferlegt, und so vergeht die Zeit angenehm, ohne daß die eine oder die andere Person besonders bemüht scheint, sie so zu machen. In der Nähe liegen immer einige Journale, Zeitungen, irgendeine neue, merkwürdige Schrift, oder ein kostbares Werk mit Kupfern, das man mit Vergnügen sieht, weil man es nicht überall trifft. Man schämt sich nicht, eine Zeitlang zu blättern, und die Uebrigen sehen nichts unhöfliches darin. Häufig entsteht eben dadurch neuer Stoff zum Gespräche. . . . In diesem Haus verlebt man wirklich ganze Abende, ohne zum Spiele seine Zuflucht zu nehmen.[34]

The informality of these events is underscored by the fact that the host appeared and disappeared at will, leaving for urgent business or taking care of routine tasks in adjoining rooms. Reimarus's teas were famous for their informal ambience. He and his family combined the normal tasks of the household with conversation and other forms of entertainment; Reimarus often participated from an adjoining room in which he prepared medicines while his wife and daughters served tea.[35]

Communities within the middle class began to differentiate themselves from other groupings by the uniqueness of their lifestyle, a fact that was noted most frequently in travelers' descriptions of regional differences. Because of its uniquely "modern" conditions, Hamburg received quite a bit of attention, which allows unique glimpses at the forms of sociability of the various layers of the middle class. The dominant middling merchant group within the middle class was at the center of attention in the descriptions of Hamburg. Alternating between admiration and—more frequently—disgust, contemporaries noted the important role that food played in the sociability of this particular group.

A distinctive feature of these merchants was their emphasis on ritualistic forms of elaborate sociability within the extended family on such occasions as baptisms, weddings, and especially funerals.[36]

Depending on their own predilections, contemporaries either praised or complained about the excessive consumption of culinary pleasures to the detriment of more cerebral forms of entertainment. A 1789 travelogue characterized the life of the merchant class as a combination of a strong work ethic on the one hand and an equally strong desire for amusements in their leisure on the other: "As attentive as the person from Hamburg is to his profits and business, as much and as sophisticated he is about living well and the pleasures of entertainment" ("So eifrig der Hamburger auf Gewinnst, und so attend er auf seine Geschäfte ist, eben so stark raffiniert und denkt er auf Wohlleben und Erlustigungen").[37] This combination conveyed a sense of modernity.[38] The variety and amount of culinary pleasures denoted the importance of the occasion, the status of the hosts, and the importance of the guests. The heavy use of meat signaled the high standard of living. Observers of the Hamburg scene frequently noted the lavish consumption of meat as a status symbol. The Hamburg merchant subclass was notorious for sparing no expense to provide a lavish spread for these special occasions. Insiders understood this as a sign of hospitality, of honoring one's guests, but outsiders regarded these cultural practices as mindless excess and despicable gluttony, where the paucity of spirited conversation had to be compensated with opulent cuisine:

> After the nuptials we went to dinner at 7, which required seven stomachs to enjoy it. O heavens! What slaughter among foul, fish, and quadrupeds must have preceded! There were quail, partridge, pheasant, capon, turkey, rabbit, deer, trout, pike, and cod—and then the mincemeat pie, pâte, compote, ragout, fricasse, entrée, well I think that even the devil and his grandmother—the first fried and the latter boiled—were present and tasty. But I can attest to the fact that there was more eating than conversing—tough sociability but tender food.

> Nach der Trauung gieng es dann zu einem Essen um 7 Uhr, das 7 Mägen erforderte, um es genießen zu können. O Himmel—welches Morden unter Vögeln, Fischen und Quadrupeden war vorher gegangen! Da waren Wachteln, Rephühner, Fasanen, Capaunen, Puter, Hasen, Rehe, Forellen, Sander, Dorsch und nun die Pasteten, Patees,

Compots, Ragouts, Fricassees, Entrements, ich glaube auch der Teufel und seine Großmutter, erster gebraten, letztere gesotten waren da und schmekten gut! Versichern aber kann ich, daß mehr gegessen als gesprochen wurde—lederne Gesellschaft, aber fleischige Speisen.[39]

Outsiders perceived the one-dimensionality of this particular form of sociability as mind-numbing and boring because it lacked contrast, innovation, and, above all, variety.

Others emphasized the unflattering effects of food and drink on the mental alertness and vivaciousness of their consumers:

How seriously they examined each dish! How much delight entered the faces when a new course was brought, how swiftly even the most stimulating conversation about exchange rates was abandoned as soon as the desired portion was on the plate, the energy with which they chewed and chewed! The faces changed by the quarter hour, the eyes became duller and duller, the cheeks more and more bloated, the tongue heavier and heavier. They were continuously served new wines but these could not provide levity of spirit. A heavy sense of satiety overtook the thus-laboring guests.

Mit welchem Ernst man jede Schüssel betrachtete! Welche Verklärung in den Gesichtern aufging, wenn eine neue Tracht aufgesetzt ward; wie angelegentlich man selbst das anregendste Gespräch vom Wechselcours abbrach, sobald nur die ersehnte Portion auf dem Teller lag, mit welchem Eifer man kauete und kauete!—Von Viertelstunde zu Viertelstunde veränderten sich die Gesichter: immer blöder wurden die Augen, immer gedunsener die Wangen, immer schwerer die Zunge. Vergebens wurden unaufhörlich neue Weine gereicht: nicht geistiger Rausch des Getränks, der schwere, irdische der Sattheit bemächtigte sich der arbeitenden Gäste.[40]

The emphasis on one kind of activity—the layering of similar practices and objects—produces the same reaction, which in its sameness lacks the power to stimulate. Its monotony is tedious and fails to give pleasure. Furthermore, the predominance of the sensual and the material, along with the conversation's mundane topic of exchange rates, struck outside observers as inferior forms of entertainment lacking esprit and culture. Of course, many observers were intellectuals who valued less materialistic forms of pleasure, but even merchants from other regions considered dining as a form of entertainment to occupy one's leisure unique to the Hamburg merchant identity.[41]

In contrast to the ridiculed forms of entertainment representative of the middling merchants, a much-admired model for the variants in sociability could be found in the forms of entertainment taking place in the country estate of the wealthy Hamburg merchant George Heinrich Sieverking (1751–99) and his wife, Johanna Margarete Reimarus (1762–1832). For these representatives of the Hamburg elite, exquisite—not opulent—dinners were an important part of the evening's entertainment, yet this was only one of many features. Conversation, leafing through books, looking at artwork alone or in small groups, and enjoying the vistas and variety of the surprising features of the garden and the interior design occupied the main part of the evening. The variety of activities and their newness is perceived as stimulating, creating the sensation of pleasure.[42]

The mix of business associates, visitors, and friends not only allowed for general conversations on a variety of topics but also provided space for a more leisurely discussion of relevant business subjects in a wider context—in modern parlance, for networking. This further places Habermas's separation of the private and the public in question. These forms of sociability with their particular forms of communication seem to be an important part of the formation of group identity. The fact that Habermas largely ignored these forms of sociability is hardly surprising, as the majority of eighteenth-century commentators clearly reacted more favorably to forms of sociability where the intellectual and cultural aspects dominated over the sensual pleasures or over an overtly economic orientation of the conversation.

In the description of the Sieverkings' cosmopolitan gatherings, the mix of public and private functions as well as the transcendence of class barriers becomes apparent. Not only members of the extended family and friends but also business associates gathered for dinner, conversation, and entertainment. While the networking function (the discussion of exchange rates mentioned above or similar business-related topics) is still quite important, it is done in a less direct manner. This elite group differentiated itself not only through the much larger scope of these forms of sociability but also through the more refined and sophisticated meals. This meant less emphasis on the amount of food and the predominance of the most expensive items (meat) and more emphasis on refinement and selection tailored to the individual tastes of the guests. Observers note that each person could select what and how much he or she wanted to eat and drink and that dinner took no more than one hour because the dishes were served simultaneously rather than in a formal sequence. This allowed for a greater variety of activities and decreased the importance of the crassly material and sensual while increasing the pleasures provided by the mode of presentation and the general ambience. The mingling of business associates and other (often international) visitors increased the spectrum of topics, which ranged from current events and travel to the arts and letters, creating a more cosmopolitan, open aspect of identity formation for this elite layer of the merchants:

> I [Böttiger] have dined there on two Sundays. The first time there were 80, the second time 70 places set in two large dining rooms and they were not enough. For the strangers this might be a delightful spectacle. It is a *congregatio gentium* like on judgment day and a mix of tongues like in the Whitsunday epistle. Both times the last heir of the Gonzagas, a prince without a country but with a lot of intelligence and a decidedly democratic mind, was present. There were rich Dutch women glittering with jewelry, while the lady of the house did not rely on external glitter. She had on a simple taffeta chemise dress (because she had just attended the baptism of the garden neighbor's Reichard's ninth child) the first time and a simple calico dress the second time. There was an Englishman from Liverpool next to a democrat from Bordeaux, next to a demoiselle Feraud, who had fought side by side with Dumouriez and emigrated with him, and next to her engrossed in pleasantries was Barthelemy, the brother of the man from Basel and agent of the republic. Further up was a Swedish consul who had just returned from Morocco, engaged in conversation with a couple of English Jews from St. Domingo and an American from New Jersey.

Ich [Böttiger] habe zwei Sonntage da gespeist. Das erste mal waren 80, das zweite Mal 70 Couverts in zwei großen Speisesälen gelegt und noch waren überzählige Gäste. Für den Fremden selbst mag dies ein ganz angenehmes Schauspiel sein. Es ist eine congregatio gentium wie am jüngsten Gericht und eine Zungenvermischung wie in der Pfingstepistel. Da war beide Mal der letzte Sprößling aus dem Hause Gonzaga, ein Prinz ohne Land aber mit vielem Verstand und erklärter Demokrat, gegenwärtig. Da waren ein paar reiche Holländerinnen, die von Juwelen glänzten, während die Frau vom Hause das erste mal in einer einfachen Taftchemise (weil sie eben bei ihrem Gartennachbarn dem Kapellmeister Reichard das neunte Kind aus der Taufe gehoben hatte), das zweite Mal in einem ganz gewöhnlichen Kattunkleide allen erborgten Glanz demüthigstolz verschmähte. Da saß ein Engländer aus Liverpool neben einem Republikaner aus Bordeaux, neben ihnen eine Dlle. Feraud, die an Dumouriez' Seite focht und mit ihm emigrierte, und neben ihr in scherzhaftem Gespräche Barthelemy, ein Bruder des Baseler und Agent der Republik. Weiter oben ein schwedischer Konsul, der aus Marroko zurückgekehrt war, in Unterredung mit einem paar englischen Juden aus St. Domingo und einem Amerikaner aus New-Yersey.[43]

As discussed in chapter 5, housewives played the most important role not only in the material preparation of these forms of sociability but also in orchestrating the forms of entertainment. They not only planned and organized the presentation of food and drink but also made the reading materials, letters, artworks, and other conversation pieces available and, above all, subtly directed the conversation by drawing all guests into groupings and making them feel comfortable. This required an enormous general knowledge of the culture of the time, especially literature and the arts but also current events. Housewives also had to be familiar with the fashionable rituals associated with the pleasures of sociability—for example, with the ceremony of presenting tea—and conduct them with elegance. They had to select and acquire fashionable objects such as the modern tea-brewing machine to serve tea at the table, the fashionable tea service, and the table linens that round out the experience. The tea ceremonies, in particular, seem to have been a marker of sociable leisure par excellence, as tea is associated with the attributes "intellectual," "ostentatiously leisured," "luxurious," and "nonfunctional" ("intellektuell . . . ostentativ müßig, luxeriös . . . nicht funktional").[44]

The successful hostess possessed excellent social skills. The mix of guests from various social classes and communities within them required particular social and psychological skills to bridge the gaps of demeanor, customs, and behaviors.[45] She carefully orchestrated and timed the entry of guests, offered guidance in the most suitable participation in conversations and other activities, facilitated the most favorable display of the individuality of the guests, and provided suitable food and drink that took the individual tastes and preferences into account. Her ability to ease all guests into the conversation by fostering a sense of successful communication created a sensation of psychological well-being, which is experienced as pleasurable. The reputation of the famous salonnières rested largely on these skills.[46]

The successful hostess was able to discover the individual strengths of her guests and to highlight them in conversation. The acknowledgment and acceptance of each guest's personality and individuality lessened the stress associated with social situations and created a relaxed atmosphere as the prerequisite for pleasurable forms of entertainment. Only the hostess's diligent acquisition of the necessary social and organizational skills and of an extensive general education could make these cultural practices look like effortless entertainment providing pleasure.

Sociability as a forum for entertainment has to be seen as linked to other instances of entertainment discussed in this study. The enjoyment of spas and (landscape) gardens was also significantly enhanced by sociability. Both were removed from the usual local context and limited in duration. The spas attracted a heterogeneous clientele and allowed for the mingling of members of various classes and communities within them. The moment of novelty and the stimulating departure from the familiar rendered these forms of entertainment pleasurable, as we will discuss in chapter 8.

For many families, the summer spent in the country or the garden was characterized by more informal patterns of sociability. Families (or many times the women) invited relatives and friends for simple meals, conversation, and the enjoyment of the natural surroundings. Of course, the forms and extent of the gatherings in the country could vary. Not all were simple affairs, as we have seen. The villa of the Sieverkings was also considered a house in the country, but it offered elaborate festivities. In larger gardens there was often also space for dancing and even small theatrical performances and the fashionable pastime of living pictures, which we will discuss below.[47]

Overall, these forms of sociability are less about creating the much-discussed bourgeois intimacy than they are about integrating the family into its larger social context. In addition, they help to define one's position and status within this community. Even if they mimic familial structures in their informalities (as the Reimarus example showed), they nevertheless foster important ties in the communities in question, be it the business or the scientific community. Despite the fact that they were leisure activities and considered entertainment, the "networking" that took place was partly "work" and partly social responsibility. Suggesting the significant burden of this "work of culture," van Dülmen describes, for example, the relief of the young wife of a Göttingen professor when summer came and she no longer had to formally entertain every Sunday evening and instead could move the gathering to the garden, where invitations took on a more informal air.[48]

A more distinct and well-researched subcategory of sociable entertainment is the salon culture of the late eighteenth century, especially the cosmopolitan salons in the urban centers such as Berlin or the gatherings of the elite in the unique culture of Weimar. They could differ significantly in the level of luxurious consumption, ranging from simple bread and tea to oysters and fine wine. Critics see the level of consumption as the only difference within the various forms of the salon. The salons were distinguished primarily by the financial means of the hostess (or her husband), the degree of luxury, and the extent of openness to strangers. Their common goal was to attract the most interesting people. Compared to the forms of sociability discussed above, the salon was more structured. It centered around a woman from the cultural elite and focused on cultural activities. At times it could compete with other salons and other social events in town. In Johanna Schopenhauer's long-standing salon in Weimar (1806–29), for example, we can see a core group of mostly prominent members of society, intellectuals, and artists—the *Bildungselite*—assembled in regular intervals on certain days of the week.[49] The schedule of her salon was coordinated with other social activities in Weimar (e.g., the theater) and represented an important part of its overall social life. These fixed evenings could display different characteristics, as Goethe writes about Johanna Schopenhauer's gatherings, which are often referred to as salons but which resemble other forms of sociability that we have discussed above. Even between her Thursday and Sunday gatherings there seem to have been differences, supporting the argument that cultural practices ranged across a continuum: "The Thursday gatherings offered a large variety of entertainments, while the smaller Sunday meetings were more focused."[50] Goethe's letter reflects on the unique group dynamics of both salons by differentiating between the forms of entertainment in larger and smaller groups. The first provide pleasant stimulation by the variety and breadth of impulses they offer, whereas the latter encourage more intensity and require more intellectual work and concentration from the participants.

The regular schedule of the salon was augmented by other forms of sociability that could include the regulars of the salon. Dinners, parties for special occasions, and evenings devoted to concerts enriched the activities during the social season, which ranged from October to May (travel, spas, and the visit to summer residences completed the year).

Overall, the salon displays some structural features that are similar to the more general forms of sociability. In the light of recent studies on sociability (Peter, Gaus, Mauser) and the forms of sociable entertainment discussed above, the borders between general forms of sociability and the form of sociability of the salon have to be seen as less clearly defined. I would argue that the range of cultural practices that the habitués engaged in was not limited to conversation, as the older literature suggest. Indicative of these older positions, Petra Wilhelmy's dissertation on the Berlin salons (1780–1914) defines this important institution in cultural history as a "free, informal sociability based on conversation about literary, artistic or political topics" ("freie, ungezwungene Geselligkeit, deren Grundlage die Konversation über literarische, künstlerische oder politische Themen bildet").[51]

As in the more loosely assembled occasions for sociability, the space for entertaining in the home of the salon hostess was not organized around one center where all guests assembled. Instead, spaces for entertaining tended to be distributed throughout several rooms, all open to each other. Visitors could mingle by the tea table, next door at the piano, or in yet another room at a table filled with art supplies that invited active participation. Johanna Schopenhauer describes the forms of sociability she organized and engaged in as a significant enhancement of the care of the self and her mental well-being:

> This evening I produced a transparent moonlight scene with Meyer . . . the others stood around in the other room engaged in conversation, Conta and Bardua occasionally sang a song, and Goethe alternated between our table where I worked with Meyer, or participated in the conversation of the others.

> Ich fabricirte den Abend noch mit Meyern einen transparenten Mondschein . . . die übrigen standen umher und conversierten im zweiten Zimmer, Conta und die Bardua sangen zwischen durch ein Liedchen, und Göthe gieng ab und zu bald an meinen Tisch wo ich mit Meyern arbeitete, bald nahm er theil an jenem Gespäch.[52]

The architectural layout of the house (contemporary tastes favored a number of public rooms—the music room, drawing room, sitting room, parlor, etc.—that could be opened to each other to accommodate these forms of sociability) encouraged mingling in small groups and allowed for a variety of different activities to take place at the same time, providing for limited (or more extensive) engagement with particular activities. The freedom to regulate the intensity of involvement allowed these activities to be experienced as pleasurable forms of entertainment. Control over the investment of energy, self-discipline, effort, and the degree of participation sets entertainment apart from the discipline of work and the activities associated with *Bildung*.

Schopenhauer's salon offered a range of activities that oscillated between high and low levels of involvement. Proportionally, in salons, activities that come close to the discipline of *Bildung* might have taken up more time than the general forms of sociability discussed above, where the guests were not all members of the cultural elite. The salons tended to be frequented by professional writers, musicians, and painters. These professional members read from their works, performed, or gave lectures on topics of their expertise. At the same time, they also participated as dilettantes in other fields and engaged in group activities—making music, singing, giving dramatic readings, performing living pictures, drawing, and creating decorative art objects (the fashionable transparent screen illuminated from behind [*transparenten Mondschein*]). Members could experience pleasurable variation by switching between consumption and production, between quasi-expert professional contributions and *Liebhaberei.*[53] The group experienced the "team approach" to the creation of decorative objects—from inception and planning to design and execution to display of the finished object—as a highly pleasurable activity that encouraged playful creativity and freed the participants from professional discipline. Compared to the modern solitary experience of artistic production, the group experience provided a stimulating contrast:

> The common project is a wonderful thing that one begins and executes together with enthusiasm; there is no more substantial and beautiful tie of sociability. I always have plans for projects to complete with my friends, this way there is always a reason for getting together, discussing, planning, and brainstorming as if the fate of the world depended on it, though in the end it is only a fireplace screen. But it is not the fireplace screen itself, it is eternal art, which is ever changing its form but yet remains the same and which brings us together and the fact that I love art, and the fact that I am lucky enough to be somewhat talented, that makes me happy in the love of these special people.

> Es ist eine herrliche Sache um solche gemeinschaftlichen Arbeiten die man mit Lust und Liebe gemeinschaftlich anfängt und ausführt; es giebt kein schönres festres Band fürs gesellige Leben, ich habe immer mit meinen Freunden so etwas vor, und das giebt ein Zusammenkommen, ein Berathen, ein Ueberlegen, als hinge das Wohl der Welt daran, am Ende wirds ein Ofenschirm. Aber es ist nicht der Ofenschirm, es ist die einzige ewige Kunst, die ewig die Form wechselt und doch eine und dieselbe bleibt die uns zusammenführt und das mir die das Glück ward die Kunst zu fühlen und zu lieben, auch nicht ganz ungeschickt zu üben, das ist's, was mich jezt in der Liebe dieser vorzüglichen Menschen so glücklich macht.[54]

Johanna Schopenhauer confirms several premises of this study. She perceives these forms of cultural entertainment as situated on a continuum of culture. She sees art as all-encompassing and not as divided into distinct realms of professional and dilettante practice. She also attests to the suggestion that playful creativity—engagement in the planning, design, and creation of an artifact—is perceived as a pleasurable stimulation that enriches everyday life and propels people to repeat the desirable activities in ever-new manifestations, driving the quest for an increase in cultural activity and consumption. The fact that these manifestations of cultural consumption are not limited to solitary pursuits but derive much of their pleasure from a sense of community is also addressed. The company of interesting people becomes part of the care of the self, ensuring mental health and providing a profound sense of well-being, even happiness, as the tone of Schopenhauer's comments suggests.

The wealthy Jewish salons in Berlin were also highly desirable sites for entertainment because of their open character, their extensive national and international connections, and their members' coming from the middle and upper classes (lower nobility). Schleiermacher, in an August 4, 1798, letter to his sister, emphasized the international flair of the Jewish salons, where people of (social) talent would be welcome and could excel, entertain, and be entertained. This was mainly due to the extraordinary talent of the Jewish women, who are—according to Schleiermacher—conversant in many topics and possess one or more artistic talents themselves.[55] Newer research on the salon has modified the traditional assumption that a salon was only a regular, domestic, home-based informal gathering for conversation.[56] Newer studies interpret the complex net of a variety of activities inside and outside the domestic sphere as salon culture. Gaus writes: "Salons are defined as spaces for communicative exchange whereby—depending on its specific character—games, art and literature could stimulate communication" ("Salons definierten sich als Freiräume zur kommunikativen Auseinandersetzung, wobei, je nach ihrer Eigenart, etwa auch Spiele, Kunst und Literatur die Kommunikation fördern konnten").[57] This moves the forms of sociability and the forms of the salons closer together. Gaus confirms that the salon culture consisted of many different forms of social entertainment, shared by a group of regulars, which could not only gather informally on a *jour fixe* at the home of the hostess but that this loose circle of habitués informally met on the promenades, at the theater, and at intimate or large gatherings. Rachel von

Varnhagen's famed salon, which attracted members of the nobility and the elite, actors, singers, authors, and members of the military and clergy, met in several different locations inside and outside her home and seemed to have taken place less regularly and frequently than Schopenhauer's.[58]

These fluid, impromptu forms of entertainment made use of all the opportunities that cities large and small could offer. The promenade depicted on the cover of this volume is but one example of such a gathering place in a smaller city. In the large urban centers like Berlin, people could informally meet on the fashionable promenade (*Unter den Linden*) and the urban parks (*Tiergarten*). This could then evolve into a visit for conversation, a meal, and visits to the theater, concerts, or other forms of public entertainment such as recitations (*Deklamatorien*), popular lectures and readings. Berlin's Tiergarten became a famous and infamous example of such a semipublic gathering place for people of all walks of life—infamous not only because "respectable" people gathered there but because it was a rendezvous for hetero- and homosexuals and a place where male and female prostitutes conducted business (Berlin housed a large garrison that was home to young males of the lower ranks).[59]

The new urban spaces are sites of both potential isolation and new forms of entertainment; they expanded the traditional social parameters of the household, work, and the familiarity of the neighborhood. Venturing into unfamiliar urban spaces creates a sense of anonymity that can be perceived as either isolating or liberating. The firm rules of propriety regulating conduct in familiar surroundings can be momentarily suspended. The unfamiliar spaces and their forms of entertainment offer independence from the individual's habitual mentalities, from social, psychological, and intellectual traditions. This break with personal, social, and symbolic systems, offering freedom from one's past, necessitated (or offered the opportunity for) the creation of new social formations. These had to fill the void of tradition and family history. The array of cultural entertainment opportunities in the urban centers and the forms of sociability they invited represented new social contexts. Unlike the extended family context, these modern forms of sociability could be entered into at will. They offered a new voluntary social grounding based on common interests. These excursions into unfamiliar territory were perceived as pleasurable because they offered stimulation through new impressions, visual titillation, and the excitement of the new or different. Strolling through these spaces tantalized the senses through the sights (the organization of the space and its integration into the city), sounds, and smells of the town. At the same time, this form of entertainment—far from being a truly destabilizing experience of an extended exclusive immersion into the unfamiliar—represents only a momentary sojourn from which people return to the safety of the familiar. Lacking danger, it can thus be experienced as pleasurable. To sample the extraterritoriality of these unfamiliar urban spaces in the company of acquaintances is even more entertaining, as it allows for verbal exchange about the novelty of this experience. The gradual integration of storefronts and shop windows displaying their goods for casual passersby further enhanced the pleasure of the experience, as these goods were visually attractive objects for viewing and desiring (see the above discussion of the shopping experience as pleasurable consumption).

New quarters of the city—for example, Friedrichstadt—reflected and facilitated these forms of mobility necessary for the various forms of entertainment; cobbled streets and indoor and outdoor coffeehouses allowed for more public activity. Coupled with more practical fashions, these material and design changes increased mobility. "Die Schleppen," a satirical playlet in the *Journal,* points to the incompatibility of fashionable clothing (the train of dresses and silk shoes) and the traditionally unpaved streets, which turned into extended fields of foul-smelling mud in inclement weather (1:120–31). New cultural practice—that is, innovation in city planning and architectural layout—literally paved the way for other cultural innovations and altered practices. The redesigning of public environments influenced and was influenced by the new forms of semipublic entertainment as an extension of the domestic sphere.

Most sizable cities contained areas where people could assemble, "spread out, breathe open, healthy air, and enjoy the beauty of the sky and landscape. Such spots are excellent additions to any city if they are adorned with lawns, fountains, and columns and are edged by trees and handsome buildings."[60] Landscape designers advocated the establishment of other green spaces close to the city walls where city dwellers could conveniently enjoy the outdoors, go for walks, get their exercise, and socialize in the fresh air. These public parks should contain broad walkways where people can stroll around together, converse, and see and be seen. Benches, shelters, and structures where refreshments are served enhance the experience of the park, and fishing, boating, and concerts provide additional layers of entertainment. The Prater and Augarten in Vienna, the Tiergarten in Berlin, and the Karlsaue in Cassel represented such modern spaces in the German states.

THE VISUAL ARTS AND MUSIC AS PART OF DOMESTIC ENTERTAINMENT

The Visual Arts

As we discussed above, the increase and popularity of the periodical press changed reading practices. It also created an increased interest in publication on the visual arts (*Kunstzeitschriften* and *Kunstlehrbücher*),[61] rendering art more accessible to a broader middle-class (lay) audience. They provided information for specialists and interested laypersons in the form of documentation on individual artworks, information on collections and exhibits, artists' biographies, lists of works, and news from the art world as well as reviews of art books and purchase information.[62] Not only did specialized publication on art and art history increase the interest in the visual arts, but the many illustrated periodicals also contributed significantly. The entertainment quality of periodicals was greatly enhanced by the inclusion of illustrations by famous artists. The most famous illustrator of his time, Daniel Nikolaus Chodowiecki, conceptualized many of his works as twelve coordinating pieces so that they could be used as frontispieces for monthlies or calendars (*Monatskupfer*). Hogarth's works became especially popular illustrations for pocketbooks and calendars.

The *Göttinger Taschen-Kalender* contained generous illustration of, among others, the latest fashions and *Monatskupfer,* a series of etchings with mythological (1802), historical (i.e., depictions of scenes with famous Romans; 1801), or moral subject matter, with brief explanations. The publications also taught the art of "reading" etchings, as was the case with Hogarth's famous social and moral critiques. The *Göttinger Taschen-Kalender* reprinted individual portions of the etchings and explained these "close-ups" one by one. Among the etchings was the famous "Die Biergasse und das Brantweingäßchen" ("Beer-street and Gin-lane," 1795).[63]

One of the most ambitiously illustrated projects of the time was Bertuch's *Bilderbuch für Kinder* (1790–1830), a comprehensive encyclopedia; its thirty-six volumes contained more than 1,185 plates, which were comprised of 6,000 detail illustrations.[64] Conveying information, stimulating the gaze, and fostering the pleasure of looking, this publication raised the bar for book illustrations. Pictures not only convey information and facilitate understanding of complicated concepts but also sensualize abstract concepts. One form of cognition complements the other. In addition, illustrations stimulate the imagination and provide amusement.[65] Although the scientific press still discredited the illustration as a mere helpmate, as a means to convey scientific information, the popular press departed from the devalorization of the image. Bertuch was convinced that the illustrations in his *Bilderbuch* caught the eye of his young audience and created curiosity, which was then satisfied by the word.[66] Overall, his focus on images as important ingredients for the book played an important role in fostering visual culture. The increased popularity of journals, almanacs, and pocketbooks, which changed the faces of literature and reading practices, is paralleled by an increase in publication on the visual arts, rendering art more accessible to a broader middle-class (lay) audience and creating significant interest in the visual arts.

This increased interest in the visual arts not only changed the visual appeal of the domestic environment but also became part of middle-class entertainment and sociability as a topic for conversation and as dilettante practice, as we have seen in Johanna Schopenhauer's salon activities. These activities fostered not only the reception and viewing of the visual arts but also its creation by individuals or groups.

The visual arts as part of everyday culture led not only to more private collections (the predominant model up to this point) opening their doors to the public but also to the establishment of public collections. As eighteenth-century autobiographies tell us, it was common practice among intellectuals, writers, and artists to visit private art collections when they traveled. In writings on art collected in his *Schriften zur Kunst,* Goethe not only tackled theoretical topics but also commented on collections in Dresden and Venice and offered detailed discussions on the Weimar art exhibits of 1801–4.[67] Here he explained the mythological paintings, listing and organizing motifs and their significance. The illustrations introduced the paintings to audiences who were unable to travel to these collections and furthered interest in the visual arts. Designed to enhance the taste formation in the visual arts, Goethe's periodical *Propyläen* (1789–1800) focused on Greek antiquity and its neoclassical heirs. With their prescriptive gesture of high culture, the focus of these writings was not on entertainment. The *Propyläen* met with only limited financial success.

Overall, in the last decades of the century a larger range of people—not only the intellectual elite—became interested in the visual arts as one aspect of their cultural literacy. With the creation of catalogs, the reading public gained more information and access to collections. At the same time, these catalogs (1778 saw the production of a complete catalog of the Düsseldorf gallery, showing its contents wall by wall) created a desire to visit the collections. Johann Heinrich Merck wrote: "It is impossible to page through these descriptions and illustrations without feeling the strongest urge to travel to Düsseldorf and view these treasures for one's self."[68] The visits to galleries themselves became a new form of entertainment, as one form of cultural practice creates others.

These new audiences, in turn, were often inspired to begin their own collections to the extent that their finances allowed. The substantial increase in etchings in particular was caused by this popularization of the visual arts. As most middle-class collectors could not afford originals of famous artists, especially not paintings, they instead purchased either original paintings of lesser artists or drawings and etchings.[69] The fact that the *Intelligenzblatt* of the *Journal des Luxus und der Moden* and other periodicals offered information on the availability and cost of these items is a further indicator that the middle class's interest in art included an interest in its acquisition. Reproductions of famous artworks by the flourishing printmaking trade made the images available for ever wider consumption. "Gallery descriptions like Heinse's, together with catalogs, art periodicals, and the reproductions of famous works," writes James Sheehan, "helped develop an audience for the visual arts within the small but significant literary public that had begun to remake German culture in the eighteenth century. From these publications about art, individuals acquired a surrogate experience of the gallery in the privacy of their homes."[70] Members of the middle class became collectors. Beyond the financial aspect, the tastes of middle-class collectors began to determine the style and subject matter of an ever greater portion of the art market. Portraiture and domestic scenes along with landscape and still life became favorite genres of this new and diverse lay audience. The disinterest in mythological painting could be explained by a lack of specialized humanistic education;[71] there were, however, attempts to explain mythological painting to a broader audience, such as Goethe's discussion and description of the Weimar art exhibits.

Another reason for the limited interest in mythological and historical paintings might have been the practice of treating artworks as part of the interior design of the bourgeois home. For this purpose, not only was the large scale of historical and mythological paintings prohibitive, but, more importantly, the self-conscious subject matter did not lend itself to serve as a backdrop for the middle-class lifestyle and therefore did not integrate well into the rest of the interior design. It would have demanded the kind of attention that was not desirable in the domestic setting used for family life or leisurely cultural pursuits.

The demand for new "decorative" forms of visual arts, in turn, produced new academies or painting schools. Here artists were trained to produce these specific genres, which further increased the availability of decorative items for the home.[72] In addition, the strong interest in the visual arts was accompanied by a recreational dilettante practice of the visual arts—especially drawing and landscape painting—as part of the cultural lifestyle of the upper middle class. Drawing lessons were part of an upper-middle-class education, and instruction books were designed and marketed to extend this form of entertainment beyond the elites by making it more affordable.[73]

The cultural practice of (decorative) art production and consumption represented another instance of the layering of entertaining activities to heighten pleasure. The example of the Englishman in *Die Wahlverwandtschaften* embodies this trend. He is not only a connoisseur of the beautiful vistas that the culturally enhanced landscape (see the next chapter) provided, but he captures them in drawings assisted by the technology of a *camera obscura*.[74] His numerous travels yield an extensive collection of landscapes, which—like the later travel photography—made distant and various impression readily available. This practice yielded a "pleasant and interesting" ("angenehm und interessant") collection.[75] His extensive compilation (*Portefeuille*) creates stimulation for himself, as he is able to conjure up experiences that are removed in time and space, thus enriching his experience of the here and now. Paving the way for the photograph, his ever-increasing collection of impressions fixed in landscape paintings could make the memory available for later and repeated consumption. In addition, he is able to entertain his hosts with his pictures and his explanations.[76] In addition to experiencing the pleasure of looking, they delight in the activity as a kind of convenient, comfortable armchair travel as they let a variety of landscapes pass by. The layering of aesthetic pleasure and the pleasure of novelty in geographic variety is further enhanced by a historical dimension in the stimulation achieved through learning about or remembering historically significant moments.[77] The image of movement in the steady stream of visual impressions suggests a proto-filmic flooding of the mind and senses, which is perceived as pleasurable. This practice bears some resemblance to two other forms of visual pleasure discussed below: the panorama and diorama and the spectacle of the living pictures.

Music

In addition to offering publications for the professional musician, the periodical press was also an important distribution medium for inexpensive sheet music, thereby furthering the interest in music as an active and passive form of domestic entertainment.[78] Journals also discussed and announced new musical pieces and offered extensive lists of availability, such as the *Journal*'s "Uebersicht neuer Musikalien" (4:343–54). Especially the *Göttinger Musenalmanach* (1770–1804) and the *Almanach der deutschen Musen* (1775, 1777, 1778, 1781) contain examples of the fashionable genre of the *Lied* (art song), which created the basis for an important form of entertainment within the community of family and friends: communal singing tradition in the domestic sphere (*Hausmusik*).[79] It also offered information on and depictions of musical instruments, such as the piano, which became especially popular during this time and soon became a status symbol in the bourgeois household. The guitar, another favorite of the time, could not only be used to accompany singing in the home but was also portable enough to be taken into the garden or nature.

Even the most ambitious almanacs contained musical scores. They were printed in a larger format than the book itself and could be folded out (e.g., in Schiller's *Musen-Almanach für das Jahr 1796*)[80] next to poems by Goethe, Hölderlin, Sophie Mereau, Schiller, and A. W. Schlegel.[81] Schiller's *Musen-Almanach für das Jahr 1797* and the provocative *Xenien-Almanach* (which appeared with a new publisher, Johann Friedrich Cotta) contained musical pieces with text and scores, as did his *Musen-Almanach für das Jahr 1798*. Especially the piano and

211

the guitar gained in popularity because they fostered and were enabled by the new interest in the *Lied*. At the same time, these instruments became signifiers of one's cultural position or status within the middle class.

Fostering interest, the collections of songs for domestic sociability[82] and the specialized print media created an audience for musical performances and aided in taste formation. With the aid of primers such as Daniel Gottlob Türk's *Klavierschule oder Anweisung zum Klavierspiele für Lehrer und Lernende* (Piano primer for teachers and students) (1789),[83] laypersons could learn to play an instrument. The inclusion of sheet music in almanacs and pocket books providing inexpensive sheet music by the major composers of the day fostered the *Hausmusik* culture and assisted in the aestheticization of domestic sociability and its cultural entertainment.[84] This phenomenon also paved the way for a different kind of music consumption: the more passive enjoyment of professionally performed concerts. In addition to the participatory pleasure of *Hausmusik,* the modern, more anonymous, nondialogic, and nonparticipatory indulgence in music began to take hold.

The fashionable practice of musical performances and singing in the domestic sphere as a form of entertainment extended beyond the middle class to the members of the nobility, especially in those courts heavily influenced by middle-class advisers such as the Weimar court. In those circles the border between lay musicians and professionals was blurred, as both lay and professional performers provided the musical entertainment. Members of the middle class as well as the members of the court regarded music as an important part of their cultural identity and as a mark of good taste, and portraits and depictions of domestic scenes often included musical instruments. The domestic painting of Wieland and his family situated him in a domestic space with the objects (a piano with opened musical scores, paintings, statues, busts, folios) that signal his status as a highly cultured man.[85] Even members of the middle class who were not in the public limelight opted to be depicted with musical instruments, as the painting *Stickerin mit abgelegter Gitarre* (Woman doing needlepoint and a guitar) (1811) shows.[86] A young woman facing the window away from the viewer in a simple room, her face visible in the mirror, is engaged in decorative needlework. In the background we see a guitar and opened sheet music. These cultural artifacts were part of the middle-class character and showed how its members wanted to be (re)presented to the public. These forms of entertainment became part of their lifestyle and identity.

Music as entertainment extended beyond the interior domestic spaces into nature—the domestic garden, the landscape garden, and the park—as instruments and musical scores accompanied people into these outdoor spaces. Music heightened the enjoyment of nature in the circle of like-minded company, creating yet another layer of pleasure. Instruments designed primarily for outdoor use became fashionable. The aeolian harp (*Äolsharfe*) was considered nature's instrument because the wind produced the unique sounds on this stringed instrument. Influenced by English models, the aeolian harp was installed in the landscape gardens of the time and added an aural dimension to the visual pleasures of the cultured nature of the landscape garden. It underscores the pensive mood that the solitary enjoyment of the garden provides. Other instruments included the French horn (*Waldhorn*) and various forms of harmonicas, which were considered especially suitable to create a desirable ambience and mood. They were integrated into outdoor festivities and, for example, at the court in Weimar they often became part of the outdoor performance of *Singspiele*.[87] The French horn in particular is associated with distant vistas "fading into twilight while the sound of a hunting horn stirs sympathetic melancholy,"[88] a mood that is evoked in Eichendorff's "Sehnsucht nach der Ferne" and which find its way into Hirschfeld's *Theory of Garden Art*: "While his eye lingers, intoxicated by the beauty of these visions, the majestic music of French horns fills the air with the heart-lifting echo and completes the soul's rapture."[89] The characters in Goethe's *Die Wahlverwandtschaften* pause in their other forms of sociable entertainment within beautiful nature to heighten the sensation of pleasure by enjoying the sound of the French horns.[90] Again, the entertainment factor seemed to be enhanced by a layering of activities or stimuli—the visual beauty of nature, the creation of a certain atmosphere by the aural pleasure of music, resonating with the mood of the individual or enhancing the dynamic of the social circle.

From autobiographical texts we know that Goethe and Wieland had musicians come to their gardens to perform for their private entertainment as a form of relaxation and stimulation. Using the pleasures of music in nature as a form of self-medication, Goethe in a letter to Frau von Stein writes that he had clarinetists play for him while he strolled in his garden. And while he appreciated the beauty of the moment, it was not enough to soften his heart.[91] This is only one of many examples for the tendency of the bourgeoisie—including the intellectuals whose theoretical positions dismiss the entertainment function of culture—to create a lifestyle replete with the pleasures of cultural consumption. Goethe, in particular, was quite sensitive to the function of *Alltagskultur* for the psychological and physical well-being of the self, as his interest in his garden, his personal environment, and other lifestyle issues attests.

Overall, the engagement with the arts (both visual and music) as forms of sociable entertainment in the form of reading and learning about them, engaging in artistic practice, and in conversational exploration created the dialogically constructed discourse on the arts that laid the groundwork for the formation of a range of aesthetic experiences. In the discussion with others (in conversation or in reading and writing about art), the bourgeoisie developed its cultural taste as a mutually developed sense of judgment. The self differentiated its own taste in the discussion with others, in the engagement with consensus values, norms, and shared ways of thinking. After all, the prized ideal of individuality and bourgeois subjectivity and originality can only emerge when it is gauged against the normative.[92] The entertaining engagement with cultural practices within the context of sociability and the pleasure of exploration it provides allowed laypersons and experts to engage freely, generating a potentially infinite range of meanings and opinions, as everyone has the right to talk about aesthetic practices. The cultural public sphere was created by an unlimited discussion of aesthetic taste and a dynamic practical engagement with and consumption of the arts. The interplay of individual judgments and shared norms—of the individual and the collective—avoids closure and thus creates the dynamic of cultural consumption. As the interest in cultural practices increased, its forms also increased and offered different ways of enjoying them. The art museum and the concert hall began to offer new forms of cultural pleasures that relied less on social engagement and more on solitary stimulation by the artifact.

The pleasures of cultural consumption could be heightened by layering (i.e., music in the garden, reading or painting in nature or in the garden) cultural activities and enjoying these layered pleasures as solitary or sociable entertainment. Entertainment, not mastery, was the ultimate goal of these cultural practices.[93]

The Spectacle of the Female Body as Parlor Game

Attitudes and Living Pictures

Attitudes (*Attitüden*) and living pictures (*Lebende Bilder* or *tableaux vivants*) exemplify a culmination of many trends in the entertainment culture of the time. Their function as amusement and pastime and the sense of astonishment they evoked provided the kind of variety, novelty, and surprise that could keep boredom at bay. Karl August Böttiger likened them to a delicious morsel of "Confect" consumed as a dessert, a visual and sensual indulgence ("Augen und Sinnenlust").[94] At the same time, these forms of entertainment represented a practical engagement with the visual arts within the context of sociability. They were practiced in various settings, from (semi)professional and public performances to informal social sites; the latter ranged from large, important public settings (Vienna Congress), to salons, to simple family venues.[95] Especially the attitudes not only enchanted the casual performers and their audience but also fascinated a culturally sophisticated audience (actors to intellectuals and cultural critics as well as artists and writers) because they could be enjoyed on several levels. For the latter audience, the genre also participated in the redefinition of mimesis that loomed large in the aesthetic debates of the time.[96] Especially artists, theater and art buffs, and academics formed a captive audience in a range of social settings: salons, private residences, and public meeting halls in European cities.

Famous performers or orchestrators of the attitudes and living pictures included Mme. de Genlis (1746–1830) in France; Lady Hamilton, née Emma Harte (1765–1815), in England and Italy;[97] and Henriette Hendel-Schütz (1772–1849) and Elise Bürger (1769–1833) in Germany. The most famous performer was Lady Hamilton (who served as a model for Bürger and Hendel-Schütz), who showcased her mimic talents as part of the cultural and artistic entertainment in Sir Hamilton's residence in Naples. Her mimoplastic talents attracted the attention of many famous contemporaries, but especially visual artists (Wilhelm Tischbein, Friedrich Rehberg, Angelika Kauffmann, Elizabeth Vigée-Lebrun) and those writers interested in visuality (Goethe, Herder).[98]

Furthermore, these performances are quintessential forms of entertainment as they weave together multiple cultural practices: the preoccupation with theater, the appeal of the visual arts, the fascination with the body, its language and its clothing, the playful masquerade, the delight of allowing the immoderate gaze to wonder freely over interesting textures, and the enchantment of the playful recognition of cultural icons. Both attitudes and living pictures depicted images that the participants recognized from other media—from illustrated books or periodicals or from famous paintings.[99] Beyond the entertainment that the presentation itself provided for spectators and performers, the planning of the presentation with others as a part of sociability, the perusal of sources of inspiration, the selection and aesthetic design of the event with its costumes, and finding the most suitable backdrop and lighting were other important factors in the entertainment value of this cultural practice.[100]

A series of poses based on antique statues, mythological or religious figures, or free poses denoting a certain mood or sentiment, attitudes traditionally centered around an individual female performer's body. They are defined as the art of "representing plastic works of art by mimic means, gestures and draping, and transforming their local and existing life into a successive temporal one."[101] The female body in simple white, loose-flowing dress[102] in an arrested scene onstage or in the parlor fascinated contemporary eighteenth- and early-nineteenth-century audiences. The *Conversationslexikon* from 1816 foregrounds the visual pleasure associated with attitudes:

> With this French technical term we denote . . . the position and arrangement of living figures, primarily at rest. But because art, based on its purpose, selects only meaningful subjects, the poses and positions of the figures—not only that of the body and their proportion in itself or its coloring (in terms of its pictorial quality)—also have not only to be meaningful and show themselves as a visually pleasing image to the trained and educated eye but also to show life in a meaningful and interesting condition.

> Mit diesem französischen Kunstausdrucke bezeichenet man . . . die Stellung oder Lage lebendiger Figuren, vorzüglich in Zuständen der Ruhe. Weil aber die Kunst vermöge ihres Zwecks, nur bedeutungsvolle Gegenstände wählt, so müssen auch diese Stellungen und Lagen der Figuren nicht nur Formen der Körper und ihre Verhältnisse an sich oder durch

den Reiz der Farbenbeleuchtung (in malerischer Hinsicht), in einem vortheilhaften das gebildete Auge erfreuenden Bilde zeigen, sondern auch durch alles dieses einen bedeutungsvollen und interessanten Zustand des Lebens musterhaft darstellen.[103]

Living pictures, on the other hand, imitate two-dimensional paintings. They translate the original (three-dimensional) body as object, which had been translated into a two-dimensional representation, into another three-dimensional representation,[104] which collapses the body and the image, the signifier and the signified. Related to the tableau as a dramatic device of the stage,[105] which presents a readable, picturesque, frozen arrangement of living figures, arresting the motion of the plot for a time, the living picture reenacted or imitated the stillness of well-known paintings with the help of physical bodies.[106] Goethe's *Proserpina* (created in 1776–78 and reworked for a performance in 1814–15) is an example of this fashionable trend that had led to the creation of a distinct new hybrid genre, the monodrama, a fusion of visual, decorative elements, gestures, costumes, and music.[107]

The *Conversationslexikon* (1818), referring to tableaux as three-dimensional representations of paintings by living persons, underscores their function as a part of "artistic education" ("künstlerische Uebung") and as a "rich and stimulating form of entertainment" ("sinnreiche und reizende Festspiele").[108] The spectators had to be familiar enough with the history of art to be able to recognize the image quickly. A prerequisite for this performance art was the increasing access to art in the emerging art market—the museum and its catalogs, public collection, (sales) exhibits, and the increase in reproductions (copies or facsimiles) as independent pieces or as illustrations in books and almanacs that we discussed above. In cities with famous large collections, such as Dresden, professional performances of living pictures at the theater tended to embody paintings from the local collection.[109] Both attitudes and living pictures thus also attested to the level of cultural knowledge, awareness, and interest in the visual arts.[110]

Beyond the playful cultural recognition of the original, in this kind of parlor game the audience delighted in a sense of astonishment: "They appeal to the simplest ability to appreciate the degree of similarity to the prototype." Behind the audience's astonishment about the likeness of the original and the physical representation "there lies an

217

unconscious, piquantly disturbing feeling of uncertainty in the face of this play with illusion and reality."[111] The discomfort that follows the pleasure of looking, the stimulation of the new and the surprising, is also part of the most famous fictional account of living pictures. In Goethe's *Die Wahlverwandtschaften,* the narrator comments that the audience truly felt transposed into another world, yet the presence of real instead of semblance caused "uncanny effects" ("eine Art von ängstlicher Empfindung"). The spectator is transported into a seemingly other world, creating an ambivalent pleasure situated between amazement and uncanniness.[112] Brigitte Peucker reads this play with illusion and reality as a "testing ground for theories of representation involving the relation of the image to materiality."[113] Peucker focuses on the living picture's collapse of the distance between signifier and signified: "In doing so, tableau vivant plays on two related uncanny effects: the arrested motion or 'freezing'—hence death—of the human body, on the one hand, and the embodiment or 'bringing to life' of the inanimate image on the other hand."[114] Jooss also attributes their disquieting effect to the fact that the audience is confronted with the mortal body instead of an image. Furthermore, the body is stilled as in death.[115] This aspect produces an ambivalent, disquieting kind of stimulation that is not purely pleasurable but alternates between the pleasure of looking, the titillation of surprise, and the disturbance by the uncanny that also underlies the fascination with the gothic, as we will see in the next chapter. Yet, while the uncanny represented part of the attraction of these forms of entertainment, my analysis focuses on the visual pleasure of this form of social entertainment.

In *Die Wahlverwandtschaften,* the guests—initiated by Luciane, who is portrayed as the embodiment of a restless desire for entertainment, an almost manic striving for diversions[116]—search out, plan, and design a series of elaborate reenactments of famous paintings,[117] living pictures, which showcase Luciane's beautiful body. These activities are portrayed as most suitable to her thoroughly dilettante interests.[118]

Depending on the model to be enacted, the living picture could be a simple or elaborate undertaking that indulged the senses of the spectators with its detail and coloring in costume, props, and even (architectural and painterly) background.[119] Music sometimes underscored the mood or created certain expectations. The performance could be set apart by an elaborate frame to underscore its character as an artistic composition and to provide unity to the image. They were not arranged in front of the spectators but behind a curtain or other visual barrier so that the spectator was confronted with the full immediate effect. Devoid of dramatic action and dialogue, the living pictures allowed the exclusive focus on the visual spectacle. From family entertainment to courtly divertissement and vaudeville, the spectators seemed to derive a sense of amazement at the pictures performed by the stilled material body. At times they were connected by musical intermissions, at others they represented interludes to theatrical performances. Holmström describes such a multimedia performance entertaining the participants at the Vienna Congress:

> The performance began with a symphony, after which the candles in the salon were extinguished and the curtain was raised for the first tableau, "Louis XIV aux pieds de Madame de La Vallière," after the picture by a young Viennese artist whose name is not given. The second tableau, after a painting by Guérin, was "Hippolyte se defendant devant Thésée á l'accusion de Phèdre." The evening ended with a great tableau representing Olympus, and this culminating item was accompanied by a harp solo.[120]

Taking their place among (masked) balls, concerts, theater performances and fireworks, and chivalric performances in which the participants dressed as troubadours, knights, and ladies in period costume, living pictures represented an important form of elegant entertainment for the European elites assembled for the Vienna Congress. While professionals organized and arranged the performances, the members of the nobility performed them.

On occasion the European courts turned these elite forms of entertainment into veritable revivals of *Festspiele*. Holmström discusses such a multimedia performance, *Lalla Roock,* which was given on the occasion of a visit by Grand Duke Nicholas to the Prussian court (1821). This spectacle—based on Thomas Mores's epic, which tells the story of an Indian princess on her way to her betrothed—allowed the indulgence in exotic splendor on a grand scale. The members of the court and their guests participated in its twelve living pictures arranged by the painter Wilhelm Hensel with scenery by Schinkel, which were accompanied by music by Spontini.[121]

By 1812 the cultural practice of living pictures had become a public form of entertainment for the bourgeoisie for which tickets could be purchased. In particular, the large urban centers, such as Vienna and Berlin, offered theater evenings centered around this practice, which was performed by professional actors, accompanied by music, and enhanced by stage design.[122]

Unlike the colorful spectacle of the living pictures, attitudes were performed without a painterly background—that is, in front of a neutral, monochromatic (usually black) cloth. The dress of the performer emphasized the statuary—instead of the painterly—aspects with white drapes and shawls over a simple white chemise. Not relying on color and a differentiated visual impact, their specular entertainment value must have rested elsewhere. In my opinion, their attraction stemmed, on the one hand, from exposing the (female) beautiful body to the spectator's gaze and, on the other, from the illusion of enlivening neoclassical statuary in a Pygmalion fantasy.[123] If the appeal of living pictures lay in the stimulating sensual indulgence in the costumes and their coloring and in their overall visual appeal pleasantly occupying the gaze, one reason for the enchantment of the visually more restrained attitudes lay in the contemporary preoccupation with antiquity and its art forms, especially with the Greek statue as the classical ideal.

Inspired by Greek statuary, classical aesthetics and philosophy accentuated the body by the end of the century. The statue is, after all, the "model object that literally embodies meaning, sense, spirit and interiority."[124] As the museum culture in the German states was still in its infancy during this time period, German audiences had only limited opportunity to view Greek statuary and artifacts, especially originals. In general their access to antiquity was restricted to late Greek art and to later copies of early Grecian originals in Italy and Sicily. Greece itself was, for the most part, not accessible to German travelers in the eighteenth century.[125] The largest collections of these artifacts could be found in Mannheim (Abgußsaal) and Dresden (Antikensammlung). Although actual visits were available to a rather limited audience due to the scarcity of museums, the interest in them was high and began to change the museum culture. This growing interest in visits to collections was a part of the thriving appeal of specular diversions as a form of recreation. By the end of the eighteenth century, new museums appeared and private collections opened their doors to the public (Vienna, Berlin, Düsseldorf).[126] Johann Georg Meusel included a list of all major collections in his *Teutsches Künstlerlexikon* (first published in

1778, it appeared in enlarged editions between 1808 and 1814) to let people know what was important to see. It was not only the visit to the museum that provided amusement; for the larger audience, reading about these collections in the reports and descriptions in journals and pocket books created another, albeit less direct, form of entertainment. The fashionable plaster casts and busts for the adornment of the domestic sphere also speak vividly to the interest in neoclassical art not only for edification but also for consumption as decorative objects, as, for example, Gottlieb Martin Klauer's extensive line of casts and busts suggests.[127] The nontraveling general audience had access to these art objects only through reproductions, predominantly two-dimensional copies (*Umrissstiche*). Of course, drawings and etchings had their limitations when reproducing statues and other three-dimensional art objects.

Rehberg's drawing of Lady Hamilton's performances—and with it their originals—became well known in Germany. The images she reproduced with her body were taken from "murals, reliefs, coins, pictures on vases, in short from all available artifacts from antiquity as well as representations from mythology and history."[128] Many of these artifacts were popularized not as a direct reproduction taken from the object itself but rather in the form of a reproduction of Lady Hamilton enacting or performing the artifact in question.

Possibly fueled by the more or less scandalous stories circulating about Emma Harte's (the later Lady Hamilton's) lifestyle that undoubtedly accompanied the illustrations, they must have produced an entertaining effect, a melange of a simple, immediately accessible form of art appreciation and gossip. This unique reception practice, in turn, had a much stronger impact than simply viewing a direct copy of the same art object. Harte's legendary beauty and her extraordinary skills in modeling had made her the subject of numerous paintings. The famous painters of the time—including, among others, Romney, Tischbein, Vigeé-LeBrun, and Kauffmann—sought her out to model for them. Often she was depicted in scenes from Greek mythology. These depictions in combination with the rumors and stories about her colorful life fueled the imagination and thus the interest in this art form.

On another level, attitudes could be enjoyed as aesthetic experiments that translate the ideal, model object of Greek statuary into another art form and, at the same time, reconnect it with the mortal body. They can be read either as aesthetic experimentation, which

221

reexamines the body's role and status in the semiotic network, or as a sensual spectacle that allows the gaze to be directed at the living body.[129] After all, the (female) body takes center stage in this art form, inviting the contemplative and explorative gaze. Their entertainment value is derived from an indulgence of the gaze and from a game of cultural recognition.

Attitudes and living pictures allow for a different kind of looking at the body. The open, sustained, examining gaze at the living body—and not its representation in art—is not part of conventional social relationships, which only allow fleeting surveying glances, reading the clothed body's positionality within its social context. Guided by epistemological assumptions, these brief glances were intended primarily for the social evaluation of the bodily presentation. In other words, the body is read as a social sign, which in the second half of the eighteenth century not only presents information about gender, class, and social position but also begins to present information about the personality of its wearer, as we have discussed in connection with fashion.

The purposefully lingering gaze, on the other hand, is reserved for the aesthetic reading of the represented body in art. Only very specialized circumstances allow for the visual inspection of the physical body—examples would be the visual relationship of painter and model, the seamstress and the body to be clothed, or audience and actor. Thus a prolonged gaze at the living body represents a transgression of social norms.

Playfully suspending the distinction between the living body (model/performer) and its representation (performance of the body), the attitudes created a complicated melange of aesthetic, sensual, and social responses. Unlike in the art forms of sculpture and painting, where the relationship between the model and the representation becomes disconnected and the model as a person recedes behind the work of art, which is then judged on its aesthetic merits, the relationship between body and its representation is less tentative in the art form of attitudes. In the critical aesthetic discourse on attitudes, the personality of the performer and the performance remain closely linked, as critics had difficulty grasping the aesthetics of this genre. Unlike the copy of a body in the form of a statue, the performing body was also a social body to which certain rules and conventions apply. The comments by contemporaries convey that the same rules which govern appearance as a socially significant sign are applied to attitudes as well.

In their comments on this issue, both Herder and Goethe point to the fact that attitudes convey a sense of masquerade, of feigned sentiments, of insincerity. Herder seems disturbed and irritated by the unreliability of the body as the site of fixed meaning, as a stable, decipherable sign.[130] The body is inscribed with a lie; it feigns a different meaning with every pose or attitude. Most importantly, the body's surface refuses to reveal its "truth." Herder, Schiller, and Goethe experienced this instability or unreliability as unpleasant. After all, the bourgeois concept of identity placed a premium on being oneself and acting according to one's true convictions. Like the art of acting, the performance of attitudes put this "natural" correspondence into question. Herder's critical reaction to Emma Harte's performance has a distinctly moralistic undertone. He feels betrayed by the beautiful mimicry, which he suspects to be without substance. His irritation stems from the fact that he is unable to read the body as a sign that reveals the true sentiment; outer beauty is no indicator of inner beauty.[131] This shallowness is also alluded to in the Luciane character in *Die Wahlverwandtschaften*, who excels in this performance art more than in other forms of cultural entertainment and is able to produce a beautiful image despite the fact that she is portrayed as a highly flawed character.[132]

As discussed above, one of the force fields in the self-fashioning of the bourgeoisie had been a transformation in the signification of the clothed body. While the nobility had regarded clothes as unambiguous markers that determined social rank, the bourgeoisie went beyond these epistemological presumptions directing and reading the bodily presentations. They instead engaged in a complex system of signification, constructing and decoding the unique characteristics of the clothed body in order to uncover the subjectivity of the individual. Based on the correspondence between the physical surface of the appearance and personal interior reality, even the playful disturbance of this system was perceived as unsettling. It created an enigma, a puzzle, or a game. This destabilization contained in the game of masquerade was part of the fascination of this kind of specular parlor game and quite possibly the source of its popularity as a form of entertainment.

As a parlor game, attitudes certainly derive their entertainment value in part from the pleasure of recognizing cultural icons. By visualizing how natural bodies are marked as cultural bodies by codified facial expressions and gestures as well as vestimentary codes, attitudes demonstrated how the body becomes culturally identifiable.[133] As in a modern quiz show, spectators relied on their cultural knowledge to identify the presentation in competition with others as a form of sociable entertainment. Beyond the pleasurable diversion created by the recognition, the performance could then serve as a topic of conversation, leading into other forms of sociability.

As we will see below, Goethe's more differentiated account explores the unique aesthetic quality of the performance in greater detail. His description concentrates on the performance as a piece of visual art coming to life in a Pygmalion-like manner and furthermore changing in front of the spectators' eyes. The dreamlike quality seems to stem from a sensual flooding by these ever-transforming images. Lacking a narrative quality, the impact seems less proto-filmic or theatrical, but a modern critic might be reminded of electronic morphing techniques *ante facto*. We can imagine that the astonishment and sense of wonder was similar to its modern-day virtual version.

As contemporaries pointed out, the performances produced a genre-specific effect that could not be reproduced adequately by the visual arts or by language alone. Hirt commented on the fact that for the aesthetically trained spectator the illustration could not do justice to the uniqueness of the artistic medium of the body art of attitudes. The spectator is enchanted by the grace of the pantomime and the movement from one pose to the next. The graceful lines of the body's silhouette captured in two-dimensional drawings are supplemented by the three-dimensionality of the body's surface and its ever-so-subtle movement.[134] The formal intricacies of the fluid lines invited the eye to traverse the body's surface. The intermediary function of the living body, as the earmark of the genre, fascinated its audience and spoke to an interest in the relationship between the living body and its representation.

As other cultural practices indicate, the relationship between the body and its artistic representation enthralled the cultural imagination.[135] In Rome, German travelers like Goethe had experienced a fashionable manner of displaying the body in statuary: the contemplation of statues in flickering candle- or torchlight. Foregrounding the three-dimensionality of the work of art, not only did this practice lend a lifelike quality to the ideal representation, but the illuminated surface created an illusion of movement that suggested the living body. The flickering light, alternating light with darkness, which momentarily withdraws the object from clear view, fostered the illusion of subtle movement and thus suggested an enlivening of the aesthetic object of admiration.[136]

In addition, those who observed statues in candlelight noted that foregrounding the features of the three-dimensional surface invited tactile exploration. Herder's discussion of the aesthetic properties of statues assumes that to see implies and evokes the memory of touch. The sculptor works best from experience, from the feel of the body's surface. He does not create a primarily visual object but re-creates a tactile experience that the spectator, through the initial visual encounter, translates back into a tactile perception. Reminded of the feel of the body, the spectator mentally re-creates this sensation when experiencing a statue: "The eye is only the guide, the mind of the hand; the hand alone allows for the three-dimensionality and for the meaning within them to emerge."[137] In the mind's eye, the material has to take on the texture of the warm flesh, a process Herder also conveys verbally in his essay in the use of adjectives that conjure up tactile rather than visual images. This illusion of flesh speaks to our senses: "We forget the cold surface of the stone and instead imagine the feel of the tender skin, the round knee, the soft cheek, the beautiful bosom, the soft hip, the beautiful form of the body."[138]

According to Herder, this was the reason for the preference of Greek art to depict the body in the nude or in wet garments. The uninterrupted quality of the classical body is achieved by stressing continuity of surface, line, form, and shape. In the classical body, unity, simplicity, and a continuously flowing movement from one part of the body to the next were emphasized and violent disruption and broken or abrupt parts were avoided. As Winckelmann pointed out in his *Gedanken über die Nachahmung der griechischen Wercke in der Mahlerey und Bildhauer-Kunst (On the Imitation of Greek Art in Painting and Sculpture)* (1755), the continuity of the naked form is preserved even in the clothed figures. Greek drapery was, for the most part, taken from thin and wet garments, which, of course, clasped the body and allowed the body's shape to emerge. Contemporary criticism also notes the close relationship between look and touch. Mieke Bal writes: "For one thing, the relationship between looking and touching is, according to Freud, an inherent one. Looking is for him a derivative of touching, and therefore looking is able to arouse desire by contiguity. Rhetorically speaking, then, looking is a metonymic substitute for touching."[139]

In addition to the sensuousness of the imaginary touchable quality of the work, its spiritual nature has to be akin to our own. The ensuing attraction of the minds is a "sensation close to desire."[140] In many ways, Herder's spectator, not the artist, occupies the position of Pygmalion, who experiences the statue's coming to life. Although he is careful to situate the aesthetic experience in the balance between sensual and spiritual experience, the scales seem to tip toward the sensual aspect. Of course, the living statues of the attitudes allow for the ultimate Pygmalion fantasy. The material body is instantly stilled into a work of art, only to come alive again and freeze into the next pose or representation. In attitudes, the lightweight fabrics and shawls draping the performer's body produced an effect similar to that of the wet draperies. Blurring the distinction between the artifact and the body, between culture and nature, the attitudes collapsed the model and the finished work of art, the body and its representation, into one.

Goethe's ambivalent reaction to attitudes might also stem from his negative reading of representations of the Pygmalion myth, in which he condemns the emphasis on the artist's sensual attraction to the artifact as being tinged with sexual undertones. Only "brutes" will harbor an "erotic attraction" to the artifact.[141] From the late vantage point of his fictional biography *Dichtung und Wahrheit*, he considers this uncomfortable shifting between art and life as a most embarrassing aspect of the representations of the Pygmalion myth:

> [This stage production] alternates between nature and art and misguidedly tries to reduce the latter into the former. We see an artist who has achieved perfection and yet is not satisfied with having given external form to his ideal and thus having lent it a higher life. No! it must also be dragged down into his earthly life. Through a most commonplace sensual action he wants to destroy the highest things that thought and deed can produce.[142]

> . . . denn diese wunderliche Produktion schwankt . . . zwischen Natur und Kunst, mit dem falschen Bestreben, diese in jene aufzulösen. Wir sehen einen Künstler, der das Vollkommenste geleistet hat, und doch nicht Befriedigung darin findet, seine Idee außer sich, kunstgemäß dargestellt und ihr ein höheres Leben verliehen zu haben; nein, sie soll

auch in das irdische Leben zu ihm herabgezogen werden. Er will das Höchste was Geist und Tat hervorgebracht, durch den gemeinsten Akt der Sinnlichkeit zerstören.[143]

The artistic representation of the idea takes on a qualitatively different "higher" life that should not be contaminated with the material world. The artist who cannot distinguish between the two is not fit to be called an artist.[144]

In a similar vein, the imaginary product of attitudes is contaminated by the materiality of the performer's body. A statue elicits an imaginary tactile response, a sense that one is touching the soft flesh, the rounded knee, and so forth. The spectator of an attitude, on the other hand, is denied this exclusively aesthetic experience of "as if," the pleasure of the imaginary. Instead, the sensual response is not mediated but direct, since the artifact is produced onto a living material body. The unmediated sensual response to this body art causes irritation because it hints at the lack of control over one's body, at the possibility of the failure of the symbolic.

Yet for the popular reception of attitudes as a form of entertainment, the tension between the tactile seduction and its obvious prohibition was most likely part of the attraction. Instead of physical, tactile exploration, the performance invited visual intoxication. The body of the performer became a fantasy machine offering a variety of imaginary scenarios conjuring up the cultural context of the icon or inspiring individual fantasies. Its rapid transformation from one representation to the next also offered the stimulation of a variety of images presented in rapid succession. Furthermore, it could provide desire, the desire to see more. As Susan Sontag put it: "Sight is a promiscuous sense. The avid gaze always wants more."[145]

At the heart of this minor area within the neoclassical movement was experimentation with the integration of sensual pleasure into art. As is well known, classical anthropology—for example, that of Schiller—conjectured that human beings are divided into a sensual self and a rational self. The sensuous drive seeks immediate gratification and draws the subject toward a desired object, while the rational drive turns concrete objects into formal entities. Schiller's description of the ideal beauty of the Juno statue explains this relationship. Its ideal beauty offers a harmonious equilibrium by drawing the sensual side to formal

227

and the intellectual side to material consideration.[146] The beauty of the artifact offers a conversion of the libidinal attraction into formal entities, as Andreas Gailus elaborates:

> Since the aesthetic image is both unattainable and beautiful, it incites the beholder's passions while simultaneously reinforcing his control over these passions. The beauty of the image offers the beholder a perceptual lure that stimulates his desire; yet the self-sufficient (illusion as deception) and representational (illusion as appearance) nature of the aesthetic image prompts him to divest the object of its erotic attraction and to treat it as an object of contemplation.[147]

Kept at bay by an objectifying gaze, the object becomes a mirror-reflection of the subject's power to dominate those forces that could potentially threaten his identity. The danger of dissolution threatens the spectator's identity as a *rational* person if the dependence on external and internal stimuli cannot be overcome in an act of visual objectification. In Schiller's aesthetics, art's beautiful images serve as protective shields against forces—sensual, but above all, sexual—that threaten the male subject with the dissolution of his identity and the loss of control over both the world and his drives.[148]

The living statue of the attitudes muddles these clear distinctions, and its instability and lack of permanence resist the spectator's conventional contemplative practices and thus complicate the process of examination. While the representational aspect of the aesthetic object encourages the spectator to divest the object of its erotic attraction and the ensuing desire, and to instead treat it as an object of contemplation, the beauty of the physical body turned statue resists this form of divestment. Instead it offers the spectator a different and stronger perceptual attraction that stimulates desire, disrupting the conventional process of objectification. At the same time, the danger of dissolution, of a loss of control over the libidinous drives, is accompanied by the pleasure of the abyss.

While the performance draws the (male) gaze inevitably and unabashedly to the female body, the metamorphosis from one cultural (religious/mythological) icon to the next vacillates between offering and withdrawing the female body. Because dress is one of the most important cultural implements for articulating and territorializing human corporeality (and thus for mapping erotogenic zones and for affixing a sexual identity),[149] the change in dress from one pose to the next—often achieved by a quick change of attributes such as shawls and veils—displaced the libidinal centers of erotic gravity.[150] At the same time, the body of the performer could withdraw itself from the desiring gaze by the representation of religious icons, for example that of *mater dolorosa*.[151] Destabilizing the female body as a site for the (male) erotic gaze, it created female sexuality as free-floating sexualizing of the whole body. These transformations construct female sexuality and subjectivity in ways that are at least potentially disruptive of the symbolic order that valorizes continuity and coherence.[152] Sensuality demands temporal change and sensory richness. While the sensuous drive strives for emotional intensity, the formal, that is, rational, drive seeks personal stability. The attitudes deemphasize stability while reveling in the seemingly endless potential for change and variety associated with the performer's body. The art form of attitudes resists this aesthetic reorganization of the spectator's affective structures. The performer interrupts contemplation in her switch to another pose or representation. She steps out of the gaze and disrupts the process of objectification.

The (male) spectator's pleasure might very well lie in the fantasy of a tension between successful and unsuccessful objectification. By destabilizing the process of objectification, the spellbinding spectacle of the body in the attitudes elicited both the pleasure and the horror of dissolution. Objectification serves as a protective shield against sensual and sexual forces that threaten the male subject with the dissolution of his identity and the loss of control over both the world and his drives. Attitudes then provide a pleasurable dynamic interplay between the familiar and the unfamiliar, between confirmation and transgression of expectations. Holding the pose just long enough to be read, the image captures a single moment in time only to transform into another moment in history with the shift of the body (and a few vestimentary attributes).

In the attitudes, the kinetic aspects of theater (mimic, gestural) as well as the appearance of the actor (hairstyle, costume) devoid of linguistic signs intersected with the visual impact associated with statues. The allure of the clothing used represents another facet in the erotic attraction of attitudes. The white chemise and the soft shawls, the natural long hair put up with only a comb—the eighteenth-century reinterpretation of Grecian garments—draped the female body loosely yet revealingly, merely suggesting the underlying shape of the body. Certain movements allowed the fabric to cling and thus offered glimpses at the contours of the body. Thus the performer's dress both revealed and concealed the body. Her apparel hints at the secret hidden body, thus creating an erotic spectacle. "Is not the most erotic portion of the body where the garment gapes?" asks Barthes,[153] and Nichols—from the perspective of film studies—confirms that "intermittence, the flash of skin between the folds of clothing, the game of hide-and-seek raised to an erotic level—this is what seduces."[154] Of course, the assertion that the suggestively clothed body is more erotic because it retains desire while the naked body satiates the eye had been a commonplace since Hogarth until this view was challenged to some degree by the neoclassicism of Winckelmann and his followers. The soft, revealing fabric that hints at the surface of the body invites the gaze to roam over a variety of focal points and thus offers an entertaining occupation with each new pose. In addition, the novelty of this uncommon experience and the motion involved created an "agreeable Surprise" that playfully engages curiosity and creates the desire and the drive to see more.[155]

This form of dress was influenced by innovations in the attire for painters' models. The painter Vigée-Lebrun had draped her models in shawls in the style of Raphael and Domenichino, thus creating this new convention in body-revealing clothes. She also produced two famous paintings of Lady Hamilton, in the style of Domenichino as a sibyl and in antique style as a bacchant dancing with a tambourine.[156] Combined with the influence of classical costumes, which symbolized the revolutionary virtues of simplicity and republicanism, Vigée-Lebrun surmised that her costumes influenced the fashion of her day, beginning in Paris and quickly spreading through Europe. This intersection of a number of forms of cultural expression from a variety of fields allows glimpses at the complex interchanges and transformations within the body of culture.

This example cautions us against interpreting cultural developments one-dimensionally. For example, it is simplistic to see innovations in the area of high culture (painting) as binarily opposed to phenomena of mass culture (fashion). Instead, the multilayered example of the attitudes points to the complex interweaving of various strands of cultural expression. As this example demonstrates, the exchange between high culture and popular culture is neither a necessarily adversarial nor a stable series of reductive dichotomies but rather a place of convergence.

Lady Hamilton as a culturally significant site is an important node in this interplay of mutually influential cultural practices. Her natural beauty, the ability to pose (which she had learned as a model), and the ability to take advantage of the more natural body-displaying clothing à la Vigée-Lebrun made her successful as a sought-after model and an enchanting performer of attitudes influencing the cultural imagination. In turn, pictorial representations of her in paintings and her reputation as a performer of attitudes helped to popularize these cultural innovations. Her style not only inspired the world of fashion but also contributed to a changing concept of beauty, participating in altering women's relationship to their bodies. The imitation of classical beauty, which is seemingly more natural and less disciplining than the body shaped by heavy corsets that was celebrated in earlier fashions, required that the body itself take on a new shape. The care of the body through dietic measures and exercise not only became a source of entertainment but also introduced a new standard of beauty.[157]

The playful character of this form of performance art, the game of masquerade and recognition, created a unique form of pleasure. The unexpected, the formal experiment, especially when it mixed features from various art forms (theater, painting, music, and pantomime), created interest and provoked a pleasurable response within a broad and diverse audience. At the same time, this form of visual intoxication, the spellbinding event, transforms the gaze into a commodity that could be sold to a consumer-spectator. In addition, the reproducibility of the event and its commercial availability fashioned it as a proto-photographic or even proto-cinematic event. Commentary on attitudes by one of its practitioners—Elise Bürger, in her short play "Die antike Statue aus Florenz"[158]—suggests that even objects from the realm of "high art"—albeit in the form of copies—can be (mis)used as objects provoking an erotic rather than an aesthetic response.

In Bürger's short play, the bored husband, after enjoying a performance of attitudes, begins to collect antique (female) statuary. The increasing availability of plaster casts for domestic consumption enables him to gain access to these artworks. The voyeuristic consumption of art in the privacy of his study takes him away from his family. When his wife learns that he is enamored with antique statuary and living pictures, she seizes the opportunity to take the place of a life-sized statuary that broke in transit. As her husband admires the beauty of the statue, it comes alive. This disquieting Pygmalion fantasy redirects his attention back at his wife. The wife and her confidante/sister conclude that the playful shifting of roles symbolized in attitudes and living pictures alleviates boredom by adding an element of novelty and surprise to the familiarity of marriage. A similar sentiment is voiced in a satirical report on a school for the performance art of attitudes and living pictures ("Ankündigung einer Academie der schönen Shawl-Künste") in the *Journal des Luxus und der Moden* (1811):

> The influence of these cultural practices on human happiness is obvious. A wife trained in the art of attitudes can present herself in many different ways, thus avoiding the dangers of boredom. . . . A woman thus trained is like a walking art exhibit, a portable gallery, and a living museum.

> Der Einfluß dieser Künste auf menschliche Glückseligkeit springt in die Augen. Eine in der Shawlkunst unterrichtete Frau kann sich dem Manne in allerlei Gestalten zeigen und das gefährliche Einerlei vermeiden. . . . Eine also abgerichtete Frau ist gleichsam ein wandelndes Kunstkabinet, eine Galerie portative und ein lebendiges Museum.[159]

These performances in the privacy of the parlor as cultural entertainment offer a semblance of variety within the intensity of the monogamous relationship of the couple in marriage. When art objects are taken out of their public context, copied, reproduced, and made widely available (for purchase) so that they can be viewed privately, their function changes.

The text hints at the fact that this private, isolated viewing altered and reduced the magical and religious authority of the original (statue).[160] It furthermore suggests that, used in this manner, neither the attitudes nor the reproductions of art objects representing the body would qualify as art, because this use discourages pure aesthetic pleasure. In this constellation the pleasurable response is directed at the materiality of the body and not its imaginary representation. The ideational object is contaminated by the interest in the real object, the body. The spectator's task of distancing himself from the actual physical sensations originating in the body is not performed. The materiality of the (re)presenting body destroys the illusionary effect, disallowing pure aesthetic pleasure. The qualitatively different experiences of pleasure—the aesthetic enjoyment of art on the one hand and physical pleasure on the other—are not clearly distinguished in the form of the attitudes. The performer's body contaminated the ideational object. These elements—reproducibility, commodification, the pleasure of visual intoxication—clearly delineate this phenomenon as part of entertainment, of cultural consumption as a fashionable pastime for the entertainment in ever wider private circles as part of domestic sociability of the middle class in nineteenth-century Germany.

Goethe and the Spectacle of *Attitüden*

Goethe purports to have become interested in this art form during his travels in Italy. His account of the genre of attitudes has become the most influential description of the genre. Yet we have to keep in mind that his seemingly autobiographical description of the performance (quoted below) was written years after his trip, which took place earlier than Lady Hamilton's performances. This suggests that he only heard and read about them.[161] His own highly subjective account commented only on those (neoclassical) elements that interested him in his account of this dilettante form of art. I see his interest in the genre in the context of his attempt to recapture the sensuality of his Italian experiences and transpose them into contemporary German culture.

> She is very lovely and has a good figure. He [Hamilton] has had a Grecian costume made for her that suits her to perfection, and she lets down her hair, takes a few shawls, and varies her postures, gestures, expressions, etc. until at last the onlooker really thinks he is dreaming. In her movements and surprising variety one sees perfected what so many thousands of artists would have liked to achieve. Standing, kneeling, sitting, lying, grave, sad, roguish, wanton, penitent, enticing, menacing, fearful, etc., one follows upon the other and from the other. She knows how to choose and change the folds of her veil to set off each expression, and makes herself a hundred different headdresses with the same cloth. The old knight holds up the light for her performances and has devoted himself heart and soul to his art object. He sees in her all the antiquities, all the beautiful profiles on Sicilian coins, even the Apollo Belvedere itself. This much is certain, it is unique entertainment![162]

233

Sie ist sehr schön und wohlgebaut. Er [Hamilton] hat ihr ein griechisches Gewand machen lassen, das sie trefflich kleidet, dazu löst sie die Haare auf, nimmt ein paar Shawls und macht eine Abwechslung von Stellungen, Gebärden, Mienen etc., daß man zuletzt wirklich meint, man träume. Man schaut, was so viele tausend Künstler gerne geleistet hätten, hier ganz fertig, in Bewegung und überraschender Abwechslung. Stehend, knieend, sitzend, liegend, ernst, traurig, neckisch, ausschweifend, bußfertig, lockend, drohend, ängstlich etc. Eins folgt aufs andere und aus dem andern. Sie weiß zu jedem Ausdruck die Falten des Schleiers zu wählen, zu wechseln und macht sich hundert Arten von Kopfputz mit denselben Tüchern. Der alte Ritter hält das Licht dazu und hat mit ganzer Seele sich diesem Gegenstand ergeben. Er findet in ihr alle Antiken, alle schönen Profile der sizilianischen Münzen, ja den belveder'schen Apoll selbst. So viel ist gewiß, der Spaß ist einzig.[163]

Goethe's description focuses on the visual quality of the performance. Although delighted with the beautiful face and body, he is even more fascinated with the idea of an instantaneous piece of art, with the fantasy that the vision of the artist could be translated into an art object without the resistance of the material and its technical limitations. Goethe's curious exaggeration "all the antiquities . . . even the Apollo Belvedere itself" places him in Winckelmann's footsteps by evoking the cultural context for attitudes: the revival of antiquity as the reintroduction of sensuality into contemporary eighteenth-century culture. After all, the most important statues were male nudes, many of them torsos, suggesting the impossibility that Lady Hamilton would have indeed been performing the most important works.[164] Goethe thus foregrounds the aesthetic effect produced by the attitudes, the fact that he is fascinated by the dizzying spectacle. His breathless description concentrates on the performance as a piece of visual art coming to life in a Pygmalion-like manner and changing in front of the spectators' eyes in a dizzying arrangement of stillness and movement. It is the surprising and instantaneous variation the performer's body is able to produce that fascinates Goethe.[165] The dreamlike quality stems from a sensual flooding by these ever-transforming images; unlike in the process of observing marble statues, here the sense of sight can hardly keep up with the transformation and is not allowed to fully contemplate each image. The image of the dream suggests a loss of control, of being swept away by images. With uncontrollability we associate the abandonment of the highly controlled sphere of the superego. This loss of control is, of course, also at the core of the cultural construction of sexuality in Western cultures. Because it is associated with loss of control over the environment and the drives, the sexual drive endangers identity. It is both the attraction of such abandonment and the fear of its potential for disorder that cause Goethe's ambivalent reaction.[166]

The question of how the presentation of the human body in statues achieves its lifelike quality—creating the illusion that it came alive under the gaze of the spectator—occupied the aesthetic discourse of the time.[167] Attitudes are one experimental answer to this question. Lessing's famous formulation of the "pregnant" moment in his "Laokoon" essay is, of course, also an attempt to theorize the way in which statues seem to come alive. He argued that since the visual artist is limited to depicting one moment, it has to be carefully selected because it must retain its representative character over many and prolonged viewings. Any exaggeration and distortion of the body by depicting extreme passion would repulse the viewer over longer duration.

To avoid this unpleasant effect, Lessing argues, the artist selects the moment before the decisive moment or before the culmination of the highest degree of sentiment. The spectator's imagination is called upon to complete the range of emotion.[168] The imagination supplies the vivid images of the physical manifestations accompanying these emotions, and in doing so the marble seems to come alive. The degree of engagement on the part of the spectator correlates with the degree of mental and sensual stimulation. The implication is that an exaggeration of a pose or emotion limits the spectator's participation in the completion process and thus in the mental animation of the statue.

The same argument can be made for attitudes as well. Unlike an actor, the performer does not complete a range of emotions and therefore allows the spectator the pleasure of completion. Yet by controlling the speed with which each stilled image is dissolved into the next one, the spectator loses power over this imaginary play, creating the spellbinding impression of being swept away by images. The tension between the habitual viewing practices of statues and their disruption by performativity, by changing from one pose to the (unrelated) next, creates the spellbinding effect. Just when spectators have "settled into" one image and begun to contemplate it, the vision disappears and melds into the next one, stunning them and disrupting their imaginary completion of the represented mood.

Goethe, in his discussion of the Laokoon statue, foregrounds the relationship between the pregnant moment and the illusion of movement:

> The great significance of this work lies in its presentation of a particular moment. If a sculpture is to convey to the viewer a sense of real movement, it has to portray a fleeting moment. We must be convinced that no part of the whole was in its present position just prior to this instant, and that no part will be in the same position just afterwards. If this is so, the sculpture will forever be a living image for countless millions.[169]

> Äußerst wichtig ist dieses Kunstwerk durch die Darstellung des Moments. Wenn ein Werk der bildenden Kunst sich wirklich vor dem Auge bewegen soll, so muß ein vorübergehender Moment gewählt sein; kurz vorher darf kein Theil des Ganzen sich in dieser Lage befunden haben, kurz nachher muß jeder Theil genötigt sein, diese Lage zu verlassen; dadurch wird das Werk Millionen Anschauern immer wieder neu lebendig sein.[170]

In this account, the statuary becomes interesting and pleasurable to the spectator precisely because it seems to come alive. To clarify this point, Goethe suggests that upon closing one's eyes for a moment, the spectator almost fears that the statue will look differently, will have changed positions. Thus the ideal statue is but a "fixed lightning, a wave petrified as it comes on land" ("fixierter Blitz, eine Welle, versteinert im Augenblicke da sie gegen das Ufer anströmt").[171] A similar attempt to enliven the marble was the aforementioned practice of viewing statuary in flickering torchlight.[172]

Herder focuses on the sense of touch in his theoretical account of the attraction of statues, a notion that Goethe takes up in the Fifth Roman Elegy. For Herder, sight and touch are intertwined; to see implies and evokes the memory of touch. The sculptor works best from experience, that is, from the memory of the touch of the beautiful body. For Herder, touch, the lowest but the most basic sense, is the foundation upon which the other senses are constructed. Their interplay provides an integrated impression of one's surroundings: "The eye is only a guide, only the hand's reasoning; only the hand provides a sense of dimension and a concept of the object" ("Das Auge ist nur Wegweiser, nur die Vernunft der Hand; die Hand allein gibt *Formen,* Begriffe deßen, was sie *bedeuten,* was in ihnen *wohnet*").[173] In the mind's eye, the material takes on the texture of flesh. Sight evokes the memory of touch and in effect becomes touch by moving into the nerve endings of the fingertips, which attracts our spirit in a sensation close to desire (*Wollust*).[174] The seduction of this repetition of the Pygmalion myth stems from the effect of the perceptual impressions on the imagination. It is on the wings of the imagination that the eroticized, visually stimulated touch takes flight and produces the desired effect, a sensual, pleasurable attraction close to sexual excitement.

The Enlightenment's privileging of sight as the icon of rationality became destabilized with the increasing valorization of the sense of touch (Winckelmann, Herder, Goethe). Less sharply delineated than the other senses (after all, sight, hearing, smell, and taste all have unique, confined functions), touch is singled out by Sander Gilman as a unique sense: "Touch seems to be an undifferentiated quality of the entire body, but it is, in fact, a multifunctional aspect of the skin. Touch is indeed the complex response of sensors that judge pressure, temperature, and vibration. But the receptors are not clearly differentiated by function."[175] In the epistemology of perceptions, touch was associated with a direct and unreflective empirical access to reality and became thus linked with irrationality. Gilman points out that in the iconography of Western fine arts, touch is seen as the erotic sense, and Eros as the antithesis of rationality was linked with madness.[176]

If vision produces the memory of touch at the sight of a marble statue, a similar yet unique effect must be produced when observing the living statue. Yet the visual inspection of the body's surface, which evokes the sense of touch, does not have to transform the cold marble. The skin itself evokes the memory of touch, limiting the experience by eliminating the task of mental transformation (marble into skin) yet retaining the second aspect, that is, being reminded of the sense of touch. This more direct eroticization of an actual body under the aegis of art leads, we can infer, even more directly to a sensation close to what Herder termed "lust" (*Wollust*).[177]

Stripped of some of its formal mental transformatory work, attitudes, more crassly than statues, expose the effects of the kind of art appreciation Winckelmann had initiated. His discussion of the aesthetic and sensual stimulation of the statue helped to create the powerful fantasy of the sexualized touch.

By disrupting contemplation (in moving from one pose to the next) as a form of divestment and by curtailing some of the powers of imagination (the sight of marble recalling the feel of skin), attitudes offer a more directly erotic/sexual attraction. It is experienced as less pleasurable because the pleasures of the imaginary are limited and because the performer contaminates the purity of the imaginary pleasure experienced in art appreciation.

When discussing the erotic attraction of statues, Herder and Goethe abstract the erotic touch from actual physical bodies. Only on this idealized level could the eroticization of touch be divested of its negative connotations of disease and pain. This is the expectation with which Goethe and Herder approach the representation of the body in attitudes. However, this idealization cannot be maintained in the attitudes because the reality of the individual performer intrudes. Social realities of character, identity, gender roles, morality, and its cultural manifestations in the traditional iconography spoil the indulgence in sensual fantasies. This is why Herder and Goethe feel compelled to comment on their disappointment over the discrepancy between their idealized expectations and the realities of the performer. Both use the metaphor of the dream (the site of uncontrolled abandon, which we had associated with sexuality) into which reality in the form of the woman performer intrudes. Noting her lack of sophistication, education, and moral character, Herder refers to Emma (before her marriage to Hamilton) with the technically correct yet strong language of "Hamilton's whore." In short, the social realities disrupt the dream of sensuality. The attempt to infuse contemporary culture with the sensuousness of antiquity by making the artifact "come to life," thus rescuing its seductive qualities and its role in the creation of desire for a contemporary audience, works only in the realm of art and culture. Here, desire—always unfulfilled—can drive the demand for ever-new forms of stimulation.

8

The Stimulation of Nature: Travel, Resorts, Spas, and Gardens

TRAVEL

The eighteenth century saw a significant increase in travel as a leisured "temporary displacement" for the purpose of entertainment.[1] Some contemporaries spoke of a veritable travel mania much like the maligned reading craze.[2] Both display a similar desire for ever-new stimulation in an attempt to repeat the sensation of pleasure created by the new impressions. Just as the relationship between the new print media and the material culture of fashion was a synergetic one, a mutually enhancing relationship also exists between the many forms of travel writing (i.e., letters, diaries, travelogues, descriptions and novels, and the emergent genre of guidebooks) and the material practice of travel. Travel could not have become an important form of leisure entertainment without the significant preparatory work of the print media. Travel literature provided practical information (which removed the discomfort of uncertainty from travel) while also raising certain expectations regarding the experience the traveler was likely to enjoy. This reading practice constituted an important part in the pleasures of the imaginary, the fantasies about endless possibilities, a reveling in the potential reactions of the self to these forms of stimulation.

Furthermore, travel literature provided an endless stream of stimulating fare for the armchair traveler. The change in mentalities with its new sense of space and the desire to expand the horizon stimulated the interest in travel literature. Not only did travel literature provide a means of self-improvement and a sign of one's taste and acculturation, but interest in it was further amplified by a distinct hunger for entertainment. Literature provided the pleasurable stimulation of novelty in its adventures and glimpses at new and different cultural practices. The cultural memory stored in descriptive travel accounts was supplemented by the visual memory that the interest in landscape painting had created. Not unlike travel accounts, the traveler's and (reader's) knowledge of art history creates certain expectations and pre-structures the experience. As a preparatory activity, reading travel literature had, I would argue, an ambiguous effect. On the one hand, it endowed the anticipated travel with countless opinions, fantasies, information, and expectations that could enrich the actual experience by embellishing it with culture. On the other hand, this knowledge pre-structured the experience by providing patterns of expectations and perspectives that would render original, spontaneous, and naive experiences virtually impossible. Just as the physical risks of travel were reduced through proper planning and organization, new experiences were often filtered through previous knowledge gleaned from travel literature. Extensive reading practices familiarized travelers with certain sites and also with the emotions and reactions of other travelers, thereby turning travel into a calculable event. Travel became codified and followed certain norms.[3] Already in this early phase of more extended leisure travel, the stimulation of travel seemed to have been not spontaneous and original but culturally mediated. By limiting the physical, mental, and sensual insecurities of travel, this acculturation of the experience provided the safety that established it as a fashionable form of entertainment.

My reading of leisure travel differs from recent theories of travel to varying degrees and in emphasis. Ursula Becher reads travel as a flight from everyday life into a counter-world; Rudy Koshar sees it as an attempt to find meaning beyond the everyday or, in a later study, as an attempt to come to terms with the quintessentially modern experience of displacement.[4] Orvar Löfgren considers tourism a cultural laboratory, a field of experimentation for new leisure practices, while John Urry focuses on travel as a departure from the ordinary, with particular emphasis on its visual elements.[5] My understanding of travel as a form of entertainment emphasizes the playfully stimulating effect of the estrangement from the familiar, of temporary displacement, the experience of the extraordinary and the spectacular. Unlike Löfgren, I see travel as one of many forms of entertainment, not a privileged or anticipatory version. Like Urry, I emphasize the visual excitement of travel as entertainment, which is, however, supplemented by additional forms of stimulation.

By the last decades of the eighteenth century, travel was no longer limited to the elite Grand Tour, which afforded worldly polish and sociopolitical connections to the elite male education.[6] Instead, several forms and purposes of travel flourished alongside each other: the remnants of the Grand Tour, the goal-oriented business trip, the scientific journey of discovery, the informal educational travel (*Bildungsreise*) of the modern intellectual or artist, and the emergent leisure travel for the purpose of (cultural) entertainment. The latter was dominated by the fashionable interest in the picturesque as the novel, the unexpected, the astounding, the bizarre, and the marvelous, in the varied and rich impression of the landscape creating vivid sensations, which are perceived as pleasurable stimulation.

The most accessible published travel accounts tend to be those of intellectuals and artists or writers and thus belong to the genre of *Bildungsreise*. Seeking out momentous experiences, this kind of travel was designed to enrich the self. The *Bildungsreise* was part of the process toward self-perfection and a harmonious integration of the individual and society through culture. It seeks out significant sites of culture—famous paintings and statuary, architecture, and monuments but also famous landscapes and sights—for study and enjoyment while also indulging in instances of cultural entertainment. The *Bildungsreise* thus displayed the widest range of cultural practices, from certain elements of the more elite Grand Tour, to the complex pleasures of high culture associated with the identity construction of the individual, and to the sensual pleasure derived from indulging the wandering gaze (*Schaulust*). Leisure travel could—if desired—liberate itself momentarily and at will from the need for self-cultivation (*Bildung*) and instead focus on enjoying the poetic qualities of beautiful landscapes, or it could indulge the wandering gaze, deriving pleasure from the visual stimulation. At the same time, it could provide entertainment to wider groups that did not seek *Bildung*, thus offering a range of ways to experience the unfamiliar. The pleasure derived from the forms of entertainment associated with travel compelled increasingly wider strata of the middle class to participate, thus driving this form of cultural consumption. The following examples of the forms of entertainment that travel provides are taken from accounts of leisure travel and *Bildungsreisen.*

Elise Bürger's travel sketches come closest to recording the pleasures of travel.[7] Goethe's *Bildungsreise,* described in his *Italienische Reise*—in particular in its first part (September 1786 to February 1787)—displays elements from the scientific journey of discovery and is dominated by the pursuit of *Bildung,* but it also indulges in forms of cultural entertainment. With a touch of envy, he acknowledges the leisure travelers who travel exclusively to indulge the gaze: "I . . . study more than I enjoy. . . . How fortunate those travelers are who merely look and move on" ("ich . . . studiere mehr als ich genieße. . . . Wie glücklich find' ich Reisende, die sehn und gehn").[8] This comment suggests a contemporary awareness of the existence of leisure travel as an important form of entertainment that derived the sensation of pleasure largely through a steady stream of visual stimulations. Elisa von der Recke's travel accounts—although in a different manner and to varying degrees—also display elements of both self-edification and self-culturation on the one hand and forms of entertainment on the other.[9] Although she is also interested in the cultural riches of the sites she visits, her self-proclaimed intent is didactic. Interested in the political turmoil during the Napoleonic reign, critical of perceived abuses of power, at times moralistic in tone with a strong religious undercurrent, she wants to expand the horizons of her readership.[10] She contextualizes her impressions with the appropriate history lesson or additional information, giving depth to the information she presents. Yet she also succumbs to pure visual indulgence (*Schaulust*) at the site of an especially panoramic view that invites the gaze to wander over its varied surfaces:

> Wherever we turned our gaze, the area surrounding us boasted splendor and riches. Clean, delightfully built villages and cities alternated with attractive villas on the hills, so that they seemed to be connected by stretches of gardens. Far in the distance the Apennine Mountains hid their peaks in the clouds and the foothills formed a brilliant amphitheater. The spicy fragrant air from the meadows and the blooming vineyards surrounded us with their refreshing balsam. Nature seemed to breathe gaiety and felicity.

> Wohin der Blick sich wendete, prangte die Gegend umher in

Herrlichkeit und Fülle. Saubere, niedlich gebaute Flecken und Städte, und auf den Höhen reizende Villen, wechselten nachbarlich mit einander ab, daß sie gleichsam durch große Gartenabtheilungen verbunden zu seyn schienen. Fern am Horizont bargen die Apenninen ihre Häupter in den Wolken, und die Vorberge mit ihren Weinhügeln bildeten ein glänzendes Amphitheater. Die würzhafte Luft von den Wiesen und von den in Blüthe stehenden Weinbergen her, umfloß uns erquickend mit ihrem stärkenden Balsam. Die ganze Natur scheint hier Heiterkeit und Frohsinn zu athmen.[11]

Like other occasions for the indulgence in specular pleasures discussed in this study, travel provided ample opportunity for the wandering gaze that could (momentarily) suspend the precise semiosis of the artist or scientist. The utilitarian or humanist trend to record the experience of the new sites could be abandoned in favor of an unsystematic look, glance, or gaze.

Leisure and scientific travel influence each other, even though they exhibit different goals. The former was interested in the indulgence of the gaze and in the "evocation of intuitive reactions, the latter in the study of the external singulars."[12] Barbara Stafford maintains that the scientific factual voyage differs "from all other forms of wandering" with its new forms of perception and classification and its essentially humanist, Enlightenment ideal of "spreading knowledge."[13] The extensive multivolume collection *Bibliothek der neuesten und wichtigsten Reisebeschreibungen* (Library of the Latest and Most Important Travel Accounts) was an example for the dissemination of travel descriptions utilizing the scientific gaze.[14] The scientific gaze strove to invent a new "factual" mode of literary or visual expression to convey the novelty of the discovered lands in their specificity.

Although Goethe is unable to claim original finds, traces of the spirit of discovery and scientific classification can be found throughout his travel accounts. The rock formations he encounters remind him of collections he has seen and prompt him to wish he could take samples along for his own collection.[15] His interest in botany led him to visit a famous botanist in Vicenza in the hopes of seeing his collection.[16] Goethe's speculation on the idea of an *Urpflanze* as the common source of all plant diversity is spurred on by the specular pleasure stimulated by diverse new forms: "It is agreeable and instructive to wander amidst vegetation that is foreign to us. . . . Here in this newly encountered diversity, the idea of mine keeps gaining strength, namely, that perhaps all plant forms can be derived from one plant" ("Es ist erfreuend und belehrend, unter einer Vegetation herumzugehen, die uns fremd ist. . . . Hier in dieser mir entgegentretenden Mannigfaltigkeit wird jener Gedanke immer lebendiger").[17] The sense of estrangement created by the unfamiliar is perceived as positive because it allows for new impressions that can stimulate fresh insights.

Technical and material innovations contributed to making travel a part of middle-class leisure and entertainment and to expand its practice to larger groups, including women. Travel dress as an object of material culture was but one of many objects that enabled this new form of cultural consumerism—travel for entertainment. Other items advertised or described in the *Journal*, such as more comfortable coaches or the travel pillow (1:258–59), signaled a trend of bringing as many comforts of the domestic sphere into this other social context and, in a sense, domesticating it (fig. 14). Maps and written travel guides allow travelers to access cities and landscapes without the help of hosts or guides. "Map in hand," writes Goethe, "I tried to find my

14. Hunting and leisure coach in *Journal des Luxus und der Moden* 23 (1808). Courtesy of the Bildarchiv Preußischer Kulturbesitz Berlin. Photo by Dietmar Katz.

way through the strangest labyrinth" ("Den Plan in der Hand suchte ich mich durch die wunderlichsten Irrgänge").[18] Guidebooks and maps liberated travelers from their dependence on expensive or dishonest guides.[19] Guides like the volumes by the Koblenz bookshop owner Karl Baedeker would become instrumental in fostering travel on a larger scale as they helped to organize, plan, and estimate the cost of travel and, in addition, create a "canon" of the most important sights (as the German term *Sehenswürdigkeit*, "an object worth seeing," suggests).

With the establishment of fixed routes, which the postal coaches traveled at regularly scheduled intervals, travel could be more easily planned and conducted. This service also provided the protection of travel insurance, and thus travel became less perilous. Insurance encouraged travelers to surrender their possessions to highway robbers, which led to less loss of life.[20] Guidebooks and advice books assisted travelers in finding safe accommodations, reported on the condition of the roads, calculated distances and time on the road, and gave information on prices and costs for services. The regularly scheduled postal coach, the innovations of more comfortable private coaches, published travel guides, travelogues, and descriptions of items related to travel in the periodical press (more appropriate travel dress, other innovations like the travel pillow, increasing personal hygiene, etc.) were important cultural elements that created this modern conception of travel as entertainment. The pleasures of travel depended on a degree of safety and comfort in this sanitized, tamed, and "disciplined" adventure.[21] The dangerous elements of travel and the confrontation with threatening others—highwaymen, robbers, gypsies, or native populations of exotic lands—lived on in adventure novels. The safety of the written text (ranging from travel guides and travel accounts to adventure novels) could provide an enjoyable degree of stimulation and excitement and satisfy the hunger for novelty and temporary imaginary destabilization.

A crisscrossing of various kinds of travel writing circulates in Elise Bürger's autobiographical essay "Die Gefahr und der Postknecht auf der Reise nach Trier" ("Danger and the Coachman on the Trip to Trier"),[22] which relates a close encounter with robbers. In this autobiographical travel note turned adventure tale with supernatural overtones, the narrator is on her way on a route that is too remote to be serviced by regular mail coach. However, she is able to procure the services of the mail coachman to take her to her destination after all. The sense of security of this arrangement is shattered as she reads the newspaper which, perchance, reports on recent robberies in the area that she is traveling.[23] As she is the only traveler, her growing sense of unease prompts her to leave the coach carrying some of her money and a small, unloaded pistol and knife. The coachman urges her to reenter the coach. Her hesitation whether to follow her instincts or the coachman's advice creates suspense as she (and the reader) tries to determine which is the greater danger: to be alone in an isolated forest or in the company of an untrustworthy guide. Robbers do indeed appear, but they retreat as they hear the coachman's whistle. As it turns out, the coachman's father had spared the life of one of the robbers, and in gratitude they vowed to spare the coaches driven by his son. The modern medium of the newspaper reporting on current events and the modern practice of leisure travel become fused with the adventure tale with gothic overtones of bloody crime in this autobiographical travel sketch as adventure literature. The fact that she carries weapons suggests the remnants of danger in leisure travel. On the other hand, the knife is said to be small and the weapon is unloaded, conveying an overall sense of trust in this new form of entertainment, leisure travel, which was necessary for the focus on pleasure in which danger is mainly imaginary, not real.

In many ways, leisure travel for entertainment was made possible by scientific travels, which had widened the geographical and cultural horizon for everyday culture. This kind of inventory taking and mapping mastered the wild and tamed geography through knowledge, reducing the real dangers to a level at which travel could be perceived as pleasurable. The acculturation of travel transformed the remaining sense of danger into a sense of adventure that—coupled with the stimulation of new impressions of people, places, and events—made travel a highly pleasurable event. The modern traveler was relatively insulated not only from the dangers of travel but also from the dangers of being confronted with other places and lifestyles and thus having to questions his or her own way of life.[24] The mediation through culture turned travel from an existential experience into a form of entertainment that could be consumed at will and as frequently as one liked—provided one's economic situation allowed it. This knowledge prestructured the experience by providing patterns of expectations and perspectives that rendered original, spontaneous, and naive experiences virtually impossible.

Within this domestication and taming of travel, discovery became rediscovery because it revisited the cultural icons of the educational tradition of the time. The element of novelty sprang from the traveler's individual reaction to the site, which was familiar from previous, often illustrated, travel accounts. In his desire to travel south as quickly as possible, Goethe feels he cannot do justice to providing a comprehensive account of his visits, but he is confident that his educated readers are already familiar with most details from other accounts and thus focuses on his sensual impressions: "But I am consoled by the thought that in our statistical era all this is no doubt already printed, and one can learn about it from books at one's convenience. At present I am only concerned with sense impressions, which no book, no picture, can give" ("Dabei kann ich mich trösten, daß in unseren statistischen Zeiten dies alles wohl schon gedruckt ist, und man sich gelegentlich davon in Büchern unterrichten kann. Mir ist jetzt nur um die sinnlichen Eindrücke zu tun, die kein Buch, kein Bild gibt").[25]

In particular, Goethe's visit to Rome shows the relationship between the novelty of travel and the cultural expectations that were socialized within the everyday culture of the domestic realm and the family and then enhanced, standardized, and canonized in formal education. Nevertheless, Goethe credits the everyday culture of his childhood and youth (which produces the habits and cultural currency in the pursuit of *Bildung* and social distinction) for setting the stage for his Rome experience:

> Now I see all my childhood dreams come to life; I see now in reality the first engravings that I remember (my father had hung the prospects of Rome in a corridor); and everything long familiar to me in paintings and drawings, copperplates and woodcuts, in plaster and cork, now stands together before me. Wherever I go I find something in this new world that I am aquainted with; it is all as I imagined, and yet new. And the same can be said of my observations, my thoughts. I have had no entirely new thought, have found nothing entirely unfamiliar, but the old thoughts have become so precise, so alive, so coherent that they can pass for new.

> Alle Träume meiner Jugend seh' ich nun lebendig; die ersten Kupferbilder, deren ich mich erinnere (mein Vater hatte die Prospekte von Rom auf einem Vorsaale aufge-

hängt), seh' ich nun in Wahrheit, und alles, was ich in Gemälden und Zeichnungen, Kupfern und Holzschnitten, in Gips und Kork schon lange gekannt, steht nun beisammen vor mir, wohin ich gehe, finde ich eine Bekanntschaft in einer neuen Welt; es ist alles wie ich mir's dachte und alles neu. Ebenso kann ich von meinen Beobachtungen, von meinen Ideen sagen. Ich habe keinen ganz neuen Gedanken gehabt, nichts ganz fremd gefunden, aber die alten sind so bestimmt, so lebendig, so zusammenhängend geworden, daß sie für neu gelten können.[26]

Comparing this phenomenon to the Pygmalion myth, Goethe sees his culturally socialized image of Rome come alive in the actual sensual experience of the city. He confirms that the cultural socialization and *Bildung* of the bourgeoisie no longer allow for the travel experience to be one of "true discovery" but only of rediscovery. Yet he acknowledges that the sensually stimulating and enriching impact of the site itself far surpasses the image created by the cultural imagination: "Every day a new remarkable object, every day some new great, extraordinary pictures, and a totality that is past imagining, however long one might think and dream" ("Alle Tage ein neuer merkwürdiger Gegenstand, täglich frische, große, seltsame Bilder und ein Ganzes, das man sich lange denkt und träumt, nie mit der Einbildungskraft erreicht").[27]

A different type of rediscovery can be seen in the travelers' rectifications of earlier travel accounts. Elisa von der Recke feels compelled to compare her impressions with those of earlier travel accounts in an attempt to correct misperceptions, as she, for example, considers the accounts of the infidelity and loose morals of the Roman wives exaggerated.[28] Expectations of city- and landscapes are measured against the actual experience[29] in an attempt to confirm or correct earlier accounts—not necessarily as a demonstration of her own reaction, as in Goethe's text.

Obviously, not every traveler will experience the same sights and sites in a similar manner. The degree of acculturation and preparation was commensurate with the options open to individual travelers. They could choose (or refuse) to indulge the wandering gaze or to indulge in the other forms of entertainment or to enhance and enrich the sensual impressions with their cultural knowledge and interests. The degree of expertise in travel and cultural context could serve as a means of distinction in the social differentiation of the middle class. As with other forms of cultural entertainment, a whole range of responses is possible for the stimulation of the voluntary displacement in unfamiliar sites: from a relatively immediate[30] delight in the Other that assesses and interprets the new impressions with the familiar categories of home to the highly educated approach familiar with the history, geography, ethnology, and the cultural practices of the Other. While the naive traveler might enjoy the sense of wonder and astonishment that the estrangement provides with a focus on the visual access and the emotive reactions to the artifact or landscape, the more educated traveler will have at his or her disposal a whole range of means of decoding these impressions.

Like the other forms of entertainment discussed above, travel as a symbolic practice could be used to define membership in a specific sub-community within the middle class. As a desirable part of the middle-class lifestyle, it could provide symbolic distinction. The degree of cultural competence is determined by the complexity and the level of differentiation of the classification system at one's disposal, as Bourdieu argues: "Its quality is determined by the manner in which it is able to differentiate in a series of successive classifications within the framework of all possibilities" ("Seine Qualität bemißt sich also danach, inwieweit es geeignet ist, eine Reihe sukzessiver, mehr oder weniger großer Unterteilungen im Rahmen der gesamten Vorstellungsmöglichkeiten vorzunehmen und daher mehr oder weniger grob unterteilte Klassen zu bestimmen").[31] Famous intellectuals like Goethe did not need to rely on the modern guidebooks and maps to give them access to a foreign city; they could also rely on their cultural knowledge and on expert guides. Goethe was able to explore Rome with the painter Tischbein, which allowed him a more differentiated and sophisticated access to the art of the city.

Von der Recke's response to the surprising view of Lake Alban displays a range of layers. Her initial sense of surprise and the consequent emotional stimulation are followed by cultural analysis: "But the sight of the lake itself was so surprising to me, that I felt a sweet terror. . . . The lake, a mirror bright as a crystal, is surrounded by a dense and light funnel-like vegetation of a circumference of almost three hours" ("Aber die Anschauung des Sees selbst war für mich so überraschend, daß ich mich von einem süßen Schrecken ergriffen fühlte. . . . Der See, ein krystallheller Spiegel, ist in einem Umfange von beinahe drei Stunden, mit hohen trichterförmigen, dicht und duftig bewachsenen Ufern eingefaßt").[32] After describing her emotional reaction and the physical attributes of the site, she augments this more immediate pleasure with her knowledge of the geographical area and the folklore associated with this site, thus adding a layer of more complex pleasure mediated through cultural knowledge. Furthermore, travelers could allude to the traditions in literature (Recke's invocation of Horaz's poetry in her description of the landscape around Tivoli)[33] or to their knowledge of art history to structure their experiences and give shape to their descriptions. The common knowledge of the painting that the traveler alludes to also helps the reader of the travel account imagine the verbal description of the scene: "The tied-up braids of the women, the men's bare chests and light jackets, the fine oxen they drive home from the market, the laden little donkeys, all of it constitutes a living moving Heinrich Roos" ("Die aufgebundenen Zöpfe der Frauen, der Männer bloße Brust und leichte Jacken, die trefflichen Ochsen, die sie vom Markt nach Hause treiben, die beladenen Eselchen, das alles bildet einen lebendigen beweglichen Heinrich Roos").[34] In Goethe's travels, the images of his cultural memory fuse with the actual impressions. The still life of his memory comes alive in this scene and unfolds before his eyes.

To various degrees, travelers could experience the physical landscape as they would a landscape painting, focusing on the picturesque and the varied panoramic view extending before their eyes. The picturesque in landscaping is defined by Stephanie Ross as "what is pleasing to the eye, what strikes the viewer as singular or appeals to him with the force of a painting, what is expressible in painting or would either afford a good subject for a painted landscape or help in conceiving one."[35] Likewise, von der Recke closes her detailed description of a landscape with the following remark: "The whole image represents an incomparably gigantic nature painting, which combines all the charm of loveliness with the majesty of splendor" ("Das ganze stellt ein unnachahmliches großes Naturgemälde dar, welches allen Zauber der Lieblichkeit, und alle Majestät der Pracht in sich vereiniget").[36] The viewing conventions of a certain form of landscape painting pre-structure her experience and allow her to read the landscape like a painting. Furthermore, her choice of descriptors alludes to her knowledge of contemporary aesthetical and philosophical views on beauty and echoes Schiller's discussion on the sublime. Without the cultural references to aesthetic and philosophical context, this trend of viewing the landscape as a picture led to pure indulgence in a particular view that was to characterize the leisure traveler as the early form of the tourist that Koshar describes: "For such tourists, nature had the status of a work of art, something to be admired and discerned, a 'view' to be had from the terrace of a comfortable lodge or while strolling along a forest lane, but not something to be engaged in directly."[37]

Both Goethe and von der Recke describe the obligatory visit to the Colosseum at night during their visits to Rome. While Goethe focuses on the spectacle of the illumination with its strong light and shade contrasts, von der Recke interprets the same strong contrasts ("a frightful change of light and darkness" ["ein schauerlicher Wechsel von Licht und Nacht"])[38] as reminders of the horror of the transitoriness of life. Reading the site as a reminder of past glory, she paints a picture in the fashionable gothic tradition complete with the dark ruins and the mournful sound of the night birds:

> A deep silence which was only interrupted by the groaning sound of a night bird dominated the area: this deadly silence among the ruins melancholically testified to the demise of life on these grounds, which now resemble a fantastic dreamscape.

> Ein tiefes Verstummen, welches nur durch das Geächze eines Nachtvogels unterbrochen wurde, herrschte umher: diese Totenstille unter den Trümmern zeugte schwermuthsvoll, daß der Geist der Lebendigkeit längst hinweggezogen sey von diesem Boden, der jetzt einem phantastischen Traumbilde gleicht.[39]

These pleasures—derived from a mixture of fear and delight—that von der Recke alludes to and the aforementioned formulation of "delightful horror" ("süße[r] Schrecken") had become a commonplace aesthetic reaction to the experience of landscapes by the end of the eighteenth century.

For the popularization of travel for larger groups of the middle class, travel literature and visual representation in etchings and prints were paramount and offered patterns of experience that the leisure traveler, the early tourist, used to guide his or her travels. They also created a lens through which the new experience was filtered. Traveling the Alpine region was a case in point. Such travels were still relatively dangerous and uncomfortable, but careful planning eliminated some of the danger and allowed for pleasurable elements to dominate the fear.

Yet the roots of the pleasure of the wild go back to the beginning of the century. Early experiences in travel by a few—usually males on Grand Tour—had been aided by and had, in turn, contributed significantly to creating an aesthetic paradigm shift. The rule-based aesthetics that could not have discovered an element of beauty in the disharmonious, asymmetrical, and seemingly useless phenomenon of Alpine regions[40] gave way to an appreciation of the strong effects of the wild (faculty psychology). These became popular in the wake of John Dennis's (1657–1734) concept of "delightful horror" as one of the foundational concepts of the sublime, along with Anthony Ashley Cooper, Third Earl of Shaftesbury's (1671–1713) "pleasing horror" and Joseph Addison's (1672–1719) "agreeable kind of horror."[41]

The wilderness of Alpine regions, with their irregular, threatening features and monumental proportions, traditionally had not been perceived as pleasurable. With the interest in the picturesque, the infinite quality of nature became a source of a mixed kind of pleasure composed of terror and delight. The experience of the Alps became a prime example for the new conception of the sublime. The initial terror experienced in the wilderness, perceived as the negative sensation of fear, was transformed through the mastery of this fear. This mastery produces a heightened pleasurable response in the sublime. The effect is intensified because it is a more complex reaction than pure delight due to the remnants of horrors. The wild landscapes display traces of danger as the stories of accidents and death in the rugged terrain heighten the sensation of the majestic beauty of the Alpine landscape. The surprising Alpine contrasts of ice and vegetation, winter and summer, past and present, eternity and transitoriness, and fear and delight offer a significant degree of variety and stimulation and thus are perceived as highly pleasurable, as von der Recke's reaction to the Alps suggests:

> Requiring less effort, on the way back down, we could enjoy the grand and sublime features of nature more intensely. Spring meadows next to fields of ice! Magically, the world of

the eternal ice, winter's stillness, transitions into summer's mildness. How powerfully the mind and senses feel affected and mightily elevated to the eternal source of the magic of nature. Boundlessly grand and sublime is nature's spirit in the lifeless images of death, as in the appearance of flourishing life.

Auf dem Rückweg konnten wir, wegen der mindern Anstrengung des Niedersteigens, mit mehr Empfänglichkeit der großen und erhabenen Naturgegenstände wahrnehmen. Frühlingswiesen und Eisflächen neben einander!—Wunderbar vereinigen sich hier, auf den Grenzen einer ewigen Eiswelt, winterliche Starrheit mit sommerlicher Milde. Wie gewaltig ergriffen und mächtig emporgehoben fühlt sich hier das Gemüth zu dem unerschöpflichen Quell dieser Wundererscheinungen der Natur. Unendlich groß und erhaben ist der Weltengeist in den starren Bildern des Todes, wie in den Gestalten des blühenden Lebens.[42]

This exemplary reaction to the Alps in the multilayered experience of the sublime had become paradigmatic for a world that offered many pleasures in the experience of variety, novelty, and contrasts. The popular philosopher Christian Garve regarded the variety of impressions that an Alpine landscape provides as an ideal aesthetically rich experience. He compared stepping from the variety it offers into a flat landscape with leaving an art gallery and stepping into a room with simple, unadorned walls.[43] A variety of impressions, the impact of strong sensations, and contrasts were considered pleasurable, and this aesthetics of the strong effects thus informed many cultural practices, from travel and landscape design to the gothic elements in literature and on the stage. After all, in the art of living, multiplicity "enriches and improves human life."[44] Exposing oneself to strong stimuli is part of the care of the self, as suggested by Foucault's rediscovery of ancient ethical practice with its techniques for the management of pleasure.[45] The management of pleasure was not to deny pleasure but to avoid excess.[46] I would take it one step further and argue that the management of pleasure avoids excess because the indulgence in the ever-same, even if pleasurable, would lose its stimulating edge. Instead it requires variation and innovation in a dynamic stream of new stimulation, thus avoiding the tedium of sameness (excess). The popular philosopher and garden designer Christian Cay Lorenz Hirschfeld, author of the *Theorie der Gartenbaukunst* (*Theory of Garden Art*, 1779–85), was well aware that the variety of impressions creates pleasure:

> Just as any feeling is tiresome if it persists unchanged, so amid the sweetest rapture we ourselves fall asleep if enchanted overlong. Variation or the gradual influx of new impressions helps maintain the vivacity and piquancy of sensations.

> So wie überhaupt einerlei Art der Empfindung ermüdet, wenn sie immer gleich, fortdauert, so entschlummern wir selbst in dem Genuß der süßesten Wollust, die uns zu lange bezaubert. Die Abwechlung oder der Zufluß anderer Eindrücke von einer ähnlichen oder verwandten Art erhalten die Empfindungen in ihrem wahren Leben und in ihrer Schmackhaftigkeit.[47]

In travel descriptions, those landscapes that offer the most variety seem to be perceived as yielding the most pleasure and thus find extensive descriptions. The visual tapestry of a varied landscape allows the gaze to wander, occupying the spectator in a pleasant manner. The visual stimulation of the landscape can be augmented by olfactory stimulation and the sensations of the climate—a common theme for northerners when visiting the mild climate of the Mediterranean.

Beyond the wilderness and rugged terrain of the Alps and its contrast with the surrounding loveliness of a varied landscape, the Rhine Valley with its strong contrasts alternating the rugged cliffs and the ruins on its peaks with the surrounding pleasant valleys became a favorite travel destination. The Baedeker travel guides would a few years later summarize the attraction as "its natural beauty, its many small towns and vineyards, the scenic castle ruins and cliffs, national monuments . . . and architectural treasures such as the Cologne cathedral."[48] Treasuring diversion, new impressions, and stimulation, people also began to go on pleasure trips to the carnival in Venice, trade fairs, journeys to visit family and friends, and to spas.[49]

Resorts and Spas

We also see this new interest in the wild at the core of the interest in the new seaside resorts (e.g., Heiligendamm near Rostock, 1794, and Nordeney, 1799) as sites for vigorous stimulation of the senses. Georg Christoph Lichtenberg describes the effect of the sea as an "indescribable stimulation" ("unbeschreibliche[r] Reiz") and relishes the powerful effects that the sight of the waves, their shimmering, and the rolling of their thunder have on the sensitive spectator.[50] Although the sea had previously been perceived as boring, dangerous, and repulsive, the same aesthetics that transformed the Alps into a pleasurable sublime spectacle reinterpreted the sea and made it available as spectacle. The sea stimulated the senses with its perpetual movement, its ever-changing surface, which was enhanced by the visual interest of the clouds and the sounds of the wind. The undulating surface of the water pleasantly occupied the gaze. The rocks and crevices carved out by the wind stimulated curiosity with their unusual shapes.

The emphasis on movement made the sea especially pleasurable, since "movement contains both variety and change" (Hirschfeld)—the latter we isolated as earmarks of a pleasurable sensation. Hirschfeld also considered the experience of greatness and expanse of a particular landscape as a primary predilection of the mind:

> How much the entirety of the soul expands, exerting all its strength, laboring to encompass everything when a vista to the ocean opens before us, or when on a bright winter's night the infinity of creation filled with radiant planets and burning fixed stars seems to unfold before our eyes! . . . The enjoyment of greatness provides the mind and imagination with nourishment that brings complete contentedness; the individual rises above the lowly common perspective to a higher realm of images and sensations; he feels that he is no longer mundane but rather a creature empowered to tower high above where we stand.

> Wie sehr erweitert sich nicht die ganze Seele spannet all ihre Kräfte an, arbeitet, um alles zu erfassen, wenn sich die Aussicht auf den Ocean voraus eröffnet, oder wenn in einer

hellen Winternacht die gränzenlose Schöpfung volleuchten-
der Planeten und brennender Fixsterne sich unserm Auge zu
entwickeln scheint! . . . Der Genuß der Größe giebt der Einbildungskraft und dem Geiste eine Nahrung, die eine Art
von Allgenügsamkeit mit sich führt, man erhebt sich von
dem gewöhnlichen niedrigen Stand dort hinauf zu einer
höheren Sphäre der Bilder und Empfindungen; man fühlt
es, daß man nicht mehr der alltägliche Mensch, sondern ein
Wesen von einer Kraft und Bestimmung ist, die weit über
den Punkt, auf dem wir stehen, hinausragt.[51]

The pleasures of the unbounded space,[52] the overwhelming immensity
of the sea, and its implication of danger produced an initial sense of
powerlessness, which was then overcome by aesthetic classification and
mastery of its impact, thus creating a complex sensation. Edmund
Burke had associated the perception of infinite space—infinite because
if the eye cannot see the borders of phenomena it produces an impression of unbounded space—with a sensation of pleasant danger.[53]
Because the danger exists only in the imagination, overcoming it is perceived as pleasurable. Real danger is not part of the sublime, as the
spectators only imagine themselves in danger.[54]

This mixed sensation of pleasurable stimulation and fear in the
sight of an overwhelming force of nature was heightened in resorts
when people actually took to the water under the protection of a new
invention, the bathing carts (*Badewagen*). The bathing carts provided a
sense of safety and enclosure in the expansive waters and shielded the
body in the new and unusual form of dress, the bathing costume, from
the gaze of the curious.[55] At the same time, this physical contact with
nature focused attention on the body and its sensations in a kind of
embodied aesthetics where the whole body with all its senses experienced a variety of sensory stimulations giving pleasure. As a form of
entertaining care of the body through motion and by exposing it to the
elements, especially fresh air and the water, this practice resembles the
use of traditional spas. However, in the latter the social aspects are more
dominant than the enjoyment of the forms of the sublime.

Spas offered intriguing forms of sociability. Frequenting the spas
served as an occasion to meet friends and acquaintances (and to make
new ones), as visitors often returned to the same spa year after year.
Spas thus extended the forms of sociability beyond the usual commu-

nity of the hometown, providing a place where people from all regions and from abroad could mingle.[56] At the same time, the sociability of the spa culture offered a liberating sense of anonymity away from one's usual community and its responsibilities and allowed for more social risk taking and adventure. Elise Bürger describes this form of sociabiliy:

> When one, liberated from domestic worries and work, strolls through nature and the narrowing path brings the strollers closer together, when one is certain that after one's departure the loose ribbon of a temporary association will be untied by the distance and does not remain tied, one more easily makes acquaintances that one would shy away from in one's usual domestic circle.

> Wenn man so, entbunden von häuslichen Sorgen und Mühen, im Grünen hinschlendert und die verengenden Wege die Gehenden zusammenführen, wenn man sicher ist, daß nach der Abreise das lockere Band eines augenblicklichen Bekanntwerdens, wieder aufgelöst durch die Entfernung, nicht bindend bleibt, so geht man gar leicht ein in Begegnungen, von denen man im heimischen Kreis sich scheu zurückziehen würde.[57]

Of course, we do not know what kind of social interaction the author is referring to. Is she describing a unique form of sociability devoid of the decorum and responsibility of one's usual community that allows for relatively intimate personal disclosures within a context of anonymity that can therefore remain without permanent social consequences? Is she hinting at erotic adventures prompted by the close physical proximity? Regardless of the specific nature of the social interaction, these "extra-ordinary" relationships enhanced the multiple pleasures of the spa experience by offering new perspectives and stimulation.

Beyond the wider patterns of sociability, spas provided other forms of entertainment and amusement, including dancing, small theater and music performances, reading, dining in an idyllic natural setting,[58] shopping, and enjoying nature in a sphere remote from home and work. Excursions by coach and on foot into the surrounding areas in the company of others exposed the visitors of the spa culture to a wide range of pleasures. People could enrich the walking experience with additional layers of activity based on their interests—singing, telling (travel) stories, or following their interest in botany.[59]

Offering additional visual stimulation, the merchants displaying luxury goods at the spas appealed not only to the patron's *Schaulust* but also to their self-image, which they could enhance with imaginary or actual purchases. Temporary yet sophisticated stands display the beautiful and often rare merchandise:

> How visually interesting are the glass and porcelain, and above all the jewelry shops, where cameos and exquisitely cut stones, mounted and unmounted, attract the gaze! The busy and artful lace-makers of the area, especially from Saxony, also bring their delicate wares to this site, where thousands look and hundreds buy.

> Wie sind doch die Glas und Porzellain-, und vor allen die Juwelier-Läden, wo Kamoen und prachtvoll geschnittene Steine, gefaßt und ungefaßt das Auge anziehen, so sehenswerth! Auch die behenden, kunstreichen Spitzenklöpplerinnen der Gegend bringen, besonders aus Sachsen, feine Waaren zu dieser Stelle, wo Tausende schauen, und viele Hunderte kaufen.[60]

The spa culture with its many forms of entertainment represented an early form of the modern practice of vacationing, as it combined the specular entertainments of travel with unique forms of sociability, shopping, and dining experiences in addition to cultural practices such as dancing and walking.

The more variety in the landscape and in the forms of entertainment spas provided, the more pleasure they created, because multiple sensory impressions enhanced the experience, as Elise Bürger's additive description attempts to convey:

> But on the top of the cliff . . . we were able to see and hear at the same time. . . . The view down into the little town, across onto the facing mountains, up to the blueness of the sky, all provided enjoyable views and the melodies coming from the bushes sounded lovely, and the most attractive per-

spectives that combined many different aspects could be found easily. We relished the experience and the further we penetrated through the trees into the depth of the forest, to the Findtlädters temple, where we could quietly rest and gaze into the valley, and as we continued further between the oaks, our minds, senses, and souls rejoiced and were calmed and it seemed as if God's peace rested on this mountain range to fortify the wanderer for a whole long life.

Aber auf der Spitze des Felsen . . . da konnten wir gleich sehen und hören. . . . Die Einsicht ins Städtchen, die Hinübersicht auf die gegenseitigen Höhen, die Himmelsbläue über uns, daß sah sich freudig an, und die Melodien, die aus den Zweigen tönten, hörten sich lieblich zu [*sic*], und die zusammengedrängten schönen Punkte der Aussicht ließen sich gleich auffinden! Da war uns wohl, und je weiter wir dann zwischen den Bäumen hindrangen in die Waldestiefe bis zu dem Findtlädters Tempel, wo wir so ruhig ruhen konnten und hinabblicken in's Thal, und weiter und weiter dann gingen zwischen den Eichen, ward uns immer wohler und stiller im Gemüth, und es war, als ob auf dieser Höhe der Friede Gottes ruhte, den Pilgernden zu stärken für ein ganzes, langes Leben![61]

Whether in spas or in general travel descriptions, those landscapes that offer the most variety in their panoramic displays seem to be perceived as yielding the most pleasure and thus receive extensive descriptions.

In addition to the social aspects, spas entertained with their unique landscape designs that facilitated the pleasure of walking. They had many comfortable, shady walks that encouraged people to move about in the fresh air. Their special landscape design had to provide comfortable shade, ample places to rest, and enough variation to hold the interest of the guests. Plantings and the topography of spas were designed to convey a sense of airiness, lightness, and expanse. Statues and even a temple to health added to the variety that visitors found exhilarating.[62]

In addition, resorts fueled general travel as wider strata of the middle class mounted excursions to spas for the sole purpose of entertainment, not to take the waters. Enhancing the mobility of the middle class, visitors traveling to spas could meet up with friends or relatives for socializing with people who were not part of one's everyday community in the context of excursions into nature.[63] Walks into the surrounding countryside allowed the specular pleasures to be enhanced by other sensual stimulation, the pleasures of scent and the tactile sensation of the body in motion on the walkways especially designed for this purpose: "We took a left onto the specially designed walkways that surround the city on three sides. These meaningfully designed and carefully tended walkways are full of roses, blossoms, and many bushes that alternate with the larger trees" ("Wir schlugen uns links in die vorzüglich von Rosen, Blüthen und vielfachen Gesträuchen, welche mit den erhabnern Bäumen abwechseln, erfüllten Spazierwege, die sinnvoll angelegt und sorgsam gepflegt, die Stadt auf drei Seiten umgeben").[64] The fragrances of nature kept fatigue at bay, and the walk could be interrupted for refreshments in outdoor garden inns. In their blending of sociability and biophilia—the human desire to be surrounded by nature—these excursions in nature were perceived to produce an intense sense of well-being derived from many different forms of entertainment and the pleasures they produce:

> O! if only—inspired by allowing their imagination to feel the scenes described—all people could experience the kind of pleasure that such a day spreads in our inner self, if they could feel the peace, filling the soul and inspiring us to new achievements, when a day and evening is spent in the arm of friendship and gazing at the genuinely beautiful and sublime!

> O könnten doch, durch Mitempfindung beglückt, alle Menschen die Wonne genießen, welche solch' ein Tag im Gemüt verbreitet, die Ruhe fühlen, welche die Seelen ausfüllt, und zu neuen Werken stärkt, wenn ein solcher Tag und Abend im Arm der Freundschaft und im Anblick des gediegenen Schönen und Erhabenen verlebt ist![65]

The forms of entertainment as an integral part of the middle-class lifestyle were seen as important moments for the psychological well-being of the self. With their stimulating effects they kept boredom and melancholia at bay. Providing an antidote to the disciplined structures of work and one's usual social and domestic context, the entertainment of spas and resorts—as of all travel—offered the necessary elements of variety and new impressions to momentarily destabilize the perceptions of the individual, thus offering a contrast to the stability of home. This temporary sense of displacement with its multilayered forms of stimulations was perceived as highly pleasurable and was thus sought out by increasing communities within the middle class. Resorts—not unlike landscape gardens—commodified nature as a form of entertainment and made natural phenomena accessible to larger and different groups of the middle class for the enhancement of their lifestyle and their well-being.

THE LANDSCAPE GARDEN

These changes in travel, as a pleasurable stimulation, and the changes in aesthetics—focusing of the effects of the work of art or the cultural artifact on the spectator—found an important resonance in a favorite pastime of the (upper) middle class: landscape design and garden architecture, which also created the basis for a form of entertainment for the strata of the middle class, visiting country houses. This fashionable pastime was especially popular in England, but it attracted the attention of German travelers and armchair travelers as well. Carole Fabricant reads "domestic tourism"—that is, "country house touring in England"—as a deeply hegemonic activity:

> Domestic tourism, however, was an activity that carefully orchestrated the movement of people through private sectors of the English countryside by defining the terms of their admittance onto the grounds of the wealthy, and by seducing them into an identification with the tastes and interests of the landed rich through the manipulation of voyeuristic delights and vicarious pleasures—through the illusion of shared participation in a world not in any meaningful sense their own. In this sense domestic tourism served the interests of the ruling classes, and reinforced their hegemony, by enlisting the complicity of the ruled in their fiction of their *in*clusion in an increasingly *ex*clusionary society. Domestic tourism was thus a perpetuator of false consciousness: it fostered attitudes that blocked true historical perception by masking societal contradictions and encouraging people to

261

think and act in ways that went against their own (material and class) interests.[66]

My own reading, unlike Fabricant's, is less interested in the question of "false consciousness" or of an "emerging culture industry" that precluded a "potentially revolutionary form of consciousness to emerge."[67] I read the cultural practice of visits to famous landscape gardens or the preoccupation with them in word and picture as essentially acquisitive. Visits, as a form of entertainment, not only produced specular pleasure—which could be acquired and repeated with every new visit—but also aided in taste formation. Not unlike the use of the fashion journal, the pleasure of looking at the country houses and grounds could be accompanied by an imaginary integration of some of its features into the visitor's self-image. This mental "trying on" of certain aspects of the lifestyle on display could enable the members of the middle class to integrate some of its features into their own more limited circumstances, thus driving the desire not only for repetition of this exposure to ever-new sites but also for establishing their own garden. The social dynamic is thus more complex and less clear cut and neat than the binary model of revolutionary or "true historical perception" versus "false consciousness" suggests. After all, the activity of leisured visits to country seats and pleasure gardens—or, in the German context, to the parks of the nobility open to the public—indicate a desire on the part of the visitors to enhance their lifestyle by including forms of entertainment in their leisure: traveling to the sites, enjoying the spectacle of the grounds, and indulging the gaze and the imagination. The fact that the visitors are interested in this particular kind of entertainment suggests, furthermore, that they are aware of the cultural practices and objects that can convey status and means of distinction. Thus these visits could function on the level of pure indulgence in the spectacle or like visits to museums—indulging the gaze and acquiring cultural knowledge—or they could provide the impetus for the imaginary acquisition of cultural practices for possible emulation within their circumstances. In addition, as part of a sophisticated lifestyle, this form of travel also brought status and distinction. For these reasons, the class implications are less clear cut than Fabricant suggests.

Just as we can no longer speak about an oppositional identity formation in dress around the turn of the century, the fashions in landscape design and ornamentation transcend the class barriers between

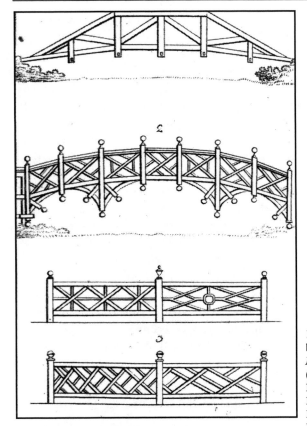

15. English garden bridges in *Journal des Luxus und der Moden* 5 (1790). Courtesy of the Bildarchiv Preußischer Kulturbesitz Berlin. Photo by Dietmar Katz.

the nobility and the (well-to-do) middle class. This distinctly German development can also be observed at the court of Weimar. Bourgeois advisers like Bertuch and Goethe transcended the class barriers and contributed significantly to a blending of tastes and values. Goethe not only assisted in planning and procuring land for the Weimar park on the Ilm but also took possession of the Roßla estate in 1798, which allowed and encouraged him to redesign its landscape and modes of utilizing the space.[68] Bertuch's assistance in the design and ornamentation of the Weimar landscape garden utilizes the same ideas he popularized in his garden magazine and in the *Journal.* In turn, he describes these courtly decorative elements from the Weimar gardens, thus in essence making them available for imitation in the middle-class garden. The result of this double strategy is a mingling of aesthetic and representational values that levels the differences between the classes. The ultimate criterion is taste (and the financial means), which can be acquired by both groups. Bridge and bench designs (along with other ornamental objects) were discussed and advertised in the *Journal* and in Bertuch's *Allgemeines Teutsches Garten Magazin* (figs. 15 and 16). They often were copies of items designed for the court, yet on occasion Bertuch also recommended to the court certain designs popularized in the *Journal*.[69]

The interest in landscape gardens ranged from reading about them, to traveling to famous gardens, to creating a landscape garden as a site for sociable entertainment and as a status symbol. As we will see, the German middle class did not limit itself to visiting the famous landscape gardens but also created gardens to enhance their lifestyle to the degree that their resources allowed. Tastes followed the English models, in which nature is not obviously dominated by formal architectural design (as in the French parks) but rather improved upon and made to resemble an idealized natural landscape. Of course the English pleasure grounds are far from natural and wild, giving only the semblance of naturalness and wilderness in a highly stylized artifice. The space was designed to produce a wide array of sensual stimulation and unique

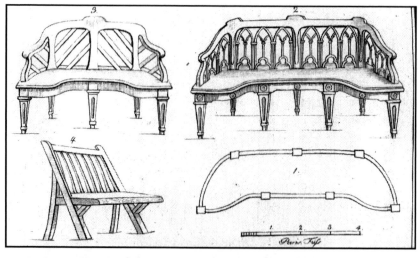

16. Garden benches in *Journal des Luxus und der Moden* 2 (1787). Courtesy of the Bildarchiv Preußischer Kulturbesitz Berlin. Photo by Dietmar Katz.

effects to entertain its visitors. A landscape that offered a variety of sites and forms was considered especially pleasurable because of its diversity. This cultural enhancement of the landscape domesticated nature while, at the same time, rendering the traces of culture invisible.[70] The creation of this semblance of nature required considerable skill in design and planning to produce the desired effect. Garden theorists like Hirschfeld thus carefully delineate the structural elements of the garden to this desired effect: the proper use of levels, swells, hollows, rocks, hills, mountains, woodlands, water, meadows, and vistas. These structures are then embellished with woody plants in groups, groves, woods, woodlands, thickets, and wilderness. Their descriptions, placement, and use and effect are complemented by the integration of flowers and grass.

The design goal of the semblance of a "natural" garden contained elements of variety and surprise, representing a type of *Gesamtkunstwerk* (multisensory artwork) in its thoughtfully assembled and arranged mixture of statuary, water features of various kinds, and illuminations (fig. 17).

The entertainment effect for the various layers of the middle class was produced by the variety of responses this kind of landscape garden

17. Waterfall in Christian Cajus Lorenz Hirschfeld, *Theorie der Gartenkunst,* vol. 1 (1779). Courtesy of Michigan State University Special Collections.

allowed. As the number of participants in cultural consumption increased, this audience was no longer willing or equipped to interpret complex emblematic meanings in every cultural area. Unlike garden art's sister arts—sculpture, painting, and architecture—in which people must learn before they can admire, gardens allow more immediate access to their beauty. "The charms of a well-designed garden are accessible to the expert and the novice without instruction or explanation" ("Allein die Reize eines wohl angelegten Gartens sind ohne Unterricht und Erklärung, den Kundigen und Unkundigen gleich empfindbar").[71] The layout of the garden path allows not only for the enjoyment of variation and diverse impressions but also for the most desirable discovery and revelation of the best vistas (while concealing any unpleasant sights).[72] The path eliminates the labor of grasping the garden's design and leads the gaze from one highlight to the next.

Alongside the scientific gaze that dominated the travels for discovery, a new form of looking—the wandering gaze—emerges. "One need only look to see here, and all that looking requires is an eye to be prepared to be charm'd."[73] Since no special code needed to be discovered, the pleasures of the landscape gardens were opened to larger segments of the middle class. This allowed for a more uninhibited experience of the garden, offering access to the less educated. At the same time, to the spectator with a trained eye it allowed a choice of viewing practices, either as discerning or recreational viewing. The use of the garden could thus result in a range of viewing pleasures. Instead of denigrating this wandering gaze as inferior, as Fabricant does,[74] I read this highly pleasurable form of entertainment that combined the delights of travel and indulged the gaze as driven by the modern need for new stimulation. Keeping the mind gently occupied, the wandering gaze delighted by offering a seemingly endless sequence of stimulation in these garden designs. Alternating the sense of closure with feelings of expansive vastness and openness and allowing for ever-new vistas to surprise the ambulatory spectator, these gardens create a kind of nature theater of ever-changing scenes.

Unlike the formal French gardens or the baroque parks, the English landscape garden no longer exclusively depended on the studious gaze of an educated elite whose members possessed the cultural preparation for an intellectual reading of the park.[75] Recognizing allusions and icons, this studious gaze is that of high culture, which takes complex pleasure in comparison, classification, and comprehensive analysis based on the received aesthetic principles of the genre in question. The spectator derived pleasure from confirming or rediscovering what he or she already knew. While the English landscape garden offered some interest for this kind of viewing pleasure—which was no longer limited to classical elements but also included fashionable icons such as the gothic elements—it paid particular attention to the creation of a variety of stimuli that appealed to the senses. Stafford writes: "It was crucial to the formulation of garden theory that the representation of entangled wilderness depended on the handling of nature in such a way as to produce dramatic, if not spectacular effects."[76] The landscaping efforts portrayed in *Die Wahlverwandtschaften* are motivated by this desire to transform the natural landscape into a culturally enhanced, more spectacular semblance of the natural. This semblance of the natural has been critiqued as a surrogate of nature.[77] There is no doubt that the seeming naturalness of the landscape is achieved by artificial—that is, carefully designed—cultural means: the vistas and views to be achieved with these manipulations loom large in the novel. In the opening passage the gardener describes Charlotte's initial landscaping efforts as successful: "You have an excellent view: the village down below, the church, whose spire you hardly notice from up there, a little to the right; and opposite, the manor-house and the gardens. . . . Then . . . the valley opens up to the right and you can see over the vast expanses of trees clear into the distance" ("Man hat einen vortrefflichen Anblick: unten das Dorf, ein wenig rechter Hand die Kirche . . . ; gegenüber das Schloß und die Gärten. . . . Dann . . . öffnet sich rechts das Tal und man sieht über die Baumwiesen in eine heitere Ferne").[78] From this modest beginning, which creates pleasing views by taking advantage of the existing social context and natural topography, the grounds grow into a significant park by the end of the novel in what seems an application of the fashionable landscape of the time (Hirschfeld). The enhancement ranges from the rocky wall (*Felswand*) (9–10), which bespeaks the fashionable predilection for the craggy, rocky, and rugged (suggesting an untamed environment); to a romantic intimate moss hut (*Mooshütte*) and seats to enjoy the view (10); to a variety of elevations embellished by various trees and bushes (28); to enhanced walkways and paths to make strolling more convenient and to provide more diverse views (64); to the construction of a second house, which is situated in such a way so that all traces of civilization—the village, and the castle—seem erased and thus offers a "different and new world" ("anderen, neuen Welt")

(65); to the creation of a large, impressive lake by combining three smaller ones (75); to the aesthetic enhancement and integration of a cemetery into the overall design (142); to the inclusion of a small chapel (143–44). These design elements are those of the fashionable landscape design of the time as it was theorized by Hirschfeld. The ultimate goal of this kind of landscape design is the stimulation that novelty, variety, and surprise provide. Both the Captain in the novel[79] and Hirschfeld in his theory consider stimulation by the new and unfamiliar an important and dynamic force driving cultural entertainment.[80]

It can be argued that with his representation of landscape design Goethe marks the historical moment when the involvement of humans with nature becomes less immediate and instead takes the form of landscape design as a form of entertainment. With this cultural practice the modern individual seeks to alter nature to eliminate the unpleasant and to heighten those effects that are considered desirable according to the historically determined ideals or fashions of design. Goethe clearly makes his audience aware of the cost (in the form of the accidents that the manipulation of the natural topography produces) of this aestheticization and acculturation. The manipulation of nature rendered people's exposure to nature less immediate, more remote and limited. While this taming of the wild and the unpredictable makes nature "safer," more convenient and accessible, and more beautiful, Goethe suggests on the one hand that the power of nature cannot be completely subdued and that its manipulation can lead to destruction and chaos. On the other hand, domestication and aestheticization lead to alienation from nature, as the linking of nature as spectacle with the motif of death suggests. The complex intertwining of the semblance of creating an image of nature in the picturesque landscape (or the stilling of the material body in the tableau) with the motif of death makes the uncanny effect amply clear. Far from simply condemning landscape design as a dilettante practice, Goethe's novel (to some degree) and his own practice of landscape design (to a larger degree) suggest that the move away from an agrarian feudal involvement with nature has to make room for a new, modern relationship to nature that brings both costs and benefits. Although the relationship to nature can only be a part—albeit a very important one—of entertainment during leisure, the sensation of pleasure that the practice of landscape design and the delight its results create are nevertheless important to the physical and mental well-being of the modern individual.

Therefore my reading takes issue with the dismissive tone of the conclusion that Bolz, for example, takes: "In *Elective Affinities* Goethe marks the historical moment when nature shrinks to become a wallpaper for the middle-class interior" ("Goethe hält in den Wahlverwandtschaften den historischen Augenblick fest, in dem Natur zur Bildtapete des bürgerlichen Interieurs zu schrumpfen beginnt").[81] His argument implies a mythical notion of authenticity that is not further described. "It would be important to resurrect the utopian heritage of Arcadia" ("Es käme . . . darauf an, das utopisch Erbe Arkadiens und seiner goldenen Zeit zu heben").[82] What would an authentic experience of nature look like under the conditions of a modern specialized and differentiated society anticipated in the novel? Is there a way to resurrect the "utopian heritage of Arcadia"? Does not the implied suggestion of an idyllic past ignore the toil and dependence on nature of the feudal farmer?

While not implying any claim to authenticity, the modern cultural practice of seeking limited access to nature is an appropriate strategy to hold the alienation of modern civilization at bay for a time. Not unlike the many other measures aiding in the care of the self, the indulgence in the spectacle of nature provides stimulation, which, in turn, is seen as vital to (mental) health. Just as the efforts in dietetics cannot solve the underlying issue of mortality, the fear of death of the modern post-Enlightenment individual, the limited and temporary access to nature in travel and the enjoyment of the picturesque landscape cannot and do not make any claim of authenticity or of transcending the alienation from nature that accompanied its demystification. Instead, they offer practical, concrete ways to enhance the quality of life in the face of modern limitations while embracing its technical and cultural advances.

The "staging" of nature in the picturesque allows a similar pleasure, created by the experience of looking, as do the elaborate stage designs (discussed in the next chapter). The spectacular site—in nature, onstage, or in the monumental panoramic art forms—trains the eye to wander, to expect a steady stream of new details maintaining the stimulation of novelty and surprise for as long as possible. The English traveler in *Die Wahlverwandtschaften* describes the self-propelling dynamic of the wandering gaze. He argues that he is accustomed to change, indeed craves it. He likens this dynamic to the experience of opera where the spectator expects a steady stream of new stage sets simply because there have been so many already: "I am used to change, in fact,

I have come to need it, just as we always expect a new stage set at the opera, since we have already seen so many" ("Ich bin an den Wechsel gwöhnt, ja er wird mir Bedürfnis, wie man in der Oper immer wieder auf eine neue Dekoration wartet, gerade weil schon so viele dagewesen").[83] The expectation of novelty, based on the earlier experience of the same, raises more expectations for stimulation and drives the desire for more. The many details of panoramic vistas, enhanced by the technical medium of the *camera obscura,* draw the eye to move from one site of interest to another and thus facilitate the pleasures afforded by the wandering gaze. The mediated images bring knowledge and pleasure.[84] The traveler's collection of images brings a semblance of the world into the domestic space of *Die Wahlverwandtschaften.*

The English landscape gardens served as models that were imitated in the German states. Painshill Park in Surrey, created by Charles Hamilton between 1738 and 1773, was an early example, boasting a steady stream of unique pictures:

> To create Painshill, Hamilton transformed three hundred acres of inhospitable moorland through intensive excavation, earth moving, and planting. The garden was laid out as a hilly four-mile circuit. Water raised from the river Mole supplied the central lake in which Hamilton built a number of islands. Painshill contained temples, monuments, and follies in various architectural styles: a Gothic temple, a Gothic tower, a ruined abbey, a Turkish tent, a mausoleum in the form of a Roman triumphal arch, a Grecian temple designed by Robert Adam, a rusticated hermitage, an elaborate grotto, and a variety of Palladian and Chinese bridges. The gardens also contained a wide variety of botanical specimens. . . . Eighteenth-century visitors to Painshill were guided around the garden in a prescribed circuit, encountering a carefully ordered sequence of monuments, scenes, and vistas.[85]

This kind of garden was imitated in principle—never quite in scale—in the German late-eighteenth-century landscape gardens. The German audience was obviously quite aware of the landscape descriptions of the English landscape garden. The sociable circle in *Die Wahlverwandtschaften* peruses the illustrated descriptions of English landscape gardens as a form of entertainment.[86] Bertuch in his descriptions of the Weimar garden in the *Journal* could simply allude to its elements—instead of describing them in detail—and no longer considered it necessary to evoke the mood that the design produced.[87]

Less elaborate but based on similar principles, the garden in Weimar displayed the familiar elements of landscape design: greatness and diversity, variation in coloring, movement, novelty, the unexpected, and contrast between meadow and woodlands. This kind of pleasure garden as a series of pictures that changed continually offered visitors carefully composed scenes with contrasting emotional tones.[88] The paths were laid out in such a way that the visitors experienced different perspectives from which to view the river and other areas of the grounds. The design of the plantings played their part in concealing a view until it appeared to its best advantage.[89]

A famous example of the stimulation through contrast and a variety of elements is the Wörlitz garden with its active volcano (active thanks to pyrotechnics), where the delightful scene with its variety of vistas changed into the horrible sight of the gaping mouth of the crater with the turn of one's body.[90]

One of most popular elements in the German landscape garden of the day was the gothic element of the gardens—for example, the

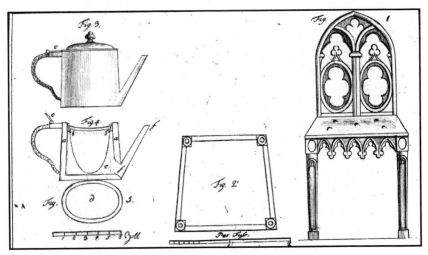

18. A gothic garden chair and an English coffeepot in *Journal des Luxus und der Moden* 3 (1788). Courtesy of the Bildarchiv Preußischer Kulturbesitz Berlin. Photo by Dietmar Katz.

271

dungeon/cavelike grotto in the park in Weimar or the gothic chapel in *Die Wahlverwandtschaften*. The "quotes" of gothic elements were similar in literary texts, theater design, and garden and interior design, and contemporaries were consequently quite familiar with them (fig. 18). In addition, this cross-genre usage of gothic elements, one evoking the memory of another, allowed for a mix of novelty and familiarity and, at the same time, increased the impact of the sensations and moods they invoked. The code of the gothic made these elements and the moods they created readable without much interpretative effort.

As an artifact, the designed landscape offered the visitor a three-dimensional space for a kinesthetic experience, an ambulatory motion through time and space. The visitor participated in reassembling the variety of individual and sometimes quite independent and contrasting scenes and vistas. At the same time, the variety of landscape features evoked a wealth of different emotions and feelings. It "requires a sentimental look in which the eye moves in and around the three-dimensional space, registering incident and contrast, generating expectation, and delighting in surprise. This garden typically contains aural as well as visual stimulation, both of which serve to animate the viewer into a sequential experience of distinct sensations."[91] The emphasis on sensations triggered by artifacts had been well established by the kinds of reading experiences I have discussed above, ones that favor the indulgence in fantasy and invite readers to insert themselves into the plot or character, into the fictional world in their imagination. This kind of garden allowed the imagination to daydream itself into the wilderness while in the safety and comfort of a cultured space. At the same time, it could become the stage for daydreams and fantasies.

The same techniques we have discussed in conjunction with texts used as triggers for sensations, which then can be elaborated into fantasies and daydreams, can be applied to the enjoyment of the landscape garden as well. It invited the visitor to not only physically and sensually explore the garden but also to revel in fantasies stimulated by the sensations it created. The "seduction of fantasy [is] created by the sentimental look, in which fantasy becomes the terrain upon which looking is played out. In this sense the screen onto which the eye projects its image in the look is fantasy itself."[92] Recalling previous sensations, the stimulation of the new trigger allows an enhancement of fantasies in which the spectator can playfully engage.

Sensations themselves are perceived as pleasurable if they are subjected to modification and variation. Variation in the design and mood of the garden can help in this human striving for entertainment. Hirschfeld argues that its absence and the lack of stimulation is perceived as detrimental to our nature:

> External things affect our feelings, modifying them in ways that are essential to our nature and seem indispensable to the soul. . . . It is, then, the arousal of agreeable sensations that is the general function of garden art; but other sensations can also be elicited by regions that are reclusive, melancholic, gloomy, romantic, solemn, and the like.

> Die Modificationen unserer Empfindung, die von den Einwirkungen der äußerlichen Dinge abhängen, scheinen selbst der Seele so untenbehrlich, daß ihre Abwesenheit eine zu beklagende Einschränkung unserer Natur seyn würde. . . . Es ist der Befug der Gartenkunst, durch eine harmonische Folge verschiedener Bewegungen, durch die Bewegungen des Großen, des Mannigfaltigen, des Neuen, des Schönen, des Wilden, des Melancholischen u.s.w. zu ergötzen.[93]

The design elements carefully created these sensations. For example, one important earmark of the landscape garden was its sense of infinity, offering unimpeded vistas that delight the mind. This required elaborate techniques to hide the fences. As early as 1731, Alexander Pope in his Epistle to Lord Burlington described the increase of pleasure associated with the infinity of landscape design: "To conceal the boundaries of a garden, by opening the garden, allows the mind even further territory. If a ha-ha [sunken fence] was indeed the critical factor in the development of the landscape garden, by opening the garden to the world beyond the ditch, it still remained just another, if more radical, manipulation of space for the delight of the human mind."[94] As a symbol, the style of the English garden embodies a sense of openness, of an endless stream of pleasurable discovery and gratification as well as the valorization of the surprising.

The landscape garden stimulated with more than just the visual, however, and this is one of the main reasons why gardens became such an important source of entertainment. They appealed to all five senses: the sense of smell is engaged by the scent of flowers, herbs, soil and mulch; one can savor the taste of fruits and herbs—or anticipate their taste; water, weather, and creatures provide aural stimulation; and weather and terrain activate the sense of touch. Furthermore, the sight of a landscape invites not only the real but also an imaginary appropriation: "Seeing a path entering the woods, we imagine ourselves following it; seeing a high wall, we imagine ourselves peering over it; seeing a distant temple or folly, we imagine ourselves exploring it."[95]

Another central feature of the enjoyment of a garden is its invitation to explore it through movement. The accumulation of pleasurable impacts by the sequenced (mobility) moments of newness (new vistas)—of moving through time and space, by being exposed to a variety of different settings, each producing unique sensations, by the repeated stimulation of the gaze, by a carefully designed effect of surprise—provided the kind of intense stimulation and the variety of impacts that were experienced as highly entertaining.

Furthermore, the sense of mobility, of the ever-changing nature of things, valorizes futurity. As futurity and mobility become associated with masculinity and modernity, the perception of nature as stable, secure (or frightening), and eternal (mother nature) loses its strength. At the same time, nature is made to be available at any given time without having to face the dangers or inconveniences of the wilderness. Nature is turned into a series of spectacles for the acquisitive gaze, and this results in a commodification of nature. As the dark side of this commodification, the stylized artificial "naturalness" also hints at a modern sense of alienation from nature. As discussed above, nature can be manipulated and can be improved upon, but it can also, by implication, be destroyed. As nature is experienced as alterable, it no longer securely grounds the individual. Just as the desire for increasingly intense erotic affinities and the promise of intensity they provide—the boundless desire embodied by modern passion in the new conception of love—bears a heavy cost with regard to social stability, the manipulation of the landscape garden to enhance its pleasures also enhances its instability, as the accidents (the mudslide and the boating accident killing the child) in *Die Wahlverwandtschaften* signify. Both mirror the dissolution of the firm social grounding of the individual in a feudal society and the modern self-fashioning of the bourgeois identity with its gains and losses.[96] The characters pay the price for the expansion of their worldview in the valorization of the (aesthetic or acquisitive) gaze with their alienation from nature and their lack of direct engagement with it.

The modern phenomenon of limitless desire, the pleasure of an uninhibited gaze (*Schaulust*), and the other forms of entertainment discussed below (the spectacle onstage, panorama, and diorama) are part of a new interest in visual pleasures, in a "universal mode of vision," the picturesque—the emphasis on the primacy of pictorial values—that united "poets, painters, travelers, gardeners, architects, connoisseurs, and dilettanti,"[97] which attempts to create a new relationship to the natural environment and derive new pleasures from it.

The picturesque was perceived as pleasurable because it contained many of the qualities we have isolated as making up pleasure—the stimulation through strong sensations, variety, novelty, surprise, the disposition that excites and feeds curiosity by a partial and uncertain concealment.[98] In addition, the pleasure of the picturesque was enhanced by the degree of taste and broad access to as many forms of cultural practice as the spectator possessed. A connoisseur, viewing the picturesque scene, is reminded of the various paintings it resembles, but later, viewing the painting, his or her thoughts turn back to the scene. Each enlivens the other, and each acquires new meaning imported by intellect and imagination and not provided by sense alone.[99]

Landscape painting and illustrations of picturesque landscapes enhanced the interest of larger segments of the middle class to participate in leisure travel to the depicted sites. The "particular pleasure of comparison and association"[100] added to the usual pleasures of travel the playful pleasure of detecting the similarities between the actual landscape and the painted one.[101] A third layer of entertainment could round out the cultural practice: the inspiration to create one's own pictures. In addition, the pictorial representations of landscape created a pictorial collection of famous landscapes that could be consumed at will—as suggested by the aforementioned scene in *Die Wahlverwandtschaften* in which the traveling Englishman paints and then collects all the landscapes he visits. Not unlike the later photography, these sketches can then serve not only to recall and record his travels but also become a form of entertainment, providing visual pleasure to others as the English traveler entertains Charlotte and Ottilie with his pictures.[102] Similarly, the novel's protagonists entertain themselves with illustrated descriptions of English landscape gardens (fig. 19).[103]

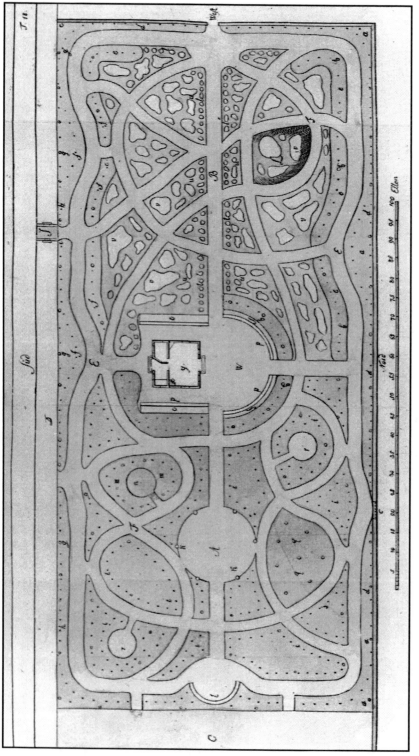

19. Plan of an English grounds in *Journal des Luxus und der Moden* 5 (1790). Courtesy of the Bildarchiv Preußischer Kulturbesitz Berlin. Photo by Dietmar Katz.

Just as in the delights that the picturesque offers, the mutual reinforcement that a variety of cultural practices produces heightens the
pleasure by involving the senses, the imagination, and the intellect. At
the same time, the implied advocacy of the breadth of cultural exposure can only be achieved if the depth of learning in one specialized
area is sacrificed. Extensive classical learning was relegated to the specialist in one area, while limited familiarity with many aspects of culture
characterized the bourgeois lifestyle. No longer requiring a formal
education, these new forms of cultural entertainment not only allowed
larger layers of the middle class to participate but also leveled the cultural playing field between men and women to some degree.

Linda Parshall's description of Hirschfeld's ideal garden is instructive not only as a model for actual gardens, which realized many of the
elements featured in his compendium, but also because it allows
glimpses at the whole range of opportunities for entertainment and the
accompanying pleasurable experiences:

> Let us follow Hirschfeld's inclination for the middle way and
> picture a garden laid out on a moderately sized piece of land,
> enough space to allow for a kilometer or so of winding path-
> ways that cross each other only rarely. Drawing near the
> property we would pass through an entryway of appropriate
> size. . . . From here a commodious roadway, perhaps a tree-
> lined alleé, would lead us toward the main house, which will
> not at first be visible, though we might catch a glimpse as the
> way bends to follow the terrain. Then the house appears,
> likely in a neo-Palladian style, positioned quite proudly in a
> cleared area with a splashing fountain in front. The grassy
> forecourt . . . might be dotted with irregular beds of fragrant
> shrubs and flowers. Standing near the facade we should
> notice inviting pathways curving across the expanses of lawn
> and leading toward picturesque borders of intermingled
> shrubs, perennials, and small trees. One path might beckon
> us enticingly, so we choose to follow it and be led away from
> art into nature and the deepening gloom of a wood. After
> some distance the pathway winds along the edge of a small
> pond, then through a sunlit clearing and back into the trees,
> where we might come upon a small chapel or perhaps a her-
> mitage, covered with birch bark. Here we would be inclined

277

to pause, resting on a shady bench, and enjoy the beauty or solemnity of the scene. . . .

Depending on the garden's scale, our stroll will take us through a variety of regions, each with its particular character—perhaps astonishment, melancholy, solemnity, or merriment. And our mood should be correspondingly affected. . . . Returning toward the main house we might encounter the ruins of a Gothic building or a horticultural garden laid out after Linnaen principles. A rustic shack nestled against a once-mighty oak will reward closer inspection when we discover it to be a library outfitted with comfortable benches, windows, and a fireplace.[104]

This description makes clear that the landscape garden procured its entertainment function from offering the utmost variety, surprise, and contrast. Indeed, Hirschfeld considered variety as providing the most pleasure in a landscape, which should provide "an endless and unmatched variety of beautiful vistas," and he suggested that plantings should be arranged in such a manner that they "compose a picture of the greatest variety."[105] Ideally, the garden yields the utmost pleasure by revealing its features a little bit at a time; it teases the spectator. To achieve this goal, the garden artist must "proceed in such a way that the observer is not satisfied all at once but is absorbed little by little and entertained for a long while."[106] Symmetry, uniformity, lack of variety, and lack of intrusions, which allow the site to be surveyed all at once, are perceived as tedious and boring. These impressions "quickly tire us and lose all their power; we want to be occupied, and we find nothing to touch us further."[107] To this end the landscape artist is to employ similar strategies as the painter: the effective composition, the use of the beautiful serpentine line, and the richness and diversity of color with its endless nuances.[108]

In addition to the visual pleasure that variety in the landscape provides, the German parks—for example, those of Weimar and Tiefurt—offered sites for sociability and refreshments:

If you worked up an appetite strolling through the park, you only have to say a word and you will be served with a light supper. Mr. Schwarz's waiters are constantly on the move and gladly serve you as swiftly in the remote areas of the park as in the close ones. Everywhere we see small groups gathering, which either dine or enjoy a bottle of punch, lemonade, or wine while censuring the passersby. This seems to encourage the latter to do the same. . . . Such are the pleasures of the Weimar Vauxhall, which on closer inspection, when compared with the garden-delights of other large cities, is not found lacking, except in the fact that it is free but costs dearly elsewhere.

Hat man sich müde, hungrig und durstig promenirt, so kostet es nur ein Wort, um sogleich mit einem kleinen Souper bedient zu werden. Die Aufwärter des Herrn Schwarz sind in beständiger Bewegung und in ihren Diensten nicht nur sehr expedit, sondern sie bedienen einem auch in den entferntesten Theilen des Parks so unverdrossen, als in dem nächsten. Man findet überall kleine Gesellschaften, die entweder soupieren, oder bey einer Bouteille Punch, Limonade oder Wein, die Vorübergehenden censieren, und wird dadurch nicht selten bewogen ein gleiches zu tun . . . [D]arin bestehen die Ergötzlichkeiten des Weimarischen Vauxhalls, der genau besehen, vor den Gartenbelustigungen aller großen Städte nichts voraus hat, als daß hier das Entre frey ist, dort aber sehr theuer bezahlt werden muß.[109]

As the sight of the forms of entertainment in the landscape gardens created the desire to procure them for oneself, the feel of this type of pleasure ground drove the middle class to re-create this experience on various scales, depending on the size of the property and the financial abilities of its owner. After all, unlike the estates of the gentry in England, the middle-class landscape garden represented sheer luxury as it did not yield the income or utilitarian use from grass, wood, and game but instead entailed significant costs for its purchase, appointment, and upkeep. Yet the luxury of a garden was increasingly coveted by the (upper) middle class as a worthwhile expense that enhanced their lifestyle significantly. Gardens brought to the bourgeois lifestyle the benefits of country life and the pleasures of variety in the seasons, providing a place where they could be enjoyed in safety, comfort, convenience, and tranquillity. In this way, the (upper) middle class was no longer limited to leisure travel to the great pleasure grounds during limited special times of the year. This trend to acquire small-scale imitations of this experience and to incorporate its pleasures into everyday life is yet another example of the transformation of lifestyle that sought to eliminate the strict demarcation between the mundane and the special occasion and instead to integrate as many forms of entertainment and the accompanying pleasure into its daily life.

The Enjoyment of the Private Garden

The interest in garden design was fueled by the interest in landscape design, and both display similar, mutually influential tastes. In certain cases both trends were fused as people tried to integrate the landscape design into the smaller setting of their domestic landscape. The English extensive landscape garden, the "pleasure grounds"[110] of the elite and the gentry, was the object of admiration and imitation. Not only the noble elite imitated these pleasure grounds in their parks—which became popular travel destinations for the upper-middle-class leisure travel—but both the English originals and the German copies became sources of inspiration for middle-class garden design on a more limited scale. The intense sensation of pleasure that the exhilaration of the landscape garden as culturally enhanced nature provided evoked the desire to make it available within the middle-class lifestyle, driving the cultural practice of gardening.[111] The gardens of the well-to-do members of the bourgeoisie could be found in close proximity to the populated and prosperous cities and commercial centers. This, in turn, enhanced not only the quality of life in the city but also the aesthetic appearance of the cityscape.[112]

Although many private middle-class gardens, especially those near the cities, were not large enough to allow the proper imitation of the English models, they nevertheless delighted in making a small space seem large through careful landscape design. The experts evoke the guiding principle of taste and advise moderation. The aesthetic can easily be combined with the useful: fruit trees can be arranged in loose and graceful groups, or they can be turned into trellises where comfortably arranged seats accommodate sociability.[113]

For the German middle class and their gardens near the cities, the natural landscape garden primarily provided a means to enhance the higher quality of life by offering additional opportunities for entertainment during leisure. Yet the aspect of status that these fashionable gardens provided did not go unnoticed by contemporaries: "The wealth that comes of successful trade soon excites the desire to distinguish oneself through expenditures on dwellings and gardens, as well as on banquets and parties. In addition, a man grown tired of the turmoil of commerce seeks out places where he can recuperate on quiet days, breathe more freely, and enjoy his own and his family's company."[114] Although the aspect of status certainly also played a role in the middle-class gardens and assisted in the differentiation of the middle class, the primary function seemed to have been its entertainment quality. The middle class took pleasure not only in the enjoyment of the garden but in its planning, creation, and maintenance. Gardens were enjoyed as part of domestic sociability or in solitary activities. The carefully designed garden appealed to all the senses. Gardens fascinated as a place "where nature itself might be fashioned into a fully dimensional and all-encompassing work of art, one capable of touching the mind, the soul, the heart, and all the senses to accomplish a true synesthesia."[115]

While gardening itself became an important form of entertainment, the emerging garden culture became the site for a whole number of additional forms of entertainment, as van Dülmen confirms:

The occupation of the work in the garden, family and social life in the garden, the retreat into "self-designed nature," were important components of what came to be known as the values of self-determination in leisure. Central for the image of a garden was the idea of freedom from external demands and concerns, a life without firm social constraints, intimate and protected. Informal dress and improvised meals were some small indicators for the levity of life in the garden. Love for nature and her "small, quiet, and uplifting delights," the enjoyment of the physical labor in contrast to one's professional work, the desire for peace and quiet found their place here. More than in the usual life in the city, people had time to enjoy family life, walks, reading and making music.

Die Beschäftigung mit Gartenarbeiten, das familiäre und gesellschaftliche Leben im Garten, der Rückzug in diese selbstgestaltete "Natur" waren eine wichtige Komponente dessen, was man mit den entstehenden Werten von Freizeit, von persönlich bestimmtem Leben verband. Wesentlich für das Bild des Gartens war die Vorstellung von Freiheit, ohne Einengung durch überkommene, oft fremdbestimmte Rücksichten und Pflichten, ohne einen festgelegten gesellschaftlichen Rahmen, ganz intim und abgeschirmt. Legere Kleidung und improvisierte Mahlzeiten im Freien waren nur kleine Zeichen für die Unbeschwertheit des Gartenlebens. Die Liebe zur Natur und ihren "stillen, herzerhebenden Freuden," das Vergnügen an der dem Berufsleben durchaus fremden Gartenarbeit, das Bedürfnis nach Stille und Einsamkeit fanden hier ihren Platz; mehr als im städtischen Alltag blieb Zeit für Freuden des Familienlebens, der Muße, für Spaziergänge, für Lesen und Musizieren.[116]

Having a spot where one "can enjoy all the benefits of country life, all pleasures of the seasons in comfort and tranquility" ("alle Vortheile des Landlebens, alle Annehmlichkeiten der Jahreszeiten"),[117] the ever-changing nature of the garden and its association with leisure, and its contrast to the discipline of work made gardens ideal sites of entertainment that both extended and altered the forms of entertainment associated with the domestic sphere.

The garden began to relate to the design of the house, whether it was the main house surrounded by a garden or the seasonal garden house at the edge of town. With the addition of unique furniture and other decorative objects designed for outdoor use, nature was transformed into an extension of the interior space (see fig. 20).

Special furniture allowed for socializing and informal entertaining in the garden. The *Journal des Luxus und der Moden* includes articles describing taking tea and coffee in the garden and the specific furniture that makes this fusion of nature and culture even more comfortable and pleasant:

> I also saw in this garden a garden chair, with a sun umbrella attached to its arm, so that the nature lover can sit close by the flower bed and enjoy the blooms or read all while enjoying a transportable shady seat, an invention which I liked very much.

Auch sah ich in diesem Garten einen Garten-Stuhl, auf

282

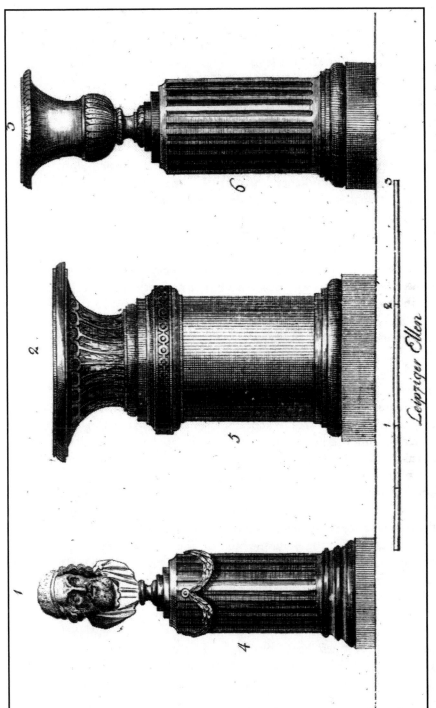

Leipziger Ellen

20. Garden decorations by Klauer in *Journal des Luxus und der Moden* 5 (1790). Courtesy of the Bildarchiv Preußischer Kulturbesitz Berlin. Photo by Dietmar Katz.

dessen Lehne ein Sonnenschirm mit etwas langer Stange steckte, und also dem Blumen-Liebhaber, der sich irgend nahe ans Blumenbeet setzten, die Flor recht genießen, oder dabey lesen wollte allenthalben einen transportablen schattigen Sitz gewährte; welche Erfindung mir sehr wohlgefallen hat.[118]

This passage evokes the entertainment quality of the comfortable and convenient pleasures of reading in a garden space, which allows the reader to enjoy simultaneously both the imaginary pleasures of the book and the sensual delights of the environment. Both the entertaining reading practices and the pleasures that the domesticated nature of the garden provides allow the risk-free indulgence in sensual pleasures from the safety of a contained space.

The delights of the garden also found their way into the interior. Flower arrangements with either fresh or artificial flowers became fashionable accessories in interior design. The *Journal* shows a table especially designed for the display of arrangements, the *Jardinière,* at times in conjunction with a birdcage (see figs. 12 and 13). One successful manufacturing company producing artificial flowers, owned by Bertuch and his wife, is well known because Christiane Goethe was employed there.

Transitional spaces such as terraces and paved walkways facilitated easy access from one area to another. Changes in architectural tastes, in particular of those houses in the country or garden houses, placed the social spaces—the library, the drawing room, and the dining room—on the ground-floor level and appointed them with large windows and doors that integrated the view onto the garden. As a backdrop to the interior design, this allowed the gaze to wander beyond the confines of the rooms. They also provided convenient access to the outdoor spaces. As an extension of the domestic interior, the outdoor spaces served as an important site for spending leisure in a pleasurable manner alone or among family, friends, and lovers. As in the spaces designed for sociability, several related areas in the garden could serve several groups of visitors simultaneously and offer a variety of forms of entertainment.

As an extension of the domestic sphere and the central site for entertainment ("geselliges Lokal"),[119] the garden became the subject of a wide range of specialized publications—van Dülmen speaks of a veritable "flood" of publications on gardening.[120] As with fashion and travel, there is an intense interrelationship between the new interest in gardening for the middle class and the explosion of publications on the subject. As with the other forms of entertainment discussed in this volume, there is a symbiotic relationship between reading about gardening and horticulture and its cultural practice. Bertuch was not only involved with landscape design and its financing for the court (his Industrie-Comptoir published more than thirty titles with a specific focus on gardening)[121] but also an avid gardener himself. He considered his garden his refuge, a place that replenished his strength by offering rest and relaxation, and the site for family life and sociability.[122] Again, the written discourse played an important role in the transformation of the bourgeois garden from a purely utilitarian space into one of aesthetic and sensual pleasures. Gardening books and periodicals facilitated this transfiguration and in themselves represent significant sources of entertainment. Hirschfeld's *Theory of Garden Art* drew the praise of Christoph Martin Wieland, who found it to be both entertaining and educational in its "mingling of genres: part musings on the joys of living close to nature, part philosophy of aesthetics, part historical survey, part travel book, part anthology, part moral and political tract."[123]

The illustrations and the descriptions of famous landscapes contributed to the formation of taste in landscape design. The *Taschenkalender auf das Jahr 1798 für Natur- und Gartenfreuden* contained essays of taste formation and the integration of architecture and garden design as well as descriptions of famous sample gardens.[124] Schiller's review of this important publication emphasizes its contribution to taste formation in landscape design. The oftentimes attractively illustrated volumes on gardening not only provided useful information that expanded the knowledge of its readers but also offered visual pleasures, allowing the eye to roam and explore while the verbal description of landscape visits stimulated the powers of the imagination. Even the illustrations "are meant to be evocative, to pique our imagination."[125] Both illustrations and descriptions allowed readers to imagine the described landscapes, plants, and objects. Despite his dissatisfaction with landscape illustrations, Hirschfeld felt that the combination of illustration and description is most conducive to producing the most pleasurable effect:

> I have commented on the inadequacy of engravings for landscape representations. Yet in works of this type they

always provide another idea, or enhance and illuminate an idea one is trying to bring forth in words, while engaging the imagination in not an unpleasant activity.

Ich habe freilich das mangelhafte der Kupferstiche bey landschaftlichen Vorstellungen überhaupt schon bemerkt. Indessen liefern sie in Werken dieser Art doch immer eine Idee mehr, oder erheben und erheitern die Idee, die man durch Worte zu erwecken sucht; zugleich geben sie der Phantasie eine nicht unangenehme Beschäftigung.[126]

Readers of garden publications could indulge in the pleasure of planning and mentally creating or redesigning their own garden spaces, and they could daydream about how they would use these spaces, thus providing entertainment for both the armchair gardener and the actual garden enthusiast. The infinite nature of the garden—always in flux, in transition, and in a state of change—represents an ideal illustration for the pleasure people derived from the stimulation of the ever changing, the oeuvre that is "always becoming" and never limits the imagination. Both evoke a sense of perpetual discovery that ideally exemplifies the dynamic essence of (cultural) consumption. The verbal description that fuels the imagination is especially valuable because it allows the flexibility and movement that capture the ever-evolving (living) landscape more than illustrations, which are, after all, static and fix the garden at a certain moment. Prompted by the verbal descriptions, the imagination can supply the element of growth, movement, and change and thus can better capture the essence of a particular landscape than landscape painting or illustrations.

New, specialized pocket books and calendars focused on gardening; they were usually intended for a general audience, such as the *Taschenkalender auf das Jahr 1798 für Natur- und Gartenfreuden: Mit Abbildungen von Hohenheim und andern Kupfern* (1798),[127] or addressed both experts and lay audiences, such as Philip Jacob Röder's *Lehrbegriff der Baumzucht und deren Veredlungsarten für Liebhaber und Landleute* (1796).[128] These publications popularized gardening methods and horticultural knowledge. The smaller-scale gardens required more attention to detail, the proper mix of shrubbery and flowers, and integration with the more utilitarian kitchen garden. Specialized publications taught how to design, plan, and maintain a garden by offering informa-

21. Primrose in Neuenhahn d.
Jüngere, *Annalen der Gärtnerey*
(1795). Courtesy of Michigan
State University Special
Collections.

tion and inspiration (fig. 21). Seed catalogs and nurseries emerged and offered the materials for the garden. Horticultural societies became popular.[129] In cities, gardening clubs emerged that occupied themselves with the cultivation and hybridization of flowers.[130] In the smaller gardens of the middle class that could not exhilarate through their expanse, the focus was on flower beds to dazzle the senses.

Beyond the enchantment of the sensual and aesthetic dimension, the garden could offer other forms of entertainment as well. In the greenhouse, hidden away from public display, the classification of plants according to genus, species, and variety provided entertainment as a hobby. The creation of new cultivars enhanced the practice of horticulture as a pastime. How-to advice ranged from offering an almanac and a calendar of the sequence in which the fruit species ripen, to giving basic information such as how to keep rabbits away from trees, to introducing new varieties of fruits and vegetables. At the same time, this particular publication offers insights into the aesthetics of design and discusses famous landscapes, such as the gardens of Hohenheim and the way these expertly designed gardens were used as sites for courtly sociability.[131] While the first periodical is an example for the more general, widely conceived interest in gardening, ranging from giving specific advice to descriptions of large parks, the second is an example for the more detailed, specific variety, offering expert advice to novices and experts. In particular, the grafting and enhancement of fruit trees with new cultivars became a favorite pastime of gardeners, not only enhancing the landscape but enriching the palate of the middle class: "That pomology is one of the supreme occupations that a garden lover can enjoy is beyond a doubt" ("Daß die Baumzucht eine der edelsten Beschäftigungen sey, die ein Liebhaber vornehmen kann, wird wohl niemand außer Zweifel ziehen").[132] Röder praises fruit as a healthy and tasty food that provides lovely beverages and vinegars and

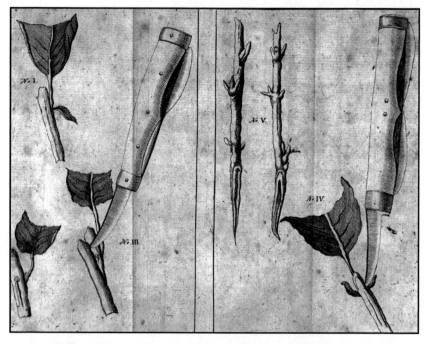

22. Pomology in Philip Jacob Röder, *Lehrbegriffe der Baumzucht und deren Veredelung für Liebhaber und Landleute* (1796). Courtesy of Michigan State University Special Collections.

can be preserved for the winter months by drying.[133] Yet he also emphasizes the pleasures of pomology as an applied science because of "the pure pleasure that is offered to us by the fusion of nature and culture, just as we can see in the variety of fruits the wisdom of the Creator" ("das reine Vergnügen, welches unsere Kunst in der Verbindung mit der Natur darbietet, so wie wir in der Mannigfaltigkeit der Früchte die Weisheit des Schöpfers bewundern lernen").[134] The techniques for the hobby horticulturist could be acquired from books giving detailed instructions often aided by illustrations. Röder even suggests the establishment of public orchards and teaching gardens for schools, where a wider public could enjoy the pleasures and insights derived from gardening and pomology in particular (fig. 22).

The increase in varieties of domestic fruits[135] and vegetables, in turn, reinforced the interest in horticulture as entertainment, driving the creation of more and more varieties. New techniques lengthened the period during which fruit and vegetables remained available. Cold frames, cellar beds, manure hotbeds, and greenhouses extended the growing season.[136] Neuenhahn in the *Annalen der Gärtnerey* and its accompanying *Intelligenzblatt* advertised the latest varieties of flower and vegetable seeds. A whole page each is devoted to herb seeds, varieties of cabbage seeds, and root vegetables. Twenty-two varieties of lettuce, fourteen kinds of leeks, eight kinds of radishes, nine kinds of peas, and sixteen kinds of beans are mentioned.

Accompanied by the increasing availability of imported spices, these new fruits and vegetables provided the prerequisites for a more complex cuisine. Both went hand in hand with an interest in cookbooks and more elaborate presentation of food gracing the middle-class table. New vegetables like broccoli, artichokes, new kinds of cabbage, and radishes found their way into German gardens and onto German tables.[137] Traditional mealtimes had been simple and hurried, but the larger variety of foods, its more elaborate preparation, and its presentation in specialized serving dishes ranging from fine china to modern stoneware required a significant time investment for preparation and consumption. This transformed mealtimes into social and cultural occasions for interaction and conversation with family members and guests. The synergetic interrelationship of these various trends (gardening and horticulture as hobby, the interest in more elaborate cuisine, the fancy table linens, graceful porcelain, etc.)—the total effect being more significant than the sum of its parts—is a notable aspect of cultural consumption enriching the middle-class lifestyle with its layering of sensual pleasures. The preeminent sense of sight beholds the shape and color of the food, flowers, fruits, and their pleasing arrangement in their respective vessels, and the sense of smell and taste of the food round out the sensory experience of mealtimes as the various senses enhance each other.

Moreover, garden publications not only aided in creating the garden but also in transforming the garden into a space for cultural entertainment: it became the site for pleasurable walks, conversations, and reading in nature alone or with friends. The importance of Goethe's garden for his mental well-being is well known. Sigrid Damm's bestseller *Christiane und Goethe* paints an interesting picture of how Goethe used the various moods of his garden with its diverse sites to entertain the people close to him.[138] He reserved certain spots in his garden for the most intimate encounters, while others signaled a more public encounter. Elise Bürger's short stories and travel accounts frequently describe the integration of traditionally domestic activities into nature. She does so by describing picnics, excursions that have the outdoor garden of an inn as one of their destinations, or elaborate nocturnal festivals replete with food, drink, and dance in the garden.[139]

The fact that many families spent the summer mostly in their gardens beyond the confines of the towns is another indication of the interest in gardening as an important form of sociable entertainment. Men usually continued their professional duties in the cities and joined their families in the evenings or on weekends. If their work allowed it, they also took advantage of the quiet environment to work in the garden. Intellectuals and writers seem to have been especially energized by working in natural surroundings.[140] Hirschfeld describes the beneficial sensual impact of a beautiful garden on the intellectual capacity. Mental activity is enhanced by objects of gentle charm, which kindle our emotions and arouse the imagination with fresh images. A break from the discipline of work to enjoy the garden sharpens and clears the mind.[141]

The entertainment value and the sense of pleasure that accompany life in the garden are seen as antidotes to the more specialized and differentiated modern life, which began to show the first signs of alienation. In contrast to the discipline of work and certain social practices, the garden offered desirable freedom, fragrances benefiting the well-being of body and soul, delightful diversions, quiet contentment, and oblivion to worldly worries.[142]

The attraction of life—work and entertainment—in the garden might stem from an anachronistic desire to overcome the separation of work and leisure while at the same time attempting to fuse nature and civilization—if only for a limited time. Goethe's relationship to his garden house seems symptomatic of these desires. By allowing the senses to be stimulated by the varying sensations, spectacles, and moods that nature provided, by listening to the body's and mind's needs for rest, nourishment, stimulation, and work instead of following the rigid artificial schedules of modern disciplined society, he was able to overcome the ills of a functionalized society for a time. Goethe, living in the garden house even in the winter and by himself, suggests this desire to be in harmony with one's own nature and the nature surrounding the self.

The association of sensibility and the celebration of "nature" in an artificial simplicity ("kunstvollen Kunstlosigkeit") inspired by the English landscape garden is an important trope in the self-definition of bourgeois identity.[143] It has its roots in the Enlightenment's critical contrast between the virtues of the country and the depravity and luxury of city life. The political edge contained in the celebration of the simple country life (Lessing's *Emilia Galotti*) becomes internalized in the celebration of living in harmony with nature as an earmark of sensibility and the private sphere. The climax and crisis of this utopian (or regressive) attempt at being in harmony with nature is exemplified in Goethe's novel *Die Leiden des jungen Werthers* (The Sorrows of Young Werther). This paradigm assumes that happiness, humanity, and self-fulfillment can be achieved in a peaceful life in nature. The discourse of sensibility resists the modernization and acceleration of the more differentiated bourgeois lifestyle by insisting on a natural rhythm of life.[144] However, as the novel suggests, the withdrawal into nature has to fail in the post-agrarian modern lifestyle of the bourgeoisie and its intellectuals and artists. Although the discourse of the garden in the popular press of the time and the compendia on garden design uses similar tropes, metaphors, and images, it no longer functions as an oppositional formation (the humanity of idyllic country life versus the artifice and lack of morality at the court and the instrumentalization of work). It no longer strives for (or believes in) the possibility of an idyllic country life but rather seeks new forms of temporary integration (or compromise), an alternating among the discipline and tedium of work, the everyday realities of life in towns and cities, and the pleasure of a less disciplined, fluid enjoyment of nature. The modern individual seeking out garden culture as a form of entertainment is painfully aware that the opportunity to live in accord with nature—that is, to let the body's natural rhythms determine activity and enjoy the sensual pleasures of nature—has to be alternated with periods of discipline, work, and the diversions of culture.

The practice of garden culture is a limited integration attempt where work is re-embedded into nature in both time and place as often as possible: in the natural surroundings the advances of civilization and self-discipline can be momentarily suspended in the garden. The summer in the garden functions as a time-out from the demands of one's normal lifestyle. Here the self can follow a more natural schedule of body and mind and work as long as one feels like it, interrupting work when the body or mind fatigues rather than according to a prescribed schedule. Designed to "delight and entertain,"[145] the garden counterbalances the discipline, effort, and tedium of work. More completely and immediately than its sister arts, painting and poetry, gardening "grips our senses, striking directly at our emotions through the presence of actual objects without filtering them through memory and imagination."[146] The pleasures of the life associated with the garden offer themselves without the work of aesthetic and cultural discernment. The forms of entertainment the garden offers are seen as an important aspect of the bourgeois lifestyle with significant benefits for the care of the self. Yet it is clear that this indulgence in the pleasure that nature offers as well as the pleasure derived from other forms of entertainment can only be momentary and fleeting. Obviously, the disciplining force of the civilizing process no longer allows the individual to return to live "in nature" or to maintain a state of sheer pleasure. Instead, the forms of entertainment described in this study represent a more modest attempt to integrate as many pockets of pleasure as possible into the middle-class lifestyle, to level out the painful opposition of work and leisure that accompanies the modern bourgeois lifestyle, and to shorten the intervals between routine and special occasions, between the tedium of the ordinary and the stimulation that the forms of entertainment provide.

Furthermore, the entertainment that the cultural practice of gardening provided to the middle class represents an attempt to minimize the dark side of modern functionalized and differentiated society. It does this by deemphasizing the strict discipline of body and mind, the limitation of narrow, specialized work, and the devaluation of sensuality. Sowing, tending, and harvesting fruits and vegetables, delighting in the visual and aromatic pleasures of one's own flowers, and preparing simple meals from the homegrown bounty requiring only minimal vessels—such practices short-circuit for a moment the chain of specialists who usually separate the producer and the consumer and momentarily suspend the usual everyday cultural consumption. Collapsing producer and consumer into one creates the illusion of a non-alienated life. The self can integrate nature and culture by opting to write, read, or think, tend the vegetables, experiment in horticulture, or indulge in the sights and sound of the garden in complete repose, suggesting a sense of completeness and wholeness—if only for a limited time. It is only possible during leisure in the summer months and for certain professions.

With modification, this model also holds true for women, who are more or less restrained by the work schedule of their husbands. A more carefully scheduled workday in the city, in turn, forced women to compartmentalize and schedule their days with more discipline as well. The summer spent in the garden, however, saw less elaborate meals and more modest forms of sociability restricted to a more intimate circle of relatives and friends. The diminished focus on the larger public community required less organizational work and allowed more time to indulge in pleasurable pastimes such as reading, needlecraft, music, and enjoying the stimulation of nature.

9
Pleasurable Diversions

DEKLAMATORIEN

New kinds of performances invited both men and women to expand the sociability of the domestic sphere for an evening of cultural entertainment in public town or meeting halls. Also an occasion to meet with friends and acquaintances and to display the latest fashions, these performances represented new cultural practices altering the conventional genres. In the so-called *Deklamatorien,* famous monologues and dialogues were isolated from well-known plays and recited independently. Many actors, such as Elise Bürger, Wilhelmine Maaß, and even the famous August Wilhelm Iffland and Karl Wilhelm Ferdinand Unzelmann, performed such recitations in larger cities. Bürger, for example, performed monologues from Goethe's *Iphigenie* and poems by Schiller. Friederike Bethmann performed scenes from *Faust,* and Maaß and Bethmann together gave the Montgomery scene from *Die Jungfrau von Orleans* at their recitals.[1] Bürger performed in Berlin, Bamberg, Nürnberg, and Cologne, among others.[2] Usually accompanied by music and theatrical gestures, she often performed in front of a relatively large audience—Bürger speaks of eight hundred people in attendance at a single performance (the occasion was a Schiller memorial tribute in the Dresdener Gewandthaus-Saal on December 30, 1805).[3] Luciane in *Die Wahlverwandtschaften,* who is portrayed as addicted to the diversions of

295

entertainment, also dabbles in the performance of *Deklamatorien,* though she possesses little talent. The association of her negatively portrayed character with this cultural practice alludes to the low aesthetic respect afforded to this form of entertainment. These performances refashioned the experience associated with theater performances. A dramatic text no longer had to be consumed or experienced in its entirety; instead, its highlights were arranged together with equally effective passages from unrelated dramatic or poetic texts, creating a new theatrical practice. By combining the most dramatic scenes from several plays, the performance heightened the degree of emotional stimulation by shortening the intervals between strong impacts. In the original plays the arch between tension and release, or stimulation and relief, is considerably wider. In a traditional performance of a play, the full range of emotions centering on one theme in its development is explored. *Deklamatorien,* on the other hand, feature a number of most likely unrelated emotions often at their peak (instead of slowly developed) that result in short intervals of strong stimulation by a variety of strong emotions. The audience is confronted with waves of unrelated, strong emotions contributing to an enhanced form of stimulation. The reproducibility and availability on demand of certain forms of stimulation are earmarks of modern forms of cultural entertainment.

Dissecting the cultural experience of a play into monologues or dialogues, the isolating focus on famous and thus recognizable passages alters the auratic quality of a work of art or literature, anticipating its technical reproduction. It is a part of leisure entertainment for an increasingly larger part of the bourgeois population. This nonprofessional mode of consumption in excerpts is an antecedent of the variety shows and as such is a phenomenon of the emergent entertainment culture in the urban centers. The admission fee for these events was lower than those of the theater and opera, thus opening cultural entertainment to larger segments of the middle class.[4]

Two mutually constitutive factors played a role in the popularization of these forms. The audience increased while the educational preparation became more pragmatic and less conducive for aesthetic experimentation, except for the intellectual elite. While still interested in the original artifact, more people opted for more readily accessible presentations in less ambitious forms of cultural entertainment in addition to traditional practices, which increased the variety of the available forms of entertainment.

Visits to the Theater

The social aspects of attending the theater as entertainment during leisure added another dimension to the theater experience. This social aspect is usually referred to in negative terms, that is, as inattentiveness to the play. Coming late, leaving early, staying only for one act or part, walking around, and eating and smoking during the performance were repeatedly criticized. These activities had become increasingly relegated to the periphery—to the intermission and the times before and after the performance. The theater had also served as a meeting place for men and prostitutes, another function of theater that had become discouraged.[5] The atmosphere of the theater was often described as that of a coffeehouse or "tobaccohouse" (*Tabagie*), with the significant difference that women were in attendance. Despite all this criticism, the theater's socializing function could never be totally suppressed. Conversation, food, and drink rounded out the entertainment provided by the play and created a pleasurable evening out—away from work on the one hand and from the domestic sphere on the other.

Visiting the theater also constituted an occasion to demonstrate one's social standing, refinement, and sophistication; in addition to displaying one's refined taste in theater as an important part of *Bildung,* the accompanying practices, such as dress, also served as an important means to distinguish oneself socially. Furthermore, displaying the latest fashion, seeing and being seen, and socializing with friends and acquaintances provided stimulation on several levels. An evening in the theater offered varied forms of entertainment and was thus highly successful in fabricating pleasure.

As demands by a larger audience for the theater as an important site of leisure entertainment increased, the theaters had to expand their repertoires. Consequently, directors not only selected more popular plays but also opted for a more accessible mode of delivery. Actors considered plays with less complex dialogues and monologues, shorter lines, and more parts a relief. Directors turned to less intricate plays because they could be mastered within the constraints of the existing company. We should remind ourselves that about three rehearsals were considered customary. This practice did not leave much room for complex interpretation, memorization, and study of body language of difficult plays. Even the Weimar Court Theater under the directorship of Goethe was said to make do with three rehearsals.

The demand for the large number of performances required a wealth of scripts and new plays. Directors turned to prolific dramatists—some writing two hundred or more plays (e.g., Karl Friedrich Hensler, Karl Meisel, Johanna Franul von Weissenthurn)—who could supply them with interesting basic scripts. They had to rely on playwrights who were able to produce plays quickly. These allowed the actors to draw on their experience (and to improvise) by including familiar plots in which situations and dramatic characters recur with considerable frequency. The range of popular genres, comedies, farces, melodramas, and the fashionable *Ritterstück* (chivalric play; a genre we will take a closer look at below) as well as musical pieces not only facilitated variety but also provided a firm structural frame for this type of scripting between scenarios and carefully crafted works.

As the history of literature and to some degree of theater is dependent on the written text, we have only an incomplete record of this tradition. Many plays produced for the immediate need of the day were not collected in the traditional manner of high cultural artifacts. Others, due to their dependence on the habitual and conventional, were considered inferior to the plays in the tradition of high culture when measured by the same standards. Both traditions—and the range of practices in between—offer different forms of entertainment in keeping with their aesthetic differences.

For artifacts to be considered as belonging to high culture they have to prize formal and thematic innovation and complexity and display a distinct poetic language. They exhibit openness, which provides intellectual challenges, provokes repeated interpretive efforts, and invites multiple attentive viewings. They can produce the kind of complex pleasure that Corngold theorized as the complicated relationship between thought and feeling, between reason and imagination, produced by a tension between the faculties.[6] The kind of pleasure and entertainment provided by high culture is thus based on intellectual activity, on negotiating ambiguity, on the detection and appreciation of formal innovation or tensions between genre expectations and the particular realization in any given text. The complexity of the response—and the kind of pleasure derived from it—is dependent on the audience's knowledge of Western cultural history with its grounding in ancient mythology and Christian traditions.

The other tradition creates a more immediate pleasure, one that can remain uninhibited by moral or cognitive interests. It requires the familiar and the customary, offering itself to immediate recognition. The solutions or resolutions advanced are often expected and lack ambiguity. Yet their formulaic structure is realized with new twists and innovative features, thus retaining interest by submitting the desirably familiar in the new, by providing novelty in familiarity. They could test bourgeois norms and values, or model and negotiate bourgeois lifestyles and patterns of behavior, while at the same time indulging the senses and the emotions. The pleasure created by the more immediate emotional and sensual response to the events onstage further offered an entertaining sense of activity—of being pleasantly occupied—without (mental) exertion. This kind of reception allowed audiences with less educational preparation to participate in the theater experience. Extending the range of entertainment opportunities, this kind of theater experience offered variety to the cultural life around 1800.

The reemergence of theater as a pleasurable spectacle consumed as leisure-time entertainment can, in a sense, be seen as a backlash against the reforms of the Enlightenment project, against the didactic pleasures of the theater as a moralizing institution.[7] The reformers' programmatic concentration on plot and characters had devalued the performative, especially the visual aspects. After all, the Enlightenment's initially didactic and then later moralizing intent had required the restructuring of the theater experience. The spectacle, the gazing at the semiotics of the body, had to be transformed into an attentive focus on the spoken word. The extensive reform movement that valued edification emphasized the text and devalued the language of the body.

Yet the commonly held notion of literary historiography describing the transformation of the theater during the course of the eighteenth century is too simplistic and one-dimensional because it ignores the differing concurrent demands made on the theater. It tends to delineate the development of theater from the crude entertainment provided by the traveling theaters into the more refined emotive pleasure of the theater of sensibility or the cerebral pleasure of the theater as moralizing institution.[8] It ignores the fact that the Enlightenment theoreticians and writers (and during our time frame the neoclassical tendencies) were, after all, a small vanguard whose vision describes an anticipated ideal situation. Only this avant-garde vision found its place in literary history, while the other strands of theater practice—lay theaters, school plays, and the private city theaters sponsored by the wealthy elites of the town who worked together with intellectuals and civil servants[9]—remained largely unrecorded.

Regardless of the programmatic changes desired and propagated by dramatists and critics and to a certain extent realized in a few plays, change is a process that could not be willed but instead evolved in a nonlinear fashion within a net of discourses. The various expectations of the dramatists and theoreticians of the diverse groups within the audience, the actors, and the directors were force fields that mutually shaped the theater experience. The theater as a site of contention shaped not only the exterior and interior architecture of the building, the seating arrangements of the audience, and the placement and design of the stage, props, costumes, and lighting but also the behavior of the audience.

During our time frame the variety of theater practices not only increased but became more visible. Berlin at the end of the eighteenth century had a diverse but relatively small group of people who were interested in the various cultural events offered throughout the year. If significant or attractive performances drew the audience to a certain event, the empty chairs in the regular houses suggested that one and the same audience was partaking in the variety of entertainment options available.[10]

The theater was only one form of specular entertainment in the larger cities. The number and kind of competing cultural events of course varied from city to city and changed at any given time. A portrait of the cultural life in Berlin from 1796 lists a theater of medium quality, a Grand Italian opera, and a masked ball during the period of the carnival as the main sources of public entertainment. Clubs and the coffee- and tobacco houses supplemented these. Other popular means of entertainment were card and board games, conversation, and outings. The middle classes passed the winter season with balls and gambling. Just a few years later, in 1811, the variety of leisure-time activities had increased significantly and included "rides, concerts, guest performances by foreign actors, puppet shows, and mechanical performances."[11] Competing for what seems to have been essentially the same audience were not only the growing establishment of lay theaters but also the guest performances from other visiting theater troupes. In 1803 a new type of puppet theater became a big draw. The life-sized puppets with their splendid, elaborate costumes and sets seem to have attracted—maybe surprisingly—the more sophisticated audiences, especially those with affinities to the romantic movement. The sense of estrangement created by the puppets foregrounded artifice, the formal aesthetic quality.[12] With the audience no longer satisfied with the predominance of the verbal/literary aspects of the play, not only did the variety of performance types increase but we also see a strong interest in the visual aspects of the theater sets.

The audience became increasingly fascinated by the visual impact of the play as a sequence of images and pictures. The listener turned into a spectator demanding ever more elaborate and innovative designs. The audience exerted its influence in reshaping the theater experience by favoring less complex plays and by taking a liking to plays with elaborate stage sets. The spectators are drawn into the visual experience by the movement of the gaze following the invitation of the visual field itself. No longer exclusively forced to recognize and respond to the unique negotiations of the conventions of genre, the spectator's gaze is free to wander and delight in the spectacle. The fashionable elaborate stage sets and costumes begin to foreground the specular elements of theater. This aesthetic of visuality opens the door for creating larger audiences, with the consequence that participation in the cultural activity of theater—as with other cultural practices dominated by visuality—no longer automatically attests to one's elite status: "One no longer sees with the educated eyes of a classically informed elite, and, correspondingly, the activity of looking itself no longer testifies to one's belonging to that elite. What begins to replace it is an aesthetic of individualism in which the sentimental look is sufficient to indicate one's being part of a republic of visuality."[13] A focus on the visual demanded less attention, concentration, and engagement with the performances, allowing instead for a less focused play of the imagination and the freedom to open oneself up to the sensual stimulation of the performance without being compelled to classify and analyze. Eventually, the diversity of plays with an increasing contingent of less complex plays resulted in the split into specific theaters with distinct repertoires, for example, the differentiation into distinct theaters for children and adults.[14] Complex moral and aesthetic edification is relegated to one type of theater frequented predominantly by experts, professional insiders, and the educated elite. Entertainment becomes the domain of popular theater, which at the same time could retain a didactic or moralizing function. Yet a few of the plays that became canonized and whose author was one of the pillars of high culture in late-eighteenth-century Germany, Friedrich Schiller, appealed to both modes of reception.

SPECTACLES

Extensive Stage Design as Pleasurable Indulgence

The tension between the various functions and forms of entertainment concerned dramatists and theoreticians and created considerable debate. The entertainment function in the traditional sense became split off from the theater as influential writers and critics were ambivalent about the theater's social function as leisure entertainment. Schiller deplores the fact that the theater is

> not the school of the nation led by the dramatists as the teacher but instead functions as a diversion to avoid debilitating boredom and depressing winter nights for the large number of loafers who want to be enriched by the foam of wisdom, the paper currency of sentiment, and gallantry for which the theater is a site of fashionable display and for the sensual pleasures of an inn.

> So lang das Schauspiel weniger Schule als Zeitvertreib ist— mehr dazu gebraucht wird die eingähnende Langeweile zu beleben, unfreudliche Winternächte zu betrügen, und das grosse Heer unserer süssen Müssiggänger mit dem Schaume der Weisheit, dem Papiergeld der Empfindung, und galanten Zoten zu bereichern, so lang es mehr für die Toilette und die Schenke arbeitet.[15]

Yet especially in his pre-Kantian essays, Schiller acknowledges the theater's function as a form of pleasurable escape, helping people to dream away the unpleasantness, boredom, and loneliness of the real world that poisons their lives when their work disgusts them, their souls are weighed down by a thousand worries, and their professional lives dampen the senses.[16] Schiller is keenly aware of the psychosocial price his contemporaries were paying for the potentially alienating specialization of modern civilization. This ambiguity in his position indicates that he understands the multiple functions and several layers of entertainment at work in the theater experience.

While Schiller in his post-Kantian essays is denouncing sensuality on the stage in theory, in practice many of his plays encourage a high degree of sensual stimulation in his use of elaborate stage sets, extensive historical costume, and music.[17] Schiller, who was not only a great theoretician but also an experienced and sensitive practitioner of theater, set new standards in his *Die Jungfrau von Orleans* with its mass processions, requiring "moving decorations" (*Wanderdekorationen*) that fascinated audiences. In response, the theater director Iffland was concerned about the heightened expectations that plays like *Die Jungfrau von Orleans* with its mass processions, elaborate stage design, and historical costumes had created. This desire for new specular thrills contributed considerably to the complexity and cost of performing these elaborate plays, forcing theater directors into large expenses to compete with other theaters and especially the opera in order to meet the expectations of the audience. *Die Jungfrau von Orleans* set a new standard of elaborate stage design that provided visual and aural stimulation to an audience hungry for new excitation through ever stronger and more surprising effects.[18] The audience came to expect the special effects of the theater machinery with its thunder and lightning and elements such as processionals, battles, and jousting matches replete with the appropriate sounds.[19]

Goethe, who was often criticized for "selling out" by catering to the need for entertainment in the productions he prepared for the Weimar Court Theater, also paid particular attention to the spectacular aspects of performances. Realizing the play's potential for spectacle, Goethe took great pains to produce Schiller's *Wallenstein's Lager* as an elaborate *Gesamtkunstwerk* for the Weimar Court Theater. Careful historical research on the Thirty Years War provided him with the inspiration for costumes and props.[20] A kaleidoscope of sight and sound greeted the audience as the curtain rose. Elaborate stage painting, a wealth of props, combined with groups of supernumeraries created a colorful living background for the dramatic action. The dramatic action itself was conceptualized as spanning the peasant's conversation with his son, the sermon of the monk as well as the grand pathos of Wallenstein's speeches.[21] The music added another layer of meaning to the visual presentation, the spoken word, and the sound effects. The multidimensional stage performance made this play successful and interesting for the audience, whose senses were indulged. The historical period of the Thirty Years War was alien enough to contemporary audiences that the relatively accurate historical props stimulated in their novelty.

The audience's desire for novelty was an important motor for the increasing specularity of the theater experience.[22] Perpetual novelty was difficult to achieve by a standing theater company with a fixed repertoire and a steady cast of actors. Since neither of these factors could readily be changed—new texts could only be introduced on a limited basis (the introduction of less complicated plays with shorter roles was one remedy to increase the repertoire)—the area of stage design provided another opportunity for innovation and novelty. Along with the selection of plays that were most suitable for an extravagant and interesting stage design, props and costumes became the means with which savvy directors like Iffland in Berlin and Zimmermann in Hamburg combated the competition that the increasing diversification of the entertainment offerings in their cities brought.[23] Opera and other specular events vied for a limited audience even in the big cities. In the late eighteenth century, the famous stage designers—for example, Angelo Quaglio (1784–1815), Friedrich Beuther (1777–1856), and Karl Friedrich Schinkel (1781–1841)—began to create sets not only for the opera but also for theatrical performances.[24] Beuther created a set for Schiller's *Maria Stuart* (Hamburgisches Hoftheater 1811), and Schinkel designed sets for Goethe's *Iphigenie* and Schiller's *Die Braut von Messina* and *Don Carlos*. With regard to opera, the most important example of an elaborate, spectacular stage design is that of Mozart's *Die Zauberflöte* (*The Magic Flute*), a visual feast of exotic Egyptian elements, with the famous set by Karl Friedrich Schinkel in Berlin (performed 18 January 1816), the Weimar performance (1817) with a set by Friedrich Beuther, and the Munich performance with a set by Simon Quaglio (27 November 1818). The audience marveled at the rich mixture of the strong sensual impact of, for example, the intensity of the seemingly never-ending night-blue sky illuminated by stars in the often-depicted set for the appearance of the Queen of the Night[25] and the magic of the special effects as the Queen of the Night seems to float on the clouds and the crescent of the moon.[26] If this set dazzled the audience with its strong contrasts of the intensity and the unique quality of blue—which most reproductions cannot adequately capture—and the sparkling illumination of the stars, another night scene depicting Sarastro's gardens fascinates by the softness of the moonlight evoking the stillness of a mild southern night. The design invites the spectator to visually explore the rich vegetation in the foreground, the colossal stature of the Sphinx and the pyramids dwarfing the temple and drawing the gaze into the soft depth of a luscious valley. The visual contrast of strong distinctions of light and dark with the soft fluidity of largely monochromatic scenes and the abundant exotic details of each of the numerous sets evoke a plethora of different moods in the spectator, spanning a sense of the overwhelming majesty of the night, to the disquieting spectacle of fire and water, to the darkness and strict geometrical lines of the temple, to the sensual indulgence in the softness of the moonlit night, and offering pleasurable stimulation through a change of atmospheres and feelings.

In order to compete with the dominant spectacle of the opera, Iffland had 362 new elaborate costumes made for the theater.[27] Plays such as Goethe's *Götz von Berlichingen,* Schiller's *Die Jungfrau von Orleans* and the Wallenstein trilogy, but also *Don Carlos* and *Die Braut von Messina,* among others, as well as a number of chivalric and historical plays, offered ample opportunity to excel in the area of stage design.[28] One could speculate that the painterly qualities of this kind of a stage set, which was, in turn, isolated and reproduced as (commemorative) prints that graced middle-class households, began to drive spectator expectations and altered theater practices (see fig. 23).

An early example of an elaborate stage design was Zimmermann's 1774 performance of *Götz von Berlichingen,* which could compete with

23. The opera *Titus* (1799), set by Giorgio Fuentes (1756–1821). Courtesy of the Theaterwissenschaftliche Sammlung Cologne University.

the stage design of the opera: "Götz was the reason for theater design and props that were especially luxurious for bourgeois drama" ("Götz war Anlaß für Ausstattungen, die für das bürgerliche Drama besonders prachtvoll waren").[29] Under the directorship of Schröder, the Hamburg theater became famous for its elaborate stage design and decorations. No other theater that did not offer opera had as much stage equipment. An increasingly voluminous set of props, furniture, decorations, and sets to accommodate the unique character of each play accompanied this trend toward a naturalistic style. Iffland dates the emergence of this taste for elaborate stage design between 1775 and 1780. Before this increase, the possessions of a theater company would ordinarily have consisted of six basic sets—"an elaborate hall, a street scene, a village, a living room, a dungeon, and a landscape with trees and bushes."[30] But with the historical plays—for example, Schiller's *Maria Stuart, Don Carlos,* and especially *Die Jungfrau von Orleans* (with sets by Beuther and Schinkel)—the elaborate historicizing stage sets and the visual diversity providing pleasure began to rival those of the opera. Approaching the status of a *Gesamtkunstwerk,* performances indulged the senses in an elaborate spectacle. Schiller's *Die Jungfrau von Orleans* caused a sensation.[31]

Extravagance in Stage Design: Schiller's *Die Jungfrau von Orleans*

The extraordinary success of *Die Jungfrau von Orleans*[32] makes it a good candidate for an examination of this kind of monumental stage design in more detail. As in literature, gothic elements were especially popular in stage design. The gothic is in many ways a culmination of the aesthetics of the sublime. Faced with the sense of magnitude conveyed by Gothic architecture, the spectator is dwarfed. Altering spectators' perceptions of the body in relationship to its environment, the painted building is significantly out of proportion with the actors onstage and seeks to emphasize their diminution in the face of larger and greater forces (fig. 24). This kind of architecture "shocks the viewer out of his normal perception of himself and distorts the magnitude of his surroundings."[33] Thus the Gothic architecture depicted onstage suggests an altered relationship between self and environment, producing the mixed sensation of terror experienced in the face of the infinity and vastness of the universe that was mastered as an aesthetic experience.

This mastery—in the sublime—produces a pleasurable response. The effect is intensified because it is perceived as more complex than pure delight due to the remnants of horror.

In the enormous partial representation of the Reims Cathedral, the entrance is monumental enough to fill the stage, yet it suggests an even more massive building by alluding to the towers in a pronounced upward movement. Gothic ornamentation frames the set. The proscenium frames the movement of the set, creating a playful tension between the containment of the frame and its transgression in the movement onstage. The staged Gothic architecture created perpetual visual interest through its frenetic, undulating pattern, producing "a maze of latticed activity, . . . 'a fantastic spaghetti-like interlace' whose puzzle asks to be unraveled, whose convolutions seem alternately to seek and avoid each other, whose component parts, endowed as it were with sensibility, captivate sight and sense in passionately vital movement."[34] It also generated a certain lack of calm, preventing relaxation, producing instead a highly stimulating visual impact. "Gothic nervousness quickens the senses as more of the mind becomes awake to more of the world."[35]

The stage painting indulges the spectator with an overwhelming feast for the eye, inviting the spectator to luxuriate in the strong visual impact of Gothic architecture. The gaze is pleasantly occupied, following the maze of lines and sweeping movements of its structural elements. The mind marvels over the counterintuitive apparent weightlessness of the stone sweeping upward rather than bearing down, creating a sense of wonder by its seeming lack of materiality.[36]

Another form of astonishing dematerialization occurs within the intricate filigree carvings that cover the walls like "a spider web, the flowing fan tracery on vaults and windows, and the clutter of ornament on exterior walls, arches, portals, and towers."[37] It busies the gaze and stimulates the senses. Weight gives way to levitation, suggesting the disembodiment of the material world. Altering "normal" perception creates the pleasures of novelty, of transforming the spectator into a reality other than the here and now. "The subject's experience of its limits and its fragility calls into question its previous conceptual boundaries."[38]

In other sets depicting gothic interiors, the illusion of light falling through the stained-glass windows and creating colors and patterns upon the stone provided not only a feast for the eye but also the

24. Contemporary undated calendar print of Schiller's *Die Jungfrau von Orleans*, set by Karl Friedrich Schinkel (1781–1841). Courtesy of the Theaterwissenschaftliche Sammlung Cologne University.

overwhelming experience of the sublime, as in the indulgence of the extraordinary magnificently overwhelming landscape. Julia Kristeva's description of the sublime illuminates this effect:

> When the starry sky, a vista of open seas or a stained glass window shedding purple beams fascinate me, there is a cluster of meaning, of colors, of words, of caresses, that are light touches, scents, signs, cadences that arise, shroud me, carry me away, and sweep me beyond the things that I see, hear, or think. The "sublime" object dissolves in the raptures of a bottomless memory. . . . I then forget the point of departure and find myself removed to a secondary universe, set off from the one where "I" am—delight and loss. Not at all short of but always with and through perception and words, the sublime is a *something added* that expands us, overstrains us, and causes us to be both *here,* as abjects, and *there,* as others and sparkling.[39]

The stage set for Schiller's *Don Carlos* captures some of this luminescence of the Gothic window (fig. 25). On the whole, the intoxication and indulgence of the gothic stage design is another means to push for greater visual interest. The *Ritterschauspiel* (chivalric drama) accommodated a wide range of these elements, which was, of course, an important reason for its popularity and appeal.

RITTERSCHAUSPIEL

The chivalric drama shares many formal elements, motifs, settings, and characters with the gothic in the visual arts and literature. The numerous depictions of stage sets of *Ritterschauspiel* attest not only to the popularity of the genre but also to the creative opportunities for stage and costume designers to ply their craft and visually indulge their audience. Only opera surpassed the chivalric plays in indulging the senses with its elaborate stage sets and costumes. Since definitions of the chivalric tend to be problematic and in need of a thorough reexamination—which, of course, exceeds the parameters of this study on its entertainment quality—a description of its features takes the place of a definition.[40] Historical accuracy is not of interest to most chivalric literature. The general interest in the past—in archaeology and antiques—was loosely labeled an interest in the Middle Ages. The historical period in question

25. Set from Schiller's *Don Carlos* (1818), sketch by Karl Friedrich Schinkel. Courtesy of the Theaterwissenschaftliche Sammlung Cologne University.

26. Castle ballroom set for the opera *Agnes von Hohenstaufen* by Spontini, sketch (1827–29) by Karl Friedrich Schinkel. Courtesy of the Theaterwissenschaftliche Sammlung Cologne University.

remains unspecified and represents an ahistorical amalgam of features from distinct eras, which seem selected strictly for their effects. Markus Krause describes the effects produced by this unspecified past as a form of "historical exoticism" ("historischer Exotismus").[41] The time of the Crusades is especially popular, as it offers honorable and effective motifs for separating and destabilizing families and couples and provides a convenient opening for the conflict driving the plot.

A cast of stock characters with characteristic and typecasting names, more or less honorable knights and ladies with their attendant knaves and ladies-in-waiting, pilgrims, hermits, clergymen, and children are shown in visually interesting situations. Their castles are under siege, battles rage (usually offstage), women flee the castle under the cover of darkness, and secret meetings with hermits or clergymen provide assistance and (false) information or obfuscate the truth.

Borrowing elements from the settings of the gothic, the action is frequently located in a gloomy fortress, castle, or ruin or outdoors in a wild and romantic landscape, such as a dark forest. In conjunction with the natural setting, violent weather—raging storms, lightning, howling winds, and racing clouds revealing and shrouding the moon—often helps to set and underscore a strong mood. The fortresses provide ample space for the integration of secret passageways, doorways, hidden chambers, hiding places, sealed vaults, dungeons, and underground catacombs. These visually varied and interesting stage sets created opportunities for an array of interesting vistas that hold the gaze of the spectator. As icons, their elements hint at unspeakable horrors and crimes and their punishment. On the narrative level, these elements provide moments of suspense and occasions for the twists and turns of the plot. With the elements of a strong, mysterious mood, suspense, and hints at the unspeakable, chivalric literature alludes to the related genre of gothic literature, which foregrounds these elements.

The gothic became immensely popular during the last quarter of the eighteenth century. It suited the tumultuous times of the American Revolution, the French Revolution, the Reign of Terror, and the beginning of the Napoleonic Wars. By 1780 gothic literature was recognized as a popular mode, and in the 1790s it became a mania.[42] Backscheider sees the gothic plays as fables of social identity in which the gothic protagonist is the concentrated locus of anxiety about power and authority. The genre offers glimpses at a nightmare version of human reason, and it exercised, released, and then contained the major personal and social anxieties of the time.[43] With respect to discussion of the gothic in the American context, earlier interpretations emphasize the psychological aspects, drawing the connection to later Freudian theories. As William Patrick Day summarizes: "For Freud, dreams are the expression of wishes unacknowledged in waking life; the Gothic fantasy is the expression of the fears and desires created, but unacknowledged, by conventional culture. Like a dream, it reveals the inner life of the individual."[44]

In Germany the debate was framed quite differently, less directly Freudian or political, not associated with specific political figures and less with directly identifiable crises and distinct issues. Instead, diffuse discontent with what was perceived as bald rationalism, with a threadbare didacticism and realism of much of the contemporary literature, and a general sense of aesthetic ennui were considered the sources for the interest and curiosity in the expansion of experience and the integration of the supernatural. In the contemporary discussions it is foremost an aesthetic issue; writers and critics bemoan the deterioration of taste as the "masses" begin to influence the production and reception of literature toward the end of the eighteenth century.[45] In the German context, the politicization of the genre is an effect of its reception history with a general tendency to characterize chivalric and gothic novels ("Ritter- und Schauerromane") as apolitical escapism.[46] Only recent feminist criticism exploring gothic and chivalric texts by women, which is informed by the significantly more advanced criticism on the English gothic tradition, points to the function of the gothic as an alternate, darker version of the family romance and its psychodynamics of identity formation.[47]

This interest in the gothic has also been explained as springing from the same need to expand the rational world as the contemporary interest in mesmerism, faith healing, and other miraculous occurrences.[48] In addition to Mesmer, one of the most famous and public cases was the colorful figure of Cagliostro, who made his rounds at European courts claiming to communicate with the spirits of the dead.[49]

This interest in an expanded reality responded to a sense of modern disorder and fragmentation caused by the perception that religion, science, and philosophical systems no longer provided the self with a sense of wholeness and unity. In this sense it is an indication of fears and anxieties about modern fragility and the vulnerability of a secular society. The glimpse at supernatural phenomena allows the imagination to go beyond the ordinariness of everyday experiences and beyond the dominant realistic modes of writing. Romance and adventure offered freedom from the merely referential, veridical world of realist texts in the Enlightenment tradition and the flood of utilitarian books and popular journals offering information on all facets of everyday life—from child rearing to gardening. The sense of adventure, the exotic location, the remote time span, the hinting at the supernatural and nonrational, the emphasis on sensual indulgence, and the ability to gratify usually repressed feelings of fear, anxiety, and violence all contributed to its popularity.

Chivalric drama shares many elements with novels in the chivalric and gothic tradition and with fairy tales, which authors like Sophie Albrecht, Benedikte Naubert, Caroline de la Motte-Fouqué, Johann August Apel, and Friedrich Laun, as well as the extensive collection *Die Blaue Bibliothek aller Nationen* (The Blue Library of All Nations, 1790–1802, 12 vols.; a selection of chivalric literature, fairy tales, and literature of the fantastic collected, translated, and edited by Friedrich Justin Bertuch), popularized in Germany.[50] Albrecht's *Graumännchen oder die Burg Rabenbühl* (The Gray Dwarf and Rabenbühl Fortress, 1799),[51] for example, combines the gothic novel with fairy-tale elements (e.g., the Rumpelstiltskin motif) and with historical elements such as the violent conversion to Christianity in the Black Forest.

These related genres accentuate the entertainment quality of the fantastic in order to, as Bertuch put it, provide "good amusing reading to entertain and nourish the spirit and to foster good taste . . . which is sought after and loved by almost all who did not spring completely misshapen from the hands of mother nature" ("gute amüsante Lectüre zur Unterhaltung und Nahrung des Geistes, und Ausbildung des Geschmacks . . . die fast alle, die nur nicht ganz verunglückt aus den Händen der Mutter Natur kamen, suchen und lieben").[52] He considers the nonrealistic literature a pleasurable way to playfully discern fact and fiction and to practice non-identificatory forms of reading. These texts delight because they create surprise and wonder by offering the innovative and extraordinary that transcends normalcy.[53] In Albrechts's *Graumännchen,* the monstrous supernatural figure of the same name sends the heroine dreams that sustain her in her darkest hour and save her from suicide. Here the role of the fantastic is to provide comforting alternate realities, as the narrator suggests with regard to the character Agnes: "[Agnes] was too poor in the real world that she would not have clung to every shred of hope that the invisible world of the imagination could provide" ("[Agnes] war zu arm in der würklichen Welt, als daß sie nicht jede Hoffnung, welche ihr die unsichtbare gab, mit vollem Glauben hätte umfassen sollen").[54] This could also be read as a poetological statement on the role of the enriching quality of fantasy and the imagination in literature that is consumed as a form of entertainment. As pleasant dreams heal and strengthen Agnes and allow her to survive the humiliation she is subjected to, the modern individual can indulge in (literary) fantasies not only to shape, plan, and reflect on his or her own possibilities but also to experience pleasure as the absence of repression and self-discipline. Of course, imagination is not completely unfettered; as Mark Turner cautions, "it is governed by principles. These principles are automatic and below the level of consciousness. . . . It is constrained by our knowledge, our experience, and our modes of cognition."[55] These modes of cognition are acquired unconsciously in basic conceptual metaphors. Common experiences help map those dimensions or experiences that are intangible.

By situating the plot in a historical past, chivalric literature (and its related genres) playfully challenges the limits of the predictable, the natural, and the possible. As these elements are limited to a few scenes or to peripheral characters, they create a pleasurable sensation of contained touches of horror and dread. Chivalric literature seems to toy with a sense of terror created by the supernatural, with the unknown, the unpredictable, the essentially threatening nature of the world. These elements provide suspense, the stimulating and insatiable desire to know that can make the mind race to imagine potential solutions or explanations. As the text provides answers and the reader compares them with his or her own, momentary equilibrium and mental rest are achieved, only to crave the destabilization of a new challenge created by the next suspenseful or unexplained element. This creates an ever greater demand for the repetition of this pattern of tension and release. The audience looks for texts or plays that offer similar patterns of stimulation that depart from predominantly intellectual stimulation and instead allow for a degree of ambiguity to remain. The phenomena that cannot be explained rationally maintain a degree of tension, making the audience eager for more of the same fare. A similar effect has been described in an early comment by Anna Laetitia Barbauld in "On the Pleasure Derived from Objects of Terror": "A strange and unexpected evil awakens the mind and keeps it on the stretch; and where the agency of invisible beings is introduced . . . our imagination, darting forth, explores with rapture the new world which is laid open to its view, and rejoices in the expansion of its powers. Passion and fancy, cooperating, elevate the soul to its highest pitch; and the pain of terror is lost in amazement."[56] Novelty and the extraordinary astonish the audience; at the same time, this "unsettling" effect is perceived as positive because the threat is contained.

Although such features as special effects, apparitions, voices, ghosts, predictions, fateful signs, premonitions, and dreams link chivalric and historical literature with the genre of the gothic, the chivalric genre uses these devices more sparingly. Fusing family drama with the gothic, it merely suggests without fully engaging the cataclysmic passions, the unspeakable crimes, or the breaking of ancient, sacred taboos that Backscheider considers to be at the heart of the struggle the gothic hero has with himself.[57]

The playful engagement and harnessing of these chilling notions of dread and terror or of the forces of evil or the supernatural that provide a momentary thrill is experienced as pleasurable. It converts fearful, anxious, or dangerous impulses into pleasure as the power of the imagination is able to control, channel, and limit the threatening emotions and impulses—which provides the same sense of empowerment that aestheticians theorized as the sublime. The suspense and dread can be experienced as pleasurable because the spectator can submit to it or withdraw from it at will.[58] At the same time, it flirts with the forbidden and the extraordinary, operates at the outer edge of the symbolic, and expands the possibility of meaning.[59]

To a lesser degree than the gothic, chivalric literature indulges its audience with fear, dread, and terror. Although it allows for the exploration and experience of the dark side of the human psyche—the violence of the family romance, diffuse fears of unseen dangers, or the threat of the supernatural—it does so within a rational historical framework. Not unlike the experience of the sublime in nature and the landscape garden, the audience is able to revel in imagined or momentary fantasies of submission to a potentially dangerous situation (or person) while enjoying a sense of power that stems from being able to withdraw from the threatening circumstance at will.

This type of literature functions as the discourse of the dark side of the human experience and gives contours, shape, and voice to the unspeakable and the suppressed. It both helps to grasp and understand evil, aggression, and fear and allows an outlet for these threatening emotions. Gothic elements and the sublime can thus be seen as a necessary and integral part of the disciplining process that Elias described.[60] As we have discussed, the Protestant ethic and its asceticism, supporting the more differentiated system of capitalism, required the internalization of social norms and self-discipline. These values are socialized in the nuclear family where authority is veiled as familial love, which discourages the direction of aggression—as a by-product of suppression and self-discipline—toward the primary love object, the parents. Consequently, aggression turns against the self in the form of auto-aggression. Elias theorizes that this particularly modern process of socialization produces severe fear and anxiety to enhance self-control and discipline.[61] Gothic elements in literature, here in chivalric literature, negotiate the topics that are taboo, for example, the violence of the family romance at the core of modern society and the accompanying repressed aggression. Both are usually excluded from discourse. Yet by speaking about this nexus, the literary imagination both accommodates and even indulges in it while at the same time mastering the negative sensations and rendering them nonthreatening.

In addition, the playful transgression inherent in speaking the unspeakable, the breaking of taboos, is experienced as intrinsically pleasurable. It not only allows the individual to come to grips with this aspect of modern socialization but allows for the indulgence in safely contained violent fantasies. A "safer" version of the feelings of aggression and auto-aggression that accompany modern self-discipline, which other discourses suppress, is aesthetically produced by gothic elements and invites indulgence in the literary fantasy of aggression. Because it is detached from the spectator's own direct source of aggression and projected onto fantastic circumstances, often quite removed from the veridical contemporary world, the sense of being overwhelmed by fear and horror that accompanies aggression can be experienced as pleasurable, as the mixed sensation of delightful horror. As in the experience of the sublime, the fear of powerlessness and dependency can be dispensed with at will and thus can actually serve as a strategy of empowerment, of overcoming fear.[62]

On the whole, chivalric literature represented an expansion of consciousness and reality. It suggests that reality might be more complex and tangled than we ordinarily think it is.[63] What Day points out for the genre of the gothic also applies to certain elements in chivalric literature, albeit to a lesser degree: the gothic fantasy articulates and thus confers some degree of acceptability upon otherwise dangerous personal fantasies. From a safe distance, the reader sees his or her own, perhaps unacknowledged, desires given shape and, further, public expression in a more or less respectable aspect of one's culture.[64] He suggests that its function is therapeutic in the sense that fantasy releases "tensions and anxieties by assigning them objects, by giving them objective expression in the text" while simultaneously producing "not an imaginative vision, but analytical distance."[65]

Many chivalric plays do not differ significantly in plot structure from bourgeois drama; they center on family conflicts and the family value system. Yet by transposing essentially modern conflicts into a less civilized (and thus less repressed), more barbaric or primitive past, the psychological costs—the violence, aggression, and sacrifice—could come into stronger relief than in the bourgeois drama, which tends to support the contemporary love paradigm with its romantic sensibility and its all-encompassing emotional power. The chivalric created what Terry Castle called a "cognitive dispensation—of a new collective absorption in the increasingly vivid, if also hallucinatory, content of the mind itself."[66] The chivalric genre with its gothic elements is able to point to the uncanny effects of refined sentiment and its stimulation of the imagination, which we have discussed in conjunction with the emergence of sensibility and the love paradigm. The highly sensitive person can become obsessed with the spectral images of those they love. Castle suggests: "One sees in the mind's eye those who are absent; one i[s] befriended and consoled by the phantoms of the beloved."[67] The intense erotic attraction prompts the individual to maintain an attachment even in the absence or the death (real or imagined) of the beloved. Adelheit von Rastenberg (in the play of the same name) retreats to the solitude of the forest to be close to her lover, whom she presumes is dead. Daydreams bring back absent lovers or those believed to be dead. Castle considers this capacity a crucial feature of the new sensibility and its erotic love paradigm: "In the moment of romantic self-absorption, the other was indeed reduced to a phantom—a purely mental effect, an image, as it were, on the screen of consciousness itself. The corporeality of the other—his or her actual life in the world—became strangely insubstantial and indistinct: what mattered was the mental picture, the ghost, the haunting image."[68] The mental image of the beloved can console in times of despair, as we will see below. The genre highlights the darker aspects of the psychodynamics of love, its dangers to the psyche through loss, rejection, and passion that engenders violence on the one hand and the destabilization of the self by an excessive hallucinary focus on the inner life celebrated by modern individualism.

The apparition of the dead also allows for the voicing of the anxieties of the modern individual regarding the death of his or her loved ones and mortality in general. Philippe Ariès has described these changing attitudes toward death from an accepted organic, integral aspect of human existence to a growing dissociation from corporeal reality and an unprecedented loathing of death by the eighteenth century and beyond. He attributes this change in mentalities to the individualistic and secular nature of modern Western social patterns, to the deemphasis of communal life in favor of intensified affective relationships to a few select others.[69] In its tendency to repress the body, the individual also retreats into denial in the face of death, for example, in the obsession with the motif of the beautiful death, "in hiding or denying the physical signs of mortality and decay."[70] There are no more obvious images of this tendency than the "beautification" of the cemetery, its rearrangement and transformation into a field of clover in *Die Wahlverwandtschaften,* which captures the spirit of the time, which turned cemeteries into landscaped gardens of remembrance, and above all, Ottilie's preservation in death, which bespeaks the modern cultural practice of embalming and mummification. Hand in hand with the denial of mortality goes the fascination with the idealized images of the dead and the comforting fantasy of meeting up with the loved ones after death—also expressed in the closing passage of *Die Wahlverwandtschaften.*[71] Although the chivalric alludes to this change in mentalities, it also includes elements where loved ones were only presumed dead and reappear, thus shifting the focus from death to ethical consideration, the issue of betrayal, or the dilemma of finding oneself married to two people.

Favorite themes in chivalric plays are a man torn between two women, a woman torn between two rivals, forced marriages, and betrayals. Compared to the bourgeois drama, chivalric plays provide ample opportunity for colorful characters, interesting historical periods, locations, customs, events, costumes, and special effects. The sentimental and realistic drama had become rather conventional by the end of the eighteenth century and provided only a limited sphere of action. Chivalric literature featured a more interesting setting that provided for more opportunities of heroic conflict for the protagonists. The heroes and heroines are not only defined through the familial realm but are also conceptualized as rulers over land and subjects. They display public and private dimensions that are often in conflict with each other. Even if the familial value system does not differ radically from that of the bourgeois tragedy and the romantic novels, the focus on the family romance is different in the bourgeois tragedy and sentimental novel on the one hand and chivalric and gothic literature on the other. If the first is about seduction and the creation and negotiation of erotic desire, the latter is about confinement in the family and the negotiation of authority by force, violence, and coercion.

As Foucault has argued, the "deployment of sexuality" over the traditional "deployment of alliance" puts massive stress on the family. The older model "is built up around a system of rules" according to which the "link between partners and definitive statutes," seeking to maintain the status quo, connects to the larger context, the economy, through "the role it can play in the transmission and circulation of wealth."[72] In contrast, the modern deployment of sexuality "operates according to the mobile, polymorphous, and contingent techniques of power" and is concerned with the "sensations of the body . . . the nature of impressions."[73] The family becomes "the interchange of sexuality and alliance: it conveys the law and the juridical dimension in the deployment of sexuality and it conveys the economy of pleasure and the intensity of sensations in the regime of alliance."[74] In this newer and more contradictory model, identity "evolves in and through the desiring self's exploration of the world, in the dynamic established between self and other, in a difficult negotiation between the pull of inner desire and outer 'reality.'"[75] Williams considers the gothic a narrative that is built on this "cultural fault line" between these older and newer organizational forms.[76]

The same holds true for the central conflict of chivalric plays, which explore the difference between a marriage based on honor and one based on love (or in the parlance of the eighteenth century, a marriage of convenience or a companionate marriage based on love [*Liebesehe*]), as in Eleonore von Thon's *Adelheit von Rastenberg* (1788),[77] Friedrich Wilhelm Ziegler's *Mathilde Gräfin von Griessbach* (1791),[78] Joseph Marius von Babo's *Oda, die Frau von zween Männern* (1791),[79] Elise Bürger's *Adelheit, Gräfinn [sic] von Teck* (1799),[80] Christian Heinrich Spieß's *Klara von Hoheneichen* (1800),[81] and Auguste von Wallenheim's (pseud.) *Klara von Leuenstein* (1806).[82] The rivalry between two men for the hand of a woman is one of the core conflicts of chivalric plays. The medieval setting allows the underlying power relationships—the violence at the core of the intimate family of (arranged) marriages—to be more clearly and directly exposed.[83] It more clearly demonstrates the ancient core of alliance structures in the modern family that shapes and nurtures those beings which it at the same time regulates and encloses. In these chivalric plays, the fathers exert their full patriarchal authority to force their daughters into marriages of alliance, which provide a maximum of power, status, and wealth for the father and by implication to the social position of his daughter. The daughters' true loves are forcefully removed (or retreat honorably) to take care of their lands or join the Crusades. The married couple has to deal with the consequences of a marriage that is not based on love. The situation is usually complicated because the husband is in love with his wife (and/or erotically desires her) while the wife is bound only by her sense of honor and duty. Count Adelburg in *Oda, die Frau von zween Männern* complains, "You are my wife in name only, not in your mind and heart" ("Du bist mein Weib im Wort, nicht im Geist und Herzen").[84] The psychological drama of the lack of a mutually fulfilling love relationship for these couples is made apparent by the lack of a common offspring (and by stepchildren). Just as Count Adelburg berates his wife, Oda, for not giving him children, Robert von Rastenberg in *Adelheit von Rastenberg* reproaches his wife, Adelheit, because she is unwilling (or unable) to give him children. Both men are unable to harness the power of love and sexuality in their marriages. Robert can only attempt to prevent it from spilling over the boundaries of the family—to keep his wife from her former lover who has returned and wants to reclaim her. He imprisons his wife in the tower, as the patriarchal symbol of male dominance. Yet Robert is unable to control sexuality. He can control neither his own desires nor Adelheit's lack of desire for him, which is the root cause of horror and destruction in the play. Count Adelburg in *Oda, die Frau von zween Männern* decides to flee the barren marriage bed and join the Crusades. Yet a series of coincidences reveals that Oda's first husband, Hermann, is still alive. As the wife of two men, she forsakes both and makes the men promise to become each other's friend and ally and father figures to her son (from her marriage to Hermann).

A similar gesture of forgiveness and reconciliation characterizes the ending of *Adelheit von Rastenberg,* where Adelheit's beloved, who has returned form the Crusades, Adelbert, and her husband, Robert, who are mortal enemies, join hands in friendship, and Adelheit presses both to be mentors to her stepson (Robert's son) after her death. As she was secretly fleeing the tower in which she was imprisoned, she was stabbed by Countess Bertha, who is madly in love with Adelbert and sees Adelheit as her rival, despite the fact that the latter has renounced him. In Bürger's *Adelheit, Gräfinn von Teck,* the heroine was also forced into a marriage with an old but rich count by her cruel and miserly father (he forced his second daughter, Marie, to join a convent against her will to avoid having to provide her dowry).

To maintain their authority over their daughters and to separate them from the men they love, these fathers resort to betrayal, secrets, false testimony, and murder for hire. In *Oda, die Frau von zween Männern* the father betrays his daughter's trust by telling her that her husband, Hermann, is dead, offering proof by paying two witnesses to tell Oda of his death, and eventually hiring a murderer to dispose of him. Keeping this secret for some time and the consequent loss of his wife begin to weigh heavily on his conscience, and he flees to a hermitage in the woods. As it turns out, the murderers did not do their job and Hermann is still alive but has also retreated into the solitude of the forest as a mad hermit.

Secrets, betrayal, and hints of madness drive these conflicts. Not only is the veil of benevolence torn from the idealized sentimental family that was just in the process of being discursively established, but chivalric plays link madness and evil to the family romance. Excessive erotic desire that is not reciprocated leads to revenge and destabilizes Hermann in *Oda, die Frau von zween Männern,* Bertha in *Adelheit von Rastenberg,* and Walter von Borburg in *Klara von Leuenstein,* rendering them mad. Madness here is seen as an uninhibited and unrepressed insistence on one's desires without regard for social norms or prohibitions.

Beyond the sense of evil emanating from these characters, which results in the death of their objects of aggression, the spectator is affected by the staging of madness in the form of a fear of the unpredictable. If characters are not governed by moral and social norms, their actions cannot be anticipated and predicted. The unforseeable suggests a general sense of danger; after all, the unpredictable comes always as a startling surprise, stripping the individual of any sense of control over the potential next move or actions of the other. The representation of madness onstage offers interesting possibilities to imagine, on the one hand, a limitless fulfillment of one's desires, and on the other hand dread of the asocial chaos and cost to others. The result is a pleasantly unstable mixed sensation of fear and desire.

Madness, secrets, and betrayal coupled with violence and desire blend in *Mathilde Gräfin von Griessbach,* making it the quintessential chivalric-gothic play. The orphaned Mathilde has a detailed, vivid nightmare on the eve of her wedding to Count Seewald von Homburg und zu Griessbach, who rescued her from the convent and raised her as his daughter. He falls in love with her and his love is reciprocated. Yet the dream creates fear and makes Mathilde question the appropriateness of this love relationship: "It cannot be a crime that a girl honors her father; it cannot be a sin if the girl loves the father in her spouse. It was gratitude that led her delightful sister, love, gently into my heart" ("Es kann kein Verbrechen seyn, daß das Kind den Vater ehret, es kann nicht Sünde seyn, daß das Mädchen in dem Vater nun den Gemahl liebt. Die Dankbarkeit führte ihre holdselige Schwester Liebe mir sanft in das Herz").[85] In her nightmarish premonition, her birth father appears as a wild lion and the beautiful gentle landscape that she had enjoyed with her beloved, Homburg, is plunged into darkness and turned into rough, wild, and rocky terrain. The gentle white doves are turned into black ravens, and only threatening lightning illuminates the darkness. As she calls out in fear to her beloved, the lion with the facial features of her father tears himself apart with a gruesome roar. As the creature dies, a small blue snake emerges form the lion's heart and slithers toward Mathilde, who is not afraid of the snake but takes it in her arms. As the snake drives its venom into her heart, she awakens.

The nightmare revolves around a cluster of family secrets. It is not only an expression of her desire to know about the secret of her origin and the secret of the origin of Homburg's brooding nature, but also an intuitive grasp of the past and its secrets of which she has no conscious knowledge. As it turns out, in alluding to the secrets and metaphorically betraying them, the dream also foretells her fate as a direct result of her past.

Konrad, Count Homburg's seemingly trusted vassal, is in reality Mathilde's brother, who has joined the household to take revenge. He had learned that Homburg was the young knight who killed his father in battle for Griessbach's fortress and territory. As a young and overeager knight, Homburg had not obeyed the chivalric code and shown mercy to a defeated enemy. As a mature man, he came to deeply regret his action and repents by serving as a benevolent and charitable ruler. However, Mathilde was not aware of the reason for his somber disposition. Konrad has chosen Homburg and Mathilde's wedding day to take revenge. He first tries to separate the lovers, but Mathilde refuses to give up on Homburg. Upon learning the secret of his guilt, she vows not to consummate their marriage but to instead embark on a pilgrimage with Homburg to the Holy Land immediately after the wedding. However, Konrad is consumed by hatred and revenge to the verge of madness and is thus unpredictable. After the suspenseful twists and turns of the plot, he kills Homburg following the wedding.

These chivalric plays challenge the discursive celebration of the stability of the family in the sentimental family romance as the primary social space for achieving individual happiness and unquestioned solidarity and protection. Here the family is shown as a place of confinement, power relationships, psychological tyranny, dependency, and a potential for violence. The plays not only acknowledge the dark side of the family romance but, by staging and evoking that dark side, allow a safely distanced experience of the horrors of confinement. At the same time, speaking about the taboo is already a form of transgression and thus pleasurable by imagining a refusal of discipline, restraint, and obedience.

Another major element that fascinated spectators of chivalric (and historical) plays was the effective and interesting visual and imaginary impact of the spectacle, in which the setting, the time frame, and individual motifs visually defamiliarize the piece enough to provide excitement.[86] Just as on the narrative and thematic levels, the audience's delight on the specular level of the performance stems from the dynamic mixture of the familiar and the unfamiliar, of order and security on the one hand and anxiety and tension on the other.

Ingenious and skillful technological innovations producing special effects often contribute significantly to the enjoyment of a performed text. Bürger makes use of special technical effects by including a ghostly apparition that warns Adelheit of the danger to her infant son at the hands of Stauffeneck. Pyrotechnics, for example, impart a powerful and instantaneous kind of stimulation and enjoyment that "delivers excitement and relieves boredom. Such effects often 'carry' a large part of the fantasy and bear great responsibility for absorbing the spectator in its 'world,' thereby contributing the necessary condition of the spectators' experiencing the imaginary world without continually comparing it to their own lived experience or 'reality.'"[87] In addition, the play creates visual interest and pleasure in the variety of its settings. It opens in a garden where Marie and her attendant and confidante gather herbs, then switches to an informal domestic space, an interior scene in her mother's house, then to a more formal space, a hall in the same household where the family portraits are displayed. In *Klara von Leuenstein,* indoor scenes such as the *Rittersaal* (a place for male comradery and kinship with its unique rustic furniture and drinking implements) alternate with outdoor scenes of transit from one fortress to the next. In *Mathilde Gräfin von Griessbach,* the violence of the period is expressed by decorating the hall with weapons. Each scene offers new vistas, furnishings, and props to hold the gaze of the audience. The scenes shift between nature and architecture. The scenes of home and garden alternate with spaces of the wild and dangerous forest. In *Adelheit, Gräfinn von Teck* and *Klara von Hoheneichen* the spectator is confronted with secret underground passageways and haunted towers that were used as dungeons and torture chambers. All offer ample opportunity for suspenseful action and high drama. The secret passageway deep in the bowels of the embattled castle is also at the center of the happy end in *Klara von Hoheneichen.* Klara's impending forced marriage to the ruthless Heinrich von Thüringen, who had killed her first husband to gain access to her, is foiled at the last minute. The friendly forces of Klara's former fiancé Ursmar von Adelungen, who still loves her, gain entrance into the fortress where she is held captive through the secret passageway.

Similarly, the image of the dungeon is a favorite stage set at the time. The long-lost lovers in Spieß's *Klara von Hoheneichen* meet in a dungeon. The visual notion of the prison with its "towering halls and stone courts, its vaulted crypts, grills, spikes, and torture machines," receding into a labyrinth of shadow and space, "was the invention of the stage."[88] It also became the subject of numerous depictions. It provides an opportunity for strategic, interesting lighting, for plays of dark shadows and light, as we know from numerous illustrations of stage sets where the dungeon was one of the most important stock sets with a wide range of visual interpretations. They come in a range of sizes and degrees of gruesomeness replete with instruments of torture and confinement hinting at the degree of pain inflicted as just—or unjust— punishment for unspeakable crimes. All visual representations display a degree of descent suggested by dominant, often multiple flights of stairs crisscrossing, dividing, or framing the scene. They metaphorically

27. Dungeon (ca. 1850), sketch by Lorenzo Quaglio II (1793–1869). Courtesy of the Theaterwissenschaftliche Sammlung Cologne University.

suggest the moral decline of the person justly punished or, more often, that of the punisher who falsely accuses and punishes to rid him- or herself of an unwanted person, or the theme of descent from a higher to a lower world. In addition to the vertical movement, the horizontal axis becomes equally important and produces a feeling of limit and constraint. A veritable labyrinth of massive, thick stone walls, columns, gates, doors, heavy beamed ceilings, and railings heightens the sense of enclosure and confinement. Beyond offering the opportunity for the visual interest that the play of light and shadow creates, the windows, especially those looking down into the dungeon, offer vistas for observation.[89] The spectator thus can imagine or actually observe the observers and the observed; he or she can envision the sensation that constant surveillance would create. The image of physical confinement visualizes power relationships exemplifying the might of individuals, the family, the state, or the church (fig. 27).

As a specular event offering varied strong stimuli, these scenes drew the eye of the spectator along its strong lines crisscrossing the image from detail to detail at a restless pace. The visual experience is created by the motion of the eye, which is incited to follow the varied patterns and lines of the presented image, hurrying the eye along. Being occupied without the more disciplined and strenuous work of critical discernment was one of the pleasures created by the wandering gaze—the other pleasures being those of the imagination and fantasy stimulated by the image. The objects of horror—the torture devices, the stakes, the darkness and dampness—incited the imagination to envision the terror of its inhabitants. As in so many instances of the

325

pleasurable wandering gaze, we suspect an intertwining of imaging and imagining in which the fantasy becomes the screen onto which the image is projected. No longer shackled by the critical, discerning gaze, the image appeals primarily to the senses and the emotions and frees the imagination to indulge in fantasies.

In outdoor scenes, predominantly taking place in the forest, the natural forces of the weather as well as darkness and light create visual interest and a certain ambience and mood. During their encounter in the wilderness of the forest, Adelbert attempts to physically force his embraces on Adelheit. Darkness destabilizes her concept of reality as she steps out from the tower into the forest. In the absence of clear vision, she senses danger. Darkness allows a different sense of reality to emerge. Adelheit senses rather than sees danger. At the same time, the cover of darkness enables the jealous Bertha to hide long enough to wait for an opportunity to kill Adelheit, whom she perceives as her rival. Assassination plots and dishonorable acts are plotted and executed under the cover of darkness. Konrad incites his hired hands to storm the castle to take revenge on Homburg at night, which even the hired men refuse as dishonorable. What is hidden in the darkness can be perceived as more disturbing than what the audience sees clearly, thus creating speculation and suspense.

The forest is also home to another stock element of chivalric literature, the hermitage. While this element displays Rousseauesque reminiscences as a motif in the literature (as in landscape gardens and landscape painting) of the eighteenth century in general, in chivalric literature it is often associated with evil monks misusing religion for their own sinister purposes (Bürger) or is linked to penitence for previous guilt (Thon). Linked to a dark secret, the hermit provides an element of suspense because he either complicates the plot by lies (Bürger) or offers insights that provide the protagonists with the truth (Thon). In *Oda, die Frau von zween Männern,* the penitent father figure fled from his castle to a hermitage to atone for the sin of having his daughter's husband, Hermann, killed. Here, Oda finds him as she is searching for her (second) husband, Count Adelburg, who no longer wants to torture himself and Oda by insisting on the arranged marriage in which he was unable to win her heart. Upon stumbling onto the hermitage and eventually learning her father's identity, Oda is able to forgive him. The dark forest is a site for the dark brooding of a bad conscience and guilt (Oda's father) and of bitterness and auto-aggression (Hermann). After

Hermann returned and learned that Oda had remarried he also took refuge in a dwelling in the no-man's-land of the forest, isolated from society.

Chivalric plays frequently make use of contrasting settings and moods, a feature they share with the gothic. The contrasts magnify reality between the extremes. Both alternate scenes of rapid action and movement with the stillness of tableau, stimulating the senses and the intellect by shifting between a focus on the symbolic iconography of the tableau, which invites the lingering gaze and contemplation, and its destabilization in the following action. In addition, as Linda Bayer-Berenbaum points out, "the constant presence of polar opposites prevents us from mistaking any single dimension for the whole, and with respect to density, as opposed to scope, the mind is unable to tolerate extremes for very long. We either avoid, or forget, the unbearable or become accustomed to it, yet persistent contrast discourages adjustment, because in the clash between two states we can adjust to neither, and thus any dulling of the senses is averted."[90] The tableaux set accents and emphasize certain scenes, thus making them more memorable by allowing the full impact of the multifaceted image to be absorbed by the spectator. These stilled images are particularly significant because they elucidate, modify, and supplement the meaning of the verbal text. Despite the tragic ending of Thon's and Babo's plays, the moral order is reconfirmed in a tableau where the husband, son, and former rival realize and admit the errors of their ways and vow to repent. The happy ending of Bürger's play confirms the comforting vision of family in its concluding tableau. In both plays the final tableaux visually affirm a sense of community and the essential goodness of human nature despite its manifest violations on the plot level.

Although many of these plays do not contain explicit stage directions, we can infer from the context and settings—and know from other plays and from illustrations of stage sets and productions—that the setting of a castle or fortress might contain a number of interesting props such as pieces of furniture, unusual fixtures that create a unique ambience different from contemporary life. They could hold the interest of the spectator like the objects in a museum. A similar argument can be made for the use of historical costumes, which render the play interesting because of their novelty. These historical costumes also influenced fashion in clothing (or perhaps fashion and costume mutually influenced each other). Chivalric costume found its way into the

Journal des Luxus und der Moden in the context of the debate on the desirability of a national costume as an expression of patriotic sentiment and national pride in the wake of the Napoleonic Wars. This cultural interchange is another example of the various strands making up the complex tapestry of modern entertainment culture (fig. 28).

By the end of the century, theater—as one important form of entertainment—occupied the leisure of the middle class to a considerable degree. Yet it had to compete with an ever greater variety of opportunities for entertainment. Rivaling theater as entertaining spectacle and social gathering place were new cultural forms and practices such as the perspectival performances (panorama and diorama), daguerreotype, and other forms of specular pleasures.

PERSPECTIVAL PERFORMANCE

The painted background of the stage set, especially landscapes, became more detailed and elaborate. Stage designs utilized both mechanical devices and three-dimensional objects to add dimension and movement to the experience of the stage. Independently moving bands of painted clouds on a rolling device, for example, created not only depth but also the illusion of movement and time. The famous stage designer Louis Catel created ways to produce multiple layers of stage design that could be moved independently. Behind the layer of the landscape, cut out at its contours, the sky was painted on a large canvas that could be rolled up to simulate the movement of cloudscapes; the movability of the landscape layer allowed as much or as little of the sky to show as was desired.[91] Catel also suggested that it would be more realistic if the scene changes were not interrupted by the curtain but instead by lowering the lights to complete darkness, which, given the lighting technology of the time, was nearly impossible to achieve. His reasoning was that darkness between the various images mimicked how natural perception changes from one image to the next.[92] He was interested in a strong, sensational effect. The mirage of the new scene was to appear out of nothing—in this case, darkness—to produce surprise and astonishment. Other forms of experimentation included special lighting techniques, pyrotechnics, and lifting and lowering devices. By integrating as many optical illusions as possible, interesting special effects held the audience's interest.

Much to the chagrin of the literary and theater critics, these special effects, especially the cloudscapes, caused quite a stir and many

28. National costume in *Journal des Luxus und der Moden* 30 (1815). Courtesy of the Württembergische Landesbibliothek Stuttgart.

times were rewarded with rousing applause. Their critics observed that these visual innovations distracted from the dramatic text as the primary site for producing the meaning of the play. These elements strained against the postulate of formal closure, according to which all the theatrical elements (e.g., costumes, stage sets, props) take a subservient role to the dramatic text. The emphasis on one of these theatrical elements was considered disruptive of the unity, the even weighting of elements to create a harmonious whole. Yet the audience seems to have been fascinated by special effects. This enchantment was in part due to the novelty of the effect in question. Special effects were also a form of technical enigma, like a magician's trick, whose machinations were not readily apparent to the lay audience.

Technical possibilities not only altered the theater experience but also created new theatrical forms. One such experimental form was the so-called silent theater, which focused on the architecture and the landscapes while the characters were painted onto the moving decorations. Accompanied by music underscoring the mood, they became a popular form of entertainment at the turn of the century.[93]

A range of forms transgressed the boundaries of genre, creating a number of hybrid genres located between painting and theater and even between musical performances, theater, and painting. The celebrated architect Karl Friedrich Schinkel, for example, first established his fame as a painter of perspectival-optical pictures (*perspektivisch-optische Bilder*) between 1807 and 1815.[94] Gropius was another famous name associated with panoramic design. In the 1790s, Hamburg saw such performances by the theater principal E. M. Freese. In Munich, for example, the theater architect Quaglio of the famous theater design dynasty assisted in producing a panorama as an outdoor exhibit on the occasion of the marriage ceremony of members of the nobility in 1810. Not only the large cities Munich, Hamburg, and Berlin but also the smaller cities began to see performances of these new cultural spectacles. In 1814 the transparent diorama created by the Munich court painter Schnitzler representing Moscow in flames was presented—accompanied with music—in Augsburg. Schinkel created a diorama on the same subject.[95]

Johann Adam Breysig, professor of fine art, painter of stage decorations, and propagator of the panoramic forms, envisioned an ultimate theater space that would make use of the insights gained from panorama. Utilizing all technical skills and optical illusions from

330

panorama, he conceptualized a round theater building with a rounded panoramic stage that the spectators could observe from multi-tiered boxes on the opposing round wall. He envisioned this form of stage design as an appropriate setting for many different kinds of plays.[96]

Panorama

Panorama takes this kind of design one step further by eliminating actors and plot. It represented the "theatricalization of a mode of representation."[97] Panorama is a "pictorial representation of a whole view visible from one point by an observer who in turning around looks successively to all points of the horizon."[98] A panorama usually presents a spatial static detailed pictorial representation of a scene. It can be arranged in front of the spectator or, in the more elaborate ones, surrounding the spectator. Utilizing optics and perspective, illusionistic coloration and lighting, and integrating physical three-dimensional objects, the panorama represented historical scenes or landscapes with an amazing degree of realism.[99] Of course, in order to achieve the semblance of careful imitation of nature it "distorted the spatial sense and the dimensional reality of the natural world" with the aid of "highly effective devices that gave observers the illusion that they were placed at the ideal center of the scene."[100]

The pleasure produced by this form of visual entertainment has been characterized as derived from a "naive delight in looking, an interest to see unfamiliar, historical, and exotic things,"[101] and with curiosity delighting in the visually unusual experience and the hunger for visual media.[102]

The gaze and the physical movement of the spectator create their own foci and points of interest from an array of possibilities. At times, another dimension of representation is added in the form of one or more layers of foreground cutouts or three-dimensional objects, which create a sense of perspective and three-dimensionality. As an experimental form, the panorama emerged at the end of the eighteenth century, and its heyday occurred during the nineteenth century.

A "fusion of nature and artifice,"[103] the first crude form of panorama, by the Irishman Robert Barker (1739–1806), depicted the cityscape of Edinburgh (1788). At roughly the same time, Breysig described his ideas of a panoramic spectacle in his *Sketches* of 1799:

Some ten or more years ago, I hit upon the idea of a hall for concerts, balls, etc. to be used in the evening or at night, and to be disposed in a very particular way, so that people could be in it as if out of doors. The edifice would have a circular interior and a vaulted form, like a hollow sphere. No windows for illumination, but merely concealed apertures for circulating the air. The cupola and the round walls would depict a free open scene, whose visual point would be the center of the vault. The best possibility would be a garden scene, since it would offer the chance of a lovely illumination. The entrance could be real doors on painted constructions (pavilions), which would make it seem as if the people entering were actually coming out of these buildings into the outdoors.[104]

The artifice allowed for the creation of virtual nature made available for the convenient consumption in the safety and comfort of an enclosed space. Altering both space and time, this artifice could extend and alter not only the days by turning night into day but also the seasons, creating perpetual spring or summer. Panoramas with a historical subject could bring the past into the present. Creating a "superspace," it produced a landscape in which all desirable traits could be assembled while not including the less attractive aspects and inconveniences of, for example, weather, animals, and dirt. The landscape prospects used in these installations also drew inspiration from the landscape architecture of the English-style landscape garden, in which a carefully orchestrated sequence of vistas and events in the form of fountains, lakes, and grottoes provided variety and kept the visitor's interest. The goal was to "improve" on nature while maintaining the semblance of naturalness. As in the landscape prospects, the perspective and other technical considerations of lighting and arrangement had to be carefully controlled to achieve this seeming naturalness in artifice.[105] Here the insights from landscape painting, panorama design, and landscape architecture converged and influenced each other. In the *Journal* we find an illustration of a panoramic landscape, depicted from above in an awkward bird's-eye view that clearly presented the visual artist with significant problems of representation in his attempt to negotiate the peculiar three-dimensionality of the space on the two-dimensional plane (fig. 29). The illusionistic artifice of the panorama in the imitation of reality or even hyperreality is applied to nature itself in its artifical enhancement as a living panorama.

Theater painting and props were only one source of influence for these art forms. The other seems to be the tradition of fresco paintings, the murals and ceiling paintings of churches. Panoramas can be regarded as a secularization of those subgenres in painting; instead of religious topics, they focus on a variety of themes from religious historical topics such as the city of Jerusalem under Emperor Herodot and the Crucifixion to battle scenes on land and sea or altercations from colonial history. These realistically painted portions of the panorama did not differ significantly from the gigantic paintings gracing cathedrals and castles. These had also combined material elements from architecture with painted architecture and painted landscapes and skyscapes. However, instead of opening the sky to portray the realm of the divine or of mythology as the church paintings did, the modern panorama was a predominantly secular event focusing on earthly, realistic topics.[106] Jooss links panorama and diorama with illusionistic painting, yet she also sees a similarity between the living pictures in their problematization of the relationship between reality and semblance. Both practices also represent an unconventional reception of high art. Contemporary critics of the panorama expressed the same kind of unease that living pictures had elicited: the uncanny effect of the stilled (no movement and no sound), uninhabited landscape.[107] The attempt at creating a living panorama through landscape design and the careful placement of the viewer tried to overcome this limitation. After all, it was composed of the elements of the material landscape with its variation of colors, weather conditions, changes in temperature, and seasonal changes. The drawbacks were the limited subject matter and the spatial limits that prevented it from becoming a mass phenomenon that was available as a form of entertainment in all seasons and all times of the day, as was the urban indoor experience of the theatrical panorama. This subgenre of the panorama, landscape panorama, was thus more closely related to the experience of travel, in which travelers began to seek out panoramic vistas that allowed the gaze to roam over a huge expanse with many details and a variety of shapes and forms from a fixed vantage point.

The panorama altered the viewing conventions dominating the Enlightenment, which were characterized by the concept of framing

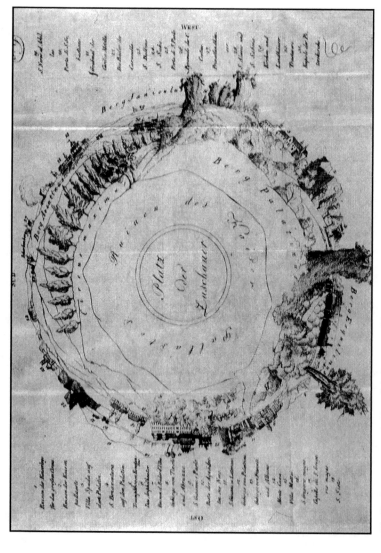

29. Garden panorama in *Journal des Luxus und der Moden* 16 (1801). Courtesy of the Thüringische Universitäts- und Landesbibliothek Jena.

(*Rahmenschau*). The latter limited the field of vision to produce a sense of clarity of view of an object, as sight was perceived as the keenest sense during the rational tendencies of the eighteenth century.[108] This was achieved by providing a frame, limiting the wealth of visual information, and thus foregrounding the object in question by showing the object as static and by providing a focus that allowed for the immediate overview, undisturbed by details.[109] The panorama made this frame disappear in the attempt to bridge the space on which the spectator stands and the picture with realia that became part of the depicted scene, creating an impression of limitless expanse, innumerable points of interest without a focal point, thereby freeing the gaze to wander. Stephan Oettermann, while also crediting the panorama with effecting the decisive break with traditional viewing conventions, does so for other reasons. While this study is interested in the entertainment effect of the new medium, Oettermann focuses on its function as a teaching tool (*Lernmaschine*) that does away with all physical constraints to allow the cool and distanced gaze, not clouded by subjectivity—in short, the scientific gaze—to emerge, which was rendering humans godlike.[110] Renzo Dubbini also attributed some of the attraction of these illusionistic forms to "satisfying a curiosity whetted by technical innovation."[111] While the curiosity in how the effects are achieved is certainly part of the appeal, I would question the quasi-scientific objectivity of the medium, not in its construction and design but in its effect on the spectator. On the contrary, the image itself with its myriad highlights allows for a highly subjective wandering gaze to be pulled almost at random over the surface of the image. The viewer is free to linger or hurry, to gaze intently at details or to scan the surface, experiencing an extensive yet not predetermined array of points of interest and stimulation.

Of course, panorama's invitation to an undisciplined wandering gaze resulted in its reputation as a mere entertainment device, which, just like other spectacles, was "thoughtlessly sucked in by the eyes" and "separated from those non-visual and informative methods that supposedly convey truths to the mind."[112] Constructing a similar dichotomy as in the reading debate, which pried apart the "trivial" from the "serious" engagement with literature, a discourse separating "deep from shallow looking, of investigation from gaping, continued apace as the century unfolded."[113]

As the new genre had no critical history, spectatorship of the panorama did not require any previous knowledge and educational background. While the traditional ceiling paintings and murals, which could be regarded as its ancestors in the visual arts, could also be viewed naively, their intended effect was religious and/or moral edification. The older forms, furthermore, relied on a distinct iconography requiring a specific knowledge. The modern panorama, on the other hand, assumed naive viewing as the norm, which could or could not be augmented by additional information. The gaze became liberated to follow its own interests and indulge in the pleasure of the specular sense without additional cognitive demands.

Just like its predecessor the mural, the panorama—due to its huge format—was produced by a team of artists and craftsmen (after 1850 this was significantly aided by the technology of the slide projector), separating the eye and hand of the artist. Because the traditional mural was fully integrated into the overall design of architecture of the specific site, the association with artisanry and craft rather than solitary artistry and art was hardly an issue. However, as the painting developed into a spectacle that was made available to a general audience for an entrance fee, the artisanal and technical aspect became foregrounded. This commercial aspect contributed to its lower status as entertainment.

The most important and favored objects were taken from nature or geography: landscapes and especially cityscapes depicting the famous cities of the world. The panorama in Vienna, which opened in 1801, offered depictions of London, Vienna, Prague, Gibraltar, Paris, and St. Petersburg. Breysig did huge-scale versions of his *Italian Sketches: View of Rome from the Ruins of the Imperial Villa;* they were exhibited in a wooden rotunda in Berlin (1800). The Cosmorama (dioramic and panoramic exhibition), established in 1820 in London's Regent Street, lists the following exhibits: "Fire and Smoke in Motion around the Houses of Parliament producing an effect strikingly true to the reality," "A View of Mont Blanc," "Colossal Statues of Memnon in the Plain of Thebes at the rising of the Sun," "Mount St. Bernard with a view of the celebrated monastery," "Baden, in the Dutchy of Baden with dioramic effects of light and shade," and "The City of Grand Cairo in Egypt."[114]

Panoramas were to become even more important mass-media events in the nineteenth century, serving as tourist- and entertainment-oriented showpieces of great cities and objects of financial speculation. Visitors came from afar and paid for the pleasure of being astonished and amazed by the spectacle of deception in which nature was re-created by artifice and technology. This form of entertainment represented a costly, high-stakes commercial venture, a risky business undertaking due to the danger of fire because of the use of artificial light.[115]

As their popularity and thus their audience grew, panoramas increasingly were installed in permanent structures, in round buildings, in which a platform in the middle allowed the visitors an unlimited view along the continuous mural. A cupola with glass allowing light to enter covered them. The space between the platform and the mural was covered by transitional objects and appropriate terrain.[116]

A well-documented example from a later period than the one under investigation here is the seascape painter Hendrik Wilhelm Mesdac's Den Haag panorama (1881). It shows a beach scene with a fishing village and Den Haag in the background, complete with fishing boats, horsemen, bathers in bathing carts, flaneurs, and even a railroad. The mural was fourteen meters tall and had a painted surface of seventeen square meters. The space between the spectators' platform and the mural painting was in this case covered with dunes and objects commonly found at the beach, increasing the desired realistic effect. The only movement in this scene was created by the ambulatory spectator's selection of focal points. The modern heirs to this cultural practice are displays in museums or certain types of decorations in store windows, where painted scenes provide the background for artifacts or natural objects on display.[117] Our contemporary panoramic cameras allow the spectator to capture the expansive vistas.

Overall, the entertainment panorama began to change "how people looked at things. . . . It is thus perfectly logical that soon the demand should arise to assign temporality to the visual event."[118] In the diorama, the panorama seemed to come alive with the help of mechanical movement and changes in lighting.

Diorama

If the spectator's gaze provides the movement in the panorama, the diorama creates its own illusion of movement and temporal evolution. This technique affected both stage design and painting conventions. Philip James de Loutherbourg (1740–1812), who became known for his creation of the effects of fire, wind, and water onstage, made "changes in the landscape . . . by the use of optical and mechanical devices, by shifts of scenery, by manipulating the direction from which the light came, and by the use of colored filters."[119] Despite its close affinity to the theater, the diorama also became an important form of entertainment in its own right.

Relying on the "sign language of light," the diorama seemed to animate the depicted scenes.[120] Moving objects provide an even higher degree of stimulation to the eye than static objects, as the eye is stimulated by changes in its field of vision. Jean Starobinski describes this phenomenon as "impatient energy that inhabits the gaze and desires something other than what it is given. It [the eye] lies in wait, hoping that a moving form will come to a standstill or that a figure at rest will reveal a slight tremor."[121] The diorama provided both: moments of stillness alternated with the movement that light and shadow add to a panoramic painting. Consequently, it offered an enhancement in the desire for the pleasurable stimulation of the visual sense.

Painting the thin layers of oil-soaked cotton that served as the canvas front and back was one way of creating this effect. Taking optical principles into account, specific lighting techniques also created the illusion of temporal change and movement.[122] A description of the diorama at Regent's Park, depicting the "Interior of the Church of Santa Croce at Florence," recorded the expected viewing experience: "The visitors are requested particularly to observe all the modifications of effect which, as if by magic, are gradually alternated—from the brilliancy and sunshine of noon—to the darkness and obscurity of midnight, as well as the extraordinary appearance of artificial illumination by means of chandeliers and candelabras, which will be seen gradually to become ignited, by the sole effect of colour, and the powerful opposition of light and shade."[123] The surprise and sense of wonder implied by magic and the creation of illusion are the elements that are experienced as entertaining.[124] Its central feature, metamorphosis itself—"the spectacle of form in flux"—"was essentially . . . a liberation of form in the flow of light and color." The audience was mesmerized by this form of scenic art, in which pictures "gradually grow out of another in mysterious fashion."[125] These pleasures were not limited to large-scale ventures for the public. They were also commissioned and utilized by wealthy middle-class businesspeople for private consumption and for advertisement purposes. Wilhelm Gropius produced a Christmas exhibit for the merchant Gabain in Berlin (1807) for which he commissioned Schinkel to produce a transparent diorama.[126]

Like many other cultural practices discussed in this study, this form of entertainment was linked to other cultural practices. This layering created new forms by fusing the effects in order to enhance the sensation of pleasure, for example, in enhancing the landscape with the help of the artificial means of dioramic principles. Dubbini credits Carmontelle (Louis Carrogis) with achieving a new level of creating artificial landscapes by transforming real landscapes "by means of large, translucent, illuminated backgrounds":

> Carmontelle called for a union between a new form of theatricality in representation and the artificiality in garden design. He accomplished that aim, in particular in the central pavilion of the Parc Monceau and in the windows of the gallery, where he put up translucent draperies decorated with landscapes. Changes of light outside the gallery made the scenes seem animated, even giving the impression of a different climate, as when they showed a radiant summer landscape in the middle of winter.
>
> Carmontelle placed enormous painted scenes lighted by sunken torches throughout the gardens he designed. In the flickering light viewers could contemplate country villages, fantastic gardens, costumed figures, statues, architectural constructions, and ruins. Seasonal variations were suggested by conventional colors; red for autumn, cold muted colors for winter. The passage of time from dawn to dusk or the rising moon could be suggested by a change in lighting. Special effects such as flames were highlighted by creating contrast between those portions of the design and the dark surrounding figures.[127]

In addition to these large-scale public and semipublic installations, the design principles of diorama also influenced decorative items for private consumption in the domestic sphere. An example was backlit furniture, the so-called moonlight transparent (*Mondschein-Transparent*), as a fashionable decoration for women's bedrooms, boudoirs, or sitting rooms (fig. 30). A suitable landscape painting or a garden scene was painted on a thin canvas and illuminated from the back either by the moonlight or by candlelight.[128] The *Journal* also mentions the transparent illustrations of famous Saxon castles, which were originally illustrations in a book on the same subject matter but were enlarged and made transparent and then displayed in the author's home (3:269).

But the phenomenon was by no means a predilection of the dilettante—even though, because they were so different from conventional paintings, academic painters considered them "simple experiments or curious applications of illusionistic painterly effects."[129] The landscape painter Philipp Hackert also produced and experimented with luminous landscapes, which Goethe describes with his customary ambivalence, with a mixture of fascination with the sensual effects and concern about how to evaluate this phenomenon with strictly artistic criteria. Goethe gives a detailed description of how Hackert created these moonlight views:

> "The whole of the landscape is first painted in tempera on a sheet of paper; afterward, he cuts out separately the large masses that are to appear in it, such as mountains, buildings, ships, etc. These are then colored and pasted onto the sheet. A knife is used to scrape the paper until it is very thin in places where the water is to reflect the rays of the moon most intensely, and the lighter parts of the landscape are covered with an alcohol-based liquid. All the rest is colored, except the parts reserved for the moonlight effects and the disk of the moon, which are left completely white." Hackert

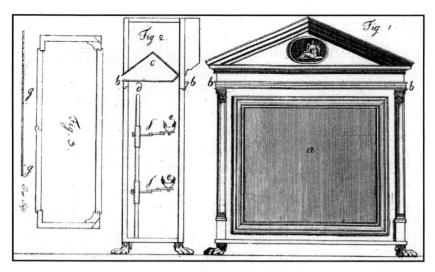

30. Moonlight transparency in *Journal des Luxus und der Moden* 14 (1799). Courtesy of the Bildarchiv Preußischer Kulturbesitz Berlin. Photo by Dietmar Katz.

would then take the sheet prepared in this manner and insert it between two pieces of glass that formed one side of a box. Inside the box he would place lamps and angled them to throw light on the picture. The lamplight flickering through the transparency would set up a play of reflections that animated the scene. Goethe notes that Hackert had placed a landscape of this sort over the door to his studio, adding that it was by no means an amusement, but rather a "true work of art."[130]

Other related systems of optical theatrical performances became fashionable all over Europe during the course of the century, and their production increased markedly in England between 1820 and 1830. Dubbini notes: "The images were printed in black and white, then were colored (by various processes), arranged within a theater-like viewing box to which backgrounds, frames, and architectural ornamentation could be added. They were viewed with the aid of optical filters, mirrors, or other devices that determined what the viewer would see."[131]

Franz Nikolaus König, a Swiss artist, had created an optical theater the size of a wardrobe for projecting transparent pictures, the diaphanorama (1815). Translucent images painted in watercolor or oil were illuminated by "light sources that could be made to vary in intensity and color."[132] His most popular scenes were Swiss landscapes, views of Berne and Lucerne by moonlight, and the Grindelwald glacier. Louis Jacques Mandé Daguerre recognized König's importance for his own diorama, which used "more sophisticated techniques to control light, which made for a smoother flow of images, and he introduced duration into his performances as well as motion."[133] Daguerre opened the first hall for diorama spectacles in Paris in 1822. Inside a circular darkened viewing area between converging galleries, the audience watched "images painted on large transparent cloth backdrops hung at the end of each gallery and lit by both reflection and refraction. The viewing area turned to face first one gallery, then the other. Shifting between images made rapid scene changes possible without awkward pauses and enables spectators to remain comfortably seated."[134] By 1834 he had perfected the "double-effect diorama," in which the objects in the various scenes seemed to change and figures seemed to appear and disappear.[135] Audiences were most awed by performances such as "The Valley of Goldau (Landslide)":

The changes in the scene in the latter were so striking that they provided a coherent and dramatic narrative. A tranquil initial image of the alpine town shifted to images of impending disaster: the inhabitants could be seen fleeing in terror as lightning flashed in the sky and houses collapsed. Dawn finally rose over a desolate view of houses in ruins, crushed by enormous rock masses that have fallen from the mountains.[136]

Dubbini attributes their entertainment value to the appeal of the playful engagement of a scientific gaze:

Spectators felt that their capacity to perceive the world expanded when they looked at an image enlarged and brought to life by an optical device. Their excited gaze could explore scenes in unknown cities, marvels of nature, or picturesque corners of the world; they could linger over the sight of a burning ship in a famous port and thrill to brilliant flames that seemed almost real, thanks to effects of light and movement.[137]

At the same time, he credits these spectacles with seducing the larger public to a new sort of curiosity about places, which could play an important role in the perception of their historical sense of place.[138] My own reading places the scientific aspects and the playful involvement as secondary to their effect on the viewing conventions. These forms of specular entertainment have in common that the spectator was freed from a traditional aesthetic response to a formally structured and framed artifact such as a painting, etching, drawing, or the stage. The richly detailed panoramas and dioramas allowed the gaze to wander freely, selecting its own foci, creating its own aesthetic structures if desired or simply scanning the vast tapestry of visual impressions. Nothing obstructed or directed the gaze. With regard to the large-scale panoramas or dioramas, especially those established within specifically designed architectural structures, the spectator was not even limited to a specific vantage point from which to observe the whole. Instead, the observer had to move around to experience the fluidity of the design in the round buildings where the spectator is in the middle and the artifacts surround him or her. The genre extended an open invitation to be explored freely and anonymously. The spectator moves within a mass of other spectators, spending as much or as little time with the artifact as is desired. One's attention span and level of interest determine the exposure to it. Furthermore, there is no prescribed or right or wrong way or appropriate or inappropriate time commitment to experience it. This free-flowing reception also allows, even encourages, the kind of communication and conversation while experiencing the artifact that the theater had worked so hard to discourage.

The enclosing artificial nature forbade even the faintest hint of a frame and required negating the pictorial character in any way, thus giving the illusion of the creation, not of pictorial art, but of a second artificial nature.[139] The goal was not to create a work of art but rather a new and different man-made copy of nature.[140] This further distances the spectator from traditional viewing expectations associated with pictorial art, in particular landscape painting. Instead they offer a simulated experience of a famous landscape or city magically transported and made accessible to a nontraveling audience.

Panoramas and dioramas introduced the masses to an exotic world, one that had become accessible through travel and tourism but was usually out of reach for most people. Both travel for entertainment and these experimental forms of depicting the cultural landscape opened the most fascinating landscapes to audiences previously excluded from such experiences. The viewing practices in established venues made panoramas products of the emergent cities. Along with illustrated journals and newspapers and anthropological and other exhibits, they introduced a broader audience to big cities, foreign countries, and exotic worlds, offering them a pleasant diversion from everyday routines. In a time of increased interest in history and foreign and exotic locations, the panorama was an up-to-date and suitable medium, creating its special effects with all possible means of illusion based on scientific principles and technical innovations. Careful preparation and exactitude, topographical surveys, proportions in the proper perspective, and true-to-life portraits were among the individual elements that were necessary for the creation of the mirage.

A form of passive travel, panoramas and dioramas provided stimulation to "picture-hungry" and "motif-craving" viewers who took pleasure in being amazed and seduced by the mirage of this artifice of nature.[141] The middle-class demand for entertainment made the grand scale of these costly artifacts possible.[142] As extensive travels and touristic undertakings were not yet a mass phenomenon, these media offered the semblance of travel. For a large segment of the middle class, viewing these spectacles and reading about travels to exotic lands was the more pleasurable activity in a time when traveling was inconvenient and expensive.

Like travel, these forms of specular entertainment involve an indulgence in visual pleasures. In the forms of entertainment we have explored, a visual component is central, both as the sensual pleasure of looking and as the construction and consumption of images through imag(in)ing. As a non-appetitive distant sense, the ocular sense is capable of "much finer discrimination, and hence presents greater possibilities for pleasurable stimulation."[143] Unlike travel, these illusionistic panoramic views offer a sense of totality of vision that was gradually disappearing, especially in the cities. The modern metropolis, for example, no longer lent itself to being viewed in its totality.

If the Enlightenment had used depiction in order to present information and knowledge in an entertaining manner, the didactic impulse dominated the playful one. Nevertheless (or maybe because of this association with didacticism), late-eighteenth-century high culture privileged the logocentric word over the image. The cognitive nature of language was regarded as superior to the less complex sense of sight, thus denigrating the mere passive gazing at the spectacular object. The last decades of the eighteenth century saw the fruits of the earlier efforts in this massive education project: the creation of silent readers who acquired knowledge through the written word. The solitary ingestion of abstracted information in the natural sciences and the introspective reading of literature established themselves as accepted forms of knowledge transfer. Images became associated with irrational visual amusements and ignorant sensuality and were therefore opposed. Entertainment had, for the most part, been banned from serious educational pursuits and relegated to the realm of inconsequential leisure. Yet just as the Enlightenment had begun to make inroads in building a market-centered, middle-class-oriented print culture to replace an aristocratic, predominantly visual culture on the one hand and a mostly oral culture in the lower classes on the other and had created the serious and solitary reader, these monolithic tendencies unraveled at the edges. We observe a resurgence of the sensual and visual in cultural practices, described in this study.

The ensuing dichotomy pits spectacle as being without discipline against the rule- and system-based forms of language and writing. "Manifold entertainment, thoughtlessly sucked in by the eyes, is separated from those non-visual and informative methods that supposedly convey truths to the mind."[144] This denigration of the scopic drive, which is after all preverbal, is one reason for the devaluation of the gaze and the art forms that primarily address it.[145] The preverbal child establishes its place in its surroundings by sight. Seeing seems to provide immediate access to our external world. Beyond collecting images, the gaze establishes relations. A sense of naïveté associated with the scopic drive has remained an undercurrent of aesthetic valorizations until today.

Furthermore, vision as a means of gaining access to information is linked with lack of effort, work, and discipline, whereas certain forms of reading and especially writing are associated with mental labor, effort, and restraint. Because of this "effortlessness," looking became an ideal form of entertainment. It provided release for intellect and mind and offered new stimuli, while occupying idle hours and thus avoiding boredom.[146] These discussions imply that repeated stimulation was perceived as pleasurable and that artifacts privileging the senses, especially sight, made little intellectual demands on the spectator. The pleasure produced by the senses—especially sight—was predicated on the absence of intellectual labor, which suggests at the same time that mental work is intrinsically unpleasant, further cementing the connection between entertainment and facile sensual stimulation.

Despite the "suppressed premise maintaining the inferiority of images (and conversely, the superiority of texts)," the eighteenth century was preoccupied with the visual realm, and the end of the century experienced an increase in experimental forms focusing on visuality.[147] At the same time, we detect increasing anxiety regarding the trend toward pleasurable, merely curious watching associated with these experimental genres foregrounding the sensual allure of vision. Cultural critics attempted to reaffirm rational, language-driven observation, while they denigrated superficial watching as geared toward the less educated. Enjoyable watching became separated from deliberate observation, paralleling the ever-present distinction between entertainment through the pleasures of the "lower" senses and the intellectual enjoyment of high culture.

Conclusion

THIS STUDY EXPLORED THE changes in the self-fashioning of the German middle class around 1800. These transformations of mentality were effected by the culture of sensibility, which had expanded the individual's consciousness through self-observation. It enabled people to pay attention to the most minute sensations, feelings, and reactions, creating an intense experience of the self. This fabrication of the prized individualism produced a decisive change in mentalities, departing from ascetic values dominating middle-class values earlier in the century and moving toward an endorsement of pleasure and entertainment.

The modern enhanced capacity to take pleasure in sensations themselves and in imaginary pleasures enabled individuals to conjure up the pleasurable sensation in the absence of actual stimuli. Desiring rather than having as the main focus of pleasure-seeking and daydreaming about (virtual) possibilities became an important affective motor for cultural consumption by linking the desired products or practices with one's self-image. Once the desired object or practice has been integrated into one's self-image or has been consumed, the cycle of desire and longing begins anew. By its very nature momentary, desire requires a steady stream of new or changing objects. Just as desire and passion as fleeting emotions crave perpetual renewal and the need to be re-created, newness becomes highly prized. The desire for new stimulation, for novelty, is the dynamo at the core of all forms of entertainment and is responsible for the increase and diversity of cultural practices. This spiral of desire and disillusionment, which requires frequent stimulation

347

of the senses, produced cultural consumerism and manifested itself in two distinct yet related strands: on the one hand, an interest in material culture, an appetite to adorn the body and its surroundings with fashionable goods; on the other, an interest in new forms of nonmaterial cultural practices and a hunger for new cultural practices and innovations in traditional genres that stimulate through innovation and variety. It is therefore the change and variety of sensations—rather than any inherent quality—that yield pleasure to the consumers of cultural products and practices.

These changes were linked to the differentiation of social life, most notably the dissociation of work and family life. As the activity that is contrasted with the strain of business activity, entertainment compensates for the toil of work with the pleasures of intellectual and/or sensual stimulation. The tension between duty and the desire for more leisure entertainment produced a new middle-class lifestyle that retained the rigors of the business day while simultaneously adopting many leisure practices not unlike those of the nobility, thus extending the day well into the night. The bourgeoisie created a unique form of domestic culture that fused the areas of consumption with those of (high) culture in the interplay of the symbolic and socioeconomic aspects of the fashionable middle-class lifestyle.

The increase in variety allowed consumers a larger selection of cultural practices and artifacts. Each new activity and product implied the potential for another, producing an escalating, self-generating system that insisted on its own transitoriness. The transitory nature of these cultural practices and objects was contained in the valorization of novelty, in the term *fashion,* which contained the seeds of its own demise in a quasi-self-regulatory system open to contingencies.

The emergent print culture, particularly the periodical, was vital in establishing an interest in material culture and in making these objects and practices part of the system of culture. The dynamics of the objects of material culture, their emphasis on change and innovation, in turn, influenced print culture itself, which reacted by offering a greater variety of specialized publications and adding features such as illustrations that were prompted by the objects of material culture described in its pages.

The periodical print media helped to produce and mirror the complex entertainment needs of the middle class, which displayed a wider variety of pleasurable responses to cultural objects and practices.

With the help of the periodical print culture, readers learned to select the kind of pleasure they desired at any given moment of leisure: the specular pleasure derived from the illustrations and the aesthetic appearance of the volume itself; the stimulation of fantasies and daydreams of adventure and love stories; the indulgence in strong emotions; the shudder of the supernatural; or the more cerebral pleasures that the avant-garde pieces offered.

The obsession with novelty—the desire for new impressions and sensations—is at the root of fashionable adornment of the self and its environment. Innovation providing stimulation is perceived as a source of pleasure in bourgeois society. Fashion visualizes the interrelationship among luxury items, economics, and the journal print culture in an exemplary manner and is therefore representative of many forms of cultural consumerism and entertainment, defining the middle class. Fashion plays a visible part in this system of subtle cultural distinctions structuring the growing and rather amorphous middle class. This structuration process plays itself out, for example, in the tension between cultural capital (taste) and economic capital (wealth). The fashion system illuminates the social mobility inherent in the new understanding of culture, which was theoretically accessible to everyone. The forms of sociability and their unique cultural practices and fashionable pastimes underscored this process of cultural distinction.

As a by-product of increasing social differentiation and social mobility, the use of culturally significant goods and practices could serve to express and read social identity in an increasingly anonymous society, setting the stage for the modern society which was to become a cohesive society of strangers. Cultural objects and practices carried messages, requiring individuals to acquire the object code to decipher these messages, in essence shaping individuals as consumers. With taste as their organizing principle, cultural entertainment and consumption became central in assigning status and cultural capital. After all, the upper middle class did not define itself solely through education, high culture, and economic strength but also through the forms of everyday culture, the pleasurable cultural enrichment of everyday life in these forms of entertainment.

Cultural socialization in the forms of entertainment plays a crucial—albeit often unacknowledged—role in identity construction. After all, the material capital of the domestic environment created the favorable conditions for the acquisition of cultural capital. It provided

349

important groundwork (Bourdieu's *habitus*) for the acculturation of its members. Within the various forms of middle-class sociability, leisure-time entertainment connects the domestic sphere with its larger social context (and in certain cases potentially with the sphere of work). At the same time, everyday cultural practices (in their material and non-material manifestations) serve as the necessary preconditions for the socialization and acculturation that make high culture possible.

Travel and the new interest in garden culture could not have become an important form of leisure entertainment without the significant preparatory work of the print media. Not only did the change in mentalities, with its new sense of space and desire for expanding one's horizons, literally and figuratively stimulate the interest in travel literature as a means of self-improvement of one's taste and acculturation, but the interest in travel literature was also enhanced by a distinct hunger for entertainment, which literature provided in the form of adventures and by allowing glimpses at new and different cultural practices, providing the pleasurable stimulation of novelty.

In the landscape garden, the accumulation of pleasurable impacts by the sequenced (mobility) moments of newness (new vistas), of moving through time, by being exposed to a variety of different settings, each producing unique sensations, by the repeated stimulation of the gaze, and by a (carefully designed) effect of surprise provided the kind of intense stimulation and the variety of impacts contemporaries experienced as highly entertaining.

The popularity of this new way of looking, the wandering gaze, is reflected in the new forms of specular entertainment, the interest in elaborate stage sets and in the spectacles of panorama and diorama. Rich in detail, the surfaces allow the gaze to be pleasantly occupied without requiring any formal organization or structuring of the viewing experience. Decidedly undisciplined, the gaze spontaneously reacted to the stimuli of the viewing environment, offering an alternate mode of looking that was not primarily interested in gathering information or assisting in cognitive processes.

Overall, I argued that the middle-class lifestyle was not based solely on literature and critical discourse, as Habermas suggests, but rather included a whole range of cultural practices and many forms of cultural consumption, which represented different yet also important aspects of the formation of a cultural public sphere. My focus was on the material landscape of the domestic sphere, which expresses not only the status of its inhabitants but their lifestyle as mirrored in the cultural objects and practices as an important aspect of middle-class identity formation and group differentiation. After all, the emergence of a functionalist society was enabled and stabilized by a more loosely organized form of sociability fostering certain general and flexible, self-regulating forms of communication without prescribing specific values. The impact of the forms of cultural entertainment and the (cultural) consumerism associated with it produces a consensus-based modern hegemonic social order. It relies on internalized, self-regulatory sociocultural norms that fashion the strands of everyday life. Regulated by taste, they derive their dynamic from the pleasure that the forms of entertainment created.

Notes

Introduction

1. Roland Barthes, *The Pleasure of the Text*, trans. Richard Miller (1973; New York: Hill & Wang, 1975), 53.
2. The emphasis on pleasure can be inferred from the considerable anxiety it produced in the cultural elite and in the criticism of high culture, which resulted in a sustained debate on the reading craze and the perceived split into high culture and mass culture.
3. Nancy Fraser, "Rethinking the Public Sphere: A Contribution to the Critique of Actually Existing Democracy," in *The Phantom Public Sphere*, ed. Bruce Robbins (Minneapolis: University of Minnesota Press, 1993), 10–11.
4. Catherine Cusset, *No Tomorrow: The Ethics of Pleasure in the French Enlightenment* (Charlottesville: University Press of Virginia, 1999); Roy Porter and Marie Mulvey Roberts, eds., *Pleasure in the Eighteenth Century* (New York: New York University Press, 1996), x. Although the first study is primarily concerned with the moral dimension of pleasure, the latter comes closer to my own focus on the social implications of entertainment and pleasure. While focusing on some of the same issues, such as consumption and the pleasure of terror, the book does not offer (due to its collection format) a comprehensive, integrated theoretical account of the conception of pleasure in England. In addition, it offers a broader focus, extending its analysis also into the moral and ethical dimension with topics such as the luxury of "Doing Good," examining benevolence in the Royal Humane Society, etc.
5. Theodor W. Adorno, *Ästhetische Theorie*, 10th ed. (Frankfurt: Suhrkamp, 1990).

6. Theodor W. Adorno and Max Horkheimer, *Dialectic of Enlightenment,* trans. John Cumming (New York: Continuum, 1972).

7. Stanley Corngold, *Complex Pleasure* (Stanford: Stanford University Press, 1998).

8. Martha Woodmansee, *The Author, Art, and the Market: Readings in the History of Aesthetics* (New York: Columbia University Press, 1994), 4.

9. Friedrich Justin Bertuch and Georg Melchior Kraus, eds., *Journal des Luxus und der Moden,* abridged edition, ed. Werner Schmidt, 4 vols. (Rpt.; Hanau: Müller and Kiepenheuer, 1967–70), 2:253. Unless otherwise noted, the quotes from the *Journal* are taken from this modern abridged four-volume reprint to facilitate access. Volume and page are given parenthetically in the text and notes.

10. Joseph Addison, "The Pleasures of the Imagination," in Joseph Addison and Richard Steele, *The Spectator,* ed. Donald Bond, vol. 3 (Oxford: Clarendon, 1965), nos. 411–21, pp. 535–82.

11. Johann Wolfgang von Goethe, "Über den Dilettantismus," in *Schriften zur Literatur,* vol. 14 of *Gedenkausgabe der Werke: Briefe und Gespräche,* ed. Ernst Beutler (Zurich: Artemis, 1954), 729–57.

12. "[W]irkt bildend"; "Ausbildung des Sehorgans die komplizierteren Formen zu bemerken" (ibid., 730). Translations are mine unless otherwise noted.

13. "Der Dilettant [hat] immer nur ein halbes [Interesse], er treibt alles als ein Spiel, als Zeitvertreib, hat meist noch einen Nebenzweck, eine Neigung zu stillen, der Laune nachzugehen." Ibid., 735.

14. Ibid., 754.

15. Charles Batteux, *Principes de la litterature,* vol. 1 (Paris: Saillant & Nyon, 1774), 11–12.

16. Niklas Luhmann, *Liebe als Passion: Zur Codierung von Intimität,* 3rd ed. (Frankfurt: Suhrkamp, 1983).

17. Colin Campbell, *The Romantic Ethic and the Spirit of Modern Consumerism* (New York: Basil Blackwell, 1987).

18. See also August Langen, *Anschauungsformen in der deutschen Dichtung des 18. Jahrhunderts: Rahmenschau und Rationalismus* (1934; rpt., Darmstadt: Wissenschaftliche Buchgesellschaft, 1965); and Barbara Maria Stafford, *Artful Science: Enlightenment Entertainment and the Eclipse of Visual Education* (Cambridge: MIT Press, 1994).

19. Alison Light, *Forever England: Femininity, Literature, and Conservatism between the Wars* (London: Routledge, 1991), 13.

20. Deidre Shauna Lynch, *The Economy of Character: Novels, Market Culture, and the Business of Inner Meaning* (Chicago: University of Chicago Press, 1998), 146.

21. See also ibid., 190.

22. Jürgen Kocka, ed., *Bürger und Bürgerlichkeit im 19. Jahrhundert* (Göttingen: Vandenhoeck & Ruprecht, 1987).

23. Wolfgang Kaschuba, "Deutsche Bürgerlichkeit nach 1800: Kultur als symbolische Praxis," in *Bürgertum im 19. Jahrhundert: Deutschland im europäischen Vergleich,* vol. 3, ed. Jürgen Kocka (Munich: dtv, 1988), 10.

24. Pierre Bourdieu, *Die feinen Unterschiede: Kritik der gesellschaftlichen Urteilskraft* (Frankfurt: Suhrkamp, 1979).

25. Eric Dorn Brose, *German History, 1789–1871: From the Holy Roman Empire to the Bismarckian Reich* (Providence: Berghahn Books, 1997), x.

26. Kaschuba, "Deutsche Bürgerlichkeit nach 1800," 12.

27. Harro Segeberg, *Literatur im technischen Zeitalter: Von der Frühzeit der deutschen Aufklärung bis zum Beginn des Ersten Weltkriegs* (Darmstadt: Wissenschaftliche Buchgesellschaft, 1997), 19.

28. Andrea van Dülmen, *Das irdische Paradies: Bürgerliche Gartenkultur der Goethezeit* (Cologne: Böhlau, 1999).

29. Ibid., 119.

30. J. H. Plumb, "Part III: Commercialization and Society," in *The Birth of Consumer Society: Commercialization in Eighteenth-Century England,* ed. Neil McKendrick, John Brewer, and J. H. Plumb (London: Hutchinson, 1982), 327.

31. Stafford, *Artful Science,* e.g., 47–58.

32. Gerhard Tanzer, *"Spectacle müssen seyn": Die Freizeit der Wiener im 18. Jahrhundert* (Vienna: Böhlau, 1992).

33. Joachim Whaley, "The German Lands before 1815," in *German History since 1800,* ed. Mary Fulbrook (London: Arnold, 1997), 15–37, 16.

34. W. Daniel Wilson, "Enlightenment's Alliance with Power: The Dialectic of Collusion and Opposition in the Literary Elite," in *Impure Reason: Dialectic of Enlightenment in Germany,* ed. W. Daniel Wilson and Robert C. Holub (Detroit: Wayne State University Press, 1993), 366–67.

35. To be sure, the state determined admittance to, controlled qualifications for, and regulated the job market of the educated upper middle class.

36. Whaley, "German Lands before 1815," 28.

37. "Without consumer goods, certain acts of self-definition and collective definition in this culture would be impossible." Grant McCracken, *Culture and Consumption: New Approaches to the Symbolic Character of Consumer Goods and Activities* (Bloomington: Indiana University Press, 1988), xi.

38. Benedict Anderson, *Imagined Communities: Reflections on the Origin and Spread of Nationalism* (London: Verso, 1983), 13–15.

39. Ernest Gellner, *Nations and Nationalism* (Ithaca: Cornell University Press, 1983), 27–28.

40. "Decisions and arguments about leisure were decisions and arguments

about power and about control, that is to say they were political." Hugh Cunningham, *Leisure in the Industrial Revolution c. 1780–1880* (London: Croom Helm, 1980), 12.

41. For Bertuch's biography see Wilhelm Feldmann, *Friedrich Justin Bertuch* (Saarbrücken: Carl Schmidtke, 1902); and Gerhard Kaiser, "Friedrich Justin Bertuch: Versuch eines Portraits," in *Friedrich Justin Bertuch (1747–1822): Verleger, Schriftsteller, und Unternehmer im klassischen Weimar,* ed. Gerhard R. Kaiser and Siegfried Seifert (Tübingen: Niemeyer, 2000), 15–39.

42. See also Christina Kröll and Jörn Göres, eds., *Heimliche Verführung: Ein Modejournal, 1786–1827* (Düsseldorf: Goethe Museum, 1978); and Doris Kuhles, "Das 'Journal des Luxus und der Moden' (1786–1827): Zur Enstehung seines inhaltlichen Profils und seiner journalistischen Struktur," in Kaiser and Seifert, *Friedrich Justin Bertuch,* 489–98.

43. Arjun Appadurai, *The Social Life of Things: Commodities in Cultural Perspective* (Cambridge: Cambridge University Press, 1989), 32.

44. Cultural practices are part of the larger context of the utopian project—and subject to the same contradictions—of creating a "civil society," a modern secularized society composed of free individuals who peacefully and rationally negotiate cooperation, without "too much social inequality and without the tutelage of the authoritarian state." Jürgen Kocka, "The Difficult Rise of a Civil Society," in Fulbrook, *German History since 1800,* 498–99. The strict distinction between public and private life, the emphasis on the family, on individual rights, on a (literary) public sphere, an arena for public debate—all these institutional arrangements required different social relations based on individual achievements in education and work instead of birth and privilege. "Certain cultural attitudes defined differences between the sexes, certain aesthetic values and a clear notion of superiority *vis-a-vis* the natural world—should become universal. This was a culture, which had been pioneered and emphasized in bourgeois circles, in the emerging *Bürgertum*. At the same time, the project of a civil society claimed universal application. In principle it aimed at freedom, equal chances and participation *for all*" (ibid., 499). This, of course, was also its basic contradiction: despite its claim for universality, it was tied to a very small elite group.

Chapter 1

1. Lynch, *The Economy of Character,* 4.

2. Immanuel Kant, *Critique of Judgement,* trans. J. H. Bernard (New York: Haffner, 1951).

3. Woodmansee, *Author, Art, and Market,* 32; Jonathan Hess, *Reconstituting the Body Politic: Enlightenment, Public Culture and the Invention of Aesthetic*

Autonomy (Detroit: Wayne State University Press, 1999), 18.

4. Stephen Heath and Gilligan Skirrow, "An Interview with Raymond Williams," in *Studies in Entertainment: Critical Approaches to Mass Culture,* ed. Tania Modleski (Bloomington: Indiana University Press, 1986), 4.

5. Martin Greiner, *Die Entstehung der modernen Unterhaltungsliteratur: Studien zum Trivialroman des 18. Jahrhunderts* (Reinbek: Rowohlt, 1964); Marion Beaujean, *Der Trivialroman im ausgehenden 18. Jahrhundert* (Bonn: Bouvier, 1964).

6. Dana Polan, "Brief Encounters: Mass Culture and the Evacuation of Sense," in Modleski, *Studies in Entertainment,* 169.

7. Tania Modleski, "The Terror of Pleasure: The Contemporary Horror Film and Postmodern Theory," in Modleski, *Studies in Entertainment,* 157.

8. This would require a more extensive study of aesthetic theory, since, e.g., Adorno's argument that there can be no continuum from "bad to medium and good" art in the tradition of Hegel's dictum of art as the manifestation of truth would have to be dealt with. Adorno, "Prologemona," *Ästhetische Theorie,* 464–66.

9. Polan, "Brief Encounters," 170.

10. Modleski, "The Terror of Pleasure," 157.

11. Max Weber, *The Protestant Ethic and the Spirit of Capitalism,* trans. Talcott Parsons (London: Unwin University Books, 1930).

12. Stuart Hall, "Encoding and Decoding in the Television Discourse," Stencilled Occasional Papers, no. 7 (Birmingham, England: Centre for Contemporary Cultural Studies, 1973).

13. Christa Bürger, *Textanalyse als Ideologiekritik: Zur Rezeption zeitgenössischer Unterhaltungsliteratur* (Frankfurt: Athenäum, 1973); Andreas Huyssen, "Mass Culture as Woman: Modernism's Other," in Modleski, *Studies in Entertainment,* 188–207.

14. Adorno, "Paralipomena—Theorien über den Ursprung der Kunst," *Ästhetische Theorie,* 466–67.

15. Herbert Marcuse, "Über den affirmativen Charakter der Kultur," in *Kultur und Gesellschaft,* vol. 1 (Frankfurt: Suhrkamp, 1965), 56–101, here 88. For a discussion see also C. Bürger, *Textanalyse als Ideologiekritik,* 11–12.

16. Lionell Trilling, "The Fate of Pleasure: Wordsworth to Dostoyevsky," *Partisan Review,* summer 1963, 182.

17. Ibid., 178.

18. Huyssen, "Mass Culture as Woman."

19. This view still surfaces; the elaborate close reading of Goethe's *Wahlverwandtschaften* by Werner Schlick in *Goethe's* Die Wahlverwandt-schaften: *A Middle-Class Critique of Aesthetic Aristocratism* (Heidelberg: Winter,

2000) engages in this vilification as it belabors the point that the "real" nobility and the fictional characters in this novel are given to vacuous entertainment.

20. Hans Magnus Enzensberger, "Constituents of a Theory of the Media," in *The Consciousness Industry: On Literature, Politics, and the Media* (New York: Seabury, 1974), 95–128. Cf. also Fredric Jameson, "Reification and Utopia in Mass Culture," *Social Text* 1 (1979): 130–48; and Richard Dyer, "Entertainment and Utopia in Mass Culture," in *Genre: The Musical: A Reader,* ed. Rick Altman (London: Routledge & Kegan Paul, 1991), 175–89.

21. McKendrick, Brewer, and Plumb, *The Birth of Consumer Society;* Campbell, *Romantic Ethic;* McCracken, *Culture and Consumption;* John Brewer and Roy Porter, eds., *Consumption and the World of Goods* (London: Routledge, 1993).

22. McCracken, *Culture and Consumption,* 4.

23. Ibid., 11.

24. Norbert Elias, *Über den Prozeß der Zivilisation: Soziogenetische und psychogenetische Untersuchungen,* 2 vols. (Frankfurt: Suhrkamp, 1989).

25. McKendrick, Brewer, and Plumb, *The Birth of Consumer Society;* Campbell, *Romantic Ethic,* 288.

26. McCracken, *Culture and Consumption,* 22.

27. Russell Berman, *Cultural Studies of Modern Germany: History, Representation, and Nationhood* (Madison: University of Wisconsin Press, 1993), 10.

28. Jürgen Habermas, *Strukturwandel der Öffentlichkeit* (1962; Frankfurt: Suhrkamp, 1990), 69–75; see also the discussion on Habermas in Hess, *Reconstituting the Body Politic,* 105–9.

29. Habermas, *Strukturwandel,* 76.

30. Jochen Schulte-Sasse, "Das Konzept bürgerlich-literarischer Öffentlichkeit und die historischen Gründe seines Zerfalls," in *Aufklärung und literarische Öffentlichkeit,* ed. Christa Bürger, Peter Bürger, and Jochen Schulte-Sasse (Frankfurt: Suhrkamp, 1980), 83–115; and Dorothea von Mücke, *Virtue and the Veil of Illusion: Generic Innovation and the Pedagogical Project in Eighteenth-Century Literature* (Stanford: Stanford University Press, 1991).

31. Hess, *Reconstituting the Body Politic,* 117.

32. Jürgen Habermas, *Der philosophische Diskurs der Moderne* (Frankfurt: Suhrkamp, 1988).

33. Erich Schön, *Der Verlust der Sinnlichkeit oder Die Verwandlung des Lesers: Mentalitätswandel um 1800* (Stuttgart: Klett-Cotta, 1987), 305–6; and also, confirming Schön, Roberto Simanowski, *Die Verwaltung des Abenteuers: Massenkultur um 1800 am Beispiel Christian August Vulpius* (Göt-

tingen: Vandenhoeck & Ruprecht, 1998), 105.

34. Rolf Engelsing, *Der Bürger als Leser: Lesergeschichte in Deutschland, 1500–1800* (Stuttgart: Metzler, 1974), 221.

35. Simanowski, *Die Verwaltung des Abenteuers*.

36. See also, e.g., Ulrike Weckel, Claudia Opitz, Olivia Hochstrasser, and Brigitte Tolkemitt, eds., *Ordnung, Politik, und Geselligkeit der Geschlechter im 18. Jahrhundert* (Göttingen: Wallstein, 1998), or Detlef Gaus, *Geselligkeit und das Gesellige: Bildung, Bürgertum, und bildungsbürgerliche Kultur um 1800* (Stuttgart: Metzler, 1998), both of which pay attention to these multiple public spheres.

37. Bourdieu, *Die feinen Unterschiede*, 17–19. He links both also to political power—a dimension that is not of immediate interest to my argument.

38. Pierre Bourdieu, "The Genesis of the Concepts of Habitus and Field," trans. Channa Newman, in *The Field of Cultural Production: Essays in Art and Literature,* ed. and intro. Randal Johnson (New York: Columbia University Press, 1993), 5.

39. Pierre Bourdieu, *In Other Words: Essays towards a Reflective Sociology,* trans. Matthew Adamson (Cambridge and Stanford: Polity Press and Stanford University Press, 1990), 111, 222.

40. Pierre Bourdieu and Jean-Claude Passeron, *Reproduction in Education, Society, and Culture,* trans. Richard Nice, Sage Studies in Social and Educational Change no. 5 (London: Sage, 1977), 76.

41. Bourdieu, *Die feinen Unterschiede*, 23–24; Pierre Bourdieu, "Outline of a Sociological Theory of Art Perception," in *The Field of Cultural Production*, 215–37, 228.

42. Pierre Bourdieu, "The Market of Symbolic Goods," in *The Field of Cultural Production*, 113.

43. The language of the cultural practices—their object code—can serve as a means by which society both encourages and endures change. By conceptualizing new ways of seeing oneself that are outside and contrary to existing cultural definitions, the process assists in incorporating these changes into the existing cultural context and in diffusing their destabilizing potential. For example, portraiture, which glorified the representation of the individual in its realistic portrayal of members of the middle class and their families, often with special focus on children, soon made its way into the aristocratic circles as well. Painting was an important medium for depicting the wishes, needs, and yearning of society and for satisfying the growing desire to be pictured (as the photograph serves us today). "Middle-class consumer culture thus made inroads into traditional art forms and altered them to suit their needs and desires for new self-representation. The object-code is Janus-faced. It looks away from

innovation and toward it. It looks away from tradition and toward it. It serves both as an instrument of change and an instrument of continuity." McCracken, *Culture and Consumption*, 137.

Chapter 2

1. I understand class as a complex exchange between economic forces and cultural identity. Cf. Carroll Smith-Rosenberg, "Writing History: Language, Class, and Gender," in *Feminist Studies Critical Studies*, ed. Theresa de Lauretis (Bloomington: Indiana University Press, 1986), 34. It is discursively constructed and undergoes constant redefinition.

2. Simon Richter, in his introduction to *Unwrapping Goethe's Weimar: Essays in Cultural Studies and Local Knowledge*, ed. Burkhard Henke, Susanne Kord, and Simon Richter (Rochester: Camden House, 2000), refers to this Other to high culture as "hybrid" culture (5).

3. In Schiller's concept of *Spiel*, humans are called upon to achieve the integration of two fundamental impulses. The first draws the individual toward sensuous experience, the second to (rational) control. The interplay between these two impulses or drives is his concept of *Spieltrieb*, which allows us to take pleasure in the beautiful as a symbol of reconciliation. Friedrich Schiller, "Ueber die ästhetische Erziehung," in *Schillers Werke Nationalausgabe: Philosophische Schriften*, ed. Benno von Wiese, vol. 20 (Weimar: Hermann Böhlaus Nachfolger, 1962), 309–421, esp. 355–60.

4. But this development did not take the same course for men and women. The early Enlightenment had theorized members of both sexes as essentially equal rational beings who fulfill different roles in society. Silvia Bovenschen, *Die imaginierte Weiblichkeit: Exemplarische Untersuchungen zu kulturgeschichtlichen und literarischen Präsentationsformen des Weiblichen* (Frankfurt: Suhrkamp, 1979). But due to complex changes in the family (from the whole house to the intimate nuclear family) and the net of cultural, political, and economic discourses in which these changes were theorized, late-Enlightenment thinkers accentuated the "natural" difference between the sexes (*Geschlechtscharaktere*). For a summary see Heidi Rosenberg, *Formen der Familie* (Frankfurt: Suhrkamp, 1982), Karin Wurst, *Familiale Liebe ist die "wahre Gewalt": Zur Repräsentation der Familie in G. E. Lessings dramatischen Werken* (Amsterdam: Rodopi, 1988), and the important discussions in Ute Frevert, ed., *Bürgerinnen und Bürger* (Göttingen: Vandenhoeck & Ruprecht, 1988). A series of binary oppositions described the "natural" characteristics of the sexes which essentially were seen to complement each other: women were depicted as passive, reactive, emotional, compassionate, modest, and relational; men were characterized as active, rational, intellectually independent,

and self-directed (Bovenschen, *Die imaginierte Weiblichkeit,* 241 n. 336). These philosophical and anthropological delineations influenced and were supported by a gender-specific concept of education. See Helga Meise, *Die Unschuld und die Schrift: Deutsche Frauenromane im 18. Jahrhundert* (Berlin: Guttandin & Hoppe, 1983), 35–50.

5. However, the central ideological principle of intellectual and artistic independence—associated with various forms of cultural critique—had problematic implications for woman writers, whose lives were, after all, marked by discourses of dependence such as the legal, economical, educational, medical, and moral discourses.

6. Schön, *Verlust der Sinnlichkeit,* 41.

7. Norbert Elias, *Die Höfische Gesellschaft* (1969; Frankfurt: Suhrkamp, 1983), 85.

8. Gert Mattenklott and Klaus Scherpe, eds., *Literatur der Bürgerlichen Emanzipation im 18. Jahrhundert* (Kronberg: Scriptor, 1973). Gert Mattenklott and Klaus Scherpe, eds., *Westberliner Projekt: Grundkurs 18. Jahrhundert. Die Funktion der Literatur bei der Formierung der bürgerlichen Klasse Deutschlands im 18. Jahrhundert* (Kronberg: Scriptor, 1974). Schulte-Sasse, "Das Konzept bürgerlich-literarischer Öffentlichkeit"; Bürger, Bürger, and Schulte-Sasse, *Aufklärung und literarische Öffentlichkeit.*

9. Reinhard Koselleck, *Kritik und Krise: Eine Studie zur Pathogenese der bürgerlichen Welt* (1959; Frankfurt: Suhrkamp, 1973).

10. Antonio Gramsci, *Selections from the Prison Notebooks,* ed. Quintin Hoare and Geoffrey Nowell Smith (London: International Publishers, 1971), 55–60, 160–61.

11. Ibid., 57.

12. Morag Shiach, *Discourse on Popular Culture: Class, Gender, and History in Cultural Analysis, 1730 to the Present* (Oxford: Polity Press, 1989), 17.

13. Jürgen Kocka, "The European Pattern and the German Case," in *Bourgeois Society in Nineteenth-Century Europe,* ed. Jürgen Kocka and Allen Mitchell (Oxford: Berg, 1993), 6.

14. Robert Lee, "'Relative Backwardness' and Long-Run Development: Economic, Demographic, and Social Changes," in Fulbrook, *German History since 1800,* 87 n. 1. See also Richard Sylla and Gianni Toniolo, eds., *Patterns of European Industrialization: The Nineteenth Century* (London: Routledge, 1991).

15. Whaley, "German Lands before 1815," 17.

16. Georg Bollenbeck, *Bildung und Kultur: Glanz und Elend eines deutschen Deutungsmusters* (Frankfurt: Insel, 1994), 53–54.

17. Dorn Brose, *German History,* 114.

18. Ibid.

19. Bollenbeck, *Bildung und Kultur,* 92.

20. Jürgen Müller, "Crumbling Walls: Urban Change in Eighteenth-Century Germany," *German Studies Review* 19, no. 2 (1996): 227; Dieter Hein, "Umbruch und Aufbruch: Bürgertum in Karlsruhe und Mannheim, 1780–1820," in *Vom alten zum neuen Bürgertum: Die mitteleuropäische Stadt im Umbruch, 1780–1820,* ed. Lothar Gall (Munich: Oldenbourg, 1991), 447–515; Lothar Gall, *Von der städtischen zur bürgerlichen Gesellschaft, Enzyklopädie deutscher Geschichte,* vol. 25 (Munich: Oldenbourg, 1993).

21. J. Müller, "Crumbling Walls," 227.

22. Kaschuba, "Deutsche Bürgerlichkeit nach 1800," 10.

23. McCracken, *Culture and Consumption,* xi.

24. Reinhard Koselleck, *Vergangene Zukunft: Zur Semantik geschichtlicher Zeiten* (Frankfurt: Suhrkamp, 1992), 12.

25. Schön, *Verlust der Sinnlichkeit,* 246.

26. Ibid., 249.

27. Ibid., 240–41.

28. "Man kann den Kaffee als *das* bürgerliche Stimulansgetränk bezeichnen, durch welches das Bürgertum seine natürliche Physiologie umschuf zur bürgerlichen zweiten Natur." Wolfgang Schivelbusch, *Das Paradies, der Geschmack und die Vernunft: Eine Geschichte der Genußmittel* (Munich: Hanser, 1980), 13–14. Translated as *Tastes of Paradise: A Social History of Spices, Stimulants, and Intoxicants* (New York: Vintage Books, 1993), 38.

29. For a summary see Wurst, *Familiale Liebe,* 44–53 passim.

30. Elisa von der Recke, *Familien-Scenen oder Entwickelungen auf dem Maskenballe* (1794; Leipzig: Fleischer, 1826), 81.

31. "Lassen Sie es uns nicht vergessen, daß der Mann für den Staat lebt, daß er Erhalter und Stütze seiner Familie ist. Tausend Verdrießlichkeiten begegnen ihm in den Geschäften, unzählige Kränkungen erhält er im Umgange mit Menschen. So gereizt, aufgerieben und in Mißmuth versetzt, eilt er zur Gefährtin seines Lebens: was Wunder, wenn das erste, was ihm zuhause aufstößt, und nach seinem Sinne nicht ist, seinen gereizten Nerven auffällt, und bei ihm in Mißmuth ausbricht! Muß da nicht die sanfte Liebe alles, was ihn drücken konnte, mit heiterer Duldung aus dem Wege räumen?—Ja, meine Julie, wir müssen um den Gefährten unsers Lebens dann einen Himmel zu schaffen suchen, der es ihn vergessen lehrt, daß der Mensch diese schöne Gottes-Welt dem Menschen so oft zur Hölle macht." Ibid.

32. G. J. Barker-Benfield, *The Culture of Sensibility: Sex and Society in Eighteenth-Century Britain* (Chicago: University of Chicago Press, 1992), xxv.

33. Ibid.

34. "Die funktionale Konzentration des Sozialsystems Familie auf zwischen-menschliche Beziehungen und intimer Liebesbeziehung erfolgt entlang der Dichotomisierung von Natur und Kultur, die als Dualismus von Öffentlichkeit und Privatheit interpretiert wird." Siegfried Schmidt, *Die Selbstorganisation des Sozialsystems Literatur im 18. Jahrhundert* (Frankfurt: Suhrkamp, 1989), 114.

35. Kaschuba, "Deutsche Bürgerlichkeit nach 1800," 21.

36. Ibid., 25.

37. Establishing boundaries between work and leisure time served as another means to distinguish the bourgeoisie from the nobility. In the absolute state, the tasks of the members of the nobility were not separated into leisure and work.

38. "Nicht um eine Abschaffung des Vergnügens überhaupt ging es den Aufklärern, auch nicht um eine Einschränkung nur in Hinsicht auf die optimale Ausnutzung menschlicher Arbeitskraft, sondern im Kern tritt immer wieder ihr Bemühen hervor, die Lebensverhältnisse nach klaren Richtlinien zu ordnen, zu vereinheitlichen, Rhythmen von Alltag und Fest regelmäßiger zu gestalten und zu nivellieren—nur eine stetige Lebensweise führt nach ihrer Meinung zum Glück; der aufgeklärte Staat, der seine Untertanen zur Glückseligkeit führen will, hat die Aufgabe, Bedingungen zu schaffen, daß dies auch möglich wird!" Tanzer, *"Specta-cle müssen seyn,"* 112.

39. "Die Freiheit verwirklicht sich in einer eigenen, von der Arbeitszeit abge-hobenen Zeit. Ein Recht auf eine solche Zeit der Freiheit haben alle Menschen in gleichem Maße. Diese Zeit der Freiheit soll der 'Auf-klärung' des Menschen dienen. Diese Aufklärung verwirklicht sich vor allem in Bildung und Genuß. Als notwendige Voraussetzung zu Bildung und Genuß kommt für den arbeitenden Menschen noch Erholung von der Arbeit als Inhalt der Freizeit hinzu." Ibid., 13.

Chapter 3

1. Mentalities describe cognitive, ethical, and affective dispositions that can be further differentiated into period-, class-, and gender-specific disposi-tions within other fields, such as one's profession, family, or local situa-tion. The individual is placed at the point of convergence where the var-ious discourses and social systems meet.

2. I will translate *Empfindsamkeit* as "sensibility," well aware that the two are not exactly synonymous.

3. Barker-Benfield, *The Culture of Sensibility*, xvii.

4. "Das Vergnügen bey unsern sinnlichen Vorstellungen von jeder Art, giebt uns unsre Idee von dem natürlichen Guten oder der Glückseligkeit, und daher werden alle Gegenstände, die geschickt sind, dieses Vergnü-

gen zu erregen, unmittelbar gut genennet." *Franz Hutchesons Unter-suchungen unserer Begriffe von Schönheit und Tugend in zwo Abhandlungen . . .* übersetzt von J. H. Merck (Frankfurt and Leipzig, 1762), 112–13, qtd. in Gerhard Sauder, *Empfindsamkeit (I) Voraussetzungen und Elemente* (Stuttgart: Metzler, 1974), 77.

5. Karl Daniel Küster, "Empfindsam," *Sittliches Erziehungslexikon . . .* (Magdeburg, 1773), 47, qtd. in Sauder, *Empfindsamkeit (I),* 9.

6. "Fähig, leicht sanfte Empfindungen zu bekommen, fähig leicht gerührt zu werden; für das gemeinere und vieldeutige empfindlich." Johann Christoph Adelung, *Grammatisch-Kritisches Wörterbuch der hochdeutschen Mundart,* 2nd ed., 4 vols. (Leipzig, 1793–1801), 1:1800.

7. Van Dülmen, *Das irdische Paradies,* 221, 156–76. Many families spent the summer months in their beloved gardens away from the city. As soon as the weather allowed, a veritable exodus began as bedding, household items, kitchen utensils, toys for the children, and other necessities were transported to the garden. Usually located just outside the city and furnished with a more or less elaborate garden house, it allowed the family to be closer to nature and to live more informally.

8. Ibid., 14.

9. "'[D]enn jedes neue Gefühl zieht die Aufmerksamkeit auf einen neuen Gegenstand, und vermehrt also nicht allein den Umfang der Dinge, die uns interessieren, sondern lehrt uns dabey allemal eine neue Seite von uns selbst kenen . . . von je mehr verschiedenen Gefühlen wir also betroffen und gerührt werden . . . desto mehr Ausdehnung bekömmt unser Selbstgefühl, unser Bewußtsein, und der Begriff, welchen wir von unserem Ich haben.'" Karl Franz von Irwing, *Erfahrungen und Untersuchungen über den Menschen,* 4 vols. (Berlin, 1777–85), 2:216–17, qtd. in Sauder, *Empfindsamkeit (I),* 212.

10. "In dem historischen Augenblick, in dem das Subjekt nicht mehr im Zeichen einer gesellschaftlichen oder funktionalen *Bestimmtheit* definiert werden kann, eröffnet sich der Raum des Unbestimmten, der Formen der Projektion und der Selbstreflexion mit sich bringt, die für biographisches Schreiben zentral sind. Dabei spielt die Steigerungsfähigkeit (im Sinne von Perfektibilität und Selbstvervollkommung) eine ebenso große Rolle wie das stete Umkreisen der Einheit von Identität und Differenz bzw. der Differenz von Allgemeinem und Besonderem." Wilhelm Voßkamp, "Individualität—Biographie—Roman," in *Lebensläufe um 1800,* ed. Jürgen Fohrmann (Tübingen: Niemeyer, 1998), 257–58.

11. Around 1800, the term *Jünglingsalter* would have been used. Bettine von Arnim summed this tendency up: "I know what youth is: heartfelt, undistracted perception of the self." *Bettine von Arnims und Clemens*

Brentanos Frühlingskranz (Frankfurt: Insel, 1985), 310.

12. Günter Oesterle, "Youth—A Romantic Concept? Introduction," in *Jugend: Ein romantisches Konzept?* ed. Günter Oesterle (Würzburg: Königshausen & Neumann, 1997), 35.

13. Literature is the site where "das Versprechen komplexer, risikoreicher, innovativer Erfahrungs-und Erlebensmöglichkeiten ganzheitlicher Art, in denen kognitive, moralische und hedonistische Momente integriert bleiben (bzw. werden) können." Schmidt, *Selbstorganisation,* 21.

14. See also Schön, *Verlust der Sinnlichkeit,* 24.

15. Ibid., 25.

16. Ibid.

17. Nikolaus Wegmann, *Diskurse der Empfindsamkeit: Zur Geschichte eines Gefühls in der Literatur des 18. Jahrhunderts* (Stuttgart: Metzlersche Verlagsbuchhandlung, 1988), 86.

18. Wurst, *Familiale Liebe,* 38–40.

19. "Die Empfindsamkeit, zurückgenommen auf die Familie, entlastet andere Teilbereiche der Gesellschaft—wie z.B. Wirtschaft und Justiz— von individuellen Glücks- und Bedürfnisansprüchen, die einem effizienten Funktionsablauf nur hinderlich sein müssen." Wegmann, *Diskurse der Empfindsamkeit,* 125.

20. Elke Clauss, *Liebeskunst: Untersuchungen zum Liebesbrief im 18. Jahrhundert* (Stuttgart: Metzler, 1993), 9–10.

21. Luhmann, *Liebe als Passion;* Jutta Greis, *Drama Liebe: Zur Entstehungsgeschichte der modernen Liebe im Drama des 18. Jahrhunderts* (Stuttgart: Metzler, 1991), 1–13.

22. Greis, *Drama Liebe,* 21.

23. "Sexualität aber haftet der Verdacht des Chaotischen, Unberechenbaren, Unkalkulierbaren an—im Hintegrund steht immer das Bild der (außerehelichen) galanten 'Wollust.' Daher bedroht der Sexus latent die Ordnung der familiären Empfindsamkeit, das System Liebe-Ehe." Ibid., 107.

24. Wegmann, *Diskurse der Empfindsamkeit,* 111.

25. Greis, *Drama Liebe,* 140–41.

26. "Der Moment der Heirat, die, dem zentralen Prinzip der empfindsamen Liebe gemäß, durch freie Liebeswahl zustandekommen muß, wird zum einzigen Augenblick weiblicher Selbstverfügung. Liebe wird zum zentralen Daseinserlebnis. . . ." Ibid., 173.

27. Sigrid Damm, *Cornelia Goethe* (Weimar: Aufbau, 1988).

28. Helga Gallas, "Ehe als Instrument des Masochismus oder 'Glückseligkeitstriangel' als Aufrechterhaltung des Begehrens," in *Untersuchungen zum Roman von Frauen,* ed. Helga Gallas and Magdalene Heuser (Tübingen: Niemeyer, 1990), 66–75.

29. In the middle class, the responsibilities for men rested primarily on their role as economic provider and legal head of the family, that of women on their supervision of the family and household.

30. "Es wird unterschieden zwischen dem sexuellen Bedürfnis, das auf Befriedigung aus ist und eine Angelegenheit der Allgemeinheit darstellt, und einem sinnlichen Begehren, das wenigen vorbehalten ist, höchsten Genuß verschafft, aber nichts mit realer Befriedigung zu tun hat. . . . Gerade dadurch kann die Liebe bewahrt werden, wird ewig. Liebe und vor allem Begehren und Sexualität fallen so auseinander, sie sind nicht vereinbar." Gallas, "'Glückseligkeitstriangel,'" 69.

31. Michel Foucault, *The History of Sexuality*, vol. 1, *An Introduction* (New York: Vintage House, 1980), 105–8.

32. "Nicht-Befriedigung der sinnlichen Leidenschaft führt zu erotischem Begehren, sich enthalten um zu genießen." Gallas, "'Glückseligkeitstriangel,'" 73.

33. Ibid.

34. Christiane Karoline Schlegel, *Düval und Charmille* (Leipzig: Weidmanns Erben und Reich, 1778), reprinted in *Frauen und Drama im achtzehnten Jahrhundert,* ed. and intro. Karin A. Wurst (Köln: Böhlau, 1991), 96–140.

35. Karin A. Wurst, "Spurensicherung: Elise Bürgers Einakter *Die Antike Statue aus Florenz* (1814) als Beispiel dramatischer Experimente an der Jahrhundertwende," *Goethe Yearbook* 8 (1996): 210–37.

36. "In der Ehe kann es Freundschaft, Zärtlichkeit und Befriedigung se- sueller Bedürfnisse geben, aber kein sinnliches Begehren; ich füge mit Jaques Lacan hinzu: da man nicht begehren kann, was man hat." Gallas, "'Glückseligkeitstriangel,'" 70.

Chapter 4

1. Woodmansee, *Author, Art, and Market,* 6.

2. Johann Georg Sulzer, *Allgemeine Theorie der schönen Künste,* vol. 2 (Leipzig: Weidmannsche Buchhandlung, 1792), 55.

3. Edmund Burke, *A Philosophical Inquiry into the Origins of Our Ideas of the Sublime and Beautiful* (1757; rpt., Notre Dame: University of Notre Dame Press, 1968), 91, 43.

4. Ibid., 39.

5. Ibid., 57–87 passim.

6. "Ein Äquivalent der Unendlichkeit auf der Seite der Formen war aus- geschlossen. Allenfalls auf dem Wege der Assoziation ließ es sich in der Objektwelt wiederfinden. Das Unendliche gibt es immer nur als seine Assoziation, für seine Darstellung in Kunst und Literatur wird das bedeuten: im Zitat. . . . Ästhetisch zum Programm raffiniert, prägt es die

neuen Kunstformen und ihre Techniken als Kombination der Prinzipien Wirkung und Zitat." Hans von Trotha, *Angenehme Empfindungen: Medien einer populären Wirkungsästhetik im 18. Jahrhundert vom Landschaftsgarten bis zum Schauerroman* (Munich: Fink, 1999), 16.

7. Von Trotha summarizes the implications: "Die Revolution der Raumerfahrung bedurfte einer Revolution der Auffassung des Menschen von sich selbst im Raum. Eine Umwertung der Erschütterung war in einer veränderten Wahrnehmung, einer Neuordnung der Rahmenbedingungen auf der Seite des erfahrenden und reflektierenden Subjekts zu leisten. Die Erschütterung, der Schreck war die Erfahrung; die neue Bewertung hatte ein begleitender Gedanke zu leisten. . . . Dem erschreckenden Gedanken folgte die geistige Erhebung darüber, die ein neues Selbstbewußtsein begründen half. . . . In Oxymora wie 'delightful Horror' (John Dennis), 'agreeable Horrour' (Joseph Addison), 'Wohlgefallen aber mit Grausen' (Kant), 'Schauerliche Lust' (Schiller) fand es seinen sprachlichen Ausdruck" (ibid., 19). Schiller's definition of the sublime (*Das Erhabene*) theorizes this mixed sensation when the individual is faced with an overwhelming (natural) phenomenon: "*Erhaben* nennen wir ein Objekt, bey dessen Vorstellung unsre sinnliche Natur ihre Schranken, unsre vernünftige Natur aber ihre Ueberlegenheit, ihre Freyheit von Schranken fühlt; gegen das wir also *physisch* den Kürzeren ziehen, über welches wir uns aber *moralisch* durch Ideen erheben." Schiller, "Vom Erhabenen," in *Schillers Werke Nationalausgabe*, 20:171–95. Christian Begemann also sees the root of the enhanced pleasure that nature provides in the fear of nature which becomes transformed into pleasure through mastery: "Das Selbstbehauptungserlebnis gegenüber dem entgrenzten Raum wurde immer auch als Selbstbehauptungserlebnis gegenüber der Natur konstruiert. Raum und Natur werden gemeinsam erschlossen. Die Entdeckung des Erhabenen hatte so Anteil an dem im 18. Jahrhundert sich vollziehenden Dreischritt von 'Naturfurcht, Naturbeherrschung, Naturgenuß.'" Christian Begemann, *Furcht und Angst im Prozeß der Aufklärung* (Frankfurt: Athenäum, 1987), 97.

8. Von Trotha, *Angenehme Empfindungen*, 23.

9. Friedrich Schiller, "Zerstreute Betrachtungen über verschiedene ästhetische Gegenstände," in *Schillers Werke Nationalausgabe*, 20:222. His fourth category, "das Gute," is not of relevance in our context.

10. Despite the fact that he considers the role of art to please and entertain (*vergnügen*), it is lacking crucial elements: "Das *Angenehme* vergnügt nur die *Sinne*. . . . Es gefällt durch seine Materie, denn nur der Stoff kann den Sinn afficieren. . . . Das Schöne gefällt zwar durch das Medium der Sinne, . . . aber es gefällt durch seine Form der Vernunft, wodurch es sich

vom Angenehmen unterscheidet. . . . Das Gute wird gedacht, das Schöne betrachtet, das Angenehme bloß gefühlt." Ibid.

11. Karl Phillipp Moritz, *Schriften zur Ästhetik und Poetik: Kritische Ausgabe,* ed. Hans Joachim Schrimpf, vol. 7 (Tübingen: Niemeyer, 1962), 5.

12. Woodmansee, *Author, Art, and Market,* 21.

13. Addison, "The Pleasures of the Imagination," no. 411, in *The Spectator,* 3:539.

14. Erin Mackie, introduction to *The Commerce of Everyday Life: Selections from* The Tatler *and* The Spectator, ed. Mackie (Boston: St. Martins Press, 1998), 31.

15. Addison, "The Pleasures of the Imagination," no. 411, in *The Spectator,* 3:535–36.

16. Hartmut Böhme, "Hamburg und sein Wasser im 18. Jahrhundert," in *Hamburg im Zeitalter der Aufklärung,* ed. Hans-Gerd Winter and Inge Stephan (Berlin: Dietrich Reimer, 1989), 63.

17. Woodmansee, *Author, Art, and Market,* 97. As Woodmansee discusses, there is a similar development in England, as Coleridge feels compelled to not condemn the merchants' lack of interest in the arts but instead to acknowledge their desire for diversion by offering them a "stimulant, which though less intense is more permanent, and by its greater divergency no less than duration, even more pleasurable" (220–21). See also her complete discussion on the uses of Kant in England (111–47).

18. Jacob Grimm and Wilhelm Grimm, *Deutsches Wörterbuch,* vol. 6 (Leipzig: S. Hirzel, 1885), 184.

19. Ibid., 2779–80.

20. Ibid., 2772.

21. See Barker-Benfield, *The Culture of Sensibility,* 23.

22. Jacob Grimm and Wilhelm Grimm, *Deutsches Wörterbuch,* vol. 12, pt. 1 (Leipzig: S. Hirzel, 1951), 463–71, here 463.

23. *Trübners Deutsches Wörterbuch,* ed. Walther Mitzka, vol. 7 (Berlin: de Gruyter, 1956), 448.

24. Grimm and Grimm, *Deutsches Wörterbuch,* 12:467.

25. Ibid., 469.

26. *Trübners Deutsches Wörterbuch,* 449.

27. "Vergnügen ist im allgemeinen das behagliche, zufriedene gefühl, das wohlbehagen, in folge angenehmer anregung. es ist aber mitunter auch diese anregung selbst, das einzelereignis, das jenes gefühl hervorbringt [*sic*]." Grimm and Grimm, *Deutsches Wörterbuch,* 12:469.

28. Campbell, *Romantic Ethic,* 60.

29. Wolfgang Binder, *Aufschlüsse: Studien zur deutschen Literatur* (Zurich: Artemis, 1976), 55; see also the discussion in Wegmann, *Diskurse der Empfindsamkeit,* 87.

30. Campbell, *Romantic Ethic,* 69.
31. The ability to enjoy, savor, and delight in sentiments is not limited to positive sensations. The experience of suffering or melancholic thoughts also produces a desirable sensation, as we can see in the frequent reference to tears as a signifier for a desired state of heightened sensibility.
32. Campbell, *Romantic Ethic,* 69.
33. Addison, "The Pleasures of the Imagination," no. 411, in *The Spectator,* 3:537.
34. My reading of the Eros and Psyche myth differs from other readings. Traditionally it has been read as a symbol of man's soul. Erich Neumann read it as the embodiment of the Jungian "feminine" nature. He essentially sees her as a failing by necessity because she is female and thus subordinate. Neumann, *Amor and Psyche: The Psychological Development of the Feminine,* trans. Ralph Mannheim (Princeton: Princeton University Press, 1971). His phallocentrism has been critiqued by Lee Edwards, *Psyche as Hero: Female Heroism and Fictional Form* (Middletown, Conn.: Wesleyan University Press, 1984), and Rosemary Franklin, "The Awakening and the Failure of Psyche," *American Literature* 56 (1984): 510–26. Anne Williams's discussion of female individuation, which focuses on the nature of the tasks Psyche has to accomplish, emphasizes the cooperative nature of her individuation: "The Psyche myth, however, proposes a different idea about the nature and function of ties to others, culminating in Eros. Such ties are necessary, not merely to survival, but to reaching the highest, best condition of human existence." Williams, *The Art of Darkness: A Poetics of the Gothic* (Chicago: University of Chicago Press, 1995), 148.
35. Campbell, *Romantic Ethic,* 77.
36. Barker-Benfield, *The Culture of Sensibility,* 68.
37. Campbell, *Romantic Ethic,* 85, 86.
38. "Der emotiv-kognitive Vorgang der Signifikation werde somit zur eigentlichen Quelle des Lustgewinns. Man könnte dies als einen 'lustvollen' Wechsel von der Körperlichkeit (im Sinne realer Anwesenheit) zur Existenz als Zeichen (im Sinne selbsterschaffener Anwesenheit in der Phantasie) nennen—und im Grunde steckt gerade im Vorgang der Verkörperung des Zeichen, in der 'Zeugung' einer Welt die genuine Lust der Lektüre." Simanowski, *Die Verwaltung des Abenteuers,* 127.
39. Jochen Schulte-Sasse argues: "Zwischen der Strukturanalyse des empfindsamen Fühlens bei Mendelssohn und der modernen Analyse des Kitschgenusses ergeben sich für uns zunächst auffällige Übereinstimmungen: Das empfindsame Gefühl habe zwar auch eine Beziehung auf das Objekt, weil ja von diesem die gefühlsauslösende Wirkung ausgehe,

wesentlicher sei jedoch die Beziehung auf das Subjekt, d.h. die subjektive Reaktion auf das angeregte Fühlen" (38–39). "Der Optimismus der Empfindsamkeit, der in dieser Deutung des Selbstgenusses als eines fundierten Aktes für soziales Verhalten deutlich wird, mußte in diesem Maße brüchig werden, wie der Selbstgenuß *an sich* als lustvoll erstrebt wurde" (41). Schulte-Sasse, *Die Kritik an der Trivialliteratur seit der Aufklärung: Studien zur Geschichte des Kitschbegriffs* (Munich: Fink, 1971), 38–41.

40. Wolfram Mauser, "Die 'Balsam=Kraft' von innen: Dichtung und Diätik am Beispiel des B. H. Brockes," in Mauser, *Konzepte aufgeklärter Lebensführung: Literarische Kultur im frühmodernen Deutschland* (Würzburg: Königshausen & Neumann, 2000), 233–74, 256.

41. "Die Glückserwartung, die man an diese Freude knüpfte, stand, zumal im 18. Jahrhundert, in unmittelbarem Zusammenhang mit der bürgerlichen Leistungsethik. Für die sich ausbreitende Professionalisierung aller Arbeitsbereiche war 'Freude an der Arbeit' eine der wichtigsten Voraussetzungen. Gesundheit und Freude, die mit der Arbeit einhergehen, fanden zunehmend dort Beachtung, wo der Einzelne für Leistung konditioniert werden sollte; und Leistung war mehr denn je der Schlüssel zu Erfolg und Anerkennung in der bürgerlichen Welt." Ibid., 262.

42. Johann Wolfgang von Goethe, *Die Wahlverwandtschaften,* vol. 9 of *Gedenkausgabe der Werke, Briefe und Gespräche,* ed. Ernst Beutler (Zurich: Artemis, 1954), 9–275.

43. Hans Rudolf Vaget, *Dilettantismus und Meisterschaft: Zum Problem des Dilettantismus bei Goethe: Praxis Theorie, Zeitkritik* (Munich: Winkler, 1971), 18–19.

44. Ibid., 25.

45. "[E]in empfänglicher aber unschöpferischer Kunstfreund." Ibid., 28.

46. *Goethes Werke und Briefe,* ed. Erich Trunz and Karl Robert Mandelkow, vol. 9, 4th ed. (Hamburg: Wegner, 1960), 539.

47. Vaget, *Dilettantismus und Meisterschaft,* 57.

48. Johann Wolfgang von Goethe, "Brief an Karl August vom 11. 8. 1787," *Briefe der Jahre 1786–1814,* vol. 19 of *Gedenkausgabe der Werke, Briefe und Gespräche* ed. Ernst Beutler (Zurich: Artemis, 1954), 88.

49. Vaget, *Dilettantismus und Meisterschaft,* 88. Vaget also clearly sees the *Freitagsgesellschaft* as a dilettante enterprise (90) and explains the positive tone that Goethe takes with his pedagogical impulse to foster the cultural life in Weimar. Therefore the kind of polemical critique that is part of the later dilettantism sketch cannot easily be aligned with the pedagogical impulses.

50. Johann Wolfgang von Goethe, "*Propyläen* Einleitung," in *Schriften zur Kunst,* vol. 13 of *Gedenkausgabe der Werke, Briefe und Gespräche,* ed. Ernst

Beutler (Zurich: Artemis, 1954), 138.

51. Vaget, *Dilettantismus und Meisterschaft,* 51.

52. Ibid., 188.

53. He saw "den Nutzen und Schaden sowohl für das Subjekt als auch für das Ganze der Gesellschaft in einem höchst prekären Verhältnis stehen und die Goethe ganz mit der Hintergründigkeit des Eingeweihten zeichnet, einer Mischung von Betroffenheit und Sympathie, Verstehen und Sorge." Ibid., 217.

54. Campbell, *Romantic Ethic,* 63.

55. Johan Huizinga, *Homo Ludens: Vom Ursprung der Kultur im Spiel* (1938; Hamburg: Rowohlt, 1987), 37.

56. Schiller, "Ueber die ästhetische Erziehung," 410.

57. Ibid., 323–27.

58. "Gerne will ich Ihnen eingestehen, daß so wenig es auch den Individuen bey dieser Zerstückelung ihres Wesens wohl werden kann, doch die Gattung auf keine andere Art hätte Fortschritte machen können." Ibid., 326.

59. "Es muß also falsch seyn, daß die Ausbildung der einzelnen Kräfte das Opfer ihrer Totalität notwending macht; oder wenn auch das Gesetz der Natur noch so sehr dahin strebte. So muß es bey uns stehn, diese Totalität in unsrer Natur, welche die Kunst zerstört hat, durch eine höhere Kunst wieder herzustellen." Ibid., 328.

60. "Er soll empfinden, weil er sich bewußt ist, und er soll sich bewußt seyn, weil er empfindet"; "daß die Zeit einen Inhalt habe"; "daß keine Veränderung sey." Ibid., 353.

61. "Der Spieltrieb also, als in welchem beyde verbunden wirken, wird das Gemüt zugleich moralisch und physisch nöthigen; er wird also, weil er alle Zufälligkeit aufhebt, auch alle Nöthigung aufheben, und den Menschen, sowohl physisch als moralisch, in Freyheit setzen." Ibid., 354.

62. Ibid., 360

63. Ibid., 404.

64. Campbell, *Romantic Ethic,* 90.

65. McCracken, *Culture and Consumption,* 111.

66. Ibid., 115.

67. Chandra Mukerji, *From Graven Images: Patterns of Modern Materialism* (New York: Columbia University Press, 1983), 12.

68. McCracken, *Culture and Consumption,* xi.

69. In his essay "The Dressing Gown," Diderot explains how the introduction of a new object, the elegant dressing gown, forced him to reconstruct his whole study to conform to the symbolic significance of this new object. See ibid., 118–29.

70. "Die Kleidung bestimmt das Ameublement der Zimmer, die Tafel, den

Umgang, die Equipage, die Bedienten und dergleichen. Es muß alles akkordiren, sonst nimmt sichs nicht aus." *Journal* 1 (October 1786): 352.

71. Campbell, *Romantic Ethic,* 90.
72. "Es ist bekanntlich Plan und Zweck dieses Journals . . . Teutschland auf seinen eigenen Kunstfleiß aufmerksamer zu machen." *Journal,* 1:81–82.
73. Neil McKendrick, introduction to McKendrick, Brewer, and Plumb, *The Birth of a Consumer Society,* 1.
74. Barker-Benfield, *The Culture of Sensibility,* xxii.
75. Lee, "'Relative Backwardness' and Long-Run Development," 62.
76. McKendrick, Brewer, and Plumb, *The Birth of a Consumer Society,* 101.
77. Initially the imports from England were dominant. Josiah Wedgewood, the most important importer, had revolutionized advertisement, marketing, and transportation. By employing French-, German-, Italian-, and Dutch-speaking clerks, he was able to capture foreign markets. As a sign of demand and clever marketing, he accelerated his imports to the German states between 1767 to 1793. He received orders from Dessau and Leipzig in 1774; Bonn and Dresden, 1775; Vienna, 1781; Hamburg and Stuttgart, 1783; Dorpat and Straßburg, 1785; Danzig, 1787; Lübeck, Mittau, Nüremberg, and Riga, 1788; Darmstadt, Mainz, and Mannheim, 1789; Göttingen and Regensburg, 1790; Ansbach, 1791; Cologne and Memmingen, 1793. Ibid., 134; see 141 for a discussion of Wedgewood's innovative marketing techniques.
78. Rita Bake, "Zur Arbeits- und Lebensweise Hamburger Manufakturarbeiterinnen im 18. Jahrhundert," in Stephan and Winter, *Hamburg im Zeitalter der Aufklärung,* 357–58.
79. McKendrick, Brewer, and Plumb, *The Birth of a Consumer Society,* 14.
80. Campbell, *Romantic Ethic,* 89.
81. Karin A. Wurst, "'Wilde Wünsche': The Discourse of Love in the Sturm and Drang," in *Literature of the Sturm and Drang,* ed. David Hill (Rochester: Camden House, 2003), 220.
82. Richard Payne Knight, *Analytical Inquiry into the Principles of Taste* (London: Payne and White, 1805), 145.
83. "Köstlichkeiten des stillen Lebens." *Journal,* 3:111.
84. This suggests that the *Journal* allowed both sides on the controversial concept of entertainment to be heard.
85. Elias, *Höfische Gesellschaft.*
86. "Drey Classen der Societät aber sind es vorzüglich, denen Luxus am leichtesten gefährlich wird; der Kaufmann, der Handwerker, das Gesinde." *Journal,* 1:26.
87. Qtd. in Wolfgang Griep, "'Die Handlung steht im Flor . . .': Über das Bild Hamburgs in Reisebeschreibungen aus dem 18. Jahrhundert," in

Stephan and Winter, *Hamburg im Zeitalter der Aufklärung,* 28.

88. Addison and Steele, *The Spectator,* 3:527 (no. 409, June 19, 1712).

89. J. H. Plumb, "The Commercialization of Leisure," in McKendrick, Brewer, and Plumb, *The Birth of Consumer Society,* 265.

90. "Fragmente, über Luxus, Bürger-Tugend und Bürger-Wohl für hamburgische Bürger, die das Gute wollen und können, gelesen am 17. Nov. 1791," in *Verhandlungen und Schriften der hamburgischen Gesellschaft zur Beförderung der Künste und nützlichen Gewerbe,* vol. 4 (Hamburg, 1797), 164–65.

91. Wolfram Mauser, "Glückseligkeit und Melancholie: Zur Anthropologie der Frühaufklärung," in Mauser, *Konzepte aufgeklärter Lebensführung,* 234.

92. Ibid., 235.

93. Brockes qtd. in Mauser: "'Schau, höre, fühle, riech und schmecke nur, / Mit Andacht ihren [der Natur] Ton!' (II, 263), dann findest du zu Gott und zur Gesundheit deiner Seele." Mauser, "Die 'Balsam=Kraft' von innen," 253 n. 20.

94. "Man litt im 18. Jahrhundert nicht an der Melancholie, weil äußere Faktoren der Erfüllung entgegenstehen, wie Lepenies vermutet, sondern an der Erfahrung, daß es *das eigene Ich* ist, das der Erfüllung von Vollkommenheitsvorstellungen im Wege steht oder stehen kann. Dieses Bewußtsein eines inneren Verfehlens ist ungleich schmerzhafter, als es die Folgen äußerer Hemmnisse je sein könnten." Mauser, "Glückseligkeit," 216.

95. Ibid., 220.

96. "Freude, Fröhlichkeit und Lust können bewirken, daß der Mensch zu einer der Natur gemäßen Lebensordnung findet. Die theoretische Begründung einer solchen 'Kur' formuliert nicht die Poesie, sondern das medizinisch-diätische Schrifttum der Zeit, dessen unmittelbare Vorgeschichte in das 17. Jahrhundert zurückreicht." Wolfram Mauser, "Anakreon als Therapie? Zur Medizinisch-diätetischen Begründung der Rokokodichtung," in Mauser, *Konzepte aufgeklärter Lebensführung,* 303.

Chapter 5

1. Campbell, *Romantic Ethic,* 77.

2. "Wer wird es tadeln, wenn der Mann, der mehrere Stunden des Tages den wichtigen Dingen aus irgend einem Theile der Wissenschaften nachgedacht hat, nun ein Buch zur Hand nimmt, aus dem er freylich keine wichtigen Wahrheiten lernen kann, das ihm aber doch Vergnügen und Unterhaltung zu gewähren, ihn wenn man so sagen darf, mit seinen Hauptwissenschaften wieder auszusöhnen, oder allenfalls auch nur seine Neugierde zu befriedigen im Stande ist. . . . Wer kann es Unrecht finden,

daß derjenige Theil unsers Geschlechts, welchem die ihm zugetheilten Geschäfte weit mehr müßige Stunden übrig lassen, als den Männern, und dessen lebhafter Geist, und wirksame Einbildungskraft nur selten und ungerne bey lauter ernsthaften Gegenständen verweilt, seine übrige Zeit mit Lesen solcher Bücher ausfüllet, die der weiblichen Lebhaftigkeit und ihren feinern Empfindungen angemessen sind? Nein, unser Geist bedarf, so wie unser Körper, Erholungen und Ruhepunkte; er kann ohne Gefahr einer gänzlichen Erschlaffung nicht immer mit ernsthaften und anstrengenden Gegenständen sich beschäftigen. Wie manche Tagesstunden würden aber viele Menschen in der traurigsten Geschäftslosigkeit hinbringen müssen, wenn sie nicht ihre Zuflucht zu einem unterhaltenden Buch nehmen könnten?" 1795; "Warum lieset man Bücher? und was hat man dabey zu beobachten?" qtd. in Schön, *Verlust der Sinnlichkeit*, 244.

3. Other earmarks of trivial literature include emphases on interesting characters and the language of passion. Dietrich Naumann, "Das Werk August Lafontaines und das Problem der Trivialität," in *Studien zur Trivialliteratur*, ed. Heinz Otto Burger (Frankfurt: Klostermann, 1968), 84.

4. ". . . denn der größte Theil des lesenden Publikums, wenigstens dessen, das obgedachte Mode-Lektüre unter seine tägliche Nahrung und Nothdurft rechnet, ist und bleibt im Stande der Kindheit, ließt nie, um sich zu unterrichten, sondern blos um die Amme zu ersetzen, die ihnen nun keine Mährchen mehr erzählt, und entweder die Imagination zu spannen, oder die Bedürfnisse des Herzens einzulullen; folglich wird sich ihre Lieblings-Lektüre immer entweder im Kreise des Wunderbaren oder der Empfindungen auch Empfindeley herumdrehen; zuweilen diese oder jene Modification, dieß oder jenes Colorit davon annehmen, selten aber sich ganz aus dieser Bahn entfernen." *Journal*, 1:372–73.

5. Victor Nell, *Lost in a Book: The Psychology of Reading for Pleasure* (New Haven: Yale University Press, 1988), 170.

6. Ibid., 176.

7. D. E. Berlyne and K. B. Madsen, eds., *Pleasure, Reward, Preference: Their Nature, Determinants, and Role in Behavior* (New York: Academic Press, 1973), 9.

8. See Schön, *Verlust der Sinnlichkeit*, 99–122.

9. Nell, *Lost in a Book*, 75.

10. The actor and writer Elise Bürger, who was briefly married to Gottfried August Bürger, produced ballads that were clearly influenced by those of G. A. Bürger. For a discussion of the ballad as a pawn in the culture wars of the 1790s, when Schiller used Bürger's ballads as negative examples of a populism no longer possible and desirable, see Woodmansee, *Author, Art, and Market*, 59–67, and Friedrich Schiller, "Über Bürgers

Gedichte," in *Schillers Werke Nationalausgabe: Philosophische Schriften*, ed. Herbert Meyer, vol. 22 (Weimar: Böhlaus Nachfolger, 1958), 245–64.

11. York-Gothart Mix, *Die deutschen Musenalmanache des 18. Jahrhundert* (Munich: Beck, 1987), 147. See also Woodmansee, *Author, Art, and Market,* 58.

12. Schön, *Verlust der Sinnlichkeit,* 119.

13. Fritz Nies, "Bilder von Bildung und Verbildung durch Lesen," in Fohrmann, *Lebensläufe um 1800,* 208.

14. Ibid., 204.

15. Mix, *Die deutschen Musenalamanache,* 42.

16. Nies, "Bilder," 207.

17. Schön, *Verlust der Sinnlichkeit,* 162–63.

18. Goethe was known for his practice of peripatetic reading in his garden. Van Dülmen, *Das irdische Paradies,* 224.

19. Sometimes professional acting careers were launched in these lay theaters. Sophie Albrecht, for example, discovered her love for acting in one of these private amateur performances. Wurst, *Frauen und Drama,* 69; see also Berit C. R. Royer, "Sophie Albrecht (1757–1840) im Kreis der Schriftstellerinnen um 1800: eine literatur- und kulturwissenschaftliche Werk Monographie" (Diss., University of California, Davis, 1999), 50–52.

20. Van Dülmen, *Das irdische Paradies,* 224.

21. For a recent publication on this topic, see Hans-Wolf Jäger, ed., *"Öffentlichkeit" im 18. Jahrhundert* (Göttingen: Wallstein, 1997).

22. Exceptions are the various works by Mix dealing with the topic of his dissertation, *Die deutschen Musenalmanache des 18. Jahrhunderts.*

23. Heinrich Bosse, "Die gelehrte Republik," in Jäger, *"Öffentlichkeit" im 18. Jahrhundert,* 61.

24. Ibid., 66.

25. For a recent revisiting of the emergence of the literary marketplace and its modes of distribution see Simanowski, *Die Verwaltung des Abenteuers,* 98–102. Not much new evidence has been discovered since the seminal empirical studies by Engelsing, Schenda, and Schön; their statistical evidence is recycled in the newer studies. Engelsing, *Der Bürger als Leser;* Rudolf Schenda, *Volk ohne Buch: Sozialgeschichte der populären Lesestoffe, 1770–1910* (Frankfurt: Vittorio Klostermann, 1970); Schön, *Verlust der Sinnlichkeit.*

26. Christian Gottlob Kayser, *Vollständiges Bücherlexikon. Schauspiele* (Leipzig, 1836), qtd. in Schulte-Sasse, *Die Kritik an der Trivialliteratur,* 46. See also the discussion in Erich Schön, "Weibliches Lesen: Romanleserinnen im späten 18. Jahrhundert," in Gallas and Heuser, *Untersuchungen zum Roman von Frauen um 1800,* 20–40.

27. Anthony La Vopa, *Grace, Talent, and Merit: Poor Students, Clerical Careers, and Professional Ideology in Eighteenth-Century Germany* (Cambridge: Cambridge University Press, 1988).

28. A good survey is offered by *Vom Almanach bis Zeitung: Ein Handbuch der Medien in Deutschland, 1700–1800,* ed. Ernst Fischer, Wilhelm Haefs, and York-Gothart Mix (Munich: Beck, 1999).

29. Johann Georg Meusel, *Lexikon der vom Jahre 1750–1800 verstorbenen teutschen Schriftsteller,* 15 vols. (Leipzig, 1802–16).

30. York-Gothart Mix, "Ohne Taschenbuch und Almanach in die Moderne—Otto Julius Bierbaums *Moderner Musen Almanach* (1839–94) im medienhistorischen Kontext," in *Literarische Leitmedien: Almanach und Taschenbuch im kulturwissenschaftlichen Kontext,* ed. Paul Gerhard Klussmann and York-Gothart Mix (Wiesbaden: Harassowitz, 1998), 189.

31. Mix, *Die deutschen Musenalmanache,* 36.

32. York-Gothart Mix, "Der Literaturfreund als Kalendernarr: Die Almanachkultur und ihr Publikum," in Mix, *Almanach und Taschenbuchkultur,* 82.

33. Huyssen, "Mass Culture as Woman," 198.

34. Woodmansee, *Author, Art, and Market,* 75.

35. Daniel Purdy, "Weimar Classicism and the Origins of Consumer Culture," in Henke, Kord, and Richter, *Unwrapping Goethe's Weimar,* 44.

36. The question of how the participation of certain groups, such as women, influenced these discourses themselves deserves further and larger-scale critical attention than is possible in this study. Women are often singled out as a distinct group whose cultural participation—most importantly, their participation in the reading practices of the time—is theorized as dilettante.

37. Rolf Grimminger, "Die Utopie der vernünftigen Lust: Sozialphilosophische Skizze zur Ästhetik des 18. Jahrhunderts bis zu Kant," in Bürger, Bürger, and Schulte-Sasse, *Aufklärung und literarische Öffentlichkeit,* 128.

38. As Pikulik put it: "Das empfindsame Fühlen ist als Reflexion des Fühlens auch ein Fühlen des Fühlens, insofern das Bewußtsein, zu fühlen, sich selbst als Gefühl äußert" (79). Lothar Pikulik, *"Bürgerliches Trauerspiel" und Empfindsamkeit* (Köln: Böhlau, 1966).

39. Sulzer, *Allgemeine Theorie der schönen Künste,* 144.

40. Ibid., 752.

41. Ibid., 751–52.

42. Johann Gottfried Hoche, *Vertraute Briefe* (Hanover: Chr. Ritcher, 1794), 24.

43. Moritz, *Schriften zur Ästhetik und Poetik,* 201.

44. Ibid., 7.

45. Marcus Herz, *Versuche über den Geschmack und die Ursachen seiner Verschiedenheit,* 2nd ed. (1776; Berlin, 1790), 94–95.

46. Goethe, *"Propyläen* Einleitung," 148.

47. Schiller, "Über das Pathetische," in *Schillers Werke Nationalausgabe,* 20:199.

48. Immanuel Kant, *Kritik der Urteilskraft,* vol. 10 of *Werkausgabe,* ed. Wilhelm Weischedel (Frankfurt: Suhrkamp, 1977), 131.

49. Ibid., 124.

50. Corngold, *Complex Pleasure,* 52.

51. Ibid., 55, 56.

52. Ibid., 8.

53. Ibid., 12.

54. Ibid.

55. Friedrich Schlegel, *Seine prosaischen Jugendschriften,* ed. Jacob Minor, vol. 1 (Vienna: Konegen, 1882), 112.

56. Hoche, *Vertraute Briefe,* 74; Johann Christoph Friedrich Bährens, *Ueber den Werth der Empfindsamkeit besonders in Rücksicht auf die Romane* (Halle, 1786), 14.

57. Bährens, *Ueber den Werth der Empfindsamkeit,* 36.

58. *The Collected Dialogues of Plato,* ed. Edith Hamilton and Huntington Cairns (New York: Pantheon, 1961), 624.

59. Goethe, "Über den Dilettantismus," 754.

60. "Diese hohe Gleichmütigkeit und Freyheit des Geistes, mit Kraft und Rüstigkeit verbunden, ist die Stimmung, in der uns ein ächtes Kunstwerk entlassen soll, und es giebt keinen sicherern Probierstein der wahren ästhetischen Güte." Schiller, "Ueber die ästhetische Erziehung," 380.

61. Schulte-Sasse, *Die Kritik an der Trivialliteratur,* 93.

62. Schlegel, *Seine prosaischen Jugendschriften,* 87–88.

63. With regard to women, reading was frequently associasted with masturbation and as such became the object of voyeuristic images or caricatures. Examples include the illustration no. 7 by F. Hubert titled "Dieser Dame ersetzt 'Die Kunst des Liebens' den Liebhaber—ein Schelm, wer Arges dabei denkt!" in Schön, *Verlust der Sinnlichkeit,* 7; and the anonymous illustration no. 11, "Luxury of the Comforts of a Rumpford, London 1801," in Nies, "Bilder," 222.

64. Maria Anna Antonia Sternheim (Marianne Ehrmann), der Verfasserin der *Philosophie eines Weibs, Leichtsinn und gutes Herz oder die Folgen der Erziehung* (Strasbourg: Heinrich Heitz, 1786), reprinted in Wurst, *Frauen und Drama,* 188–251.

65. Barker-Benfield, *The Culture of Sensibility,* 340.

66. Sulzer, *Allgemeine Theorie der schönen Künste,* 419.

67. This is not an invention of the late nineteenth century and the concept

of modernism, as Huyssen seems to suggest, although he hints at an earlier tradition: "It is indeed striking to observe how the political, psychological, and aesthetic discourse around the turn of the century consistently and obsessively genders mass culture and the masses as feminine, while high culture, whether traditional or modern, clearly remains the privileged realm of male activities." "Mass Culture as Woman," 191.

68. Johann Wolfgang Goethe, *Gespräche mit Eckermann*, vol. 24 of *Gedenkausgabe der Werke, Briefe und Gespräche*, ed. Ernst Beutler (Zürich: Artemis, 1949), 448.

69. Ibid., 173.

70. C. Bürger, *Leben Schreiben*, 28. "Schillers Dilettantismusdefinition ist über den Gegensatzreihen aktiv/produktiv/wirkend zu passiv/rezeptiv/leidend konstruiert und stimmt mit Humboldts Auffassung des Gegensatzes von männlich und weiblich nahezu wörtlich überein" (28 n. 19).

71. Ibid., 29.

72. "Ausübung der Kunst nach Wissenschaft, Annahme einer objektiven Kunst, Schulgerechte Folge und Steigerung, Profession und Beruf." Goethe, "Über den Dilettantismus," 748.

73. "Schiller had the good thought to have a house solely for tragedies and also to perform one play per week for men alone. Yet this would require a very large residence and was not achievable in our limited circumstances" ("Schiller hatte den guten Gedanken, ein eigenes Haus für die Tragödien zu bauen, auch jede Woche ein Stück bloß für Männer zu geben. Allein dies setzte eine sehr große Residenz voraus und war in unsern kleinen Verhältnissen nicht zu realisieren"). Goethe, *Gespräche mit Eckermann*, 106.

74. Ibid.

75. Christine Battersby, *Gender and Genius* (Bloomington: Indiana University Press, 1989), 3.

76. This symbolic erotic relationship between creator and text is a recurrent image. See also Sandra Gilbert and Susan Gubar, *The Madwoman in the Attic: The Women Writer and the Nineteenth-Century Literary Imagination* (New Haven: Yale University Press, 1979), 13.

77. Schön, *Verlust der Sinnlichkeit*, 32.

78. Hans Friedrich Foltin, "Karl Gottlieb Cramers 'Erasmus Schleicher' als Beispiel eines frühen Unterhaltungs- oder Trivialromans," in Burger, *Studien zur Trivialliteratur*, 80–81.

79. Schön, *Verlust der Sinnlichkeit*, 32.

80. "Nimm ein Stück nach dem andern, in der Reihe, ließ es aufmercksam durch, und wenn es dir auch nicht gefällt, ließ es doch. Du mußt dir Gewalt anthun . . . und nicht nur Vergnügen beym Lesen suchen. Wenn

du es gelesen hast; so mach das Buch zu und stelle Betrachtungen darüber an." Johann Wolfgang Goethe, *Briefe der Jahre 1764–1786,* vol. 18 of *Gedenkausgabe der Werke, Briefe und Gespräche,* ed. Ernst Beutler (Zürich: Artemis, 1949), 27.

81. Goethe, *Gespräche mit Eckermann,* 138.

82. Schulte-Sasse, *Die Kritik an der Trivialliteratur,* 121.

83. J. W. Appell, *Die Ritter-, Räuber-, und Schauerromantik: Zur Geschichte der deutschen Unterhaltungsliteratur* (Leipzig: Wilhelm Engelmann, 1859), 5.

84. Christa Bürger, *Der Ursprung der bürgerlichen Institution Kunst im höfischen Weimar: Literatursoziologische Untersuchungen zum klassischen Goethe* (Frankfurt: Suhrkamp, 1977), 109.

85. Schmidt, *Selbstorganisation,* 340–41; and Marlies Prüsener, "Lesegesellschaften im 18. Jahrhundert," *Börsenblatt für den deutschen Buchhandel,* no. 10 (1972): 229–34.

86. "[Z]u eigen, zu tief und zu männlich" for the "zuckersüßen Schwätzer[n] und Schwätzerinnen." Schiller, "Anthologie auf das Jahr 1782," in *Schillers Werke Nationalausgabe,* 22:135. See also Goethe, *Gespräche mit Eckermann,* 138, 448.

87. Appell, *Ritter-, Räuber-, und Schauerromantik,* 5

88. Johann Heinrich Merck in Wieland's *Teutsche[m] Merkur,* September 1776, 261.

89. Carl Müller-Fraunreuth, *Die Ritter- und Räuberromane* (Halle, 1894; facsimile edition, Hildesheim: Olms, 1965), 109–10.

90. Ibid., 94.

91. Ibid., 1.

92. Ibid., 64.

93. Gustav Sichelschmidt, *Liebe, Mord, und Abenteuer: Eine Geschichte der Unterhaltungsliteratur* (Berlin: Haude & Spener, 1969), 65–66.

94. Ibid.

95. Ibid., 12; Kurt-Ingo Flessau, *Der moralische Roman: Studien zur gesellschaftskritischen Trivialliteratur der Goethezeit* (Köln, Graz: Böhlau, 1968), refers to trivial literature as a mirror of its time (40).

96. Sichelschmidt, *Liebe, Mord, und Abenteuer,* 22.

97. Greiner, *Die Entstehung der modernen Unterhaltungsliteratur,* 80.

98. Hans Friedrich Foltin, "Zur Erforschung der Unterhaltungs- und Trivialliteratur, insbesondere im Bereich des Romans," in Burger, *Studien zur Trivialliteratur,* 265.

99. Peter Nusser, *Trivialliteratur* (Stuttgart: Metzler, 1991).

100. Winfried Fluck, *Populäre Kultur: Studienbuch zur Funktionsbestimmung und Interpretation populärer Kultur* (Stuttgart: Metzler, 1979), 61.

101. Jochen Schulte-Sasse, "Gebrauchswerte der Literatur: Eine Kritik der ästhetischen Kategorien 'Identifikation' und 'Reflexion,'" vor allem in

Hinblick auf Adorno," in *Zur Dichotomisierung von hoher und niederer Literatur,* ed. Christa Bürger, Peter Bürger, and Jochen Schulte-Sasse (Frankfurt: Suhrkamp, 1984), 62–107, 89.

102. Contemporary sources such as the long-running *Journal des Luxus und der Moden* make a point of describing regional differences. In fact, one of the *Journal*'s goals as a national publication was to familiarize readers with the customs, perceived regional characteristics, and habits of other parts within the German states.

103. I am not interested in the distinction among these publications; instead, I would like to emphasize their common features. For a thorough discussion on the genre of almanac, see the works by York-Gothart Mix, especially, his *Die deutschen Musenalmanache des 18. Jahrhunderts,* in which he also provides an overview of the relevant research (16).

104. Kirsten Belgum, "A Nation for the Masses: Production of Identity in the Late-Nineteenth Century Popular Press," in *A User's Guide to German Cultural Studies,* ed. Scott Denham, Irene Kacandes, and Jonathan Petropoulos (Ann Arbor: University of Michigan Press, 1997), 164.

105. "Der Herausgeber dieser Sammlung ist so unermüdet, die Welt mit Compilationen zu beschenken, daß wir ihn fast einen Blumenkrämer in der Gelehrtenrepublik nennen mögten, der täglich auf den Fluren unsrer schönen Literatur umherwandelt, und für das geehrte Publicum nach Stand, Geschlecht und Alter verschiedene Sträuschen bindet." *Neue Unterhaltungen* Hamburg 1 (June 1774): 89–95, 89.

106. After the completion of this manuscript, a complete set of illustrations from the *Journal* appeared in *Journal des Luxus und der Moden, 1786–1827, Analytische Bibliographie mit sämtlichen 517 schwarzweißen und 976 farbigen Abbildungen der Originalzeitschrift,* ed. Doris Kuhles, 3 vols. (Munich: Saur, 2003). This publication allows a more thorough appreciation of the visual impact of this central publication for taste formation.

107. Marie-Kristin Hauke, "'Wenns nur Lärmen macht . . .': Friedrich Justin Bertuch und die (Buch-) Werbung des späten 18. Jahrhunderts," in Kaiser and Seifert, *Friedrich Justin Bertuch,* 374.

108. Bertuch argued that science heeds its calling only when it leads to practical applications that enhance the quality of life. F. J. Bertuch, "Über die Wichtigkeit der Landes-Industrie-Institute für Deutschland" (1793), qtd. in Helmut Holtzhauer, *Friedrich Justin Bertuch: Zum 150. Todestag am 3. April 1972* (Weimar: Weimarer Stadtmuseum, 1972), 22.

109. Michael Diers, "Bertuchs Bilderwelt: Zur populären Ikonographie der Aufklärung," in Kaiser and Seifert, *Friedrich Justin Bertuch,* 438.

110. More than forty periodicals originated in Bertuch's publishing house alone. Uta Kühn-Stillmark, "Zum Verlagsprofil des Landes-Industrie-Comptoirs und des Geographischen Instituts unter Friedrich Justin

Bertuch in den Jahren 1791 bis 1822," in Kaiser and Seifert, *Friedrich Justin Bertuch*, 419.

111. For a more extensive listing of titles see Mix, *Die deutschen Musenalmanache*, 160–79.

112. *Almanach für Damen* (Tübingen: Cotta, 1801).

113. *Karrikaturen Almanach mit 9 illuminierten Blättern nach Hogarth und Lichtenberg* (Hamburg: Vollmer, 1801).

114. E. A. W. Zimmermann, *Almanach der Reisen, oder unterhaltende Darstellung der Entdeckungen des 18then Jahrhunderts in Rücksicht auf Länder- Menschen- und Produktenkunde für jede Klasse von Lesern* (Leipzig: Fischer, 1814).

115. Solbrig's *Almanach der Travestieen und Parodieen* (Leipzig: Franz, 1816).

116. *Hamburger Taschenbuch der Moden und des Luxus* (Hamburg: Vollmer, 1802).

117. *Taschenbuch von Wieland und Goethe* (Tübingen: Cotta, 1804).

118. *Taschenbuch, für Freunde u. Freundinnen des Carnevals mit Illuminierten Kupfern* (Leipzig: Leo, 1804).

119. *Das goldne ABC für Herren und Damen ausser der Ehe: Ein Taschenbuch* (Berlin: Hayn, 1809).

120. Friederike Baronin de la Motte Fouque, *Legenden* (Berlin: Realschul-Buchhandlung, 1813).

121. Solbrig's *Taschenbuch der Deklamation* (Leipzig: Franz, 1814).

122. *Taschenbuch für Mineralwassertrinker* (Nürnberg: Baur und Raspe, 1820).

123. *Leipziger Taschenbuch für Frauenzimmer: Zum Nutzen und Vergnügen auf das Jahr 1804* (Leipzig: Böhme, 1804).

124. Jan Knopf, "Kalender," in *Von Almanach bis Zeitung: Ein Handbuch der Medien in Deutschland 1700–1800*, ed. Ernst Fischer, Wilhelm Haefs, and York-Gothart Mix (Munich: Beck, 1999), 122.

125. *Taschenkalender auf das Jahr 1798 für Natur- und Gartenfreuden: Mit Abbildungen von Hohenheim und andern Kupfern* (Tübingen: Cotta' schasche Buchhandlung, 1798).

126. Nies, "Bilder," 203.

127. Mix, who evaluated the few subscription lists available as well as inventories of private collections, comes to the following conclusion about the readership of almanachs: "83.4% belonged to the educated middle class, 7.2% to the nobility and officers, and 9.4% could not be identified by class. The majority of readers (84.91%) were not professionally involved with literature. Only 15.01% of the readership belonged to the group of intellectuals, professors, and teachers." Mix, *Die deutschen Musenalmanache*, 124–25.

128. "Das Buch als Träger menschlichen Wissens und menschlicher Erfahrung sollte *handhabbar* sein und an jedem Ort und in jeder Stunde als *Vade-*

mecum genutzt werden können." Ibid., 41.

129. Ibid., 41–42.

130. One of these volumes is housed at the Literaturarchiv Marbach.

131. Qtd. in Paul Gerhard Klussmann, "Das Taschenbuch im literarischen Leben der Romantik und Biedermeierzeit: Begriff, Konzept, Wirkung," in Klussmann and Mix, *Literarische Leitmedien,* 56.

132. Stephan Füssel, "Almanache und Kalender aus der Verlagsproduktion Georg Joachim Göschen (1752–1828)," in Klussman and Mix, *Literarische Leitmedien,* 67.

133. See Belgum's recent study *Popularizing the Nation: Audience, Representation, and the Production of Identity in* Die Gartenlaube *(1853–1900)* (Lincoln: University of Nebraska Press, 1998).

134. Newspapers became another form of reading that depended on novelty and helped to foster a new sense of time: "Jezt aber ist wirklich der Fall eingetreten, wo eine neue, allgemeine und weit mächtigere Mode Lectüre, als alle vorhergehenden, sich nicht allein über Teutschland, sondern über ganz Europa verbreitet hat, alle Stände und Classen der Societät anzieht, und fast jede andere Lectüre verdrängt, und dies ist die Lektüre der Zeitungen und fliegenden politischen Blätter." *Journal,* 1:373.

135. "Especially, but not exclusively for women, excessive newspaper consumption is a sign of a pathological *politicomania,* an indulgence in sensationalism or superficiality." Nies, "Bilder," 210. For a recent analysis of the famous and long-running newspaper *Cotta'sche Allgemeinen Zeitung,* see Günter Müchler, *"Wie ein treuer Spiegel": Die Geschichte der Cotta'schen Allgemeinen Zeitung* (Darmstadt: Wissenschaftliche Buchgesellschaft, 1998).

136. Reprinted in Mix, *Die deutschen Musenalmanache,* appendix 7.

Chapter 6

1. For a comprehensive account of his many cultural and economic activities see Kaiser and Seifert, *Friedrich Justin Bertuch.*

2. See also Kröll and Göres, *Heimliche Verführung;* and Kuhles, "Das 'Journal.'" Michael Knoche refers to a European readership ("europaweite Ausstrahlung"). Knoche, "Vorwort," in Kuhles, *Analytische Bibliographie,* vii.

3. "4 Rthr in Golde" (Schön, *Verlust der Sinnlichkeit,* 315). The *Journal* had 1,488 (1786) and 1,765 (1789) subscribers according to Friedrich Bertuch Nachlaß, Goethe-Schiller Archiv, Weimar (N.F. 867/II), and yielded handsome profits.

4. Kuhles, "Das 'Journal,'" 489.

5. Bertuch was a renowned figure in the cultural world in Weimar. A well-educated businessman, writer, and translator in his own right, Bertuch

became financial adviser at the ducal court in Weimar under Karl August. His background in economics and finance and his connections at the court combined with his background in arts and letters to make him a knowledgeable editor who not only edited this sophisticated fashion magazine but also served as coeditor—together with Wieland and Christian Gottfried Schütz (professor of literature in Jena)—of the highly regarded *Allgemeine Literaturzeitung* (General Literary Newspaper, 1785–1803 in Jena and 1804–49 in Halle), whose contributors included Goethe, Schiller, Kant, Fichte, and Alexander von Humboldt, among others. He also published the *Bilderbuch für Kinder* (12 vols., 1790–1830) and other culturally significant titles. However, the *Journal* remained the most notable publication for a general upper-middle-class audience. The wide range of contributors and correspondents provided the necessary variety and breadth to make it desirable reading material. The original contained some 40,000 pages and over 1,500 illustrations (the four-volume reprint contains only 1,500 pages). For a description of the *Journal*'s physical appearance see Kuhles, "Das 'Journal,'" 491–92. In addition to the stature of the editor, timing made this venture more successful than earlier attempts. I see a reason for the lack of responsiveness to earlier fashion journals in the general condemnation of luxury in the early wave of middle-class oppositional identity formation, when the consumption of luxury items and entertainment was generally associated with the nobility.

6. Before Bertuch became a famous publisher he was a businessman, and he and his wife, Caroline, were active in manufacturing. One example is the manufacture of artificial flowers for decorative purposes in fashion and the home. He also founded the Landes-Industrie-Comptoir (1791). Under the Bertuchs' guidance the small manufacturing business grew from employing a few women to around fifty; the owners advertised the decorative luxury objects at the trade fairs in Leipzig and Frankfurt. Not only did this Weimar enterprise provide an opportunity for local impoverished women to earn money and support their families, but its success established an alternative to imported luxury goods and therefore stimulated the local and regional economy. Caroline Bertuch's receipts mention the following objects: "bouquets of elegant flowers for ladies' hats, a basket filled with a miniature landscape with flowers, and diverse other artificial flowers" ("Bouquets feine Blumen zu einigen Damens Hüthen, Korb von Landschaft mit Blumen garniret und verschiedene andere Blumen") (1782–1783 Staatsarchiv [A I 113 Bl. 36 and Bl. 83]). See also Sigrid Damm, *Christiane und Goethe: Eine Recherche* (Frankfurt: Insel, 1998), 73–79. In addition, Bertuch's publishing business provided employment to the colorists who finished the prints.

7. Daniel Purdy, "The Veil of Masculinity: Clothing and Identity via Goethe's *Die Leiden des jungen Werthers,*" *Lessing Yearbook* 27 (1996): 103–29.

8. Ibid., 105.

9. Purdy, "Weimar Classicism," 37–38.

10. Beyond their aesthetic appeal, their verbal and visual information could also be utilized as models for patterns. As patterns or models, the fashion magazines replaced the more expensive and cumbersome miniature mannequins (sporting the latest fashion) or the older costume books. In the sixteenth century, costume books became popular. These described and depicted fashionable variations in dress in different regions and no doubt contributed toward a speeding up of the fashion process. It was only in the fifteenth and sixteenth centuries that it began to seem shameful to wear outdated clothes, and those who could afford to do so discarded clothing simply because it had gone out of style. Elizabeth Wilson, *Adorned in Dreams: Fashion and Modernity* (London: Virago, 1985), 20. The increased use of the fashion doll, the often life-sized wooden mannequin, modeling not only the latest fashions but the fashionable hairstyle and accessories, made the information on fashion more portable and thus more accessible to larger groups of people. From its Paris-based exclusive origins at the beginning of the century to the London more mass-based use (of smaller and cheaper paper dolls) in the last decades it made its way to Germany in an emulation of English cultural values. These paper dolls with their fashionable wardrobes could be easily and economically distributed and could help women study good and bad taste. Yet the true popularization of fashion in the German states took place only when the subject and depiction of fashionable clothing became a topic in the periodical press. See also McKendrick, Brewer, and Plumb, *The Birth of Consumer Society,* 43–47, on the use of the fashion doll: "It was original, cheap and effective. It was capable of almost endless variety. It could penetrate many different social levels. As an advertisement it had good survival value, for even when discarded by mothers it was taken up by children as a toy, and so could begin the indoctrination of the next generation of fashion consumers—teaching even in infancy the importance and intricacies of fashion awareness" (45–46).

11. Veblen assumes that the main motivation of fashion is the emulation of the clothing of the upper classes by the lower tiers, in the spirit of social climbing. Thorstein Veblen, *The Theory of the Leisure Class* (New York: MacMillan, 1899), and also in Veblen, "Theorie der feinen Leute," in *Die Listen der Mode,* ed. Silvia Bovenschen (Frankfurt: Suhrkamp, 1986), 106–55, esp. 141–51.

12. This study also does not follow the other dominant range of arguments that consider fashionable change as a result of the manipulation of the media as advertiser for the capitalist marketplace. First explored in the classic economic study by Werner Sombart ("Wirtschaft und Mode: Ein Beitrag zur Theorie der modernen Bedarfsgestaltung," in *Grenzfragen des Nerven- und Seelenlebens,* vol. 12 [Wiesbaden: Bergmann, 1902], rpt. in Werner Sombart, "Wirtschaft und Mode," in Bovenschen, *Die Listen der Mode,* 80–105), it culminated in Adorno's characterization of fashion. Adorno was talking about fashion in the larger sense of changing trends (in art) as alienation par excellence because he considers it as sheer manipulation by industrial capitalism. Adorno, *Ästhetische Theorie,* 468. As discussed above, his influential argument of mass culture as an ideological stratagem is not altogether suitable as an explanatory model for the late eighteenth and early nineteenth century.

13. "It is precisely this inconstancy of the goddess 'fashion,' which changes her appearance with every new moon, that we decided to produce this periodical as a monthly so that we could quickly inform about new trends in all branches of luxury and give detailed descriptions of color and design of new trends in fashion and inventions as they are produced in France, England, Germany, and Italy" ("Eben diese Unbeständigkeit der Göttin Mode, die fast mit dem Monde ihre Gestalten wechselt, und immer unter neuen erscheint, ist Ursach, daß wir dieses Journal blos zum fliegenden Blatte machten, um nur immer zeitig genug Nachricht, genaue Beschreibung, Farbe und Zeichnung von jeder neuen Mode und Erfindung, so wie sie in Frankreich, England, Teutschland und Italien erscheint, in welchem Zweige von Luxus es sey, zu liefern.") *Journal,* 1:29–30.

14. Johann Wolfgang von Goethe, *Elective Affinities,* trans. Judith Ryan, in *Goethe's Collected Works,* vol. 11 (New York: Suhrkamp, 1988), 121; Goethe, *Die Wahlverwandtschaften,* 52.

15. In the debate, the *Journal* advocated the more "progressive" position against this instrument of female confinement, advocating a more active, healthy lifestyle. The position against the corset had been the topic of some debate and was the theme of a competition, which the scientist Sömmering and an anonymous entry won; they were published by Salzmann in 1788 as *Ueber die Schädlichkeit der Schnürbrüste; zwey Preisschriften, durch eine von der Erziehungsanstalt zu Schnepfenthal aufgegebene Preis-Frage veranlaßt* (Leipzig: Crusius, 1788).

16. "Wir übergaben daher die Vertheidigung der Schnürbrüste gleichfalls einer Dame von Geist, die glückliche Mutter mehrerer gesunder und schön gewachsener Kinder ist, und die durch ihre Erfahrung und hellen

Verstand sich vollkommen zu der, von unserer anonymen Correspon-
dentin verlangten Richterin qualifizierte, und baten um ihr Urtheil."
Journal, 1:109.

17. "Genie, Caprice und Zufall sind meistens ihre Schöpfer; Durst nach
Neuheit und Abwechslung, oft Hang zur Singularität, und meistens
Speculationen der Manufackturen machen sie unbeständig und schnell
wechselnd." Ibid., 1:29.

18. "Nun wird ein aufmerksamer Beobachter unserer elegantesten Damen
gewiß schon bemerkt haben, daß sie bald eine Mode ablegen, die sie mit
allen und jeden theilen sollen." Ibid., 85.

19. Georg Simmel, "Die Mode," in Bovenschen, *Die Listen der Mode*, 184.

20. Anne Hollander, *Sex and Suits* (New York: Knopf, 1994), 16.

21. See also Purdy, "Weimar Classicism," esp. 47–48.

22. Friedrich Justin Bertuch, *London und Paris* (Weimar: Verlag des Industrie-Comptoirs, 1799), no. 3, 189–97.

23. McCracken, *Culture and Consumption*, 27.

24. Erin Mackie, *Market à la Mode: Fashion, Commodity, and Gender in* The
Tatler *and* The Spectator (Baltimore: Johns Hopkins University Press,
1997), 59.

25. Ibid., 82.

26. Georg Christoph Lichtenberg, *Briefwechsel*, ed. Ulrich Joost and Albrecht
Schöne (Munich: Beck, 1983), 27–28.

27. Sophie von La Roche, *Sophie in London, 1786, Being the Diary of Sophie v.
La Roche*, trans. Clare Williams (London: Jonathan Cape, 1933), 87.

28. Ibid., 141.

29. Bertuch, *London und Paris*, no. 3, 190.

30. "I never manage to go to my destination without stopping at a store to
look at something I had not noticed before or even to go inside and buy
something" ("es [gelingt] mir nimmer, daß ich meines Weges gehen
kann, ohne an einem Laden stehen zu bleiben, und etwas vorher nicht
bemerktes zu begucken, oder wohl gar hinein zu gehen und zu kaufen").
Ibid.

31. The *Journal* (3:370) describes the decorations of a grocery store where
the food was displayed to evoke visual pleasure.

32. In 1804 Herder writes: "Pernicious fashion journals undermine domestic
prosperity through their constantly changing demands and create vanity
and thus are harmful to health, morality, and all better usefulness" ("Ver-
derbliche Modejournale, die durch stets veränderten Aufwand den häuslichen Wohlstand untergraben, und wie sie das Gemüt eitel machen, so
der Gesundheit, Moralität und aller besseren Zweckhaftigkeit schaden").
This is qtd. in the "Einleitung" to the *Journal* (1:15) as an example of the
kind of argumentation that the magazine is confronted with.

33. "One must admit that objective [*rein*] observations are rarer than one thinks. Our feelings, views, and judgements become part of pure experience so quickly that we cannot long maintain our position as impartial observers but instead soon begin forming opinions. Yet, we should attribute importance to these opinions only to the extent that we can trust the nature and training of our mind as a basis for them." Johann Wolfgang von Goethe, "Introduction to the *Propylaea*," in *Essays on Art and Literature*, trans. Ellen von Nardroff and Ernest von Nardroff (New York: Suhrkamp, 1986), 79.

34. For a more detailed look at Klauer's plaster casts in the context of Weimar culture see Catriona MacLeod, "Floating Heads: Weimar Portrait Busts," in Henke, Kord, and Richter, *Unwrapping Goethe's Weimar*, 65–84 + 12 ill.

35. *Allgemeines Teutsches Garten-Magazin oder gemeinnützige Beiträge für alle Theile des praktischen Gartenwesen*, vol. 3, ed. Friedrich Justus Bertuch (Weimar: Industrie-Comptoir, 1809), 3–4.

36. Autobiographical accounts as well as sales records and advertisements allow glimpses at the variety of toys available, ranging from puppet theaters to dolls with cut-out clothes, rocking horses, and pets.

37. Diers, "Bertuchs Bilderwelt," 441.

38. The other trend that allowed the playfulness of fashion to become the topic of analysis is postmodern thinking, which relativized the dogmatic positions of the social movements of the late 1960s and 1970s, as Gert Mattenklott argued in an interview with Vischer on the topic of fashion. Gert Mattenklott, "Friedrich Theodor Vischer im Gespräch: Auch ein Beitrag zur Philosophie der Mode," in Bovenschen, *Die Listen der Mode*, 366–67.

39. See also Gesa Dane, *"Die heilsame Toilette": Kosmetik und Bildung in Goethe's "Der Mann von fünfzig Jahren"* (Göttingen: Wallstein, 1994), 116–20.

40. During the Napoleonic era (1806–15) this more constructivist concept of culture becomes more dominant. Some contributors to the *Journal* link this trend with the nationalist tendencies that emerge under, e.g., the guise of the national costume debate (*Tracht*). The advocates of national costume suggest that it would not only unite the German people but delineate their difference from the French (enemies). After the defeat of Napoleon, national costume was advocated by many patriots as a sign of the hard-won political independence that should be underscored through cultural independence. Bertuch himself remained committed to the self-regulatory system of fashion, which he saw as a guarantee for economic growth and thus the strength of a nation.

41. Bertuch quotes Herder's discussion of clothing and women's role in this

form of cultural signification in his *Kalligone*. Herder also emphasizes the constructedness of the clothed, adorned body. Clothes are more than a window to the individual, hidden self. They do more than hint at the secret concealed self; how we see and consequently dress ourselves influences how we act and how others act toward us. Qtd. in *Journal*, 2:45–46.

42. "The desire to please and to distinguish oneself is the spirit that is intimately linked to the essence of human nature in all peoples on this earth. Merely the materials used and the external signs are different. The more wealthy and cultivated a nation is, the more comfortable, tasteful, and varied are her fashions" ("Der Wunsch zu gefallen, und sich auszuzeichnen, ist der Geist, der mit dem Grundstoffe der menschlichen Natur bey allen Völkern der Erde innigst verwebt ist. Nur Materie und Zeichen sind verschieden. Je reicher und verfeinerter eine aufgeklärte Nation ist, desto bequemer, schöner, geschmackvoller und mannigfältiger sind auch ihre Moden"). Ibid., 1:29.

43. McCracken, *Culture and Consumption*, 60.

44. Elizabeth Wilson, "Fashion and the Postmodern Body," in *Chic Thrills: A Fashion Reader*, ed. Juliet Ash and Elizabeth Wilson (Berkeley: University of California Press, 1993), 6.

45. E. Wilson, *Adorned in Dreams*, 35.

46. Van Dülmen, *Das irdische Paradies*, 192.

47. E. Wilson, *Adorned in Dreams*, 35.

48. Ibid., 122–23.

49. La Roche, *Sophie in London*, 123.

50. Winfried Löschburg, *History of Travel* (Leipzig: Interdruck, 1979), 81.

51. Lynch, *The Economy of Character*, 145.

52. McCracken, *Culture and Consumption*, xi.

53. Marshall Sahlins, *Culture and Practical Reason* (Chicago: University of Chicago Press, 1976), 203.

54. McCracken, *Culture and Consumption*, 22.

55. "The women work, the master of the house joins them occasionally from his adjacent study, and he has the unique ability to bring things from his study that have a connection to the conversations taking place and which one consequently examines with pleasure and interest" ("Die Frauenzimmer arbeiten, der Herr des Hauses geht aus seiner nahegelegenen Studierstube ab und zu, und hat die ganz eigene Kunst aus der letzteren oft etwas herbeyzubringen, das sich auf die jedesmalige Unterredung bezieht, und das man mit Vergnügen und Interesse sieht"). Brigitte Tolkemitt, "Knotenpunkt im Beziehungsnetz der Gebildeten: Die gemischte Geselligkeit in den offenen Häusern der Hamburger Familien

Reimarus und Sieverking," in Weckel et al., *Ordnung, Politik, und Gesellligkeit,* 182.

56. *Journal* 3 (September 1788): 385.

57. Christian Garve, "Über die Moden," in *Versuche über verschiedene Gegenstände aus der Moral, der Literatur und dem gesellschaftlichen Leben* (1792; rpt. Hildesheim: Olms, 1985), 241.

58. Angelika Emmrich and Susanne Schröder, "Weimarer historische Interieurs: Zum Ameublement im Journal des Luxus und der Moden," in Kaiser and Seifert, *Friedrich Justin Bertuch,* 508.

59. See, for example, *Journal* 1 (July 1786): 266 and plate XXII for a depiction of light fixtures.

60. Ibid., 266.

61. Dane, *"Die heilsame Toilette,"* 62–63.

62. Ibid., 50–51.

63. *Grundriß einer auserlesenen Literatur für die physisch=medizinische Aufklärung, zur Begründung der Felicität im Staate, in der Gesellschaft und im häuslichen Leben; Nach Anleitung und Ordnung des Faustischen Gesundheitskatechismus, wie auch zur Begleitung der Hufland'schen Makrobiotik und der Salzmannschen Werke: vom menschlichen Elende und vom Himmel auf Erden,* bearbeitet von W(ilhelm) J(ulius) A(ugustinus) Vogel (qtd. in Dane, *"Die heilsame Toilette,"* 59).

64. Van Dülmen, *Das irdische Paradies,* 9.

65. Christian Cayus Lorenz Hirschfeld, *Theorie der Gartenkunst* (1779–1785), 5 vols. in 2 (Hildesheim: Olms, 1973), 3:39. Unless otherwise noted, translations are from *The Theory of Garden Art: C. C. L. Hirschfeld,* ed. and trans. Linda B. Parshall (Philadelphia: University of Pennsylvania Press, 2000).

66. Qtd. in van Dülmen, *Das irdische Paradies,* 153.

67. As far as I can tell, the *Journal* did not discuss bathing costumes, which occupied moralists in other countries in connection with seaside resorts.

68. ". . . the ladies become easily fatigued when going for a walk; also dancing, which might be quite useful under certain circumstances, is highly uncomfortable in full dress and becomes unhealthy because the body—weighted down by clothes and unable to move freely—is heated to perspiration and exhaustion" (". . . die Damen werden im Spatzierengehen sogleich zu sehr ermüdet; auch das unter manchen Umständen nützliche Tanzen wird im vollen Putze beschwerlich und nachtheilig, weil der mit Kleidungen beschwerte und eingepresste Körper, keine freyen Bewegungen mehr macht, bis zum Schweiße erhitzt und ermüdet wird"). *Journal,* 1:105.

69. J. C. Flügel, *The Psychology of Clothes* (London; Hoarth, 1930), rpt. trans.

excerpt in Bovenschen, *Die Listen der Mode,* 208–63.

70. Mackie, *Market à la Mode,* 168.

71. E. Wilson, *Adorned in Dreams,* 117.

72. Friedrich Theordor Vischer, "Mode und Zynismus," rpt. in Bovenschen, *Die Listen der Mode,* 45.

73. E. Wilson, *Adorned in Dreams,* 117; Kaja Silverman, "Fragments of a Fashionable Discourse," in Modleski, *Studies in Entertainment,* 145–46.

74. "The bourgeoisie prided itself on its sobriety, good taste and refinement—by contrast with an aristocracy that often seemed course, profligate and immoral. In Germany the very notion of 'civilization' was organized around this sense of superiority by which the educated middle class elevated itself to a sphere that was morally—if not financially—superior to that of the landowning classes." E. Wilson, *Adorned in Dreams,* 118.

75. Jennifer Craik, *The Face of Fashion: Cultural Studies in Fashion* (New York: Routledge, 1994), 13.

76. As women come to see themselves as objects to be observed, they see themselves through the male gaze, thus erasing more direct desire directed at the male body. This is an important process in the creation of femininity and its celebrated value of passivity. Considering fashion as a vehicle for fantasy, Elizabeth Wilson argues that clothes are an indispensable part of the production of the social self (*Adorned in Dreams,* 264).

Chapter 7

1. Wurst, *Frauen und Drama,* 58–59.

2. Sophie von La Roche, *Briefe an Lina* (Speier, 1785; facsimile rpt., Eschborn: Dieter Klotz, 1993).

3. For an overview on La Roche's concept of female education see Monika Nenon, *Autorschaft und Frauenbildung: Das Beispiel Sophie von LaRoche* (Würzburg: Königshausen & Neumann, 1988).

4. La Roche, *Briefe an Lina,* 61.

5. Ibid., 57.

6. Elise Bürger, who perceived her marriage to Gottfried August Bürger as stifling, insisted on keeping up her correspondence with her acquaintances, much to the chagrin of her husband, who considered this a waste of time. According to him, her time would be better spent supervising their household and taking care of their child, whereas she considered her correspondence and other forms of entertainment with her friends (reading together, going on picnics, dancing, etc.) as important forms of sociability and therefore as part of her identity. *Bürgers unglückliche Liebe: Ehestandsgeschichte von Elise Hahn und Gottfried August Bürger,* ed. Hermann Kinder, 2nd ed. (Frankfurt: Insel, 1987), esp. 79–110.

7. I want to thank Clint Goodson of Michigan State University for bring-

ing the text to my attention.

8. Wolfram Mauser, "Geselligkeit: Eine sozialethische Utopie des 18. Jahrhunderts," in Mauser, *Konzepte aufgeklärter Lebensführung*, 31.

9. Ibid., 39.

10. *Der Gesellige, eine moralische Wochenschrift*, ed. Samuel Gotthold Lange and George Friedrich Meier, rpt. Wolfgang Martens, 6 books in 3 vols. (Hildesheim: Olms, 1987).

11. Mauser, "Geselligkeit," 39.

12. Jacob Grimm and Wilhelm Grimm, *Deutsches Wörterbuch*, vol. 4 (Leipzig: S. Hirzel, 1887), 4047.

13. Justus Möser, "Versuch einiger Gemälde unserer Zeit, vormals zu Hannover als ein Wochenblatt ausgetheilet" (Hannover, 1747), in Möser, *Sämtliche Werke historisch-kritische Ausgabe in 14. Bänden*, ed. Werner Kohlschmidt, vol. 1 (Oldeburg, Berlin, 1944), 58.

14. Mauser, "Geselligkeit," 43.

15. Adolph Freiherr Knigge, *Über den Umgang mit Menschen*, ed. Karl-Heinz Göttert (Stuttgart: Reclam, 1991), 12.

16. Emanuel Peter, *Geselligkeiten: Literatur, Gruppenbildung, und Kultureller Wandel im 18. Jahrhundert* (Tübingen: Niemeyer, 1999), 112.

17. Wolfgang Martens, "Geselligkeit im *Gesellige* (1748–50)," *Gesellige Vernunft: Zur Kultur der literarischen Aufklärung, Festschrift für Wolfgang Mauser zum 65 Geburtstag*, ed. Ortud Gutjahr et al. (Würzburg: Königshausen & Neumann, 1993), esp. 176–80.

18. Wolf Lepenies, *Melancholie und Gesellschaft* (Frankfurt: Suhrkamp, 1992); Hannah Arendt, *Rahel Varnhagen: Lebensgeschichte einer deutschen Jüdin aus der Romantik* (Munich: Piper, 1959), trans. Hannah Arendt, *Rachel Varnhagen: The Life of a Jewess*, ed. Liliane Weissberg, trans. Richard and Clara Winston (Baltimore: Johns Hopkins University Press, 1997); Inge Hoffmann-Axthelm, "'Geisterfamilie': Studien zur Geselligkeit der Frühromantik" (Diss., Berlin, 1970). See the discussion on the genesis of the salon in Gaus, *Geselligkeit und das Gesellige*, 15–25.

19. Mauser, "Geselligkeit," 44.

20. Feilchenfeldt qtd. in Gaus, *Geselligkeit und das Gesellige*, 21.

21. Ibid., 35.

22. Ibid., 472.

23. Ibid., 75.

24. The class contrast, which characterizes the nobility as the embodiment of the inferior dilettante culture, is less important than often surmised, most recently by Werner Schlick in *Goethe's* Die Wahlverwandtschaften, 3.

25. Gaus, *Geselligkeit und das Gesellige*, 54–55.

26. La Roche, *Briefe an Lina*, 57.

27. Gaus, *Geselligkeit und das Gesellige*, 77.

28. Rudolf Weil, *Das Berliner Theaterpublikum unter A. W. Ifflands Direktion (1796 bis 1814)* (Berlin: Selbstverlag der Gesellschaft für Theatergeschichte, 1932), 67.

29. "Es ist bekannt, daß Schiller's unsterbliche Jungfrau von Orleans, in Hinsicht des Ganzen, wozu auch die Costums und Decorationen vorzüglich gehören, nirgends so vollkommen gegeben wurde, als auf dem großen National-Theater in Berlin. Vorzüglich prächtig und überraschend ist der ganze Krönungszug zur Cathedrale in Reims. Daher war es eine gute Idee, diesen festlichen Zug, wie er auf dem Theater ausgeführt wird, in einem Kunstblatte darzustellen, welches in Imperial Folio, unter der oben stehenden Aufschrift, vor kurzem in Berlin erschienen ist. ... Das Kunstblatt ist in Contouren radiert; die Gebäude und die Menschengruppen haben einen Aquatinta-Ton erhalten, und dann ist das Ganze in Aquarell auf das sorgfältigste coloriert." *Journal,* 3:136–37. The *Journal* participates in popularizing what it considers this key scene in its depiction as an aquatint etching.

30. Gaus, *Geselligkeit und das Gesellige,* 103.

31. "The 'groupings' are only loosely and spontaneously formed and can be rearranged quickly, but this allows that men and women, young and old, married and unmarried people, can pursue their individual interests within a common framework. Yes, even the informal retreat of individuals with a book or other activities (drawing or others) in the same room does not disturb sociability as such. Furthermore, it is part of the middle-class and democratic identity of these forms of sociability that there is 'complete equality' and that everybody is 'made to feel comfortable.' This was achieved by the informality with which all could come and go, play, listen to music, dance or read, as they please" ("Die 'Fraktionierungen' sind natürlich nur lose, ad hoc und jederzeit aufhebbar, aber sie ermöglichen doch, daß im selben Rahmen neben Männern und Frauen auch Junge und Alte, Verheiratete und Unverheiratete spezifischen Interessen nachgehen können. Ja, sogar eine gewisse lockere Absonderung einzelner mit einem Buch oder einer anderen Beschäftigung wie einer Zeichnung o.ä. innerhalb derselben Räumlichkeit sprengt nicht den geselligen Rahmen als solchen. Es gehört zum bürgerlichen, demokratischen Selbstverständnis dieser Gesellschaften, daß 'eine vollständige Gleichheit' herrschte und 'die Geselligkeit allen gemütlich' machte; und dazu gehörte auch, daß 'in allem, im Kommen und Gehen, im Spiel, Musik und Tanz oder Lesen für sich oder mit anderen, ... die größte Freiheit herrschen sollte"). G. H. Sieverking, *Lebensbild eines hamburgischen Kaufmanns aus dem Zeitalter der französischen Revolution* (1913), qtd. in Schön, *Verlust der Sinnlichkeit,* 187–89.

32. Gaus, *Geselligkeit und das Gesellige,* appendix IV: Friedrich Parthey

[1907], 465–66.

33. Ibid., 36–37.
34. Carl Gottlob Kuettner, *Reise durch Deutschland, Dänemark, Schweden, Norwegen und einen Theil von Italien, in den Jahren 1797. 1798. 1799.* Erster Theil (Leipzig 1801), 237–39, qtd. in Tolkemitt, "Knotenpunkt im Beziehungsnetz der Gebildeten," 181.
35. Karl Wilhelm Böttiger, *Literarische Zustände und Zeitgenossen,* qtd. in Horst Gronemeyer, "Klopstocks Stellung in der Hamburger Gesellschaft," in Stephan and Winter, *Hamburg im Zeitalter der Aufklärung,* 291–92.
36. See Griep, "'Die Handlung,'" 24.
37. Johann Hermann Stöver qtd. in ibid., 27. Others consider the bourgeois lifestyle of the Hamburg merchants excessive. Ibid., 27–31.
38. Of course, it should be added that the common negative cliché associated with Hamburg is that its inhabitants display an excessive focus on business and money and that their forms of entertainment consist largely of physical indulgences: "Weiber, Gärten, Schmäuse und Familienzeremonien sind der Gelehrten wie der Kaufleute meiste Beschäftigung." Christlob Mylius qtd. in ibid., 24.
39. Jakob Friedrich Langerfeld qtd. in ibid., 26.
40. Anon. qtd. in ibid.
41. Langerfeld (qtd. above) was a merchant from Braunschweig; ibid.
42. "Die Tafel ist gut, fein und reichlich, aber nicht übermäßig besetzt. Bei Tische wird nach der vernünftigen französischen Sitte, von allen Schüsseln zugleich gegessen. Jeder nimmt sich, oder läßt sich geben, von welcher Schüssel er will; und so wird es möglich, daß eine Gesellschaft von 40 Personen in einer Stunde abgegessen haben können, wenn sie wollen. Jeder fordert sich Wein, welchen er will, und theilt denen mit, die mit ihm gleichen Geschmack haben. . . . Jeder steht vom Tische auf, geht zu einem Andern, zu Mehreren, zu Allen, wie es ihm einfällt, und solange es ihm gefällt. Jeder verläßt den Tisch ganz, wann es ihm gefällt. Er geht dann in den Garten, besieht Kupferstiche, Gemälde, durchblättert Bücher, setzt sich mit einem Buche an einen Lieblingsort, oder fährt gar stillschweigends in die Stadt zurück." Johann Ludwig Ewald (1799) qtd. in Tolkemitt, "Knotenpunkte im Beziehungsnetz der Gebildeten," 192.
43. Karl August Böttiger, *Literarische Zustände und Zeitgenossen,* ed. Karl Wilhelm Böttiger (1795; Leipzig, 1838), 21–22.
44. Gaus, *Geselligkeit und das Gesellige,* 341.
45. Ibid., 343–51.
46. Irmgard Roebling, "'Frühlingsmomente eines geselligen Vollgenusses': Geselligkeit als kritische Intersubjektivität im Kreis der Rahel Levin," in

Gutjahr et al., *Gesellige Vernunft,* 248.

47. Van Dülmen, *Das irdische Paradies,* 184.

48. Ibid., 181.

49. Regulars at Schopenhauer's salon were Goethe, the Bertuch family, Johannes Daniel, Caroline Falk, Henrich Meyer, Friedrich Wilhelm Riemer, Johan Stephan Schütze, Friedrich Hildebrandt von Einsiedel, Johanne Karoline Amalie von Ludecus, and Friedrich Anton von Conta and his sister. At times they were joined by Christoph Martin Wieland, Karl Ludwig Fernow, Caroline Bardua, Georg Friedrich von Gerstenbergk, and Karl von Holtey. Astrid Köhler, *Salonkultur im klassischen Weimar: Geselligkeit als Lebensform und literarisches Konzept* (Stuttgart: Verlag für Wissenschaft und Forschung, 1996), 91.

50. "Bei Frau Hofrath Schopenhauer sind der Donnerstag und der Sonntag jeder auf seine Art interessant: der erste wegen vieler Sozietät, wo man eine sehr mannigfaltige Unterhaltung findet; der zweite, wo man wegen kleinerer Sozietät genötigt ist, auf eine konzentrierte und konzen trierende Unterhaltung zu denken." "Goethe an Knebel, Weimar den 25. November 1808," in *Gedenkausgabe der Werke, Briefe und Gespräche,* 19:571.

51. Petra Wilhelmy, *Der Berliner Salon im 19. Jahrhundert (1780–1914),* Veröffentlichungen der Berliner Historischen Kommision Bd. 73 (Berlin: de Gruyter, 1989), 24–26. It might very well be that the longer historical period she examines leads her to reconfirm the focus on conversation. As the Schopenhauer example shows, for the decades around 1800 it is too restrictive.

52. *Die Schopenhauers: Der Familienbriefwechsel von Adele, Arthur, Heinrich Floris, und Johanna Schopenhauer,* ed. and intro. Ludger Lütkehaus (Zurich: Haffmans, 1991), 135.

53. Goethe, *Die Wahlverwandtschaften,* 30.

54. *Die Schopenhauers,* 141.

55. Appendix 4, text 7, Gaus, *Geselligkeit und das Gesellige,* 472.

56. For a description of the conventional wisdom see Heyden-Rynch: "Im weitesten Sinne stellt der Salon eine zweckfreie, zwanglose Geselligkeitsform dar, deren Kristallisationspunkt eine Frau bildet. Die Gäste, die sich regelmäßig und ohne besondere Aufforderung zu einem Jour fixe einfinden, die sogenannten Habitués, pflegen miteinander einen freundschaftlichen Umgang. Sie gehören verschiedenen Gesellschaftsschichten und Lebenskreisen an." Verena von der Heyden-Rynsch, *Europäische Salons: Höhepunkte einer versunkenen weiblichen Kultur* (Munich: Artemis & Winkler, 1992), 16.

57. Gaus, *Geselligkeit und das Gesellige,* 123.

58. Roebling, "'Frühlingsmomente eines geselligen Vollgenusses,'" 245.

59. Paul Derks, *Die Schande der heiligen Päderastie. Öffentlichkeit in der deutschen Literatur, 1750–1850* (Berlin: Rosa Winkel, 1990), 130–32. See also Gaus, *Geselligkeit und das Gesellige,* 186–87.
60. Hirschfeld, *Garden Art,* 406.
61. For an overview see Heide Hollmer and Albert Meier, "Kunstzeitschriften," in Fischer, Haefs, and Mix, *Von Almanach bis Zeitung,* 157–75.
62. Ibid., 167.
63. Other examples were "Leichtgläubigkeit, Aberglauben und Fanatismus" (1787); "Hogarth's Leben des Liederlichen, mit Zeichnungen der vorzüglichsten Köpfe erläutert" (1785); "Heirath nach der Mode" (1786); "Ausmarsch der Truppen nach Finchley" (1789); "Folgen der Emsigkeit und des Müssiggangs" (1792); and "Frankreich und England" (1794). Many times, the illustrations create their moralizing satirical impact by contrasting desirable and undesirable activities or states of mind as in the juxtaposition of content/discontent, pleasant/unpleasant, or smart/stupid (1795); by offering a cultural critique in a series of etchings depicting the progression in a day from morning to night in the country, the city, and with the upper class (1797); by depicting the stages of a woman's life in various social settings (1798 and 1799); by contrasting the development of a good and a bad soldier (1800); and by contrasting the cultural effects of war and peace. The publications flourished under the editorship of Lichtenberg, who was also responsible for enlisting Chodowiecki and featuring him prominently.
64. Diers, "Bertuchs Bilderwelt," 438–39.
65. "Beyond the didactic and informative function, Bertuch takes the aesthetic use value of images and the enjoyment of viewing of his readers into consideration." Ibid., 442.
66. He is at the core of the controversy between visual (sensual) and print (rational) culture that Barbara Stafford describes in *Artful Science.*
67. Goethe, *Schriften zur Kunst,* 83–91 (Venice), 91–108 (Dresden).
68. Qtd. in James Sheehan, *Museums in the German Art World: From the End of the Old Regime to the Rise of Modenism* (Oxford: Oxford University Press, 2000), 24–25.
69. Astrid Grieger, "Kunst und Öffentlichkeit in der zweiten Hälfte des 18. Jahrhunderts," in Jäger, *"Öffentlichkeit" im 18. Jahrhundert,* 121–22.
70. Sheehan, *Museums in the German Art World,* 25.
71. Grieger, "Kunst und Öffentlichkeit," 122.
72. Decorative painting extended to other objects such as porcelain and glassware, furniture, etc.
73. Grieger, "Kunst und Öffentlichkeit," 132–33, 135.
74. Goethe, *Die Wahlverwandtschaften,* 210.

75. Ibid., 211.

76. ". . . und unterhielt sie durch das Bild, teils durch die Auslegung." Ibid.

77. "Sie freuten sich, hier in ihrer Einsamkeit die Welt so bequem zu durchreisen, Ufer und Häfen, Berge, Seen und Flüsse. Städte, Kastelle und manches andere Lokal, das in der Geschichte einen Namen hat, vor sich vorbeiziehen zu sehen." Ibid.

78. For an overview on the periodicals specializing in music see Axel Beer, "Musikzeitschriften," in Fischer, Haefs, and Mix, *Von Almanach bis Zeitung*, 233–47. Volume 27 (March 1812) of the *Journal* contained examples of fashionable sheet music, the "Chor zu Romeo und Juliet."

79. See also Gerhard Sauder, "Almanach-Kultur und Empfindsamkeit," in Klussman and Mix, *Literarische Leitmedien*, 16–30.

80. Friedrich Schiller, *Musen-Almanach für das Jahr 1796* (Neustrelitz: Michaelis, 1796).

81. Mix, *Die deutschen Musenalmanache*, 73.

82. See Gabriele Busch-Salmen, "Private gesellige Zirkel und 'musikalische Unterhaltungen,'" in Gabriele Busch-Salmen, Walter Salmen, and Christoph Michel, *Der Weimarer Musenhof: Literatur, Musik und Tanz, Gartenkunst, Geselligkeit, Malerei* (Stuttgart: Metzler, 1998), 94–95.

83. Daniel Gottlob Türk, *Klavierschule oder Anweisung zum Klavierspiele für Lehrer und Lernende*, ed. Erwin R. Jacobi (Leipzig, Halle, 1789; rpt. Kassel: Bärenreiter, 1962).

84. Mix, *Die deutschen Musenalmanache*, 113.

85. George Melchior Kraus, *Chr. M Wieland mit seiner Familie*, 1774/75, oil on canvas, in Busch-Salmen, Salmen, and Michel, *Der Weimarer Musenhof*, 85 (unpaginated).

86. George Kersting, *Stickerin mit abgelegter Gitarre*, 1811, oil on canvas, ibid., 107.

87. See Gabriele Busch-Salmen and Walter Salmen, "Gärten und Parks als 'tönende Natur' und Musizierräume," in Busch-Salmen, Salmen, and Michel, *Der Weimarer Musenhof*, 29–60, esp. 58–60.

88. Linda B. Parshall, introduction to Hirschfeld, *Garden Art*, 34.

89. Hirschfeld, *Garden Art*, 220.

90. "Waldhörner ließen sich in diesem Augenblick vom Schloß herüber vernehmen, bejahten gleichsam und bekräftigten die guten Gesinnungen und Wünsche der beisammen verweilenden Freunde. Stillschweigend hörten sie zu, indem jedes in sich selbst zurückkehrte, und sein eigenes Glück in so schöner Verbindung doppelt empfand." Goethe, *Die Wahlverwandtschaften*, 27.

91. Qtd. in Salmen-Busch and Salmen, "Gärten und Parks," 34.

92. William Ray put forward a similar argument regarding the discursive formation of consensus procedures in his presentation "Speaking of Beauty:

The Aesthetic Disclosure of the Subject," Midwest American Society for Eighteenth-Century Studies (Iowa City, November 9–12, 2001).

93. In *Die Wahlverwandtschaften,* Goethe explores this emerging form of practical cultured engagement with regard to a number of practices. Music is one of them. The limited skills that characterize Eduard's flute playing were probably more the norm than the exception in the use of music as a form of domestic sociable entertainment. Ottilie displays similar traits: "Sie [Ottilie] hatte seine Mängel so zu den ihrigen gemacht, daß daraus wieder ein Art von lebendigem Ganzen entsprang, das sich zwar nicht taktgemäß bewegte, aber doch höchst angenehm und gefällig lautete. Der Komponist selbst hätte seine Freude daran gehabt, sein Werk auf eine so liebevolle Weise entstellt zu sehen" (68). See also Eduard's reaction to criticism: "er war sich eines kindlichen Strebens ohne die mindeste Anmaßung bewußt. Was ihn unterhielt, was ihn erfreute sollte doch mit Schonung von Freunden behandelt werden" (103).

94. Karl August Böttiger, "Plastisch-mimische Darstellungen," *Abend-Zeitung* no. 11–12, Dresden, January 14–15, 1818.

95. See also the art-historical study by Birgit Jooss, *Lebende Bilder: Körperliche Nachahmung von Kunstwerken in der Goethezeit* (Berlin: Reimer, 1999), 218–24.

96. "Die autonom gewordenen Künste begannen ihre mimetische Bindung an die Wirklichkeit abzubauen. Nicht mehr die Repräsentation der tatsächlich vorhandenen Welt, sondern die Präsentation eigener ästhetischer Welten standen nun im Zentrum des Interesses." Ibid., 252.

97. "The fashion for *tableaux vivants* was historically connected with the species of performance called 'attitudes,' whose leading exponent was that meteor of the age of the French Wars, Emma Lady Hamilton. Abetted by the collector and classical enthusiast, Sir William Hamilton, she virtually invented the form, having profited by the prior experience of sitting for an infatuated George Romney in a vast range of personae and passions. Romney painted her as Circe, Calypso, Euphronyne, a Sybil, a Bacchante, Saint Cecilie, Lady Macbeth, Cassandra . . ." Martin Meisel, *Realizations: Narrative, Pictorial, and Theatrical Arts in Nineteenth-Century England* (Princeton: Princeton: University Press, 1983), 338.

98. The German artist Friedrich Rehberg drew a series of attitudes which were in turn engraved by Piroli. Published in Rome in 1794, the work attracted immediate attention in Germany; it was reviewed by the archaeologist Alois Ludwig Hirt in *Der Teutsche Merkur* in 1794, and Karl August Böttiger published his article "Tischbeins Vasen, Lady Hamilton's Attitüden von Rehberg" in the *Journal* 10 (February 1795): 58–85.

99. Jooss's *Lebende Bilder* contains a number of paintings that were copied and thus found their way into the practice of living pictures such as, e.g., the paintings that served as the models in Goethe's *Die Wahlverwandtschaften:* Nicolas Poussin's *Esther von Ahasverus* (ca. 1645; plate 22), Gerard Terborch's *Die väterliche Ermahnung* (ca. 1654–55; plate 24), and Jaques-Louis David's *Belisar bittet um Almosen* (1784; plate 26).

100. Goethe, *Die Wahlverwandtschaften* 170–74.

101. Kirsten Gram Holmström, *Monodrama, Attitudes, Tableaux Vivants: Studies on Some Trends of Theatrical Fashion, 1770–1815* (Stockholm: Almquist & Wiksell, 1967), 119.

102. All etchings and verbal descriptions of attitudes depict the clothing as of the typical neoclassicist white, which foreground the statue-like qualities of the representation. However, the paintings of Elisabeth Vigeé-LeBrun of Emma Harte, the later Lady Hamilton, depict her in the same poses as bacchant and sibyl as Rehberg's drawings but in dark colors, the sibyl in a bright red chemise and medium-blue draperies across her legs, the bacchant in dark brown draperies. It is likely that Vigeé-LeBrun altered the coloring to enhance the painterly effect.

103. *Allgemeine deutsche Real-Encyklopedie für gebildete Stände: Conversationslexikon,* vol. 1 (Leipzig: Brockhaus, 1816), 354–55.

104. "Übertragung der illusionistischen Dreidimensionalität eines zweidimensionalen Werkes in die 'reale' Dreidimensionalität"; Jooss, *Lebende Bilder,* 24.

105. Ibid., 44–82.

106. Meisel, *Realizations,* 47.

107. Jooss, *Lebende Bilder,* 52.

108. "Tableaux nennt man die plastische Darstellung von Gemählden durch lebende Personen, welche jetzt theils als künstlerische Uebung, theils als sinnreiche und reizende Festspiele beliebt sind." *Conversationslexikon,* vol. 9 (1818), 611.

109. Karl August Böttiger, "Van Dycks Landleben," *Abend-Zeitung,* Dresden, no. 218 (1817).

110. Jooss, *Lebende Bilder,* 223.

111. Holmström, *Monodrama, Attitudes, Tableaux Vivants,* 216.

112. Goethe, *Die Wahlverwandtschaften,* 171.

113. Brigitte Peucker, "The Material Image in Goethe's *Wahlverwandtschaften,*" *Germanic Review* 74, no. 3 (1999): 171.

114. Ibid., 209–10.

115. Jooss, *Lebende Bilder,* 240–41.

116. Goethe, *Die Wahlverwandtschaften,* 163.

117. Ibid., 156–72.

118. Ibid., 168–69.

119. Ibid., 171.

120. Holmström, *Monodrama, Attitudes, Tableaux Vivants,* 226–27.

121. Ibid., 227.

122. These mixed performances could also be used as benefits for a variety of humanitarian causes, as in an example from Vienna: we learn that a group of women from the nobility organized an evening of music, recitations, and living pictures, a so-called academy (*Akademie*) for the benefit of poor orphans. *Morgenblatt für gebildete Stände,* February, 22, 1815, 180.

123. In a 1795 piece for the *Journal,* Böttiger describes Lady Hamilton's "enchanting" "play of pantomime": "Ihr Anzug, wenn sie vor einem auserlesenen Kreis ihrer Freunde diese Verwandlungen vornimmt, ist ein ganz einfaches langes weißes Gewand, unter der Brust mit einem kunstlosen Bande gegürtet, ganz wie die Tunika der Alten. Außer diesem hat sie nichts, als einen sehr weiten, freien indischen Schaal oder Schleier, den sie, so wie es die Beschaffenheit der jedesmal hervorzubringende Attitüde fodert, mit einer wunderbaren Behendigkeit und Geschicklichkeit bald lang von ihrem schönen Haar herabfließen, bald in dem schönen Faltenwurf an diesen oder jenen Theil des Körpers sich anschließt, bald leicht flattern, bald nur die Füße bedecken läßt. Kurz dies ist der Zaubermantel einer Fee, durch dessen meisterhaften und auf den malerischen Effekt berechneten Gebrauch sie eine unendliche Mannigfaltigkeit von Bekleidungen hervorzubringen versteht. 'Das Vortheilhafte dieser Kleidung, sagt uns ein urtheilsfähiger Augenzeuge, welche ihre schlanke Gestalt nur leicht verhüllt; ihre langen castanienbraunen Haare, die in einem Nu nach jeder Art von Stellung sich richten; die Gesichtszüge, welche jeden Ausdruck bestimmt zeichnen und durch eine leise Spannung festhalten; und endlich die Mannigfaltigkeit der Stellungen selbst, dieß alles formiert ein in seiner Art einziges Schauspiel.'" *Journal* 10 (February 1795): 79.

124. Veronica Kelly and Dorothea von Mücke, "Introduction: Body and Text in the Eighteenth Century," in *Body and Text in the Eighteenth Century,* ed. Kelly and von Mücke (Stanford: Stanford University Press, 1994), 18.

125. August Langen, "Attitüde und Tableau in der Goethezeit," *Jahrbuch der deutschen Schillergesellschaft* 12 (1968): 201.

126. Walter Grasskamp, *Museumsgründer und Museumsstürmer: Zur Sozialgeschichte des Kunstmuseums* (Munich: Beck, 1981), 30–41. See also Sheehan, *Museums in the German Art World.*

127. MacLeod, "Floating Heads," 67.

128. Langen, "Attitüde und Tableau," 211.

129. "Ich sehe nämlich, wie entfernt man vom wahren Sentiment jeder edlen Art doch so ein glücklicher Affe sein könne." Herder to his wife, February 21, 1789, qtd. in ibid., 213.

130. While one can easily imagine that the specular feast of the attitudes and their playful quality were attractive to a general audience, one wonders what made this (body) art form interesting to artists, art and theater buffs, and intellectuals. What is the latter group's attraction beyond the specular/spectacular voyeuristic pleasure? Their interest in this art form and the pleasure derived from it seems to stem from its spirit of experimentation. The attitudes lent themselves to an exploration of issues raised in the fields of anthropology, aesthetics, and even technology by contemporary theoretical debates on the one hand and their practical applications on the other. In this case, technology came into play in the innovations in and experimentation with lighting techniques. But more importantly, attitudes embodied the practical application of theoretical queries into the intricacies of the pleasurable aesthetic response to a work of art. Especially the relationship between the body and its representation in the visual arts was of central interest at the time. Therefore the level of interest in statues was high in the second half of the eighteenth century. This fascination with the body and its representation is intricately linked to the new appreciation of antiquity, or more accurately, the German theoreticians' own vision of antiquity, based on a rather restrictive sample of Greek art.
Certainly, the technical aspects of display and lighting were of interest to a specialist audience. The attitudes were usually performed in a room covered with dark cloth to form a nondistracting canvas to set off the performer's body. Hamilton went so far as to have a box constructed in the shape of a picture frame covered with black velvet as the backdrop for some of Lady Hamilton's performances. About the performances of Hendel-Schütz we know that a new form of stage lighting focused the light of eighty candles (reflected by a silver-plated device) from the side onto the performer's body (Langen, "Attitüde und Tableau," 221). While the audience sat in a darkened room, the light illuminated the performer's body, which was placed on a dark cloth serving as the canvas for the presentation. The play of light and shadow accentuated the rounded surfaces of the body in a fashion similar to the contemporary practice of illuminating statues with torch or candlelight.

131. Ibid., 213.

132. Goethe, *Die Wahlverwandtschaften*, 169–70.

133. Peter Brooks, *Body Work: Objects of Desire in Modern Narrative* (Cambridge: Harvard University Press, 1993), xii.

134. "Zwar begreift wohl ein jeder von selbst, dass gerade der mächtigste

Zauber in dieser Pantomime, *die Grazie der fortschreitenden Bewegung,* die schnellen überraschenden Uebergänge aus einer Stellung in die andere, die unbeschreibliche Regsamkeit und Bewegsamkeit aller Theile des schönen Körpers, die Zartheit der Schwingungen und Umrisse, durchaus durch kein Mittel der bildenden Kunst ausgedrückt werden können." Hirt qtd. in Holmström, *Monodrama, Attitudes, Tableaux Vivants,* 187.

135. Herder's essay on "Plastik" (1778) discusses the statue as art form; Lessing's "Laokoon" distinguishes between verbal and visual arts; and Winkelmann attempted to bring the beauty of the Hercules torso of Belvedere (1759) to life with language. See Karin Wurst, "Spellbinding: The Body as Art/Art as Body in *Attitüden,*" *Lessing Yearbook* 32 (2001): 151–81.

136. "Das flackernde Licht der Fackel verlieh den Statuen Bewegung, die—als etwas dem Lebenden immanentes—gleichgesetzt wurde mit 'Anmut und Leben.' Darüberhinaus erhielten sie durch die verstärkte Licht-Schatten-Wirkung auch malerische Qualitäten." Jooss, *Lebende Bilder,* 242.

137. "Das Auge ist nur Wegweiser, nur die Vernunft der Hand; die Hand allein gibt *Formen,* Begriffe deßen, was sie *bedeuten,* was in ihnen *wohnet.*" Herder, "Plastik: Einige Wahrnehmungen über Form und Gestalt aus Pygmalions bildendem Traume," in *Herders Sämmtliche Werke,* ed. Bernhard Suphan (Berlin: Weidmannsche Buchhandlung, 1892), 8:39.

138. "Eine Statue muß *leben:* ihr Fleisch muß sich beleben: ihr Gesicht und Mine sprechen. Wir müssen sie anzutasten glauben und fühlen, daß sie sich unter unsern Händen erwärmt. Wir müssen sie vor uns stehen sehen, und fühlen, daß sie zu uns spricht. Sieh da zwei Hauptstücke der Sculptur *Fleisch und Geist!*

1. *Fleisch.* Seine Illusion ist offenbar fürs Gefühl. Das Auge tritt in die Spitzen der Finger: wir vergessen die kalte Oberfläche, als obs Malerei wäre: wir sehen nicht, wir fühlen die zarte Haut, das runde Knie, die sanfte Wange, die schöne Brust, die weiche Hüfte—den schönen Umriß des Körpers." Herder, "Studien und Entwürfe zur Plastik: 1. Von der Bildhauerkunst fürs Gefühl," *Herders Sämmtliche Werke,* 8:88.

139. Mieke Bal, *Reading "Rembrandt": Beyond the Word-Image Opposition* (Cambridge: Cambridge University Press, 1991), 150.

140. "Es ist nicht blos genug, daß sich alles unter unsern Händen erwärme: es muß ein *Geist* in diesem Fühlbaren wohnen, der unmittelbar zu unserm Geist spreche: durch eine Sympathie, durch eine Anziehung, die sich der Wollust nähert." Herder, "Studien und Entwürfe zur Plastik," 91.

141. "Die Tradition sagt: daß brutale Menschen gegen plastische Meisterwerke von sinnlichen Begierden entzündet wurden." Goethe, "Diderots

Versuch über die Malerei," *Schriften zur Kunst,* 212.

142. Goethe, *From My Life: Poetry and Truth,* trans. Robert Heitner, *Goethe's Collected Works,* vol. 4 (New York: Suhrkamp, 1987), 363.

143. Goethe, *Aus meinem Leben: Dichtung und Wahrheit,* vol. 10 of *Gedenkausgabe der Werke, Briefe und Gespräche,* ed. Ernst Beutler (Zurich: Artemis, 1954), 536.

144. ". . . kein echter Künstler verlangt sein Werk neben ein Naturprodukt, oder gar an dessen Stelle zu setzten; der es täte, wäre wie ein Mittelgeschöpf aus dem Reiche der Kunst zu verstoßen, und im Reiche der Natur nicht aufzunehmen. Dem Dichter kann man wohl verzeihen, wenn er, um eine interessante Situation in der Phantasie zu erregen, seinen Bildhauer in eine selbst hervorgebrachte Statue wirklich verliebt denkt, wenn er ihm Begierden zu derselben andichtet, wenn er sie endlich in seinen Armen erweichen läßt. Das gibt wohl ein lüsternes Geschichtchen, das sich ganz artig anhört; für den bildenden Künstler bleibt es ein unwürdiges Märchen. Die Tradition sagt: daß brutale Menschen gegen plastische Meisterwerke von sinnlichen Begierden entzündet wurden; die Liebe eines hohen Künstlers aber zu seinem trefflichen Werk ist ganz anderer Art; sie gleicht der frommen heiligen Liebe unter Blutsverwandten und Freunden. Hätte Pygmalion seiner Statue begehren können, so wäre er ein Pfuscher gewesen, unfähig eine Gestalt hervorzubringen, die verdient hätte, als Kunstwerk oder als Naturwerk geschätzt zu werden." Goethe, "Diderots Versuch über die Malerei," 212.

145. Susan Sontag, *The Volcano Lover: A Romance* (New York: Anchor Books Doubleday, 1992), 71.

146. Schiller, "Ueber die ästhetische Erziehung," 360, letter 15. "Durch die Schönheit wird der sinnliche Mensch zur Form und zum Denken geleitet; durch die Schönheit wird der geistige Mensch zur Materie zurückgeführt, und der Sinnewelt wiedergegeben." Ibid., 365, letter 18.

147. Andreas Gailus, "Of Beautiful and Dismembered Bodies: Art as Social Discipline in Schiller's 'On the Aesthetic Education of Man,'" in Wilson and Holub, *Impure Reason,* 160.

148. Ibid., 162.

149. Silverman, "Fragments of a Fashionable Discourse," 139–52.

150. Ibid., 147–48.

151. Goethe's famous description in *Dichtung und Wahrheit* makes no mention of the religious themes which were an important part of Harte's and Hendel-Schütz's performances—an indication that this aspect did not interest him.

152. Silverman, "Fragments of a Fashionable Discourse," 147–48.

153. Barthes, *The Pleasure of the Text,* 9.
154. Bill Nichols, *Ideology and Image* (Bloomington: Indiana University Press, 1981), 123.
155. Addison, "The Pleasures of the Imagination," no. 412, in *The Spectator,* 3:541.
156. Holmström, *Monodrama, Attitudes, Tableaux Vivants,* 118–19.
157. See also my article "Designing the Self: Fashion and the Body," in *Body Dialectics in the Age of Goethe,* vol. 55 of *Amsterdamer Beiträge,* ed. Holger Pausch and Marianne Henn (Amsterdam: Rodopi, 2003), 47–66.
158. Reprinted in Wurst, "Spurensicherung."
159. *Journal* 26 (March 1811): 147–50.
160. In this case, the original representation of a vestalin (priestess) is copied and read as an erotic icon. If Bürger's spectator wishes that his object of admiration reveal more of her body, he is clearly not interested in the religious aspect.
161. Goethe could not have seen Emma Harte perform attitudes in 1787 because they were developed later; it seems he constructed his description from conversations and descriptions by others, mixing them with the descriptions of performances of others like Hendel-Schütz (in 1800 in Weimar). See also Waltraud Maierhofer, "Goethe on Emma Hamilton's 'Attitudes': Can Classicist Art Be Fun?" *Goethe Yearbook* 9 (1999): 222–52.
162. Goethe, *Italian Journey,* trans. Robert R. Heitner, ed. Thomas P. Saine and Jeffrey Sammons, in *Goethe's Collected Works,* vol. 6 (New York: Suhrkamp, 1989), 171.
163. Goethe, *Italienische Reise,* vol. 11 of *Gedenkausgabe der Werke, Briefe und Gespräche,* ed. Ernst Beutler (Zurich: Artemis, 1954), March 17, 1787, 228–29.
164. The description of this scene—an older, aristocratic male holding the light (carrying a torch?) for a young, lower-class, uneducated girl—also serves as an ironic distancing device, dismissing the art form as sensual dilettante and an artistically naive form of cultural revival.
165. Lacking a narrative quality, the impact seems less proto-filmic or theatrical, but a modern critic might be reminded of electronic morphing techniques *ante facto.* We can imagine that the sense of wonder this created was similar to that of its modern-day technological version.
166. He notes: "daß mir unsere schöne Unterhaltende doch eigentlich als ein geistloses Wesen vorkommt, die wohl mit ihrer Gestalt bezahlen, aber durch keinen seelenvollen Ausdruck der Stimme, der Sprache sich geltend machen kann." Goethe, *Italienische Reise,* May 27, 1787, 363. As if to distance himself from his fascination with the beautiful spectacle, he

reminds us that as a woman she does not measure up to his ideal image of women as a mixture of physical attractiveness, education, a beautiful soul, and sentiment.

167. In his *History of Ancient Art* (*Geschichte der Kunst des Alterthums,* 1764), Winckelmann's description of beauty in statuary also cautions against too much expressiveness because emotion alters the facial features and the body's posture, adversely affecting the beauty of form.

168. Gotthold Ephraim Lessing, "Laokoon: oder Über die Grenzen der Mahlerey und Poesie," in *Sämtliche Schriften,* ed. Karl Lachmann and Franz Muncker (Stuttgart: Göschen, 1893), 19.

169. Goethe, "On the Laocoon Group," in *Essays on Art and Literature,* trans. Ellen von Nardroff and Ernest H. von Nardroff, ed. John Gearey, vol. 2 (New York: Suhrkamp, 1986), 17–18.

170. Goethe, "Über Laokoon," *Schriften zur Kunst,* 166.

171. Ibid.

172. Jooss, *Lebende Bilder,* 241–42.

173. Herder, "Plastik," 39.

174. Ibid., 88–89, 91.

175. Sander Gilman, *Sexuality: An Illustrated History; Representing the Sexual in Medicine and Culture from the Middle Ages to the Age of AIDS* (New York: Wiley, 1989), 10.

176. Ibid., 40.

177. Herder, "Studien und Entwürfe zur Plastik," 91.

Chapter 8

1. Leisure travel has met with the same critical disdain as other forms of entertainment. As Rudy Koshar summarizes: "One of the central problems of much scholarship on leisure travel is that it has treated tourists as malleable dupes cowed by the commercialized itineraries of a bourgeoning tourist industry" (204). His reservations with reference to travel in the nineteenth and twentieth centuries are even more apt for our time frame. See also his overview. Koshar, *German Travel Cultures* (Oxford: Berg, 2000), esp. 1–18. Koshar's analysis regards travel as a form of leisure that potentially allows the individual to make sense of an existential fact of modern life: the consciousness of displacement (8). He sees this as a hermeneutical search for depth (12).

2. See the discussion in Simanowski, *Die Verwaltung des Abenteuers,* 141.

3. Ibid., 149.

4. Ursula Becher, *Geschichte des modernen Lebensstils. Essen-Wohnen-Freizeit-Reisen* (Munich: Beck, 1990), 197–98, 204–5. Rudy Koshar, "'What Ought to Be Seen': Tourist Guidebooks and National Identities in Modern Germany and Europe," *Journal of Contemporary History* 33 (1998):

339; Koshar, *German Travel Cultures*, 8.

5. Orvar Löfgren, *On Holiday: A History of Vacationing* (Berkeley: University of California Press, 1999), 7; John Urry, *The Tourist Gaze: Leisure and Travel in Contemporary Societies* (London: Sage, 1990).

6. "The Grand Tour's sites were determined in large part by the political interests of the European aristocracy and the 'managerial classes' of the developing nation states. Diplomatic and official relationships often decided where the scion of an aristocratic family would tour, or whom the aspiring state official would meet. Even when the cultural pull of Italy or Greece shaped itineraries, participants in the Grand Tour understood that their activity prepared them for later diplomatic or political service." Koshar, *German Travel Cultures*, 55.

7. Elise Bürger, *Lilienblätter und Zypressen-Zweige* von Theodora (Frankfurt: Heller und Rohm, 1826), 78–178.

8. Goethe, *Italienische Reise*, Rome, December 13, 1786, 161.

9. In addition to the obvious differences between Goethe and von der Recke, the disparity in age gave the descriptions a different quality. Goethe was under forty, and von der Recke (1754–1833) was fifty. She labels herself as past the prime of her life ("über den Mittag meines Lebens hinaus"), and her gesture is one of taking stock, of preparing for what she considers a serious and difficult part of her life. *Tagebuch einer Reise durch einen Theil Deutschlands und durch Italien (1804–1806) von Elisa von der Recke*, ed. Hofrath Böttiger, 4 vols. (Berlin: Nicolaische Buchhandlung, 1817), 1:x. Goethe's tenor, on the other hand, is one of youthful anticipation of an important stage in his life that will bring even greater personal rewards for his future: "Die Wiedergeburt, die mich hier von innen heraus umarbeitet, wirkt immer fort." *Italienische Reise*, December 20, 1786, 163.

10. "Ueberdem aber glaubte ich, noch einen inneren Beruf zu vernehmen, der mich aufforderte, meine Beobachtungen, wie gering auch ihre Wirkung ausfallen möge, den Zeitgenossen darzulegen, um die Aufmerksamkeit der Unbefangenen gewissen Bestrebungen zuzuwenden, die eine Verfinsterung unseren höchsten, heiligsten Angelegenheiten erzielen. . . ." Von der Recke, *Tagebuch einer Reise*, 4:iv.

11. Ibid., 239.

12. Barbara Maria Stafford, *Voyage into Substance: Art, Science, Nature, and the Illustrated Travel Account, 1740–1840* (Cambridge: MIT Press, 1984), 4.

13. Ibid., 25, 40.

14. *Bibliothek der neuesten und wichtigsten Reisebeschreibungen zur Erweiterung der Erdkunde nach einem systematischen Plane* bearbeitet, und in Verbindung mit einigen anderen Gelehrten gesammelt und herausgegeben von M. Spengler und T. Ehrmann Bd. 15 (Weimar: Landes-

Industrie Comptoir, 1804). Here reports—some in translation—from discoveries are collected and made available to the reading public.

15. Goethe, *Italienische Reise*, September 14, 1786, 41. Johann Karl Wilhelm Voigt (1752–1821), for example, sold such rock collections. "Collecting and traveling were intimately related troughout the history of modern tourism." Koshar, *German Travel Cultures*, 21. See also Löfgren, *On Holiday*, 17.

16. Goethe, *Italienische Reise*, September 21, 1786, 58–59.

17. Goethe, *Italian Journey*, 53–54; *Italienische Reise*, Padua, September 27, 1786, 65.

18. Goethe, *Italian Journey*, 63; *Italienische Reise*, October 3, 1786, 80.

19. Koshar, *German Travel Cultures*, 30.

20. Klaus Laermann, "Raumerfahrung und Erfahrungsraum: Einige Überlegungen zu Reiseberichten aus Deutschland vom Ende des 18. Jahrhunderts," in *Reise und Utopie: Zur Literatur der Spätaufklärung*, ed. Hans Joachim Piechotta (Frankfurt: Suhrkamp, 1976), 73.

21. Simanowski, *Die Verwaltung des Abenteuers*, 150.

22. Elise Bürger, "Die Gefahr und der Postknecht auf der Reise nach Trier," *Lilienblätter und Zypressen-Zweige*, 153–63.

23. Ibid., 154.

24. Simanowski, *Die Verwaltung des Abenteuers*, 150.

25. Goethe, *Italian Journey*, Trent, September 11, 1786, 25; *Italienische Reise*, Trient, September 11, 1786, early morning, 27.

26. Goethe, *Italian Journey*, Rome, November 1, 1786, 104; *Italienische Reise*, Rom, November 1, 1786, 137.

27. Goethe, *Italian Journey*, November 10, 1786, 110; *Italienische Reise*, November 10, [1786], 146.

28. Von der Recke, *Tagebuch einer Reise*, March 16, 1806, 1:74.

29. ". . . denn der wohlklingende Name *Tivoli*, den ich so oft und immer in Begleitung lieblicher Bilder aussprechen hörte, hatte natürlich in meiner Phantasie eine romantisch anmuthige Vorstellung hervorgebracht, gegen welche freilich die unansehnliche Stadt selbst, getrennt von ihren reizenden Umgebungen, widerwärtig abstechen mußte." Ibid., May 14, 1806, 151.

30. I agree with Pierre Bourdieu, who cautions that immediate naive access to artifacts is merely a myth: "Es gibt keine Wahrnehmung, die nicht einen unbewußten Code einschlösse; dem Mythos vom 'reinen Auge' als einer Begnadung, wie sie allein der Einfalt und der Unschuld zuteil wird, kann nicht nachdrücklich genug widersprochen werden." Bourdieu, *Zur Soziologie der symbolischen Formen*, trans. Wolfgang Fietkau, 6th ed. (1974; Frankfurt: Suhrkamp, 1997), 162.

31. Ibid., 172–73.

32. Von der Recke, *Tagebuch einer Reise,* May 28, 1806, 1:183–84.

33. Ibid., May 12, 1806, 160.

34. Goethe, *Italian Journey,* September 11, 1786, 26; *Italienische Reise,* September 11, 1786, 28. Heinrich Roos (1631–73) was a Dutch painter famous for animal scenes.

35. Stephanie Ross, *What Gardens Mean* (Chicago: University of Chicago Press, 1998), 124.

36. Von der Recke, *Tagebuch einer Reise,* May 29, 1806, 1:186.

37. Koshar, *German Travel Cultures,* 59.

38. Von der Recke, *Tagebuch einer Reise,* May 6, 1806, 1:131.

39. Ibid.

40. Von Trotha, *Angenehme Empfindungen,* 39.

41. Joseph Addison, *Anmerkungen über verschiedene Teile von Italien* (Altenburg: Paul Emanuel Richter, 1752), and especially Edmund Burke's *A Philosophical Inquiry into the Origins of Our Ideas of the Sublime and Beautiful* (1757) and their heirs in the German aesthetic discourse, Barthold Heinrich Brockes (1680–1747) and Albrecht von Haller (1708–77). Qtd. in von Trotha, *Angenehme Empfindungen,* 19. For a genesis of the sublime, which goes beyond the scope of this study, see Begemann, *Furcht und Angst,* and Carsten Zelle, *Angenehmes Grauen: Literaturhistorische Beiträge zur Ästhetik des Schrecklichen im achtzehnten Jahrhundert* (Hamburg: Felix Meiner, 1987).

42. Von der Recke, *Tagebuch einer Reise,* July 21, 1806, 1:363.

43. "Meine Empfindung ist mir deutlich, daß wenn ich aus dem Gebirge in die Ebene komme, es mir zu Muthe ist, als wenn ich eine Gemähldegalerie verlassen hätte, und in ein Zimmer mit nackten Wänden oder mit einfachen Tapeten behangen, einträte." Christian Garve, *Popularphilosophische Schriften über literarische, ästhetische, und gesellschaftliche Gegenstände,* ed. Kurt Wölfel, facsimile rpt., vol. 2 (Stuttgart: Metzler, 1974), 1073.

44. Alexander Nehamas, *The Art of Living: Socratic Reflections from Plato to Foucault* (Berkeley: University of California Press, 1998), 10.

45. Michel Foucault, *The History of Sexuality,* vol. 3, *The Care of the Self,* trans. Robert Hurley (New York: Random House, 1986), 89.

46. Nehamas, *The Art of Living,* 177–78, 179.

47. Hirschfeld, *Gartenkunst,* 1:155; *Garden Art,* 147.

48. Koshar, *German Travel Cultures,* 56.

49. Löschburg, *History of Travel,* 81.

50. "Anblick der Meereswogen, ihr Leuchten und das Rollen ihres Donners." Georg Christoph Lichtenberg, "Warum hat Deutschland noch kein großes öffentliches Seebad?" in *Georg Christoph Lichtenberg Schriften und Briefe,* ed. Wolfgang Promies, 2nd ed. (Munich: Beck, 1973), 3:96.

51. Hirschfeld, *Gartenkunst,* 1:162; *Garden Art,* 152.

52. Stafford, *Voyage into Substance,* 356.

53. See the discussion in Begemann, *Furcht und Angst,* 116.

54. Schiller, "Vom Erhabenen," 178.

55. Löfgren, *On Holiday,* 116–20.

56. Elise Bürger, "Mein Aufenthalt in Karlsbad und in Franzensbrunn, im Jahre 1815," *Lillienblätter und Zypressen-Zweige,* 136–37.

57. Ibid., 136.

58. "Es war im Dorfe Hammer, wohin wir nicht allein der Forellen zu lieb, nein! Weit mehr des lieblichen Plätzchens wegen, oft spazierten . . ." Ibid.

59. Elise Bürger, "Ein Sommermorgen in Baden-Baden 1808," *Lilienblätter und Zypressen-Zweige,* 86.

60. Elise Bürger, "Mein Aufenthalt," 139.

61. Ibid., 135–36.

62. Hirschfeld, *Gartenkunst,* 5:85; *Garden Art,* 414–17.

63. Elise Bürger, "Einer meiner schönsten Tage in Frankfurt am Main," *Lilienblätter und Zypressen-Zweige,* 104–11.

64. Ibid., 105.

65. Ibid., 111.

66. Carole Fabricant, "The Literature of Domestic Tourism and the Public Consumption of Private Property," in *The New Eighteenth Century: Theory, Politics, English Literature,* ed. Felicity Nussbaum and Laura Brown (1987; New York: Routledge, 1991), 257.

67. Ibid.

68. Richard Faber, "Parkleben: Zur sozialen Idyllik Goethes," in *Goethes Wahlverwandtschaften: Kritische Modelle und Diskursanalysen zum Mythos der Literatur,* ed. Norbert W. Bolz (Hildesheim: Gerstenberg, 1981), 96.

69. Emmrich and Schröder, "Weimarer historische Interieurs," 508–9. While the authors discuss elements of interior design, it stands to reason that the same pattern of mutual influence also existed for the elements of outdoor design. Bertuch had been charged with supervising the design of the park construction in Weimar (1787–96). See also Angelika Schneider, "Friedrich Justin Bertuch—Ein Beförderer der Gartenkunst," in Kaiser and Seifert, *Friedrich Justin Bertuch,* 629–57.

70. Hirschfeld, *Gartenkunst,* 2:86; *Garden Art,* 233.

71. Hirschfeld, *Gartenkunst,* 1:157; *Garden Art,* 149.

72. Hirschfeld, *Gartenkunst,* 2:130; *Garden Art,* 251.

73. Peter de Bolla, "The charm'd eye," in Kelly and von Mücke, *Body and Text in the Eighteenth Century,* 94.

74. "The tourist was encouraged to rely on appearances and fleeting surfaces, on sights that could be apprehended in a single glance rather than ones

that required intensive scrutiny or reflection, thereby threatening to become tedious and burdensome, or to slow down the progress of one's crowded itinerary, by engrossing the attention for too long." Fabricant, "Literature of Domestic Tourism," 260.

75. "Such exclusivity depends upon the continuing educational and social elitism which trains the eye to rest on the object of attention, peering studiously until it gives up its meanings. It is a gaze founded in knowledge, a knowing eye that teases out allusions and delights in the play of wit." De Bolla, "The charm'd eye," 94.

76. Stafford, *Voyage into Substance*, 6.

77. Norbert W. Bolz, "Ästhetisches Opfer: Die Foren der Wünsche in Goethes *Wahlverwandtschaften*," in Bolz, *Goethes* Wahlverwandtschaften, 77.

78. Goethe, *Elective Affinities*, 93; Goethe, *Die Wahlverwandtschaften*, 9. Page numbers for the following examples are given parenthetically in the text.

79. "After all, don't we all enjoy taking a long drive to drink coffee or eat fish that we would not have enjoyed so much at home? We like to have a little change and to see different things" ("Macht man nicht gern eine entfernte Spazierfahrt, um einen Kaffee zu trinken, einen Fisch zu genießen, der uns zuhause nicht so gut geschmeckt hätte? Wir verlangen Abwechslung und fremde Gegenstände"). Goethe, *Elective Affinities*, 130; Goethe, *Die Wahlverwandtschaften*, 66.

80. Hirschfeld, *Gartenkunst*, 1:155; *Garden Art*, 147–48.

81. Bolz, "Ästhetisches Opfer," 78.

82. Faber, "Parkleben," 147.

83. Goethe, *Elective Affinities*, 223; Goethe, *Die Wahlverwandtschaften*, 213.

84. Jochen Hörisch, "Die Dekonstruktion der Sprache und der Advent neuer Medien in Goethes *Wahlverwandtschaften*," *Merkur* 52 (1998): 826–39.

85. Ross, *What Gardens Mean*, 85.

86. Goethe, *Die Wahlverwandtschaften*, 57.

87. Susanne Müller, "Über Englische Gärten, französische Landsitze und den 'Park bey Weimar': Die Gartenkunst im *Journal des Luxus und der Moden*," presentation at the symposium "Das *Journal des Luxus und der Moden*: Kultur um 1800," Jena 2000.

88. Ross, *What Gardens Mean*, 87.

89. Other gardens playfully alluded to paintings or copied certain aspects of a painting within the limits of the genre (garden). It was fashionable to re-create a garden in the "Old Master" cast of many eighteenth-century landscape paintings. To this effect tourists of the time imposed these subdued tonalities on the natural landscape by viewing it through a "Claude glass." Ibid., 98.

90. Von Trotha, *Angenehme Empfindungen,* 295.

91. De Bolla, "The charm'd eye," 94.

92. Ibid.

93. Hirschfeld, *Gartenkunst,* 1:155; *Garden Art,* 147.

94. Qtd. in von Trotha, *Angenehme Empfindungen,* 120.

95. Ross, *What Gardens Mean,* 166.

96. Helmut Schneider's interpretation of Goethe's *Die Wahlverwandtschaften* discusses the parallel relationship between garden design, the modern concept of love, and the process of modernization dissolving feudal society. "Für diesen epochalen Vorgang der Moderne, der den globalen Hintergrund des Romans bildet, steht die ästhetische Vergegenständlichung der unmittelbaren Naturumgebung, die das von Charlotte initiierte und von den anderen Figuren in leidenschaftlichem Eifer aufgenommene Projekt der Umgestaltung des alten Schloßgartens ausmacht. Was die Ehethematik auf der sozial- und kulturgeschichtlichen Ebene bedeutet, nämlich die Auflösung der altständischen-vormodernen Ehe und ihre Transformation in die romantische Liebesbeziehung, das spiegelt sich auch in Natur und Landschaft; den Wahl*verwandt*schaften entsprechen die Wahl*land*schaften." Helmut Schneider, "Wahllandschaften: Mobilisierung der Natur und das Darstellungsproblem der Moderne in Goethes *Wahlverwandtschaften,*" in *Rereading Romanticism,* ed. Martha Helfer (Amsterdam: Rodopi, 2000), 287.

97. David Watkin, *The English Vision: The Pictoresque in Architecture, Landscape, and Garden Design* (London: John Murrey, 1982), vii.

98. Ross, *What Gardens Mean,* 133.

99. Ibid., 137.

100. Malcom Andrews, *The Search for the Pictoresque: Landscape Aesthetics and Tourism in Britain, 1760–1800* (Stanford: Stanford University Press, 1989), 39.

101. Ross, describing this kind of "picturesque tourism" in England, mentions specific guidebooks that suggested the proper angles and perspectives from which to produce such paintings and that taught the conventions of landscape painting—albeit in a rather rigid and conventionalized form. *What Gardens Mean,* 126.

102. Goethe, *Die Wahlverwandtschaften,* 211.

103. Ibid., 57.

104. Parshall, "Introduction," 6–9.

105. Hirschfeld, *Garden Art,* 85, 123.

106. Ibid., 133.

107. Ibid., 134.

108. Ibid., 142–44.

109. V. Neuenhahn d. Jüngere, ed., *Annalen der Gärtnerey: Nebst einem Intel-*

ligenzblatt für Garten- und Blumen-Freunde (Erfurt: Keysersche Buchhandlung, 1795), 51.

110. The early-nineteenth-century landscape designer John Claudius Loudon explained the unique situation of England with its advanced position in agricultural development: "As the lands devoted to agriculture in England were, sooner than in any other country in Europe, generally enclosed with hedges and hedgerow trees, so the face of the country in England, sooner than in any other part of Europe, produced an appearance which bore a closer resemblance to country seats laid out in the geometrical style; and for this reason, an attempt to imitate the irregularity of nature in laying out pleasure grounds was made in England sooner than in any other part of the world." Qtd. in Tom Williamson, *Polite Landscapes: Gardens and Society in Eighteenth-Century England* (Baltimore: Johns Hopkins University Press, 1995), 3.

111. "Indeed, here these pleasures are heightened and multiplied exactly to the degree that reason and taste employ the charms of cultivation to render a garden superior to the untouched landscape" ("Ja diese Vortheile und Ergötzungen erhöhen und vervielfältigen sich hier in diesem Grade, in welchem Vernunft und Geschmack bemüht sind, einen Garten durch Reize der Cultur über eine sich selbst überlassene Gegend zu erheben"). Hirschfeld, *Gartenkunst,* 1:154; *Garden Art,* 146.

112. Hirschfeld, *Gartenkunst,* 5:47; *Garden Art,* 397.

113. Hirschfeld, *Gartenkunst,* 5:57–62; *Garden Art,* 401.

114. Hirschfeld, *Garden Art,* 398.

115. Parshall, "Introduction," 1.

116. Van Dülmen, *Das irdische Paradies,* 6.

117. Hirschfeld, *Gartenkunst,* 1:154; *Garden Art,* 146.

118. *Journal* 4 (May 1789): 226.

119. Goethe, "Über den Dilettantismus," 730.

120. Van Dülmen, *Das irdische Paradies,* 30–32.

121. A. Schneider, "Friedrich Justin Bertuch," appendix 3, 652–54,

122. Ibid., 649.

123. Parshall, "Introduction," 5.

124. A list of suitable publications of interest to the middle class nonprofessional gardener and garden designer ("Garten-Miscellen"; "Gartenliteratur") rounded out the informational aspect of the publication.

125. Parshall, "Introduction," 48.

126. Hirschfeld, *Gartenkunst,* 1:xiii; *Garden Art,* 69.

127. *Taschenkalender auf das Jahr 1798 für Natur- und Gartenfreuden: Mit Abbildungen von Hohenheim und andern Kupfern* (Tübingen: Cotta'sche Buchhandlung, 1798). This is a small pocket book, slightly larger than palm-sized, densely printed with small lettering and containing illustrations and

a large fold-out etching of the gardens at the Hohenheim castle. Its price is given as 1 Rthlr 4gr, sächsisch oder 2 fl.rheinisch.

128. Philip Jacob Röder, ed., *Lehrbegriff der Baumzucht und deren Veredlungsarten für Liebhaber und Landleute* (Coburg: Rudolph August Wilhelm Ahl, 1796).

129. Williamson, *Polite Landscapes*, 114.

130. A. Schneider, "Friedrich Justin Bertuch," 646.

131. The interest in landscape gardening was of course not limited to the bourgeoisie; the new designs replaced the more formal designs at the courts as well. The mixed society in Weimar, e.g., was famous for their interest and engagement in landscape design and the enjoyment of this cultivated nature. Wieland, Johann Friedrich Reichardt (1752–1814, court conductor under Fredrick the Great and Friedrich Wilhelm II in Potsdam and later musical adviser to Goethe in Weimar), and Goethe were all passionate about their private gardens. See Busch-Salmen, Salmen, and Michel, *Der Weimarer Musenhof*, esp. 33–36.

132. Röder, *Lehrbegriff der Baumzucht*, 1; see also van Dülmen, *Das irdische Paradies*, 66–75.

133. Röder, *Lehrbegriff der Baumzucht*, 10.

134. Ibid., 11.

135. A. Schneider, "Friedrich Justin Bertuch," 643–44.

136. Van Dülmen, *Das irdische Paradies*, 75–81.

137. A. Schneider, "Friedrich Justin Bertuch," 647.

138. Damm, *Christiane und Goethe*.

139. For example, in her prose narratives in *Lilienblätter und Zypressen-Zweige*.

140. "Schriftsätze und Predigten wurden im Garten aufgesetzt, Briefe und sogar Bücher hier geschrieben. Die heitere, unbeschwerte Atmosphäre in der umgebenden Natur war für viele geistig Arbeitende geradezu ein Stimulans, das zu neuem kreativen Elan verhalf." Van Dülmen, *Das irdische Paradies*, 164.

141. Hirschfeld, *Gartenkunst*, 5:74; *Garden Art*, 409.

142. Hirschfeld *Gartenkunst*, 1:155–56; *Garden Art*, 147.

143. Wegmann, *Diskurse der Empfindsamkeit*, 91.

144. "Zur freien und unverfälschten Natur zählt wesentlich eine Zeiterfahrung, die ganz auf den Genuß und Nachvollzug der natürlichen Tages- bzw. Jahreszeiten abstellt." Ibid., 95.

145. Hirschfeld, *Garden Art*, 148.

146. Ibid., 149.

Chapter 9

1. Weil, *Das Berliner Theaterpublikum*, 59.

2. Ibid.; Elise Bürger, *Gedichte: Als erster Band ihrer Gedichte, Reise-Blätter,*

Kunst- und Lebens-Ansichten (Hamburg: Conrad Müller, 1812).

3. Bürger, *Lilienblätter und Zypressen-Zweige,* 197.

4. Weil, *Das Berliner Theaterpublikum,* 56.

5. Ibid., 91 n. 102.

6. Corngold, *Complex Pleasure,* 8.

7. Leading up to the eighteenth century, the performances of the traveling troupes had taken place in the context of special times in the calendar, at fairs, holidays, court festivals, and special celebrations ranging from carnival to weddings of the nobility. Removed from the humdrum of everyday life, the performances were part of leisure-time recreation with its indulgence of the senses. They offered release from the ever increasing disciplining of the body and its sensual pleasures. The demonization of these performances and their consequent transformation into occasions for edification that became integrated into the everyday practices of the middle class signified an important step in the civilizing process taking place during the eighteenth century. Based on the suppression of the senses, discipline and eventually self-discipline became favored virtues propagated by the vanguard of Enlightenment theoreticians. They wanted to channel and integrate the entertainment factor of theater and to make it a more regular feature of leisure that alternated with the demands of work, thus easing its burden.

8. See also Susanne Eigenmann, *Zwischen ästhetischer Raserei und aufgeklärter Disziplin: Hamburger Theater im späten 18. Jahrhundert* (Stuttgart: Metzler, 1994).

9. "Festzuhalten bleibt eine breite Verbürgerlichung des Theaterwesens seit dem letzten Drittels des 18. Jahrhunderts, die sich mit der zahlenmäßigen Zunahme der Theater in bürgerlichen Städten und deren Trägerschaft oder Kontrolle durch die stadtbürgerlichen Eliten belegen läßt." Frank Möller, "Zwischen Kunst und Kommerz: Bürgertheater im 19. Jahrhundert," in *Bürgerkultur im 19. Jahrhundert: Bildung, Kunst, und Lebenswelten,* ed. Dieter Hein and Andreas Schulz (Munich: Beck, 1996), 24.

10. Actually determining the composition of the audience is fairly complicated and does not readily lend itself to generalizations. Considering the specific situation of individual theaters might provide some context. Historical and geographical specificity needs to be balanced with a determination of general trends. If we take the two specific cases of Berlin and Hamburg, similarities and differences emerge. The lists of ticket holders indicate that in Berlin the audience was fairly small when compared with the large population size (Berlin had 160,000 inhabitants in 1796 and the theater had at most a capacity of 1,200 persons, with some reports indicating as few as 800). Judging by these lists, the audience seems to

have consisted of members from all classes. Free tickets (*Freibillet;* Weil, *Das Berliner Theaterpublikum,* 66), made available at certain times, enabled even members of the lower classes to attend the theater. At the same time, it seems that the same audience more or less constituted the spectatorship for many of the entertainment events.

11. Weil, *Das Berliner Theaterpublikum,* 39. Usually the opera drew a large audience. In this particular instance the opera was not as big a competitor because most of the seats were reserved for the members of the court and their guests. The few tickets available for purchase by the middle class were, however, sought after and highly valued. On the few occasions when extra performances were given for the general audience, the theater noticed its impact by the number of empty seats. However, the same held true for those times during the carnival when masked balls drew the crowds away from the theater (*Nationaltheater;* ibid., 43).

12. Schiller comments: "We almost feel tempted to advocate the puppet shows again and encourage the citizens to implant Garrick's art into the wooden heroes so that the attention of the audience, which is usually divided into three—content, author, actor—focuses less on the third and more on the first" ("Beinahe möchte man den Marionetten wieder das Wort reden, und die Maschinisten ermuntern, die Garrikischen Künste in ihre hölzerne Helden zu verpflanzen, so würde doch die Aufmerksamkeit des Publikums, die sich gewöhnlicher massen in den Inhalt, den Dichter und Spieler dritteilt, von dem letztern zurücktreten, und sich mehr auf dem ersten versammeln"). Schiller, "Ueber das gegenwärtige teutsche Theater," *Schillers Werke Nationalausgabe,* 20:81. On the other end of the spectrum of this experimental aesthetics were those puppet theater performances that took place in inns, where they were an integral part of the entertainment for the lower classes. Servants, soldiers, and apprentices partook of this form of entertainment in an evening of dance, drink, and conversation. Weil, *Das Berliner Theaterpublikum,* 54. For the nobility a whole array of cultural spectacles, activities, and events supplemented those of the theater and the opera, festivities containing a whole range of elaborate special effects. These luxurious spectacles incorporated such elements as portable volcanoes, grottoes, landscapes with palm trees, springs, rivers, water nymphs among the reeds, and fortresses bursting into flames, deceiving the senses and blurring the borders of nature and artifice. Paul Zucker, *Die Theaterdekoration des Klassizismus: Eine Kunstgeschichte der Bühnenbilder* (Berlin: Rudolf Kaemmerer, 1925), 34–35. Masquerades where the members of the court transformed themselves into peasants and celebrated harvest festivals and make-believe peasant weddings were popular forms of entertainment.

13. De Bolla, "The charm'd eye," 108.

14. Eigenmann, *Ästhetische Raserei,* 42.

15. Schiller, "Ueber das gegenwärtige teutsche Theater," 81–82.

16. "Wenn Gram an dem Herzen nagt, wenn trübe Laune unsre einsamen Stunden vergiftet, wenn uns Welt und Geschäfte anekeln, wenn tausend Lasten unsre Seele drücken, und unsre Reizbarkeit unter Arbeiten des Berufs zu ersticken droht, so empfängt uns die Bühne—in dieser künstlichen Welt träumen wir die wirkliche hinweg, wir werden uns selbst wieder gegeben, unsre Empfindung erwacht, heilsame Leidenschaften erschüttern unsre schlummernde Natur, und treiben das Blut in frischeren Wallungen." Friedrich Schiller, "Was kann eine gute stehende Schaubühne eigentlich wirken?" in *Schillers Werke Nationalausgabe,* 20:100.

17. The entertainment value of theater is derived from the multi-sensory flooding, as Paula Backscheider observed with regard to gothic drama: "Gothic drama undoubtedly succeeded as mass art so prodigiously because it managed to unite nearly unprecedented spectacle and excitement with the elements we now know consumers find most satisfying in entertainment art. It depended upon spectacular settings, mood music, and acting in specific styles as much as—or even more than—it did upon a predictable set of characters, conflicts, icons, and resolutions." Backscheider, *Spectacular Politics: Theatrical Power and Mass Culture in Early Modern England* (Baltimore: Johns Hopkins University Press, 1993), 167.

18. Commentary on "Die Jungfrau von Orleans," *Zeitung für die elegante Welt* no. 57, May 13, 1802, 455.

19. Heinrich August Ottokar Reichard, "Uebersicht des heutigen Zustandes des teutschen Schaubühnen-Wesens," *Journal* 4 (February 1789): 72.

20. Goethe researched the history of the Thirty Years War extensively for the production of *Wallenstein's Lager.* Hans Knudsen, *Goethes Welt des Theaters: Ein Vierteljahrhundert Weimarer Bühnenleitung* (Berlin: Tempelhof, 1949), 67 (the well-known illustration can also be found there).

21. In Cotta's *Allgemeine Zeitung,* the performance of part 1 of the *Wallenstein* trilogy in Weimar is discussed: "'heitere, militärisch klingende Musik habe den Auftakt gegeben; und, noch ehe der Vorhang in die Höhe ging, hörte man ein Lied singen'—und eines, in das bezeichnenderweise Goethe zwischen Schillers Strophen auch eigene eingefügt hatte. Bald war das Theater aufgedeckt, und es erschien vor den Augen des Zuschauers das bunte Gewimmel eines Lagers." Qtd. in *Bretter, die die Welt bedeuten: Entwürfe zum Theaterdekor und zum Bühnenkostüm: Ausstellung der Kunstbibliothek Berlin Staatliche Museen Preußischer Kulturbesitz* (Berlin: Dietrich Reimer, 1978), 143. "Man sieht: Goethe hat den gemalten Prospekt, die Statistengruppe und die zahlreichen Requi-

siten zu einem kaleidoskopartigen Miteinander verbunden und damit Schritt für Schritt sich verwandelnden, gleichsam lebendigen Hintergrund verwoben, vor dem sich nun die einzelnen Szenen des 'Lagers' vom schlauen Gespräch des Bauern mit seinem Sohn über die aufrüttelnde Kapuzienerpredigt bis zum alle tragischen Möglichkeiten des großen Feldherrn und seines Heerlagers eröffnenden Schluß hin abspielten" (ibid.). Despite the indulgence in the sensual, Goethe makes every effort to subordinate it to the overall design of the play in his description of the first performance in Weimar (1799). The most substantial part of the description refers to plot and character, while the few paragraphs on costumes and designs are placed at the end of the essay: "Die Direktion sparte keinen Aufwand, durch Dekorationen und Kleidung den Sinn und Geist des Gedichts würdig auszuführen und die Aufgabe, das barbarische Kostüm jener Zeit, welches dargestellt werden mußte, dem Auge gefällig zu behandeln und eine schickliche Mitte zwischen dem Abgeschmackten und dem Edlen zu treffen, so viel es möglich sein wollte zu lösen." Johann Wolfgang Goethe, "Die Piccolomini: Wallensteins erster Teil," *Schriften zur Literatur,* 59.

22. An older form of visual pleasure in the theater, the elaborately painted curtain, which was still in use at many theaters, could be used to round out the visual pleasure. It indulged the gaze before the performance got under way. The monumental paintings encouraged the ocular sense to wander over the richly detailed curtain like the child does in a children's book. Karl Bachler, *Gemalte Theatervorhänge in Deutschland und Österreich* (Munich: Bruckmann, 1972), 72.

23. For a detailed description of the theater situation in Hamburg see also Eigenmann, *Ästhetische Raserei.*

24. In the history of theater and theater design in late-eighteenth- and early-nineteenth-century Germany, the most important genre is the opera, not drama, as theater catalogs and historical collections such as the Theaterwissenschaftliche Sammlung at the University of Cologne and the collections at the Theatermuseum in Munich show. Opera is, of course, a central instance of entertainment during our time frame, pleasuring the senses of sight and sound, and thus could have commanded a chapter in this study. My decision not to include an extended analysis of opera was based on the fact that the spectacular operas of the time are well known and well researched in the history of theater and music.

25. Reproductions of the famous set for the appearance of the Queen of the Night—one by Schinkel and the other by Quaglio—can be found in the exhibition catalog *Vom Himmel durch die Welt zur Hölle: Ausstellungsspektakel in zehn Stationen (5. Juni 1988–1. November 1988),* ed. Elmar Buck et al. (Köln: Theatermuseum, 1988), 227, 228.

26. A contemporary observer of the Berlin performance (set by Schinkel) describes the impact: "In the very background, on the horizon of this star-filled sky, a dark, cavernous space is surrounded by borders of light. Behind this, in the center of the curtain, the Queen of the Night hovers on the illuminated crescent of the moon, as if emerging from the ocean waves, and steps from there onto the stage. The moon, now resting above the clouds, gives this scene, fleeting as an apparition, a magical quality" ("Ganz im Hintergrund, am Horizont dieses Sternengewölbes hat sich ein dunkles, von Lichtsäumen umfaßtes Gewölbe gelagert; hinter ihm, im Mittelpunkt der Gardine, schwebt die Königin der Nacht, auf der glänzend erleuchteten Mondsichel stehend, wie aus den Fluten des Meeres empor und schreitet von da aus über das Gewölb hinaus auf die Bühne. Der nun über den Wolken ruhende Mond macht in dieser ganzen, nur wie eine flüchtige Erscheinung vorübergleitende Szene, einen magischen Effekt"). Qtd. in *Das Bühnenbild im 19. Jahrhundert* (Munich: Theatermuseum München, 1959), 11.

27. "Hinsichtlich der Kostümgestaltung sah Iffland den Hauptgesichtspunkt in der Konkurrenz zur Oper. Um bestehen zu können, ließ er 362 prunkvolle Kostüme machen." *Bretter, die die Welt bedeuten,* 146.

28. "Überhaupt war der Götz und die ganze Flut der Ritterschauspiele ein mächtiger Anlaß zur Bereicherung des Fundus der bürgerlichen Schauspielhäuser." Zucker, *Die Theaterdekoration des Klassizismus,* 13.

29. Ibid.

30. "Vorher habe der Fundus einer solchen Bühne nur aus einem Prachtsaal, einer Straße, einem Dorf, etlichen bürgerlichen Zimmern, einem Kerker und etlichen Hügeln und Gebüschen bestanden." Ibid., 14.

31. The *Berlin Bürgerblatt,* January 29, 1802: "Schiller's *Jungfrau von Orleans* caused a sensation. Our experts have not quite found an explanation for this significant phenomenon and only express their astonishment in fragmentary comments" ("Allgemein war die Sensation, welche Schiller's *Jungfrau von Orleans* erregt hat. Unsere wirklichen Kunstrichter finden noch keine Erklärung über dieses große Phänomen und drückten nur einstweilen in abgebrochenen Worten ihre Verwunderung aus"). Qtd. in *Bretter, die die Welt bedeuten,* 146.

32. With regard to the sensational Berlin performance of Schiller's *Jungfrau von Orleans* on November 23, 1801, under Iffland at the National Theater, Karl Friedrich Zelter (1758–1832), director of the music academy in Berlin, writes: "The splendor of our performance of the piece is more than majestic; the fourth act contains more than 800 people, and the music and everything else has such a formidable effect that the audience reacts ecstatically every time it is performed. The cathedral and all the decorations, which consist of a long hall through which the procession

enters the church, is in the Gothic style" ("Die Pracht der Aufführung unserer Darstellung dieses Stückes ist mehr als kaiserlich; der vierte Akt desselben ist hier mit mehr denn 800 Personen besetzt und, Musik und alles andere inbegriffen, von so eklatanter Wirkung, daß das Auditorium jedesmal in Ekstase gerät. Die Kathedrale mit der ganzen Dekoration, welche in einem langen Säulengange besteht, durch den der Zug in die Kirche geht, ist im gothischen Stil"). Ibid., 145.

33. Linda Bayer-Berenbaum, *The Gothic Imagination: Expansion in Gothic Literature and Art* (Rutherford, N.J., and London: Fairleigh Dickinson University Press and Associated University Presses, 1982), 55.

34. Ibid., 48.

35. Ibid.

36. "In order to minimize the heavy quality of stone and stress its spirituality, Gothic architecture adopted flying buttresses and pointed arches to facilitate a towering, vertical structure unimpaired by internal supports. As a result, solid wall space could be reduced and great windows accommodated. The height and the open spaces achieved counteract the natural weight of the stone, and the thrust of steep pinnacles opposes the pull of gravity. The joining of pillars to the cross ribs of the vaults through attached columns draws the structure up in a sweeping movement. The pillars do not appear to be supporting weight or to be pressing down, but rather soaring upward." Ibid., 52. Gothic art dematerializes its composition in order to spiritualize its material components.

37. Ibid., 55.

38. Williams, *Art of Darkness*, 76.

39. Julia Kristeva, *Powers of Horror: An Essay in Abjection*, trans. Leon S. Roudiez (1980; New York: Columbia University Press, 1982), 12.

40. I do not agree with Krause, who assumes that the "canon" of chivalric dramas in essentially set, and it is unlikely that new plays would be added: "Zu diesen [den bedeutendsten Autoren] zählen vor allem Schröder, Iffland und Kotzebue sowie Joseph Marius von Babo und Joseph August Graf von Törring. Die heute noch zumindest dem Literarhistoriker geläufigen Namen sind übrigens diejenigen der auch zu ihrer Zeit bekanntesten Trivialdramatiker; 'Neu'—oder 'Wiederentdeckungen' dürften auf diesem Gebiet kaum möglich sein." Markus Krause, *Das Trivialdrama der Goethezeit, 1780–1805: Produktion und Rezeption* (Bonn: Bouvier, 1982), 92. Krause ignores, e.g., the contribution that women authors have made to the genre. My study thus purposefully departs from his "canon" and instead chooses a different set of chivalric plays by male and female authors.

41. Ibid., 201. Krause compares the sentimental family drama and the *Ritterschauspiel* with a focus on the social and moral implications of the play.

As is the case for most of the German criticism on the "trivial" tradition, his attention is on the ideology of the plays.

42. Backscheider, *Spectacular Politics*, 149. Backscheider interprets the gothic as dealing with the uncertainties of power relationships seen from the perspective of the powerless: "What has gone berserk in this world, of course, is power. And British people felt they lived in such a place" (163).

43. Ibid., 189, 151.

44. William Patrick Day, *In the Circles of Fear and Desire: A Study of Gothic Fantasy* (Chicago: University of Chicago Press, 1985), 177.

45. Müller-Fraunreuth, *Die Ritter- und Räuberromane*, 1.

46. The following example is representative of this type of argument, which was forwarded as late as the 1970s and even when the interest in the so-called trivial literature grew as part of the trend toward the democratization of literature in light of the student movement's critique of the elitist concept of literature. "Im Unterschied zu der Enge der bürgerlichen Welt eröffnet der Räuberroman die Illusion der Freiheit und der Ungebundenheit; im Unterschied zu der platten Alltäglichkeit dringt die ungezügelte Phantasie im Geisterroman ins Unwirklich-Gespenstische, und im Unterschied zu der sozialrevolutionären Unruhe in den Jahrzehnten vor und nach der Französischen Revolution wendet sich der Ritterroman mit einer kraftgenialischen Gebärde zurück in die Vergangenheit statt vorwärts in die Zukunft. Denn das alles sind ja Möglichkeiten und Ventile, den Unmut, das Unbehagen und die Unzufriedenheit auf eine harmlose und unschädliche Weise abzureagieren. Je wilder und zügelloser sich die Phantasie in diesen Romanen austobt, desto eher findet sich der phantastische Träumer mit der nüchternen Wirklichkeit ab." Greiner, *Die Entstehung der modernen Unterhaltungsliteratur*, 80.

47. Anne Williams, in *The Art of Darkness*, gives an exemplary gender-aware reading of the dark side of the family romance. Her study is influenced by Freud, Lacan, and Kristeva. With regard to German literature there is considerably less critical activity; see, e.g., Karin A. Wurst, "Elise Bürger and the Gothic Imagination," *Women in German Yearbook* 13 (1997): 11–27; Royer, "Sophie Albrecht," esp. 236–71; and especially Silke Arnold-de Simine, *Leichen im Keller: Zu Fragen des Gender in Angstinszenierungen der Schauer- und Kriminalliteratur (1780–1830)* (St. Ingbert: Röhrig Universitätsverlag, 2000). The latter also gives a a more detailed overview of the research on the gothic (see esp. 21–45). These analyses focus on prose texts.

48. Müller-Fraunreuth, *Die Ritter- und Räuberromane*, 64.

49. Elisa von der Recke, who after personal trauma had enlisted the help of

Cagliostro to find solace in communication with her dead child and brother (1779), later wrote the decisive treatise exposing him as a fraud. Charlotta Elisabeth Konstantia von der Recke, *Nachricht von des berüchtigten Cagliostro Aufenthalte in Mitau im Jahre 1779 und von dessen magischen Operationen* (Berlin: bey Friedrich Nicolai, 1787).

50. There was a significant literary transfer between the English and German women writers producing in the gothic tradition. Bendikte Naubert and Margarethe Liebeskind translated works by Ann Radcliff and Sophia Lee, and in turn Naubert was one of the most frequently translated writers of the time in England. Although Arnold-de Simine mentions the relationship, the interconnectedness and especially the influence of the German gothic and chivalric tradition on the more famous English literature has not been explored in sufficient detail. Of course, such an extended comparative study is beyond the scope of the present volume. For a recent overview see Marshall Brown, "Gothic Readers versus Gothic Writers," *Eighteenth-Century Studies* 35, no. 4 (2002): 615–59.

51. Sophie Albrecht, *Graumännchen oder die Burg Rabenbühl: Eine Geistergeschichte altdeutschen Ursprungs* (Hamburg and Altona: Buchhandlung der Verlagsgesellschaft, 1799).

52. Friedrich Justin Bertuch, "Ankündigung der Blauen Bibliothek aller Nationen," in *Blaue Bibliothek aller Nationen,* ed. Friedrich Justin Bertuch, vol. 1 (1790), n.p.

53. "Bertuch schätzt, wie sein eigenes 'Märchen vom Bilboquet' zeigt, das raffiniert ironische Spiel von Fiktion und Faktum, von Distanz und Affinität als Unterhaltungswert. Er bezieht sich beim Wunderbaren im Sinne der Wirkungsästhetik auf den Effekt, auf 'das innerweltliche Vergnügen an der Verblüffung, am Überraschenden, Fremden, Kühnen, Außerordentlichen, Seltsamen, Neuen, Normensprengenden, den Erwartungshorizont des Gewöhnlichen Überschreitenden, Verwunderungswürdigen.'" Angela Borchert, "Übersetzung und Umschrift: Spätaufklärerische Kulturpolitik am Beispiel von Friedrich Justin Bertuchs Märchensammlung 'Die Blaue Bibliothek aller Nationen,'" in Kaiser and Seifert, *Friedrich Justin Bertuch,* 182.

54. Albrecht, *Graumännchen,* 49–50.

55. Mark Turner, *Death Is the Mother of Beauty: Mind, Metaphor, Criticism* (Chicago: University of Chicago Press, 1987), 16.

56. Anna Laetitia Barbauld, "On the Pleasure Derived from Objects of Terror," qtd. in David Richter, "The Reception of the Gothic Novel in the 1790s," in *The Idea of the Novel in the Eighteenth Century,* ed. Robert Uphaus (East Lansing: Michigan State University Press, 1988), 122.

57. "This man, and it seems to always be a man, is 'gothic' because he is pushing the absolute limits of what the audience imagines to be possible

in nature." Backscheider, *Spectacular Politics,* 163.

58. Ibid., 170.

59. Kristeva, *Powers of Horror,* 11.

60. ". . . der Aufbau der Ängste [ist, K.A.W.] nichts anderes als der psychische Widerpart der Zwänge, die die Menschen kraft ihrer gesellschaftlichen Verflechtung auf einander ausüben. Die Ängste bilden einen der Verbindungswege—einen der wichtigsten—über den hin sich die Strukturen der Gesellschaft auf die individuellen psychischen Funktionen überträgt. Der Motor jener zivilisatorischen Ängste bildet eine ganz bestimmte Veränderung der gesellschaftlichen Zwänge, die auf den Einzelnen einwirken, ein spezifischer Umbau des ganzen Beziehungsgewebes und darin vor allem der Gewaltorganisation." Elias, *Prozeß der Zivilisation,* 2:446.

61. Ibid., 317.

62. "Die Theorien des Erhabenen sind Angstabwehrstrategien . . . , [eine] Tendenz, aus einem Schreckensbild, aus einem Gefühl der das Angst, Machtlosigkeit und Abhängigkeit die eigene Größe abzuleiten und die eigentliche Schwäche auf das schreckenerregende *Andere* zu projizieren . . ." Arnold-de Simine, *Leichen im Keller,* 130.

63. Day, *In the Circles of Fear and Desire,* 63.

64. Ibid., 64.

65. Ibid., 73.

66. Terry Castle, "The Spectralization of the Other in the Mysteries of Udolpho," in Nussbaum and Brown, *The New Eighteenth Century,* 237.

67. Ibid., 234.

68. Ibid., 237.

69. Philippe Ariès, *The Hour of Our Death,* trans. Helen Weaver (New York: Knopf, 1981).

70. Castle, "The Spectralization of the Other," 242.

71. Goethe, *Die Wahlverwandtschaften,* 243. "The fear of death—the desire to stay its effect, to preserve the body—is repeatedly attached to the problem of representation in this novel. Here, at least in part, is one reason for Goethe's prohibition against the making of exact copies, for they produce the uncanny effects that underline rather than cover over the relation of representation to death." Peucker, "Material Image in Goethe's *Wahlverwandtschaften,*" 202.

72. Foucault, *History of Sexuality,* 1:106.

73. Ibid., 106–7.

74. Ibid., 108.

75. Williams, *Art of Darkness,* 95.

76. Ibid.

77. Eleonore von Thon, *Adelheit von Rastenberg* (Weimar: Hoffmannsche

Buchhandlung, 1788), rpt. in Karin A. Wurst, ed. and intro., *Eleonore von Thon, Adelheit von Rastenberg,* Text and Translations Series (New York: MLA, 1996).

78. Friedrich Wilhelm Ziegler, *"Mathilde Gräfin von Griessbach:* Ein Trauerspiel in fünf Aufzügen aus den Zeiten des Faustrechts," *Deutsche Schaubühne* 11 (1791): 99–178.

79. Joseph Marius von Babo, *"Oda, die Frau von zween Männern:* Ein Trauerspiel," *Deutsche Schaubühne* 6 (1791): 223–310.

80. Elise Bürger, *Adelheit, Gräfinn [sic] von Teck: Ritterschauspiel in fünf Aufzügen* (1799; Jena: Voigtsche Buchhandlung, 1812).

81. Christian Heinrich Spieß, *Klara von Hoheneichen: Ritterschauspiel in vier Aufzügen* (Prag und Leipzig: n.p., 1800).

82. Auguste von Wallenheim, *Klara von Leuenstein: Ein Schauspiel aus den Ritterzeiten* (1806), *Neueste deutsche Schaubühne* 6 (1806): 49–120.

83. These texts project the contemporary eighteenth-century concepts of modern love and marriage onto the earlier historical period, when love and marriage were clearly separated. The family alliance model that would have dominated the historical time of the Crusades is ahistorically fused with the concept of the modern *Liebesehe* based on erotic love, indicating that the interest is on the modern, complex fusion of love and marriage and its many contradictions. See also Wurst, *Familiale Liebe,* and Karin A. Wurst, "'Wilde Wünsche': The Discourse of Love in the Sturm und Drang," in *Literature of the Sturm und Drang,* ed. David Hill (Rochester: Camden House, 2003), and "Women Dramatists in Late-Eighteenth-Century Germany: The Hazards of Marriage as Love Match," *Seminar* 38, no. 4 (2002): 313–31.

84. Babo, *"Oda, die Frau von zween Männern,"* 233.

85. Ziegler, *"Mathilde Gräfin von Griessbach,"* 108.

86. One could speculate that the canonized examples and models of bourgeois tragedy in high culture—Lessing's *Miß Sara Sampson* and especially *Emilia Galotti*—take place in the realm of the English gentry and an Italian court not only for ideological reasons but also for practical theatrical reasons. The settings of both plays provide ample opportunities for visually interesting scenes.

87. Backscheider, *Spectacular Politics,* 238.

88. Meisel, *Realizations,* 283–84.

89. "Disciplinary power . . . is exercised through its invisibility; at the same time it imposes on those whom it subjects a principle of compulsory visibility. . . . It is the fact of being constantly seen, of being able always to be seen, that maintains the disciplined individual in his subjection." Michel Foucault, *Discipline and Punish: The Birth of the Prison,* trans. Alan Sheridan (New York: Vintage, 1979), 187.

90. Bayer-Berenbaum, *The Gothic Imagination,* 22–23.

91. "Er [Louis Catel] schlägt nämlich für die Darstellung ziehender Wolken eine Leinwand vor, die über zwei Walzen geht. Die Gegend selbst sey auf einer Fläche gemacht und auf ihrer äußersten Kontur ausgeschnitten. Hinter dieses ausgeschnittene Bild sey die Malerei der Luft auf einer beweglichen Decke angebracht, die sich aufrollen läßt. . . . So wird man, wenn das Bild sich in die Höhe hebt, immer mehr an Gewölck von der Tiefe heraus bis auf die sichtbare Bildfläche bringen können." Zucker, *Die Theaterdekoration des Klassizismus,* 19.

92. ". . . 'denn wenn man die Augen schließt und der Phantasie erlaubt, Bilder herbeizuführen, so erscheinen diese in finsterer Nacht hintereinander.'" Catel qtd. in ibid.

93. "Endlich muß noch bemerkt werden, daß Servandoni auch der Erfinder sogenannter 'stummer Schauspiele' ist, also der Anreger der späteren Dioramen und Panoramen. . . . Die Figuren waren dabei als Staffage fest auf die wandelnden Dekorationen gemalt. Die Vorstellungen wurden von Musik begleitet und erfreuten sich regelmäßig großen Beifalls des Publikums." Ibid., 8–9.

94. They not only made him famous but also attracted the attention of the Prussian court and led to his employment as a civil service architect (*preußischer Baubeamter*). Ibid. 20.

95. Ibid.

96. At the same time, he was also known for his classicist and very restrained stage designs, the relief stage, presumably reserved for tragedy. An audience seeking entertainment is offered more opportunities in an elaborate panoramic space than in a relatively Spartan stage that favors the classicist relief and minimizes specular sensual indulgence in an abundance of colors, shapes, and special effects.

97. Renzo Dubbini, *Geography of the Gaze: Urban and Rural Vision in Early Modern Europe,* trans. Lydia G. Cochrane (Chicago: University of Chicago Press, 2002), 4.

98. Dolf Sternberger, *Panorama of the Nintheenth Century,* trans. Joachim Neugroschel (New York: Urizen Books, 1977), 1.

99. "Es versuchte in einem Rundblick von 360 Grad mittels perspektivischer Projektion und Farbgebung unter Zuhilfenahme von plastischen Elementen und durch besondere Beleuchtungseffekte, historische Szenen oder Landschaften mit großer räumlicher Wirkung möglichst täuschend zu vermitteln. Der Betrachter wurde durch seinen Standort in das geschaffene Kunstwerk so integriert, daß ihm die Realität nicht mehr als direkter Vergleich zur Kunst zur Verfügung stand. Er sollte glauben, nicht die gemalte, sondern die reale Natur zu sehen." Jooss, *Lebende Bilder,* 244.

100. Dubbini, *Geography of the Gaze*, 4.
101. "Naive Schaufreude, das Interesse, fremde, historische, exotische Dinge kennenzulernen, und sich darüber hinaus eine 'amüsante' Augenfreude zu bereiten, lassen sich aus der Beliebtheit derartiger Vorführungen ablesen, die im übrigen vielen Kunstausstellungen unter Verfolgung änlicher Strategien große Konkurrenz machten." Jooss, *Lebende Bilder,* 245–46.
102. "Sie müssen im Zusammenhang mit der Neugier am visuellen, ungewohnten Erlebnis und dem Bedürfnis nach bildhaften Medien gesehen werden, die mit den allgemeinen technischen und sozialen Entwicklungen jener Zeit einhergingen." Ibid., 246.
103. Sternberger, *Panorama of the Ninetheenth Century,* 186.
104. Qtd. in ibid., 186 n. 1.
105. "Der Zweck dieser neuen Art von Malerei soll seyn, zu zeigen, wie weit die Kunst die Blendwerke der Täuschung treiben kann. Und in der That versichern Alle, die es gesehen haben, daß die Aehnlichkeit einer Nachbildung mit der Naturwahrheit nicht weiter gehen könne. Um diesen Zweck zu ereichen, hat der Maler nicht allein alle Hülfsmittel der Linien- und Luftperspective erschöpft; er hat auch alle körperliche Umgebungen entfernt, um die Täuschung nicht durch die Vergleichung mit der Naturwahrheit zu zerstören." Johann August Eberhard, "Ueber das Panorama," *Journal* 17 (December 1802), qtd. in Jooss, *Lebende Bilder,* 244.
106. "Das Panoram ist aktuell und welthaltig. Im Zeitalter des Historismus, der das ganze Erbe der Menscheitsgeschichte benutzt, ist es ein Ort des Präsens, der Gegenwart, und der diesseitigen Weltsicht. Es setzt auf die Mittel der Illusion aber es möchte nichts Überwirkliches glauben machen, sondern einzig und allein die Welt abbilden. Mit dieser Tendenz steht es in einem lehrreichen Gegensatz zu den letzten großen Rundumgemälden der Kunstgeschichte. Als die ersten Panoramenmaler am Ende des 18. Jahrhunderts in London ihre Arbeit aufnahmen, wurden in großen Teilen des katholischen Europa leistungsfähige Malermannnschaften arbeitslos, die vorher die Decken von Kirchen und Schlössern ausgemalt hatten. Ihr Auftrag und ihre Kunst war es gewesen, mit Mitteln der Illusionsmalerei das Dach aufzureißen und den Blick in einen tiefen und von vielerlei göttlichen Wesen bevölkerten Himmel zu lenken. Um den Übergang von realer Architektur und Skulptur über gemalte Architektur und Figur in die Wolken und Lüfte ihrer himmlischen Gefilde gleitend und täuschend zu gestalten, bedienten sie sich kaum anderer Mittel, als sie den späteren Panoramamalern zur Verfügung standen." Wolfgang Kemp, "Die Revolutionierung der Medien: Lithographie, Photographie, Diorama, Panorama," "Funkkolleg moderne Kunst," Saarländischer Rundfunk: Hauptabteil Kulturelles Wort.

Sendung October 23–29, 1989.

107. To Johann August Eberhard, this effect is unpleasant: "So bringt es . . . die täuschende Wirkung hervor, die aber . . . bald in hohem Grad peinlich, widerlich und endlich unerträglich wird. . . . Meine Theorie der Täuschung macht mir diese Wirkung vollkommen wahrscheinlich. Nach ihr muß das Panorama gerade desto unangenehmer auf uns wirken, je vollständiger seine Wirkung ist. Die vollständigste ist, wenn wir sogar den Schein des Kunstwerkes für die völlige Naturwahrheit halten müssen. Gerade in dieser Vollständigkeit der Illusion liegen mehrere Gründe ihrer Widerlichkeit." Eberhard qtd. in Jooss, *Lebende Bilder,* 244–45. His discomfort stems from the absolute silence, the lack of movement, the destabilized sense of perception that fails to clearly distinguish between reality and artifice, and the impossibility of resisting the illusion. Ibid., 245.

108. "Der dem Verstande zu übermittlende Erkenntnisgegenstand verlangt geeignete Gestalt: begrenzten Umfang, klare Übersichtlichkeit, geschlossene Form. . . . Es besteht daher im Rationalismus des 18. Jahrhunderts die Tendenz, den jeweiligen Apperzeptionspunkt, den kleinen Ausschnitt der schärfsten und deutlichsten Wahrnehmung abzusondern, einzufassen und losgelöst zu betrachten. Dadurch erhält das Anschauungsobjekt die Form des kleinen umrahmten Bildes." Langen, *Anschaungsformen,* 7–8.

109. Ibid., 8–9.

110. Stephan Oettermann, *Das Panorama: Die Geschichte eines Massenmediums* (Frankfurt: Syndikat, 1980), 12–13.

111. Dubbini, *Geography of the Gaze,* 116.

112. Barbara Maria Stafford, *Good Looking: Essays on the Virtue of Images* (Cambrige: MIT Press, 1996), 196.

113. Ibid., 192.

114. Appended Facsimile of an Advertisement of the Cosmorama in 209 Regent Street, London. *Diorama: Regent's Park: Description of the Two Pictures Now Exhibiting,* by M. Bouton (London: Schulze and Co., n.d.).

115. Due to the sheer size and precarious nature of the artifacts, they did not survive as historical objects. I was only able to find verbal descriptions and a few depictions of the originals. Of the hundreds of panoramas popular in the nineteenth century, only twelve have survived. Kemp, "Die Revolutionierung der Medien," 22.

116. Kemp describes a building designed for a panorama: "Eingang und Kasse, dann führen ein verdunkelter Gang und eine Treppe in die Mitte des großen Rundbaus, zur Besucherplattform, von der man die Rundleinwand in dem plastisch gestalteten Vordergund betrachten kann. . . . Diese Panoramen sind eigene Gebäude, spezielle Architekturen, man

muß sich vorstellen, daß ein Rundbau, eine große Rundarchitektur diese Leinwand aufnimmt. Darüber gibt es ein Glasdach, das das Licht hineinläßt. Es ist nur natürliches Licht in diesen Panoramen möglich. Und in der Mitte dieses großen Rundes befinde sich also die Besucherplattform. . . . Der Blick nach oben ist durch ein großes Schirmdach abgeschnitten. Der Blick nach unten ist uns verwehrt durch dieses Terrain, das sich rings um diese Plattform befindet, ein Terrain, das aus scheinbar echten Dünen gebildet ist. Wir haben hier Sand, Strandgut liegen, und das ganze soll, und tut es auch, sich übergangslos mit der Illusion der Leinwand verbinden." Ibid., 1.

117. Kemp writes: "Nach dem Sinn dieser illusionistischen Malerei und Architektur würden wir uns also auf einer Düne des Strandbades Schweningen befinden. Schweningen, das ist etwa 10 Kilometer von dem Standort entfernt, an dem wir uns tatsächlich befinden, nämlich Den Haag. Auf einer Düne mit Blick über die Nordsee, über das Fischerdorf und frühe Strandbad des Jahres 1881, über die Stadt Den Haag am Horizont. Das alles erfüllt mit Leben, es ist ein Sommertag, Fischerboote haben angelandet, bergen ihren Fang, andere stechen in See. Es gibt eine Kavalkade von Reitern. Es gibt Badekarren, die ihre Badegäste ins Meer entlassen. Es gibt Flaneure auf der Strandpromenade, es gibt Leben im Dorf, es gibt Verkehr, eine Eisenbahn." Ibid., 1.

118. Dubbini, *Geography of the Gaze*, 82.

119. Ibid., 120.

120. Sternberger, *Panorama of the Ninetheenth Century*, 9.

121. Jean Starobinski, *The Living Eye*, trans. Arthur Goldhammer (Cambridge: Harvard University Press, 1989), 3, translation of *L'Oeil vivant* (1961) chapters 1–3; 4–7 *L'Oeil vivant II: La Relation critique* (1970).

122. Technical descriptions and sketches of the diorama are found in *Das Daguerreotyp und das Diorama oder genaue und authentische Beschreibung meines Verfahrens und meiner Apparate zu Fixierung der Bilder der* Camera obscura *und der von mir bei dem Diorama angewendeten Art und Weise der Malerei und der Beleuchtung, von Louis Jacq. M. Daguerre* (Stuttgart: Metzlersche Buchhandlung, 1839), which is accompanied by a sales bill (Verkaufs-Anzeige) for replicas of the Daguerre's apparati by the mechanic Carl Geiger in Stuttgart, making them available for experts and dilettantes (*Sachkenner* and *Liebhaber;* unpaginated).

123. *Diorama: Regent's Park*, 3.

124. Other descriptions illustrate this genre further: "The spectator sits in a small amphitheater; the scene appears covered with a curtain enshrouded in darkness. Little by little, however, this darkness gives way to a twilight and the scene commences on the curtain itself: A landscape or prospect emerges more and more distinctly thereupon, the dawn lightens, the

scene grows lively, trees loom out of the shadows, the outlines of mountains, of houses become visible, human and animal figures appear in the foreground which turns brighter and brighter as if from the rising sun; day has broken. The sun mounts higher and higher; through the open window of a house one sees a kitchen fire gradually blazing up; in a corner of the countryside, a group of bivouacking soldiers sit around a mess-kettle under which the fire is increasing bit by bit; a smithy heaves into view, and its smoldering fire seems to be fanned more and more by an unseen bellows. After a while, and the spectator's interest has no yard-stick for the brevity of time, the daylight wanes, while the red glow of the artificial fire gains in strength; the twilight returns and then at last comes night. Soon, however, the moonlight re-enters into its rights, the landscape is once again visible in the soft tints of the illuminated night, a ship's lantern kindles in the boat anchored in the foreground of a harbor; the candles on the altar in the background of an excellent church prospect light up, the herofore invisible congregation is shone upon by rays from the altar; or lamenting people stand on the edge of the avalanche whose devastations are moonlit in the same place where hitherto Mount Ruffi formed the backdrop of the charming Swiss countryside of Goldau." Qtd. in Sternberger, *Panorama of the Ninetheenth Century,* 188–89 n. 1.

125. Meisel, *Realizations,* 184.
126. "Vor dem landschaftlichen Teil des Bildes standen die Staffagefiguren dioramenartig ausgeschnitten, sie wirkten im wesentlichen wohl als Silhouette. Außerdem waren vor dem einzelnen Hintergrundsbild stark durchbrochene Prospekte aufgestellt, die den plastischen Eindruck des ganzen erhöhten. Hinter den einzelnen Bildteilen war die Beleuchtung angebracht, die durch die transparenten ölgetränkten Teile des Papiers hindurchschimmerte. Die Vorführung des Ganzen wurde von Musik begleitet." Zucker, *Die Theaterdekoration des Klassizismus,* 20.
127. Dubbini, *Geography of the Gaze,* 118–19.
128. The *Journal* describes (and offers illustrations of) backlit decorative luxury items for the bedroom: "a delightful moonlit landscape or garden scene" ("eine solche von vollem Monde beleuchtete liebliche Landschaft oder Gartenscene"), "a piece of furniture with an insertable moonlit scene, which can be illuminated from behind" ("Möbelstück mit einlegbarer Mondscheinscene, die von hinten mit Wachslampen illuminiert werden") and creates a romantic ambience (2:179–80).
129. Dubbini, *Geography of the Gaze,* 226 n. 7, with reference to Goethe.
130. Ibid., 117–18.
131. Ibid., 115.
132. Ibid., 121.

133. Ibid., 121–22.
134. Ibid., 123.
135. Ibid., 16.
136. Ibid., 127.
137. Ibid., 115–16.
138. Ibid., 132.
139. Sternberger, *Panorama of the Ninetheenth Century,* 9.
140. Ibid., 13.
141. Ibid., 51, 13.
142. Ibid., 11.
143. Campbell, *Romantic Ethic,* 67.
144. Stafford, *Good Looking,* 196.
145. The scopic drive has its inception at a very early age, before the oedipal stage and even prior to the acquisition of language, at a stage of psychic development (Lacan's mirror stage).
146. "The lure of recreation was consonant with Locke's and Rousseau's sensationalist view that people preferred to have their sense organs continuously exercised to avoid boredom." Stafford, *Artful Science,* 55.
147. Stafford, *Good Looking,* 46.

Bibliography

Primary Sources

Addison, Joseph. "The Pleasures of the Imagination." *Joseph Addison and Richard Steele, The Spectator.* Vol. 3, nos. 411–21, pp. 535–80. Ed. Donald Bond. Oxford: Clarendon Press, 1965.

Adelung, Johann Christoph. *Grammatisch-Kritisches Wörterbuch der hochdeutschen Mundart.* 4 vols. 2nd ed. Leipzig, 1793–1801.

Albrecht, Sophie. *Graumännchen oder die Burg Rabenbühl. Eine Geistergeschichte altdeutschen Ursprungs.* Hamburg and Altona: Buchhandlung der Verlagsgesellschaft, 1799.

Allgemeine deutsche Real-Encyklopedie für gebildete Stände. Conversationslexikon. Vol. 9. Leipzig: Brockhaus, 1818.

Allgemeines Teutsches Garten-Magazin oder gemeinnützige Beiträge für alle Theile des praktischen Gartenwesens. Vol. 3. Ed. Friedrich Justus Bertuch. Weimar: Industrie-Comptoir, 1809.

Almanach für Damen. Tübingen: Cotta, 1801.

Anon. "Die Jungfrau von Orleans." *Zeitung für die elegante Welt,* Breslau, April 18, 1802, 454–55.

"Apologie des Thee's: Von einem französischen Thee-Trinker." *Journal des Luxus und der Moden* 22 (March 1807): 203–4.

Arnim, Bettine von. *Bettine von Arnims und Clemens Brentanos Frühlingskranz.* Frankfurt: Insel, 1985.

Babo, Joseph Marius von. *"Oda, die Frau von zween Männern:* Ein Trauerspiel." *Deutsche Schaubühne* 6 (1791): 223–310.

Bährens, Johann Christoph Friedrich. *Ueber den Werth der Empfindsamkeit besonders in Rücksicht auf die Romane.* Halle, 1786.

Batteux, Charles. *Principes de la litterature.* Vol. 1. Paris: Saillant & Nyon, 1774.

Bertuch, Friedrich Justin. "Ankündigung der Blauen Bibliothek aller Nationen." In *Blaue Bibliothek aller Nationen,* ed. Friedrich Justin Bertuch, vol. 1 (1790), n.p.

————. *Bibliothek der neuesten und wichtigsten Reisebeschreibungen zur Erweiterung der Erdkunde nach einem systematischen Plane.* Ed. M. Spengler und T. Ehrmann. Bd. 15. Weimar: Landes-Industrie-Comptoir, 1804.

————. *London und Paris.* Weimar: Verlag des Industrie-Comptoirs, 1799.

Bertuch, Friedrich Justin, and Georg Melchior Kraus, eds. *Journal des Luxus und der Moden.* Abridged edition. Ed. Werner Schmidt. 4 vols. Rpt. Hanau: Müller and Kiepenheuer, 1967–70.

Böttiger, Karl August. *Literarische Zustände und Zeitgenossen.* Ed. Karl Wilhelm Böttiger. 1795. Leipzig, 1838.

————. "Plastisch-mimische Darstellungen." *Abend-Zeitung.* Dresden nos. 11–12 (1818).

————. "Tischbeins Vasen, Lady Hamilton's Attitüden von Rehberg." *Journal des Luxus und der Moden* 10 (February 1795): 58–85.

————. "Van Dycks Landleben." *Abend-Zeitung.* Dresden no. 218 (1817): n.p.

Bouton, M. *Diorama: Regent's Park: Description of the Two Pictures Now Exhibiting.* London: Schulze and Co., n.d.

Bürger, Elise. *Adelheit, Gräfinn von Teck: Ritterschauspiel in fünf Aufzügen.* 1799. Jena: Voigtsche Buchhandlung, 1812.

————. "Einer meiner schönsten Tage in Frankfurt am Main." Bürger, *Lilienblätter und Zypressen-Zweige,* 104–11.

————. *Gedichte: Als erster Band ihrer Gedichte, Reise-Blätter, Kunst- und Lebens-Ansichten.* Hamburg: Conrad Müller, 1812.

————. "Die Gefahr und der Postknecht auf der Reise nach Trier." Bürger, *Lilienblätter und Zypressen-Zweige,* 153–63.

————. *Lilienblätter und Zypressen-Zweige* von Theodora. Frankfurt: Heller und Rohm, 1826.

————. "Mein Aufenthalt in Karlsbad und in Franzensbrunn, im Jahre 1815." Bürger, *Lillienblätter und Zypressen-Zweige,* 135–44.

————. *Mein Taschenbuch, den Freundlichen meines Geschlechts geweiht.* Pirna: Friese, 1802.

————. "Ein Sommermorgen in Baden-Baden 1808." Bürger, *Lilienblätter und Zypressen-Zweige,* 81–87.

Burke, Edmund. *A Philosophical Inquiry into the Origins of Our Ideas of the Sublime and Beautiful.* 1757. Rpt. Notre Dame: University of Notre Dame Press, 1968.

Daguerre, Louis Jacques Mandé *Das Daguerreotyp und das Diorama oder genaue und authentische Beschreibung meines Verfahrens und meiner Apparate zu*

Fixierung der Bilder der Camera obscura *und der von mir bei dem Diorama angewendeten Art und Weise der Malerei und der Beleuchtung.* Stuttgart: Metzlersche Buchhandlung, 1839.

Ehrmann, Marianne. *Leichtsinn und gutes Herz: Oder die Folgen der Erziehung.* Strasbourg: Joh. Heinrich Heitz Univ. Buchdr., 1786. Rpt. in Karin A. Wurst, *Frauen und Drama im achtzehnten Jahrhundert,* 188–251. Cologne: Böhlau, 1991.

Der Gesellige, eine moralische Wochenschrift. Ed. Samuel Gotthold Lange and George Friedrich Meier. Rpt. Wolfgang Martens. 6 books in 3 vols. Hildesheim: Olms, 1987.

Goethe, Johann Wolfgang von. *Aus meinem Leben: Dichtung und Wahrheit.* Vol. 10 of *Gedenkausgabe der Werke, Briefe und Gespräche.* Ed. Ernst Beutler. Zurich: Artemis, 1954.

———. "Brief an Karl August vom 11. 8. 1787." In *Briefe der Jahre 1786–1814,* 87–90. Vol. 19 of *Gedenkausgabe der Werke, Briefe und Gespräche.* Ed. Ernst Beutler. Zurich: Artemis, 1954.

———. "Diderots Versuch über die Malerei." In *Schriften zur Kunst,* 201–53. Vol. 13 of *Gedenkausgabe der Werke, Briefe und Gespräche.* Ed. Ernst Beutler. Zurich: Artemis, 1954.

———. *Elective Affinities.* Trans. Judith Ryan. Vol. 11 of *Goethe's Collected Works.* New York: Suhrkamp, 1988.

———. *From My Life: Poetry and Truth.* Trans. Robert Heitner. Vol. 4 of *Goethe's Collected Works.* New York: Suhrkamp, 1987.

———. *Gespräche mit Eckermann.* Vol. 24 of *Gedenkausgabe der Werke, Briefe und Gespräche.* Ed. Ernst Beutler. Zürich: Artemis, 1949.

———. *Goethes Werke und Briefe.* Ed. Erich Trunz and Karl Robert Mandelkow. Vol. 9. 4th ed. Hamburg: Wegner, 1960.

———. "Introduction to the *Propylaea.*" In *Essays on Art and Literature,* trans. Ellen von Nardroff and Ernest von Nardroff, ed. John Gearey, 3:78–90. New York: Suhrkamp, 1986.

———. *Italian Journey.* Trans. Robert R. Heitner. Ed. Thomas P. Saine and Jeffrey Sammons. Vol. 6 of *Goethe's Collected Works.* New York: Suhrkamp, 1989.

———. *Italienische Reise,* 9–612. Vol. 11 of *Gedenkausgabe der Werke, Briefe und Gespräche.* Ed. Ernst Beutler. Zurich: Artemis, 1954.

———. "On the Laocoon Group." In *Essays on Art and Literature,* trans. Ellen von Nardroff and Ernest H. von Nardroff, ed. John Gearey, 3:15–23. New York: Suhrkamp, 1986.

———. "*Propyläen* Einleitung." In *Schriften zur Kunst,* 135–56. Vol. 13 of *Gedenkausgabe der Werke, Briefe und Gespräche.* Ed. Ernst Beutler. Zurich: Artemis, 1954.

———. *Schriften zur Kunst.* Vol. 13 of *Gedenkausgabe der Werke, Briefe und*

Gespräche. Ed. Ernst Beutler. Zurich: Artemis, 1954.

———. "Über den Dilettantismus." In *Schriften zur Literatur,* 729–54. Vol. 14 of *Gedenkausgabe der Werke, Briefe und Gespräche.* Ed. Ernst Beutler. Zurich: Artemis, 1954.

———. "Über Laokoon." In *Schriften zur Kunst,* 161–74. Vol. 13 of *Gedenkausgabe der Werke, Briefe und Gespräche.* Ed. Ernst Beutler. Zurich: Artemis, 1954.

———. *Die Wahlverwandtschaften,* 9–275. Vol. 9 of *Gedenkausgabe der Werke, Briefe und Gespräche.* Ed. Ernst Beutler. Zurich: Artemis, 1954.

Das goldne ABC für Herren und Damen ausser der Ehe: Ein Taschenbuch. Berlin: Hayn, 1809.

Grimm, Jacob, and Wilhelm Grimm. *Deutsches Wörterbuch.* Leipzig: Hirzel, 1854–1919.

Hamburger Taschenbuch der Moden und des Luxus. Hamburg: Vollmer, 1802.

Herder, Johann Gottfried von. "Plastik: Einige Wahrnehmungen über Form und Gestalt aus Pygmalions bildendem Traume." In *Herders Sämmtliche Werke,* ed. Bernhard Suphan, 8:1–87. Berlin: Weidmannsche Buchhandlung, 1892.

———. "Studien und Entwürfe zur Plastik: 1. Von der Bildhauerkunst fürs Gefühl." In *Herders Sämmtliche Werke,* ed. Bernhard Suphan, 8:88–115. Berlin: Weidmannsche Buchhandlung, 1892.

Herz, Marcus. *Versuche über den Geschmack und die Ursachen seiner Verschiedenheit.* 2nd ed. 1776. Berlin, 1790.

Hirschfeld, Christian Cayus Lorenz. *Theorie der Gartenkunst.* Leipzig: Weidmanns Erben und Reich, 1779.

———. *Theorie der Gartenkunst.* Rpt. 5 vols. in 2. 1779–85. Hildesheim: Olms, 1973.

———. *The Theory of Garden Art: C. C. L. Hirschfeld.* Ed. and trans. Linda B. Parshall. Philadelphia: University of Pennsylvania Press, 2001.

Hoche, Johann Gottfried. *Vertraute Briefe.* Hanover: Chr. Ritscher, 1794.

Journal der Moden. Ed. Friedrich Justin Bertuch and Georg Melchior Kraus. Vol. 1. Gotha: Ettingersche Buchhandlung, 1786.

"Journal des Luxus und der Moden": 80 Colorierte Kupfer aus Deutschlands erster Modezeitschrift. Ed. Christina Kröll. Düsseldorf: Goethe Museum, 1979.

Journal für Literatur, Kunst, Luxus und Mode. Ed. Heinrich Döring. Vols. 31–41. Weimar Industrie-Comptoir, 1816–26.

Journal für Literatur, Kunst und geselliges Leben. Ed. Stephan Schütz. Vol. 42. Weimar Industrie-Comptoir, 1827.

Journal für Luxus, Mode und Gegenstände der Kunst. Ed. Carl Bertuch Vols. 28–30. Weimar Industrie-Comptoir, 1813–15.

"Die Jungfrau von Orleans." *Zeitung für die elegante Welt* no. 57, May 13, 1802, 454–55.

Kant, Immanuel. *Critique of Judgement.* Trans. J. H. Bernard. New York: Haffner Press, 1951.

———. *Kritik der Urteilskraft.* Vol. 10 of *Werkausgabe.* Ed. Wilhelm Weischedel. Frankfurt: Suhrkamp, 1977.

Karikaturen Almanach mit 9 illuminierten Blättern nach Hogarth und Lichtenberg. Hamburg: Vollmer, 1801.

Knigge, Adolph Freiherr. *Über den Umgang mit Menschen.* Ed. Karl-Heinz Göttert. Stuttgart: Reclam, 1991.

Knight, Richard Payne. *Analytical Inquiry into the Principles of Taste.* London: Payne and White, 1805.

La Roche, Sophie von. *Briefe an Lina.* Speier, 1785. Facsimile rpt., Eschborn: Dieter Klotz, 1993.

———. *Sophie in London, 1786, Being the Diary of Sophie v. La Roche.* Trans. Clare Williams. London: Jonathan Cape, 1933.

Leipziger Taschenbuch für Frauenzimmer: Zum Nutzen und Vergnügen auf das Jahr 1804. Leipzig: Böhme, 1804.

Lessing, Gotthold Ephraim. "Laokoon: oder Über die Grenzen der Mahlerey und Poesie." In *Sämtliche Schriften,* ed. Karl Lachmann and Franz Muncker, 9:1–173. Stuttgart: Göschen, 1893.

Lichtenberg, Georg Christoph. *Briefwechsel.* Ed. Ulrich Joost and Albrecht Schöne. Munich: Beck, 1983.

———. "Warum hat Deutschland noch kein großes öffentliches Seebad?" In *Georg Christoph Lichtenberg Schriften und Briefe,* ed. Wolfgang Promies, 3:95–102. 2nd ed. Munich: Beck, 1973.

Meusel, Johann Georg. *Lexikon der vom Jahre 1750–1800 verstorbenen teutschen Schriftsteller.* 15 vols. Leipzig, 1802–16.

Möser, Justus. "Versuch einiger Gemälde unserer Zeit, vormals zu Hannover als ein Wochenblatt ausgetheilet" (Hannover 1747). In Möser, *Sämtliche Werke historisch-kritische Ausgabe in 14. Bänden.* Vol. 1. Ed. Werner Kohlschmidt. Berlin: Oldenborg, 1944.

Neuenhahn d. Jüngere, V., ed. *Annalen der Gärtnerey: Nebst einem Intelligenzblatt für Garten-und Blumen-Freunde.* Erfurt: Keysersche Buchhandlung, 1795.

Pockels, Carl Friedrich. *Versuch einer Charakteristik des weiblichen Geschlechts: Ein Sittengemälde der Menschen, des Zeitalters und des geselligen Lebens.* Bd. 1–4 Hanover, 1797–1801.

Recke, Charlotta Elisabeth Konstantia von der. *Nachricht von des berüchtigten Cagliostro Aufenthalte in Mitau im Jahre 1779 und von dessen magischen Operationen.* Berlin: bey Friedrich Nicolai, 1787.

Recke, Elisa von der. *Familien-Scenen oder Entwickelungen auf dem Maskenballe.* 1794. Leipzig: Fleischer, 1826.

———. *Tagebuch einer Reise durch einen Theil Deutschlands und durch Italien*

(1804–1806) von Elisa von der Recke. Ed. Hofrath Böttiger. 4 vols. Berlin: Nicolaische Buchhhandlung, 1817.

Reichard, Heinrich August Ottokar. "Uebersicht des heutigen Zustandes des teutschen Schaubühnen-Wesens." *Journal des Luxus und der Moden* 4 (February 1789): 58–75.

Röder, Philip Jacob, ed. *Lehrbegriff der Baumzucht und deren Veredlungsarten für Liebhaber und Landleute.* Coburg: Rudolph August Wilhelm Ahl, 1796.

Schiller, Friedrich. "Anthologie auf das Jahr 1782." In *Schillers Werke Nationalausgabe: Philosophische Schriften,* ed. Herbert Meyer, 22:132–35. Weimar: Böhlaus Nachfolger, 1958.

———. *Musen-Almanach für das Jahr 1796.* Neustrelitz: Michaelis, 1796.

———. *Musen-Almanach für das Jahr 1797.* Tübingen: Cotta, 1797.

———. *Musen-Almanach für das Jahr 1798.* Tübingen: Cotta, 1798.

———. *Schillers Werke Nationalausgabe.* Ed. Julius Peterson, Liselotte Blumenthal, Benno von Wiese, Norbert Oeller, and Siegfried Seidel. 42 vols. Weimar: Hermann Böhlaus Nachfolger, 1953–85.

———. "Über Bürgers Gedichte." In *Schillers Werke Nationalausgabe: Philosophische Schriften,* ed. Herbert Meyer, 22:245–64. Weimar: Hermann Böhlaus Nachfolger, 1958.

———. "Über das Pathetische." In *Schillers Werke Nationalausgabe: Philosophische Schriften,* ed. Benno von Wiese, 20:196–221. Weimar: Hermann Böhlaus Nachfolger, 1962.

———. "Ueber das gegenwärtige teutsche Theater." In *Schillers Werke Nationalausgabe: Philosophische Schriften,* ed. Benno von Wiese, 20:79–86. Weimar: Hermann Böhlaus Nachfolger, 1962.

———. "Ueber die ästhetische Erziehung." In *Schillers Werke Nationalausgabe: Philosophische Schriften,* ed. Benno von Wiese, 20:309–412. Weimar: Hermann Böhlaus Nachfolger, 1962.

———. "Vom Erhabenen." In *Schillers Werke Nationalausgabe: Philosophische Schriften,* ed. Benno von Wiese, 20:171–95. Weimar: Hermann Böhlaus Nachfolger, 1962.

———. "Was kann eine gute stehende Schaubühne eigentlich wirken?" In *Schillers Werke Nationalausgabe: Philosophische Schriften,* ed. Benno von Wiese, 20:87–100. Weimar: Hermann Böhlaus Nachfolger, 1962.

———. "Zerstreute Betrachtungen über verschiedene ästhetische Gegenstände." In *Schillers Werke Nationalausgabe: Philosophische Schriften,* ed. Benno von Wiese, 20:222–40. Weimar: Hermann Böhlaus Nachfolger, 1962.

Schlegel, Friedrich. *Seine prosaischen Jugendschriften.* Ed. Jacob Minor. Vol. 1. Vienna: Konegen, 1882.

Die Schopenhauers: Der Familienbriefwechsel von Adele, Arthur, Heinrich, Floris, und Johanna Schopenhauer. Ed. and intro. Ludger Lütkehaus. Zurich:

Haffmans, 1991.

Solbrig's *Almanach der Travestieen und Parodieen.* Leipzig: Franz, 1816.

Solbrig's *Taschenbuch der Deklamation.* Leipzig: Franz, 1814.

Spieß, Christian Heinrich. *Klara von Hoheneichen: Ritterschauspiel in vier Aufzügen.* Prag und Leipzig, 1800.

Taschenbuch für Mineralwassertrinker. Nürnberg: Baur und Raspe, 1820.

Taschenbuch für Freunde u. Freundinnen des Carnevals mit Illuminierten Kupfern. Leipzig: Leo, 1804.

Taschenbuch von Wieland und Goethe. Tübingen: Cotta, 1804.

Taschenkalender auf das Jahr 1798 für Natur- und Gartenfreuden. Mit Abbildungen von Hohenheim und andern Kupfern. Tübingen: Cotta'sche Buchhandlung, 1798.

Thon, Eleonore von. *Adelheit von Rastenberg.* Weimar: Hoffmannsche Buchhandlung, 1788. Rpt., Karin A. Wurst, ed. and intro., *Eleonore von Thon, Adelheit von Rastenberg.* Text and Translations Series. New York: MLA, 1996.

Trübners Deutsches Wörterbuch. Ed. Walther Mitzka. Vol. 7. Berlin: de Gruyter, 1956.

Türk, Daniel Gottlob. *Klavierschule oder Anweisung zum Klavierspiele für Lehrer und Lernende.* Ed. Erwin R. Jacobi. Leipzig: Halle, 1789. Rpt. Kassel: Bärenreiter, 1962.

Varnhagen von Ense, K. A. *Galerie von Bildnissen aus Rahel's Umgang und Briefwechsel.* Leipzig: Gebr. Reichenbach, 1836.

Verhandlungen und Schriften der hamburgischen Gesellschaft zur Beförderung der Künste und nützlichen Gewerbe. Vol. 4. Hamburg, 1797.

Wallenheim, Auguste von. *Klara von Leuenstein: Ein Schauspiel aus den Ritterzeiten* (1806). *Neueste deutsche Schaubühne* 6 (1806): 49–120.

Ziegler, Friedrich Wilhelm. *"Mathilde Gräfin von Griessbach:* Ein Trauerspiel in fünf Aufzügen aus den Zeiten des Faustrechts" (1791). *Deutsche Schaubühne* 11 (1791): 99–178.

Zimmermann, E. A. W. *Almanach der Reisen, oder unterhaltende Darstellung der Entdeckungen des 18then Jahrhunderts in Rücksicht auf Länder- Menschen- und Produktenkunde für jede Klasse von Lesern.* Leipzig: Fischer, 1814.

Secondary Sources

Adelson, Leslie. *Making Bodies, Making History: Feminism and German Identity.* Lincoln: University of Nebraska Press, 1993.

Adorno, Theodor W. *Ästhetische Theorie.* 10th ed. Frankfurt: Suhrkamp, 1990.

———. *Negative Dialektik.* 8th ed. Frankfurt: Suhrkamp, 1994.

Adorno, Theodor W., and Max Horkheimer. *Dialectic of Enlightenment.* Trans. John Cumming. New York: Continuum, 1972.

Anderson, Benedict. *Imagined Communities: Reflections on the Origin and Spread of Nationalism.* London: Verso, 1983.

Andrews, Malcom. *The Search for the Picturesque: Landscape Aesthetics and Tourism in Britain, 1760–1800.* Stanford: Stanford University Press, 1989.

Appadurai, Arjun. *The Social Life of Things: Commodities in Cultural Perspective.* Cambridge: Cambridge University Press, 1989.

Appell, J. W. *Die Ritter-, Räuber-, und Schauerromantik: Zur Geschichte der deutschen Unterhaltungsliteratur.* Leipzig: Wilhelm Engelmann, 1859.

Arendt, Hannah. *Rahel Varnhagen: Lebensgeschichte einer deutschen Jüdin aus der Romantik.* Munich: Piper, 1959. Trans. Hannah Arendt, *Rachel Varnhagen: The Life of a Jewess.* Ed. Liliane Weissberg, trans. Richard and Clara Winston. Baltimore: Johns Hopkins University Press, 1997.

Ariès, Philippe. *The Hour of Our Death.* Trans. Helen Weaver. New York: Knopf, 1981.

Armstrong, Nancy, and Leonhard Tennenhouse, eds. *The Ideology of Conduct: Essays on Literature and the History of Sexuality.* New York: Methuen, 1987.

Arnold-de Simine, Silke. *Leichen im Keller: Zu Fragen des Gender in Angstinszenierungen der Schauer- und Kriminalliteratur (1780–1830).* St. Ingbert: Röhrig Universitätsverlag, 2000.

Ash, Juliet, and Elizabeth Wilson, eds. *Chic Thrills: A Fashion Reader.* Berkeley: University of California Press, 1993.

Bachler, Karl. *Gemalte Theatervorhänge in Deutschland und Österreich.* Munich: Bruckmann, 1972.

Backscheider, Paula. *Spectacular Politics: Theatrical Power and Mass Culture in Early Modern England.* Baltimore: Johns Hopkins University Press, 1994.

Bake, Rita. "Zur Arbeits- und Lebensweise Hamburger Manufakturarbeiterinnen im 18. Jahrhundert." In *Hamburg im Zeitalter der Aufklärung,* ed. Inge Stephan and Hans-Gerd Winter, 357–72. Berlin: Dietrich Reimer, 1989.

Bal, Mieke. *Reading "Rembrandt": Beyond the Word-Image Opposition.* Cambridge: Cambridge University Press, 1991.

Barker-Benfield, G. J. *The Culture of Sensibility: Sex and Society in Eighteenth-Century Britain.* Chicago: University of Chicago Press, 1992.

Barthes, Roland. *The Pleasure of the Text.* Trans. Richard Miller. 1973; New York: Hill & Wang, 1975.

Battersby, Christine. *Gender and Genius.* Bloomington: Indiana University Press, 1989.

Batteux, Charles. "Les beaux arts reduits," *Principes de la litterature.* Vol. 1. Göttingen and Leyden, 1764.

Bayer-Berenbaum, Linda. *The Gothic Imagination: Expansion in Gothic*

Literature and Art. Rutherford, N.J., and London: Fairleigh Dickinson University Press and Associated University Presses, 1982.

Beaujean, Marion. *Der Trivialroman im ausgehenden 18. Jahrhundert.* Bonn: Bouvier, 1964.

Becher, Ursula. *Geschichte des modernen Lebensstils: Essen-Wohnen-Freizeit-Reisen.* Munich: Beck, 1990.

Becker-Cantarino, Barbara. *Der lange Weg zur Mündigkeit: Frau und Literatur (1500–1800).* Stuttgart: Metzler, 1987.

Beer, Axel. "Musikzeitschriften." In *Von Almanach bis Zeitung: Ein Handbuch der Medien in Deutschland, 1700–1800,* ed. Ernst Fischer, Wilhelm Haefs, and York-Gothart Mix, 233–47. Munich: Beck, 1999.

Begemann, Christian. *Furcht und Angst im Prozeß der Aufklärung.* Frankfurt: Athenäum, 1987.

Belgum, Kirsten. "A Nation for the Masses: Production of Identity in the Late-Nineteenth-Century Popular Press." In *A User's Guide to German Cultural Studies,* ed. Scott Denham, Irene Kacandes, and Jonathan Petropoulos, 163–80. Ann Arbor: University of Michigan Press, 1997.

———. *Popularizing the Nation: Audience, Representation, and the Production of Identity in* Die Gartenlaube *(1853–1900).* Lincoln: University of Nebraska Press, 1998.

Berlyne, D. E., and K. B. Madsen, eds. *Pleasure, Reward, Preference: Their Nature, Determinants, and Role in Behavior.* New York: Academic Press, 1973.

Berman, Russell. *Cultural Studies of Modern Germany: History, Representation, and Nationhood.* Madison: University of Wisconsin Press, 1993.

Binder, Wolfgang. *Aufschlüsse: Studien zur deutschen Literatur.* Zurich: Artemis, 1976.

Böhme, Hartmut. "Hamburg und sein Wasser im 18. Jahrhundert." In *Hamburg im Zeitalter der Aufklärung,* ed. Hans-Gerd Winter and Inge Stephan, 57–92. Berlin: Dietrich Reimer, 1989.

Bolla, Peter de. "The charm'd eye." In *Body and Text in the Eighteenth Century,* ed. Veronica Kelly and Dorothea von Mücke, 89–111. Stanford: Stanford University Press, 1994.

Bollenbeck, Georg. *Bildung und Kultur: Glanz und Elend eines deutschen Deutungsmusters.* Frankfurt: Insel, 1994.

Bolz, Norbert W. "Ästhetisches Opfer: Die Foren der Wünsche in Goethes *Wahlverwandtschaften.*" In *Goethes* Wahlverwandtschaften: *Kritische Modelle und Diskursanalysen zum Mythos der Literatur,* ed. Bolz, 64–90. Hildesheim: Gerstenberg, 1981.

———, ed. *Goethes* Wahlverwandtschaften: *Kritische Modelle und Diskursanalysen zum Mythos der Literatur.* Hildesheim: Gerstenberg, 1981.

Borchert, Angela. "Übersetzung und Umschrift: Spätaufklärerische Kulturpolitik am Beispiel von Friedrich Justin Bertuchs Märchensammlung 'Die Blaue Bibliothek aller Nationen.'" In *Friedrich Justin Bertuch (1747–1822): Verleger, Schriftsteller, und Unternehmer im klassischen Weimar,* ed. Gerhard R. Kaiser and Siegfried Seifert, 169–94. Tübingen: Niemeyer, 2000.

Bosse, Heinrich. "Die gelehrte Republik." In *"Öffentlichkeit" im 18. Jahrhundert,* ed. Hans-Wolf Jäger, 51–76. Göttingen: Wallstein, 1997.

Bourdieu, Pierre. *Distinction: A Social Critique of the Judgement of Taste.* Trans. Richard Nice. 1979. Cambridge: Harvard University Press, 1984.

———. *Die feinen Unterschiede: Kritik der gesellschaftlichen Urteilskraft.* Frankfurt: Suhrkamp, 1979.

———. "The Genesis of the Concepts of Habitus and Field." Trans. Channa Newman. In Bourdieu, *The Field of Cultural Production: Essays in Art and Literature,* ed. and intro. Randal Johnson, 1–25. New York: Columbia University Press, 1993.

———. *In Other Words: Essays Towards a Reflective Sociology.* Trans. Matthew Adamson. Cambridge and Stanford: Polity Press and Stanford University Press, 1990.

———. "The Market of Symbolic Goods." In Bourdieu, *The Field of Cultural Production: Essays in Art and Literature,* ed. and intro. Randal Johnson, 112–41. New York: Columbia University Press, 1993.

———. "Outline of a Sociological Theory of Art Perception." In Bourdieu, *The Field of Cultural Production: Essays on Art and Literature,* ed. and intro. Randal Johnson, 215–37. New York: Columbia University Press, 1993.

———. *Zur Soziologie der symbolischen Formen.* Trans. Wolfgang Fietkau. 6th ed. Frankfurt: Suhrkamp, 1997.

Bourdieu, Pierre, and Jean-Claude Passeron. *Reproduction in Education, Society, and Culture.* Trans. Richard Nice. Sage Studies in Social and Educational Change, no. 5. London: Sage, 1977.

Bovenschen, Silvia. *Die imaginierte Weiblichkeit: Exemplarische Untersuchungen zu kulturgeschichtlichen und literarischen Präsentationsformen des Weiblichen.* Frankfurt: Suhrkamp, 1979.

———, ed. *Die Listen der Mode.* Frankfurt: Suhrkamp, 1986.

Braudel, Fernand. *Civilization and Capitalism, Fifteenth–Eighteenth Century.* Vol. 1, *The Structures of Everyday Life;* vol. 2, *The Wheels of Commerce;* vol. 3, *The Perspective of the World.* New York: Harper & Row, 1985.

Bretter, die die Welt bedeuten: Entwürfe zum Theaterdekor und zum Bühnenkostüm: Ausstellung der Kunstbibliothek Berlin Staatliche Museen Preußischer Kulturbesitz. Berlin: Dietrich Reimer, 1978.

Brewer, John, and Roy Porter, eds. *Consumption and the World of Goods.* London: Routledge, 1993.

Brooks, Peter. *Body Work: Objects of Desire in Modern Narrative.* Cambridge: Harvard University Press, 1993.

Brown, Marshall. "Gothic Readers versus Gothic Writers" *Eighteenth-Century Studies* 35, no. 4 (2002): 615–59.

———. *Preromanticism*. Stanford: Stanford University Press, 1991.

Bruford, Walter. *Germany in the Eighteenth Century: The Social Background of the Literary Revival*. Cambridge: Cambridge University Press, 1949.

Das Bühnenbild im 19. Jahrhundert. Munich: Theatermuseum München, 1959.

Bürger, Christa. *Textanalyse als Ideologiekritik: Zur Rezeption zeitgenössischer Unterhaltungsliteratur*. Frankfurt: Athenäum, 1973.

———. *Der Ursprung der bürgerlichen Institution Kunst im höfischen Weimar: Literatursoziologische Untersuchungen zum klassischen Goethe*. Frankfurt: Suhrkamp, 1977.

Bürger, Christa, Peter Bürger, and Jochen Schulte-Sasse, eds. *Aufklärung und literarische Öffentlichkeit*. Frankfurt: Suhrkamp, 1980.

Burger, Heinz Otto, ed. *Studien zur Trivialliteratur*. Frankfurt: Klostermann, 1968.

Bürgers unglückliche Liebe: Ehestandsgeschichte von Elise Hahn und Gottfried August Bürger. Ed. Hermann Kinder. 2nd ed. Frankfurt: Insel, 1987.

Busch-Salmen, Gabriele. "Private gesellige Zirkel und 'musikalische Unterhaltungen.'" In Gabriele Busch-Salmen, Walter Salmen, and Christoph Michel, *Der Weimarer Musenhof: Literatur, Musik, und Tanz, Gartenkunst, Geselligkeit, Malerei*, 85–108. Stuttgart: Metzler, 1998.

Campbell, Colin. *The Romantic Ethic and the Spirit of Modern Consumerism*. New York: Basil Blackwell, 1987.

Castle, Terry. "The Spectralization of the Other in the Mysteries of Udolpho." In *The New Eighteenth Century: Theory, Politics, English Literature*, ed. Felicity Nussbaum and Laura Brown, 231–53. New York: Routledge, 1991.

Clauss, Elke. *Liebeskunst: Der Liebesbrief im 18. Jahrhundert*. Stuttgart: Metzler, 1993.

The Collected Dialogues of Plato. Ed. Edith Hamilton and Huntington Cairns. New York: Pantheon, 1961.

Corngold, Stanley. *Complex Pleasure*. Stanford: Stanford University Press, 1998.

Craik, Jennifer. *The Face of Fashion: Cultural Studies in Fashion*. New York: Routledge, 1994.

Cunningham, Hugh. *Leisure in the Industrial Revolution c. 1780–1880*. London: Croom Helm, 1980.

Cusset, Catherine. *No Tomorrow: The Ethics of Pleasure in the French Enlightenment*. Charlottesville: University Press of Virginia, 1999.

Damm, Sigrid. *Christiane und Goethe: Eine Recherche*. Frankfurt: Insel, 1998.

———. *Cornelia Goethe*. Berlin: Aufbau, 1988.

Dane, Gesa. *"Die heilsame Toilette": Kosmetik und Bildung in Goethe's* Der Mann von fünfzig Jahren. Göttingen: Wallstein, 1994.

Dawson, Ruth. "Women Communicating: Eighteenth-Century German Journals Edited by Women." *Archives et Bibliothèques de Belgique* 54 (1983): 95–111.

Day, William Patrick. *In the Circles of Fear and Desire: A Study of Gothic Fantasy.* Chicago: University of Chicago Press, 1985.

Derks, Paul. *Die Schande der heiligen Päderastie: Homosexualität und Öffentlichkeit in der deutschen Literatur, 1750–1850.* Berlin: Rosa Winkel, 1990.

Diers, Michael. "Bertuchs Bilderwelt: Zur populären Ikonographie der Aufklärung." In *Friedrich Justin Bertuch (1747–1822): Verleger, Schriftsteller, und Unternehmer im klassischen Weimar,* ed. Gerhard R. Kaiser and Siegfried Seifert, 433–45. Tübingen: Niemeyer, 2000.

Dorn Brose, Eric. *German History, 1789–1871: From the Holy Roman Empire to the Bismarckian Reich.* Providence: Berghahn Books. 1997.

Dubbini, Renzo. *Geography of the Gaze: Urban and Rural Vision in Early Modern Europe.* Trans. Lydia G. Cochrane. Chicago: University of Chicago Press, 2002.

Dyer, Richard. "Entertainment and Utopia in Mass Culture." In *Genre: The Musical: A Reader,* ed. Rick Altman, 175–89. London: Routledge & Kegan Paul, 1991.

Edwards, Lee. *Psyche as Hero: Female Heroism and Fictional Form.* Middletown, Conn.: Wesleyan University Press, 1984.

Eigenmann, Susanne. *Zwischen ästhetischer Raserei und aufgeklärter Disziplin: Hamburger Theater im späten 18. Jahrhundert.* Stuttgart: Metzler, 1994.

Elias, Norbert. *The Civilizing Process:* vol. 1, *The History of Manners;* vol. 2, *Power and Civility;* vol. 3, *The Court Society.* New York: Pantheon, 1978, 1982, 1983.

———. *Die Höfische Gesellschaft.* 1969. Frankfurt: Suhrkamp, 1983.

———. *Über den Prozeß der Zivilisation: Soziogenetische und psychogenetische Untersuchungen.* 2 vols. Frankfurt: Suhrkamp, 1989.

Emmrich, Angelika, and Susanne Schröder. "Weimarer historische Interieurs: Zum Ameublement im Journal des Luxus und der Moden." In *Friedrich Justin Bertuch (1747–1822): Verleger, Schriftsteller, und Unternehmer im klassischen Weimar,* ed. Gerhard R. Kaiser and Siegfried Seifert, 501–18. Tübingen: Niemeyer, 2000.

Engelsing, Rolf. *Analphabetentum und Lektüre: Zur Sozialgeschichte des Lesens in Deutschland zwischen feudaler und industrieller Gesellschaft.* Stuttgart: Metzlersche Buchhandlung, 1973.

———. *Der Bürger als Leser: Lesergeschichte in Deutschland, 1500–1800.* Stuttgart: Metzler, 1974.

Enzensberger, Hans Magnus. "Constituents of a Theory of the Media." In *The*

Consciousness Industry: On Literature, Politics, and the Media, 95–128. New York: Seabury, 1974.

Faber, Richard. "Parkleben: Zur sozialen Idyllik Goethes." In *Goethes Wahlverwandtschaften: Kritische Modelle und Diskursanalysen zum Mythos der Literatur,* ed. Norbert W. Bolz, 91–168. Hildesheim: Gerstenberg, 1981.

Fabricant, Carole. "The Literature of Domestic Tourism and the Public Consumption of Private Property." In *The New Eighteenth Century: Theory, Politics, English Literature,* ed. Felicity Nussbaum and Laura Brown, 254–75. 1987; New York: Routledge, 1991.

Feldmann, Wilhelm. *Friedrich Justin Bertuch.* Saarbrücken: Carl Schmidtke, 1902.

Ferguson Ellis, Kate. *The Contested Castle: Gothic Novels and the Subversion of Domestic Ideology.* Urbana: University of Illinois Press, 1989.

Fischer, Ernst, Wilhelm Haefs, and York-Gothart Mix, eds. *Vom Almanach bis Zeitung: Ein Handbuch der Medien in Deutschland, 1700–1800.* Munich: Beck, 1999.

Flessau, Kurt-Ingo. *Der moralische Roman: Studien zur gesellschaftskritischen Trivialliteratur der Goethezeit.* Köln, Graz: Böhlau, 1968.

Fluck, Winfried. *Populäre Kultur: Studienbuch zur Funktionsbestimmung und Interpretation populärer Kultur.* Stuttgart: Metzler, 1979.

Flügel, J. C. *The Psychology of Clothes.* London: Hoarth, 1930. Rpt. trans. "Die Psychologie der Mode." Excerpt in *Die Listen der Mode,* ed. Silvia Bovenschen, 208–63. Frankfurt: Suhrkamp, 1986.

Foltin, Hans Friedrich. "Karl Gottlieb Cramers 'Erasmus Schleicher' als Beispiel eines frühen Unterhaltungs- oder Trivialromans." In *Studien zur Trivialliteratur,* ed. Heinz Otto Burger, 57–81. Frankfurt: Klostermann, 1968.

———. "Zur Erforschung der Unterhaltungs- und Trivialliteratur, insbesondere im Bereich des Romans." In *Studien zur Trivialliteratur,* ed. Heinz Otto Burger, 242–70. Frankfurt: Klostermann, 1968.

Foucault, Michel. *Discipline and Punish: The Birth of the Prison.* Trans. Alan Sheridan. New York: Vintage, 1979.

———. *The History of Sexuality.* Vol. 1, *An Introduction.* Trans. Robert Hurley. New York: Vintage House, 1980.

———. *The History of Sexuality.* Vol. 3, *The Care of the Self.* Trans. Robert Hurley. New York: Random House, 1986.

Franklin, Rosemary. "The Awakening and the Failure of Psyche." *American Literature* 56 (1984): 510–26.

Fraser, Nancy. "Rethinking the Public Sphere: A Contribution to the Critique of Actually Existing Democracy." In *The Phantom Public Sphere,* ed. Bruce Robbins, 10–11. Minneapolis: University of Minnesota Press, 1993.

Frevert, Ute, ed. *Bürgerinnen und Bürger.* Göttingen: Vandenhoeck & Ruprecht, 1988.

Friedberg, Anne. *Window Shopping: Cinema and the Postmodern.* Berkeley: University of California Press, 1993.

Füssel, Stephan. "Almanache und Kalender aus der Verlagsproduktion Georg Joachim Göschen (1752–1828)." In *Literarische Leitmedien: Almanach und Taschenbuch im kulturwissenschaftlichen Kontext,* ed. Paul Gerhard Klussmann and York-Gothart Mix, 65–82. Wiesbaden: Harassowitz, 1998.

Gall, Lothar. *Von der städtischen zur bürgerlichen Gesellschaft, Enzyklopädie deutscher Geschichte.* Vol. 25. Munich: Oldenbourg, 1993.

Gailus, Andreas. "Of Beautiful and Dismembered Bodies: Art as Social Discipline in Schiller's 'On the Aesthetic Education of Man.'" In *Impure Reason: Dialectic of Enlightenment in Germany,* ed. W. Daniel Wilson and Robert C. Holub, 146–65. Detroit: Wayne State University Press, 1993.

Gallas, Helga. "Ehe als Instrument des Masochismus oder 'Glückseligkeitstriangel' als Aufrechterhaltung des Begehrens." In *Untersuchungen zum Roman von Frauen,* ed. Helga Gallas and Magdalene Heuser, 66–75. Tübingen: Niemeyer, 1990.

Garve, Christian. *Popularphilosophische Schriften über literarische, ästhetische und gesellschaftliche Gegenstände.* Ed. Kurt Wölfel. Facsimile rpt., vol. 2. Stuttgart: Metzler, 1974.

———. "Über die Moden." In *Versuche über verschiedene Gegenstände aus der Moral, der Literatur und dem gesellschaftlichen Leben.* 1792. Rpt. Hildesheim: Olms, 1985.

Gaus, Detlef. *Geselligkeit und das Gesellige: Bildung, Bürgertum, und bildungsbürgerliche Kultur um 1800.* Stuttgart: Metzler, 1998.

Gellner, Ernest. *Nations and Nationalism.* Ithaca: Cornell University Press, 1983.

Gilbert, Sandra, and Susan Gubar. *The Madwoman in the Attic: The Woman Writer and the Nineteenth-Century Literary Imagination.* New Haven: Yale University Press, 1979.

Gramsci, Antonio. *Selections from the Prison Notebooks.* Ed. Quintin Hoare and Geoffrey Nowell Smith. London: International Publishers, 1971.

Grasskamp, Walter. *Museumsgründer und Museumsstürmer: Zur Sozialgeschichte des Kunstmuseums.* Munich: Beck, 1981.

Greenblatt, Stephen. *Renaissance Self-Fashioning: From More to Shakespeare.* Chicago: University of Chicago Press, 1980.

Greiner, Martin. *Die Entstehung der modernen Unterhaltungsliteratur: Studien zum Trivialroman des 18. Jahrhunderts.* Reinbek: Rowohlt, 1964.

Greis, Jutta. *Drama Liebe: Zur Entstehungsgeschichte der modernen Liebe im Drama des 18. Jahrhunderts.* Stuttgart: Metzler, 1991.

Grieger, Astrid. "Kunst und Öffentlichkeit in der zweiten Hälfte des 18. Jahrhunderts." In *"Öffentlichkeit" im 18. Jahrhundert,* ed. Hans-Wolf Jäger, 117–35. Göttingen: Wallstein, 1997.

Griep, Wolfgang. "'Die Handlung steht im Flor . . .': Über das Bild Hamburgs in Reisebeschreibungen aus dem 18. Jahrhundert." In *Hamburg im Zeitalter der Aufklärung,* ed. Inge Stephan and Hans-Gerd Winter, 16–41. Berlin: Dietrich Reimer, 1989.

Grimminger, Rolf. "Die Utopie der vernünftigen Lust: Sozialphilosophische Skizze zur Ästhetik des 18. Jahrhunderts bis zu Kant." In *Aufklärung und literarische Öffentlichkeit,* ed. Christa Bürger, Peter Bürger, and Jochen Schulte-Sasse, 116–32. Frankfurt: Suhrkamp, 1980.

Gronemeyer, Horst. "Klopstocks Stellung in der Hamburger Gesellschaft." In *Hamburg im Zeitalter der Aufklärung,* ed. Inge Stephan and Hans-Gerd Winter, 284–304. Berlin: Dietrich Reimer, 1989.

Habermas, Jürgen. *Der philosophische Diskurs der Moderne.* Frankfurt: Suhrkamp, 1988.

———. *The Structural Transformation of the Public Sphere.* Trans. Thomas Burger and Friedrich Lawrence. Cambridge: MIT Press, 1989.

———. *Strukturwandel der Öffentlichkeit.* 1962; Frankfurt: Suhrkamp, 1990.

Hall, Stuart. "Encoding and Decoding in the Television Discourse." Stencilled Occasional Papers, no. 7. Birmingham, England: Centre for Contemporary Cultural Studies, 1973.

Hauke, Marie-Kristin. "'Wenns nur Lärmen macht . . .': Friedrich Justin Bertuch und die (Buch-) Werbung des späten 18. Jahrhunderts." In *Friedrich Justin Bertuch (1747–1822): Verleger, Schriftsteller, und Unternehmer im klassischen Weimar,* ed. Gerhard R. Kaiser and Siegfried Seifert, 369–80. Tübingen: Niemeyer, 2000.

Heath, Stephen, and Gilligan Skirrow. "An Interview with Raymond Williams." In *Studies in Entertainment: Critical Approaches to Mass Culture,* ed. in Tania Modleski, 3–17. Bloomington: Indiana University Press, 1986.

Hein, Dieter. "Umbruch und Aufbruch: Bürgertum in Karlsruhe und Mannheim 1780–1820." In *Vom alten zum neuen Bürgertum: Die mitteleuropäische Stadt im Umbruch, 1780–1820,* ed. Lothar Gall, 447–515. Munich: Oldenbourg, 1991.

Hess, Jonathan. *Reconstituting the Body Politic: Enlightenment, Public Culture, and the Invention of Aesthetic Autonomy.* Detroit: Wayne State University Press, 1999.

Heyden-Rynsch, Verena von der. *Europäische Salons: Höhepunkte einer versunkenen weiblichen Kultur.* Munich: Artemis & Winkler, 1992.

Hirsch, Marianne, Ruth Perry, and Virginia Swain. Foreword. In *In the Shadow of Olympus: German Women Writers around 1800,* ed. Katherine R.

Goodman and Edith Waldstein, vii–xi. Albany: SUNY Press, 1992.

Hoff, Dagmar von, and Helga Meise. "Tableux vivants: Die Kunst- und Kultform der Attitüden und lebenden Bilder." In *Weiblichkeit und Tod in der Literatur,* ed. Renate Berger and Inge Stephan, 69–86. Cologne: Böhlau, 1987.

Hoffmann-Axthelm, Inge. "'Geisterfamilie': Studien zur Geselligkeit der Frühromantik." Diss., Berlin, 1970.

Hollander, Anne. *Sex and Suits.* New York: Knopf, 1994.

Hollmer, Heide, and Albert Meier. "Kunstzeitschriften." In *Von Almanach bis Zeitung: Ein Handbuch der Medien in Deutschland 1700–1800,* ed. Ernst Fischer, Wilhelm Haefs, and York-Gothart Mix, 157–75. Munich: Beck, 1999.

Holmström, Kirsten Gram. *Monodrama, Attitudes, Tableaux Vivants: Studies on Some Trends of Theatrical Fashions, 1770–1815.* Stockholm: Almqvist & Wiksell, 1967.

Holtzhauer, Helmut. *Friedrich Justin Bertuch: Zum 150. Todestag am 3. April 1972.* Weimar: Weimarer Stadtmuseum, 1972.

Hörisch, Jochen. "Die Dekonstruktion der Sprache und der Advent neuer Medien in Goethes *Wahlverwandtschaften.*" *Merkur* 52 (1998): 826–39.

Horkheimer, Max. "Art and Mass Culture," *Studies in Philosophy and Social Science* 9, no. 2 (1941): 290–304.

Huizinga, Johan. *Homo Ludens: Vom Ursprung der Kultur im Spiel.* 1938. Hamburg: Rowohlt, 1987.

Huyssen, Andreas. "Mass Culture as Woman: Modernism's Other." In *Studies in Entertainment: Cultural Approaches to Mass Culture,* ed. Tania Modleski, 188–207. Bloomington: Indiana University Press, 1986.

Jäger, Hans-Wolf, ed. *"Öffentlichkeit" im 18. Jahrhundert.* Göttigen: Wallstein, 1997.

Jameson, Fredric. "Reification and Utopia in Mass Culture." *Social Text* 1 (1979): 130–48.

Jooss, Birgit. *Lebende Bilder: Körperliche Nachahmung von Kunstwerken in der Goethezeit.* Berlin: Reimer, 1999.

Kaiser, Gerhard. "Friedrich Justin Bertuch: Versuch eines Portraits." In *Friedrich Justin Bertuch (1747–1822): Verleger, Schriftsteller, und Unternehmer im klassischen Weimar,* ed. Gerhard R. Kaiser and Siegfried Seifert, 15–39. Tübingen: Niemeyer, 2000.

Kaschuba, Wolfgang. "Deutsche Bürgerlichkeit nach 1800: Kultur als symbolische Praxis." In *Bürgertum im 19. Jahrhundert: Deutschland im europäischen Vergleich,* ed. Jürgen Kocka, 3:9–44. Munich: dtv, 1988.

Kelly, Veronica, and Dorothea von Mücke. "Introduction: Body and Text in the Eighteenth Century." In *Body and Text in the Eighteenth Century,* ed. Veronica Kelly and Dorothea von Mücke, 1–20. Stanford: Stanford

University Press, 1994.

Kemp, Wolfgang. "Die Revolutionierung der Medien: Lithographie, Photographie, Diorama, Panorama." "Funkkolleg moderne Kunst," Saarländischer Rundfunk: Hauptabteil Kulturelles Wort. Sendung October 23–29, 1989.

Klussmann, Paul Gerhard. "Das Taschenbuch im literarischen Leben der Romantik und Biedermeierzeit: Begriff, Konzept, Wirkung." In *Literarische Leitmedien: Almanach und Taschenbuch im kulturwissenschaftlichen Kontext,* ed. Paul Gerhard Klussmann and York-Gothart Mix, 47–64. Wiesbaden: Harassowitz, 1998.

Klussmann, Paul Gerhard, and York-Gothart Mix, eds. *Literarische Leitmedien: Almanach und Taschenbuch im kulturwissenschaftlichen Kontext.* Wiesbaden: Harassowitz, 1998.

Knopf, Jan. "Kalender." In *Von Almanach bis Zeitung: Ein Handbuch der Medien in Deutschland, 1700–1800,* ed. Ernst Fischer, Wilhelm Haefs, and York-Gothart Mix, 121–36. Munich: Beck, 1999.

Knudsen, Hans. *Goethes Welt des Theaters: Ein Vierteljahrhundert Weimarer Bühnenleitung.* Berlin: Tempelhof, 1949.

Kocka, Jürgen. "The Difficult Rise of a Civil Society." In *German History since 1800,* ed. Mary Fulbrook, 498–99. London: Arnold, 1997.

———. "The European Pattern and the German Case." In *Bourgeois Society in Nineteenth-Century Europe,* ed. Jürgen Kocka and Allen Mitchell, 3–99. Oxford: Berg, 1993.

———, ed. *Bürger und Bürgerlichkeit im 19. Jahrhundert.* Göttingen: Vandenhoeck & Ruprecht, 1987.

Köhler, Astrid. *Salonkultur im klassischen Weimar: Geselligkeit als Lebensform und literarisches Konzept.* Stuttgart: Verlag für Wissenschaft und Forschung, 1996.

Kontje, Todd. *Women, the Novel, and the German Nation, 1771–1871: Domestic Fiction in the Fatherland.* New York: Cambridge University Press, 1998.

Koschorke, Albrecht. "Alphabetisation und Empfindsamkeit." In *Der ganze Mensch: Anthropologie und Literatur im 18. Jahrhundert,* ed. Hans-Jürgen Schings, 605–28. Stuttgart: Metzler, 1994.

Koselleck, Reinhard. *Kritik und Krise: Eine Studie zur Pathogenese der bürgerlichen Welt.* 1959. Frankfurt: Suhrkamp, 1973.

———. *Vergangene Zukunft: Zur Semantik geschichtlicher Zeiten.* Frankfurt: Suhrkamp, 1992.

Koshar, Rudy. *German Travel Cultures.* Oxford: Berg, 2000.

———. "'What Ought to Be Seen': Tourist Guidebooks and National Identities in Modern Germany and Europe." *Journal of Contemporary History* 33 (1998): 323–40.

Krause, Markus. *Das Trivialdrama der Goethezeit, 1780–1805: Produktion und Rezeption.* Bonn: Bouvier, 1982.

Kristeva, Julia. *Powers of Horror: An Essay in Abjection*. Trans. Leon S. Roudiez. 1980. New York: Columbia University Press, 1982.

Kröll, Christina, and Jörn Göres, eds. *Heimliche Verführung: Ein Modejournal, 1786–1827*. Düsseldorf: Goethe Museum, 1978.

Kuhles, Doris. "Das 'Journal des Luxus und der Moden' (1786–1827): Zur Enstehung seines inhaltlichen Profils und seiner journalistischen Struktur." In *Friedrich Justin Bertuch (1747–1822): Verleger, Schriftsteller und Unternehmer im klassischen Weimar*, ed. Gerhard R. Kaiser and Siegfried Seifert, 489–98. Tübingen: Niemeyer, 2000.

———, ed. *Journal des Luxus und der Moden, 1786–1827: Analytische Bibliographie mit sämtlichen 517 schwarzweißen und 976 farbigen Abbildungen der Originalzeitschrift*. 3 vols. Munich: Saur, 2003.

Kühn-Stillmark, Uta. "Zum Verlagsprofil des Landes-Industrie-Comptoirs und des Geographischen Instituts unter Friedrich Justin Bertuch in den Jahren 1791 bis 1822." In *Friedrich Justin Bertuch (1747–1822): Verleger, Schriftsteller, und Unternehmer im klassischen Weimar*, ed. Gerhard R. Kaiser and Siegfried Seifert, 417–30. Tübingen: Niemeyer, 2000.

Laermann, Klaus. "Raumerfahrung und Erfahrungsraum: Einige Überlegungen zu Reiseberichten aus Deutschland vom Ende des 18. Jahrhunderts." In *Reise und Utopie: Zur Literatur der Spätaufklärung*, ed. Hans Joachim Piechotta, 57–97. Frankfurt: Suhrkamp, 1976.

Langen, August. *Anschauungsformen in der deutschen Dichtung des 18. Jahrhunderts: Rahmenschau und Rationalismus*. 1934. Rpt., Darmstadt: Wissenschaftliche Buchgesellschaft, 1965.

———. "Attitüde und Tableau in der Goethezeit." *Jahrbuch der deutschen Schillergesellschaft* 12 (1968): 194–258.

La Vopa, Anthony. *Grace, Talent, and Merit: Poor Students, Clerical Careers, and Professional Ideology in Eighteenth-Century Germany*. Cambridge: Cambridge University Press, 1988.

Lee, Robert. "'Relative Backwardness' and Long-Run Development: Economic, Demographic, and Social Changes." In *German History since 1800*, ed. Mary Fulbrook, 61–87. London: Arnold, 1997.

Lepenies, Wolf. *Melancholie und Gesellschaft*. Frankfurt: Suhrkamp, 1992.

Light, Alison. *Forever England: Femininity, Literature, and Conservatism between the Wars*. London: Routledge, 1991.

Löfgren, Orvar. *On Holiday: A History of Vacationing*. Berkeley: University of California Press, 1999.

Löschburg, Winfried. *History of Travel*. Leipzig: Interdruck, 1979.

Luhmann, Niklas. *Liebe als Passion: Zur Codierung von Intimität*. 3rd ed. Frankfurt: Suhrkamp, 1983.

Lynch, Deidre Shauna. *The Economy of Character: Novels, Market Culture, and the Business of Inner Meaning*. Chicago: University of Chicago Press, 1998.

446

Mackie, Erin. Introduction. *The Commerce of Everyday Life: Selections from* The Tatler *and* The Spectator, ed. Mackie, 1–32. Boston: St. Martins Press, 1998.

———. *Market à la Mode: Fashion, Commodity, and Gender in* The Tatler *and* The Spectator. Baltimore: Johns Hopkins University Press, 1997.

MacLeod, Catriona. "Floating Heads: Weimar Portrait Busts." In *Unwrapping Goethe's Weimar: Essays in Cultural Studies and Local Knowledge,* ed. Burkhard Henke, Susanne Kord, and Simon Richter, 65–84. Rochester: Camden House, 2000.

Maierhofer, Waltraud. "Goethe on Emma Hamilton's 'Attitudes': Can Classicist Art Be Fun?" *Goethe Yearbook* 9 (1999): 222–52.

Maler, Anselm. *Exotische Welten in populären Lektüren.* Tübingen: Niemeyer, 1990.

Marcuse, Herbert. "Über den affirmativen Charakter der Kultur." In *Kultur und Gesellschaft,* 1:56–101. Frankfurt: Suhrkamp, 1965.

Martens, Wolfgang. "Geselligkeit im *Geselligen* (1748–50)." In *Gesellige Vernunft: Zur Kultur der literarischen Aufklärung, Festschrift für Wolfgang Mauser zum 65 Geburtstag,* ed. Ortud Gutjahr et al., 174–85. Würzburg: Königshausen & Neumann, 1993.

Mattenklott, Gert. "Friedrich Theodor Vischer im Gespräch: Auch ein Beitrag zur Philosophie der Mode." In *Die Listen der Mode,* ed. Silvia Bovenschen, 355–73. Frankfurt: Suhrkamp, 1979.

Mattenklott, Gert, and Klaus Scherpe, eds. *Literatur der Bürgerlichen Emanzipation im 18. Jahrhundert.* Kronberg: Scriptor, 1973.

———. *Westberliner Projekt: Grundkurs 18. Jahrhundert. Die Funktion der Literatur bei der Formierung der bürgerlichen Klasse Deutschlands im 18. Jahrhundert.* Kronberg: Scriptor, 1974.

Mauser, Wolfram. "Anakreon als Therapie? Zur Medizinisch-diätetischen Begründung der Rokokodichtung." In *Konzepte aufgeklärter Lebensführung: Literarische Kultur im frühmodernen Deutschland,* 301–29. Würzburg: Königshausen & Neumann, 2000.

———. "Die 'Balsam=Kraft' von innen: Dichtung und Diätik am Beispiel des B. H. Brockes." In *Konzepte aufgeklärter Lebensführung: Literarische Kultur im frühmodernen Deutschland,* 244–74. Würzburg: Königshausen & Neumann, 2000.

———. "Geselligkeit: Eine sozialethische Utopie des 18. Jahrhunderts." In *Konzepte aufgeklärter Lebensführung: Literarische Kultur im frühmodernen Deutschland,* 17–49. Würzburg: Königshausen & Neumann, 2000.

———. "Glückseligkeit und Melancholie: Zur Anthropologie der Frühaufklärung." In *Konzepte aufgeklärter Lebensführung: Literarische Kultur im frühmodernen Deutschland,* 211–43. Würzburg: Königshausen & Neumann, 2000.

————. *Konzepte aufgeklärter Lebensführung: Literarische Kultur im frühmodernen Deutschland.* Würzburg: Königshausen & Neumann, 2000.

McCarthy, John A. "The Art of Reading and the Goals of the German Enlightenment." *Lessing Yearbook* 16 (1984): 79–94.

McCracken, Grant. *Culture and Consumption: New Approaches to the Symbolic Character of Consumer Goods and Activities.* Bloomington: Indiana University Press, 1988.

McKendrick, Neil. Introduction. In *The Birth of a Consumer Society: The Commercialization of Eighteenth Century England,* ed. Neil McKendrick, John Brewer, and J. H. Plumb, 1–6. London: Hutchinson, 1984.

McKendrick, Neil, John Brewer, and J. H. Plumb, eds. *The Birth of a Consumer Society: The Commercialization of Eighteenth-Century England.* London: Hutchinson, 1984.

Meise, Helga. *Die Unschuld und die Schrift: Deutsche Frauenromane im 18. Jahrhundert.* Berlin: Guttandin & Hoppe, 1983.

Meisel, Martin. *Realizations: Narrative, Pictorial, and Theatrical Arts in Nineteenth-Century England.* Princeton: Princeton University Press, 1983.

Messer-Davidow, Ellen. "'For Softness She': Gender Ideology and Aesthetics in Eighteenth Century England." In *Eighteenth-Century Women and the Arts,* ed. Frederick M. Keener and Susan E. Lorsch, 45–55. New York: Greenwood Press, 1988.

Miller, Norbert. "Mutmaßungen über Lebende Bilder." In *Das Triviale in Literatur, Musik, und Bildende Kunst,* ed. Helga de la Motte-Haber, 106–30. Frankfurt: Klostermann, 1972.

Mix, York-Gothart. *Die deutschen Musenalmanache des 18. Jahrhunderts.* Munich: Beck, 1987.

————. "Der Literaturfreund als Kalendernarr: Die Almanachkultur und ihr Publikum." In *Almanach und Taschenbuchkultur des 18. und 19. Jahrhunderts,* ed. Mix. Wiesbaden: Harrassowitz, 1996.

————. "Ohne Taschenbuch und Almanach in die Moderne—Otto Julius Bierbaums *Moderner Musen Almanach* (1839–94) im medienhistorischen Kontext." In *Literarische Leitmedien: Almanach und Taschenbuch im kulturwissenschaftlichen Kontext,* ed. Paul Gerhard Klussmann and York-Gothart Mix, 183–99. Wiesbaden: Harassowitz, 1998.

Modleski, Tania. "The Terror of Pleasure: The Contemporary Horror Film and Postmodern Theory." In *Studies in Entertainment: Critical Approaches to Mass Culture,* ed. Tania Modleski, 155–66. Bloomington: Indiana University Press, 1986.

————, ed. *Studies in Entertainment: Critical Approaches to Mass Culture.* Bloomington: Indiana University Press, 1986.

Möller, Frank. "Zwischen Kunst und Kommerz: Bürgertheater im 19.

Jahrhundert." In *Bürgerkultur im 19. Jahrhundert: Bildung, Kunst, und Lebenswelten,* ed. Dieter Hein and Andreas Schulz, 19–33. Munich: Beck, 1996.

Moritz, Karl Phillipp. *Schriften zur Ästhetik und Poetik: Kritische Ausgabe.* Ed. Hans Joachim Schrimpf. Vol. 7. Tübingen: Niemeyer, 1962.

Müchler, Günter. *"Wie ein treuer Spiegel": Die Geschichte der Cotta'schen Allgemeinen Zeitung.* Darmstadt: Wissenschaftliche Buchgesellschaft, 1998.

Mukerji, Chandra. *From Graven Images: Patterns of Modern Materialism.* New York: Columbia University Press, 1983.

Müller, Jürgen. "Crumbling Walls: Urban Change in Eighteenth-Century Germany." *German Studies Review* 19, no. 2 (1996): 106–18.

Müller, Susanne. "Über Englische Gärten, französische Landsitze und den 'Park bey Weimar': Die Gartenkunst im *Journal des Luxus und der Moden.*" Presentation at the symposium "Das Journal des Luxus und der Moden: Kultur um 1800." Ereignis Weimar-Jena: Kultur um 1800.

Müller-Fraunreuth, Carl. *Die Ritter- und Räuberromane.* Halle, 1894. Facsimile ed., Hildesheim: Olms, 1965.

Naumann, Dietrich. "Das Werk August Lafontaines und das Problem der Trivialität." In *Studien zur Trivialliteratur,* ed. Heinz Otto Burger, 82–100. Frankfurt: Klostermann, 1968.

Nehamas, Alexander. *The Art of Living: Socratic Reflections from Plato to Foucault.* Berkeley: University of California Press, 1998.

Nell, Victor. *Lost in a Book: The Psychology of Reading for Pleasure.* New Haven: Yale University Press, 1988.

Nenon, Monika. *Autorschaft und Frauenbildung: Das Beispiel Sophie von LaRoche.* Würzburg: Königshausen & Neumann, 1988.

Neumann, Erich. *Amor and Psyche: The Psychological Development of the Feminine.* Trans. Ralph Mannheim. Princeton: Princeton University Press, 1971.

Nichols, Bill. *Ideology and Image.* Bloomington: Indiana University Press, 1981.

Nickisch, Reinhard. *Brief.* Stuttgart: Metzler, 1991.

———. "Die Frau als Briefschreiberin im Zeitalter der deutschen Aufklärung." *Wolfenbütteler Studien zur Aufklärung* 3–4 (1976–77): 29–65.

———. *Die Stilprinzipien in den deutschen Briefstellern des 17. und 18. Jahrhunderts: Mit einer Bibliographie zur Briefschreiblehre (1474–1800).* Göttingen: Vandenhoeck & Ruprecht, 1969.

Nies, Fritz. "Bilder von Bildung und Verbildung durch Lesen." In *Lebensläufe um 1800,* ed. Jürgen Fohrmann, 202–22. Tübingen: Niemeyer, 1998.

Nusser, Peter. *Trivialliteratur.* Stuttgart: Metzler, 1991.

Oesterle, Günter. "Youth—A Romantic Concept? Introduction." In *Jugend: Ein romantisches Konzept?* ed. Oesterle, 31–43. Würzburg: Königshausen

& Neumann, 1997.

Oettermann, Stephan. *Das Panorama: Die Geschichte eines Massenmediums.* Frankfurt: Syndikat, 1980.

Parshall, Linda B. Introduction. *The Theory of Garden Art: C. C. L. Hirschfeld,* ed. and trans. Parshall, 1–54. Philadelphia: University of Pennsylvania Press, 2001.

Paulson, Ronald. *Popular and Polite Art in the Age of Hogarth and Fielding.* Notre Dame: University of Notre Dame Press, 1979.

Pawlowicz, Peter H. "The Letter Theme: Fragonard and the Image of Women." In *Eighteenth-Century Women and the Arts,* ed. Frederick M. Keener and Susan E. Lorsch, 189–200. New York: Greenwood Press, 1988.

Pelz, Annegret. *Reisen durch die eigene Fremde: Reiseliteratur von Frauen als auto-geographische Schriften.* Cologne: Böhlau, 1993.

Perry, Gill, and Michael Rossington. Introduction. In *Femininity and Masculinity in Eighteenth-Century Art and Culture,* ed. Perry and Rossington, 1–17. Manchester: Manchester University Press, 1994.

Peter, Emanuel. *Geselligkeiten: Literatur, Gruppenbildung, und Kultureller Wandel im 18. Jahrhundert.* Tübingen: Niemeyer, 1999.

Petzold, Dieter, and Eberhard Späth, eds. *Unterhaltungsliteratur. Ziele und Methoden ihrer Erforschung.* Erlangen: Universitätsbund Erlangen-Nürnberg, 1990.

Peucker, Brigitte. "The Material Image in Goethe's *Wahlverwandtschaften.*" *Germanic Review* 74, no. 3 (1999): 195–213.

Pfotenhauer, Helmut. *Literarische Anthropologie: Selbstbiographien und ihre Geschichte—am Leitfaden des Leibes.* Stuttgart: Metzlersche Verlagsbuchhandlung, 1987.

Pikulik, Lothar. *"Bürgerliches Trauerspiel" und Empfindsamkeit.* Cologne: Böhlau, 1966.

Plaul, Hainer. *Illustrierte Geschichte der Trivialliteratur.* Hildesheim: Olms, 1983.

Plumb, J. H. "The Commercialization of Leisure." In *The Birth of Consumer Society: Commercialization in Eighteenth-Century England,* ed. Neil McKendrick, John Brewer, and J. H. Plumb, 265–85. London: Hutchinson, 1984.

———. "Part III: Commercialization and Society." In *The Birth of Consumer Society: Commercialization in Eighteenth-Century England,* ed. Neil McKendrick, John Brewer, and J. H. Plumb, 265–334. London: Hutchinson, 1984.

Polan, Dana. "Brief Encounters: Mass Culture and the Evacuation of Sense." In *Studies in Entertainment: Critical Approaches to Mass Culture,* ed. Tania Modleski, 167–87. Bloomington: Indiana University Press, 1986.

Porter, Roy, and Marie Mulvey Roberts, eds. *Pleasure in the Eighteenth Century.*

New York: New York University Press, 1996.

Prüsener, Marlies. "Lesegesellschaften im 18. Jahrhundert." *Börsenblatt für den deutschen Buchhandel*, no. 10 (1972): 229–34.

Purdy, Daniel. *The Tyranny of Elegance: Consumer Cosmopolitanism in the Era of Goethe*. Baltimore: Johns Hopkins University Press, 1998.

———. "The Veil of Masculinity: Clothing and Identity via Goethe's *Die Leiden des jungen Werthers*." *Lessing Yearbook* 27 (1995): 103–30.

———. "Weimar Classicism and the Origins of Consumer Culture." In *Unwrapping Goethe's Weimar: Essays in Cultural Studies and Local Knowledge*, ed. Burkhard Henke, Susanne Kord, and Simon Richter, 36–57. Rochester: Camden, 2000.

Richter, David. "The Reception of the Gothic Novel in the 1790s." In *The Idea of the Novel in the Eighteenth Century*, ed. Robert Uphaus, 117–37. East Lansing: Michigan State University Press, 1988.

Roebling, Irmgard. "'Frühlingsmomente eines geselligen Vollgenusses': Geselligkeit als kritische Intersubjektivität im Kreis der Rahel Levin." In *Gesellige Vernunft: Zur Kultur der literarischen Aufklärung, Festschrift für Wolfgang Mauser zum 65 Geburtstag*, ed. Ortud Gutjahr et al., 243–62. Würzburg: Königshausen & Neumann, 1993.

Rosenberg, Heidi. *Formen der Familie*. Frankfurt: Suhrkamp, 1982.

Ross, Stephanie. *What Gardens Mean*. Chicago: University of Chicago Press, 1998.

Royer, Berit C. R. "Sophie Albrecht (1757–1840) im Kreis der Schriftstellerinnen um 1800: eine literatur- und kulturwissenschaftliche Werk Monographie." Diss., University of California, Davis, 1999.

Sahlins, Marshall. *Culture and Practical Reason*. Chicago: University of Chicago Press, 1976.

Sauder, Gerhard. "Almanach-Kultur und Empfindsamkeit." In *Literarische Leitmedien: Almanach und Taschenbuch im kulturwissenschaftlichen Kontext*, ed. Paul Gerhard Klussmann and York-Gothart Mix, 16–30. Wiesbaden: Harrassowitz, 1998.

———. *Empfindsamkeit (I) Voraussetzungen und Elemente*. Stuttgart: Metzler, 1974.

———. *Empfindsamkeit (II) Quellen und Dokumente*. Stuttgart: Metzler, 1980.

Schenda, Rudolf. *Volk ohne Buch: Studien zur Sozialgeschichte der populären Lesestoffe 1770–1910*. Frankfurt: Vittorio Klostermann, 1970.

Schiefer, Karl. *Elise Bürger: Ein Beitrag zur deutschen Literatur und Theatergeschichte*. Diss., Frankfurt am Main, 1921.

Schivelbusch, Wolfgang. *Das Paradies, der Geschmack und die Vernunft: Eine Geschichte der Genußmittel*. Munich: Hanser, 1980.

Schlick, Werner. *Goethe's Die Wahlverwandtschaften: A Middle-Class Critique of Aesthetic Aristocratism*. Heidelberg: Winter, 2000.

Schmidt, Siegfried. *Die Selbstorganisation des Sozialsystems Literatur im 18. Jahrhundert.* Frankfurt: Suhrkamp, 1989.

Schneider, Angelika. "Friedrich Justin Bertuch—ein Beförderer der Gartenkunst." In *Friedrich Justin Bertuch (1747–1822): Verleger, Schriftsteller, und Unternehmer im klassischen Weimar,* ed. Gerhard R. Kaiser and Siegfried Seifert, 629–57. Tübingen: Niemeyer, 2000.

Schneider, Helmut. "Wahllandschaften: Mobilisierung der Natur und das Darstellungsproblem der Moderne in Goethes *Wahlverwandtschaften.*" In *Rereading Romanticism,* ed. Martha Helfer, 285–300. Amsterdam: Rodopi, 2000.

Schön, Erich. *Der Verlust der Sinnlichkeit oder Die Verwandlung des Lesers: Mentalitätswandel um 1800.* Stuttgart: Klett-Cotta, 1987.

———. "Weibliches Lesen: Romanleserinnen im späten 18. Jahrhundert." In *Untersuchungen zum Roman von Frauen um 1800,* ed. Helga Gallas and Magdalene Heuser, 20–40. Tübingen: Niemeyer, 1990.

Schulte-Sasse, Jochen. "Gebrauchswerte der Literatur: Eine Kritik der ästhetischen Kategorien 'Identifikation' und 'Reflexion,' vor allem in Hinblick auf Adorno." In *Zur Dichotomisierung von hoher und niederer Literatur,* ed. Christa Bürger, Peter Bürger, and Jochen Schulte-Sasse 62–107. Frankfurt: Suhrkamp, 1984.

———. "Das Konzept bürgerlich-literarischer Öffentlichkeit und die historischen Gründe seines Zerfalls." In *Aufklärung und literarische Öffentlichkeit,* ed. Christa Bürger, Peter Bürger, and Jochen Schulte-Sasse, 12–38. Frankfurt: Suhrkamp, 1980.

———. *Die Kritik an der Trivialliteratur seit der Aufklärung: Studien zur Geschichte des Kitschbegriffs.* Munich: Fink, 1971.

Segeberg, Harro. *Literatur im technischen Zeitalter: Von der Frühzeit der deutschen Aufklärung bis zum Beginn des Ersten Weltkriegs.* Darmstadt: Wissenschaftliche Buchgesellschaft, 1997.

Sheehan, James. *Museums in the German Art World: From the End of the Old Regime to the Rise of Modernism.* Oxford: Oxford University Press, 2000.

Shiach, Morag. *Discourse on Popular Culture: Class, Gender, and History in Cultural Analysis, 1730 to the Present.* Oxford: Polity Press, 1989.

Sichelschmidt, Gustav. *Liebe, Mord, und Abenteuer: Eine Geschichte der Unterhaltungsliteratur.* Berlin: Haude & Spener, 1969.

Silverman, Kaja. "Fragments of a Fashionable Disourse." In *Studies in Entertainment,* ed. Tania Modelski, 139–52. Bloomington: Indiana University Press, 1986.

Simanowski, Roberto. *Die Verwaltung des Abenteuers: Massenkultur um 1800 am Beispiel Christian August Vulpius.* Göttingen: Vandenhoeck & Ruprecht, 1998.

Simmel, Georg. "Die Mode." In *Die Listen der Mode,* ed. Silvia Bovenschen, 179–207. Frankfurt: Suhrkamp, 1979.

Smith-Rosenberg, Carroll. "Writing History: Language, Class, and Gender." In *Feminist Studies Critical Studies,* ed. Theresa de Lauretis, 31–54. Bloomington: Indiana University Press, 1986.

Sombart, Werner. *Luxury and Capitalism.* Trans. W. R. Dittmar. Ann Arbor: University of Michigan Press, 1967.

———. "Wirtschaft und Mode: Ein Beitrag zur Theorie der modernen Bedarfsgestaltung." In *Grenzfragen des Nerven- und Seelenlebens.* Vol. 12. Wiesbaden: Bergmann, 1902. Rpt. Werner Sombart, "Wirtschaft und Mode." In *Die Listen der Mode,* ed. Silvia Bovenschen, 80–105. Frankfurt: Suhrkamp, 1986.

Sontag, Susan. *The Volcano Lover: A Romance.* New York: Anchor Books Doubleday, 1992.

Sperber, Jonathan. "Bürger, Bürgertum, Bürgerlichkeit. Bürgerliche Gesellschaft: Studies of the German (Upper) Middle Class and Its Sociocultural World" (review article). *Journal of Modern History* 69, no. 2 (1997): 271–97.

Stafford, Barbara Maria. *Artful Science: Enlightenment Entertainment and the Eclipse of Visual Education.* Cambridge: MIT Press, 1994.

———. *Good Looking: Essays on the Virtue of Images.* Cambridge: MIT Press, 1996.

———. *Voyage into Substance: Art, Science, Nature, and the Illustrated Travel Account, 1740–1840.* Cambridge: MIT Press, 1984.

Starobinski, Jean. *The Living Eye.* Trans. Arthur Goldhammer. Cambridge: Harvard University Press, 1989. Transation of *L'Oeil vivant* (1961) chapters 1–3; 4–7. *L'Oeil vivant II: La Relation critique* (1970).

Stephan, Inge, and Hans-Gerd Winter, eds. *Hamburg im Zeitalter der Aufklärung.* Berlin: Dietrich Reimer, 1989.

Sternberger, Dolf. *Panorama of the Nineteenth Century.* Trans. Joachim Neugroschel. New York: Urizen Books, 1977. Translation of *Panorama oder Ansichten vom 19. Jahrhundert.* Hamburg: Classen, 1955.

Sulzer, Johann Georg. *Allgemeine Theorie der schönen Künste.* Vol. 2. Leipzig: Weidmannsche Buchhandlung, 1792.

Sylla, Richard, and Gianni Toniolo, eds. *Patterns of European Industrialization: The Nineteenth Century.* London: Routledge, 1991.

Tanzer, Gerhard. *"Spectacle müssen seyn": Die Freizeit der Wiener im 18. Jahrhundert.* Vienna: Böhlau, 1992.

Tolkemitt, Brigitte. "Knotenpunkt im Beziehungsnetz der Gebildeten: Die gemischte Geselligkeit in den offenen Häusern der Hamburger Familien Reimarus und Sieverking." In *Ordnung, Politik, und Geselligkeit der*

Geschlechter im 18. Jahrhundert, ed. Ulrike Weckel, Claudia Opitz, Olivia Hochstrasser, and Brigitte Tolkemitt, 167–202. Göttingen: Wallstein, 1998.

Trilling, Lionel. "The Fate of Pleasure: Wordsworth to Dostoevsky." *Partisan Review,* summer 1963, 73–106.

Turner, Mark. *Death Is the Mother of Beauty: Mind, Metaphor, Criticism.* Chicago: University of Chicago Press, 1987.

Urry, John. *The Tourist Gaze: Leisure and Travel in Contemporary Societies.* London: Sage, 1990.

Vaget, Hans Rudolf. *Dilettantismus und Meisterschaft: Zum Problem des Dilettantismus bei Goethe: Praxis Theorie, Zeitkritik.* Munich: Winkler, 1971.

Van Dülmen, Andrea. *Das irdische Paradies: Bürgerliche Gartenkultur der Goethezeit.* Cologne: Böhlau, 1999.

Veblen, Thorstein. "Die Mode der feinen Leute." In *Die Listen der Mode,* ed. Silvia Bovenschen, 106–55. Frankfurt: Suhrkamp, 1979.

———. *The Theory of the Leisure Class.* New York: MacMillan, 1899.

Vischer, Friedrich Theodor. "Mode und Zynismus." Rpt. in *Die Listen der Mode,* ed. Silvia Bovenschen, 33–79. Frankfurt: Suhrkamp, 1979.

Von Mücke, Dorothea. *Virtue and the Veil of Illusion: Generic Innovation and the Pedagogical Project in Eighteenth-Century Literature.* Stanford: Stanford University Press, 1991.

Von Trotha, Hans. *Angenehme Empfindungen: Medien einer populären Wirkungsästhetik im 18. Jahrhundert vom Landschaftsgarten bis zum Schauerroman.* Munich: Fink, 1999.

Voßkamp, Wilhelm. "Individualität—Biographie—Roman." In *Lebensläufe um 1800,* ed. Jürgen Fohrmann, 257–61. Tübingen: Niemeyer, 1998.

Ward, Albert. *Book Production, Fiction, and the German Reading Public, 1740–1800.* Oxford: Clarendon Press, 1974.

Watkin, David. *The English Vision: The Pictoresque in Architecture, Landscape, and Garden Design.* London: John Murrey, 1982.

Weber, Max. *The Protestant Ethic and the Spirit of Capitalism.* Trans. Talcott Parsons. London: Unwin University Books, 1930.

Weckel, Ulrike, Claudia Opitz, Olivia Hochstrasser, and Brigitte Tolkemitt, eds. *Ordnung, Politik, und Geselligkeit der Geschlechter im 18. Jahrhundert.* Göttingen: Wallstein, 1998.

Wegmann, Nikolaus. *Diskurse der Empfindsamkeit: Zur Geschichte eines Gefühls in der Literatur des 18. Jahrhunderts.* Stuttgart: Metzlersche Verlagsbuchhandlung, 1988.

Weil, Rudolf. *Das Berliner Theaterpublikum unter A. W. Ifflands Direktion (1796 bis 1814).* Berlin: Selbstverlag der Gesellschaft für Theatergeschichte, 1932.

Wellbery, David E. "The Pathos of Theory: *Laokoon* Revisited." In *Intertextuality: German Literature and the Visual Art from the Renaissance to the Twentieth Century,* ed. Ingeborg Hoesterey and Ulrich Weisstein, 47–63. Drawer, S.C.: Camden House, 1993.

Whaley, Joachim. "The German Lands before 1815." In *German History since 1800,* ed. Mary Fulbrook, 15–37. London: Arnold, 1997.

Wilhelmy, Petra. *Der Berliner Salon im 19. Jahrhundert (1780–1914).* Veröffentlichungen der Berliner Historischen Kommision Bd. 73. Berlin: de Gruyter, 1989.

Williams, Anne. *The Art of Darkness: A Poetics of the Gothic.* Chicago: University of Chicago Press, 1995.

Williamson, Tom. *Polite Landscapes: Gardens and Society in Eighteenth-Century England.* Baltimore: Johns Hopkins University Press, 1995.

Wilson, W. Daniel. "Enlightenment's Alliance with Power: The Dialectic of Collusion and Opposition in the Literary Elite." In *Impure Reason: Dialectic of Enlightenment in Germany,* ed. W. Daniel Wilson and Robert C. Holub, 364–84. Detroit: Wayne State University Press, 1993.

Wilson, Elizabeth. *Adorned in Dreams: Fashion and Modernity.* London: Virago, 1985.

———. "Fashion and the Postmodern Body." In *Chic Thrills: A Fashion Reader,* ed. Juliet Ash and Elizabeth Wilson, 3–16. Berkeley: University of California Press, 1993.

Woodmansee, Martha. *The Author, Art, and the Market: Readings in the History of Aesthetics.* New York: Columbia University Press, 1994.

Wurst, Karin A. "Designing the Self: Fashion and the Body." In *Body Dialectics in the Age of Goethe,* vol. 55 of *Amsterdamer Beiträge,* ed. Holger Pausch and Marianne Henn, 47–66. Amsterdam: Rodopi, 2003.

———. "Elise Bürger and the Gothic Imagination." *Women in German Yearbook* 13 (1997): 11–27.

———. *Familiale Liebe ist die "wahre Gewalt": Zur Repräsentation der Familie in G. E. Lessings dramatischen Werken.* Amsterdam: Rodopi, 1988.

———. "The Self-Fashioning of the Bourgeoisie in Late Eighteenth-Century German Culture: Bertuch's *Journal des Luxus und der Moden.*" *Germanic Review* 72, no. 3 (1997): 170–82.

———. "Spellbinding: The Body as Art/Art as Body in *Attitüden.*" *Lessing Yearbook* 32 (2001): 151–81.

———. "Spurensicherung: Elise Bürgers Einakter *Die Antike Statue aus Florenz* (1814) als Beispiel dramatischer Experimente an der Jahrhundertwende." *Goethe Yearbook* 8 (1996): 210–37.

———. "'Wilde Wünsche': The Discourse of Love in the Sturm and Drang." In *Literature of the Sturm and Drang,* ed. David Hill, 217–40. Rochester: Camden House, 2003.

————. "Women Dramatists in Late-Eighteenth-Century Germany: The Hazards of Marriage as Love Match." *Seminar* 38, no. 4 (2002): 313–31.

————, ed. and intro. *Frauen und Drama im achtzehnten Jahrhundert*. Köln: Böhlau, 1991.

Zelle, Carsten. *Angenehmes Grauen: Literaturhistorische Beiträge zur Ästhetik des Schrecklichen im achtzehnten Jahrhundert*. Hamburg: Felix Meiner, 1987.

Zucker, Paul. *Die Theaterdekoration des Klassizismus: Eine Kunstgeschichte des Bühnenbildes*. Berlin: Rudolf Kaemmerer, 1925.

Index